Convention Sales and Services
Seventh Edition

Milton T. Astroff
Marketing Consultant

James R. Abbey, Ph.D.
Professor Emeritus
College of Hotel Administration
University of Nevada, Las Vegas

Waterbury Press

Disclaimer

This publication is designed to provide accurate and authoritative information in regard to the subject matter covered. It is sold with the understanding that the publisher is not engaged in rendering legal, accounting, or other professional service. If legal advice or other expert assistance is required, the services of a competent professional person should be sought.
— *From the Declaration of Principles jointly adopted by the American Bar Associaqtion and a Committee of Publishers and Associations.*

Contents

4 Selling the Association Market

5 Selling the Corporate Meetings Market

(handwritten annotation in margin: Small meetings)

6 Selling Other Markets

7 Selling to the Meetings Market

Green meetings & Social Responsibility

8 Advertising to the Meeting Planner

9 Negotiations and Contracts

Part II Convention Services

10 The Service Function

11 Guestrooms

12 Preparing for the Event

13 Function Rooms and Meeting Setups

14 Food and Beverage Service

15 Audiovisual Requirements

16 Admission Systems and Other Services

17 Exhibits and Trade Shows

18 Convention Billing and Post-Convention Review

Appendix I

Appendix II

Appendix III

Index

Introduction

Successful hotel executives must have a complete grasp of convention sales and service, which offers an opportunity to go after *desired* guests, not just numbers. No one can progress to executive ranks today without a full understanding of the role meetings and convention business plays in hotel profitability, so this lucrative market merits careful study by both students and those already in the field.

Convention Sales and Services is designed to serve as both a primer and a guide to those who are already involved in this exciting segment of the hospitality field. The first six editions of this book have been tested on the firing line in university classrooms and in hotel sales offices throughout the world. Most gratifying have been the critiques of seasoned industry professionals who have commented, "Yes, this is just the way it's done... large or small, those properties that are successful follow the procedures as laid out in your text."

To maintain that level of credibility, the contents of this seventh edition have been substantially updated. Based on the suggestions of professors, students and industry professionals, a number of improvements have been made in this text. The discussions of many topics have been rewritten to update them and to make them more comprehensive. These revisions are based on current trade journal articles, seminar notes, book reviews, and input from industry leaders.

New or expanded sections, providing the latest research information and current industry practices, have been added to every chapter, and new photographs and forms enhance the content. These additions include several examples of standardized forms developed for industry-wide use by the Convention Industry Council (CIC) as well as a more comprehensive glossary of key terms (taken from the updated meetings glossary available in its entirety on the CIC's website — www.conventionindustry.org). It also warrants mention that there has been a change in the industry during the writing of this book – as of August 2, 2005, the International Association of Convention and Visitors Bureaus (IACVB) has changed its name to the Destination Marketing Association International (DMAI).

Part I offers practical insight into the different kinds of meetings and conventions, the types of organizations that stage such events, and the people who hold the key to site selection. It also provides advice and suggestions on how to reach and sell to these important groups and people. Material also includes how to analyze a hotel property to determine which segments of the market may be sold and serviced successfully and how to organize a staff to go after desired business. Practical advice is also given on how to finalize an event through negotiations and letters of agreement.

Part II deals with the convention service itself. Once the client has been sold on holding his or her event in a hotel, its staff must ensure that the event flows smoothly. Each convention is a custom production, and skilled, knowledgeable people are needed for its execution. Repeat business is essential for the success of any hotel, and professional convention service is absolutely necessary for a hotel to compete for its share of business.

Text Features

Our purpose is to present convention management in a readable style. Each chapter contains numerous cross-referenced illustrations, actual industry examples, and quotes from successful hotel sales and service managers to enhance comprehension and encourage retention of the text material. Several case studies are also included in the text and in Appendix III to illustrate the practical application of principles presented and provide ample opportunity for group "brain-storming."

It is our goal to make this material readily understandable and usable. Toward that end, we have added "Best Practices" industry examples to each chapter and periodic sections on "Putting It All Together." The initial "Putting It All Together" sections provide case study examples of how concepts discussed in the text can be used to create successful sales and marketing strategies and to execute successful functions. In later chapters, students will be given the opportunity to test their knowledge, using the concepts discussed in the chapter to solve hypothetical problems themselves.

End of Chapter Material

A chapter summary and study questions follow each chapter. These questions help the reader pull together and integrate the basic concepts of the chapter. In addition, these questions give the reader an opportunity to see how his or her own values will affect the way management principles will be applied.

End of chapter materials also include "Key Terms" (a glossary of the terms introduced — and bolded — in each chapter), "Additional References" (a listing of other written, and sometimes electronic, material that provides additional, in-depth information on topics covered in the chapter), and a listing of "Internet Sites" for the firms and organizations mentioned in each chapter.

Instructional Support Package

A comprehensive Instructor's Manual to assist teachers in the classroom use of the text is available. The Instructor's Manual provides a Chapter Overview, Suggested Lecture Outline, Class Activities, including Suggested Guest Speakers and Individual/Group Work, Audiovisual Supplements and Test Questions and an indexed answer key for each chapter as well as Class Exercises and Case Studies (with answers to discussion questions) for a number of chapters.

Transparency Masters

A complete series of transparency masters has also been prepared for the instructor. To a large degree, the study of convention sales and service is a study of forms. The charts, exhibits and figures from the text have been enlarged and reproduced in a separate manual available to educators.

Convention Sales and Services will detail how the hospitality industry is responding to this market, and show you how selling to or servicing the conventions and meetings market offers the opportunity for you to enjoy an exciting and rewarding career with practically limitless potential.

James R. Abbey, Ph.D., CHA
Las Vegas, Nevada

Acknowledgements

This text could not have been written without the assistance of numerous industry professionals who contributed their knowledge, expertise, and practical advice. Many of them have been profiled at the beginning of the chapters of this text (and within selected chapters), but it is impossible to list everyone who helped to make this work comprehensive, up-to-date, and practical. You are all greatly appreciated.

The author also thanks the hospitality publications, firms, and individuals who contributed not only their expertise, but also granted permission for the use of their forms, exhibits, and advertisements to enhance the text of this book.

And, the author wishes to express his gratitude to his Las Vegas-based assistants who contributed to the production of this book. Donna Merrill, who has worked on a number of editions of this book as well as on the author's Hospitality Sales and Advertising texts, assisted in the editing of this text, typed additions and corrections, proofread the book in its various stages, and has edited and typed the accompanying Instructor's Manual. Robert Wais, a talented graphic artist and the author's electronic publishing expert, scanned numerous new illustrations and exhibits, designed graphics, and is responsible for the layout of this text and for the cover design for both the sixth and seventh editions of Convention Sales and Services.

Convention Sales and Services

Part I

Convention Sales

Learning Objectives:

This portion of your text introduces you to the nature and scope of today's growing and changing meetings market. When you have studied this chapter, you will:

- Be able to identify organizations involved in the advancement of professionalism in the convention and meetings industry.

- Be able to identify the types of meetings held and tell when and why each is typically used.

- Know the types of organizations that hold meetings and detail specific requirements of each.

- Be able to describe the various types of meeting facilities.

- Be aware of the current trends that are impacting the meetings industry industry, especially the role of third-party meeting planners and the increased use of technology.

Outline

The Convention and Meetings Industry Today

The Scope of Today's Meetings Market

- Types of Meetings
- Who Holds Meetings
- Types of Group Customers
- Types of Meeting Facilities

Trends in the Meetings Industry

- Globalization
- Second-Tier Cities
- The Growth of Convention Centers
- Third-Party Meeting Planners
- Increased Use of Technology
- Revenue Management
- Complicated Contracts

Summary

The Meetings Market: Types of Meeting Customers

Keith Patrick
Director of Convention Services
Pinehurst, Inc., North Carolina

"Meeting terminology is important...Those in the hotel business who aspire to be true professionals seek to understand the differences in order to help the meeting planner produce a successful event...As a convention sales or service professional, you'll be working with an ever-increasing professional group of people referred to as meeting planners or convention managers...Only by knowing the groups and the purpose of their meetings can you service them toward the accomplishment of their goals...."

1 Introduction to the Convention, Meetings and Trade Show Industry

Only four decades ago, the hospitality industry looked at servicing the conventions and meetings market as a "necessary evil," and meetings and convention business was regarded as a fairly insignificant market segment. Except for a few resort destinations, such as Miami Beach, Las Vegas and a handful of premier hotels in the nation's larger cities, there were few locations suitable for large meetings.

The few meetings held were typically conventions or small business meetings. Convention delegates were usually white males attending primarily for the food and fun. Activities for spouses—who were usually wives—were scarce, and since people didn't travel much, the convention was looked upon as a "perk"—a mini-vacation of sorts.

Few hotels had convention departments to assist in meeting planning or to solicit convention business, and the position of convention service manager was a rarity. Most meetings business was handled by the property's sales department, which handled sporadic requests from non-professional meeting planners, such as secretaries or clerical support staff.

Today, meetings and convention business may account for as much as 70 percent of the sales volume in major hotels, while smaller properties generally realize 15 to 20 percent of their business from the group segment. In this chapter, we will provide an introduction into today's dynamic meetings market and discuss how this growing and increasingly profitable market segment is impacting the hotel industry.

The Convention and Meetings Industry Today

The conventions and meetings industry is vastly different today. Projections based on the most recent study commissioned by the Convention Industry Council (CIC) discloses that the average association delegate spends $266 per day and that approximately $115 billion dollars annually is generated directly from meeting, conventions, expositions and incentive travel (see Figure 1.1).[1] And, this figure is only a fraction of the $315 billion—supporting nearly four million jobs—generated indirectly from the convention business; local transportation companies, hotel suppliers, retail stores and other businesses all benefit (see Figure 1.2).

While leisure travelers may represent larger numbers for the hospitality industry, meeting attendees—who frequently travel on an expense account—bring in the lion's share of revenue in addition to benefiting properties by filling "soft spots" and generating word of mouth business. Therefore, the lucrative convention and meetings market is becoming an increasingly important—and competitive—target market.

To take advantage of the profitable meetings and conventions market, it is important to become aware of the trends that have affected it over the past few years.

One of the most important factors impacting the convention industry has been the increase of female business travelers. As a result of the growth of this market segment, which is generally more discriminating and security conscious than the typical male business traveler, many properties have offered additional amenities. Premium shampoos and lotions, hair dryers and makeup mirrors, all-female floors accessed by special keys or cards, improved lighting in parking lots and additional security measures are just some of the services now offered to meet the female traveler's needs. Areas such as open atrium lobbies and business floors with conference space have been added to provide female business travelers an alternative to meeting with male clients or associates in their rooms or a hotel bar. Hotel bars, too, have changed. Many have adopted an open format in lobby areas, making them more inviting for casual patronage and providing a more secure and relaxed setting for business contacts.

Figure 1.1 WHERE ASSOCIATION DELEGATES SPEND MONEY.

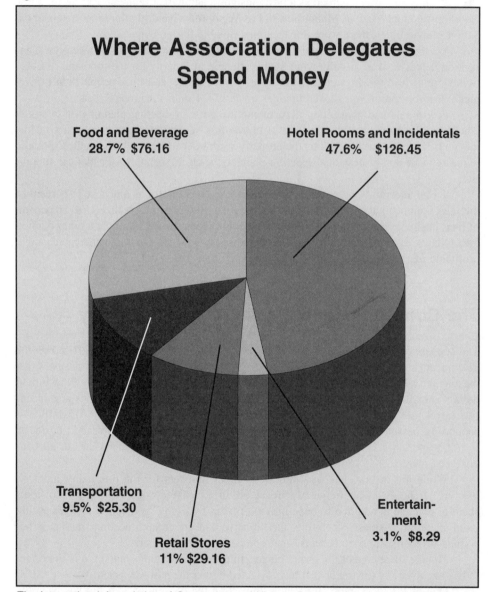

Where Association Delegates Spend Money

Food and Beverage
28.7% $76.16

Hotel Rooms and Incidentals
47.6% $126.45

Transportation
9.5% $25.30

**Entertain-
ment**
3.1% $8.29

Retail Stores
11% $29.16

The International Association of Convention and Visitors Bureaus determined that the average association meeting delegate spent approximately 266 dollars per day at national and international conventions. It is important to note that this survey includes only association delegates; corporate delegates can be expected to spend an additional twenty to thirty dollars per day more, as many are on expense accounts and usually entertain potential clients while attending meetings and conventions. **Source: Adapted from the International Association of Convention and Visitors Bureaus' Expenditure and Impact Survey (EXPACT). Used with permission.**

Figure 1.2 THE ECONOMIC IMPACT OF THE MEETINGS INDUSTRY.

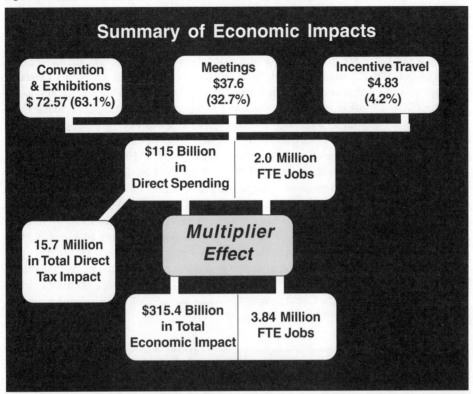

While direct spending from meetings totaled $115 billion, supporting 2 million full-time equivalent (FTE) jobs, the total impact of the meetings market business has an even larger, more far-reaching effect on the nation's economy. As a result of meetings and conventions, the demand for auxiliary goods and services also rose, generating a total of $315.4 billion, supporting 3.84 million FTE jobs.
Source: Updated from "The Economic Impact of Conventions, Expositions, Meetings & Incentive Travel Study", conducted by Deloitte & Touche for the Convention Industry Council (CIC).

No longer are conventions attended primarily by males. According to recent figures, as many as 39 percent of association meeting attendees and 35 percent of corporate meeting attendees are women. So today's accompanying spouses are often husbands instead of wives!

Meeting and convention attendees are also just as likely to be single as married, and are typically younger (25 to 40 years of age) and more affluent than convention delegates of two decades ago. But despite increased spending power, meetings are no longer attended primarily for fun; in most cases, meeting attendance must be considered worthwhile enough to justify the expense and time away from the office.

The economy has also played an important part in changing the meetings and convention market. For example, the previous 80 percent deduction for business meals and entertainment has been reduced to 50 percent, forcing meeting planners and convention delegates to "cut corners" and look for the best deals. This trend, in addition to deregulated airlines and increased competition for meetings and convention business in the hospitality industry, has resulted in increased negotiation for group transportation, discounted room rates, low- or no-cost meeting space and inclusive packages. Contracts for hotel services are now the norm, and many corporations and associations are signing multiple-meeting contracts. This trend not only provides a savings to the organization (contracts usually guarantee a percentage off the rack rate in exchange for multiple business), but also gives the advantage of having only one contract for multiple events.

Many hotel contracts are negotiated by meeting planners who, unlike the meeting planning clients of the past (who typically had little knowledge of the requirements for a successful meeting), are highly trained professionals. Twenty years ago, the Convention Industry Council (CIC) administered its first certification exam to just a handful of meeting planners who had taken its educational courses. Today, over 10,000 meeting professionals hold the CIC's Certified Meeting Professional designation, and additional courses and certifications are offered by a number of other organizations as well (see box titled "Meeting Industry Professional Certifications"). Certified Association Executives (CAE) are trained by the American Society of Association Executives (ASAE), while the International Association for Exhibition Management (IAEM) offers the Certified Exhibition Manager (CEM) program. Also, professional groups such as Meeting Professionals International (MPI), the Professional Convention Management Association (PCMA), and the Society of Incentive Travel Executives (SITE) have been formed—and joined in force by meeting planners—for additional training and networking. A Certified Meeting Manager (CMM) program, for example, is offered by Meeting Professionals International (MPI). This program, begun in Europe at the request of meeting planners who wanted a more comprehensive educational program, was recently approved for the U.S. Viewed as a graduate curriculum for meeting planners, the CMM program provides senior-level certification on a global scale.

MEETING INDUSTRY PROFESSIONAL CERTIFICATIONS

Certified Association Executive (CAE)
Certification program offered by the American Society of Association Executives. Certification designed to elevate professional standards, enhance individual performance and designate those who demonstrate knowledge essential to the practice of association management.

Certified Exhibition Manager (CEM)
An exhibition management professional, as officially designated by the International Association of Exhibition Management.

Certified Hospitality Sales Professional (CHSP)
A certification program offered by the American Hotel & Lodging Educational Institute.

Certified Hotel Administrator (CHA)
A certification program offered by the American Hotel & Lodging Educational Institute.

Certified Incentive Travel Executive (CITE)
A designation offered by the Society of Incentive & Travel Executives (SITE).

Certified Manager of Exhibits (CME)
An exhibit industry professional, as officially designated by the Trade Show Exhibitors Association.

Certified Meeting Professional (CMP)
Certification program offered by the Convention Industry Council. This designation certifies competency in 27 areas of meeting management through application and examination.

Certified Special Events Professional (CSEP)
Accredited designation offered by the International Special Event Society. This designation is earned for professional achievement in event management.

Certified Meeting Manager (CMM)
Managed by Meeting Professionals International, this certification is aimed at the more experienced meeting planner.

Destination Management Certified Professional (DMCP)
The Association of Destination Management Executives has developed a certification, modeled after the CMP, for its members.

Certified Hospitality Marketing Executive (CHME)
Certification program of the Hospitality Sales & Marketing Association International.

Certified Destination Management Executive (CDME)
Offered to senior level members of the International Association of Convention and Visitors Bureaus.

Certified Government Meeting Professional (CGMP)
A special designation given to planners of government events after a comprehensive education program. Includes most of the same modules that are in the CMP course, but with a government operations slant.

Increasingly, people within an industry seek to become "certified" or "licensed" in the skills of their profession. While certification is not essential, many meetings planners and suppliers recognize the importance of education, and take advantage of opportunities to improve their skills and update their knowledge through programs offered by their professional associations. The meetings industry is filled with an "alphabet soup" of certifications, many of which are earned at the association's regional conventions, at regional seminars or through courses offered over the Internet. Many of the industry leaders who have contributed to this text have completed one or more of the certification programs listed above.

The Scope of Today's Meetings Market

Despite rising costs for transportation and hospitality services, more and more meetings are being held. They are held for a variety of purposes: to keep abreast of today's ever-changing technology; to keep sales goals on track; to meet for group motivation and rewards; and many more. No longer are meetings limited to a few annual conventions that simply require a large ballroom for a general session and a few food functions or small business meetings where attendees are informed by a speaker armed only with a flip chart and a few marking pens. Today's attendees—and planners—expect a lot more. Hotel business centers that are complete with computers, fax machines and sophisticated communications equipment have become commonplace; state-of-the-art audiovisual equipment is expected; and many conventions have taken on the appearance of lavish productions—complete with exotic foods and decor—to attract attendees. Picture an event on the scale of a Broadway production with an anticipated run of just a week or even a few days, with a professional cast and production people, and the budget committed to accomplish a presentation on this level, and you then have an idea of the scope of many of today's meetings.

This boom is a far cry from the meetings picture following September 11, 2001. During the early 2000s, the meetings market suffered a dramatic slump, as people were hesitant to travel great distances, especially by air. During that time, properties were willing to make a number of concessions to attract meetings business.

In today's booming meetings market, however, the supply cannot keep pace with the demand. Beverly Kinkade, vice president and director of association sales for the Sheraton Corporation, says,

> "Small meetings are up, and so is training activity...Convention attendance is up in all industries...There is greater demand across the board."[2]

Now planners are seeing how economic cycles play a vital role in how hotels respond to group business. The greater demand, which is due in part to there having been virtually no growth in the upscale and luxury property category, has resulted in:

- tighter availability of rooms, especially at peak times
- stricter enforcement of cancellation and attrition penalties
- fewer concessions on food and beverage functions
- less flexibility in "comp" allotments; and
- tougher negotiations of other amenities

Bruce Harris, president of Conferon, the nation's largest independent meeting planning company, says,

> "When the economy got better, the pendulum switched to a sellers' marketplace. Prices went up, and the need to make concessions went down. Hotels are putting an end to some of the 'ridiculous' concessions, certain things they felt they had to do to book business despite the fact that they hurt their ability to be profitable."[3]

Although more convention hotels are being built, it is still a seller's market, and today's contracts and negotiation issues generally favor hotels. Planners continue to face higher rates, reduced flexibility with dates and stiffer penalties if they fail to fill space. But, the industry is highly cyclical, and a wise hotelier knows that business lost today may be business lost tomorrow, when it is needed. Hotels are looking to hold on to future group business by working with planners, often suggesting flexibility with dates; groups looking for value as well as availability, for example, are urged to consider off seasons rather than peak periods for their meetings.

You still face a great deal of competition in selling your site and facility for today's meeting. If you land a piece of business, you remain very much involved. You have a strong vested interest in the success of the convention. If it goes well and you gain the approval of the event sponsors and attendees, you stand a better chance of getting the repeat business and recommended business that is so very important in the career of anyone in the hospitality business. To successfully compete in the marketplace, it is important to know:

- the types of meetings held
- who plans and holds meetings
- the types of group planners with whom you'll deal, and
- the types of properties that can successfully accommodate different meeting groups

Types of Meetings

In the interest of simplicity, we will use the term *convention business*. But we are actually dealing with an entire spectrum of meetings of all types. It would be simpler if all events were just called *meetings*; after all, that's what they basically are. But that's not the way it is. There are a number of not-quite synonyms for the term, with nuances of difference.

Convention. The most commonly used term in the field is **convention**. The dictionary tells us that a convention is a meeting of delegates for action on particular matters. These may be matters of politics, trade, science, or technology, among others.

Today's convention usually involves a general session and supplementary smaller meetings. Conventions are produced both with and without exhibits. Most conventions have a repetitive cycle, the most common of which is annual. Giving market reports, introducing new products, and mapping of company strategy are some common objectives of a convention. The general session usually requires a ballroom or large auditorium for the whole group. Specific problems are discussed in smaller groups, using a number of small breakout rooms.

Conference. A *conference* is a near-synonym for a convention, usually implying much discussion and participation. The word convention is used in trade circles for regular meetings of a general nature. The term conference is used frequently in technical and scientific areas, although it is used in trade as well. The differences are those of semantics rather than execution. A conference program commonly deals with specific problems or developments and may or may not have smaller breakout meetings. Conferences may be small or large in attendance.

Congress. The term *congress* is most commonly used in Europe and in international events. It usually refers to an event similar to a conference in nature. Oddly enough, only in the United States is the term used to designate a legislative body. Attendance at a congress varies a great deal.

Forum. A meeting featuring much back-and-forth discussion, generally led by panelists or presenters, is often called a *forum*. Much audience participation is to be expected, with all sides of a question aired by both panelists and the audience. Two or more speakers might take opposing sides and address the audience rather than each other.

A moderator will summarize points of view and lead the discussion. The audience is usually allowed to ask questions, so a number of microphones must be supplied by the hotel.

Symposium. A *symposium* is similar to a forum, except that conduct seems to be more formal in a symposium. Whether by individuals or panels, the method is one of presentations. Some audience participation is anticipated, but there is generally less of the give-and-take that characterizes a forum.

Lecture. The *lecture* is even more formal or structured, using individual presentation, often by just one expert. It may or may not be followed by questions from the audience. Lectures vary widely in size.

Seminar. The *seminar* format tries to get away from the idea of a presenter or presenters addressing an audience from a platform. A seminar usually involves much participation, much give-and-take, a sharing of knowledge and experience by all. It usually is under the supervision of a discussion leader. This format obviously lends itself to relatively small groups; when such a meeting grows, it generally changes to a forum or symposium.

Workshop. The *workshop* format calls for general sessions involving only small groups that deal with specific problems or assignments. Whether or not the term is used, the workshop format is commonly used by training directors for skill training and drills. The participants actually train each other as they share new knowledge, skills, and insights into problems. Obviously, it is characterized by face-to-face dealing, with a great deal of participation by all.

Clinic. Used a great deal in training activity, the *clinic* offers drills and instruction in specific subjects. It is almost always limited to small groups interacting with each other on an individual basis.

Retreat. A *retreat* is usually a small meeting, typically in a remote location, for the purpose of bonding, intensive planning sessions, or simply to "get away from it all."

Institute. Conferences, seminars and workshops are often offered by an *institute*, which is frequently established within a trade or profession to offer extended educational and training opportunities. The term is often used to suggest further meetings on the same topic. For example, an institute might offer continuing training programs every quarter of the year.

Panel. The *panel* calls for two or more speakers offering viewpoints or areas of expertise. It is open for discussion among the panelists, as well as with the audience. A panel is always guided by a moderator and may be part of a larger meeting format.

Exhibitions and Trade Shows. An *exhibition* usually describes an event held in conjunction with another meeting, such as a convention. The exhibition format is used for display, usually by vendors of goods and services, and has a built-in audience since it is held as part of a convention (see Figure 1.3).

The term **trade show** is used to describe a show that is held for its own sake. In Europe such exhibits, generally held without any type of program, are called *trade fairs.*

Another term used interchangeably is *exposition.* Most industrial, professional, and scientific trade shows are not open to the public. When large scale exhibitions are open to the public, they are referred to as *consumer shows* (examples are home shows, flower and garden shows, auto shows and boat shows) and a modest admission fee is typically charged. Because consumer shows are designed to attract a local clientele, they do not generate a large amount of room revenue for community hotels.

But the trade show concept is often attractive to meeting planners, whose meeting costs can be defrayed by the revenues generated from exhibitors, who are charged for their booth or table space. And, the concept of a "marketplace" showcasing a vast array of new equipment, technology, and ideas often boosts delegate attendance. An interesting convention program coupled with the showcase of the trade show combines to form a strong

Figure 1.3. TRADE SHOW EXHIBITION.

This floor at the Las Vegas Hilton shows a typical trade show exhibit. The convention service manager and the meeting planner have created a master layout that the decorator follows to partition areas for each exhibitor. Such exhibits are of extreme importance to the financial well-being of the trade association.

magnet, drawing increased delegate attendance benefiting show organizer, exhibitor and attendee.

In the past few years, trade shows have increased in scope, with some—such as the Consumer Electronics Show (CES) or annual or bi-annual home builders shows – attracting thousands of attendees. This growth has resulted in a new industry substructure which includes trade show planning specialists, convention planning services, and auxiliary firms supplying trade show equipment and labor.

Persons and companies who sponsor and manage trade shows often hold membership in the International Association for Exhibition Management (IAEM). IAEM has over 3,000 members who plan nearly 5,000 shows and exhibitions annually.

Meetings. All the terms we've defined represent meetings of a sort. When none of the terms seems to apply, the event can always be called simply a *meeting*. This is particularly true when all the attendees are members of a single organization, meeting to discuss organizational affairs, such as stockholder meetings, board of directors meetings, etc. These can attract both a local and an out-of-town clientele, and range from a few attendees to large groups. It is important to understand these various differences in terminology in order to grasp the kind of event the client is trying to produce and to help the meeting planner to effectively carry it out. Much of it has to do with the projection of a desired image. While meeting descriptions are not scientific terms, but loose, often interchangeable ones, proper terminology can help people work together to achieve a tone or image for an event, and in that sense terms are important. For example, a *seminar* connotes something more cerebral than a *convention*. A *conference* in Chicago may be termed a *congress* in Geneva. A *conference* conjures up a picture of a small group in shirt-sleeves, while a *lecture* promises a more formal presentation to a passive audience. Accurate communication is needed in the convention business, and the ability to use proper terminology is important. Those in the field should understand the various terms used to describe meetings and use them correctly to achieve the professionalism expected by today's more sophisticated meeting planners.

Who Holds Meetings

Once you have determined that convention business, whatever the terminology, is worth going after, the next question deals with determining who holds meetings. Corporations and associations represent the two major types of meeting sponsors. But nonprofit organizations, such as governmental agencies, labor unions, and fraternal and religious organizations also hold conventions, meetings and trade shows. For convenience, we have broken today's convention business into three major categories:

- Corporations
- Associations
- Nonprofit organizations

Corporations. The corporate meeting is of extreme importance. Such meetings can be likened to an iceberg. A small tip protrudes above the surface while a huge mass floats beneath it. Companies have no need or desire to publicize their meetings, but meet they do. And often. They hold small meetings, large meetings, and middle-sized meetings. Business executives stress communications, and one of the most fundamental methods of intracompany communications is the meeting. Company meetings are a prime part of the market and growing rapidly.

Attending conventions and conferences is very definitely a part of professional and business activity. Such expenses as transportation, lodging, food, entertainment of clients, and registration fees are tax-deductible as business or professional expenses. Companies that stage meetings for dealers or their own staffs may deduct the cost of such events as business expenses. This has been a strong stimulant to meetings and conventions. It is also a strong factor in site selection, as those who attend look to such business trips as quasi-vacations.

Insurance companies are important to the hotel sales manager because they are such prolific meeting sponsors. There are continuing training programs for personnel. The prize, however, is the incentive trip for their top salespeople. These deluxe events are produced in various sizes and durations. Such trips are free to the attendee but are not planned exclusively for recognition and recreation. Most insurance companies schedule training and sales technique workshops in conjunction with such trips. Incentive trips are promoted a year in advance and therefore require more advanced planning. However, so many insurance company meetings are produced in such a variety of sizes and types that the insurance company meeting planner is a prime contact for hotels from the large property to the small inn.

Associations. The most visible convention organizers are the many associations throughout the country—indeed throughout the world because many of them are truly international. Associations vary in size and nature. Their scope ranges from small regional organizations through statewide associations to national and international ones. Perhaps the best-known group to hotel sales managers is the American Society of Association Executives (ASAE). This group's membership consists of key decision makers who play major roles in the selection of cities and hotels for their own associations' conventions. Associations can be divided into several general categories:

- Trade associations
- Professional and scientific associations
- Technical societies

Trade Associations. Trade associations are usually considered the most lucrative form of meeting business because their members are composed mostly of executives who have made it in business. Such conventions are often held in conjunction with exhibits.

A good example of such a group in the hospitality industry is the National Restaurant Association, which meets annually in Chicago with more than 110,000 in attendance. Big industrial suppliers of kitchen equipment and restaurant supplies do a great amount of entertaining during the convention.

It is a rare trade that doesn't have at least one association. Many have several national ones, involving different levels of the trade. It is common for the manufacturers in a trade to have their own association; the wholesalers and distributors to have theirs; and the retailers, still a third.

The photographic industry shows this pattern. There is the Photographic Marketing Association, whose members are retailers and photofinishers. They hold an annual convention of national status followed by a regional one six months later. The National Association of Photographic Manufacturers is a smaller group made up exclusively of domestic manufacturers. Its members meet once a year, while its boards and committees meet more frequently. The Photographic Manufacturers and Distributors Association has the broader membership base made up of foreign and domestic companies. In addition, there are a number of regional associations of independent camera dealers that hold regional exhibits and meetings. All of these organizations are trade associations.

Professional and Scientific Associations. The numerous associations in the professional and scientific fields are also inveterate meeting holders. Their subject matter ranges far and wide, but they all share a love for meetings. Each profession has its national association as well as state chapters.

The American Medical Association and the American Bar Association are well known to almost everyone. The Hospitality Sales Marketing Association International (HSMAI) is a good example in the hospitality industry, meeting annually for a major get-together and holding a number of regional and state workshops throughout the year.

Technical Societies. Associations also are found among technical professions. The Society of Motion Picture and Television Engineers holds two national conventions a year. The Professional Photographers of America holds a national event annually, and most states have chapters that hold annual conventions of their own. In addition, there are specialty groups such as wedding photographers and newspaper photographers that have their own associations and conventions. Think of any profession or career and you'll find at least one association. Librarians, teachers, hospital administrators, engineers—all have associations.

Nonprofit Organizations. There are many nonprofit organizations that just don't fit into the above slots, but they take no back seat when it comes to meetings. We have all seen political conventions on television. The camera shows the main floor, but think of the demand for smaller meeting rooms, suites, food functions, and so on. The story is repeated on a more modest scale on the state and regional level. All add to the market.

Hotels house weekend seminars on sex and marital problems, women's roles in the world, and social problems, to mention a few. The meetings of nonprofit organizations are just like those of other associations, and should be sold and serviced just like them.

Government Agencies. Many branches of the government have a need to hold meetings off government premises for government employees or with the public. The Department of Agriculture, the Department of Commerce, the World Health Organization, and the United Nations affiliates are prolific meeting planners.

These agencies are funded in a variety of ways. Chambers of Commerce are usually membership organizations that are privately funded. The Department of Agriculture, of course, spends public money. The labels are not important so long as you understand how they operate, what their meeting needs are, and how you can sell and serve them efficiently.

(A word may be in order here. There is a love for acronyms among associations and governmental agencies that can drive the outsider up the wall. Each association seems to feel that the world is focused on it and that everyone knows what XYZ stands for. It also leads to crossed lines. Take AMA. It can refer to the American Medical Association or the American Management Association, both prolific meeting holders. It takes a bit of caution. Listen carefully and take good notes. Take nothing out of context. Soon, you'll talk in acronyms, too.)

Labor Unions. Labor unions have become one of the most important economic forces in the world. The largest unions are in the construction, manufacturing, mining, and transportation fields.

Labor unions are organized on four levels: local, state and regional, national, and international. Each level represents countless meetings and conventions, providing a fertile market for hotels. Most union members spend slightly less than the average convention delegate, but they still provide hotels with a sizable piece of business.

Large labor union conventions are similar to political conventions. They are held annually or biannually and include committee meetings, debates, speeches, and guest speakers.

SMERF Groups. The industry has coined an acronym for certain nonprofits—the term SMERF (which stands for social, military, educational, religious and fraternal) has come to represent a major market segment for many properties because of the large number of room nights these groups occupy each year—largely during property slack times.

SMERF groups have three common characteristics: they are very price sensitive; they are more likely to book meetings during the hotel's off-season; they very often have nonprofessional planners who change from year to year.

Religious groups, for example, are not traditionally big spenders, but they are a viable market. Denominations hold regional and national meetings as well as seminars and ministerial workshops. Their events frequently begin on Monday and close on Thursday, providing weekend resort properties with midweek business.

Educational associations, too, are typically price sensitive, but they can be prime sources of business. Educational groups not only hold a number of national meetings, but every state has at least one teachers' association as well. In addition, educational business is particularly attractive to hotels as these groups frequently meet during the slow summer months.

Veterans' groups and military associations can also be good business, especially for resorts. Many of these groups have large annual conventions as well as both large and small reunions, and attendees may be bigger spenders than those in other SMERF groups.

14

Although "big spenders" are not the norm (attendees tend to double and triple up in rooms, eat most meals off-property, and spend little money in lounges), SMERF groups are proving to be increasingly important for properties.

Barbara McDonald, national account manager for Sheraton Corporation's Chicago sales office says:

> "SMERF business used to be the lowest rated business. The perception has been that these meetings are groups like fraternity chapters coming to have a beer brawl in your hotel, and that's just not so. The SMERF market is just as important as the corporate and other markets because the SMERF groups fill our down time. It's that simple. Also, small SMERF business can lead to much larger business. If a CEO comes in with his fraternity and likes the hotel, you could have just landed another piece of business."[4]

According to Warren Breaux, assistant vice president of national sales for Hyatt Hotels Corporation:

> "Hotels must have at least 70 percent occupancy to get a return on the investment of building the property. The four-and-a-half months worth of weekends, holidays, and seasonally distressed times are very difficult to fill, but this is a market that can help fill it. We would certainly rather fill our rooms at a reasonable, yet lower, rate than let these rooms go vacant. But we can't use that philosophy 365 days a year."[5]

SMERF groups do not follow a normal business schedule, and shop for the best rates, but they provide an excellent source of revenue during slack times. A property that can offer discount rates—and is willing to assist the largely nonprofessional meeting planners—can find that SMERF groups may make a considerable impact on the property's revenues.

Types of Group Customers

Since group meetings customers represent so many different types of organizations, from trade and professional associations to corporations and businesses to SMERF groups, you will likely work with different types of meeting planners with varying degrees of expertise. Meeting planners fall into four basic groups:

Full-time meeting planners. Large national associations and corporations that look to convention revenues to financially support their organizations are most likely to staff full-time, professional meeting planners. These planners know exactly what is required to stage a successful event and will be thorough and timely in presenting information and instructions to the hotel.

Single event or part-time planners. These meeting planners typically work for smaller companies or associations that do not have enough meeting activity to warrant a full-time meeting planner. The experience of these planners will vary; some will have little or no knowledge of the mechanics of running a meeting and will look to your hotel for assistance. It will be necessary to provide these planners with a timetable of the hotel's needs and deadlines and to assure them of your commitment to helping them stage a successful event. Other part-time planners have extensive knowledge of the meetings process. It is important, therefore, to ascertain the planner's knowledge and experience and to respond accordingly.

Committees. Many associations, fraternal and nonprofit groups have committees that are involved in initial suggestions for meetings, screening of meeting sites and the actual planning of meetings. As with single event or part-time planners, the experience of committee members may vary and the hotel may be faced with multiple or conflicting decisions. You can minimize potential problems by suggesting that one person be put in charge and by offering your hotel's expertise in helping to make decisions.

Third-party planners. An increasing number of meetings are being booked by third parties, such as meeting management firms, association management companies and travel agents. If this is the case, you will be dealing with an intermediary, not directly with the company or association holding the meeting. Most of these third parties are experienced planners, but there may be cases in which you will need to assist the intermediary in making decisions about the event. If problems arise, you should first deal directly with the intermediary; you must use discretion regarding contacting the group that the intermediary represents, only going to the group after exhausting all other avenues (and thoroughly documenting your attempts to resolve problems).

While the above profiles will help you to determine how much assistance might be needed from the hotel, each group and each planner is different. All meeting planners, regardless of their level of expertise, expect you to get to know them, their group and the purpose of their meetings so that you can best meet their needs.

Types of Meeting Facilities

When the term "meeting site" is mentioned, hotels and resorts typically come to mind (downtown, suburban and resort hotels host about 70 percent of all meetings). But hotels encompass a wide variety of choices. There are resort hotels, downtown hotels, suburban hotels, airport hotels and large motels and motor hotels, and some are better suited for holding varying types of meetings. Airport hotels, for example, are excellent choices when the planner needs to get attendees to a central, convenient location (see Figure 1.4), and these hotels may be an excellent choice for one-day or overnight meetings. Resorts, which are often the choice for annual conventions and incentive trips, offer a respite from the work world and appeal to attendees with families. But there are now a number of alternatives to "traditional" hotel and resort venues.

Planners who wish to book into a hotel can now opt for all-suite or boutique hotels or book their meetings into other, "nontraditional" venues, such as conference centers, cruise ships and college campuses. In this section, we will take a look at some of these alternatives and see how they are impacting the hotel industry.

All-Suite Hotels. All-suite hotels were originally positioned to attract two market segments: business travelers who wanted "more than a room" and the relocation market. All-suite hotels, with their separate living rooms, complimentary "perks" such as breakfasts and cocktail hours, and homey atmospheres serve as "temporary residences," and are espe-

Figure 1.4. AIRPORT HOTELS.

Boardrooms for 10, banquets for 1000 & airport convenience for everyone.

Equidistance to both coasts, walking distance to Denver's Stapleton Airport & complimentary airport transporation combine to make The Registry Hotel a smart choice for savvy meeting planners. And it's Registry's superb Convention Services Staff & versatile, professional approach to meetings, banquets and receptions that keep them returning. Plus, 25 luxurious meeting rooms totaling 26,000 sq. ft., including our stunning 9,700 sq. ft. ballroom. At Registry, we aim to please all the people all the time.

The **REGISTRY** *Hotel*

Denver, Colorado at Stapleton Airport
303-321-3333

Airport hotels are often chosen for one-day or overnight meetings. While some airport hotels offered limited meeting space in the past, most, such as The Registry Hotel near Denver's Stapleton Airport, have expanded their meeting facilities, making them more attractive to groups. This hotel is within walking distance to the airport; some airport hotels are actually part of the airport complex.
Courtesy of The Registry Hotel. Used with permission.

cially attractive because their features are available at rates competitive with standard hotel rooms. But many meeting planners are attracted by the features offered by all-suite hotels.

First, all-suite hotels are ideal for board meetings and small training sessions as each suite can serve as a small breakout room, and the atmosphere is conducive to conducting both business and personal conversations. Second, all-suite hotels solicit the smaller markets that are virtually ignored by the larger properties; larger properties are often perceived to be more interested in serving groups of 200 or more, while groups of 50 or less seemed to get far less of the hotel staff's attention. Third, the worries about room assignments are eliminated—every attendee is offered a suite and therefore receives VIP treatment. In addition, meeting planners of small, regional meetings find that attendees are willing to pay for the perceived value of a suite over a conventional hotel room.

Many chains are targeting the small meetings market by developing all-suite properties. Embassy Suites, a forerunner in the development of all-suites properties, has formed a national group and meeting planning service department and offers a toll-free number to planners arranging meetings for groups of 300 or less (see Figure 1.5). Marriott also offers all-suite properties (with approximately 3,000 sq. ft. of meeting space) to accommodate groups of 300 or less to attract small corporate meetings.

Conference Centers. **Conference centers**, which are typically designed to accommodate meetings of between 20-300 people and generally host groups averaging 35 attendees, differ from hotels in several ways. First, the *design* of conference centers typically differs from meeting facilities offered by hotels and resorts. Meeting rooms are situated away from high traffic areas to minimize distractions, and offer conveniently located

Figure 1.5. ALL-SUITE HOTELS.

This advertisement promotes the benefits of Embassy Suites to meeting planners. Once simply characterized as offering two-room suites and a free breakfast, all-suite hotels have expanded to meet the needs of meeting planners. Embassy Suites, for example, promotes its fully equipped meeting rooms, conference suite, and the attention of its staff to both large and small meetings.

breakout areas that are constantly refreshed. Since many conference sessions run for several hours, meeting rooms are designed for endurance and comfort and are equipped with commonly used audiovisual equipment (see Figure 1.6).

Most conference centers, since they are geared toward meetings and study, offer guestrooms that provide extra work and study space, and their onsite facilities may include

Figure 1.6. MARKETING A CONFERENCE CENTER TO THE MEETINGS MARKET.

This advertisement for Canada's Deerhurst Resort, billed as "One of Canada's Premier Conference Resorts," highlights the special meetings amenities offered by the facility. Unlike hotels, which must keep function space flexible, conference centers are dedicated to meetings, and can offer 24-hour holds on meeting rooms and focus on the special needs of meeting planners, such as the PC hookups and cork strips for hanging visual aids mentioned in this ad.

small offices, libraries and computer centers. Even the dining rooms are designed to facilitate small group interaction. Most feature half walls, large plants and other decor that offer privacy. And, to provide for greater flexibility, most offer buffet meals rather than set menus.

Conference centers also differ from hotels in terms of *pricing policy*. Most conference centers offer their own version of the *Full American Plan*, a *package* price, available either per day or per person, that includes rooms, meals, breaks, meetings rooms, audiovisual equipment and other needs. This "one-stop shopping" for a **complete meeting package** eliminates unexpected charges and is considered a real value by many meeting planners.

Planners also appreciate that conference center *bookings* can be made on a 24-hour basis. Therefore, if a meeting runs longer than expected, the group doesn't have to be concerned about incurring additional, often exorbitant, rental costs or having to vacate to accommodate another group.

Today, the largest independent conference centers are Dolce International (see "Best Practices" box), which operates conference center resorts in the United States, Canada and France, and Benchmark Hospitality. But many hotels have also gotten into the conference center business. Both the Hilton and Marriott chains are active in the conference center market.

The International Association of Conference Centers (IACC) was founded to assist properties in targeting the conference center market. IACC members include conference centers and related firms and suppliers. To qualify for membership in the IACC, a property must derive a minimum of 60 percent of its business from meeting-related activities and must offer a "total and balanced meeting environment."

Other types of facilities chosen by meeting planners may include boutique hotels, condominium resorts, convention centers, cruise ships and college and university facilities. Cruise ships, for example, can be a popular choice for incentive meetings, and, as with conference centers, the cost of meals is included in the fee. The Radisson chain launched the *Radisson Diamond*, a ship designed solely to handle the group market, in 1992. While it merged with Seven Seas Cruises in 1995 and is no longer devoted strictly to the meetings market, meetings still account for about a third of the ship's business.

Meeting planners with limited budgets can opt for holding meetings at college and university campuses. While facilities, equipment and such features as dining options and recreational amenities may vary, these settings can provide a casual, focused atmosphere.

Today's meeting sites offer a wide variety of choices, advantages and disadvantages. No matter what type of facility is selected by the meeting planner, however, the principles outlined in this text can be applied to all venues.

Best Practices

Dolce International: Managing Conference Centers

Dolce International, which owns and manages 20 conference centers in the United States, Canada and Europe, differentiated itself from its growing competition by offering more products and services while still helping clients to save money. To do so, the company introduced Dolce Conference Solutions, which broadens the firm's services to include transportation and other amenities, such as in-room gift items.

The firm teamed with three travel partners, American Airlines, Avis and Empire International (a ground transportation operator), to enable it to offer significant discounts on airfare, rental cars and ground transportation as well as such services as one point of contact within 30 minutes and one integrated proposal within one business day.

This "one-stop shopping" approach, which was launched with a direct mail campaign, a press release, a brochure and on the company's website, proved popular from the start, with 103 of 280 visitors to the website asking for Conference Solutions elements.

Source: Harvey Chipkin, "Success Stories That Inspire," HSMAI Marketing Review, Spring 2002, p. 11.

Trends in the Meeting Industry

The expanding convention business has been—and will continue to be—impacted by a number of recent trends. Properties and managers who wish to continue to successfully compete for the meetings dollar should be aware of the impact of the following trends.

Globalization

The unprecedented events of the past two decades—the breakup of the former Soviet Union, the opening of trade in European bloc countries, the passage of the North American Free Trade Agreement, and the establishment of the European Economic Community, to name just a few—opened up a vast new market for the convention industry. Potential business was no longer limited to 240 million Americans, but a global village of five billion people with growing economies. **Globalization** has impacted the convention industry in two significant ways.

First, despite a generally sluggish economy, the lifting of restrictions ushered in a boom in world tourism and business travel, increasing attendance at more meetings and conventions at domestic properties.

Second, the economy was ripe for foreign hospitality interests to buy domestic properties.This means there is additional competition for both foreign and domestic convention business, resulting in the need for more creative marketing on the part of domestic properties to attract international business—and keep domestic meetings and conventions.

Second-Tier Cities

As costs for hotel rooms and transportation continue to rise in many major cities, budget conscious meeting planners search for more economical sites. Milwaukee, Wisconsin; Birmingham, Alabama; and Charlotte, North Carolina, are just a few examples of what has become known in the industry as **second-tier cities**.

Meeting planners who face the challenge of "selling" attendees on these seemingly less exotic locations usually find attractive incentives. In Charleston, West Virginia, for example, delegates can go white water rafting or take a cruise on the *West Virginia Belle* during their free time—activities that cannot be enjoyed in Chicago or New York. Attendees for the most part have responded favorably to these diverse activities, and have also noted the friendliness of the people living in second-tier cities. And, all of this is usually enjoyed at a much lower cost than attendees would pay to meet in a larger city.

In addition to lower room rates—and often lower transportation expenses—second-tier cities often offer better service. Besides being enthusiastic about new business, and "rolling out the red carpet," hotels in many second-tier cities often focus on one meeting at a time.

The growth in the choice of second-tier cities has led to the building of convention centers in many of these cities to better serve smaller association and corporate business meetings with larger facilities and up-to-date communications and audiovisual equipment.

The Growth of Convention Centers

The nation's exhibit and meeting space has doubled over the past ten years, largely due to new or expanded convention centers. First-tier cities, including Chicago, Atlanta, Orlando, San Diego, Las Vegas and Los Angeles, have expanded or built additional, modernized facilities. Second-tier cities, such as Mobile, Alabama; Providence, Rhode Island; and suburbs of New York, New Orleans and Atlanta have also built new centers to attract state and regional groups and national groups with local connections.

Most convention centers are publicly owned and are supported by taxes on hotel rooms. Known as hotel occupancy, room or bed taxes, these fees vary considerably. High room taxes are often a factor in site selection, and can price a city out of a planner's budget.

Other convention facilities are privately owned. The Sands Expo and Convention Center in Las Vegas, for example, is the largest privately owned facility in the nation. It already boosts over 1,900,000 square feet of exhibit space and 125 meeting rooms, and additional expansion is planned.

There are, of course, differences in how public and private convention centers operate and how they solicit and service business (see Figure 1.7). This has changed dramatically over the past few years with the increase of convention centers. The overbuilding of convention centers has resulted in some centers resorting to provide cash or other incentives to book business. In Atlanta, for example, the Georgia World Congress Center opened its $282 million expansion in 2003. Although the new, expanded facility was expected to be a gold mine for the city's convention business, the city is now resorting to compensating some groups to rent its space. When the National Association of Home Builders, the city's biggest convention, cancelled shows planned for 2007 and 2008, the city offered the group $2 million to keep its 100,000 plus members coming to Atlanta; the group's leaders decided that $10 million would have been a more realistic number.

Still, despite increased competition, convention centers are attractive to large groups that need extensive exhibit space, and hotels can share in the business that convention centers bring in by working with these facilities to provide products and services from hotel rooms to catered events. In Chapter 7, we will discuss how hotel sales people can effectively work with convention centers to maximize hotel revenues.

Third-Party Meeting Planners

Today, it is not always easy to identify the meeting decision maker. While hotel salespeople formerly dealt almost exclusively with corporate and association meeting planners, third-party planners (either independents or meeting management firms) are becoming more prevalent in the industry.

Corporate downsizing, the increased complexity of negotiations in a seller's market, and increased use of Internet technology has many organizations looking *outside* their staffs for meeting planning services. Since these intermediaries are hired "out-of-house," a new industry buzzword— *outsourcing*—has been coined. Corporations typically outsource to such intermediaries as travel agents, destination management companies and incentive travel houses. Associations and nonprofits generally look to meeting management companies or association management companies to assist them with their meeting needs. Therefore, as a hospitality salesperson, your customers will not only be association or corporate executives, but also the meeting management firms that represent them.

Despite the growing number of third-party planners, these intermediaries differ greatly in services and expertise. Some offer only assistance in site selection. Others assist with contract negotiation, on-site logistics and special event management. Still others provide complete management for the association or corporation. Most important to hotel properties, these third-party planners act as liaisons, bringing their clients' needs for sleeping rooms, food and beverage and meeting facilities to hotels. Jeff Heckard, with the Westin Innsbrook Resort in Palm Harbor, Florida, says:

> "Our hotel books a lot of business from third-party planners located all over the U.S.: corporate, association, SMERF and non-profits."[6]

Figure 1.7. MARKETING A CONVENTION CENTER TO MEETING PLANNERS.

Aren't they a *perfect* couple?

With the combined resources of 364 premiere hotel rooms, meeting space to accommodate 10 to 9,000 people, a 20,000 square foot ballroom, and a 2,400 car parking garage, The Rhode Island Convention Center Complex featuring The Westin Hotel Providence (which recently enjoyed a $10,000,000 renovation) is a match made in 'meetings heaven'. For added convenience, the two facilities are connected by a covered walkway so you never have to step outside, and we're ten minutes from a major airport.

The Rhode Island Convention Center has won the Prime Site Award from Facilities Magazine nine years running, while the Westin Hotel has won the Successful Meetings' Pinnacle Award for 2003, is the only Providence hotel to receive a AAA Four Diamond Rating, and has won a coveted spot on the 2003 Condé Nast Traveler Gold List.

Call to find out more about this perfect combination.

THE RHODE ISLAND CONVENTION CENTER
An SMG Managed Facility

THE WESTIN
PROVIDENCE

For information call John McGinn at 401.458.6001 or Sheila Westerfield at 401.598.8245, or visit our websites: **www.riconvention.com** or **www.westin.com**

To make convention centers a more attractive choice for meeting planners, many are attached to an "anchor" hotel. This ad for The Rhode Island Convention Center and The Westin Providence promotes the combined resources of the two entities. And, as is the case with convention centers/anchor hotels in other cities, such as Minneapolis, the two facilities are connected by a covered walkway, ensuring accessibility even in inclement weather.

Third-party planners can be broken down into several categories:

- Meeting Management Firms
- Association Management Companies
- Destination Management Companies
- Incentive Travel Houses
- Travel Agents

Meeting management firms. *Meeting management firms* are private contractors (companies or individuals) who provide planning services directly to a client. Increasingly, planners are leaving their associations and corporations to set up shop as independents. Such planners are generally easy to work with because they are experienced. They function as intermediaries, and are paid a fee, which can vary. Some independent meeting planners simply assist corporate in-house meeting planners; others are responsible for the entire execution of the meeting. Interestingly, these companies often employ former hotel salespeople who know how to negotiate with hotels.

The largest of the meeting management companies are Conferon, Maritz McGettigan and HelmsBriscoe. To demonstrate the importance of meeting management firms, Conferon (and the clients it represents) were the largest single group customer of Starwood, Hyatt, Marriott and Radisson hotels last year. These companies often team up with similar businesses (especially Internet companies) to offer a more comprehensive package of planning, housing, and reservations. Conferon, for example, has licensed the technology of Passkey.com, a large housing company that is replacing many convention and visitor center housing bureaus, to enable them to more easily interface with the hotel community.

Meeting management companies search out hotel sites and aid their clients in conducting meeting programs (the sidebar titled "Delegating Tasks" illustrates the services most often offered to meeting groups by third-party planners). These third-party planners make their money by charging a flat fee to the meeting organization or by seeking a commission from the hotel.

In years past, many hotels agreed to pay commissions to meeting management firms. In today's sellers' market, hotels are reluctant to pay commissions to these third parties, but will do so during slow periods when business is needed.

Delegating Tasks

WHAT SERVICES DO THIRD-PARTY PLANNERS PROVIDE FOR YOUR ORGANIZATION?

Facility research and selection	51%
Planning entertainment, social and sports functions	51%
Negotiating with facilities	50%
On-site staffing	49%
Destination research and selection	48%
Transportation arrangements	40%
Vendor research and subcontracting	28%
Trade-show planning	19%
Planning incentive travel programs	13%
Negotiating with airlines	8%

Source: M&C Research survey of 430 meeting planners; reprinted in Meetings & Conventions, April 2005, p. 28.

Association management companies. *Association management companies* work for smaller associations that do not employ a full time professional staff. In most cases, employees of these firms work through the board of directors of associations to manage meetings and plan conventions and other activities. Often these firms provide management services for two or more associations.

SmithBucklin and Associates, the largest of the association management firms, manages the affairs, including annual meetings, for several meeting and event organizations. Recently, the Insurance Conference Planners Association (ICPA) shut down its Vancouver, British Columbia office and became a SmithBucklin client. The ICPA joins the Center for Exhibition Industry Research (CEIR), a source for trade show statistics and education, and the Society of Incentive and Travel Executives (SITE), both of which have also turned over their management to SmithBucklin.

Destination management companies. These firms offer convention and meeting services at the host city. **Destination management companies** may arrange for room accommodations, restaurant reservations, airport shuttle service, entertainment, technical services (teleconferences, audiovisual presentations, etc.), and special programs for attendees and spouses.

Most destination management companies remain "behind the scenes," assisting the meeting planner with the details of the meeting. This type of firm knows the host city, and can provide in-depth information on the destination, both in terms of suppliers and extra convention activities (special sight-seeing tours, etc.). In Europe, a destination management company is generally called a **professional congress organizer.**

The Growth of the Destination Management Industry

Karen Gorden
President, Activity Planners

After air travel allowed greater numbers of participants to attend conventions at a national level, Ground Operators began offering transportation and later "Ladies Programs" for the wives of attendees...Ground Operators later added special events and themed parties to their list of services...As the role of these "local experts" grew, the industry began referring to them as Destination Management Companies, and these DMCs continued to expand their role in the meeting, convention and travel industry...As corporate meetings and retreats became more common, many DMCs added additional services, such as motivational speakers, educational seminars, and personalized merchandise and gift items, making them a "one-stop shop" for meeting planning...Since the role of DMCs is to keep their city "fresh" in the eyes of repeat visitors, DMCs continually updated their services and style and, recognizing a need for regulation and standardization, created the Association of Destination Management Executives (ADME) in June 1995. The non-profit, non-partisan, international trade association defines DMCs as "Professional services companies possessing extensive local knowledge, expertise, and resources, specializing in the design and implementation of events, activities, tours, transportation and group logistics."...The growth from Ground Operator to Destination Management Company in just over 30 years is only the beginning. With developments in technology, such as the World Wide Web, the average traveler is more educated than ever before, making the job of the DMC a continuous challenge to keep abreast of the ever-changing demands of the marketplace.

Incentive travel houses. *Incentive travel houses* deal directly with arranging incentive travel packages for corporations wishing to reward or motivate their staffs or their customers. These packages are usually "first class," and involve an exotic or popular resort location. They typically include a number of "perks" and special amenities not commonly associated with regular hotel and travel packages. Chapter 6 provides an extensive discussion of the workings of the incentive travel market and the role incentive travel houses play in this segment of the meetings market.

Travel agents. Some travel agents have expanded their traditional role of selling package tours, transportation and guestroom services to offer meeting planning services to corporate accounts. Mega travel agencies, such as BTI America (with 100 meeting planners), McGettigan Partners (150 planners in three offices) and American Express (48 planners) plan everything from board meetings to trade shows.

This transition came naturally, as travel agents were able to keep abreast of changing airline price structures and routes, and many corporate meeting planners are now turning to travel agents to arrange everything from transportation to rooms to meeting space. Since not all travel agents are experienced in meeting planning, corporate clients must carefully select those who have this expertise, and properties may have to work more closely with those who are just learning the meetings field. This association can prove extremely profitable, however, both in terms of meetings business and other individual and group bookings at the property.

A highly controversial subject between hotels and travel agents is the question of commissions on convention business. Generally, a hotel will pay a commission of approximately 10 percent to an agent who books an *independent* or *tour guest* into the hotel. However, *convention rates* are usually quoted *net* and not commissionable further. What this means is that the hotel will not pay a commission to a travel agent for booking a convention delegate.

Increased Use of Technology

New advances in computer, telephone and video technology have radically changed the ways hotels do business and communicate with clients. This new technology includes:

- The Internet
- Fax capability, including Broadcast fax and fax-on-demand
- E-mail
- Video Conferencing
- In-room Technology
- Bar Coding

Internet. Leading this trend is an increasing use of *the Internet,* a worldwide system of computer networks providing easy access to thousands of "pipelines" of database information. The Internet is being used by properties, meeting planners and other property business sources.

Meeting planners now use the Internet to search for properties that meet their requirements, "tour" properties, and even auction their event for the best price. At Plansoft.com, for example, meeting planners can search a database of more than 14,000 meeting venues and then forward a RFP (request for proposal) to the desired property. Other sites offering searchable databases can be found at the end of this chapter. Some sites offer meeting facilities only, while others offer direct access to other service providers, such as transportation companies and other key suppliers.

While many meeting planners still rely on site visits to make a final decision, an increasing number are viewing properties through the "virtual tours" offered on hotel web sites. These tours, which vary in their degree of sophistication, are replacing brochures

Meeting Planner Profile

Today's meeting planners spend thousands of hours a year planning events from simple training meetings to huge conventions involving thousands of participants and hundreds of exhibitors. It is an exciting and varied career, and one which is constantly evolving. So who is the "typical" meeting planner of today?

According to a survey conducted by *Meetings & Conventions* magazine, today's professional meeting planner fits the following profile:

- Female (62% versus 38% male)
- Works in a department with a dozen other people
- Has been at the same job for nine years
- Earns $55,000 a year (salaries range from $25,000 to $100,000 or more; (50% of all meeting planners make $30,000 to $59,999)

Duties typically include: budgeting; site selection; negotiating with hotels, airlines and vendors; program planning; trade show and exhibit planning; food and beverage selection; hotel and ground transportation arrangements; and post-meeting evaluation, including surveys of participants and an evaluation of the facility and service provided at each function.

In order to stay on top of market conditions, most belong to one or more professional associations, and find the following skills most useful for their profession: excellent oral and written communication and organizational skills; leadership qualities; flexibility; and the ability to handle pressure.

Joan Eisenstodt, a meeting manager with over 30 years of experience, suggests that you ask yourself the following questions to determine if you have what it takes to become a successful meetings professional:

- Do you like to plan parties, work schedules, your day, and so forth?
- Do you have a date book or personal digital assistant (PDA) that you update regularly and that includes everything you need to do for weeks or months in the future?
- Do you like to organize your bedroom, car, workplace, and so on? Is your idea of fun organizing a closet for someone?
- Are you very organized, almost to the point of obsession?

(including video brochures) and even CD-ROMs as an effective way to present a property. If the planner likes what he or she sees, it only takes the click of a mouse to contact the hotel for additional information or a RFP.

One of the newest Internet applications is auctioning meetings. StarCite Inc. offers auctions in which hotels bid on business descibed by planners during a 15-minute on-line auction. At the end of the auction, the planner can select a hotel from among the bidders or the lowest bid wins (the outcome depends on the auction's format). StarCite reported that in their auctions participating meeting planners could save an average of 10-32 percent over opening bids -- which opened 25-40 percent below current market prices.

Hotels are also using the Internet to create a presence for their properties, link to other sources of meeting planning business, and conduct market research. Hotel chains use corporate web sites to link their properties; a meeting planner can log on to the corporate site and call up a number of locations. But even small properties, realizing that they are now advertising to a global market, are developing web sites.

In addition to the value of having an individual presence on the Web, many hospitality properties are benefiting from alliances with other entities that service the meetings market. Hotels can be featured on or linked to web sites hosted by their destination cities, their local convention and visitors bureau, or other firms and organizations that offer services to the meetings industry, such as Expedia (expedia.com). A detailed discussion on how the Internet is used to market properties will be presented in Chapter 8.

Last, but certainly not least, the Internet can be used as a powerful research tool. Hotels can use the Internet to research their competition, their target markets, and current economic trends that impact business. Logging on to a competitor's web site provides a wealth of information on its facilities and ability to service meetings. Accessing a particular corporation or association can yield contact information and pertinent facts about meeting history. As an added benefit, the Internet can provide the names of businesses and associations that were not even previously considered by the property.

To keep pace with the changes brought about by technology, today's hotel salespeople are expected to be computer literate. Not only will they be using the Internet for research and bookings, they will most likely use computerized applications for most aspects of the sales and service process (see Chapter 3).

Fax capability, including Broadcast Fax and Fax-on-Demand. While some thought *fax transmissions* would become obsolete due to the popularity of e-mail, fax is still a powerful tool for communicating with meeting planners. *Broadcast fax* is used to send updates on the property and other announcements to meeting planners at regular intervals. *Fax-on-demand* provides a source for meeting planners for meeting room specs, open dates, banquet menus and other meeting-related information by simply dialing a property's fax number. Fax is still an easy and fast way to transmit an existing document.

E-mail. *E-mail* (electronic mail) is becoming increasingly popular for communicating both inter-office and inter-property and with meeting planners and other possible sources of business. The advantage of e-mail over fax (which is simply a copy of a document) is that e-mail can be edited; a meeting planner can be e-mailed a copy of a contract, for example, edit it and return it to the hotel with a minimum of effort. Further information on applications of both fax and e-mail will be presented in Chapters 3 and 8.

Video conferencing. *Video conferencing*, also called *teleconferencing*, has been in use for some time, using satellites to link groups and speakers. New technology has greatly enhanced transmission quality and sound, and has led to other improvements, including multimedia presentations, video-enhanced speakers, instant replay, and "live projection" (projecting a close-up image of the speaker onto a large video screen to bring him or her "closer" to the audience). Additional information on audiovisual technology is provided in Chapter 15.

In-room technology. *In-room technology* already includes the availability of fax machines, voice mail services and computer hookups in guestrooms. Some hotels offer a separate Internet connection that will not tie up the room telephone line, but many meeting planners now demand wireless and high-speed Internet access in guestrooms. Other applications include in-room video checkout, voice or electronic control of thermostats and lighting levels, in-room television channels that offer "tours" of the property and display convention programs and other pertinent information to guests, and other innovations.

Brian Beamish, a supplier of voice-processing systems, states,

> "Soon the widespread telephone technology will be linked to computer
> networks on the information superhighway. I can see an E-mail message
> from the Internet triggering the light on the telephone to indicate there's
> a message waiting. Similarly this could also work voice-to-text. Some-

one could send out a message over the Internet by simply speaking into the phone."[7]

Bar coding. *Bar coding* is currently being used to "code" room keys and for ease in convention registration and accessibility, and it is increasingly being used for inventory control of audiovisual and other convention related equipment (see Chapters 15 and 16).

Revenue Management

Over the past few years, hotels have joined the ranks of airlines and cruise ships in using yield management -- setting room prices based on demand. With today's technology, prices can be revised instantaneously as availability and demand warrant (this concept will be discussed further in Chapter 3).

While this strategy has proven effective in filling rooms, hotels generally realize revenue from a number of sources. Hotels today are interested in more than rates, dates, and space. They are basing pricing on demand, but applying the approach to all the property's profit centers, not just guestrooms. Hotels are now evaluating a group's spending patterns and potential for meeting space and food and beverage before booking them.

Kostas Trivizas, director of revenue management for the Savoy Group, London, explains:

> "Hotels receive combined requests for meeting rooms, food and beverage, guestrooms, and all of these requests come with a different profit margin, so you want to find the right mix that optimizes the one profit margin at the end for all the departments together. This requires specific forecasting -- demand for guestrooms with meeting rooms, meeting rooms with banqueting rooms, or banqueting rooms alone, or meeting rooms alone...Often what happens is that yield managers end up trying to do tactical optimizing -- last minute close up of rates...revenue management gets to the root, such as correctly formulating pricing issues."[8]

Mr. Trivizas feels that revenue management is one of the most challenging aspects in the industry, and predicts that revenue management director positions, which are marketing driven, will become more commonplace.

Already, hotel chains are evaluating convention and meeting groups with revenue management software. Salespeople input estimates of room revenue and catering revenue in dollars per night, suite and hospitality revenues, arrival and departure patterns, room to function space in square feet per night, and date requirements of prospective meetings. The software then evaluates the business according to what is already on the books, historical trends, and forecasts of potential bookings. Meeting groups are assessed on their ability to meet revenue expectations in food and beverage, audiovisual, recreational usage, telephone revenues, and even retail spending.

Complicated Contracts

According to Roger Dow, a longtime executive with Marriott International who became president and CEO of the Travel Industry Association of America in January 2005, planners of 25 years ago had three basic questions, "How does your space look, will I fit, and will you give me good service?" Today, however, hoteliers are focusing more on the bottom line, and protecting themselves with contracts that include attrition clauses, due diligence and other measures to minimize losses from cancellations and other issues arising from group business.

Dow says that both sides are putting far more time and energy into contracts rather than the old concerns of space and service, creating a tension that did not exist in the days before contracts became a matter of prime importance. Dow says:

> "The handshake and the relationship are still there, but then comes the 30-page contract."[9]

Some meeting planners today feel that they spend an inordinate amount of time on legal issues. Deidre Ross, CMP, director of conference services for the American Library Association, says:

> "I feel like an attorney. I'm looking at contracts all the time...It didn't seem to be that legal when I started. It was friendlier, and even though people have good relationships now, when it's a contract it's a contract. We didn't even used to use that term – we called it a letter of agreement."[10]

Most organizations now have attorneys who look over hotel contracts, and more meeting planners are being taught the nuances of contract negotiation, especially when it comes to cancellation clauses and attrition. Some organizations, such as the American Cancer Society, are asking their major hotel suppliers to create "umbrella contracts" to help to eliminate potential problems, and that organization as well as other organizations and meeting planners are hoping that the process of doing business will become less complicated.

Summary

As you can see from this overview of the convention and meetings industry, there are a number of factors that must be taken into consideration after the decision has been made to solicit this lucrative market segment. To successfully compete for meetings business, you must have a working knowledge of the various types of meetings and the groups that typically hold them, be aware of the types of facilities that can best sell and service the various segments within the meetings market, and stay abreast of trends impacting the industry to enable you to develop effective strategies for attracting meetings business.

In the next chapter, we will take a look at the most important factor in successfully obtaining meetings business—planning—and learn how to successfully market a property. Subsequent chapters will detail establishing a sales office for maximum efficiency, will outline specific strategies for reaching each of the subsegments of the meetings market, and will discuss the issues most important to meeting planners today.

Endnotes:

1. EXPACT 2004 Convention Expenditure and Impact Study.
2. Amy Tiebel, "What Buyers Need to Know in a Seller's Market," *Convene*.
3. Ibid.
4. Dara Wilson, "SMERF GROUPS: Second-Class No Longer," *Association Management*.
5. Ibid.
6. Barbara Ann Cox, "The Third-Party Meeting Planner is an Asset to the Hotelier," *Florida Hotel and Motel Journal*, June 2002, p. 32.
7. Deborah McKay-Stokey, *Future Hotelier*.
8. "Profit Performance: A primer for mastering revenue management," *World Hospitality*, February 2000, p. 4.
9. Dave Kovaleski, "The Meeting Industry Grows Up," *Corporate Meetings & Incentives*, March 2005, p. 28.
10. Ginny Phillips, "Legal-Sized Planners," *pcma convene*, June 2004, p. 55.

Additional References:

*   <u>Fundamentals of Destination Management and Marketing</u>, Richard Harrill, Editor, American Hotel and Lodging Association, 2005.
    www.ei-ahla.org
*   "The Impact of Technology on Today's Meetings," *Meetings and Conventions* magazine supplement.
    www.meetings-conventions.com
*   Meeting News Handbook — Selecting a Meeting Site.
    www.meetingnews.com/handbook.htm
*   <u>Professional Meeting Management, 4th Edition</u>, Professional Convention Management Association.
    www.pcma.org
*   "Recommendations for Industry Best Practices," Professional Convention Management Association Task Force on Third-Party Practices.
    www.pcma.org
*   "Utilization of the Internet: The Meetings Industry" — Independent study by J.D. Powers and Associates for Meeting Professionals International.
    www.mpiweb.org

Internet Sites:

For more information, visit the following Internet sites. Internet addresses can change without notice. If a site is no longer available at the address listed below, a search engine can be used to find the new address or additional, related sites.

Alliance of Meeting Management Companies – www.ammc.org
Association of Exhibition Organisers (United Kingdom) – www.aeo.org.uk
Association of German Trade Fair Industry – www.auma-fairs.com
Benchmark Hospitality – www.benchmark-hospitality.com
British Exhibition Contractors Association – www.beca.org.uk
China Council for Promotion of International Trade – www.ccpit.org
Conferon – www.conferon.com
Convention Industry Council (CIC) – www.conventionindustry.org
Dolce International – www.dolce.com
European Federation of Conference Towns – www.efct.com
Helms Briscoe – www.helmsbriscoe.com
Hilton Hotels – www.hilton.com
Hong Kong Exhibition and Convention Organisers and Supplies Association – www.exhibitions.org.hk
Independent Meeting Planners Association of Canada – www.impaccanada.com
International Association of Conference Centers (IACC) – www.iacconline.org
International Association of Convention and Visitors Bureaus (IACVB) – www.iacvb.org
International Association of Professional Congress Organizers – www.iapco.org
International Congress and Convention Association – www.icca.nl
Meeting Professionals International (MPI) – www.mpiweb.org
Netherlands Convention Bureau – www.nlcongress.nl
Professional Convention Management Association (PCMA) – www.pcma.org
SmithBucklin – www.smithbucklin.com
StarCite, Inc. – www.starcite.com/index/htm
Switzerland Convention & Incentive Bureau – www.myswitzerland.com

Study Questions:

1. Why is it important for hotel people to understand the differences between various types of meetings? After all, aren't all the definitions synonymous?
2. Distinguish between a congress and a conference, a symposium and a workshop, a trade show and a consumer show.
3. As a convention sales or service manager, what are the types of meeting planners you might be working with? How are these planners different?
4. How do conference centers differ from hotels?
5. Why are many meeting planners choosing second-tier cities for their conventions?
6. What are the characteristics of SMERF groups?
7. Describe the competitive advantages of all-suite hotels in the meetings industry.
8. Briefly describe the important and changing role of third-party meeting planners in the meetings market.
9. Explain how technology is reshaping the relationship between meeting planners and hotel salespeople.
10. What is revenue management and how is it affecting the way hotels sell and service the meetings industry?

Key Terms:

All-suite hotel. A hotel that features rooms larger than typical guest rooms, with a living or working space separate from the bedroom(s).

Complete meeting package. An all-inclusive pricing plan offered at conference centers.

Conference center. A property specifically designed to handle group meetings. Conference centers are often located outside metropolitan areas and may provide extensive leisure facilities.

Convention. A meeting of delegates for action on a particular matter. Usually involves a general session and supplementary smaller meetings. Conventions are produced with and without exhibits.

Destination management companies. Professional management companies specializing in the design and delivery of convention events, activities, tours, staffing, and transportation, utilizing local knowledge, expertise, and resources.

Globalization. The international consolidation of big business and the growing trend for countries to allow free transfer of goods and services across national boundaries.

Professional Congress Organizer (PCO). European term for DMC (Destination Management Company). Local supplier who can arrange, manage and/or plan any function or service an event.

Second-tier cities. Smaller cities and suburbs of major cities that offer the meeting planner an attractive location and at the same time provide less costly accommodations and transportation.

Trade show. An exhibition with displays, generally held within a trade industry or discipline. May be independent or in conjunction with a convention. Not open to the general public.

Learning Objectives:

This portion of your text covers the importance of developing a marketing plan in order to compete successfully in the meetings market. When you have studied this chapter, you will:

- Be able to explain the difference between sales and marketing and tell why marketing is essential to the success of hotels and restaurants.

- Be familiar with the ideas, terminology and steps associated with developing and implementing a marketing plan.

- Be familiar with such marketing concepts as market segmentation, positioning and target marketing.

- Be able to explain how objectives and action plans are developed as part of a marketing plan.

Outline

The Difference Between Sales and Marketing

The Importance of Marketing

The Marketing Plan

The Four Steps of the Marketing Plan

    Step #1 - Conducting Marketing Research

    Step #2 - Selecting Target Markets and Positioning the Property

    Step #3 - Establishing Objectives and Action Plans

    Step #4 - Reviewing and Monitoring the Marketing Plan

Putting a Marketing Plan into Action

Summary

Charles Walhaven
Director of Convention Services, Meetings.com
Nashville, TN

"Knowing what aspects of your meeting facility are most important to meeting groups is essential...The foundation of any marketing plan is the property analysis...A property analysis is a written, unbiased self-appraisal used to assess the strengths and weaknesses of your hotel...Experience your property from a meeting planner's point of view...Your creativity and knowledge of your properties capabilities will help you meet the needs of your target markets."

2

Developing a Marketing Plan

In Chapter 1, we saw that the convention business is a potentially lucrative market segment that can be serviced by almost any type of property. But this does not mean that a hotel should just plunge headlong into attempting to capture all the convention business it can handle. Going after convention business without a sense of what the property can deliver may lead to costly mistakes, including misdirected advertising, fruitless sales calls or, worst of all, poor service.

Serious consideration must be given to a property's overall goals and how the convention business fits into them. A true managerial approach to marketing should lead to realistic objectives that can be measured. A good plan, in fact, *demands* clearly defined objectives, with careful thought given to methods, policies and procedures.

In this chapter, we will present a practical step-by-step approach to planning a marketing program. The case study of the Rolling Green Resort will be used to explain key marketing concepts. Many of the figures and examples in this chapter are related to this case study, so it is important that you not only read the text but also review these examples for a better understanding of each application.

The marketing plan will be our base. We will refer to it often, so it is necessary to grasp the concept thoroughly.

The Difference Between Sales and Marketing

Before we explore the foundation for convention sales and marketing, there is an important question that needs to be addressed: What exactly is **marketing**? Some people think that marketing and **sales** are synonymous. Others think that marketing is no different than the age-old sales and promotion concept; they consider the combination of sales, advertising, promotion and merchandising to be marketing. Neither is correct.

There is a clear distinction between marketing and sales. The terms are not synonymous – sales and marketing are *not* equal; marketing is more than sales. Being market-minded is much broader than being simply sales-minded. Marketing is strategic and directive. It is goal-oriented, and the goals are concise and measurable. It is the groundwork, the research, the *plan* on which sales promotion is based (see box titled "The Difference Between Sales and Marketing").

The practice of marketing—combining, blending, integrating and controlling all of the factors that have an influence on sales—is not new. Many firms have recognized the importance of their customers and have successfully catered to their changing needs. The conscious application of marketing theory, however, is relatively new to the hospitality industry. Until recently, hotel marketing was never thought of in the same light as industrial marketing. It was not considered that a hotel might be similar to a consumer product.

In the recent past, the demand for hotel rooms was far greater than the supply; there simply were not enough rooms to go around. It didn't matter what type of rooms were built; the customer had no alternative choices. A marketing plan that was customer-oriented was not needed to sell the product.

But the hospitality industry of today is far different. The city that once had a single inn now has four or five new hotels, each of them unique. Where formerly the demand exceeded the supply, the reverse is now true in many markets.

Now, the lodging industry is realizing that its problems are not unlike those of companies specializing in tangible products. Thus, many hotels are attempting to come to grips with what marketing means in an effort to apply marketing management principles. Hotels that wish to effectively compete must become marketing-oriented. The future belongs to those who are customer-oriented, those who are in the business of meeting the changing needs of the public -- not just in the business of maintaining hotel rooms.

THE DIFFERENCE BETWEEN SALES AND MARKETING

MARKETING

Focuses on market analysis, planning and control of changing market variables.

Focuses on long-term trends and creating new products, markets and strategies for future growth.

Focuses on profit planning, including determining the optimum market segment mix.

SALES

Focuses on field work and desk work to sell to the consumer.

Focuses on short-term considerations—today's products, markets, consumers and strategies.

Focuses on volumes and quotas, current sales, bonuses and commissions.

The Importance of Marketing

Like other industries, the hospitality industry is subject to both controllable and uncontrollable variables that will affect sales efforts. External variables, such as weather conditions, fuel shortages and airline strikes, are largely uncontrollable. Other market variables, however, are inherent to all properties and can be controlled through marketing strategies to attract and retain new and repeat business.

These controllable variables, called the **marketing mix**, consist of "four Ps"—product, place, promotion and price. *Product*, in the hospitality industry, consists both of physical facilities—guestrooms, banquet space, meeting facilities and recreational amenities—and of more intangible factors—such as service and the vacation or meeting experience itself. Since a large part of the hospitality product is intangible (you are often selling a property's atmosphere), most marketing strategies will emphasize *benefits* rather than the more tangible physical *features* offered by a property (this concept will be discussed in greater detail in the sales chapter of this book). *Place* refers to the accessibility of the products to its consumers. Hospitality products, of course, do not have to be distributed to the consumer; instead, the consumer must travel to them. This accessibility may be facilitated by marketing strategies which involve intermediaries, such as meeting planners, tour operators and travel agents.

Promotion includes both persuasion (getting the consumer to buy) and communication (developing a relationship with the client). In the hospitality industry, communication plays an especially important part in determining exactly what a meeting planner wishes to purchase and is just as important as the actual promotion of the property. *Price,* the fourth factor, is one of the crucial concerns of the marketing mix. Since price is often an important consideration when dealing with the meetings market, this variable should be taken into consideration when establishing room rates for the varying market segments (see Figure 2.1).

Many properties employ a *marketing manager* to plan, direct and control all of these factors. It is his or her job to establish programs, policies and objectives to adapt to changing customer needs. The marketing manager must know and understand such concepts as capital markets, break-even analysis and cost control, as his or her function includes establishing long- and short-range sales goals.

The marketing manager's job begins with planning. He or she must constantly plan new ways and activities to adapt to the changing needs of the customer while providing continuity to the hotel and improving its image and salability.

The Marketing Plan

While the fast-paced and ever-changing nature of the hospitality industry seems to be better suited to short-term sales efforts rather than long-term marketing strategies, there are many advantages to long-range marketing planning. Having a detailed, written plan creates an awareness of the problems and obstacles faced by the property and helps managers to think ahead to make better use of the property's resources. In addition, a written **marketing plan** sets responsibilities, coordinates efforts and helps evaluate the results of marketing and sales efforts. As an added bonus, the research done in the early stages of developing the marketing plan can identify opportunities to increase revenues in some market segments and point out previously ignored segments.

To be most effective, a marketing plan should cover a *three-year period*. While many properties feel that a yearly marketing plan is enough, a twelve-month plan may restrict sales efforts to already established guest bases. Many corporations and associations make meeting commitments well beyond one year, and short term sales goals may eliminate the opportunity to capture a larger share of the lucrative conventions and meetings business.

A three-year plan, of course, may be broken down into yearly segments with specific goals for each time period. Periodic review of the plan is essential, especially if there are drastic changes in the economy or personnel, enabling advertising and direct sales efforts to be adjusted to adapt to these changes.

The marketing plan will serve as the property's "road map," and should include programs to attract business to each of the property's **revenue centers**—rooms, banquet facilities, restaurants, and so on. Because these programs should complement rather than compete with one other, it is important to define specific objectives for each revenue center, and to be sure that these objectives—and strategies for attaining them—are understood by each staff member.

While the director of sales or the marketing manager is ultimately responsible for the property's marketing plan, many properties have recognized the benefit of a team effort in the development of effective sales strategies. In a marketing team, or "sales committee" approach, representatives from each revenue center provide detailed information on the workings of their departments and offer specific strategies for review. This type of team effort not only gives the director of sales or marketing manager better insights on how to best promote or improve day-to-day operations, but also provides an excellent way to sell the entire property.

For example, Tammis Anderson, general manager of the Hassa Yampah Inn, actively involves all her department heads in the development of the marketing plan. Every year, the

Figure 2.1. THE IMPORTANCE OF PRICE IN PROMOTING THE HOSPITALITY PRODUCT.

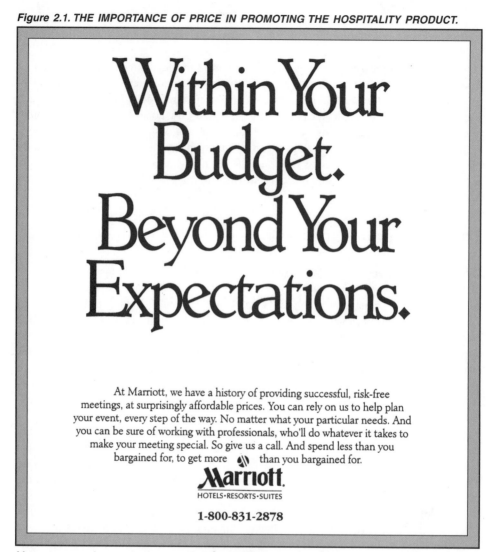

Many sources of group business, including associations, government groups, the SMERF market and small corporations, are especially price-sensitive. This ad addresses the consumer's concern over price — while still promoting the services offered by the property at an affordable cost.

department heads "retreat" for a few days off property to ponder the current year's results and the opportunities that may present themselves in the coming year. The department heads are then held accountable for goals that are agreed upon and they monitor the marketing plan to ensure that it is being executed, adjusting it periodically based upon changing market conditions. This marketing committee approach has resulted in revenue increases in all of the property's profit centers for every period over the past two years.[1]

The Four Steps of the Marketing Plan

No matter what approach is taken, a marketing plan consists of four basic steps (see Figure 2.2):

- Conducting market research
- Selecting target markets and positioning the property
- Establishing objectives and action plans
- Reviewing and monitoring the marketing plan

To ensure a better understanding of these steps, we will be using the fictitious Rolling Green Resort as a case study (see Rolling Green Resort Case Study).

Step #1 — Conducting Market Research

Before you sell any product, you must know its strengths and weaknesses in order to determine how to best promote it. This is where the first step of the marketing plan, conducting market research, is invaluable. In selling the hospitality product, it is not enough to know what your property has to offer; you must also determine what competition you face and what trends in the marketplace may affect future sales and marketing efforts. In order to determine how to best position your property in the marketplace, it will be necessary for you to gather research information so you may conduct a:

- Property analysis
- Competition analysis
- Marketplace analysis

The findings from these three types of research will be used as the foundation to plan the most effective marketing strategies for your property, and will set the stage for the

Figure 2.2. THE FOUR STEPS OF THE MARKETING PLAN.

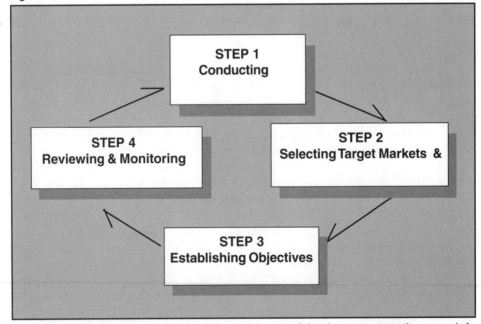

In today's highly competitive hospitality industry, it is essential to have a systematic approach for increasing sales. A well-developed marketing plan serves as a blueprint for the sales effort, and provides an effective sequence that minimizes wasteful effort. Marketing plan development, therefore, is a never-ending process. After one marketing plan cycle has been completed, results are evaluated and the process returns to the research portion of the marketing cycle to ensure that up-to-date sales guidelines and strategies are employed.

The Rolling Green Resort Case Study

The 320-room property is located forty miles north of St. Louis, a metropolis of over three million people. Situated on the banks of the Pritchard River, it is in a renowned vacation area featuring high wooded hills, picturesque fruit and dairy farms, country estates, historic battlefields and a national cemetery. A small community nearby, Forest Glen, serves as a shopping center for the approximately 1,200 rural residents of the valley.

The resort is about two miles off U.S.16, a main four-lane north-south highway that is fairly heavily traveled by tourists going south in the winter and north in the summer. This transient trade constitutes the bulk of the resort's business, which is good in the peak summer months and for a few weeks in the winter. But business is generally poor in the spring, fall and late winter months.

The Rolling Green Resort's revenues currently consist primarily of room sales to individuals and a minimal amount of banquet business—despite the fact that the property has an excellent dining room and boasts a ballroom that can accommodate 600 people on the second floor. Both the first-floor dining room and the ballroom overlook the river, and both feature charming outside patio/balcony areas. On the lower level, there are several rooms of varying sizes which are now being used only for storage.

Property recreational amenities include a large swimming pool, three lighted tennis courts and riding stables. The resort is in close proximity to a number of riding, hiking and biking trails, and bicycle rentals are available in Forest Glen. In addition, there is a small dock that is adequate for three or four small boats and can be used for fishing, although the resort does not offer any organized river activities.

The general manager of the resort is an elderly gentleman who knows the hotel business, but he is unable to come up with any ideas to increase occupancy. The property's board of directors has appointed you as their marketing manager, and it is your job to create a marketing plan that will meet the property's goals of attracting additional business—perhaps including the meetings market, which has not previously been targeted—and increasing occupancy during the slow periods.

targeting of specific market segments and the development of marketing strategies designed to sell the property to each.

Property Analysis. A **property analysis** involves an honest appraisal of exactly what a property has to offer. Since this analysis will form the base of information from which virtually every marketing and advertising decision will be made, any error in judgment here will almost certainly result in mistakes in your marketing and advertising strategy. In order to most objectively judge a property, input can be solicited from variety of sources, including employees and guests. You might also try to picture the property as if you are seeing it for the first time—become a guest yourself and experience the property from a guest's perspective. Later, as you analyze other parts of the property, put yourself in the place of a meeting planner seeing the property for the first time.

While it may seem superfluous, this analysis should always be done in writing (even if you feel you know the property inside and out), and should include all of the property's revenue centers. This analysis should detail the property's strengths and weaknesses, and provide space for comments on areas that need improvement (see Figure 2.3).

The first place to start is with the property's physical appearance. Since customers, including meeting planners, form a negative or positive first impression from the appearance of the property, and appearance often plays a large part in sales promotion, a hotel with a neat eye-catching appearance (see Figure 2.4) is a step ahead of a more lackluster competitor.

First, the entrances, grounds and exterior construction should be assessed with a critical eye for improvement. What is the overall general appearance? Is there ample parking? Are outside areas well-lighted and secure? The exterior of the property

Figure 2.3. SAMPLE PROPERTY ANALYSIS FORM.

PROPERTY ANALYSIS - ROLLING GREEN RESORT			
AREA	**STRENGTHS**	**WEAKNESSES**	**RECOMMENDATIONS**
Exterior	Attractive and appealing, newly designed entrance Clean, good repair, freshly painted	Lack of seating/relaxing area near entrance Dumpster area visible from west wing	Veranda entrance could be more inviting with addition of comfortable chairs Construct fence to conceal trash area
Meeting rooms	Ballroom can accommodate 600 persons Ballroom overlooks river	Rooms on main level are not utilized	Convert storage rooms to meeting and function space
Parking	Convenient to rooms Lot has perimeter fence and landscaping	Driveway is in need of repair Perimeter fence is too low for security purposes Very narrow driveways at hotel entrance Difficult to enter driveway because of traffic	Repair asphalt cracks in drive Research feasibility of widening entrance
Rooms	Comfortable, modern decor Easy to keep clean Cable television Easily accessible Refrigerator in each room Effective air-conditioning	Not entirely secure Little consistency in door locking systems Small bathrooms	Install stronger window locks Install high quality door latch mechanisms Rent out less desirable rooms last
Reputation	Friendly, clean hotel, modern, charming Courteous staff Moderate priced rooms	Positioning is as an average facility More individual than group business Not a well known property	Use slogan or marketing strategy Involve hotel in more community support
Location	Riverfront Accessible to Expressway Popular vacation/resort area	Far from downtown and airport Two miles off main road	Develop shuttle system for groups Billboard advertising on highway

To provide the best source of information possible about a property, a property analysis should be written out, and include an objective look at the property's strengths and weaknesses. This is only one of several pages in the Property Analysis. Similar comparisons should be done for every area that can affect the property's profitability, including restaurants, lounges, room service, catering, convention services, shops, recreational amenities, housekeeping, bell staff, reservations, and accounting and billing, as well as other influences, such as local attractions, pricing and brand awareness. This type of analysis provides a means of taking stock of what the property has to offer, what areas need to be upgraded, and what steps can be considered to improve weaknesses.

Figure 2.4. CONVENTION HOTEL CONSTRUCTION.

Today's convention hotels are a far cry from the traditional choices of the past. The Mirage Hotel & Casino in Las Vegas, for example, attracts meeting goers with its multiple lagoons, waterfalls, and a 54-foot "volcano," and is also recognized for its 90-foot high glass enclosed atrium, a popular feature in many of today's new convention hotels. In addition to its visual appeal, the property has addressed the needs of the meetings market with a large lobby, enhanced by a 20,000 gallon saltwater aquarium. The lobby has multiple windows to ensure efficient check-in. And, meeting rooms are situated away from transient traffic and accessed by two separate lobbies that provide convenient places to meet before and after individual sessions. One lobby features a large counter that can be used for registration and message service. (Courtesy of MGM-Mirage).

FACILITIES THAT MEET THE NEEDS OF THE MEETINGS MARKET

William Cox, the architect for the Boca Raton Hotel in Boca Raton, Florida, conducted a study to determine an ideal design and layout for function rooms at convention-oriented properties. His research showed that a different type of facility was needed for servicing groups than for catering to individual guests, and he recommended the following design guidelines to the Boca Raton management:

1. A large hall capable of seating and feeding at one time the total number of guests the house is designed to accommodate.

2. Meeting rooms for groups ranging in size from 20 to 100. The total area of these rooms should equal or exceed that of the banquet hall.

3. Large and small meeting rooms that can be partitioned easily and quickly to adapt to individual group requirements.

4. Built-in audio and visual aids in each meeting room, with individual control stations in each possible subdivision of the space. The speaker should be able to control lights, sound and projection from a single station.

5. Stage facilities in the main banquet room for a single performer or production of musical shows.

6. Exhibit space with adequate electrical service, water and gas. Another special requirement: doorways must be high enough and wide enough to accommodate a tractor-trailer.

Cox's recommendations can be applied by any property seriously considering the convention business.

Source: William Cox, "Design Guidelines for Convention Resorts" (highlights from speech at meeting of the American Hotel & Lodging Association's Resort Committee).

should be evaluated in terms of traffic flow, accessibility, eye appeal and compatibility with local surroundings.

Next, make a detailed, room-by-room and facility-by-facility inspection. Are rooms clean and in good repair? What type of dining facilities are offered by the property? Are kitchen facilities modern and up to code? Do you have an on-premise lounge or nightclub? Does it offer entertainment—and what type? What is the condition of the common areas—are they clean, inviting and well-lighted?

Put yourself in the place of the meeting planner. In terms of facilities, what do you offer? Location? Adequate transportation? Ample meeting space and up-to-date audiovisual equipment? Meeting rooms that are free from distraction? A highly trained staff? A well-lighted and secured environment that will make women attendees feel more comfortable?

Hotels vying for convention business should assess their function space and what equipment they have available or can obtain from local suppliers. It is wise for a hotel to prepare a printed list of its group function business equipment, including the kind and quantity available and the locations of the specific pieces of equipment. This itemization can serve both as a selling tool when presented to a meeting planner and as an inventory list for the property.

In some cases, properties wishing to target a specific market segment, such as the meetings market, have designed special facilities to appeal to their target markets (see box titled "Facilities that Meet the Needs of the Meetings Market"). While this type of renovation may not be practical for all properties, the property analysis can give valuable clues as to what property modifications are needed to attract specific business.

And what about recreational amenities? Do you have indoor/outdoor swimming pools? Do you offer easy access to golf and tennis? Do you have an exercise facility? How good are your recreational amenities in relation to those of your competitors?

Your inspection of the Rolling Green Resort has shown the exterior to be charming and in good repair, although the wide veranda could be made even more inviting with the addition of comfortable chairs. The guestrooms, ballroom and kitchen facilities are modern and adequate, but you are determined to make better use of the wasted space on the lower level.

Your tour of the grounds has shown that the driveway to the property is in need of minor repair—and perhaps widening—and that parking facilities are minimal. The pool area is large and clean, but is probably underused; its size and convenient proximity to the kitchen facilities offer excellent possibilities for food and beverage functions.

In addition to taking stock of the physical aspects, the property analysis also takes into consideration such intangible factors as the property's reputation and quality of service. Reputation includes how the property is perceived — is it classified as an inn, hotel, resort? Is it considered upscale, budget, family-oriented? How would guests describe the atmosphere — relaxing, bustling, business-like?

As far as the Rolling Green Resort's reputation, it is perceived as modern yet charming, but —unfortunately—the property seems to be a well-kept secret. Aside from a directional sign on the highway, nothing has been done to promote the property. There is a definite need for you to get the word out.

A property's location can also be a selling point. Is it within easy access to major highways or airports? Are there other historic or scenic attractions or major amusement centers close by? Are there annual events that draw people to the area?

The Rolling Green Resort has the advantage of being located in a particularly popular vacation area—and can capitalize on a number of scenic attractions. Its location on the river can also be a selling point. Two drawbacks come immediately to mind— it is a considerable distance from the nearest airport, and, because of its location off the highway, may not be accessible year-round in inclement weather.

The last part of your property analysis helps you assess your property's current position in the marketplace by examining the property's sales history and current guest base. This part of your research, known as the **business status and trends summaries**, traces the property's past, present and potential operating statistics, including sales patterns over a three-to-five-year period (see Figure 2.5). Such analysis helps to track the "soft spots"—low business periods—inherent to hospitality sales, and can disclose sales areas that need improvement.

These charts show the history of occupancy and activity by month for all profit centers. Without this, it is difficult to determine objectives and action strategies for the coming year.

In addition to looking at room statistics, it is also necessary to determine the makeup of your property's **business mix**. How old are they? Are they singles, married couples, families? Middle-income, high-income? Sports-minded? Good drinkers? This information, which is extremely useful in planning marketing strategies, can be obtained by designing a guest questionnaire and perhaps offering an incentive (a free dinner for two, a week-end at the property, etc.) to ensure guest participation. The box titled "Guest History

Figure 2.5. THE BUSINESS STATUS AND TRENDS SUMMARIES.

MONTHLY OCCUPANCY AND AVERAGE RATE

Month	2003		2004		2005	
	Average Rate	Occupancy Percent	Average Rate	Occupancy Percent	Average Rate	Occupancy Percent
January	69.00	50.5	74.50	46.7	86.70	59.6
February	61.50	52.4	71.00	52.6	85.45	62.0
to Dec.						

BANQUET FOOD AND BEVERAGE REVENUE (in thousands)

Month	2003		2004		2005	
	Food	Beverage	Food	Beverage	Food	Beverage
January	7691	761	6541	531	14126	1646
February	10250	1614	4694	1911	17120	3361
to Dec.						

RESTAURANT FOOD AND BEVERAGE REVENUE (in thousands)

Month	2003		2004		2005	
	Food	Beverage	Food	Beverage	Food	Beverage
January	15461	8761	18640	7640	21013	9641
February	20911	11411	22611	11311	23415	11421
to Dec.						

FUNCTION ROOM REVENUE (in thousands)

Month	2003		2004		2005	
	Food	Beverage	Food	Beverage	Food	Beverage
January	1290	330	1700	410	2690	491
February	810	240	1423	467	2870	502
to Dec.						

Figure 2.5 continues on the following page

Analysis" illustrates a sample guest registration card that is typically used to obtain guest information, but more extensive surveys can also be developed.

This type of analysis of guest history and future prospect information is referred to as **consumer research**, and it can take many different forms. At the Conrad International Centennial in Singapore, Theresa Choo, director of sales and marketing, says part of her

Figure 2.5 (cont. from preceding page) THE BUSINESS STATUS AND TRENDS SUMMARIES.

GEOGRAPHIC ORIGIN OF GROUP BOOKINGS

Missouri	Number by City	Total by State	State Percent
Kansas City Springfield Joplin Jefferson City	51 36 32 24		
TOTAL		143	34 percent
etc.			

GROUP ROOM NIGHTS BY MARKET SEGMENT

Segment	Jan	Feb	Mar	Apr	May	Jun	to Dec.
Corporate Group							
Insurance	621	541					
Computer	29	59					
Incentive	43	122					
Other	—						
Association							
National	330	461					
State and Regional	461	296					
Other	69	—					
SMERF							
etc.							

This market research, which is also called an occupancy and activity analysis, traces the property's past and present operating statistics and aids in forecasting future activity. While most properties keep guestroom statistics, it is also important to monitor the activities of other revenue centers, such as restaurants and banquet operations, and to determine where the property's customer base is coming from — and when. These statistics make it easier to develop effective marketing strategies to both existing and new markets.

research includes talking with current guests, an often overlooked source of ready information. She says:

> "In the elevator, I introduce myself and try to find out what the guest needs. I invite ten guests a week to have tea with me and ask them if what we are giving as value-added perks is actually what they want."[2]

Another key area for research is the **geographic origin study**. Not only is it important to know who your guests are, but also where they come from. Identifying "feeder cities" or "catchment areas" can result in a more effective use of time and money. And, the smaller the geographic area used as categories the better. It is more useful to know, for example, that a

A Guest History Analysis:
A Valuable Key for Building Business

PLEASE PAY LAST AMOUNT

Hilton Inn St. George, Utah
1450 HILTON INN DRIVE
ST. GEORGE, UTAH 84770
(801) 628-0463

GUEST REGISTRATION 34725

Names_____

Address_____

City or Town_____ State_____ Zip_____

Firm_____

MAKE OF CAR	LICENSE No	MODEL	STATE

MY ACCOUNT WILL BE PAID BY
☐ CASH ☐ CHECK ☐ CREDIT CARD_____
TYPE AND NUMBER

I AGREE TO THE CORRECTNESS OF THIS STATEMENT AND PERSONALLY ASSUME LIABILITY

SIGNATURE
X_____

REMARKS_____

NOTICE TO GUESTS   SAFETY DEPOSIT BOXES ARE PROVIDED FOR DEPOSIT OF VALUABLES. THE HOTEL IS NOT RESPONSIBLE FOR VALUABLES NOT DEPOSITED

ARRIVED	DEPARTED	ROOM	RATE	CLERK	NO. GUESTS

Consumer research is an invaluable tool for both protecting a property's current customer base and for developing strategies to increase new and repeat business. While other guest market research, such as geographic origin, may be obtained from responses to advertising or direct mail campaigns or from post-departure guest surveys, one of your most valuable resources can be found in-house: *guest registration cards*. Guest registration cards are an effective way to determine the geographic origin of a property's guests, and offer a wealth of other information, including:

- the number and type of guests (individual business travelers, family leisure travelers, group commercial business, etc.)
- the source of the reservation (travel agent, meeting planner, guest direct, etc.)
- reservation date (which will help to determine the lead time required)
- length of stay
- room rate and revenue generated (room, food and beverage, gift shop, valet, etc.)
- personal information, including name, address, city, state and zip code (a ready-made mailing list)

This knowledge helps a property to determine which market segments (and guests) are sources for the most business, and, by learning what zip codes are producing the most business, the property can direct advertising (or rely on repeat business and target other geographic areas).

By determining guest origins, patterns, and needs, a property can develop strategies and programs to increase potential business. If, for example, guest market research reveals that 80% of the property's business comes from within the state and that these in-state guests travel an average of three week-ends a year, the property could consider quarterly mailings offering special packages to these guests to entice repeat business. A fishing tournament, a "Get-Away" week-end, etc., are just two examples of possible strategies. And, besides offering a great potential for repeat business, former satisfied guests are an invaluable source for building additional business through word-of-mouth advertising. Such referrals make it even more important to keep in touch with customers. It is costly to get a guest the first time; it is vital to get business again.

guest came from Chicago than to know that a guest came from Illinois. This breakdown by cities and even zip codes can help the property to direct advertising to those areas which are most likely to produce guests.

Geographic and zip code information can come from a number of sources, beginning with the guest registration card. Other sources of information include responses from advertising or direct mail campaigns. This information should be updated regularly to avoid a confrontation with thousands of guest registration cards at the end of the year and to ensure that the correct areas are being targeted.

Competition Analysis. In addition to analyzing your own property, it is of prime importance to know your competitors and evaluate their strengths and weaknesses in comparison to your own. First, you must know your competition. Your competitors are comparable properties in the immediate area that offer similar facilities and room rates and service similar markets. These properties, called your **competitive set**, usually include four to six properties that are the most important competition for your hotel (see Figures 2.6 and 2.7).

To completely and effectively assess your competition, fact sheets should be prepared to compare: guestroom and function room rental rates; banquet menu pricing; function room square footage and quality of meeting space; typical number of guestrooms allocated to groups (called the group room allotment); and services offered to meeting groups, i.e., audiovisual, airport shuttle, express check-in, and so on.

A **competition analysis** should be done at least quarterly, and information gathered from a variety of sources. The most useful source is a firsthand look at the competitor. Stay there, or walk through, pick up literature and study their advertising. Get literature from convention and visitors' bureaus and the chamber of commerce. Check the telephone directories, hotel chain directories and travel guides to try to determine just what features are being promoted and to whom. Internet searches can also yield extensive information. Most convention hotels host Internet sites that you can access for a fast, comprehensive analysis of competitive properties. Smith Travel Research (www.smithtravelresearch.com) is an-

Figure 2.6. COMPETITIVE RATE ANALYSIS.

COMPETITIVE RATE ANALYSIS

Hotel / Rates	Rolling Green			Arrowhead Conference Center			Hilton Inn		
	Single	Double	Suite	Single	Double	Suite	Single	Double	Suite
Rack	84-92	94-102	130+	100-105	105-110	160	102-116	102-118	140+
Corporate	80	80	120	98	104	140	88	88	130
Tour	62	72	—	—	—	—	85	92	—
Convention	78-90	88-100	120+	85-100	90-105	140	88-98	94-104	130+
Club Floor	90	100	—	—	—	—	115	125	—
Government	68	78	—	85	90	—	85	90	—

This form compares the rates of your property against those of the competition. Note that ALL types of rates are included — rack, corporate, convention, tour, club floor and government. In today's technological market, rates comparisons should also be made for website rates and rates from Internet global distribution sites. In addition to benchmarking rates, hotels also gauge competitor activities in areas such as occupancies, group bookings, guest relations, promotional programs, use of advertising, selling methods, market penetration, and market segmentation mix. To monitor these areas, fact sheets are often prepared on each competitor. This comprehensive type of analysis can point out specific areas in which your property differs from the competition and can help you to determine how to set your rates in order to better compete for specific market groups.

Figure 2.7. COMPETITIVE ANALYSIS — NEED FULFILLMENT BY MARKET SEGMENT.

COMPETITIVE ANALYSIS
NEED FULFILLMENT BY MARKET SEGMENT

Needs and Wants of Target Markets	COMPETITORS			
	Rolling Green Resort	Hilton Inn	Arrowhead Conference Center	Comments
Corporate Meetings Market				
AV equipment	1	3	3	Our acess to outside AV firms is limited
Security	3	2	2	
Training atmosphere	2	2	2	Our secluded location is a benefit to corp planners
Space on short lead time	3	2	3	
Soundproof meeting rooms	2	2	1	
Master account billing	3	2	3	
Efficient check-in, check-out	2	2	2	
	2	2	2	
	2	2	3	
Association Meetings Market				
Comp. room policy	3	2	2	We offer 1 comp for 40, rather than 1 comp for 50 rooms booked
Exhibit space	1	3	1	
Accessible location	1	3	2	
Overflow arrangements	1	3	2	
Assistance with housing	2	2	2	
Spouse programs	2	3	2	
Reasonable room rates	3	2	2	Key: 3 = superior
Recreational amenities	3	1	1	2 = average 1 = poor
Convention coordinator	3	2	2	

A competitive analysis can take many forms, including just a simple feature-by-feature comparison of the competitors' facilities with one's own. The most pertinent information can be gained by evaluating how one's property "stacks up" in specific market areas. This is one type of form used to compare the services offered to each market segment. Market segmentation is the practice of targeting segments of customers within the overall marketplace. Isolating target markets and determining how well your property fills the needs and wants of each segment is extremely helpful in finding your competitive advantages. Once determined, these advantages can be used to differentiate your property in the form of positioning. This form illustrates just two market segments. You should assess the needs and wants of all market segments you are targeting — the corporate individual traveler, the travel agent market, the incentive group market, the family market, and so on. The key is to find a "difference that makes a difference" to each targeted customer.

other site that can be used to provide competitive intelligence and historical trends. For a fee, the firm will provide industry data customized to your local market and competitive set.

This analysis of the competition can help to point out market segments that are not being serviced at your property and can provide valuable clues as to how you can change your own marketing strategies to generate additional business.

As far as the Rolling Green Resort is concerned, there is obviously no local competition for rooms, but this is a rare case in the hospitality business. In most locations — even small towns — there is at least one other competitor (and often times many more), who may offer a different type of product or may target a market segment that your own property is overlooking. The Rolling Green Resort has identified the Arrowhead Conference Center and the Hilton Inn as competitors. Both are located in the outskirts of St. Louis.

Marketplace Analysis. The **marketplace analysis**, also known as a *situation analysis,* evaluates the environment in which the property operates (see Figure 2.8) and the property's operating status in that environment. The marketplace analysis identifies factors that can affect business, such as the cost of travel and government regulation, and also includes research on the environment around the property. This latter research can include the population and projected growth of the local community, the economic trends being experienced by local industry, the traffic counts for nearby highways and airports, recreational amenities and attractions in the area, and unique area activities — such as fairs, festivals, rodeos, etc. — that attract crowds. All of these strengths can be incorporated into property promotion.

Data for the marketplace analysis can be found in census information, industry reports, periodic updates from the chamber of commerce and even the local newspaper. Becoming involved in community affairs is another way to learn what is going on in the area and how trends may affect business.

In the case of the Rolling Green Resort, the marketplace analysis may reveal that there is little going on in terms of population growth and projected changes in the economy. If you were to find out that a light industrial park was proposed nearby, however, that information would greatly impact your property.

While the research phase of the marketing plan is very important, the crucial exercise is not to merely collect data but to *interpret* property, competition and marketplace information. The key is to "boil down" the statistical information gathered in order to select appropriate market segments and to help form strategies for reaching them.

In the case of the Rolling Green Resort, for example, your research has shown that you could indeed service at least some portion of the meetings market if you were to formulate a plan to better utilize the "wasted" space on the main level. It may be viable to turn one or two rooms into attractive conference rooms, or to add a business center or other facilities — such as an exercise room or childcare center — to attract this additional business.

As you can see, the research step of the marketing plan can be an involved and time-consuming process. Therefore, some hotels hire outside experts to assist with the research step of the marketing plan. Outside consultants provide an opportunity for you to get a fresh look at what the property is doing to maximize sales. When the Ritz-Carlton Kapalua on Maui wanted to validate their sales strategy, for example, they brought in David Brudney, a hotel industry consultant.

He reports:

> "I spent an hour each with every member of the sales and marketing team and half a day with the GM; I spent a full day visiting the competition...Then I came back and did a report on why group business

Figure 2.8. THE MARKETPLACE ANALYSIS.

Part I	MARKETPLACE ANALYSIS	
OPPORTUNITIES	**EFFECTS ON BUSINESS**	
The St. Louis Airport is expanding and bringing in two new regional carriers.	Easier accessibility to the city. These airlines service several of our feeder cities.	
The local college has made arrangements with several companies to hold seminars and workshops on electronics this spring and fall.	Possible room nights from students and instructors, and meeting space for meetings, classes and seminars.	
Archaeological dig in Majestic Canyon has uncovered an ancient Indian burial ground. An influx of scientists and historians have begun a major investigation of the area. etc.	Possibility of room nights from those not wishing to sleep on site and day rooms from those who wish to shower and clean up after the dig. Also increased business in food and beverage areas.	

Part II		
PROBLEMS	**EFFECTS ON BUSINESS**	
The highway from St. Louis is scheduled to be repaired in May.	Guests will experience some delays during May. However, when construction is finished the repairs and additional lane will make access to our resort easier and faster. Also a possibility of increased restaurant business from the workers.	
A new Sheraton Hotel has been proposed. Construction is to commence late next year. etc.	This property is to be located midway between our property and St. Louis. If developed, this will be increased competition; and Sheraton is strong in the corporate market and has a good established reputation.	

This marketplace analysis looks at the environment in which your hotel operates and assesses the effects of political, economic, sociological and technological factors (these are often termed the "uncontrollable variables"). The marketplace analysis generally consists of two parts, one titled "Opportunities and Effects on Business"; the other is titled "Problems and Effects on Business." These studies detail influences (both positive and negative) that may have an effect on your business and provide a way to determine how these opportunities and challenges can impact your property. You should use this environmental scanning to monitor your environment in order to design strategies that will help you to avoid potential problems while taking advantage of the opportunities provided in your marketplace environment.

had dropped. I interviewed incentive houses and validated why incentive business had dropped."[3]

Brudney says his evaluation included questions dealing with account coverage, handling the SMERF market and group sales strategy (whether proactive calls were made, how many sales calls, how many site inspections). He also evaluated where leads were coming from, what hired parties the hotel was using to generate leads and whether or not salespeople were receiving proper direction.

Step #2 — Selecting Target Markets and Positioning the Property

After an honest self-appraisal, set reasonable, reachable targets. Be realistic because sales efforts are costly and, if done sincerely, are emotionally exhausting and the price is too high to be wasted.

How do you choose your **target markets**? The obvious first step is to target groups you are already serving. The information obtained from room reservation cards may show that a majority of your guests come from metropolitan St. Louis. If so, direct advertising there.

Next, chart the number of room nights you are currently selling to each market segment by month (see Figure 2.9). If you are realizing a high occupancy from associations or sports teams, for example, expand your efforts to those market segments.

You will also want to target markets that would be the most profitable to your hotel, not only in terms of rooms revenue but additional revenue from such sources as meeting space, food and beverage and other property profit centers. **Segment profitability** is determined by analyzing the purchasing patterns of past customers. For example, your hotel may already be targeting sports teams, but what is the profit potential of targeting executives (both international and domestic) with unlimited expense accounts?

Marketing goals should be set and hotel salespeople should be trained to target business from potentially more profitable groups. If, for example, your hotel doesn't generate acceptable revenues in its profit centers from association meeting attendees, who tend to be more price conscious, perhaps you should target other segments that tend to spend more freely on restaurant meals, recreational amenities and in the gift shop, such as business travelers on expense accounts.

Then, determine what other markets you may adequately service (see box titled "Selecting Target Markets"). A property such as the Rolling Green Resort would be an attractive destination for market segments such as honeymooners, business travelers and families. Its location and atmosphere would be ideal for "murder mystery weekends" or special educational seminars or retreats.

The conventions and meetings industry has been shown to be a lucrative market segment that should be targeted. While this particular property is probably inadequate to handle large conventions, what other segments within the convention and meetings industry can it service? What specific needs of meeting planners does it meet? Your location away from the bustle of the city may be an inducement to St. Louis businesses wishing to hold training sessions in a quiet, yet convenient, location. And, many small meetings and seminars do not require large facilities — or even have a food function. Are there state or regional associations that can be targeted? SMERF groups? Other groups that you can adequately serve?

Figure 2.9. STATE AND REGIONAL ASSOCIATIONS OCCUPANCY CHART.

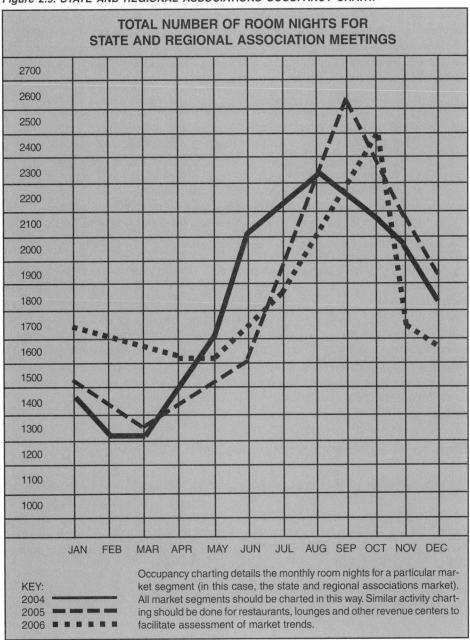

In order to determine the most effective marketing strategies, properties should chart the number of room nights they realize from each market segment they serve. This occupancy chart for the state and regional associations market sub-segment provides such information as the number of guests and peak months of occupancy, and is useful to forecast trends and direct advertising.

Due to its historic setting, the Rolling Green Resort might also appeal to historical societies, educational groups and veterans' groups. And, the nearby city of Forest Glen should not be overlooked as a potential source of business from wedding receptions, awards banquets and other community functions. Perhaps the resort could promote regional activities, such as a dairy festival, or sponsor a sports team to attract visitors to the area.

Once you have selected your target markets, you must then determine how to best *position* the property to each of them. **Positioning** refers to the perception of a property by the guest. It is a composite of the property's reputation, what it stands for and how it differs from the competition. In short, it is the property's image or uniqueness — which gives you the wherewithal to sell it to your guests. Kathleen A. Girard, vice president of marketing at the Hotel Millennium in New York City, says:

> "Knowing your product and how to position it is a fundamental key to success in the hotel business. You have to have a very strong identity from the moment you open your door, and you must not compromise it. Otherwise people get confused. You have to know who your audience is, who buys. Many hotels don't know who they are. They try to be all things to all people, and certain market segments clash. Conventions clash with the individual business traveler, for example. It's better to do a few things very well rather than do a lot of things in a mediocre manner."[4]

To effectively sell a property, your perception of it and your customers' perception of it must match (see box titled "Positioning Your Property"). An example of success in positioning is the Cadillac automobile. The name immediately conjurs up the image of a luxury car.

The property's positioning plays an important role in advertising. It enables you to create the advertising which will project the image you want for the property.

You may, for example, wish to position the Rolling Green Resort as an attractive small meetings destination. Or, you may wish to "play up" the historical significance or the tranquility of the area to attract associations or retreat business.

Step #3 — Establishing Objectives and Action Plans

One of the attractions of the convention business is that it fills many rooms at a time — and business can often be controlled to fill those rooms at the most advantageous times, such as during the off-season or slow periods. To best take advantage of marketing opportunities, however, it is necessary to set specific objectives and to develop plans to help bring about the desired results. And, since marketing goals cannot be met without sales, it is wise to look at each revenue-producing center and set goals for each.

Marketing Objectives. At the beginning of each year, research data should be used to set specific goals for each market segment. To arrive at these goals, certain questions need to be answered:

- When are the property's peak periods? In what months does business need to be increased?
- What revenue centers need more sales effort? Does the restaurant do more business during some months? Would offering family rates help to boost room occupancies?
- What market segments can be reached to increase business? What priority should each be given?
- What steps can be taken to generate additional revenues in each segment?

Marketing objectives should be set for each market segment, revenue center and revenue-producing service (the property's laundry, valet parking, gift shop, and so on). These goals must be clearly defined *in writing* so that every one involved gets the same information. In addition, the goals must be realistic yet challenging; if a property is currently experiencing an average occupancy of 65 percent, it is unrealistic to expect to set a goal of 100 percent — but the sales staff can shoot for a more reachable, yet challenging, goal of 80 percent during certain months.

Setting specific goals helps in the monitoring process. Room nights can be tracked and restaurant covers counted periodically to ensure that marketing goals are being met.

Developing Action Plans. Once objectives have been outlined, **action plans** must be developed to meet those objectives. This is the real meat of the marketing plan. There should be detailed action plans for each market segment and revenue center, and, since action plans can be compared to "mini" marketing plans, they should incorporate the following six areas:

1 *A description of the market segments or types of business to be solicited.* Will the plan target business travelers? Local associations?
2 *A specific description of the target customer.* If the target segment is local associations, this portion of the action plan will include the names, addresses and telephone numbers of local contact persons.
3 *Rates, special plans or promotions that will be offered.* This should include any discounted rates for association groups, a possible free room for a tour operator, special package rates (rooms, food service, entertainment) for groups.
4 *Specific Objectives.* Here, the objectives are clearly spelled out. The plan should not just call for "increasing room occupancies," but rather should specify the room night and revenue goals by month for the entire year. These types of objectives enable the sales department to plan strategies to meet its goals.
5 *Action Steps.* This portion of the action plan involves the actual steps that should be taken to carry out the marketing objective. Perhaps some promotional literature will be developed. An "open house" may be held to introduce the local meeting planners to your facilities. In the case of the Rolling Green Resort, you may plan an advertising campaign directed to those leisure travelers within a two-day drive of the property (see Figure 2.10.).
6 *Budgeting.* It is not enough to simply set goals. Enough money has to be allocated to help achieve them. You should go through each strategy and action step to determine what each will cost.

As you can see, action plans are specific and therefore require personalized attention. It is highly recommended that the action plans for each revenue center be assigned to specific individuals who can oversee their part of the total marketing effort and monitor the progress of their department's objectives. The Chapter Appendix provides a detailed description of how each of the six areas discussed in the marketing plan are applied in the Rolling Green's market segment plan for increasing corporate meetings.

Budgeting. As we mentioned in the discussion on developing action plans, there needs to be a specific budget set for each revenue center and for each market segment (see

Selecting Target Markets

The primary purpose of the research phase of marketing planning is to identify three to five priority needs for the property and ways to meet those needs. The study of the property, competition and marketplace (the business status and trends summaries, in particular) assist the marketing team to identify areas needing sales activity and when specific business is needed.

Once a property's priorities are identified, market segments can be selected that can meet these priorities. Hotels are always looking for ways to improve their customer mix; they must periodically evaluate their customer mix in order to drop or replace low rated segments and boost business from segments that are more profitable.

Noted industry marketing consultant Tom McCarthy suggests that properties ask the following five questions to best determine which market segments to target:

- Does the property meet the needs of this segment?
- How does the competition meet the needs of this segment? The number and quality of competitors in the area weighs heavily in determining whether or not to solicit a specific segment.
- Does this segment meet the property's needs? Look at the list of property's needs and determine whether the segment will provide the kinds of business that will satisfy those needs.
- How much business is the property getting from this segment at present? If it is getting some business from this segment, there is likely to be more out there.
- How much time and money will it take to solicit this segment vis-a-vis its long-term potential?

In today's favorable market, properties are being more selective, not only in regard to the market segments they are targeting, but even as to the particular customers they are booking. Transients pay higher rates than groups, so in periods of high demand, some meetings business is given "back burner" treatment. The type of group is also being closely scrutinized; those with substantial banquet business, for example, are of more value to hotels.

Barbara Best, National Accounts Director for Hyatt Hotels says, "Smart hoteliers want to have a mix of business, but we are trying to learn how to best manage that mix." Because of high demand, hotels can indeed be more selective—but their selectivity is often at the expense of the meetings industry. Lynn Tiras, president of International Meetings Managers in Houston, TX, says, "Hotels are looking at the whole picture to see if a particular piece of business is of value to them, and they are turning away business that doesn't have enough food and beverage or whatever.

"In some cases I can understand it, like when they don't want to tie up all their meeting space for a group that may not need any sleeping rooms or F&B, but they are going way beyond what's reasonable in some cases too."

Continues on next page

Obviously, a property must make sound business decisions, but it must be careful, too, not to jeopardize future business. Weighing out a property's priorities, current business relationships with the meetings industry, and market trends is essential to help a property to effectively manage its customer mix without jeopardizing future business.

To illustrate how these strategies are put into practice, let's go back to our case study of the Rolling Green Resort. The property's marketing team, for example, has decided not to solicit the individual government business because the segment is too rate conscious, and also determined that there is no substantial room night volume from the leisure sport fishing traveler. The marketing team instead decided on the following priorities and selected the marketing segments listed in the accompanying chart to meet the property's needs.

Market Segments Targeted to Fill Priorities

Priorities	Market Segments to be Given Emphasis to Solve Priorities
Priority #1 **Midweek Business** **Year Round** This is our area of greatest opportunity for significant increases. We have some corporate individual travelers, but if this can be expanded and coupled with the corporate meetings market targeted, we will be able to create a strong corporate base to fill this need.	• Corporate Individual • Corporate Meetings • Intensive Training Meetings
Priority #2 **Shoulder and Value Season Group** Early fall and late spring are our shoulder periods, with winter being the off season. The association market (particularly state and regional groups) have been our strongest in the past. We will concentrate our efforts in this market and also with the SMERF market to target groups into the shoulder and value seasons.	• State and Regional Associations • Educational Groups • Government Groups • Religious Groups in Preparation for Christmas and Easter Pageants • Medical Associations • Veterans Groups
Priority #3 **Banquet Business** Has not been pursued actively in the past. Efforts will be directed to maintain current customer base with increases in average check, banquet beverage revenue and to target into the weekends.	• Local Corporate Groups • Weddings - Bridal Fairs • Reunion Business • Civic Groups

Positioning Your Property

Positioning is essentially the name recognition of your property by the public, and is critical to a property's success. Just as the "golden arches" are immediately linked to McDonald's, it is imperative for a property to establish a readily recognizable image in today's competitive hospitality industry.

One example is the Peabody Hotel in Memphis, TN, whose mallard ducks have been an integral part of the property's marketing plan since the 1930s. Each day, at 11:00 a.m. and at 5:00 p.m., one drake and four mallard hens march in and out of the hotel's lobby fountain to the strains of John Philip Sousa's "King Cotton March." The ritual is so popular that the ducks have come to symbolize the property. So, although the ducks themselves generate no revenue, they are an invaluable tool in promoting the property—they appear on the property's logo, and on gift items, and are used in advertising (the ad shown here uses the ducks to detail the varied types of meetings that the hotel services).

But positioning is more than just catchy symbols or logos. In today's competitive marketplace, proper positioning enables you to:

1. Identify possible competitive advantages.
2. Select the *right* competitive advantages.
3. Deliver your property's chosen position to carefully selected target markets.

To effectively position your property, the following factors should be taken into consideration:

- *Physical Attributes* — Is your property a "classic" hotel with a colorful history? Does it feature unique construction or features — formal gardens, waterfalls, etc.? How is it different from other properties in your area?
- *Service* — How efficient is your check-in and check-out service? How long is the wait at your restaurant? Do you offer specialized service needed by guests (computers, FAX service, children's programs, etc.)?
- *Personnel* — How are your customer contact people perceived? Are they courteous and friendly? Can they communicate well and respond to guest needs?
- *Location* — Where is your property located — beachfront, mountain, mid-city, airport, etc.? Is it conveniently located (or, conversely, remote)? What aspect of your location gives you an advantage over the competition?
- *Image* — How is your property perceived by the public — luxury, family, business traveler friendly? Do you have a distinctive image that differentiates you from your competition? Does your property live up to its perceived image?

Continues on next page

Your property's projected image must effectively meet the needs and wants of each of your targeted market segments. You must find opportunities to determine and promote what each segment needs. What benefits do they seek? What needs are currently unmet — and what needs can be met or improved? What innovations are needed to attract unreached market segments? And, most important, are those additional segments worth going after?

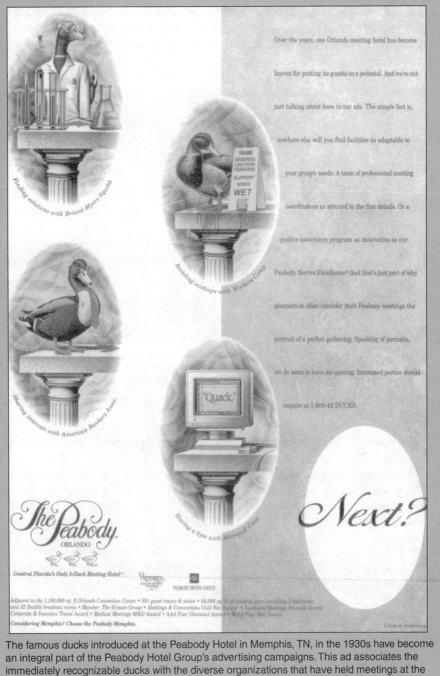

The famous ducks introduced at the Peabody Hotel in Memphis, TN, in the 1930s have become an integral part of the Peabody Hotel Group's advertising campaigns. This ad associates the immediately recognizable ducks with the diverse organizations that have held meetings at the Peabody Orlando. Courtesy of Peabody Hotels and Turkel Schwartz & Partners.

Chapter Appendix, Part VI). This type of fiscal planning ensures that there are enough dollars spent in the most effective areas.

While there are several types of budgeting, one of those most commonly used is **zero-based budgeting**. This method of allocating money is based on a "task method;" money is budgeted at levels to get the job done, but each expenditure must be justified. This approach assumes that the marketing department starts with zero dollars and that every expense is analyzed on the basis that it will yield more favorable results than spending the amount in another way.

Since this budget is based on the tasks that need to be done, *it can only be completed after an action plan has been developed.* In this way, the property can be sure that there has been enough money allocated to meet the objective. If, for example, you have determined that an extra six sales calls a month are needed in the St. Louis area, you can easily determine the amount of money needed to take care of that portion of the action plan.

Another advantage of this system is that once money has been committed to a certain department or market segment, there is some room for adjustment. If advertising costs less than estimated, for example, you may opt to increase advertising or divert the excess money into additional sales calls. In order to readily see what is available, however, a budget form must be developed that provides instant access to information (see Figure 2.11.). The budget form, when completed, is your most important budgeting tool. It not only specifies your original budget, but also breaks your budget down into spending for each market segment.

Figure 2.10. TARGETING PROSPECTIVE CUSTOMERS.

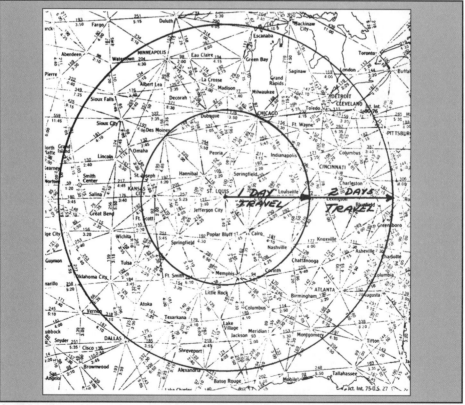

A map such as this can be used to target customers with a one- or two-day driving time from a property. This part of an action plan can be incorporated into either a direct mail or print advertising campaign to target the business or leisure travelers most likely to visit the resort. (Map by permission of Rand-McNally).

The use of computers in hotel sales offices has greatly facilitated the budgeting process. Computers can forecast based on previous and current expenditures, and provide instant printouts to let you know where you stand on dollars allocated for your marketing strategies.

Step #4 — Reviewing and Monitoring the Marketing Plan

Despite the best planning, outside influences (an energy crisis, a natural disaster, etc.) or inherent weakness in the marketing plan (unrealistic goals, lack of provision for personnel turnover, etc.) make it imperative to periodically review the marketing plan. This evaluation should be done at regular intervals — each month, each quarter or at the end of an advertising program — to ensure that marketing goals are "on track" and that money is not being wasted on strategies that are not producing the desired results.

John Hogan, director of education and cultural diversity for Best Western International, says:

> "Once the actions steps are reviewed and approved by the manager or owner, a follow-up system needs to be implemented. Each month, the action steps need to be individually reviewed. Marketing and sales plans are only effective if managers, owners and sales staff view the process as living and important. Regular reviews of tactics that do and do not work are essential to long-term success."[5]

Goals that have been clearly spelled out are easier to monitor and revise. For example, if specific goals have been set to increase room occupancies in the winter months by 15 percent or to cater an additional ten wedding receptions during the month of June, it is a simple matter to count room nights and banquet activity. Other types of monitoring can include the recording of room nights by market segment, charting and comparing room nights or restaurant covers before and after an advertising campaign, and determining what zip codes are producing the most business.

In the case of the Rolling Green Resort, for example, you may have coded newspaper advertising to determine which cities are responsible for generating additional business. If you see that there is little response from the Chicago area, you may opt to channel advertising dollars being spent there into more lucrative areas, such as the St. Louis market, or try for a better response by advertising in travel guides or specialty magazines instead.

Before "scrapping" a part of the marketing plan, however, you must ascertain if the strategy was given enough time to work (as we have learned, some corporations and associations make booking commitments years in advance and a one-time direct mailing may not bring immediate results) and determine if there could be other reasons for a lack of response (inclement weather in the Chicago area, for example, may have prohibited people from traveling). Sometimes, all it takes is a little corrective action — such as targeting a market segment during a month in which they are more likely to book — for a strategy to bring about increased business. In other cases, an evaluation may show that a more effective marketing strategy is needed to reach a particular segment. Perhaps rooms are priced too high to attract a price-sensitive group or a specific benefit offered does not have enough appeal. A periodic evaluation will point out these weaknesses and give the property an opportunity to either revise strategies or goals or to focus its marketing efforts in other directions.

This process of monitoring, evaluating and correcting is the final phase of a marketing cycle that returns once again to the research stage in order to keep abreast of market trends and new ways to reach and retain business.

Figure 2.11. SAMPLE MARKETING BUDGET FORM.

NAME OF PROPERTY

Marketing/Sales Methods		Last Year				Next Year							
Merchandising/ In-House Promotions	Actual Expenditures	Budgeted Expenditure	Variance	Budget	Allocation by Target Markets								Comments
a. Display Material	$____	$____	$____	$____	$____	$____	$____	$____	$____	$____	$____		____
b. Special Events	$____	$____	$____	$____	$____	$____	$____	$____	$____	$____	$____		____
c. Free Samples	$____	$____	$____	$____	$____	$____	$____	$____	$____	$____	$____		____
d. Prizes	$____	$____	$____	$____	$____	$____	$____	$____	$____	$____	$____		____
e. ____	$____	$____	$____	$____	$____	$____	$____	$____	$____	$____	$____		____
Subtotal	$____	$____	$____	$____									
Travel Trade Marketing													
a. Print materials	$____	$____	$____	$____	$____	$____	$____	$____	$____	$____	$____		____
b. Travel/Trade Shows	$____	$____	$____	$____	$____	$____	$____	$____	$____	$____	$____		____
c. Familiarization trips	$____	$____	$____	$____	$____	$____	$____	$____	$____	$____	$____		____
d. ____	$____	$____	$____	$____	$____	$____	$____	$____	$____	$____	$____		____
e. ____	$____	$____	$____	$____	$____	$____	$____	$____	$____	$____	$____		____
Subtotal	$____	$____	$____	$____									
Other Marketing Programs													
a. Marketing seminar	$____	$____	$____	$____	$____	$____	$____	$____	$____	$____	$____		____
b. ____	$____	$____	$____	$____	$____	$____	$____	$____	$____	$____	$____		____
c. ____	$____	$____	$____	$____	$____	$____	$____	$____	$____	$____	$____		____
Subtotal	$____	$____	$____	$____									
TOTAL	$____	$____	$____	$____									

A summary budget should be prepared combining the budgets developed for each of the market segment plans. This format is especially helpful when developing a marketing budget because it lists anticipated and actual amounts expended the previous year, provides a variance column and allocates the current budget into targeted market segments.

Putting a Marketing Plan Into Action

The marketing plan is not developed to sit on a shelf collecting dust; it should be an integral part of sales and promotional efforts and referred to often. Once the marketing plan has been prepared, it should be distributed to each department, and its objectives and how to meet them explained to all of those who are involved in particular parts of the marketing effort. Juergen Bartels, past president of Westin Hotels, says of his chain's marketing plan, "It's not a dead plan, it's a lively plan; we work from the plan everyday."

Since the marketing plan is the foundation for sales efforts, it is important that the entire sales team become especially familiar with the goals and objectives outlined. From these goals and objectives, sales goals and quotas are set and specific market segments are targeted. It is important that the sales team thoroughly understand their role(s) in the marketing effort, and utilize the research collected to position the property to potential sources of business.

In addition to the sales department, the implementation of the marketing plan will impact everyone on property. Each department should be appraised of department goals — and the strategies for achieving these goals — and should be made aware of the integral part that the department plays in the overall success of the property's sales efforts. If a marketing team approach was used to develop the marketing plan, each department's representative can serve as a "team leader" to ensure that his or her department remains on track.

For long-term success, effective and complete communication between sales and operations is essential. The sales team has to "sell" internally to the rest of the hotel staff as well as to potential guests, so regular meetings should be held with such staff as front desk personnel, housekeepers, accounting, engineering, cooks, wait staff and so on. Topics for discussion can include how groups and individuals book at the hotel, how much time and effort it takes to get groups, how future and repeat business depends on service, how the operation staff's responsiveness is essential to total guest satisfaction, how the market is competitive and how each staff member makes a difference in sales and service.[6] With this approach, line staff will understand how satisfied guests are the key to the property's profitability, which, in turn results in additional compensation and benefits to them, and they will become willing participants in the property's overall marketing efforts.

Summary

Today's meeting planner has a myriad of choices, so competition for the meetings market has become fierce. Attracting and keeping customers requires a planned, carefully researched and thought-out effort, and a written marketing plan is a must for every hospitality establishment. In this chapter, we have discussed the four steps inherent to each marketing plan and how to implement the marketing plan.

Although the marketing effort will involve the entire staff of the property, the main thrust begins in the sales department. In the next chapter, we will discuss how putting together an effective sales team, implementing workable sales procedures and organizing an efficient sales office can help the property to remain competitive and meet its marketing goals.

 Endnotes:

1. Carol Verret, "When the Crystal Ball is Cloudy; Marketing Plans for 2004," www.hotel-online.com, July 2003.
2. "Marketing Research Includes Talking to In-House Guests," *World Hospitality*, March 2000.
3. Harvey Chipkin, "The Sales and Marketing Audit: A Proven Way to Build Business," *HSMAI Marketing Review*, Summer 2003, p. 33.
4. *World Hospitality*, May 2000, p. 10.
5. John Hogan, MBA, CHA, MHS, "Marketing Plans Must Be a 'Living Being': They Cannot Sit on Shelves!," hotel-online.com, June 2004.
6. John Hogan, MBA, CHA, MHS, "Everyone Should Know What the Sales Department Does," hotel-online.com, September 2004.

Additional References:

- Heads in Beds: "Hospitality and Tourism Marketing, Ivo Raza, Prentice Hall, 2004.
  www.prenticehall.com

- Hospitality Marketing Management, Third Edition, Robert Reid and David Bojanic, John Wiley and Sons, 2001.
  www.hospitality@wiley.com

- Lessons From the Field: A Common Sense Approach to Effective Sales, Howard Feiertag and John Hogan. Available from HSMAI.
  www.hsmai.org

- Marketing Leadership in Hospitality, Third Edition, Robert Lewis and Richard Chambers, John Wiley and Sons, 2000.
  www.hospitality@wiley.com

Internet Sites:

For more information, visit the following Internet sites. Internet addresses can change without notice. If a site is no longer available at the address listed below, a search engine can be used to find the new address or additional, related sites.

Association for Convention Marketing Executives (ACME) – www.acmenet.org
Best Western International – www.bestwestern.com
Boca Raton Resort and Club – www.bocaresort.com
Conrad International Centennial – www.singapore.conradmeetings.com
Hospitality Sales and Marketing Association International (HSMAI) –
www.hsmai.org
Mirage Hotel and Casino – www.themirage.com
Ritz-Carlton Kapalua – www.ritzcarlton.com/resorts/kapalua
Smith Travel Research – www.smithtravelresearch.com

Study Questions:

1. What is the difference between sales and marketing?
2. The marketing plan should cover what time frame?
3. List the four steps in developing a marketing plan.
4. Research should be conducted in what areas before developing action plans?

5. What factors should be considered when selecting target markets?
6. What is meant by zero-based budgeting?
7. Choose two lodging properties and assess how each has positioned itself in the marketplace. Include a discussion of the following factors: physical attributes, service, personnel, location and image.

Key Terms:

Action plans. The specific steps taken to achieve marketing objectives.
Business mix. The variety or mixture of guests who stay at a property. For instance, business may consist of 20 percent association meetings, 15 percent corporate meetings, 15 percent SMERF groups, 40 percent leisure travelers and 10 percent transient guests. Also called **customer mix**.
Business status and trend summaries. Reports that assess the property's current position in the marketplace by examining the property's sales history and current guest base. Part of the property analysis.
Competition analysis. An evaluation of competition in order to identify their strengths and weaknesses in comparison to your own. Part of the market research step.
Competitive set. A group of properties that are the most important competition for a hotel in a given market.
Consumer research. Marketing research aimed at providing a profile of present and future guests.
Geographic origin study. Research identifying key feeder cities and the zip codes from which guests are generated. Part of the business status and trends summaries.
Marketing. The practice of combining, blending, integrating and controlling the factors that influence sales.
Marketing mix. The combination of the four "Ps" of marketing — product, price, place and promotion — used to achieve marketing objectives for a target market.
Marketing plan. A written guide detailing sales, advertising and promotion programs used to attract business to the property's revenue centers.
Marketplace analysis. An evaluation of the environment in which the property operates. Assesses both opportunities and problems in the marketplace, and determines how they impact the property. Part of the market research step.
Positioning. A strategy to develop the product and service as distinct in the minds of consumers. Positioning attempts to distinguish a firm from any of its competitors.
Property analysis. An evaluation of a business' facilities, services and programs to determine strengths and weaknesses. Part of the market research step.
Revenue center. A hotel division or department that sells products or services to guests, thereby directly generating revenue for the hotel. Also called **profit centers**, these may include food and beverage outlets, room service, retail stores, recreational facilities and other services, such as laundry services and valet parking.
Sales. Direct efforts through face-to-face calls, telephone calls and mailings.
Segment profitability. The profitability of a particular type of consumer or market segment. Determined by analyzing the revenues generated through the sale of

products and services to that type of consumer or segment.

Target markets. Market segments that a property singles out as having the greatest potential, and toward which marketing activities are directed.

Zero-based budget. A budget that starts at zero and requires planners to justify expenditures for each activity. The process of building a budget without the benefit of a previous year's budget.

Chapter Appendix

Sample Marketing Plan

This excerpt from a hotel marketing plan illustrates a detailed market segment plan for the corporate meetings market. The Rolling Green Resort would prepare detailed action plans for each market segment and revenue center. This third step is the core of the marketing plan. The statistics gathered on the property, the competition, the marketplace, and the target customers in the first two steps might encompass more pages in the plan, but success is based on how well the action plans are developed and implemented.

As you read this action plan, note how complete and specific it is, providing a "road map" for the coming year. The strongest marketing plans result from the input of people from all areas of the property. Therefore, brainstorming sessions with key personnel are essential to developing effective action plans.

Market Segment Plan

Corporate Meetings

I. Description

The Rolling Green Resort will aim at expanding its share of the corporate meetings market. Types of meetings sought will include: corporate sales, training and development, distributor and dealer, executive conferences, product presentations, stockholder, board and management meetings. Our property should target local, statewide and national corporations who have yearly meetings in our area.

II. Target Customers

A. Present local files.   98

B. Priority accounts — present high volume accounts and   5
   those in the area not using us at present, but are known
   to produce high volume business.

   • Pritchard Data Services
   • Harper and Associates
   • Stewart Group
   • Stubs Real Estate Investment
   • Adam and Bre Corporation

C. St. Louis Prospects

   • Companies of over 50 employees within selected SIC   120
     numbers in following zip codes:
     63111, 63137, 63128, 63104, 63121

- Companies of over 100 employees within selected SIC numbers in all other zip codes within metropolitan area — 70

D. Tri-County-St. Louis Area (other than above zip codes)

All companies with 100+ employees plus the following companies if they have less than 100 employees:

- Top 10 law firms, stockbroker-investment firms, leasing firms, relocation firms, insurance companies, advertising agencies, real estate main offices — 200

- All branch and regional offices of Fortune 500 companies — 24

- All companies of 50+ employees moving in from outside Montcalm County — 73

E. Kansas City, Springfield, Chicago (within one day drive)

- All manufacturing and insurance companies with 100+ employees — 55

- All branch and regional offices of Fortune 500 companies — 62

- MPI (Meeting Professionals International) and SCMP (Society of Corporate Meeting Professionals) members in these cities — 325

F. Four-State Region

- Top 30 seminar companies — 30

- Fortune 500 company home offices — 150

- ASTD (American Society for Training and Development) members in the four-state region. — 917

Total Target Customers — 2026

III. Rates, Special Plans, Packages and Promotions

A. Seminar/Training/Corporate Group Package:
Available on selection of specific dates.
Minimum of 25 sleeping rooms include:

	Single	Double, Per Person
Room (per person)	$80.00	$40.00
Tax (7%)	5.60	2.80
Meeting Room	4.00	4.00
Continental Breakfast	3.50	3.50
Lunch	7.50	7.50
AM/PM Refreshment Breaks	3.00	3.00
All Food Tax (7%)	.98	.98
All Food Service (15%)	2.10	2.10
	$106.68	$63.88
Above package including dinner		
Dinner	15.00	15.00
Tax	1.05	1.05
Food Service	2.25	2.25
	$125.00	$82.18

B. Extended Stay/Early Arrival

If stay is extended to include Saturdays, free unlimited use of the championship golf course and tennis facilities, along with free champagne brunch will be provided. For new bookings arriving on Sundays rather than Mondays, free welcome cocktail parties will be organized and tickets given to a local show or performance.

IV. Objectives and Goals

Based on a review of our property, the competition and marketplace, we have identified fall and spring as our most important priorities for the coming year. The corporate market is targeted as one segment to fill this need. Our objective is to increase our corporate group rooms business from 6% to 10% of our total rooms business. And to increase our annual room sales revenue from $622,542 to $669,400 (7% increase) and increase average daily rate from $72 to $79 for this segment. Monthly targets are identified below:

Room Nights and Revenue Goals From Corporate Meetings													
	J	F	M	A	M	J	J	A	S	O	N	D	Totals
Room Nights	700	850	900	800	700	600	550	550	600	750	900	600	8500 room nights
ADR	78	78	80	80	80	75	75	75	78	82	82	78	$78.75
Room Rev (000)	54.6	66.3	72.0	64.0	56.0	45.0	41.3	41.3	46.8	61.5	73.8	46.8	$669.40

V. Action Steps

A. Sales/Direct Mail

Step No.	Method	Target Customers	No.	Details	Qtr.	Sales Days	Resp.
1	Telephone	Present local files	98	Survey their satisfaction over the telephone. Give comp one-night stays to any who were dissatisfied.	1	5	AH JM
2	Telephone	Priority accounts	5	Have contact with these accounts a minimum of once a month. Include entertainment at hotel, sporting events or other local activities to build relationship.	1,2,3,4	20	AH JM
3	Personal Blitz	St. Louis prospects and those in Tri-County St. Louis area	287	Personal visits by sales staff to outline our services and deliver small gifts such as a business pen.	2,4	15	TS AH JM
4	Phone Blitz	Planners in key feeder cities of Chicago, Kansas City, Springfield and Four-State Region	1539	Promote our package and familiarize the company with our product.	1,3	25	AH TS JM
5	Direct Mail	Previous corporate meeting customers	250	Send personal thank you letters for their past business and ask them to rate satisfaction by returning post-paid questionnaire.	1	4	AH JS
6	Telephone	Previous corporate meeting customers (not returning questionnaire)	70 (est)	Survey satisfaction over the phone. Provide comp room night to any who were dissatisfied.	1	3	AH JS
7	Telephone	Tri-County St. Louis, Kansas City, Springfield and Chicago areas of of over 100 employees	340	Call for initial qualification to determine if file should be set up (at least 30 room nights per year). Set up appointments.	2	6	JM TS
8	Direct Mail	ASTD members in Four-State region	1000	Promote our package and familiarize with our product special rates, etc. Mail-in response card enclosed.	2	25	TS JM AH
9	Telephone	ASTD members in Four-State region	100	Respondents to mailing.	3	25	JM AH

B. Advertising

Media
The Trade Journal Magazine (2 col x 5 ") 12 times
Corporate Market Review (5 col x 8 ") 6 times
The St. Louis Directory — Annual

C. Merchandising
   Development of the following brochures and flyers:

	Total
Meeting Planners Informational Brochure, 4p4c	1,500
Hotel Fact Sheet (group) 8"x11" 2c	5,000
Meeting Package 4p4c	5,000

D. Public Relations and Publicity
   Contact local TV stations, major newspapers, and the Convention Authority announcing prominent corporate meetings.

VI. Budget

A. Sales
   Dues and Subscriptions
      The Trade Journal Magazine $500
      Corporate Market Review .... 350 .... $850
B. Advertising
   Media
      The Trade Journal Magazine
         2 Col x 5" @ $800 x 12x 9,600
      Corporate Market Review
         5 col x 8" @ $750 x 6x 4,500
      The St. Louis Directory
         Annual .... 1,000 ..... $15,100
   Direct Mail
      American Society for Training and
         Development (ASTD) $3,000

      Brochures and Flyers
         Informational Brochures 1,650
         Hotel Fact Sheets 1,200
         Meeting Packages 2,400
                                                    $5,250
      Production costs (ads and brochures) $5,000

      Other Selling Aids — Gifts for Blitzes $6,000
                                Total Corporate $35,200

Summary

Corporate meetings business is one of our priorities for the coming year. The estimated 8,500 room nights is 10% of total rooms business, and the $35,200 is 9.2% of total marketing budget.

Learning Objectives:

This portion of your text discusses how sales departments are organized. We will cover both the function and physical layout of a sales office, look at positions within sales and see how sales efforts are managed. We will also discuss how automation has changed the way hotel salespeople do business. When you have studied this chapter, you will:

- Understand the function of the sales office and how the sales office interfaces with other departments in the hotel.
- Be able to describe the various positions within the sales department and the duties of each.
- Understand how the director of sales manages the sales team in terms of standard operating procedures, conducting sales meetings, assigning account responsibility and evaluating the sales effort.
- Be familiar with the procedures used by sales offices to follow a sale through from prospecting to execution of the event and understand how sales office automation is being used to enhance the sales effort.

Outline

Sales Structures
- The Sales Office
- How the Sales Office Interfaces with Other Departments

The Sales and Marketing Staff
- Positions Within Sales
- Supplemental Sales Staff

Managing the Sales Effort
- Standard Operating Procedures
- Sales Meetings
- Assigning Account Responsibility
- Evaluating the Sales Effort

Sales Records and Filing Systems
- Hotel Filing Systems
- Control Books and Sales Forms

Sales Office Automation
- Advantages of Automation
- New Advances in Hotel Computer Systems
- The "Virtual" Office
- Additional Uses of Automation

Summary

Organizing the Sales Office

Beverly W. Kinkade, CHME, CMP
Vice President Industry Relations
Starwood Hotels and Resorts

"The role of the sales department in pursuing the convention business is vitally important. With today's competitive hotel environment, it is imperative to have sales policies and procedures in place to smooth the communication both within the sales office and other areas of the property. In order to reach occupancy and revenue goals, the sales office must not only be organized and staffed with enthusiastic, knowledgeable people but also have an efficient filing system, written operating procedures and an effective system for monitoring both function room and guest room bookings."

3 Organizing for Convention Sales

According to a study by Laventhol and Horwath, a consulting firm to the hospitality industry, approximately 50 percent of the lodging industry's total receipts are derived from the meetings market. But in today's highly competitive marketplace, it is simply not good enough to send salespeople out into the field to solicit meetings business. Tapping this lucrative market requires an efficient, organized sales endeavor.

This chapter deals with how to organize the sales effort by creating a sales office — both the physical plant and the personnel in it — that maximizes a property's potential to sell to and service the convention and meetings market. We will also discuss some of the positions within sales, and see how sales efforts can be structured and managed for optimum results.

Sales Structures

Two trends have greatly impacted the way hotel sales departments do business. First, acquisitions, mergers, and consolidations have occurred in the lodging industry at a record pace as companies realize the value of acquiring multiple brands and the cost savings from combining departments. In recent years, numerous acquisitions have taken place: Marriott's purchase of Renaissance and Ritz-Carlton; Starwood's take over of Sheraton, Le Meridien and Westin; Fairmont's purchase of Delta Hotels; and, Hilton's acquisition of Doubletree, Red Lion, Embassy Suites and Hampton Inns.

Today, a handful of firms own nearly 100 brands. To increase efficiency, these hotel companies are consolidating their operations and relying more on regional and national sales offices. Rather than having a dozen individual properties call on a potential client for meetings business, chains are assigning a single salesperson to represent every brand in the hotel company's portfolio to the client. This concept will be discussed in greater detail later in this chapter.

Second, marketing functions have increasingly been incorporated into sales. More hotels today are focusing on the overall bottom line, not just revenue from meetings business. While rates, dates and space are still important, more properties are evaluating a group's spending patterns and potential for revenue property-wide before booking them. This trend, called revenue management, has led to revenue management positions and departments within many sales offices, and revenue management is expected to expand throughout the industry. A detailed look at revenue management will be provided later in this chapter.

All hotels, whether they are large or small, should have some kind of sales department from which sales efforts are directed. At small properties, a salesperson usually handles all types of business. He or she may call on meeting planners, travel agents, tour operators and other sources of potential business. Still smaller hotels may have to combine sales operations under another department or even have the general manager direct the sales effort, with the GM often designating one day a week for personally making sales calls.

Regardless of size, every hotel has "non-sales" employees who could be recruited to assist in the sales effort. If a food service employee and two front desk people, for example, would each make five calls per week to qualify new prospects, fifteen calls per week -- 750 calls a year -- could be made!

Larger properties generally have a specialized sales staff and operate out of a separate sales office. It is best, if at all possible, to have full-time sales specialists for convention sales. In the largest organizations, the degree of specialization is carried still further, with salespeople assigned to market segments. One sales staffer may go after association business, another goes after corporate meetings business, still another focuses on incentive programs. Obviously, such concentration is practical only for chain operations. It is not essential to successful selling to break down the task so finely, but this should tell you that each segment of the market has its own appeal.

The Sales Office

The sales office is often the first contact a client has with the property, and first impressions can make the difference between sales success or failure. To be effective, the sales office (and effort) must be properly organized. This organization should include both a sales philosophy as well as a physical office layout conducive to generating sales.

The Function of the Sales Office. As we have said, the sales office must be established and organized to enable it to meet the overall goals and objectives of the property's marketing plan. The sales department should be structured so that group business is not only solicited but also properly serviced by being given authority over other departments that will be involved in servicing group business (see Figure 3.1).

However the sales office is organized, it is crucial that all employees understand their roles in meeting the goals set forth in the marketing plan. Property salespeople should be professional, knowledgeable and service oriented. And, all property employees, whether they be field salespeople or the receptionist at the sales office, should be aware of their importance in the marketing effort. Walk-in clients, for example, should be greeted promptly and made to feel at home, and the receptionist or secretary should be able to answer any immediate questions a visitor may have.

The Physical Layout of the Sales Office. Both the location and the appearance of the sales office are important. Sales offices should never be hidden away in the basement or an unused guest room; nor should they be located in "goldfish bowl" areas off the main lobby. Ideally, a property selling meeting and banquet facilities should locate the sales office adjacent to these areas.

The sales office should appear tasteful and professional, with a minimum of clutter, be well-lit and ventilated, and have comfortable seating and reading material available. Property information sheets and brochures, sample menus, complimentary letters from satisfied meeting planners and perhaps albums of past events or news clippings about the property are informative — and good pre-sale tools. Sales office decor can also include photographs of guest and banquet rooms and the sales and managerial staff as well as awards received by the property. This type of decor helps to familiarize the client with the property's facilities, and can also help to develop confidence in the property.

Figure 3.1. TYPICAL CONVENTION HOTEL ORGANIZATION CHART.

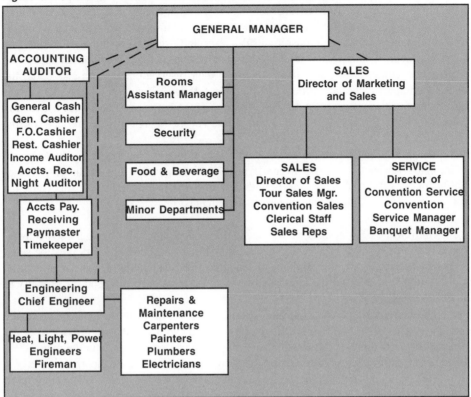

The sales department of a convention hotel usually provides information and input directly to the general manager. It is important to note, however, that the sales department, especially in convention hotels, is increasingly being given authority over other departments, such as the front desk, reservations, catering, and housekeeping, to enable it to deliver what it promises to clients.

How the Sales Office Interfaces With Other Departments

Before the hospitality industry became more marketing-oriented, the sales department was usually a separate entity responsible only for filling guestrooms and function space. Today, however, it has become imperative for not only the director of sales but also his or her staff to move into the mainstream of the day-to-day operations of the property.

Ronald Hughes, former general manager of the Palmer House Hilton in Chicago, stresses this viewpoint:

> "We have a responsibility to our salesmen and saleswomen that they become more involved in the day-to-day hotel operations, not only for the training benefit, but even more important so that their input and suggestions are built into the operation. The hotel that is market-oriented is a giant step ahead of its competition. To develop this marketing concept, the senior salesman, and especially the sales director, must be involved when we do our long range budgeting, short range forecasting, and many other basic planning functions."

In other words, management must indicate that the sales effort has a high priority and see that the director of sales has been delegated sufficient authority. To function well, the director of sales and marketing must have full authority over the banquet department, the convention services staff, advertising and sales promotion, a supporting clerical staff, and, of course, the sales staff itself. In many hotels, the reservations department is also considered an important area in relationship to sales, especially since reservationists are the first to have contact with potential clients (this relationship can be so important that some hotels, such as the Hyatt chain, have structured their reservations departments under the sales department). Negotiations between the sales staff and clients generally result in promises made. Such promises must be kept. The difference between a successful convention property with many repeat bookings and a less successful one usually reflects on the determination to live up to commitments.

This is especially true in dealing with convention and group meetings business. In addition to ensuring that guestrooms are available, it is imperative that the director of sales and his or her sales staff work closely with a number of other departments, especially the convention services and banquet/catering departments.

Convention Services. As we will see in the second part of this book, a good convention services department is essential for repeat bookings. Meeting planners must be satisfied with meeting space, the handling of functions, the availability of equipment and the service attitude of the staff in order to book repeat business or recommend the property to others (see Figure 3.2).

The convention service manager serves as the on-the-scene contact between the convention organizer and the hotel. He or she is the one who sees that all provisions of the contract are carried out, and is the one who must be prepared to cope with the requests — and emergencies — that come up as the convention nears and during the event itself.

This position is a very crucial one and should never be downgraded. The convention service manager must have sufficient stature and authority to cope with the unexpected (see Figure 3.3).

Sheraton Hotels, in recognition of the importance of convention services personnel, defines their convention and conference service professionals as follows:

> "A Convention and Conference Service Professional is a diplomat, accountant, psychologist, juggler, mind reader and goodwill ambassador with an impelling attention to detail. It's one of the most challenging and rewarding jobs in the hospitality industry.
>
> "It's challenging because you get to wear so many hats. You deal with a lot of different personalities and a lot of demands are made on you. Details and deadlines define your workday.
>
> "It's rewarding because you get to see a project through from start to finish, knowing that you helped make it all happen. You make meetings for two thousand or two dozen run like clockwork. And you make customers come back again and again, just because you did a good job."[1]

Banquet/Catering Department. Although some people feel that the banquet/catering department does not belong under the authority of the sales department, we feel that control of all function space should be overseen by one person — the director of sales. This eliminates confusion and communication problems, since choices must sometimes be made regarding who will get a function room on a certain night. This decision must be made with an eye toward the overall scheme of things, and this falls within the responsibility of the sales executive.

For the sake of argument, let's look at at what would happen if this were not the case. This partial organization chart has the banquet manager reporting indirectly to the assistant manager. When a client requests banquet space, the banquet manager will book one of the hotel's banquet rooms. While this action seems efficient enough on the surface, the sales department often needs the function rooms should any convention group be booked.

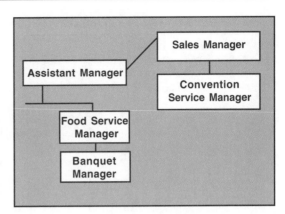

This could happen in the event of a communication breakdown. If the banquet department booked a function room and the sales department unknowingly booked the same room for a training seminar, the hotel would be placed in an embarrassing position and would most likely lose business.

The Sales and Marketing Staff

The sales staff is the first contact that many people have with a hotel. The corporate planner and the association meeting planner first establish contact through the sales office. Their first impressions are formed by the warmth, personality and public contact of the sales staff.

Positions Within Sales

While the sales effort itself should be coordinated by one person, the director of sales, there are a wide variety of positions within the sales department. While each individual on the sales staff is given certain responsibilities, it is important to remember that sales is a *team effort*. The efforts of each member must be coordinated with those of the others on the sales team for maximum results.

The Director of Marketing. The director of marketing spearheads the sales effort by setting objectives and monitoring the action plans. He or she works closely with the director of sales to ensure that goals are being met and that the sales effort is kept within budgeted limits.

The Director of Sales. The director of sales, who may be called the sales director or vice-president of sales at some properties, is responsible for executing the marketing plan formulated and accepted by top management. It is his or her job to coordinate and direct the efforts of the sales staff. All sales promotional programs must be channeled through him or her for approval. He or she works closely with the general manager or director of marketing to determine target markets and to set the budget appropriations for each market segment.

While the scope of this position is often argued, it is our belief that the director of sales should be given all the authority necessary to ensure that sales goals are met. This may include becoming involved in a number of areas, including advertising and public relations, budgeting and any other function of the hotel that directly or indirectly affects the sales effort. The salary for this position will vary depending on the type of hotel (see box titled "Typical Salaries and Bonuses for Directors of Sales").

Figure 3.2. THE IMPORTANCE OF THE CONVENTION SERVICE DEPARTMENT

This advertisement promotes a convention service staff of CMP/CMM accredited personnel who are organized and available at a moment's notice to assist inexperienced and experienced meeting planners alike. It promotes the hotel's passion to make every meeting a success as the property understands what is at stake.

The Director of Revenue Management. With today's trend toward combining sales and marketing efforts, revenue management has become increasingly important to hotels. Properties that previously relied on the director of marketing and the director of sales to realize maximum profit potential are now creating a specific position dedicated to forecasting supply and demand and researching the potential profitability of groups.

Swissôtel, for example, employs a revenue manager to decide price structure based on the date, season, day of the week, competitive situation, and the potential of the group. A state of the art computer system is at the heart of the revenue manager's decision making process, and predictions can be made for weeks -- even months -- ahead. While the position is fairly new and can be expected to change, the HSMAI expects that the position will be firmly integrated into hotel sales offices by the year 2010.[2]

Sales Managers. Depending on the size and type of property, there may be a number of additional sales managerial positions. The *convention sales manager* is responsible for soliciting convention trade for the hotel (see Figure 3.4). It is his or her job to identify and contact the associations, corporations and fraternal organizations that could use the hotel for their conventions. Convention sales are generally made through personal visits, so the convention sales manager must build a relationship of confidence with the prospective client. Due to long lead times, a convention sales manager may need three to five years to get specific convention business.

The *convention service manager,* while not always considered an actual member of the sales team, works hand in hand with the convention sales manager. His or her job is to coordinate and service the conventions booked by the property. The convention service manager takes over after the sale has been made and begins to work out the fine details with the convention group. In addition, any problems that arise during the convention will be directed through convention services. The convention service manager must work closely with all departments, coordinating the efforts of the food and beverage departments, the front office, and the banquet setup crew to see that things run smoothly in the exhibit area.

Since this is such an important position, as the convention service manager is ultimately responsible for the success or failure of a meeting, it has become increasingly common for CSM's to become certified. As we mentioned in Chapter 1, there are a number of certification programs available to ensure that CSMs provide the best in service to

TYPICAL SALARIES AND BONUSES FOR DIRECTORS OF SALES

Type of Property	Median Base Salary	Median Bonus
All-suite/Extended Stay	$ 70,355	$ 4,200
Commercial-Transient Hotel with limited meeting space	$ 94,551	$11,165
Conference Center - Meeting and Convention Oriented Properties	$105,270	$ 881
Resort Properties Targeting Leisure and Convention Guests	$111,650	$12,982

The above figures show the median annual salary and bonuses earned by the director of sales at various types of properties. Compensation for this position varies based on a number of factors, including property revenues and geographical location as well as type of property.

Figure 3.3. THE COMMUNICATION ROLE OF THE CONVENTION SERVICE MANAGER.

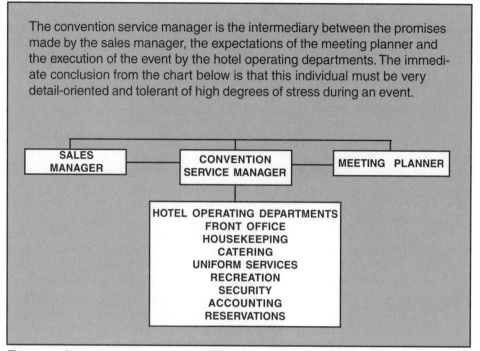

The convention service manager is the intermediary between the promises made by the sales manager, the expectations of the meeting planner and the execution of the event by the hotel operating departments. The immediate conclusion from the chart below is that this individual must be very detail-oriented and tolerant of high degrees of stress during an event.

The convention service manager acts as the on-site connection between a meeting group and the host property.

meetings groups. The "Best Practices" box in this section details just one of these programs – the Meeting Maestros Program developed by Delta Hotels in conjunction with the PCMA.

A *tour and travel sales manager* is responsible for developing group and charter business for the hotel. He or she works closely with travel agents, tour wholesalers, tour operators and transportation companies. This person is generally instrumental in putting together tour packages and must have expertise in the pricing and promotion of group packages. The tour and travel sales manager may also put together group incentive packages.

Some properties may also employ a *director of advertising and public relations* whose job it is to coordinate all promotional materials and public relations and to make the final decision on advertising media (radio, television, magazines, newspaper, billboard, direct mail).

The Sales Staff. The property's salespeople are the key to sales success. These are the people who prospect, set appointments and make personal calls on prospective clients. They must be professional, knowledgeable about the property, the competition, and their markets, and must possess excellent organizational and verbal and written communication skills. Today's sales professionals must also be computer literate as most hotels utilize computerized sales systems, and long-distance communication is often an integral part of the sales function.

Ironically, the increased use of technology sometimes impacts relationships between salespeople and clients. The use of the Internet by meeting planners to research possible sites, "virtual tours" of properties, and other technology, such as electronic transmittal of

Best Practices

Delta Hotels and the PCMA Team Up to Offer the Delta Convention Services Manager (CSM) Meeting Maestros Program.

In October 2004, Delta Hotels, which has hotels throughout Canada, launched the Delta Convention Services Manager (CSM) Meeting Maestros Program, developed and sponsored by Delta Hotels and the PCMA. The intensive three-day course focuses on the complex and changing role of the convention service manager, and features such topics as building client relations, adult learning, food and beverage, and technology.

All Delta CSMs are required to take the course, which centers around deliverables such as guaranteeing that all Delta CSMs will be PCMA-trained professionals, that meeting planners will be recognized on a personal level, and that Delta will deliver the fastest response in the industry. Sharon Bolan, director of learning and development for Delta Hotels, says,

> "We wanted it to be known that if you're planning a meeting with Delta, you will work with someone who's trained specifically for that...We wanted everyone to be trained to the same standards. So it made sense that we would look for a [standardized] training program, and PCMA was able to customize it."

Darrin Stern, who helped develop the content of the course and facilitated it, says that the course was designed by meeting managers for meeting managers. According to Stern, one of the areas of the program that generated the most discussion among participants was the section on adult learning, specifically how a room setup affects learning.

Danny Champagne, manager of convention services for the Delta Centre-Ville, says:

> "This three-day class made us realize what our clients are experiencing while they're at our property...I think that it brings new meaning to customer service for our clients. They already know that they are important to us, but the difference now is that they have the assurance that the convention services managers across Delta Hotels are devoted to their meetings and that we give guarantees to them in order to provide them with the level of service they deserve."

Source: Ginny Phillips, pcma Convene, October 2004, p. 78.

contracts have sometimes minimized face-to-face contact between meeting planners and hotel salespeople.

This makes it all the more important for salespeople to commit to building long-term relationships with customers. **Relationship marketing** -- the building and maintaining of lasting relationships with customers -- is important in today's competitive environment. Meeting planners are more likely to feel comfortable with a salesperson who has performed well in the past, and may even take familiarity and trust into consideration over other factors, including price.

Unfortunately, meeting planners are sometimes unable to work with the salesperson who assisted with a past function. The turnover of sales personnel in the hotel industry is considerably higher than turnover in other industries. According to a recent Dartnell's Sales Force Compensation Study, the annual turnover in all industries is 14.1 percent; in the hospitality industry, turnover more than doubled at 30.5 percent. And, the percentage may actually be considerably higher, as hotels do not consider transfers within the company as employee turnover.

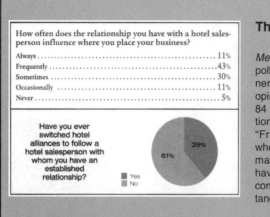

How often does the relationship you have with a hotel sales-person influence where you place your business?

Always 11%
Frequently 43%
Sometimes 30%
Occasionally 11%
Never 5%

Have you ever switched hotel alliances to follow a hotel salesperson with whom you have an established relationship?

39%
61%

■ Yes
■ No

The Importance of Relationships

Meetings & Conventions magazine recently polled hotel salespeople and meeting planners regarding how each felt about developing relationships. This chart shows that 84 percent of planners said that their relationships with hotel sales people "Always," "Frequently," or "Sometimes" influence where they book their meetings. Approximately 40 percent of planners surveyed have followed salespeople from one hotel company to another because of the importance of established relationships.

Source: Cheryl-Anne Sturken and Breadan Lynch, Meetings & Conventions, May 2004, p. 56.

Turnover is especially frustrating for meeting planners who have developed a good working relationship with salespeople and other property staff. Jackie Brave, a partner with Accenting Chicago Events and Tours, says:

"There has been so much turnover of personnel at hotels that it's hard to keep up with who is where. It's very difficult to create relationships with people who disappear at a moment's notice."[3]

The compensation structures employed by some hotels may be contributing to the problem. Some hotels opt to reward salespeople for performance, paying a commission rather than a salary, so there is a tendency for salespeople, especially younger sales people, to opt for compensation from the generation of new business rather than commit to building relationships with current customers.

But good convention salespeople are especially important to a property's success if it has targeted the group meetings market, and prior experience in sales is often desired. In many cases, students begin getting exposure to this sales area while still in school by participating in sales blitzes coordinated with a convention property.

According to a survey by David C. Bojanic and Elizabeth A. Dale:

"In the hotel industry, most sales training is done internally, with emphasis on field training. Then, as one gains experience, more classroom training is provided. Convention salespeople tend to progress through the ranks, enabling them to gain an in-depth knowledge of the hotel's products. However, one's sales training is mostly on-the-job training, working with smaller clients under close supervision and most hotels are requiring sales experience for new hires in convention sales."[4]

Clerical Support. To enable salespeople to handle the most important aspect of their jobs — selling —it is essential that a property employ a good clerical staff that can maintain careful and detailed records, make intelligent use of this data and assist in follow-up. While responsibilities may vary from property to property, the main function of the clerical staff is to provide support at the home base and to handle walk-in clients in the absence of sales personnel.

Figure 3.4. SHERATON'S JOB DESCRIPTION FOR CONVENTION SALES MANAGER POSITION

Job Title:	Convention Sales Manager
Department:	Marketing
Reports to:	Director of Sales
Basic Functions:	Reviews with Director of Sales the marketing strategy that will obtain maximum occupancy levels and average rate. Responsible for all convention group business related to the market segments as they relate to annual revenue projection.
Scope:	Sales manager will be the primary person for booking of long term convention group business with long term being more than six months out.

Work Performed: Initiate prospecting and solicitation of new accounts; manage current accounts to maximize room nights from the account in relation to the hotel marketing plan; responsible for administrative efforts necessary to perform the aforementioned.

1. Quotas for this position are:

Room nights per month	1200
Soft spot percentage	20
Phone calls per week:	
Trace:	20
Prospecting:	25
Personal calls per week	10
New accounts per week	10

   Individual to supply weekly, monthly and annual reports supporting productivity standards.
2. Probe for customer needs: rooms, suites, desired dates, day of week pattern, program agenda, food & beverage requirements and degree of flexibility in each of the aforementioned areas.
3. When available obtain information on the group's past history, i.e., previous rooms picked-up, arrival/departure pattern and double occupancy percentage.
4. Review availability of client's REQUIRED DATES AND ANY ALTERNATE DATES which should be offered. The dates presented to the customer should satisfy the customer's needs while allowing the hotel to maximize occupancy and average rate.
5. Negotiate with the customer: day/day of the week pattern, day by day room block, group rates (within guidelines as set by DOS), comps and function space.
6. Tentatively block rooms and function space in accordance with office policy.
7. Confirm in writing all aspects of the meeting. Check to ensure they received the signed contract.
8. Upon receiving the signed contract, process definite booking ticket, definite function room outline and credit application.
9. Oversee, manage and track the way in which reservations are to be made.
10. To periodically contact the customer while in-house to be certain all is in order and going well.
11. Conduct an exit interview with the customer to determine their level of satisfaction and ask for additional business.
12. Send letter of appreciation to customer.

Supervision Exercised:	Supervise and share one secretary with another individual.
Supervision Received:	Primary supervision from the Director of Sales. Initial training, and retraining as needed, also received from the Director of Sales, as well as direction as to room merchandising.

(continued)

Figure 3.4. (continued)

Responsibility & Authority:	Upon satisfactory completing rooms merchandising and operational training, the individual will have the authority to make decisions and confirm dates, room blocks and rates to the clients.
Minimum Requirements:	Bachelor of Arts or Science degree — preferably business, hotel or restaurant administration. Individual must also be professional in appearance and approach.
Experience:	Minimum of two years experience in hotel sales.
Sales Competencies:	1. Ability to negotiate. 2. Accounts strategizing. 3. Ability to prospect. 4. Ability to judge profitablility of new business. 5. Knowledge of product. 6. Knowledge of competition. 7. Ability to make presentations. 8. Ability to organize and plan. 9. Ability to utilize selling skills 10. Ability to overcome objections. 11. Ability to problem solve and make decisions. 12. Ability to write effectively.

A job description is a detailed listing of the function and organizational relationship of each employee. This job description for the convention sales manager shows the many facets of this important job and details the qualifications required for the position. Note that under "Work Performed" both room night and activity goals are stated. Top salespeople like to have their efforts measured against predetermined goals. Quality of calls is more important that quantity; therefore, room night/revenue goals are most important. However, maintaining activity goals such as number of phone calls, personal sales calls, and new accounts per week leads to more room nights booked and more revenue.

It would be penny-wise and pound-foolish to foot the considerable expense of fielding a sales staff only to skimp on the support at home. The period of sales effort before signing a convention can be very long, and salespeople must be continually in touch with the meeting planner. With today's high cost of sales calls, a follow-up system of letters and phone calls generated by a well-trained clerical staff is essential. The clerical staff will also maintain careful, detailed records of your prospects' convention activities, personnel changes and other data that may help win the sale.

Supplemental Sales Staff

It is often impractical and uneconomical for hotels to cover all the market bases with their in-house staff. To gain representation nationwide, chain properties supplement their staffs' sales efforts with *regional and national sales offices,* while independent properties turn to *independent hotel representatives* to help them with regional and national sales efforts.

Regional and National Sales Offices. National chains are reorganizing their sales function from a property basis to a regional basis. Marriott, Hilton and Starwood, for example, are merging sales departments from several properties into one central location. As this happens and the number of "unassisted" sales continues to grow as planners take advantage of Internet virtual tours and electronic transactions, individual salespeople in the future will only sell to their property's larger accounts, and sales staffs at the property level will be reduced in favor of regional sales reps.

One of the reasons for the success of regional and national offices is their use of *corporate sales staffs* in regional sales offices. The **regional sales office** serves as an intermediary between meeting planners and individual properties by providing a central information point that directs meeting planners to the property that best fits their needs.

The corporate staff solicits business for any hotel in the chain, and there are a number of advantages in this approach (see sidebar). First, a customer who has experienced good service and a successful meeting in one hotel of the chain might be induced to stay within the chain for their next meeting. Even when convention organizers have to move around the country to increase attendance, they may be sold on staying within the chain. Secondly, it is easier for a meeting planner who is scheduling ten similar meetings in

> **What Meeting Planners Say About Regional and National Sales Offices**
>
> - "They've invaluable. They open doors"
> - "They offer one point of contact for all hotels and brands within the chain."
> - "They know our company, our history, our culture, our attendees and whether or not a particular property is the right fit for our group."
> - "They tell our story to individual hotels, so we don't have to repeat basic information about ourselves."

many parts of the country to book all of them at once with a single salesperson. Once a salesperson has broken through to close a sale, the way to booking additional locations is easier. And, still another advantage comes into play when a meeting planner cannot get a free date at one hotel. The chain may be able to offer another hotel on that date, whereas an independent property loses out when firm dates cannot be met.

Several hotel chains, including Sheraton, Hyatt, and Red Lion Hotels and Inns, have developed computer systems that link their convention hotels with their regional and national sales offices. These systems give instant electronic access to group booking data, including availability, rates and dates, and, in addition, track client histories and account activity chainwide. With such information at their fingertips, many regional sales representatives are now empowered to block space, print out proposals for any hotel on the system, and book business on the spot. The hotel's director of sales is then notified by electronic mail for approval of the agreement. And, regional sales offices also serve the properties within a chain's region by providing promotional materials and public relations.

Independent Hotel Representatives. Many hotels do not feel they can adequately cover all of their market bases with an in-house sales staff; they often supplement the staff with an **independent hotel representative**. These outside individuals or firms represent the property as a "long arm" of the sales department.

Because hotels have different needs, the services provided by independent hotel representatives vary widely. In some cases, the representative may be hired simply as a field salesperson, soliciting clients who are impractical for the hotel's in-house staff to reach. Other hotels may use larger representation companies, whose services include consulting, market analysis, advertising and public relations in addition to sales.

Because of economics, independent hotel representatives usually represent more than one property. This causes many hotels to balk at the notion of being represented by such firms. Quite logically, they question having a competitor represented by the same firm. Hotel representatives answer this criticism by saying they represent properties of different sizes and market emphasis, not similar clients seeking the same clients.

Should a hotel use an independent hotel representative? If you can afford to field your own staff and it performs satisfactorily, that's fine. If you can afford only limited sales efforts, a representative may offer another dimension. What counts is the amount of sales generated.

A hotel should investigate the benefits offered by an independent hotel representative firm. Such firms usually specialize in a particular market, while overlapping to other sources of business. If your target market is the convention trade, be selective, since few firms actually specialize in this area. And, since the majority of association and trade convention groups are headquartered in Washington, DC, Chicago or New York, your chances of reaching the convention market are greatly increased if your representative has an office in one of these locations. Just two examples of such firms include the Krisam Group, headquartered in Washington, DC, and The Leading Hotels of the World, Ltd., based in New York City.

There are a number of factors that you will want to consider in making your decision (see box titled "How to Choose an Independent Hotel Representative"). In addition, you may wish to consult similar-sized properties who are using a representative you are considering. Ask them about the effectiveness of the representative, especially in regard to areas in which you feel you may have difficulties.

If you opt to go with an independent hotel representative, it is important to remember that they are generally hired on a contract basis, usually paid a fee and receive a set percentage of the volume of business they directly book for the hotel. They must be given clear guidelines on what type of business the property is soliciting and what rates the property will accept.

In other words, the hotel representative should work within the framework of the property's marketing plan, and, as an extended member of your sales force, should be thoroughly familiar with the property's facilities, rates and operating procedures. Personal visits and tours by the management should be encouraged. The representative should be

---

HOW TO CHOOSE AN INDEPENDENT HOTEL REPRESENTATIVE

Choosing an independent hotel representative is not to be taken lightly. Take the same care in hiring a hotel representative as you would in hiring an in-house executive. Here are questions to help you to determine whether an individual or firm would be an asset to your sales operation:

1. How many hotels does the firm represent? Has it extended itself so much that it may not be able to meet your needs?
2. Does the firm represent competing properties? If so, how will this affect its handling of your account?
3. Does the representative specialize in that targeted market you are seeking? Does he or she have knowledge of the group and convention business? Is the firm doing business with organizations you have targeted?
4. Does the firm have offices in the cities that are your major market areas?
5. Is the representative's staff knowledgeable about your type of operation? Does his or her staff have a hotel background?
6. How does the representative regard service? Do you want him or her to be an extension of your sales staff? Is he or she willing to be part of your team?
7. Can he or she deliver needed supporting services and advise you on brochures and other printed materials?

given organizational charts, operating manuals and materials detailing charges for meeting rooms, guestrooms and other facilities. And, most importantly, the representative should be given a copy of the property's marketing plan — with specific objectives spelled out for him or her to meet.

Managing the Sales Effort

While hiring good salespeople, whether they be in-house staff or independent hotel representatives, is an important step toward achieving sales goals, the sales effort itself must be structured and managed properly for maximum effectiveness. Managing the sales effort involves a number of areas: the development of standard operating procedures (SOPs) for salespeople and convention staff; periodic sales meetings to discuss goals and problems; the prioritizing of accounts; keeping accurate records; and, most important, the monitoring and evaluating of progress.

Standard Operating Procedures

An effective sales effort begins with standardized guidelines for each step of the sales and servicing process. Each salesperson should be made aware of the sales office's **standard operating procedures (SOPs)**. These are instructions explaining how recurring business activities should be handled.

Each hotel salesperson should have a three-ring binder containing the property's standard operating procedures on their desk in order to keep everyone "on the same page" for consistent selling. Written SOPs presented together in a manual provide a constant reference for sales and banquet personnel, and are an essential training tool for new employees. Areas that might be included in a SOP manual include:

- function book control and procedures
- guestroom control book procedures
- booking policies
- rate guidelines for high and low demand periods
- credit/deposit/cancellation policies
- policies regarding V.I.P. and complimentary rooms
- meeting room rental fees and procedures
- banquet and room reservation cut-off dates
- convention service standards and procedures
- the organizational chart and specific job descriptions for the sales department

The sales department's SOPs can be added to or amended as situations warrant, but it is important that each person involved in the sales effort be made aware of any changes. These written SOPs help to eliminate costly errors by ensuring that each member of the sales team follows the same procedures when booking and servicing groups.

Sales Meetings

Just as written procedures are important, good communication is also essential to an effective sales effort. Sales meetings are an excellent way to ensure that all people involved in the sales effort have the same information and can help to eliminate potential problems by identifying and dealing with them early.

While the number and type of sales meetings may vary, the most commonly used meetings are (1) weekly and monthly staff meetings; (2) weekly function meetings; and, (3) marketing team meetings and periodic (usually annual or semi-annual) sales meetings for all employees.

- Weekly and monthly sales or staff meetings are usually headed by the coordinator of the sales effort; this may be the director of marketing, the director of sales or the sales manager at larger properties, or the general manager at small properties. Held to discuss any changes in the sales or promotional effort, the progress on certain accounts, new and tentative bookings, sales goals and potential problems, these meetings are usually attended by all sales personnel and the heads of any departments affected by the sales efforts (convention services, banquet/catering, front desk, etc.). Since the mutual exchange of ideas and information is vitally important to any sales effort, these regularly scheduled sales meetings should also include a period of open discussion or a brainstorming session.
- Weekly function meetings generally include only the department heads involved in selling to and servicing the convention market. These meetings ensure that every area of the property is adequately covered when making commitments to groups, and help to ensure that specific business is understood and properly handled.
- Many properties hold an annual or semi-annual sales meeting for all the property's staff. The marketing plan—and each employee's role in it—is presented, and specific information, such as advertising and promotional efforts and the affect on individual departments and employees is discussed. This benefits both employee and management, providing an opportunity to obtain ideas and suggestions from employees working in day-to-day operations.

Assigning Account Responsibility

Keeping the sales staff abreast of current information and goals is only part of the management of the sales effort. It is the responsibility of the director of sales or other leader of the sales effort to ensure that accounts are being distributed and handled in the most productive and cost-effective manner for optimum results.

There are many variables in assigning responsibility. Some directors of sales feel that accounts should be assigned by market segment; if he or she has three salespeople, for example, one will be assigned to corporate meetings, one to association business and one to incentive travel. While this may seem practical on the surface, there may be drastic imbalance within the market segments. The salesperson assigned to corporate meetings, for example, may end up with more accounts than he or she can handle.

The director of sales may see this imbalance, and assign two people to cover the property's most lucrative segment. This approach, too, may present problems, since most corporations find it more comfortable to deal with only one contact person at a property.

One solution is to *assign specific accounts, rather than market segments*, to each of the salespeople; one salesperson would be responsible for all the business generated by a particular organization. This type of account assignment is beneficial to both the salesperson and the client; it provides one contact person and helps to build rapport that may generate future business. If this approach is taken, it is important to distribute accounts with particular attention to the number of accounts, their geographic area and the market segments into which they fall. In terms of numbers, it is usually considered best to assign accounts equally; if, for example, a property expects to target 900 accounts over the coming year, each of the hotel's three salespeople should be given 300 of them.

This number can vary based upon the location of the accounts. If, for example, a property can target a nearby industrial park, it is easier for a salesperson to handle these accounts than it would be for a salesperson to adequately cover accounts spread over a two state area. In this case, the salesperson covering the local area can be assigned a larger number of accounts.

The market segment factor comes into play when determining just how much business will be generated by each account. A salesperson assigned to a large corporate account, for example, can expect to cover a great deal more business — meetings, award ceremonies, the annual convention, etc. — than a salesperson assigned to an association that stages just one annual convention. In this case, or in the case of the salesperson who shows particular expertise in servicing a specific market segment, accounts can be redistributed for the best results.

Key Account Management. Once accounts have been assigned, the typical salesperson may find that he or she is looking at 300 to 400 sources of potential business. Selling to and servicing these accounts will involve making cold calls, setting appointments and following up — all activities that will generate a mountain of paperwork. So how does a salesperson decide how to handle the monumental task of effectively selling to his or her accounts? The solution is **key account management**.

Key account management involves prioritizing accounts based on their profit potential. This is important because, generally, 20 percent of a salesperson's accounts generate 80 percent of the business. Look at accounts individually to determine which ones have the highest potential for generating business and organize your time to sell and service these accounts. Key account management, then, involves ranking accounts. This is usually done on five levels:

- *Level 1* consists of all new and established accounts with a high potential for business. These are the accounts that will warrant your highest attention. As a general rule, a minimum of five personal calls and five telephone calls should be allocated to these accounts annually.
- *Level 2* consists of high potential accounts that are already providing a good share of business. Of course you want to continue to follow up on these lucrative accounts, but they don't require the same amount of personal attention and they can usually be serviced by four personal and four telephone calls annually.
- *Level 3* consists of new accounts with medium potential and established accounts that are not generating the medium potential expected of them. These accounts generally require three personal and three telephone calls each year.

Figure 3.5. KEY ACCOUNT MANAGEMENT SPREAD SHEET.

KEY ACCOUNT MANAGEMENT SPREAD SHEET

Name of account and key contact	# of times account was called on last year	# of times we expect to call on account this year	Estimate of room night potential from account
Stubbs Insurance Mark Steward	4 Personal calls 4 Telephone calls	5 Personal 5 Telephone	25 r.n. x 12 mo. @ $75 = $22,500 20 r.n. x 12 mo. @ $80= $19,200 30r.n. x 2 days x 4 @ $72=$17,280 125r.n. x3 days @ $75 = <u>$28,125</u> Total $87,105

Prioritizing accounts can be accomplished easily if a salesperson takes a look at all of his or her accounts and judges them by the same criteria. A spread sheet, such as this one, provides a place for necessary data and enables the salesperson to see the profit potential of each account at a glance. Since each of a salesperson's 300-400 accounts are assessed, the director of sales can review the spread sheets with salespeople on a periodic basis (usually the end or beginning of a year) to reassess priorities.

- *Level 4* consists of accounts with medium potential providing an acceptable level of business. These accounts are normally followed up with two personal and two telephone calls annually.
- *Level 5* consists of low potential new and established accounts that do not warrant a great deal of time. These accounts require little more than token attention, such as a personal visit while on a sales trip to a more lucrative account or a telephone call after all the other business has been handled.

The level of each account can be determined by preparing an account "spread sheet" (see Figure 3.5) and by discussing questionable accounts with the director of sales. When setting account levels, however, remember that your priorities may change as your accounts and prospects change. Perhaps a company that had a low potential level because of its distance from the property may expand into your area or an association that had previously met at another hotel chain may have become dissatisfied and is now looking for another meeting place. These scenarios, which are not that uncommon, show the necessity for qualifying each account (see box titled "Home Run Accounts") and for personally reviewing your accounts to determine how much time and effort should be spent to realize maximum sales potential.

Home Run Accounts

In most situations, there are a few accounts on which you should concentrate because these key accounts can have an immediate impact on your business. *Home run accounts* are those accounts that are likely to generate the greatest revenue.

To manage accounts properly, you must *fully qualify* the contact. Full qualification involves gathering all information necessary to place a dollar value on the account's potential business. For example, a corporation contact might state they average 25 room nights per month for their own executives, another 20 room nights for visiting clients, quarterly two-day workshops for 30 persons, and a large new product showcase annually, requiring 125 guestrooms for the three day event. From this information, it is now possible to estimate the potential dollar volume the account represents for your hotel (see Figure 3.5).

Figure 3.5. CONTINUED

KEY ACCOUNT MANAGEMENT SPREAD SHEET			
Estimate of food and beverage potential	Estimate of meeting room revenue potential	Total potential dollar value of account	Level of account priority (Level 1 through Level 5)
40% of Room Revenue = $34,842	4 Workshops - Complimentary function space Product Showcase - 1.00 per square foot for exhibit hall = $10,000	Rooms $86,105 Food & Beverage $34,842 Meeting Space $10,000	Level 1 — High Potential Account

It is also important to note that the goals set for a salesperson will affect how he or she manages accounts. Most hotels measure sales productivity and provide salespeople with bonuses and incentives based on both the amount of revenue generated and the number of room nights booked. If salespeople were measured strictly by the number of room nights booked, there would be a tendency to book business at almost any rate rather than the highest possible rate. Some properties set goals for high and low periods, for example. In this case, a fairly low priority account may provide the business needed during a slow period -- and help achieve an individual sales goal. It is also important to maintain a balance between maintaining good customer relations and prospecting for new customers. In some cases, salespeople will have sales goals based on business from current customers and business to book from new accounts. All of these variables will figure into managing accounts for maximum benefit.

Evaluating the Sales Effort

To ensure that the sales office is operating at top capacity, it is necessary to periodically review both the salespeople and the organizational structure itself. Salespeople should be monitored to determine if they are meeting their personal quotas. They should also be evaluated as to how they are using their general sales abilities — are they prospecting, developing concrete leads, following up? Do they have a good service attitude? Are they managing their time properly? These evaluations should be made at least quarterly to enable sales management to control small problems that could develop into major difficulties. One seasoned sales professional says:

> "Review the activity of a salesperson to check what's being done and to make sure the person's performance is in line with corporate or property sales procedures. Review each salesperson's weekly sales activity report with the salesperson. You also want to look at the follow-up accounts to see if the trace system is working accordingly. Pull some files to see how accounts are being handled."[5]

New salespeople should be reviewed more frequently to ensure that they are "on track." To assist in evaluations, each salesperson should maintain a **reader file**. This file contains copies of all correspondence and call reports generated by a salesperson. Each salesperson's reader file should be evaluated weekly by the director of sales.

The organizational structure of the sales office should also be reviewed to determine if current efforts make the most of the strengths of its staff and contribute to the property's bottom line. This involves taking a look at a number of factors. Are lines of communication open with both the sales staff and other departments on the property? Has authority been clearly delegated — and is the scope of that authority understood? Are duties and responsibilities being carried out? Is sales follow-up — correspondence, telephone calls, etc. — being handled properly? Is there an adequate support staff?

Sales Records and Filing Systems

A hotel sales department should have an efficient system of sales records and files. Effective sales promotion requires it. Vast amounts of client information must be documented and filed, accurately and up-to-date, if they are to be meaningful. Similarly, forms and records are valuable only if the information they contain is accessible. If you cannot locate the needed information quickly, the system isn't much good.

While most hotels today use computerized systems for record keeping and managing sales efforts, some smaller properties still use manual systems. And, if a computer system is used, it is still customary to maintain "hard copy" files and maintain a paper trail of customer business. Even when correspondence, contracts, and other paperwork inherent to sales efforts are sent electronically (e-mail or fax), they are printed out and placed in a customer file.

In this section, we will discuss the basic forms that are used for the sales function. We will first show the manual versions of each before illustrating its computerized counterpart. Later in the chapter, we will show how the computer is used to manage the service function and how technology can enhance sales efforts and profitability.

Hotel Filing Systems

The late C. Dewitt Coffman stated that "the maintenance of accurate and up-to-date file systems is the single, most important mechanical operation of any sales department. Without minutely accurate file records, the sales department is without ammunition." When selling, especially to groups, sales personnel need easily available, up-to-date information.

Methods of Filing. Most hotel filing systems, whether they are manual, computerized, or a combination of both, fall into three general categories. *Alphabetical filing* is done by the title of the organization, firm or association (or by the name of the contact person), and is often used by hotels. Many properties find this to be the easiest method of filing.

The second method of filing is by *key word of the title*. This type of filing is advantageous when the exact name of the organization is not known. For example, the Association of Petroleum and Oil Products would be filed under the word "petroleum." Or, several key words could be used (in this case, the account could also be filed under "oil"). This method can be varied by using a three-level way of classification. Accounts would be filed under such headings as Trade-Manufacturing-Shoes, Trade-Retail-Clothes and Educational-Teachers-High School.

The third method of filing is *numerical*. Each file carries an assigned account number and a corresponding set of file cards is kept by the number and name. This method is often effective for larger file systems, and while it has not always been widely used, it is becoming more popular as hotels turn increasingly to computer technology to assist in keeping account records. Most computerized systems enable the salesperson to access accounts by a number of criteria, including account number, name, key word, and other specialized searches.

Some properties prefer one method over another, and some use more than one method. Some hotels, for example, may also file master cards geographically to facilitate sales trip planning. A simple system usually tends to be superior to a complicated setup.

Elements of Filing Systems. Most hotel filing systems share three common elements:

- the master card
- the account file, and
- the tickler (trace) file

As each is explained and illustrated keep in mind that systems will vary slightly from hotel to hotel.

The **master card** serves as a summary for the sales effort. It details such information as contact names and titles, addresses, telephone numbers, month or months in which the group meets, the size of the group, where it has met in the past, who makes the initial and final site decision, and other pertinent information (see Figure 3.6). The master card serves as a data bank of prospects and is often color-coded to draw attention to specific areas. If you are going after groups in a specific area, for example, you may color-code the cards by geographic location. Or you may color-code cards based on the month of meetings to attempt to fill holes in your property's calendar. Groups can also be color-coded by size or other key factors.

Large companies having a number of divisions usually require a master card and several "trailer cards." The master card would detail information on the corporate level,

Figure 3.6. SAMPLE ACCOUNT MASTER CARD (MANUAL SYSTEM).

Jan.	Feb.	Mar.	April	May	June	July	Aug.	Sept.	Oct.	Nov.	Dec.	1 to 100	100 to 250	250 to 350	350 to 500	Over 500

Convention Group *NATIONAL LIVESTOCK DEALERS ASSO. N-02197*

Main Contact *DAVID PRITCHARD*   Title *ASSO. MANAGER*

Address   Phone

City

Other Contacts

How is Decision Made   When

Date	City	Hotel	Attend	No. of Hotel Rms.
				Exhibits
				Functions

The master card provides a summary of convention information on a 5x8-inch card. Master cards can be color coded by geographic location, month of meeting, or other category to assist salespeople in soliciting business or following up on the account.

while the trailer cards would contain contact names, meeting dates and similar information for divisions in the company. A company such as General Electric, for example, would have a number of trailer cards.

The computerized version of the master file enables the salesperson to instantly access the account and add an unlimited amount of material to each account file. The file can be broken down into several screens (or windows) that provide a variety of additional information: account history, name of contact person, etc. (see Figure 3.7). Using a computerized master file eliminates the need to make copious notes on an index card, and necessary information is immediately available on a computer terminal.

The **account file** serves as the basic group business record, and its file folder should include all correspondence and related materials (contracts, past convention programs, tear sheets from trade papers, etc.). The account file is usually a standard size file folder (see Figure 3.8), and, like the master card, it may be color-coded to draw attention to specific data.

If a file needs to be removed from the file cabinet, a guide card detailing the name of the group, its file number, the date of removal, and the initials of the person requesting the file should be placed in the file drawer in place of the file. This enables the sales staff to keep track of the file's whereabouts.

The **tickler file**, also known as a *trace file, bring-up file* or *follow-up file*, is an effective follow-up tool. Tickler files may come in various forms; some are card files with monthly dividers and card separators marked 1 through 30 or 31 (see Figure 3.9), others are accordion-style files with multi-pockets. And, there are systems designed to fit within a letter-sized file cabinet. In all of these systems, cards are filed by month and day.

The tickler file, used properly, works very well, costs little and takes little time to implement. It works this way: you make contact with a prospect who indicates that no meeting plans will be finalized until October. Obviously, you want to contact the person before then — perhaps by the middle of September — so you place a card or note or a copy of some correspondence in the pocket marked September 15. This type of system eliminates reliance on memory, and ensures good follow-up — *if* you remember to remove everything in the pocket on each day of the month!

Of course, all records should be updated when a booking has been made. And outdated copies should be removed from the follow-up file. This will avoid an automatic follow-up letter being sent. The same procedure should be taken if the association has made a booking with another hotel.

Several computerized versions of the tickler file are available. Specialized hotel software, such as Delphi, not only reminds salespeople of important dates, but also offers additional sales tools. The computerized trace report show in Figure 3.10, for example, breaks down the day's business into several categories. The salesperson can take advantage of this to prioritize his or her work and schedule each day to make the most of sales opportunities. But even salespeople who do not have access to hotel-specific software can utilize other programs, such as Microsoft Outlook, to help organize their work. The Outlook program features a daily calendar and task list.

Control Books and Sales Forms

In addition to files, the sales office utilizes a number of forms and control books in selling to and servicing the group sales business.

Figure 3.7. COMPUTERIZED MASTER CARD FILES.

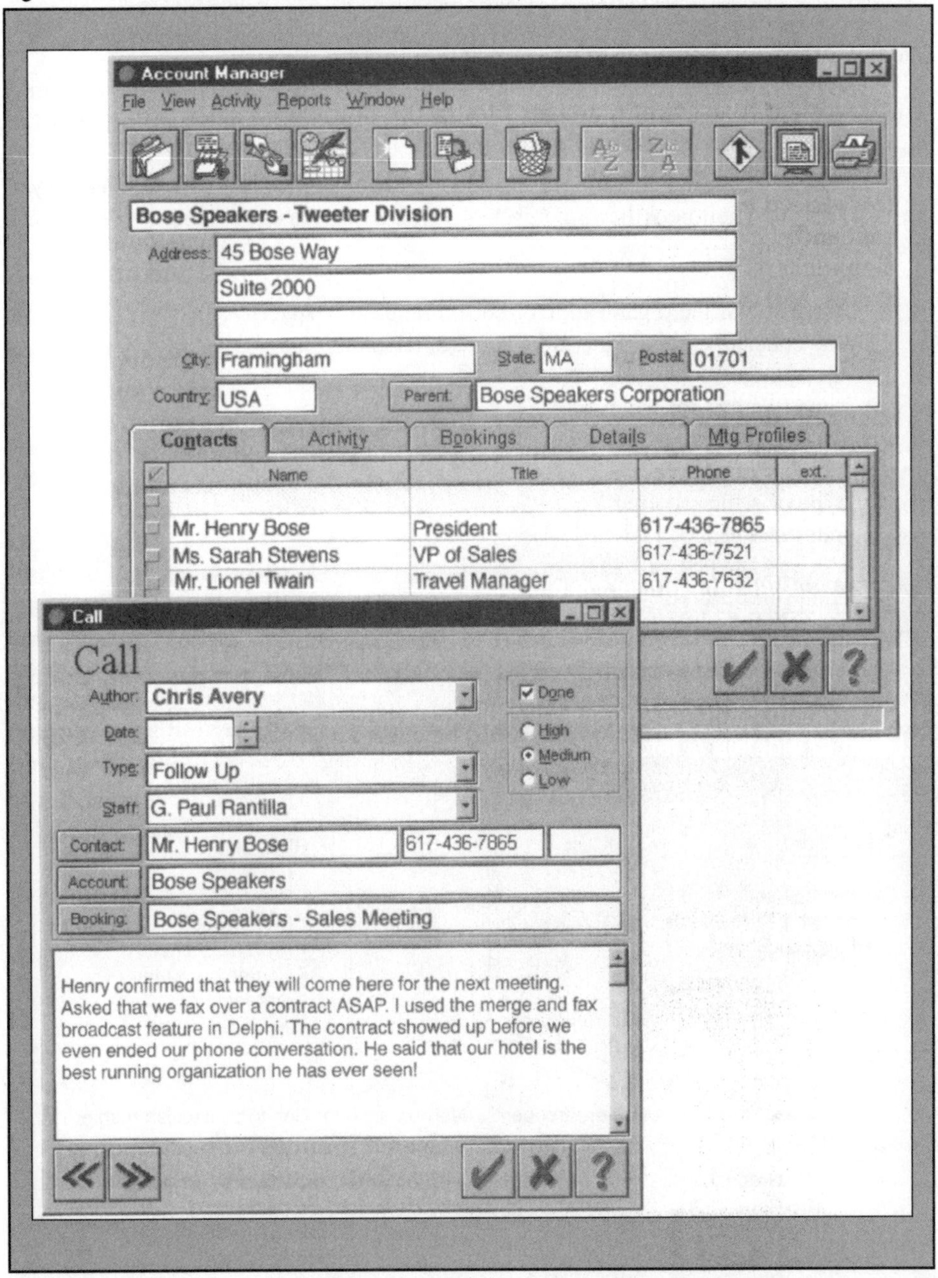

This computerized version of the account master card enables the salesperson to instantly access the account — and add an unlimited amount of material to each account's file. The file can be broken into several screens (or windows) which provide a variety of additional information — account history, name of contact person, etc. Using a computerized master file eliminates the need to make copious notes on an index card — and the need to spend a great deal of time in locating the necessary information (it can all be done at the salesperson's desk.)

Source: Delphi 7/Newmarket Software Systems, Inc., Durham, New Hampshire. For more information, browse the company's Web site at http://www.newmarketinc.com.

Control Books. In selling public and banquet space to convention groups, for example, the salesperson must be sure that the assigned space will be available. Overbooking is eliminated by the use of a hotel **function book** (see Figure 3.11).

The function book serves as the hotel's "bible" when it comes to booking meeting and banquet space, so there should only be one book to prevent mismatched entries or **double bookings**.

The most common type of function book is a large book with a page for every day of the year. The function book has a number of vertical columns, providing space for such information as:

- the name of the organization or person requesting space
- the contact person (name, title, address, telephone)
- type of function
- time required for the event
- total time required (for setup, breakdown, cleanup)
- number of attendees
- type of setup required
- rates charged

Figure 3.8. SAMPLE ACCOUNT FILE.

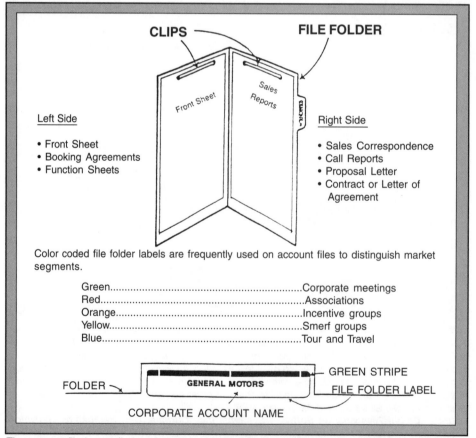

The account file is usually kept in a standard file folder and contains all of the group's information, including sales call reports, tentative and definite booking information, function sheets from past business, and correspondence generated relating to the booking. Information is placed in the file in chronological order (with the newest on top)) and secured with clips to prevent loss. Like the master file, account file folders may be color coded to call attention to specific characteristics of the group.

Figure 3.9. SAMPLE TICKLER (TRACE) FILE – MANUAL SYSTEM.

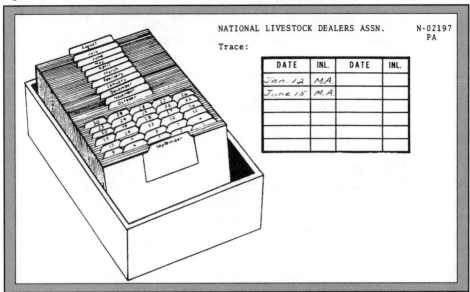

Divided into months and days of the month, the tickler file helps with account follow up. Salespeople use the tickler file to remind themselves of calls to be made or correspondence to be sent on a specific date.

- contract status
- other remarks

There should be at least one section for each meeting or function room, with space to cover specific time periods in each day. To ensure the most efficient use of the function book, all bookings should be made in pencil, the name of the group should be recorded exactly as it appears on the file to facilitate future referencing, and the starting and ending times should be recorded to enable the property to book another event if possible.

To eliminate possible errors, only one person should be given control of the function book. This may be the convention sales manager, or, at properties with a large staff, the senior sales executive. Single person control of the function book is essential; convention space cannot be sold efficiently without this control.

There may be instances in which the same space is desired by two groups. In this case, sales managers will try to determine the best "fit" for both the hotel and the group. Factors to be considered are the likelihood that the space will actually be filled, the estimated profitability of each group, the status of the group (regular client or new business), the likelihood of repeat business, the long-term profitability of each group, the possibility that one group would consider an alternate date, and the group's convention history. Only after a decision has been made will the group's name be entered into the function book.

In addition to controlling meeting space, it is also necessary to control guestrooms. Properties use a **guestrooms control book** for this; at some properties this book is referred to as the *rooms control bible.* This ensures that rooms are available for groups. This book is used by the sales department to stay aware of the number of rooms it can sell, as hotels often stipulate a maximum *group allotment* — the number of rooms available for sale to groups — to ensure that a proper market mix of group, tour and travel, and individual guest business is maintained. Demand fluctuates by time of year and by day of week so the group room allotment varies considerably. For example, the summer months are generally soft

Figure 3.10. SAMPLE TICKER (TRACE) REPORT – COMPUTERIZED SYSTEM.

The Durham Resort
Morning Report for Ralph Johnson
September 21, 1999

Rooming List Due

Group Name	Date	Day	Room Type	Agree	Block	Pickup	New Block
Mt. Hope Radiology Dept.	2/ 2/ 00	Wed	Run of House	25	25	_____	_____
	2/ 3/ 00	Thu	Run of House	25	25	_____	_____
	2/ 4/ 00	Fri	Run of House	300	300	_____	_____
	2/18/ 00	Fri	Run of House	25	25	_____	_____

Deposits Due

Group Name	Arrival Date	Trace Date	New Status/ New Trace Date
Acorn Dry Cleaning	3/ 20/ 00	1/ 10/ 00	_____ ___/___/___

Verbal Definites - Contract Due

Group Name	Arrival Date	Trace Date	New Status/ New Trace Date
Jacobs Wedding	9/ 1/ 00	1/ 15/ 00	_____ ___/___/___

Tentatives - Decision Due

Group Name	Arrival Date	Trace Date	New Status/ New Trace Date
Automobile Travelers Assn	3/ 24/ 00	11/ 20/ 99	_____/ ___/___/___
Arizona Building Company	4/ 30/ 00	12/ 20/ 99	_____/ ___/___/___

Leads - Decision Due

Group Name	Arrival Date	Trace Date	New Status/ New Trace Date
Balloon Industries	2/ 1/ 00	11/ 1/ 99	_____/ ___/___/___

Source: Delphi Newmarket Software Systems, Inc., Durham, New Hampshire

This report not only replaces the cumbersome manual tickler file, but also offers additional sales tools to the salesperson. The trace report, for example, breaks down the day's business into several categories. The salesperson can take advantage of this feature to prioritize work and schedule each day to make the most of sales opportunities.

Figure 3.11. FUNCTION BOOK RESERVATION SHEET.

U.S. Grant HOTEL

FUNCTION BOOK RESERVATION SHEET

Group Name _____   Comments _____

Contact _____   _____

Address _____   _____

Phone _____   _____

Dates In House _____   _____

A G E N D A

DAY/DATE	TIME	FUNCTION	SET-UP	# OF PEOPLE	ROOM NAME

Meeting Space Charges:

Sales Rep _____

Date _____

Option Date _____

Date Entered _____

Entered By _____

The sales or catering manager must fill out this form and submit it to the person responsible for monitoring the hotel's function space. In addition, one copy of this form will go into the account file and another copy to the salesperson's reader file.

convention months, so a 400-room hotel might only do 25 percent of its business with meeting groups and 75 percent with individual travelers.

Although these percentages may be reversed in the typically busy convention periods of spring or fall, hotels rarely, if ever, will sell the entire hotel to convention groups. Individual corporate and leisure travelers are consistent year-round producers, and selling out to a convention will alienate travelers displaced by convention groups.

The guestrooms control book's format usually consists of monthly report sheets with space for the group's name and guestroom commitment by day. These "forecast sheets" are dated and bound in book form, providing projections several years ahead.

As with the function book, all entries should be made in pencil. Often, definite bookings are listed on the upper half of the page, while tentative bookings are entered on the lower half. This technique indicates the negotiating period of convention sales.

It is extremely important for the hotel sales office and the front desk/reservations department to have good communication and contact with one another. Because both are booking business, it is imperative that room sales are not overlapped. Traditionally, reservations has reported to the front office manager, but reservations are increasingly being placed under the sales department in many convention-oriented hotels.

Most hotels also computerized their function and guestrooms control books (see Figure 3.12). This method still provides control, since only authorized personnel can add or change information (while information is being changed, the system goes into a "read only" mode until the information is updated). However, the information is readily available to salespeople, either in-house or from a remote location.

Before Hyatt Hotels updated their function books, Gordon Kerr, Hyatt's senior vice president of Management Information Systems, said:

> "Each hotel kept this giant diary with function room bookings written in it. If a customer called Hyatt headquarters in Chicago to book a function room in San Francisco, for example, the manager of the San Francisco hotel had to be called to check availability. Customers eager to book space would wait hours, or even days, to receive a reply. By that time, many would-be customers had found space elsewhere. With the computerized system, Hyatt users can check availability and book function rooms at any connected hotel from any hotel in the network."[6]

Wendy Bonvechio, director of sales and marketing, Sheraton Seattle Hotel & Towers, says:

> "Automation is very important to our business. A problem that has been completely eliminated is the inevitable double booking that occurred with the manual systems. With automation, the computer won't allow you to double book. Our customers demand automation because it is quicker, makes us more efficient and virtually eliminates mistakes. It's no longer an option, but a necessity in order to compete in today's market."[7]

Sales Forms. Once a sales commitment has been made, there are a number of forms used to follow the sale to the final execution of the function. The *tentative booking sheet* (or report) is used if a date has not been confirmed or if details have not been worked out (see Figure 3.13).

In the normal sequence of events, a convention organizer may inquire about the availability of the property on certain dates. Requirements are discussed, but perhaps there are circumstances that must be resolved before setting a definite date. Perhaps board ap-

Figure 3.12. COMPUTERIZED FUNCTION AND GUESTROOMS CONTROL BOOK.

THE RIVERVIEW HOTEL

Date printed: October 1, 20__   Time printed: 11:59 AM

DELPHI — Function Space Profile   Page: 1

Report for Oct 1 20__ to Oct 31 20__

Room Name	Time Period	We 1	Th 2	Fr 3	Sa 4	Su 5	Mo 6	Tu 7	We 8	Th 9	Fr 10	Sa 11	Su 12	Mo 13	Tu 14	We 15	Th 16	Fr 17	Sa 18	Su 19	Mo 20	Tu 21	We 22	Th 23	Fr 24	Sa 25	Su 26	Mo 27	Tu 28	We 29	Th 30	Fr 31
WASHINTN	M				D	D	D	D				D	D						T	T	T											
	L				D	D													T	T	T											
	A				D														T	T	T											
	E																		T	T	T											
ADAMS	M																		DD	DD												
	L																															
	A							T	T													DD	DD									
	E				T	T	T		T	T																						
JEFFERSON	M				D	D	D		VD	VD	VD	VD	VD	VD																		
	L											VD	VD	VD																		
	A																															
	E																															
MADISON	M												T	T	T						DD	DD	DD					T	T	T		
	L								VD	VD																		T	T	T		
	A								VD	VD				T	T	T																
	E																															
MONROE	M																		T	T	T											
	L																		T	T	T											
	A																		T	T	T											
	E																		T	T	T											
JACKSON	M					VD	VD	VD			D	D	D																			
	L					VD	VD	VD			D	D	D																			
	A																															
	E																															

Many hotels are using computerized function and guestrooms control books to provide instant access to information by sales personnel, who must often provide an immediate answer regarding the availability of function space or rooms. These reports are very similar to the manual reports kept by some hotels. The main difference is that the computer generates these reports automatically by using booking information already entered into the system. These sample reports were generated by Delphi System, software specifically designed to meet the needs of the hotel industry.   (continued)

proval is needed or, in the case of a corporate meeting, a supervisor must be consulted. The meeting planner then asks for an **option** on the space, and a *hold* is placed on the room(s).

This means that the hotel has agreed to hold the space pending final confirmation by the client (this agreement may be verbal or by letter). Some properties are cautious about tentative bookings; they do not want to lose out on other business while protecting a tentative account that may not "go definite." That is why it is important to limit the length of the hold by designating an *option date*. An option date is the date by which the client must confirm the order or release the space. If this period is too long, the hotel has severely limited its freedom to seek another customer, but the date should be long enough to enable the client to secure the necessary approval. A typical first option agreement might read:

Figure 3.12. COMPUTERIZED FUNCTION AND GUESTROOMS CONTROL BOOKS.

THE RIVERVIEW HOTEL

Date printed: August 27, 20__   Time printed: 11:41 AM

DELPHI — Group rooms Control Report for 20__ June

	1 Sun	2 Mon	3 Tue	4 Wed	5 Thur	6 Fri	27 Fri	28 Sat	29 Sun	30 Mon	Total Rooms	Total Guests	Ave. Rate	Room Revenue	Decision Date	RT	SRC	Stat	Date Entered
DEFINITES for CORP.																			
D.E.C.											500	500	124.00	62,000.00	8/27/96		TRB	D	8/27/96
Mass Bay Co											200	200	118.00	23,600.00	8/27/96		TRB	D	8/27/96
I.B.M.											90	90	125.00	11,250.00	8/27/96		TRB	D	8/27/96
Coastal Inc.											15	15	128.00	1,920.00			TRB	D	2/13/96
CORP.	0	0	0	0	0	0	0	0	0	0	805	820	122.69	98,770.00				D	
TENTATIVES for CORP.																			
Lotus Dev. Co.			5	5	5	5					20	40	145.00	2,900.00	8/27/96		SB	T	8/27/96
Crimson Trvl						6					24	48	118.00	2,832.00	8/27/96		RWH	T	8/27/96
Eastern Inc.											35	70	130.00	4,550.00	8/27/96		RWH	T	8/27/96
Lotus Dev. Co.											15	30	121.00	1,815.00	8/27/96		RWH	T	8/27/96
Intel Corp.											9	27	121.00	1,089.00	8/27/96				
Eastern Inc.											4	4	145.00	580.00	8/27/96				
CORP.	0	0	5	5	5	11	0	0	0	0	107	223	128.65	13,766.00				T	
DEFINITES for Assoc.																			
Travel Assoc.	25.	25	25								75	75	108.00	8,100.00	9/30/96		KL	D	3/10/96
N.A.F.E.											30	60	127.00	3,810.00	8/12/96		CRW	DD	8/12/96
U.S.ASSOC.											120	240	120.00	14,400.00	8/1/96		TS	D	8/10/96
U.S.ASSOC.							7	7	7	7	63	126	112.00	7,056.00			TS	D	8/10/96
U.S.ASSOC.							5				20	20	120.00	2,400.00					
ASSOC.	25	25	25	0	0	0	17	7	7	7	308	521	116.12	35,766.00				D	
TENTATIVES for ASSOC.																			
Vets Assoc.	2	2	2								6	12	121.00	726.00	8/25/96		TRB	T	8/25/96
N.A.R.R.P.	10	10									20	40	120.00	2,200.00	8/25/96		TRB	T	8/25/96
Data Systems			6	6	6	6					48	96	131.00	6,288.00	8/25/96		TRB	T	8/25/96
D.P.A.			10	10	10						30	60	145.00	4,350.00	8/25/96		TRB	T	8/25/96
Mutual Assoc.					3	3					24	48	131.00	3,144.00	8/25/96		TRB	T	8/25/96
Mont Ward Co.											40	80	100.00	4,000.00	6/24/96		EP	T	6/24/96
Newsweek											16	32	131.00	2,096.00	8/25/96		RWH	T	8/25/96
N.A.F.E.											36	72	127.00	4,572.00	8/12/96		TRB	T	8/25/96
Int'l Assoc.											8	16	118.00	944.00	8/25/96		TRB	T	8/25/96
Womens Assoc.											4	8	110.00	440.00	8/25/96		TRB	T	8/25/96
Manufact. Assn											48	96	127.00	6,096.00	8/25/96		TRB	T	8/25/96
N.A.T.C.O.							45				270	540	234.00	63,180.00	8/25/96		TRB	T	8/25/96
Dental Assoc.								2	2		4	8	110.00	440.00	8/25/96		TRB	T	8/25/96
Central Assoc.									30	30	60	120	120.00	7,200.00	8/25/96		TRB	T	8/25/96
US Yacht Club									4	4	8	16	131.00	1,048.00	8/25/96		TRB	T	8/25/96
ASSOC.	12	12	18	16	19	9	45	2	36	34	622	1244	171.58	106,724.00				T	

(Continued from preceding page) Tentative and definite bookings in the function book and guestroom control book are monitored on a regular basis. At the weekly sales meeting, discussion will center on booking activity and how to best manage the guestroom and function space inventory. The computerized function and guestrooms control books will help the sales team to look at business on the books and manage it for the benefit of both the hotel and meeting planners.

"This tentative room block is being held on a first option basis until [date]. Following this period, all space outlined above will become subject to availability unless prior arrangements for an extension have been made."

A *definite booking form* is used after business has been confirmed (see Figure 3.14). It is processed when a contract or letter of agreement has been signed and when the business is scheduled for a specific date. The form includes a number of details needed to properly

Figure 3.13. TENTATIVE BOOKING FORM.

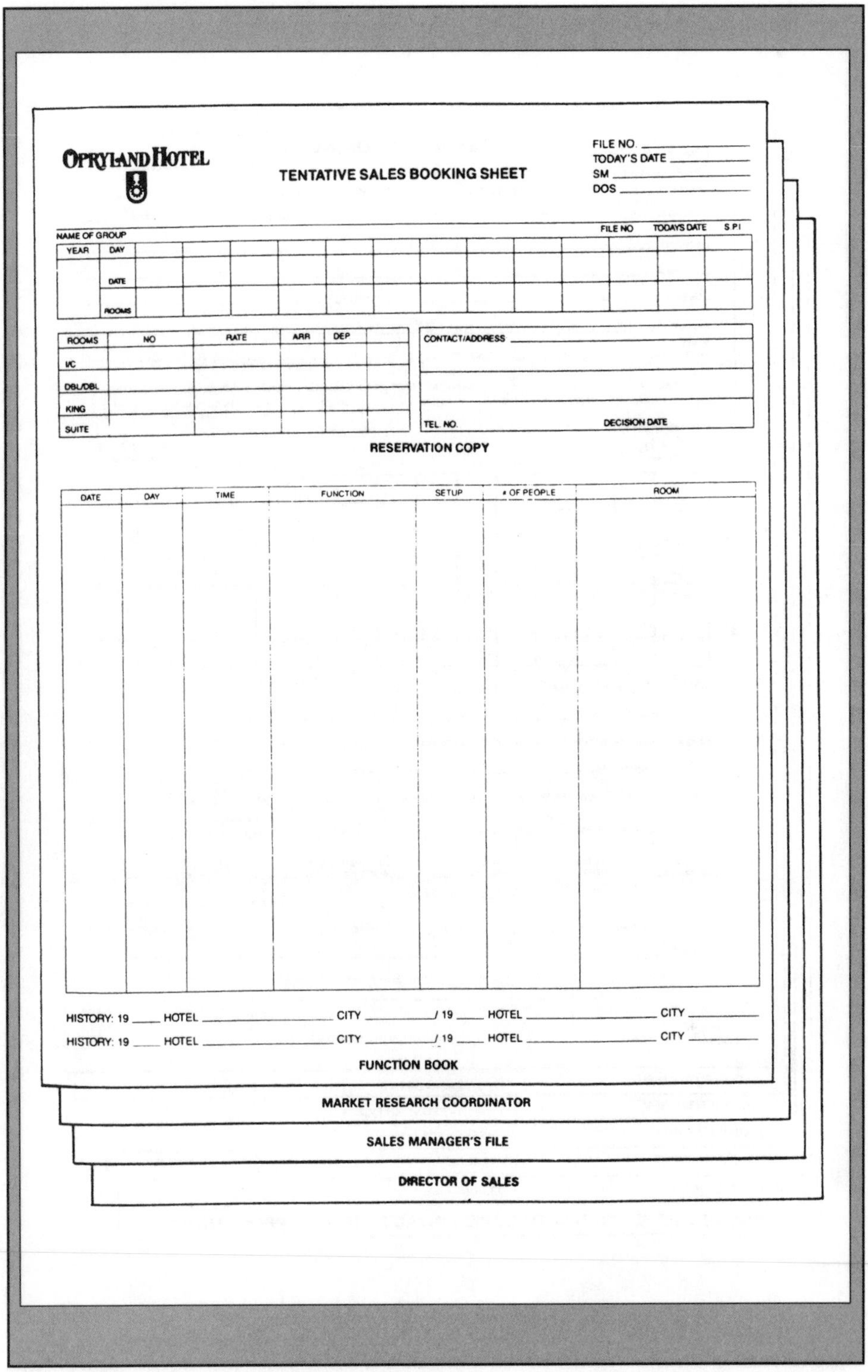

OPRYLAND HOTEL

TENTATIVE SALES BOOKING SHEET

FILE NO. ______
TODAY'S DATE ______
SM ______
DOS ______

NAME OF GROUP | FILE NO | TODAYS DATE | S.P.I

YEAR	DAY												
	DATE												
	ROOMS												

ROOMS	NO	RATE	ARR	DEP	
I/C					
DBL/DBL					
KING					
SUITE					

CONTACT/ADDRESS ______

TEL. NO. | DECISION DATE

RESERVATION COPY

DATE	DAY	TIME	FUNCTION	SETUP	# OF PEOPLE	ROOM

HISTORY: 19 ___ HOTEL ______ CITY ______ / 19 ___ HOTEL ______ CITY ______

HISTORY: 19 ___ HOTEL ______ CITY ______ / 19 ___ HOTEL ______ CITY ______

FUNCTION BOOK

MARKET RESEARCH COORDINATOR

SALES MANAGER'S FILE

DIRECTOR OF SALES

This form is used pending final confirmation of an event or function. Tentative bookings are often made when a client is interested in the space but needs to work out additional details or get approval. Using this form, tentative details are entered into the function book in the event that the function is confirmed (note the space for the option date, *the date by which a final decision must be made).*

Figure 3.14. DEFINITE BOOKING FORM.

This form is processed when a contract or letter of agreement is signed. At that time, the information on the form is entered into the function control book. Note that the form includes details of the function to enable plans to be made to service it effectively.

service the function, such as the number of attendees, setup requirements, etc. The date and details will be penciled into the function book (and guestrooms control book, if required).

Once a group "goes definite," establish a **working file** for the event. This file differs from the account file. The working file contains only the information relevant to the event. It is the file from which the convention service department works. Once the event concludes, the working file is broken down and appropriate materials are returned to the account file. Some hotels file the folders chronologically, but because the function book already lists all events in such order, you may be more comfortable filing alphabetically. It doesn't matter so long as there is some chronological system to remind the hotel of pending events.

After the convention is booked, other forms may also be necessary. In some cases, details such as a date, room requirement or guest room figure may change. It is then necessary to complete a *change form* to ensure that these changes are made. There may be many times when a piece of business which was considered definite is cancelled. In such a case, a *cancellation form* must be filed. Since there may be a number of reasons for the cancellation, some properties follow up the cancellation form with a *lost business report* that details the reason for the cancellation.

Some properties use a general form that eliminates the use of several of these forms. And, in addition to these general sales office forms, salespeople also utilize a number of forms for their individual use to track their progress in selling to accounts. These forms will be discussed in Chapter 7, where we take a look at specific selling techniques.

Sales Office Automation

Over the past several years, there have been dramatic changes in the way hotels do business. Today's advanced technology has eliminated much of the "drudge work" that was an inherent part of the sales effort. Paperwork that used to be done by hand (notes about sales calls and account requirements, for example), taking hours to prepare, update and analyze, is now readily available by calling up a screen on a computer terminal. In this section, we will take a look at how today's computer is drastically changing the face of the sales office — how it is not only helping to eliminate time-consuming paperwork, but how it is being used to personalize presentations, create lists of potential contacts, and forecast future demand for guest and meeting rooms.

Advantages of Automation

Hospitality industry professionals agree that up to 70 percent of a salesperson's time can be spent on non-sales activities, such as call tracing, checking the availability of rooms, blocking rooms and space — and simply running back and forth to filing cabinets to retrieve information. The computer has changed all that. No longer is it necessary to search for lost files or prepare reports by hand; this data is readily available on individual computer terminals.

In addition, the computer frees salespeople from the office. If a salesperson is out making calls, information can be accessed by other salespeople or the clerical staff if immediate action is required. And, pertinent information (often in the form of reports) is instantly available to other departments requiring it (the banquet/catering department, reservations, etc.).

Computers make it easy to "personalize" important documents such as contracts and correspondence. They also simplify mass mailings, generating mailing labels (often by zip code or group type) in a fraction of the time it would take a secretary to sort through records and type labels to specified target groups. Sales management uses computers to evaluate both individual and departmental performance — the computer can provide detailed reports of sales calls made, the amount of business booked and the potential area for future efforts.

New Advances in Hotel Computer Systems

While hotels have used computer systems for booking reservations for several years, only recently have sales offices been automated to provide up-to-date information to salespeople and sales management. Tim Grover, regional director of sales and marketing for Starwood Hotels and Resorts Worldwide, states:

> "For any hotel sales force automation is critical. Delphi (software for hotel sales and catering) controls more than 80 percent of the market; it is considered the 'Microsoft' of hotel sales and catering systems. They have a Windows-based version for managing sales contracts, group room blocks and catering space. It is also user-friendly and can generate a variety of reports. Delphi software also functions as an excellent contact manager. Every conversation with a client about an event is documented and accessible to our entire sales team. And, finally, it helps us manage our revenue more efficiently. Knowing what's on the books at any given time for both room sales and catering is a valuable asset that benefits both the customer and the hotel."[8]

In addition to the access to this information, we have also seen how computers are being used to eliminate the large amount of paperwork generated by the sales department. One of the most important ways in which a computer is being used, however, is to assist the sales department in organizing and analyzing information about meeting groups. Database management programs provide a way to keep a service history of all client bookings, including the expected and actual number of attendees, the number of guest rooms booked, the types of functions booked, average room rate and average check, etc. **Database marketing** becomes a simple process. If a salesperson wishes to target groups that meet in the western regions of the country, for example, the computer will produce a list of accounts that meet that criteria for the salesperson to contact (see box titled "The Hidden Opportunities with Database Marketing").

The "Virtual" Office

Besides eliminating much of the drudgery of keeping records and accessing the information necessary to sell to and service meetings business, computers are playing an increasing role in improving the efficiency of property salespeople. No longer does it take days to answer inquiries or check date availability. Nor do salespeople have to sell from their own property. Many of today's salespeople are using technological advances to create "virtual offices" — armed with a laptop computer, a cellular phone, an e-mail address and a Blackberry (a portable wireless device for receiving e-mail), they are free to go where the business is — while still maintaining close contact with their home property (see box titled "The

THE HIDDEN OPPORTUNITIES WITH DATABASE MARKETING

Database marketing allows hotels to develop personal long-term bonds with customers. Sometimes called relationship marketing or loyalty marketing, this approach departs from the mass marketing that has long been used to reach meeting planners. Few industries maintain the information about their customers that hotels keep — files that not only indicate guest requirements but make it easy to identify customers for future communications. Every hotel has account files, including information on past groups and registration cards from individual guests. The most frequently asked question is, "How long do we keep these records?" A more important question is, "What can the information in these files do for us?" The history in these files is the foundation for database marketing.

As competition has heated up in the past five or ten years, hotel operators have scrutinized marketing expenditures more carefully than ever. What they have learned is that *it's five to seven times more expensive to acquire new guests than it is to retain existing ones.* Your best customers are those who have purchased recently, purchase frequently, and deliver the greatest contribution to revenue.

Guest folios, registration cards, and group history on meeting planners form the core of your database; they allow you to personalize service to meet guest needs, thereby improving the guest experience and reinforcing loyalty.

Hotels typically use database marketing to analyze travel and spending patterns of market segments. Database programs allow you to easily trace and maintain customer controls, call up any customer record quickly, generate call-back schedules, follow-up letters and mailings as well as mail merge to individual or a large number of customers.

Establishing relationships and a dialogue with customers is fast becoming a requirement for survival in the hotel industry. Whether a hotel continues to rely solely on its guest history system or decides to invest the time and money in a more sophisticated database system, one thing is certain: Hotel managers who know the most about customers and are able to harness resources for quick response to threats and opportunities will enjoy a tremendous advantage in the competitive decade ahead. If you cannot move quickly enough, your competitor across the street surely will.

Contributed by Cindy Estis Green, President, Driving Revenue

Virtual Sales Manager"). Not only does this mean working while away on business; a number of hotel salespeople are now home-based. Sheraton, for example, estimates that about half of its 100 salespeople selling its Starwood brand are home-based, and this trend is expected to continue.[9]

Laptop computers are the main component of a virtual office. While they are portable enough to be carried in a briefcase, they provide the capability of tapping into the property or chain's computer system to check for room availability, rates and other information needed by potential clients. Most are equipped with fax modems, enabling the salesperson to check availability, generate a reply or proposal for the meeting planner, and immediately fax the document to the customer.

Swissôtel, a hotel chain with properties in the United States, Europe, Asia and the Middle East, was one of the first hospitality firms to "go virtual." Their United States national account team is equipped with laptop computers and accompanying cellular phones which enable salespeople to get immediate availability and rate information. The laptops are also used to send and receive faxes and, since they store property photos and detailed information about guestrooms and meeting space, they can be used to create customized presentations for meeting planners.

Swissôtel president and CEO Andreas Meinhold says of the system:

"In a sense, Swissôtel has packed its bag and taken itself on the road using specially adapted laptops and connectivity links. Because our

The Virtual Sales Manager

Many hotel sales managers feel chained to their properties, overseeing the day-to-day operations of their sales staffs and ensuring that meeting arrangements are met, — but not Michael Mulcahy, a sales manager for the Sheraton City Centre in Washington, DC. Four days a week, Mulcahy is in New York City, soliciting business for the hotel and communicating with the property through his laptop computer and cellular phone.

Mulcahy's laptop unit requires an electrical outlet and one telephone line. It has a built-in modem that allows Mulcahy to fax documents to the property and receive contracts and other documents in return. His cellular phone not only enables him to check messages on his voice mail, but also provides the capability to set appointments while he is in transit — whether it be in a taxicab or aboard a commuter flight.

Mulcahy feels that the arrangement is beneficial to both the property and the client: "At the bottomline, I'm giving them more personal service by being here and meeting with them, so it is to their advantage...There's nothing like being there and reviewing room availability onscreen with the client. And not only that, but taking it a step further and generating the contract and having them sign before you leave. The level of immediacy is far greater."

---

salespeople are tapped into the property-management system, they're able to operate out of their virtual office as if they were behind the front desk of any Swissôtel.

"Our account managers will be able to spend their time just selling, not focusing on administrative tasks. They can work when they want and where they want, and really spend their time focusing on our customers' needs."[10]

Electronic mail (e-mail) offers a number of advantages to salespeople. First, is its speed. No longer does it take days to send correspondence to a client and wait for a reply. With e-mail, the salesperson can send off a message or proposal, get a reply, and respond to the reply within a short period of time (unlike telephone messages, e-mail can be directly responded to as soon as it is received; there is no need to talk to the home office, hang up the phone, and look for and dial the client's number). Second, although it is private, a number of the same messages may be sent to different contacts at one time (if a salesperson wants to get the word out about a new promotion, for example, the message can be generated once and e-mailed to several potential customers). Third, e-mail allows for flexibility. A number of messages — either the same or different — can be generated at one sitting and one or all can be sent at the same time. Conversely, an e-mail recipient can pick up all of his or her e-mail messages at once and respond as time and priorities allow. Last, but certainly not least, is the versatility of e-mail. E-mail communications can range from a short note requesting specific information to a large file of text and graphics, and even software applications can be transferred via e-mail.

Most salespeople have an e-mail address, but the medium has not yet replaced the need for other high-tech communications devices, such as cellular phones, voice mail services and pagers. Other technological advances that have made it easier for today's hotel salespeople to concentrate their time on selling include computerized Rolodexes, "memo" machines, personal organizers, and electronic dictionaries, spelling checkers and translation devices. These advances can enhance efficiency and professionalism and will give the salesperson more time do what he or she was hired to do — sell rooms and meeting space by going where the business is and focusing on the needs of potential clients.

Additional Uses of Automation

In addition to automating sales records and enhancing the effectiveness of the property's salespeople, the computer and other facets of today's technology are being used to boost productivity and increase efficiency by:

- Generating daily, weekly, and monthly reports
- Providing rooms and equipment inventory
- Generating mailing lists
- Using word processing functions to generate contracts, proposals, routine correspondence, and so on.

Personalization. In terms of word processing, the computer age has also ushered in an age of personalization. Today's meeting planners want to be more than an account number. Computer data banks make it easy to personalize correspondence and even routine contracts to meet this need.

Some of the advantages of using word processing, with a special emphasis on personalization, include:

- Letters need to be written only once and can be stored on file for future use.
- Spelling can be verified with the system's dictionary, and most systems offer a grammar check as well.
- Mailing lists for meeting planning organizations can be merged with in-house lists (duplicate entries are purged, resulting in a single, clean file).
- Standard paragraphs can be recalled for insertion into proposal letters and contracts.
- Information from a previous function can be used in a follow-up letter, for example, "Do you wish to use the Monte Carlo room for your awards banquet again this year?"
- Filing is correctly done accurately, automatically and quickly, eliminating the most hated clerical job in the office.

Simple mass mailings can be effectively personalized with the name of the contact person and his or her group. This information can be merged into a routine sales letter to give the impression of a personal touch. And, as with computerized sales records, this type of automation frees the sales department's clerical people to pursue other, more productive duties, such as setting appointments or following up on accounts for salespeople.

Yield and Revenue Management. Another vital use of the computer has been in the area of market analysis. **Yield management**, which is based on the forecasted demand for function space and guestrooms, is becoming an increasingly important tool in filling both meeting rooms and guestrooms while increasing profitability for the hotel.

Although yield management has been used by airlines and cruise ships for a number of years (rates have long been based on the customer's willingness to pay), the hospitality industry was relatively slow to capitalize on this concept. With software programs designed specifically for hotels now on the market, however, yield management is becoming an increasingly important tool in determining how to fill rooms for the most profitability.

Today, most hotels constantly monitor their business mix (business travelers, leisure travelers and the meetings segment) to maximize revenues. They can forecast what rates they want over certain days and determine how much group business they want to see over specific dates.

Fred Shea, Hyatt's Chicago-based vice president of sales, says:

> "A ceiling is put in place based on what we think the transient demand will be. But it is constantly being re-evaluated. As we get closer to the group block ceiling, we begin to re-evaluate whether the rate should go up or down, based on the overall demand we are getting."[11]

Savvy meeting planners who know a hotel's target business mix for the days of their meeting can leverage that information in deciding whether to place the business early and be guaranteed their desired meeting space or wait to see if demand falls off and they can get a better rate. They are also aware that past data is the hotel's internal tool for determining how much group business a property wants to sell over particular dates. If their group traditionally has a high profitability, it is looked on as a more favorable piece of business and the planner may be able to negotiate a better rate.

Revenue management takes yield management a step farther by not only assessing a group's potential for rooms revenue but also looking at the group's projected impact on the property's overall bottom line. Kevin Kowalski, vice president, brand marketing, for Atlanta-based Crowne Plaza Hotels & Resorts, says that with increased demand hotels need to take a second look at their business mix to increase their profitability. He explains:

> "We can concentrate more on getting group business that is better value-related, and less on SMERF [social, military, educational, religious, fraternal] groups, which generate less ancillary revenue."[12]

Revenue management takes into consideration the size of the group, its spending history (not just in terms of rooms, but overall spending at the property's other revenue-producing outlets, such as restaurants and recreational facilities), and future revenues for the hotel (additional bookings by the group and individuals, referrals, and so on).

Summary

Organizing for sales is essential if a property is to capture its share of the lucrative meetings and convention market. In this chapter, we have discussed how sales are structured on a number of levels. We have detailed the importance of the physical layout of the sales office as well the relationship of the sales department with other property departments that will be involved in servicing a group's business, discussed the various positions within sales, and introduced types of supplementary sales staff, including regional sales offices and independent hotel representatives.

Managing the sales effort at any level involves utilizing a number of forms to successfully follow up on business booked and to ensure successful execution of a group's events. We have looked at a number of these forms, including the function and guestrooms control books, as well as forms that enable salespeople to manage their time and enable them to focus on key accounts. We have also seen how the computer has changed the way in which salespeople do business, making it far easier and more efficient to reach and service their customers. In the next three chapters, we will take a look at the primary sources of meetings business and see how sales efforts are specifically organized to sell to and service each segment.

Endnotes:

1. Sheraton's Convention and Conference Service Standards Manual.
2. Lalia Rach, Ed.D., "The Current and Future Marketing Professional," *HSMAI Marketing Review*.
3. Megan Rowe, "15 Things That Drive You Crazy and What to Do About Them," *Corporate Meetings & Incentives*, October 2003, p. 17.
4. David C. Bojanic and Elizabeth A. Dale, "A Survey of Convention Sales Career Opportunities," *Hospitality & Tourism Educator*.
5. Howard Feiertag, "Educated Sales Effort," *Hotel & Motel Management*, April 7, 2003, p. 16.
6. Courtesy of Hyatt Hotels Corporation Sales Automation System, Datamation.
7. William Duncan, "Booking Streamlined by Next Generation of Hospitality Software," *Convene*.
8. "How Technology is Refining Hotel Operations," *Convene*, December 1999, p. 124.
9. Beth Rogers, "Working at Home," *HSMAI Marketing Review*, Spring 2000, p. 34.
10. Laura Ross-Fedder, "Computers Empower Swissôtel Sales Staff," *Hotel & Motel Management*.
11. Cheryl-Anne Sturken, "As They See It: How Hotels Evaluate Group Business," *Meetings & Conventions*, May 2005, p. 49.
12. Ibid.

Additional References:

- Hospitality Sales: A Marketing Approach, Margaret Shaw and Susan Morris, John Wiley and Sons, 2000.

- *Journal of Convention and Exposition Management*, K.S. Chon, The Haworth Press, Inc.
  www.haworthpressinc.com

Internet Sites:

For more information, visit the following Internet sites. Internet addresses can change without notice. If a site is no longer available at the address listed below, a search engine can be used to find the new address or additional, related sites.

Delphi/Newmarket Software - www.newsoft.com
Delta Hotels – www.4deltahotels.com
Hilton Hotels – www.hilton.com
Hospitality Sales and Marketing Association International (HSMAI) -
www.hsmai.org
Hospitality Industry Technology Exposition and Conference - www.hitechshow.org
International Association of Hospitality Accountants (IAHA) - www.iaha.org
Starwood Hotels – www.starwood.com

 Study Questions:

1. How is the sales department perceived within the organizational structure of the hotel? Why is it necessary for the sales department to assume authority over other departments?
2. What three elements are crucial in structuring a sales office? Why is each important?
3. Sketch job descriptions for the various positions within the sales department. How will these vary between large and small properties?
4. What is an independent hotel representative? What considerations are important in choosing an individual or firm to effectively represent your property?
5. What are the key elements of a sales office filing system? Why is each important?
6. Discuss the importance of the function book and guestrooms control book. Why is it important that only one person control these books when a manual system is used?
7. How has computer technology changed the sales office? How is automation being used to enhance the sales effort?

 Key Terms:

Account file. A standardized folder holding the information needed to serve a client.
Database marketing. The process of using guest folios, registration cards and group history of meeting planners to develop relationships and dialogue with customers.
Double booking. Reserving space for two groups to use the same space at the same time; neither can be fully accommodated as contracted.
Function book. Master control of all banquet space, broken down on each page or screen by banquet rooms, with a page or screen for each day of the year.
Guestrooms control book. A book or computer screen used to monitor sleeping room allocations to groups.
Independent hotel representative. An individual or firm that acts as an addition to the hotel's internal sales staff.
Key account management. Prioritizing of accounts based upon their individual profit potential.
Master card. An index card that contains a summary of everything needed for a

sales effort, including the organization's name, the decision maker(s), key contacts, addresses, telephone numbers, and so on. Cards may be color coded to accent key factors. Many properties today use the computerized version of the master card.

Option. Meeting space or guestrooms that are reserved by the meeting group but not yet under contract. A hotel extends a right of first refusal to either confirm or release the space if there is demand from another group.

Reader file. A file containing copies of internal and external correspondence generated by a salesperson. Useful for reviewing the performance of the sales staff.

Regional sales office. Sales offices for chain properties that are located in places other than the property. Help promote and sell individual properties.

Relationship marketing. Marketing that views customers as assets and emphasizes retaining customers by nurturing and sustaining relationships with them.

Revenue management. The practice of assessing a group's overall profitability on the property's bottom line. Not only is the group's impact on guestrooms and meeting space revenues assessed, but also its spending in other areas (from restaurants to retail) as well as its potential for future business.

Standard operating procedures (SOPs). Written instructions explaining how business activities should be handled.

Tickler file. A follow-up file used to remind salespeople of correspondence, telephone calls, sales calls or other business activities that must be handled on a particular day. A computerized version is commonly used by today's hotel salespeople.

Working file. A file set up as soon as a booking is definite, containing information relevant to the event.

Yield management. A technique used to maximize the revenue/profit of the hotel by basing prices for guestrooms and banquet space on supply and demand.

Learning Objectives:

This portion of your text takes an in-depth look at the association market. We will discuss the types of meetings held by associations, their typical patterns, requirements for meetings, how site decisions are made and by whom, and ways to reach this lucrative market segment. When you have studied this chapter, you will:

- Be able to identify factors that association meeting planners consider when making a site selection.

- Be able to describe the kinds of meetings held by associations and the characteristics of each.

- Know the key decision makers for association meetings and what they look for in determining a meeting site.

- Be able to identify the most effective sources for finding association business.

Outline

Revenue Producers

Requirements for Association Meetings

Kinds of Association Meetings
- Annual Conventions
- State and Regional Conventions
- Conferences
- Seminars and Workshops
- Board and Committee Meetings

Characteristics of Association Meetings
- Cycle and Pattern
- Geographic Restrictions
- Lead Time
- Kind of Sites
- Voluntary Attendance
- Convention Duration
- Price

Association Meeting Decision Makers
- Association Director
- Association President and Officers
- Committee Chairperson
- Board of Directors
- Other Influences

Sources for Finding Association Business
- Directories
- Databases
- Specialized Periodicals
- Hotel Records

Summary

The Importance of the Association Market

Kathy Dixon Leone
Vice President of Sales
Boca Raton Resort and Club

"The association market provides a tremendous base of business, both in the meetings the market holds, and the meetings it can generate through the exposure a property gains by hosting its corporate membership. If serviced properly, it can provide a base of business that can be the foundation of a property's success for years to come."

4 Selling the Association Market

In the first three chapters, we've studied the importance of the convention business and the trends impacting it, the marketing plan—the cornerstone of sales—and the organization and operation of the sales office. In the next three chapters, we will take a look at the major meetings market segments in detail. The two most prominent target markets, the association and corporate meetings segments, will follow a similar outline:

- what planners look for in selecting sites,
- the kinds of meetings held and the characteristics of each type,
- key decision makers, and
- how to locate sources for business.

Other markets, including nonprofit organizations, government agencies, and other small meetings market segments will be covered in Chapter 6.

According to a Convention Industry Council study, associations spend more than $77.97 billion a year on meetings (see Figure 4.1). It comes as no surprise then that hotel chains such as Fairmont, Four Seasons, Hilton, Hyatt, Marriott and Starwood have convention properties in major cities and look to association meetings to fill 30-40 percent of their rooms annually. The historic Boca Raton Resort and Club attributes approximately 65 percent of its annual sales volume to groups and meetings. Forty percent of their sales from meetings are realized from the association market. That's a lot of business, and it warrants careful study of the kinds of meetings that associations hold and how you can capture your share of this lucrative market.

Revenue Producers

The convention is of extreme importance to the **association**. It is the single largest source of associations' non-dues revenue (see box titled "The Principal Sources of An Association's Income"). According to *Convene* magazine's Meetings Market Survey, associations derive

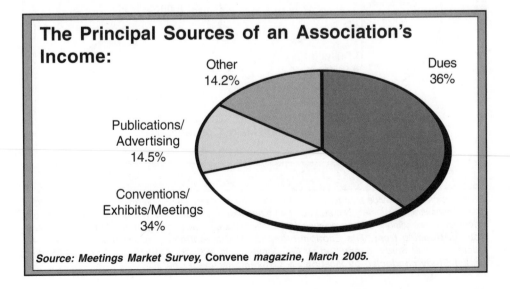

The Principal Sources of an Association's Income:

Other 14.2%

Dues 36%

Publications/ Advertising 14.5%

Conventions/ Exhibits/Meetings 34%

Source: Meetings Market Survey, Convene *magazine, March 2005.*

Figure 4.1. *ASSOCIATIONS ARE THE MOST VISIBLE CONVENTION ORGANIZERS.*

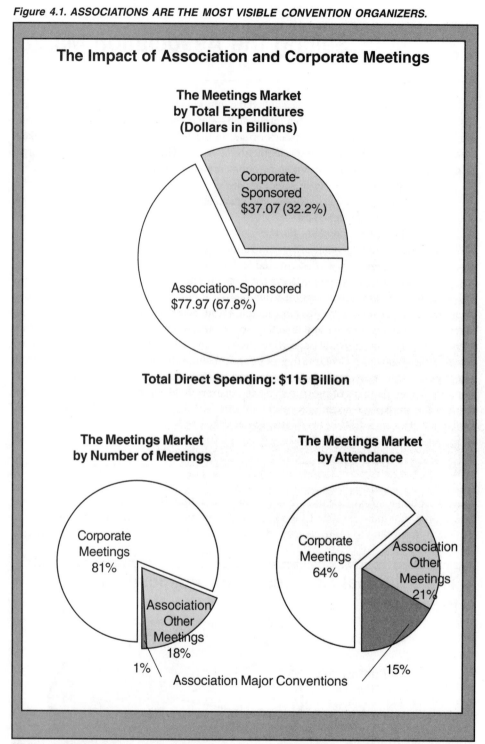

While corporations provide a larger market in total number of attendees and meetings, the spending of associations is approximately two and one-half times that of corporations. The principal reason for this difference in spending is that associations generally include a trade show as part of their conventions. **Source: Updated from "The Economic Impact of Conventions, Expositions, Meetings and Incentive Travel Study" conducted by the Conventions Industry Council and the 2004 Meeting Market Study conducted by Meetings & Conventions magazine.**

about 34 percent of their annual income from conventions and exhibitions. Membership dues range from twenty-five dollars or so to several thousand dollars annually in more affluent associations, but almost every association views its convention, meetings, and exhibits as prime sources of revenue.

Associations earn money from conventions in several ways. One is with exhibits. The group may rent the exhibit hall of a hotel or convention center for one to three dollars per square foot depending on demand and season. The association then subleases the space to exhibitors for considerably more -- up to fifty dollars per square foot in some cases.

Registration fees at such events also add to the association's coffers. When a convention "package" includes a number of meal functions, it is not uncommon for the package to cost the delegate several hundred dollars. The hotel is paid only for the actual number of meal tickets collected or the number of meals the meeting planner guarantees, which adds more to the profits of the convention since not every person attends every event.

Associations earn additional money from the advertising in their publications and programs. And when a participating company sponsors a segment of the program and picks up the tab, the association's costs are further reduced.

Thus, when you consider how important conventions are to membership retention and to revenue production, it becomes apparent that these events are absolutely essential for the well-being of an association. They constitute a major effort on an association's part, and they are planned and conducted as such.

Requirements for Association Meetings ────────

Site selection is crucial to the success of a convention. Mike Welch, executive director of the Credit Union Executives Society of Madison, Wisconsin, has said:

> "We look for good facilities, pleasant weather, an attractive location, and a city that's near the largest concentration of members. We also consider who else is going to be there and when. For instance, when our annual convention is taking place in a city, we don't want to go there for a seminar for a year or two."

Figure 4.2 details some of the other factors that meeting planners take into consideration when making a site selection. These considerations include:

Adequate Meeting Space. The organizer is always concerned about your ability to house the general assembly and smaller sessions. He or she is interested in space for workshops and committee meetings, as well as your ability to handle food functions expertly without encroaching on the meetings.

Enough Guestrooms. We don't know a single convention organizer who doesn't prefer to house the entire group in one hotel. Suites are needed in addition to singles, twins and doubles. When a single hotel can't house the entire group, two or more hotels in close proximity are the most desirable.

Adequate Exhibit Space. Exhibits mean money for the association and are an attraction for the members. Planners look for adequate exhibit space, located conveniently to housing. Hotels with exhibit facilities have an advantage. When larger exhibits require

Figure 4.2. FACTORS CONSIDERED IMPORTANT TO ASSOCIATION MEETING PLANNERS IN THE SELECTION OF A FACILITY/HOTEL.

Association Planners

Factors Considered Very Important	Major Conventions	Association Meetings
Number, size, quality of meeting rooms	88%	81%
Number, size and quality of sleeping rooms	86	68
Negotiable food, beverage and room rates	83	73
Cost of facility/hotel	84	86
Quality of food service	71	65
Efficiency of billing procedures	61	53
Meeting support services and equipment	64	53
Assignment of one staff person to handle all aspects of meeting	61	48
Availability of exhibit space	57	34
Efficiency of check-in and check-out procedures	53	46
Previous experience in dealing with facility and its staff	49	39
Number, size and quality of suites	39	15
Proximity to shopping, restaurants, off-site entertainment	35	22
Meerting rooms with multiple high-speed phone lines and computer outlets	33	24

Although the purpose of a meeting ultimately determines the facility selection criteria, the table above gives insight into general factors of importance to the association meeting planner. Negotiable rates and costs continue to be an important aspect of hotel selection for conventions and meetings.
Source: The 2004 Meetings Market Study conducted by Meetings & Conventions magazine.

exhibition halls, the preference is for setups near the hotel. Delegates prefer not to travel between hotel rooms and convention areas.

An Attractive Location. A location need not be a resort to attract different groups. Chicago gets lots of business because of its central location. That's very important to many busy groups.

Other groups may like to combine the show with other business. Your city may be in the heart of their business world. Attendance is also easier to stimulate if people don't have to travel too far. Easy driving distance may mean an extra ten percent registration. Many associations do like resort locations. You may be able to offer that, or perhaps you are located in great tourist country. Put simply, you have to offer something attractive to each group. It might be the draw of your city or destination, or your proximity to a major airport, or your reputation for superior customer service.

Service. Last, but probably most important, the meeting planners look for service. They want some assurance that you have an experienced staff that is interested in doing a good job. Each convention event is a custom job and many things can, and do, go wrong. Convention planners live with such hazards and justly feel that your staff should have the expertise and the desire to keep the show moving. Service is what brings repeat and recommended business.

Kinds of Association Meetings

The first kind of association meeting to come to mind is the *annual convention*. Certainly this is the most visible, and the largest, but there are many other occasions for associations to meet. For example, lots of planning is required in staging a convention. *Board and committee meetings* are often scheduled for this very purpose, as well as at other times for many other purposes, and may require a meeting room at a hotel property. In addition, *regional conventions, conferences, seminars and workshops* are conducted through the year by most associations (see Figure 4.3). These are all sources of good business for hotels. It is a rare property that cannot handle some kind of association business. You may not necessarily be able to handle the major events but there are many others that you can service.

Figure 4.3. SUMMARY OF TYPES OF ASSOCIATION MEETINGS OTHER THAN MAJOR CONVENTIONS.

Type of Meeting	Total Meetings	Average # Planned	Average Attendance	Average # Days Duration	Average # of Months Lead Time
Board Meetings	40,300	4.3	40	1.8	5.6
Training/Educational Seminars	66,200	7.6	153	2.1	7.0
Professional/Technical	25,000	5.5	120	2.1	7.1
Regional/Local Chapters	22,200	5.7	128	1.9	6.1
Other Meetings	12,800	4.7	163	2.1	9.9
Total/Average	116,500	14.1	121	2.0	7.1

The average association meeting planner works on over 14 meetings per year.
Source: The 2004 Meetings Market Study conducted by Meetings & Conventions magazine.

Annual Conventions

Almost every association has an annual convention. The annual convention is a ritual in associations of all types—international, national, state and regional.

Attendance varies, of course. Some conventions are truly huge affairs. The Chemical Society draws between 20,000 and 30,000; others have fewer than 100. The mean attendance is about 1,500 people. Conventions vary only in scale, maintaining similar philosophy and motivation.

The box at the top of the next page, which is from a recent market study conducted by *Meetings & Conventions* magazine, details association delegate attendance.

Since 64 percent of all national meetings and trade shows have an average attendance of 300 or less, even small properties can take advantage of this lucrative market. And, small properties can benefit from the large conventions by making arrangements with neighboring properties to handle overflow business generated by large groups.

Exhibits are a major part of association meetings, especially trade and technical societies. Two-thirds of the annual association conventions are held in conjunction with a

Delegate Attendance at Annual Convention	% of Associations
Fewer than 100	41%
100-149	7
150-299	16
300-900	15
1000+	21
	100%

Average delegate attendance:	Male	845
	Female	687
		1532

trade show or exhibit. These conventions attract 130 exhibitors using an average of 25,000 square feet of exhibit space. Exhibits are a source of essential income to associations, and very important to exhibitors, too.

There are conventions without exhibits, of course, and it is also not unheard of for a convention to stage a major program with exhibits in one hotel and another program without exhibits in another. And sometimes, an event may be held in a city because of the presence of another convention with an exhibit.

Most conventions include a **general session**, also called a plenary session, attended by everyone and a number of smaller meetings. These smaller meetings are often termed **breakout sessions**, where the group divides into smaller meetings, and **concurrent sessions**, where meeting sessions on different topics are scheduled at the same time. Sometimes, the general session runs concurrently with the exhibit hours; sometimes they run tandem so as not to compete for members' attention.

It is a rare convention without food functions. Many groups sell a complete convention package for their event. The package includes registration fees and prepaid tickets to all food functions and special events.

You can see at this point that a convention, especially a large one, calls for a number of rooms of different kinds. Large rooms are needed for the general assembly, the exhibit, and the food functions; smaller rooms for committee and board meetings, workshops, and smaller food functions; and suites and similar rooms for hospitality centers.

Often a hotel cannot handle an entire convention because of its size, so several hotels may band together to sell an association as a team. The hotel business is odd in that strong competitors often become partners in a project, and both can enjoy additional business as a result. Even a piece of a convention event may be profitable, as well as giving the hotel a foot in the door for future business (see the Copley Connection advertisement in Figure 4.4).

There is another variation of the national convention—the exhibit without convention program. These events, often called *exhibitions*, *expositions*, or *trade shows*, sometimes are not even sponsored by an association but by individual entrepreneurs or companies. These events can bring you business even if you cannot house the exhibit itself. Many an exhibition becomes the focal point of the industry or trade it serves and gives exhibitors the opportunity to hold sales meetings and dealer meetings in conjunction with the event.

Figure 4.4. THE COPLEY CONNECTION.

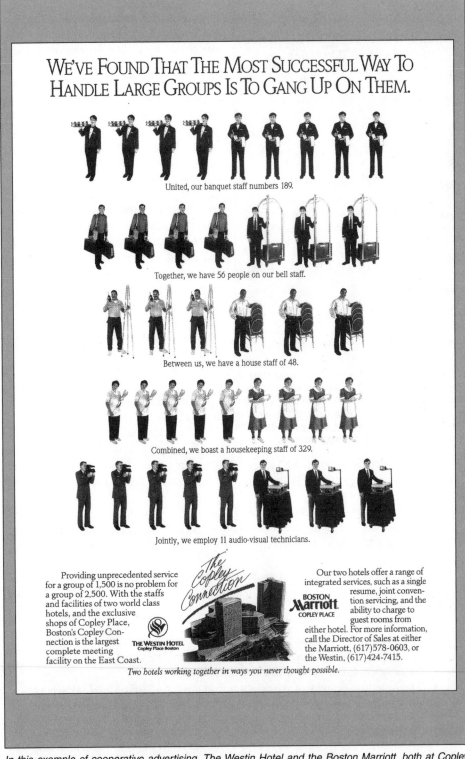

In this example of cooperative advertising, The Westin Hotel and the Boston Marriott, both at Copley Plaza, have teamed up to attract conventions and large meeting business. The properties, normally competitors, provide a range of integrated services to attract large groups.

State and Regional Conventions

State and Regional Association Planners Cite the Top Ten Attributes for Convention Site Selection		
Attribute	Percent	Rank
Proximity to hotel to meeting facility	71.4	1
Capacity of meeting rooms	65.6	2
Hotel cleanliness	62.8	3
Number of meeting rooms	61.6	4
Quality of Food and Beverage	59.8	5
Banquet space	59.0	6
Complimentary meeting space	57.3	7
Meeting room rates	56.7	8
Friendliness of hotel personnel	56.7	9
Problem-solving skills of hotel personnel	56.4	10

Source: Jeong-Ja Choi, Ph.D. and Carl A. Boger, Jr., Ph.D., "State Association Market: Relationships Between Association Characteristics and Site Selection Criteria," *Journal of Convention & Exhibition Management*, The Hawthorne Press, Inc., 2002, page 62.

The major difference between a regional convention of a national organization and one staged by a state or regional association is sponsorship (see Figure 4.5). A state association usually holds an annual meeting for its members within the state, although in recent years state organizations have ventured beyond state borders on occasion. Many national associations, even those with affiliated state chapters, hold regional conventions to supplement their national ones. Of interest is the recent growth in regional association meetings. When finances are short, many association members skip the big annual conventions, and attend smaller, shorter meetings that are closer to home. As a rule, the regional event is smaller than the national one both in attendance and size of the exhibit. Again, some regional conventions have exhibits and others don't. There is no rule of thumb.

The major difference, as far as hotel people are concerned, has to do with who makes the decisions about when and where the event will be held. The sidebar titled "State and Regional Association Planners Cite the Top 10 Attributes for Convention Site Selection" details some of the factors important in site selection. Both state and regional conventions are an important source of business for both large and small hotel properties (see Figure 4.6).

According to the *Association Meeting Trends* report, only ten percent of all state and regional conventions had an attendance of more than 1,000; 17 percent had attendance of 500 to 1,000, and 75 percent had less than 500 attendees, making this an ideal market for smaller properties.

And, since chapters of national associations meet within the state or regional boundaries, it is a market that can be reached relatively easily. Sources for locating state and regional business include:

- Chambers of Commerce and Convention Bureaus.
- The Yellow Pages of telephone directories for capital cities.
- Newspapers from capital cities or feeder cities.
- The American Society of Association Executives (ASAE). Hotel salespeople can join such groups as the Washington Society of Association Executives (WSAE) or the California Society of Association Executives (CSAE) as allied members.

Figure 4.5. STATE AND REGIONAL ASSOCIATION MARKET AT A GLANCE.

State and Regional Association Market at a Glance

Location

This segment of the association market is usually an offshoot of the national or international association. Groups usually rotate their convention among the major cities within the state or region and rely heavily upon local support for invitation. They meet four to six months before or after their affiliated national convention.

Facilities

Preferred facilities include free and ample parking as a high percentage of attendees drive. Access to means of public transportation is not critical; therefore, suburban hotels are often used. Most conventions require ballrooms for plenary sessions or banquets as well as several breakout rooms for seminars.

Price

Double occupancy is common so hotels should consider a flat rate, perhaps a compromise between the single and double rates. Attendance is voluntary so the decision maker is price-sensitive. They often will schedule their meetings during a hotel's off-periods and will schedule a Thursday arrival/ Sunday departure or Friday arrival/ Sunday departure.

Services

Preferred services include business services, such as fax machines, office copiers, typing and word processing. Other services include audiovisual equipment necessary for presentations and occasionally exhibit halls for table-top exhibits.

Decision Makers

These groups usually do not have a paid staff or a permanent office, but rather are administered by volunteers and committees on a part-time basis. The local chapters frequently submit bids or invitations to host a regional or state meeting. Because volunteer staff changes annually, it is important to actively solicit and update files frequently to determine decision makers.

Best Ways to Reach Market

Check the yellow pages under associations in all major cities (most are headquartered in capital city due to lobbying efforts). Most states have an affiliate of the American Society of Association Executives (ASAE) and publish a list of their members. Local convention and visitors bureaus and chambers of commerce will normally supply a listing of professional associations in their area. Personal contacts and direct mail are the most effective means to reach the decision makers.

Once a group has been located, it is important to remember that in many cases the meeting planners may be committees or inexperienced planners and that lead time is usually fairly short. A property that shows a willingness to assist with meeting planning will gain an edge over the competition.

Another way to solicit this market's business, which is an important source of revenue for off-peak periods, is to offer inexpensive room rates. Many attendees pay their own expenses, making room rates especially important to them. And, because spouses usually attend, a property that offers a single/double occupancy flat rate for these groups is especially attractive to this lucrative market.

Figure 4.6. MARKETING TO STATE AND REGIONAL ASSOCIATIONS.

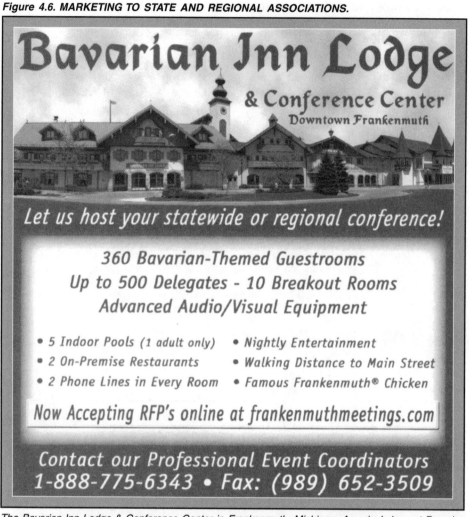

The Bavarian Inn Lodge & Conference Center in Frankenmuth, Michigan, America's largest Bavarian themed resort, is located in the heart of Michigan's "Little Bavaria." The property targets the statewide and regional conference market by promoting its meeting amenities, on-site facilities and proximity to local attractions.

Conferences

Associations have become frequent stagers of conferences, primarily to supplement the annual convention program with a specific program made timely by new developments. The recent debate over stem cell research, for example, precipitated a number of conferences.

The number of conferences held within an industry varies, of course. They have become commonplace in the technical, scientific and professional worlds. A breakthrough in an electronic process or medical treatment or a change in corporate law or tax structure brings on a rash of conferences.

Seminars and Workshops

Closely allied to the conference, but on a more modest basis, is the seminar. Association seminars are usually tied in with training and continuing education, such as the training of apprentice craftsmen, the updating of scientific and engineering personnel, or the presentation of marketing developments within an industry. Such seminars are presented around the country to small groups. Such business is within the scope of almost any hotel property.

Board and Committee Meetings

Association business regularly calls for smaller meetings. The board of directors may meet on a regular basis, not necessarily in the city of the association office. These meetings are often set in attractive locales as a way of encouraging outstanding people to serve, since they are not paid. Attendance at board meetings may range from ten to twelve to up to two hundred. The hotel chosen for such meetings is in a prime position to sell the property for the national convention, and for business emanating from the board members' own organizations.

Committee meetings may range in size from ten to fifty people and are held at varying rates of frequency. These events, too, can be serviced by hotels of any size as long as they are geared for meetings.

Characteristics of Association Meetings

Association meetings of all types follow similar patterns; understanding these patterns will help you sell them intelligently.

Cycle and Pattern

Conventions are held on a regular time cycle. The most common is annual, although about ten percent of associations hold two conventions a year and some that convene only every two years. The one-year cycle is often supplemented in a national organization with one, two or even three regional conventions on a smaller scale.

Conventions most frequently begin on Sunday and run through Wednesday or begin on Thursday and check out on Sunday (see Figure 4.7). The reason for this pattern is the airfare savings realized with a Saturday night stayover. These Saturday night stayovers, required by most airlines to qualify for reduced airfares, have boosted the occupancies of many downtown hotels that previously saw weekends as their slowest periods. Meetings and conventions that previously began on Mondays have moved registration to Sundays whenever possible so attendees can take advantage of the lower airfares. For some resort properties, however, the Saturday overnight requirement has had a negative effect, driving conference business to the end of the week. Jim Tierney, Vice President of Marketing, Amelia Island Plantation Resort, says:

> "With the drastic reduction in airfare when people stay overnight on Saturday, demand for conference business has—during the last few years—shifted to the weekends. This costs my resort and other resorts like us significant room revenue. Conferences that are booked on group

Figure 4.7. MONTHLY AND DAILY MEETING PATTERN OF ASSOCIATIONS.

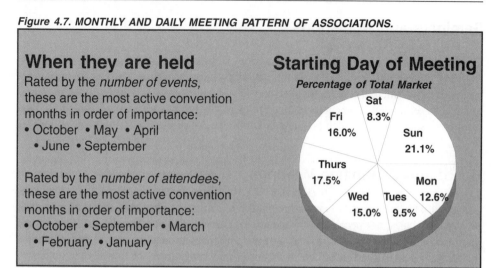

When they are held

Rated by the *number of events*, these are the most active convention months in order of importance:
• October • May • April
  • June • September

Rated by the *number of attendees*, these are the most active convention months in order of importance:
• October • September • March
  • February • January

Starting Day of Meeting
Percentage of Total Market

Sat 8.3%
Fri 16.0%
Sun 21.1%
Thurs 17.5%
Mon 12.6%
Wed 15.0%
Tues 9.5%

Source: By permission of Successful Meetings *magazine.*

rates that are lower than our daily rate take the place of social or transient guests that generally pay a higher room rate on weekends. Then to attract conference business Sunday through Thursday, we find ourselves having to negotiate deeper discounts than we might normally offer because the airfares are higher and that adds significantly to the meeting planners' overall costs. We, therefore, lose revenue at both ends of the week."[1]

A strong geographic pattern is also indicated. Jeff Sacks, CMP, an executive with Conferon, the world's largest meeting management company, states:

"A smart organization will rotate its annual convention across the map. This strategy not only allows you to meet in all regions where your membership is based, but it also benefits membership growth and recruitment in addition to keeping the meeting fresh in terms of climate, attractions, time zones, and cost of attending."[2]

Most associations alternate between the East and West in site selection. The most popular variation calls for a midwestern city every two years, with eastern and western cities alternating during the other two years. Typical examples follow:

	2004	2005	2006	2007	2008
National Conventions					
ABC Assn.	New York	Los Angeles	Washington	Denver	Boston
XYZ Assn.	Chicago	New York	St. Louis	Las Vegas	Milwaukee
Regional Conventions					
ABC Assn.	San Diego	Atlanta	Phoenix	Miami	San Francisco
	Cleveland	Kansas City	Cincinnati	St. Louis	New Orleans
XYZ Assn.	Los Angeles	Dallas	Philadelphia	Boston	Miami
	Atlanta	Seattle	San Diego	Detroit	Los Angeles

The important factor is the area of the country, not the specific city. The pattern may call for a Midwest location, which would be St. Louis, Chicago, Cincinnati or others. The Southeast could be served with Atlanta, Miami, Tampa or Memphis. Much depends on the geographic interests of the association members. If there is no special interest factor, the site selectors attempt to provide an interesting place to serve as an additional attraction.

The scheduling of regional events calls for a frank recognition that some members will not travel too far for the event. One association executive told us that his records show a hard core of regulars come to the convention every year no matter where it is held. This group is supplemented by members who come from within three hundred miles. Obviously, he holds regional conventions to keep his members involved. Perusal of the meeting pattern should show you when the group would next consider your part of the country.

Geographic Restrictions

Many state organizations, as part of their constitutions, have limited site selections to within their own states. This is also true of regional associations. There may be further restrictions because of the narrow interests of the program or the nature of the association's business.

There has been some deviation from such rigid limitations in recent years. One device that association executives have used to break out of the pattern is a reciprocal agreement with another state organization. Thus a Colorado chapter might meet in Massachusetts one year and the Massachusetts chapter would meet in Colorado. This satisfies the political aspects of catering to local businesses while providing a novel site to stimulate attendance.

Lead Time

Association conventions are planned well in advance, with a **lead time** of two to five years the norm for the meeting, a lead time of one and a half to two years for state and regional events and somewhat less than a year for other types of association meetings. Even decisions finalized two years in advance are the result of research and discussion that took up to five years. The larger the convention, the greater the lead time. Meeting planners are well aware that every hotel is not suitable for their convention. They want time to visit the site, check with past clients, and check other alternatives before making the decision.

This long lead time can be frustrating for the new hotel or the new hotel sales manager, but it is the pattern for associaton conventions. And the clear pattern enables you to decide when you can best propose your property to have the best chance of success.

Kind of Sites

Association business does not all go to the same kind of property. This is hardly surprising, considering the many kinds of associations and societies and the many types of meeting events they hold. Requirements and preferences could scarcely be expected to be uniform, but it is a rare hotel property that cannot serve some sort of association event.

Meetings are held in various types of facilities, depending on the size, nature and duration of meetings. Types of meeting facilities commonly used by associations include downtown hotels, airport hotels, suburban hotels, resorts, convention centers, conference centers, college/university campuses and the association's headquarters (see box titled "Types of Facilities Used").

Types of Facilities Used		
	For Conventions	For Other Association Meetings
Downtown hotels	65%	73%
Resort hotels (not including golf resorts)	17%	40%
Suburban hotels	16%	41%
Suite hotels	11%	18%
Airport hotels	9%	32%
Golf resorts	8%	19%
Gaming facilities	8%	9%
Residential conference centers	2%	9%
Nonresidential conference centers	1%	8%
Cruise ships	1%	1%
Other facilities	4%	30%
Did not use overnight accommodations	1%	3%

Source: **Meetings & Conventions'** *2004 Meetings Market Report.*

The kind of site selected generally reflects the group size, degree of sophistication and members' affluence. Obviously, a 200-room hotel would not be considered for a 500-person convention, unless it is in cooperation with other hotels. The basic requirements must be met—an auditorium for the main assembly, exhibit space if needed, support rooms for committees' and exhibitors' meetings.

We have discussed geographic considerations. Add to that ease of transportation and how the association executive feels about it. It is hard, for example, to find a more accessible place than the hotels near O'Hare Airport at Chicago. If the executive believes that such a site would draw more attendance, he or she may choose it.

There are other geographic factors involved. Many convention organizers want the vacation element working for them. How many extra registrations can a site such as Toronto or Las Vegas or Colorado Springs draw? That's the name of the game. There are many ways to enliven a regularly scheduled convention. Good, stimulating programming is the ideal way, but it's very hard to execute. It is often easier to stage the event at a lovely resort and keep your people happy by exposing them to "the good life."

Sports also play a role in site selection. Golf, tennis, swimming and boating are factors considered by convention planners as they analyze their people. Some fervent golfers on the board may very well swing the decision to a property with a famous course and favorable climate.

Voluntary Attendance

It should be clear by now that the association convention planner has to *attract* members to the annual event. One might think that business and professional interests would suffice as a magnet. Undoubtedly they do draw a certain number, but there are an indeterminate number of fence sitters. Should they go this year or should they skip it? This is where site attraction plays such an important role, and the meeting planner is aware of it.

The option to attend is the member's own. He or she may demand that both business needs and vacation desires be satisfied. If your property or region has tourist attractions, you should make sure that these are all part of your presentation. Whether it is the opera at the Lincoln Center or shopping at Saks Fifth Avenue in the Big Apple, exploring the winding streets of Québec City (the only fortified city in North America), or white-water rafting in Vancouver, British Columbia, a hotel's attraction is more than just its decor and facilities. Learn what positive aspects of your property you can project. Sales may depend on it.

As a bonus, records show that spouses come too when the site is attractive. That results in double occupancy revenues and longer stays. Vacations with tax-deductible expenditures also help turn out the members.

Convention Duration

The average duration of a convention is three to five days (see Figure 4.8). This is generally true for national events, although smaller affairs may last only two or three days. Seminars, committee meetings and the like can last just a day or two. Most conventions with exhibits meet no fewer than three days. There is quite a lot of additional business to be picked up as a result of such conventions as many exhibiting firms hold sales meetings just before the

Figure 4.8. AVERAGE DURATION OF ASSOCIATION MEETINGS.

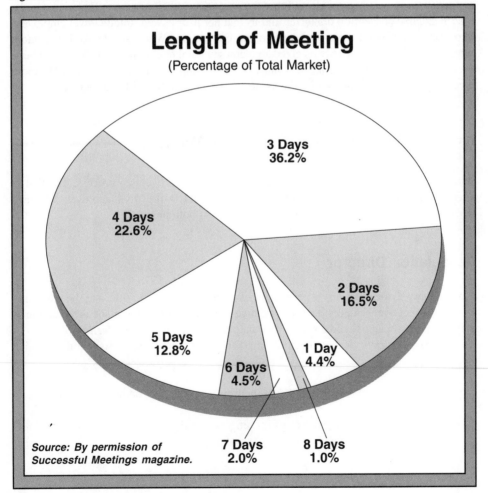

Length of Meeting
(Percentage of Total Market)

- 3 Days 36.2%
- 4 Days 22.6%
- 2 Days 16.5%
- 5 Days 12.8%
- 1 Day 4.4%
- 6 Days 4.5%
- 7 Days 2.0%
- 8 Days 1.0%

Source: By permission of Successful Meetings magazine.

event. This is true, too, for the association's board of directors and many committees. Look also for small associations among delegate groups who meet each year at the major convention.

Price

Your rate schedule is an important consideration for the association executive. We refer to your guestroom rates, not so much to your charges for meeting rooms, food functions, etc., although they will be reflected in the overall registration fee and charges for individual events. Guestroom rates must be aligned with the kind of people expected to attend. This is where the full range of hotels comes into play.

Many a convention organizer sticks with the traditional downtown hotels because of price. The older properties, built years ago at lower costs and lower mortgages, often can offer lower rates. That means nothing to some associations. But to others, it can mean the difference between choosing your property and rejecting it. Price can be a factor. Keep in mind that it is not always the most important one, even though it is always brought up.

Here, too, some study of where the group has met will help. If its history discloses successful years at places such as the Fairmont in San Francisco, the Plaza in New York and the Four Seasons in Ottawa, you can feel pretty sure that the convention organizer wants the best places for his or her people and that they are accustomed to paying the price. On the other hand, one convention organizer told us that her people were middle-level employees who traditionally paid their own way to the convention. When she booked at a more expensive place, she invariably received an increased number of complaints from members.

There is no right price level. It must suit the group you are trying to sell. Or, more accurately, it must suit the picture the association executive has of his or her people.

Association Meeting Decision Makers

Selection of the convention site—both city and hotel—is a two-step process. The first is screening all suggestions and solicitations; the second is the final approval. We have separated the two because not all people are active in both phases.

Association Director

Almost every association has a permanent executive person. The title may be executive secretary, executive vice president or executive director. Usually, he or she is the administrator of the association, and a very important person to hotel people. *Meetings & Conventions* magazine's most recent meetings market report found that association executive directors typically:

- Spend more than half (60.6%) of their professional time on meeting planning activities;
- Have been arranging meetings for ten years; and,
- Are female (77%) and about 45 years of age.

Your sales effort starts with this decision maker. A well-run sales staff of a hotel or convention bureau will treasure a file on each association and its key people; the list always starts with the executive director (see Figure 4.9).

Figure 4.9. TYPICAL JOB TITLES OF ASSOCIATION DECISION MAKERS.

Job Title	Association Planners
Events/Conventions/Conference Planner/ Coordinator/Manager/Director	29%
President/Executive Vice President	19
Meeting Planner/Coordinator/Manager/Director	20
Assistant to Executive	5
Treasurer	1
Director of Education	7
Marketing Director/Coordinator/Officer	1
Board Member/Program Director/Member Services	4
Other	24
Total	100%

Source: The 2004 Meetings Market Study conducted by Meetings & Conventions magazine.

The executive director is a key person for the initial screening of suitable convention sites and swings great influence over the final selection as well (see box titled "Executive Directors Speak Out About How Sites Decisions are Made"). After all, this executive enjoys a continuity in office that the elected officials do not have. The elected officials may serve for a year or two and then pass on the reins to the next team. But the executive director continues in office, and does so with the backing of the key members of the association.

The executive director doesn't work alone, however, especially in larger organizations. Since most of the administrative work has nothing to do with the convention activities, the executive director often has a staff member specifically assigned to convention planning. In the largest organization, this person may have a staff of his own. This convention planner thus is another person you should consider as very important when you make your presentation. He or she reports to and works closely with the executive director. Often the executive appoints a site selection committee to do **site inspections**. This group visits cities and hotels and is responsible for securing convention space arrangements for the association.

Small associations that cannot afford a full-time executive may choose to hire the services of **association management companies**. These organizations function as the executive and office staff for a number of associations that otherwise would have to make do with volunteers. In this way the associations enjoy professional management at costs they can afford.

There are approximately 200 association management organizations in business today, managing the affairs of over 500 national associations and more than 1,000 state and regional associations. The two largest association management companies are Smith Bucklin (www.smithbucklin.com) and Association Management Group (www.amg-inc.com).

**Executive Directors Speak Out About
How Site Decisions are Made**

Garis Distelhorst, National Association of College Stores:
"Our process is collaborative. The meetings staff screens proposals and prepares a list of four or five cities. At that point, my role is to determine if there are any that wouldn't work and to suggest any destination not on the list that we might want to do additional research on. We try to follow an East/West/Central rotation. We focus on second-tier cities that are going to treat our meeting as a big deal...."

Ron Moen, American Association of Orthodontists:
"Preliminary screening is the responsibility of the director of meetings. Actual site reviews of two or three cities on the short list are conducted by the director, myself, and the member of the board who will be president in the year that the meeting will be held. A committee of the board rubber stamps our recommendation...when it's unanimous...."

Dan Weder, Institute of Food Technologists:
"The recommendation comes to me. I visit cities in the running and make the site decision. While it ultimately goes to the executive committee for approval, in 30 years they've never failed to ratify a selection."

Source: Drs. J. Dana Clark, Catherine Price and Suzanne Murrmann, "Collaborative 'Buying Centers': How Associations Choose Destinations," Convene.

If an association employs an association management company, you may find yourself dealing with one man or woman responsible for several convention bookings. The advantage to you is that when selling to these organizations you are not talking about a group coming back in four or five years. One of their clients may be interested in your property later in the same year. Many of these management organizations specialize in one or two industries. If your hotel's history shows a concentration of certain types of associations, such as automotive or computer groups, it would be wise to link with those association management organizations that represent these types of associations.

The trade association representing association management organizations is called the International Association of Association Management Companies (IAAMC). This group holds an annual meeting and trade show, and is an ideal target market for smaller lodging properties (see Appendix I for their address).

There are independent companies that fill this role as well. The Alliance of Meeting Management Companies (www.ammc.org) and the Independent Meeting Planners Association of Canada (www.impca.canada.com) are two examples of independent companies. Convention management companies work either for a negotiated fee or a percentage of the registration fees as an incentive to stimulate attendance. Such management firms obviously are important. They influence site selection and are also the people who work with the hotels to execute the meeting. They are also a factor in getting other business.

Association President and Officers

The power of the president varies greatly among associations. As mentioned, the president usually serves for a year or two. He or she may serve as an honorary figurehead or may flex a great deal of muscle. You really have no choice but to pay a lot of attention to this key person. In almost all cases, keep in mind that he or she shares in the initial screening of a selection site and is certainly in on the final decision.

When you build your files on association personnel, take notes on the vice presidents and secretary/treasurers as well. These officers are future years' presidents. A recent study suggests:

> "It is not uncommon in associations to have a new chairperson every year. Often, this chairperson has substantial power over staff and other members...Such power may include the ability to affect the list of sites initially being considered and one that is eventually chosen as the convention location in the future. Because of the lead time necessary to plan major conventions or trade shows, many of these meeting sites are picked years in advance. At the same time, many associations also know in advance who the association president will be in any given year. Either tradition or bylaws regulate much of the decision power on site selection to the person who will be president during the year of a particular convention. Therefore, marketing strategies not only need to be aimed at the current chair or president, they need to identify and court future leaders. A long term relationship between the hospitality marketer and the association chair(s)-to-be can impact how they use their influence in your favor for the year they are in power."[3]

Committee Chairperson

Certain committee heads get involved in the initial suggestions and screening. This depends on the nature and structure of the organization and the subject of the event. They most definitely are a factor in site selection for seminars dealing with the committee's subject matter.

You can see that a fair number of hands get involved in creating the original list of proposed places and in the preliminary screening to narrow down the choices. If you are eliminated in the final selection, it may mean loss of business that year, but you may well be in line for a booking when the cycle brings the association back to your part of the country. There may also be some consolation prizes in the form of selection for lesser events such as committee meetings or seminars.

Board of Directors

The final list is usually presented to the board of directors for the final selection. It is worth emphasizing that the recommendations of the executive director usually are accepted. Some get their way all the time; some must deal more politically and tactfully. But the executive director remains the single most important person you must sell to get association business. He may not rule autocratically, but he manages to get his way most of the time. You may lose the business at the directors' meeting, but without the support of the executive director, you never even get that far. Generally, *all* the finalists meet with the director's approval.

Other Influences

It is common practice in many scientific and technical societies for local chapters to make an **association bid** for the national event. That is not to say they *bid* in the sense of offering money. Rather, they request the honor of playing **local host** to the national group and offer their efforts to make the convention a success. This is especially true with international societies; an invitation from a national chapter is required before a location is considered.

Hotel salespeople are aware of this practice. We know of cases in which a local delegate to an international congress has been approached by a convention bureau or hotel. An appeal is made to his local pride and to any other emotions that can be brought to bear. It is not uncommon in such cases for the bureau or hotel to bear the costs of the delegate's travel, a hospitality suite and the presentation to the board. It is wise to assure the delegate that the bureau or hotel would supply clerical support to enable the delegate to fulfill his role of host.

It doesn't always require such effort. Appeals to local delegates or chapters often bring results merely because of civic pride and a willingness to help local businesses. Look around your city and make friends with people in local association chapters. At the very least, you may pick up a local banquet or one-night meeting.

It is important when you enlist the aid of local members to impress upon them that you and your establishment are fully capable of handling the business. They may very well feel uncertain about the wisdom of getting involved and perhaps fear the embarrassment of a debacle at the national convention. But then you have to convince any prospect at any level that you and your staff are competent and interested in doing a good job. Those are the two key points you must make over and over — that your staff has the *expertise* and the *desire* to do whatever must be done to execute the meeting properly.

In addition to the decision makers who have direct involvement in their association, *third-party planners* have become increasingly influential in site selection. As we discussed in Chapter 1, many of today's meetings are planned by third-party intermediaries, including meeting management firms, independent meeting planners, and travel agents (both individuals and mega-agencies). In many cases, these third-party planners are involved in searching out hotel sites and, due to their familiarity with the industry, their recommendations highly influence their association clients -- especially when the intermediaries will be coordinating and executing the event.

Many of these third-party planners, however, seek a commission from the hotels they recommend. When hotels were struggling to fill rooms it became customary to pay a ten percent commission (the percentage of the room rate traditionally paid to travel agents) to meeting management firms. In a good economy, however, an increasing number of properties are balking at paying commissions. Therefore, meeting management companies, such as Conference Direct (www.conferencedirect.com) and Conferon (www.conferon.com) are sometimes charging the associations for their services.

Sources for Finding Association Business ———————

Associations are readily located, fortunately. The national ones seem to be clustered in a relatively few cities. The Washington, D.C. area is home to more associations (3,500) than any other city, with New York City (1,900) and Chicago (1,200) placing second and third. Other major U.S. headquarter cities include Austin, Indianapolis, Los Angeles, Milwaukee, Oklahoma City, Philadelphia and Richmond. In Canada, sources for association business can generally be found in Ottawa and in the capitals of the provinces.

Directories

Several volumes offer detailed listings of associations. One is *Who's Who in Association Management,* published by the American Society of Association Executives, 1575 Eye Street, NW, Washington, DC 20005. It lists approximately 7,000 associations. The list is available for sale and, under certain circumstances, for direct mail rental. It is a valuable reference.

Other directories include the *National Trade and Professional Associations of the United States* and its companion publication, *State and Regional Associations of the United States.* Each offers over 7,000 listings. The publisher is Columbia Books, Inc., 1212 New York Avenue NW, Suite 330, Washington, DC 20005. The publisher will rent the list for direct mail use and will supply various breakdowns and services at prices quoted on request.

The *Encyclopedia of Associations* (and its companion, *Geographic Index of Associations*) is published by Gale Research Company, 835 Pnobscot Building, Detroit, MI 48226. Contact the publisher for prices.

National Associations of the United States lists all the national associations, membership totals, and officers and addresses. It may be obtained by writing to the Superintendent of Documents, U.S. Government Printing Office, Washington, DC 20402.

Successful Meetings magazine publishes two directories. The *Directory of Conventions* lists more than 19,000 coming events in the convention field. It offers such excellent details as convention sponsor, dates, whether there is an exhibit, estimated attendance, headquarters facilities, name, title and address of the executive in charge and reports on the scope of the meetings. The second directory, *The Exhibit Schedule*, includes more than 11,000 listings of major events around the world. It includes full data, as in the *Directory of Conventions*. Contact the publisher for prices and more information on either of these products at Successful Meetings, 633 Third Ave., New York, NY 10017.

The Salesman's Guide publishes directories of association, corporate and incentive meeting planners (see Figure 4.10). Each listing includes the names and titles of the meeting planners, their addresses, number of conventions and meetings held, past and future sites, months held, and the type of facility utilized. These directories can be ordered from Douglas Publishers (phone 1-800-223-1797).

Databases

A number of databases are available to assist hotels in target marketing to the association planners. Associations, publications and independent organizations are making important facts and figures available to enable interested hotels to better identify true prospects for their particular property.

Successful Meetings magazine offers a useful marketing service for the hotel field called the *SM/Databank*. The magazine has stored data on the history of more than 300,000 meetings held by some 28,000 associations over the past twenty-five years. The database includes information on events planned by associations. You may obtain information about prospects that fit your preferred client profile, such as the time of the week in which a group meets, time of year, geographic pattern, size of the group, whether it has exhibits, where it has met previously and where it is scheduled to meet in the future.

The Professional Convention Management Association (PCMA) has developed their new *American Meetings Databank* (see Figure 4.11). This database functions as a centralized source of meetings information for both meeting planners and suppliers.

Figure 4.10 SAMPLE OF INFORMATION PROVIDED BY DIRECTORIES.

36 **CALIFORNIA – HUNTINGTON BEACH**

ASSOCIATION	MEETING PLANNERS	CONVENTION BOOKINGS	■ TYPE OF MEETING	† NO MEETINGS PER ANNUM	MONTHS HELD	NO OF DAYS	* NO OF ATTENDEES	O TYPE OF FACILITY
UNITED STATES LIFESAVING ASSN (USLA) PO BOX 366 HUNTINGTON BEACH, 92648 714-536-5283/FAX: 714-374-1500	BILL RICHARDSON (Pres) *Speaker Exhibit Space*	05/93 Florida Keys 11/93 Chicago 05/94 Seattle Booked 6 mos in advance	C			3	B	DAR
WESTERN ECONOMIC ASSN INTL (WEA) 7400 CTR AVE # 109 HUNTINGTON BEACH, 92647 714-898-3222/FAX: 714-891-6715	ELDON J DVORAK (Exec Vp) VERONICA M DVORAK (Dir Of Conf)	06/91 Seattle 06/94 Vancouver 07/92 San Francisco 07/95 San Diego 06/93 Lake Tahoe *Far East* Booked 1 yr in advance *South Pacific* OC	C M	 1		3-4	E	DRC
WYCLIFFE BIBLE TRANSLATORS (WBT) P O BOX 2727 HUNTINGTON BEACH, 92647 714-969-4600/FAX: 714-969-4661	RON OLSON (Assoc Dir) GERALD ELDER (Treas) *Speaker*	OC	M	12	V	3	A	
THE ELECTRICAL MANUFACTURING & COIL WINDING ASSN INC PO BOX 278 IMPERIAL BEACH, 91933 619-575-4191/FAX: 619-575-5009	CHARLES E THURMAN (Exec Dir) *Speaker*	10/91 Boston 10/93 Chicago 09/92 Cincinnati 09/94 Chicago 06/93 Hong Kong *Far East* Booked 2-3 yrs in advance OC	C M	 2-3		3-4 3	E A	AC
AMERICAN COLLEGE OF TRIAL LAWYERS (ACTL) 8001 IRVINE CTR DR STE 960 IRVINE, 92718 714-727-3194/FAX: 714-727-3894	ROBERT A YOUNG (Exec Dir)	Booked 2-3 yrs in advance						
INTERIOR DESIGN EDUCATORS COUNCIL (IDEC) 14252 CULVER DR SUITE A331 IRVINE, 92714 714-551-1622	CANDEE ERWIN (Exec Secy) *Exhibit Space*	04/92 Alexandria	M	6	4	4	C	D
MOTORCYCLE INDUSTRY COUNCIL (MIC) 2 JENNER ST SUITE 150 IRVINE, 92718 714-727-4211	PAMELA AMETTE (Vp) CATHY WILSHIRE (Asst Prog Dir) *Speaker*	02/94 Cincinnati 02/95 Cincinnati Booked 2 yrs in advance	C M	 1	 10	1 3	A U	C C
MULTI LEVEL MARKETING INTL ASSN. (MLMIA) 119 STANFORD CT IRVINE, 92715 714-854-0464/FAX: 714-854-7687	DORIS WOOD (Pres.) *Exhibit Space*	09/91 Toronto 06/92 Orange County *Canada* 02/93 Orange County *Europe* *Far East* Booked 3-5 mos in advance OC	C M	 4	 1, 4, 7, 10	4-5 2-3	B U	AR
NATIONAL ASSN OF NAMEPLATE MANUFACTURERS (NAME) 17300 RED HILL AVE STE 100 IRVINE, 92714 714-261-9588/FAX: 714-261-2594	JAMES A KINDER (Exec Vp) LINDA BRADY (Dir Of Educ) *Speaker Exhibit Space*	03/93 Naples 10/94 St Louis 09/93 New Orleans 03/95 Palm Springs 03/94 Scottsdale *Mexico* Booked 2 yrs in advance *Caribbean* OC	C M	 1		1-2 4-5	D B	D DR
NATIONAL MIDAS DEALERS ASSN (NMDA) 14795 JEFFREY RD STE 202 IRVINE, 92720 714-551-1289/FAX: 714-551-0621	MYRON P GORDON (Exec Dir) FRANK MAGLIOCCO (Assoc Exec Dir) *Exhibit Space*	10/91 Las Vegas 09/94 Boca Raton 11/92 New Orleans 10/93 Colorado Springs *Canada* Booked 2-3 yrs in advance OC	C M	 10	 1, 2, 3, 4, 5, 6, 7, 8, 9, 10, 11, 12	4 1-4	C U	DR A

■ TYPE OF MEETING (C) Convention Data (M) Smaller Meetings & Seminar Data
† MONTHS HELD (1) Jan (2) Feb (3) Mar (4) Apr (5) May (6) June (7) July (8) Aug (9) Sept (10) Oct (11) Nov (12) Dec (P) Spring (S) Summer (F) Fall (W) Winter (V) Various
* NUMBER OF ATTENDEES (U) Under 50 (A) 51-100 (B) 101-200 (C) 201-500 (D) 501-1000 (E) 1001-5000 (F)Over 5000
O TYPE OF FACILITY (D) Downtown (A) Airport (R) Resort (C) Convention Center

The Nationwide Directory of Association Meeting Planners, *available from The Salesman's Guide, lists the names and titles of over 10,000 meeting planners from over 6,500 major associations. The directory details the number of meetings held annually, the months in which they are held, the approximate number of attendees, and the geographic location of the meetings. Of special interest to hotel salespeople: the type of facilities used by each group.*
Source: Salesman's Guide.

Figure 4.11. SAMPLE OF DATABANK INFORMATION.

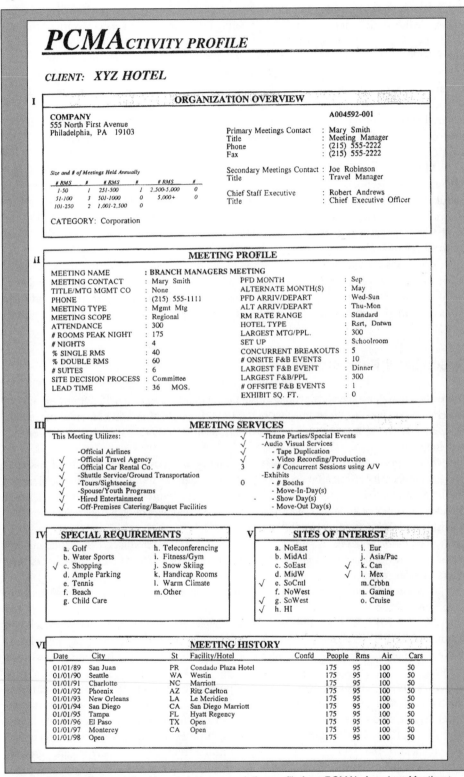

Sample of information contained in a prototype association profile from PCMA's American Meetings Databank.

Most recently, the International Associations of Convention and Visitors Bureaus (IACVB) has ended its code of confidentiality regarding information provided by member bureaus. All historical and demographic meeting information in its new Meeting Information Network (MINT) is now accessible through their local bureaus. This database contains some 28,000 meeting profiles going back over the past four years and the future site-selection information for nearly 14,500 organizations. The report includes the decision maker's name, history of past meetings, start and end dates, registered attendance, number of guestrooms used, number of meeting rooms used and square footage of exhibit space required. Approximately 1,500 new histories are added yearly. This information is invaluable, providing a factual convention operations history of these leading convention organizations.

Most meeting planners are eager to verify information for these databases on their organizations' meetings for two reasons. First, this history provides them with information useful in negotiating with hotels. Second, planners recognize that database information allows hotels to target their prospects, eliminating misdirected efforts and reducing the number of cold calls from suppliers who do not have enough rooms and/or meeting space for their meetings.

Databases provide a valuable service in building your prospect file for sales campaigns. One subscriber to databases says, "We feel it is an innovative way to find pre-qualified profiles and a really efficient way to pursue business. By receiving the profiles, we save hours of time that would otherwise be spent on cold calls."

Specialized Periodicals

There are a number of periodicals that serve the market (see Figure 4.12). Some go only to association personnel; others are distributed to both association and corporate personnel. Their advertisers are hotels, convention bureaus, airlines and other suppliers in the convention industry.

Association Management is published monthly by the American Society of Association Executives. Its circulation consists of the members of this prestigious organization. The list is available for rental for direct mail under specific circumstances. The Association Directory & Buying Guide lists members with address and telephone numbers which makes it most useful. Vendors may join the society as associate members.

Association Meetings is published six times a year. It is circulated to full-time managers of societies and associations as well as volunteer/member part-time managers, and others. A sales lead service is available to advertisers.

Convene is published ten times annually by the Professional Convention Managers Association (PCMA).

Meeting News is a monthly tabloid newspaper. Its circulation includes association personnel. The tabloid provides a reader service card to key ads and to supply sales leads. Its New Names service offers the names of meeting planners in that function for less than one year.

Meetings & Conventions is a monthly publication whose circulation also contains association personnel. Its circulation is available for rental for direct mail. Advertisers get a reader service card system plus a sales lead service in the association and corporate fields.

Medical Meetings magazine, published eight times annually, concentrates on a specific segment of the field. The circulation is formed from medical societies and associations, biomedical corporations, hospitals and medical centers, and government and foundation organizations. They, too, offer a reader sales lead system.

Figure 4.12. SPECIALIZED PERIODICALS FOR THE MEETINGS MARKET.

There are a number of publications directed to meeting planners. Some are generalized publications that appeal to a wide variety of planners, while others are available only to those who are members of the organization that sponsors a publication. Hotel salespeople can subscribe to and read many of these publications to gain a better understanding of meeting planners and their needs.

Successful Meetings, a monthly magazine, also includes association personnel in its circulation, as well as corporate planners. Advertisers receive the SM Convention Research Bulletin published weekly. It provides information about groups planning meetings. *Successful Meetings* publishes SM Tip Flash, which supplies advertisers with sales leads. Their list may be rented for direct mail.

These are prominent publications but not the only ones. Others are listed in Appendix I. Information as to the particular segment each serves should be obtained from the publishers.

Hotel Records

If you are newly assigned to a hotel convention sales staff, one of the first things to do is to closet yourself with the function books and other records from the past few years. Much can be learned from them. How many groups met in your house but never returned? It is amazing how many times business is lost because no one followed up and pressed for more business.

Your hotel records will also offer clues to personnel changes. If a group didn't return, a new executive director could offer another chance. You could call and indicate that his group had met successfully at your hotel and perhaps persuade the group to book again. You also should try to find out where the previous director is now located. After all, he or she selected your hotel previously and may be amenable to doing so again. No sales staffer should rely on a past customer's memory to bring him or her back. Sales life is not that easy. You must go after business.

Keep in mind that the easiest prospect is a satisfied past customer. If the meeting went well, you have an excellent prospect. If it did not go smoothly, it is imperative to find out why. It could be something that you must prevent from happening with other clients or it may be something that you have already corrected and you could then press for business. Some of the best business relationships result from clearing up past grievances, many of which could have been eliminated in the first place had sales executives better understood the needs of association meeting planners. To minimize problems with members of this market segment, some hotel chains are offering specialized training to their sales personnel (see "Best Practices" box).

Hotel records may also lead to other prospects gleaned from local small bookings. A dinner meeting handled solely by the banquet manager may indicate only a local chapter. But this small bit of business of dinner for twenty or so may be just the Trojan horse you need to penetrate the state or national parent organization. Much can be learned from the members themselves. At least, a follow-up phone call will increase the chances for more local business.

It is important to realize that much association business must be cultivated over the long haul, so don't get discouraged. The road to that major booking may have to go through many minor bits of business before you score the big one, or before scoring at all. Maintain a good follow-up system; keep after target associations, and you'll get your share.

Summary

In this chapter, we have discussed the importance of the associations market to hotels and identified some of the factors that hospitality firms need to consider if they wish to target this market segment. It is essential to know the types of meetings that associations hold, the characteristics of these meetings (cycle and pattern, geographic restrictions, lead time, kinds of sites desired, and price considerations), and to determine the key decision makers and how to reach them. A hotel that "does its homework" can attract business that will fill rooms and bring revenue to the property's other facilities in what would normally be slack months and may generate significant repeat business from association meeting attendees.

In the next chapter, we will discuss the corporate meetings market. While some corporate meetings may seem similar to those held by associations at first glance, there are major differences to consider that will enable your property to target this primary source of meetings business.

Best Practices

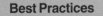

Marriott Hotels & Resorts and the PCMA Team Up to Help Hotel Sales Executives Think Like Association Meeting Planners

The Certified Association Sales Executive (CASE) Marriott/PCMA Program is an intensive nine-week course designed exclusively for hotel sales executives who sell to the association market. Louis Nicholls, senior account executive for Marriott International and a CASE graduate, says:

> "This course specifically targets issues that pertain to our industry and our day-to-day roles in it."

The CASE program, which has been open to all Marriott employees involved in association sales since 2002, gives the sales executives the opportunity to "get inside the heads" of their association clients through a combination of online learning, instructor-led training and first-hand experience with association personnel. Jessica van der Gaast, a senior account executive at the San Francisco Marriott, who had never been on the association side of meeting planning, says:

> "I had the opportunity to observe the roles and responsibilities for each staff member of the association, sit in on important meetings, and observe first-hand the decision-making process and structure of the organization. I had one-on-one discussion time with each staff person, including the executive director, and learned about current technology and changes in society in terms of how they affect the organization and its strategic planning."

Through this course, hotel salespeople get a real sense of how associations operate in terms of structure and timing issues. This understanding helps them to see associations as valuable business and be able to offer solutions to help this segment meet their objectives.

Source: Ginny Phillips, "Creating a Niche," Convene, *October 2004, p. 76.*

Endnotes:

1. "Resort Committee Seeks Members to Address Saturday Overnight Airfare Issue", *HSMAI Update*.
2. Jeff Sacks, CMP, "Site Selection," www.pcma.org/templates/Conferon/charts/Ch2_1.htm, January 11, 2003.
3. J. Dana Clark, Michael R. Evans, and Bonnie J. Knutson, "Selecting a Site for an Association Convention: An Exploratory Look at the Types of Power Used by Committee Members to Influence Decisions," *Journal of Hospitality & Leisure Marketing*.

Additional References:

- Contemporary Hospitality Marketing, William Lazer and Robert Layton, Educational Institute, AHLA. www.ei-ahla.org

- Destination Marketing For Convention and Visitors Bureaus, Second Edition, Richard Gartrell, Kendall/Hunt Publishing.

Internet Sites:

For more information, visit the following Internet sites. Internet addresses can change without notice. If a site is no longer available at the address listed below, a search engine can be used to find the new address or additional, related sites.

American Society of Association Executives (ASAE) - www.asaenet.org
Association Directory – www.assoconline.com
Association Management - www.asaenet.org/publications/amcurrent/index/html
Association Meetings - www.meetingsnet.com
"Association Management Companies" (directory) - www.asaenet.org
Canadian Society of Association Executives – www.case.org
Convene - www.pcma.org/pub/convene.rtm
Convention Industry Council (CIC) - www.conventionindustry.org
International Association of Association Management Companies - www.iaamc.org
International Association of Convention and Visitors Bureaus - www.iacvb.org
International Society of Meeting Planners - www.iami.org/ismp.html
Meetings and Conventions - www.meetings-conventions.com
Meetings in the West - www.meetingsweb.com
Professional Convention Management Association (PCMA) - www.pcma.org
Successful Meetings - www.successmtgs.com

Study Questions:

1. Conventions are extremely important to associations for financial reasons. Explain why.
2. What kinds of meetings do associations hold? What type of facilities are best suited to each?
3. How do state and regional association meetings differ from the national association meetings?
4. Identify the monthly and daily meeting pattern of association meetings.
5. Attendance for association conventions is voluntary. How important is price to association executives? What implications does this have on a hotel's sales efforts?

6. What individuals in the association make the site selection decision?
7. List sources for locating associations.

Key Terms:

Association. A group of people joined together for a common purpose.

Association bid. A regional chapter requests the honor of hosting a national convention.

Association management companies. Firms that function as the executive and office staff for a number of associations.

Breakout session. Small group sessions within the meeting, formed to discuss specific topics.

Concurrent session. Meeting sessions on different topics scheduled at the same time.

General session. The main meeting attended by the majority of the association members. Also called **plenary session**.

Lead time. The time between the booking and the actual meeting date.

Local host. A group of local people who carry out the strategies and policies established for the organization of an event held in their geographic area. Also called an **organizing committee**.

Site inspection. Tour of the property conducted by representatives of the association or corporation in order to determine whether the hotel is suitable to host the meeting/event.

Learning Objectives:

This portion of your text takes a look at the corporate meetings market. We will discuss the kinds of meeting held by corporations and what factors are considered in staging corporate meetings, the key decision makers for company meetings, and how to locate sources of corporate business. When you have studied this chapter, you will:

- Be able to identify factors that corporate meeting planners consider when making a site selection.

- Be able to describe the types of meetings held by companies and tell how these meetings differ from meetings staged by associations.

- Know the characteristics and requirements for company meetings of all types.

- Be able to identify key corporate decision makers and detail ways in which sources of business can be located.

Outline

Requirements for Corporate Meetings
Kinds of Company Meetings
- National and Regional Sales Meetings
- New Product/Dealer Meetings
- Professional/Technical Meetings
- Management Meetings
- Training Meetings
- Stockholder/Public Meetings
- Incentive Meetings

Characteristics of Company Meetings
Corporate Meeting Decision Makers
- Full-time Meeting Planner
- Company President
- Marketing and Sales Executives
- Advertising and Sales Managers
- Other Corporate Executives
- Passenger Traffic/Corporate Travel Managers
- Procurement (Purchasing) Managers
- Training Director
- Meeting Specialists/Third-Party Planners

Sources for Finding Corporate Business and Decision Makers
- Special Meeting Publications
- Trade Directories
- Trade Associations
- Internet Sites
- Convention and Visitors Bureaus
- Lateral Referral and Account Penetration

Summary

Selling to the Corporate Meetings Market

Helmut Knipp
President and Chief Operating Officer
Lexington Management Corporation

*"**Qualify** and **Quantify** are two of the most important steps in the solicitation of any account. You have to know the potential an account has before you can make intelligent rate and solicitation decisions. With our salespeople, we stress the importance of doing research on our customers...Two other areas require mentioning. One is to take outstanding care of the customers you have...It is much more costly and time-consuming to find new customers than it is to take care of existing ones...The second area is prospecting. A salesperson must make new contacts all the time... Ask your existing customers for other contacts in their business or trade. Read the newspapers and trade journals for leads and prospects...."*

5

Selling the Corporate Meetings Market

oday's corporation is a complex organization. The geographic marketing range has grown to the point that most companies now market nationally or internationally. The structure of larger companies is more detailed and multifaceted than ever before. Modern executives who received their training with such companies in mind are keenly aware of the vital need for *communication*. Meetings remain a most basic form of communication within companies. You are concerned solely with those company meetings that take place off company premises, and there are enough of them to satisfy any enterprising hotel sales staff.

If the association convention business represents the best-known and most visible segment of the meetings field, corporate meetings offer the greatest potential for growth. A recent study by *Meetings & Conventions* magazine found that more than half of the corporate planners surveyed expected to hold more meetings than they previously held in past years. Although the volume of corporate business is greater than that of the association segment, corporate business is not as visible. Since company meetings are varied and are controlled by a wider variety of personnel, they are harder to dig out. But they offer a great deal of group business potential that no hotel should ignore.

Fortunately, hotel marketing people do not have to decide which segment of the market — associations or corporations — to sell. The two are a digestible mix, and a successful property enjoys its share of both kinds. The ratio of each really reflects upon the kind of property you have, what you are equipped to handle, and where you are located. While some hotel features and benefits appeal to both markets, there are significant differences (see Figure 5.1). Examine your hotel with an eye to what corporate meeting planners want and the kinds of meetings they hold.

Requirements for Corporate Meetings

The factors that make a hotel attractive for association events hold true for most corporate meetings too. Keep in mind that corporate meetings vary a great deal in size, scope and purpose. It is important, therefore, to match the planner's needs with the hotel's facilities.

Quality Food Service. Food and beverage functions are major contributors to the success or failure of corporate meetings. Long after other meeting details are forgotten, corporate attendees remember an elegant banquet, a unique refreshment break or an unusual theme party.

Hotels can increase the comfort level in this area by having staff that assures the meeting planner of the property's attention to all the details of food and beverage functions. Mark Beaupre, executive chef at the 1,000-room JW Marriott Orlando Grande Lakes in Orlando, Florida, always meets with meeting planners beforehand and says:

> "...The idea is to build relationships, especially if the meeting is, say, three years away. I assist the sales managers, and that really adds to the comfort level of the person responsible for the event. By the time the group gets here, I have talked with and e-mailed him or her many times.

Figure 5.1. COMPARISON OF ASSOCIATION AND CORPORATE MEETING GROUPS.

FACTOR	ASSOCIATION	CORPORATION
Attendance	Voluntary	Mandatory
Decision making	Decentralized; often committee	Centralized (usually one person)
Number of meetings	Fewer, but larger attendance	More, but fewer attendees per meeting
Potential for Repeat Business	Some, but must rotate sites	High
Room Block	Must track reservation pickup closely	Stable
Spouse Attendance	Common	Seldom
Exhibits	Frequent; heavy demand for hospitality suites	Less frequent
Site Selection	Need to build attendance with attractive locations; sometimes political	Seek convenience, service and security
Geographic Pattern	Rotate geographically	No set pattern
Lead Time	Long (usually two to five years)	Short (often less than one year)
Billing Format	Individual Folios	Master Account
Risk of Cancellation	Minimal	Higher; penalty clauses and advance deposits are common
Arrival/Departure	More likely to have early arrivals	Few early arrivals or departures
Price	More price concsious; generally good negotiators	Less price-sensitive
Convention and Visitors Bureau Involvement	Frequently utilize convention bureaus, especially with citywide conventions	Seldom contact convention bureau
Reservation Procedures	Generally use postal reply cards or Housing Bureau	Frequently provide a rooming list
Attrition Concerns	Over 50% of association meeting planners cite attrition as a major issue in contracts	Only one in four corporate planners mention attrition as a concern

During the event, every evening I sit with the planner over a glass of wine, and we talk about that day and the one to follow."[1]

Corporate meeting planners consistently rate quality of food service as very important in choosing a hotel or facility (see Figure 5.2). The planner of today is continually encouraging the staff to surpass a previous year's convention program. To gain its share of repeat business, a hotel must continue to upgrade menus, contribute to the uniqueness of each event and create an occasion that will be long remembered.

Adequate Meeting Space. It is hard to hold a meeting efficiently if the meeting rooms are too small—or too large (although surplus area may be screened off). When you go after company business, discuss room requirements in detail. The main room may need support from a number of small rooms. If your layout shows these nearby, you have a strong selling point. The traffic flow pattern of the meeting is very important.

In addition to room layout, many of today's corporate meeting planners require "high tech" equipment and Internet access in both meeting rooms and guestrooms. Since most corporate meetings are about productivity and businesspeople most generally come to these meetings armed with their laptops, hotels that wish to capture this market segment

Business Class Rooms

In response to the increasing number of business travelers, hotels began offering business centers equipped with computer equipment, FAX machines, copiers and secretarial services. The drawback to business centers, however, was that many were not accessible on a 24-hour basis, making it difficult for individual business travelers and corporate meeting attendees to attend to business after hours.

Some hotels met this need by creating business floors with 24-hour access to office equipment and supplies, while some hotel chains designed guestrooms specifically for business travelers and corporate meeting attendees, who often retreat to their rooms at the end of the day's sessions to work. These "business class" rooms usually include large desks (often stocked with business amenities such as paper clips, writing implements, Post-it notes, etc.), in-room computer hookups and FAX machines, a desk telephone, enhanced lighting and ergonomic desk chairs.

Among the chains offering rooms with these special features are Hyatt (the Hyatt Business Plan), Clarion (Biz Class Office Rooms), Sheraton (Corporate Club Rooms), Westin (the Guest Office), and Delta (Business Zone Guestrooms). These rooms are usually available at a slightly higher charge than regular sleeping rooms, but are becoming increasingly popular with business travelers and are an attractive advantage when marketing a property to the corporate meetings market.

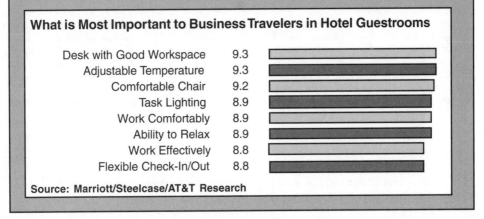

What is Most Important to Business Travelers in Hotel Guestrooms

Desk with Good Workspace	9.3
Adjustable Temperature	9.3
Comfortable Chair	9.2
Task Lighting	8.9
Work Comfortably	8.9
Ability to Relax	8.9
Work Effectively	8.8
Flexible Check-In/Out	8.8

Source: Marriott/Steelcase/AT&T Research

must offer such services as High-Speed Internet Access (HSIA) and/or Wi-Fi, wireless technology that allows attendees to log on to the Internet using radio frequencies (wireless technology is commonly offered in lobbies and other public areas as well as in meeting rooms and some guestrooms). The Internet is frequently used for demonstrations and business applications at corporate meetings, and attendees tap into the Internet to maintain productivity while on the road, including keeping in contact with customers via email. In many cases, hotels are charging a daily fee (which can be a separate charge or included in the room rate) for both wired and wireless Internet access or "bundling" these services with other amenities, such as a continental breakfast and newspaper for Concierge Level service.

Service. Companies meet for good reason, and they don't want problems. They want service — good service. They want what was promised, and on time. The reward is repeat business. Except for incentive programs, corporate meetings promise the most repeat business. Many planners mention good service first when asked what they look for in a meeting site.

Enough Guestrooms. No company likes to split up at a meeting, chancing the "loss" of attendees during the walk or cab ride to the meeting site. They prefer to house everyone under one roof. This is a difficult problem to overcome if you can't offer it but your

Figure 5.2. FACTORS CONSIDERED IMPORTANT TO CORPORATE MEETING PLANNERS IN THE SELECTION OF A FACILITY/HOTEL.

Factors Considered "Very Important"	Corporate Planners
Number, size, and quality of meeting rooms	84%
Cost of hotel or meeting facility	82
Negotiable food, beverage and room rates	79
Quality of food service	76
Number, size and quality of sleeping rooms	74
Availability of meeting support services and equipment, such as audiovisual equipment	59
Efficiency of billing procedures	58
Assignment of one staff person to handle all aspects of meeting	54
Previous experience in dealing with facility and its staff	53
Efficiency of check-in and check-out procedures	49
High-speed Internet access	42
Meeting rooms with multiple high-speed phone lines and computer outlets	40
Number, size and quality of suites	30
Proximity to airport	28

Corporate austerity programs, coupled with a greater awareness of the size of meeting expenditures, have caused corporate planners to rank the cost of a hotel or meeting facility and negotiable food, beverage and room rates high on their list of factors for site selection. The quality of food service, which was formerly their first priority, moved to fourth place on their list.
Source: The 2004 Meetings Market Report conducted by Meetings & Conventions magazine.

competitor can. Hotels combine presentations to large groups but the first choice is invariably a single hotel housing all attendees.

Convenient Location. Location is very important to the corporate meeting planner. Travel means company money. Time spent traveling and at the meeting itself means time off the job. That's a prime factor. A convenient location is a strong sales asset. Company planners use downtown hotels, airport hotels, and suburban locations, especially for regional meetings and training sessions.

Attractive Location. Business officials have a clear image of their company, and they want to meet in a hotel consistent with that image. This does not necessarily mean a posh place, but an attractive place.

For incentive trips, it goes without saying that the hotel and the area must have tourist attractions. The basic concept is to reward those who meet targeted goals. The prize selected must stimulate extra effort. The approach for incentive meetings is quite different from that of sales meetings, but the two are often intertwined. A working sales meeting requires solely a *suitable* hotel site; an incentive meeting requires a most *desirable* one.

Security. Corporate meetings are private affairs to a far greater extent than most conventions. The discussions are not meant for the ears of people outside the company, and, because of the increasing competition in the marketplace — especially in the computer and other high tech fields, security has become an even more important issue for corporate meeting planners. If your property understands this need for additional security and can offer viable solutions, you will have a far greater chance of securing corporate meetings business.

Sheraton's New Club Rooms. Responding to customer research, ITT Sheraton has introduced a guestroom with more flexible work space. The workspace includes the HP Office Jet, a combination fax/copier/printer.

Folding vinyl partitions and meeting rooms right off busy lobbies leave corporate planners cold. As does unrestricted access to meeting rooms and areas in which equipment and displays will be stored. In some cases, the planner may even worry about communications sent to the property's fax machine or the security of the property's phone system.

If you hope to handle this type of high-level meeting, you must be prepared to answer these concerns. First, offering a layout of the traffic pattern of the property can be an asset if the group's meeting and storage facilities will be isolated from the main flow of traffic. Second, you may offer additional security measures, such as one or two trusted employees to freshen meeting rooms and watch over unoccupied facilities. Third, the business may be so attractive that you will want to go to the extra expense of hiring outside security guards or setting up a dedicated fax line for the group. If the company will be the only group meeting in the hotel at that time, you have an additional selling advantage. This is an asset for the smaller properties, turning what may be considered a liability (small size) into a positive attraction. This is also a strong selling point for resort properties; the remoteness of a location may be an additional sales point for the security conscious client.

Kinds of Company Meetings

Corporate meeting business has been increasing more rapidly than any other market. Hundreds of thousands of meetings are held all over the country throughout the year, and the spectrum of meetings attended is broad. Among the prevalent types of company meetings are:

- National and regional sales meetings
- New product introduction/dealer meetings
- Professional/technical meetings
- Management meetings
- Training meetings
- Stockholder/public meetings
- Incentive meetings

Each will be considered in detail but Figure 5.3 summarizes several key characteristics. The most widely attended meetings are for professional/technical purposes and training, each type totaling over 8 million attendees. On average, the highest attendance is at new product introduction meetings (162 attendees) and the lowest at training (64 attend-

Figure 5.3. SUMMARY OF TYPES OF CORPORATE MEETINGS.

Type of Meeting	Off-premise Meetings	Average # Planned	Average Attendance	Average # Days	Average # of Months Lead Time
Management Meetings	213,800	8.9	61	2.3	3.5
Group Incentive Trips	35,600	3.9	144	4.4	8.2
Training Seminars	249,500	7.4	64	2.9	3.7
National/ Regional Sales Meetings	169,300	6.6	118	2.8	3.8
Professional/ Technical Meetings	115,800	8.5	111	2.3	5.3
New Product Introductions	44,500	4.8	162	2.2	3.7
Stockholder Meetings	8,900	1.7	142	1.9	5.2
Other Meetings	17,800	5.9	136	2.4	9.1
Total/Average	855,200	17.1	112	2.8	5.5

Note that the average lead time for corporate meetings is less than one year, the attendance is generally less than 100 persons, and the duration of most corporate meetings is two to three days.
Source: The 2004 Meetings Market Report conducted by Meetings & Conventions magazine.

ees) and management meetings (61 attendees). The average number of off-premises meetings planned yearly by corporate planners is 17.1.

The kinds of companies holding meetings are diverse. Insurance, banking and investment groups, automotive and other industrial and manufacturing concerns are just a few of the prospects for the corporate meeting business. It would be more difficult to find any sizable organizations that do not hold meetings — and lots of them.

National and Regional Sales Meetings

The best-known company meeting, and one of the largest sectors of the corporate meetings market, is the **sales meeting**. The nature of a national sales organization makes it a natural for meetings. These events are scattered throughout the country. With new products and new sales developments appearing all the time, there is constant need to meet face to face with the sales team, at every level. There are national sales meetings with everyone present, meetings of regional sales managers, and regional sales meetings run by regional sales managers.

In order to same money and maximize company productivity, many firms today are combining meetings or holding different meetings back-to-back at the same property. When companies use the same hotel for back-to-back meetings, they not only save on hotel rooms, food and beverage and on-site staff costs, but they can also save money by using the same off-site venues, entertainment, speakers, production equipment and ground transportation.

In some cases, companies will combine a large sales meeting with smaller meetings either the day before or the day after the "main event." In other cases, companies use the same facility for both training meetings and incentive trips. David Lutz, president of the Twinsburg, Ohio-based meeting planning firm, Conferon, says:

> "We're seeing it [combining meetings] happen to a much greater degree
> than ever before, and we're seeing it across industry segments."[2]

Attendance at national sales meetings averages about 150 for three to four days. Regional sales meetings are smaller, averaging 65 in size over two to three days.

The reasons for the sales meetings are many, often dealing with several objectives. The annual sales meeting may involve new product introduction, new company policy and suggested sales techniques to overcome problems, or it may simply be a morale builder and stimulator to cap a successful year and to start work on the next one. Sales meetings come in all sizes, at any time of the year, and all mean good, regular, repeat business for hotels.

Sales meetings are generally staged and controlled within the sales and marketing departments of each division of a company.

New Product Introduction/Dealer Meetings

Sales executives often hold national and regional events to meet with dealers or distributors. New product introduction is very important in these meetings too. The introduction of new sales and advertising campaigns calls for carrying the message out to the hinterlands. The very heart of the sales and marketing philosophy is to sell your own staff first and then your distributors and dealers and their staffs, and to work them up to new levels of enthusiasm. This approach results in many meetings around the country.

As in the case of the sales meetings, **dealer meetings** can be very small, such as a cocktail reception for a dozen or so one evening, or great affairs involving thousands and running three to five days. The Ford Motor Company spent several million dollars for a live Broadway-type stage show, combined with multimedia presentation, at the large Las Vegas Convention Center. The affair called for several days of rehearsals and two weeks of back-to-back charter flights from all parts of the country. The production was worthy of any on Broadway, yet had a run of only two weeks. If the objective of the meeting is achieved, the meeting is a success and the cost accepted as necessary and worthwhile.

Dealer meetings, in addition to being attended by sales personnel, also attract top company management, stockholders and the press. Since these meetings are often "gala affairs," they provide an excellent opportunity to "show off" the property and to book additional business from both the company personnel and from "outside" attendees. There is no better sales presentation than a successful execution of a meeting on premises. This is the opportunity to display your hotel at its best.

Professional/Technical Meetings

The need to update technical personnel increases every year. The volume of technical development and innovation is hard to envision. In only the last 100 years — just four generations — man has created the automobile, the airplane, the spaceship, the laser, and the transistor. An engineer or scientist cannot afford to stop learning or he or she will soon be obsolete. To give you some idea of the scope, General Electric has some 30,000 engineers, representing an enormous investment in technical talent that requires constant up-dating. It is a resource that needs to be safeguarded against personnel obsolescence.

Company **professional/technical meetings** often take the seminar and workshop formats. Independent consultants, educators and even vendors are invited to demonstrate and lecture.

Management Meetings

Just as sales and technical personnel meet, so do all levels of executives. Far-flung organizations mean that there is a need even at the top for executives to get together for discussion.

Such meetings may be regular events, such as board meetings, or may be called in response to a special situation. These are usually small meetings, but they call for the finest in accommodations and service. An important characteristic of such meetings for hotel salespeople is that each attendee is a potential customer for meetings within his or her own division or company.

Management meetings most commonly last for two days and follow no special locations rule, ranging from convenient downtown or airport locations to remote resorts and lodges.

Training Meetings

Training of personnel on all levels is an important activity of the larger corporations. Companies may conduct training in technical skills such as welding, machinery repair and maintenance. Computer systems result in more training sessions. Sales personnel receive training, as do executives.

About half of training directors conduct programs off company premises. These **training meetings** are held on a regular basis and usually run about three days. Attendance is usually small. Most training groups number fewer than 100, and most are nearer 60. Groups of ten to 15 are not at all rare, so even small hotels can handle these meetings.

That is not to say that training directors are satisfied by just any facility; they have firm criteria. They do, however, deal with small groups that are easily accommodated. They want meeting rooms with permanent walls instead of screen dividers, rooms good for audio-visual use, easy access to meeting rooms without distraction from other hotel activities, and prompt service for food functions such as refreshment breaks and lunches. Well-lighted and well-ventilated rooms with adequate space for either classroom or U-shaped seating (there is often a preference for extra-wide 24- or 30-inch tables), and guestrooms with well-lighted work space (desks or large tables) are especially attractive to training meeting planners.

Training directors do not need prestigious locations and impressive surroundings. They are more likely to choose hotels that are convenient to airports, highways and parking. Training directors have no need to change locations to stimulate attendance or interest. They make excellent customers because they tend to come back to hotels that have worked out well. Dependability, reasonable prices and good service all count a great deal toward repeat business.

Many hotels and motels have done well with this kind of business, to the point of having almost permanent commitment of certain meeting rooms and a constant use of a minimum number of guest rooms by a single company. Chains, too, find such business good because trainers often call for similar setups by a team in central locations around the country.

Regular business bookings can also be picked up when personnel become acquainted with a property while attending a training session.

An odd characteristic of training meetings is the frequent reluctance to use the term *training*. At lower levels, employees look for training and will regard it as an added benefit and frequently stick with an employer that offers it. But sales and middle-level people at times resent the thought that they *need* further development. The situation is dispelled by tact, so don't be surprised to see *workshops, seminars,* or *management development* or simply *meetings* being booked by training directors.

The position of training director has broadened in many companies over the years. Today, you may find your key decision maker under a title reflecting involvement with *human resources.*

Stockholder/Public Meetings

Companies find it necessary at times to hold meetings for non-employees. These typically fall into the category of **stockholder/public meetings**. The annual stockholders meeting can range from a mere formality attended by a handful to a fairly active one-day event involving a goodly number, with lunch and refreshment breaks. These seem to vary with the economic climate.

Public relations and industrial relations departments also hold meetings and exhibits to tell their stories. They, too, add their bit to the growing number of corporate meetings.

Incentive Meetings

Each year, as millions of people exceed their business goals or quotas, many are rewarded by a trip — trips that collectively mean close to $6 billion to the travel industry. Up to 45 percent of that figure is spent on hotels alone. Meetings are included in 80 percent of all incentive trips and those meetings are called **incentive meetings**.

Incentive travelers may be suppliers, dealers, customers, salespeople or other employees. They must qualify in some way to participate.

What do incentive customers want? Above all, they look for first-class service. Companies offer these trips as rewards to top performers, so they want them treated in a special way.

For hotels that can deliver what these customers want, the benefits are substantial. First, bookings are guaranteed. This means easy forecasting and a break-even factor that's minimal compared to other markets. Second, incentive participants typically make use of all hotel facilities, such as restaurants, bars and room service. Third, incentive meetings mean high-dollar revenues. Average room rates are usually higher, with double occupancy most common, and they spend more on banquets than do many other meeting segments. Because this market is so lucrative, an extended discussion is included in the next chapter.

Characteristics of Company Meetings

Any meeting should have a clear objective, a logical attendance group, and a site and structure to suit the event. When we discuss characteristics of company meetings, keep in mind that we are talking about many different *kinds* of meetings — all sizes and shapes, instigated by many causes, planned and executed with rare exception by a variety of people.

But this very difficulty in describing a "typical" meeting should be most encouraging to hotel staffs. It is a most unimaginative hotel salesperson, or a particularly primitive hotel property, who cannot come up with some part of this market that can be sold and serviced well. This is the time to ignore what facilities you may lack and concentrate on what you *have*. Select that portion of the market that you can target and call your own. Think in terms of your own sales campaigns and the kinds of hotel properties that can handle the situations discussed in this chapter.

Time Cycle

Corporations tend to meet midweek and throughout the year. Company meetings seem to follow a demand schedule instead of the fixed-time cycle that is common with associations. A meeting is planned and executed as need arises. After all, a company meeting doesn't require the time needed by associations to build attendance. A simple directive from the top brass is all that is needed to ensure that everyone will attend the meeting.

Lead Time

The planning period for company meetings is relatively short, rarely longer than a year. In the case of incentive trips, some consideration about general area may be made some eight

Figure 5.4. WHEN CORPORATE MEETINGS ARE HELD.

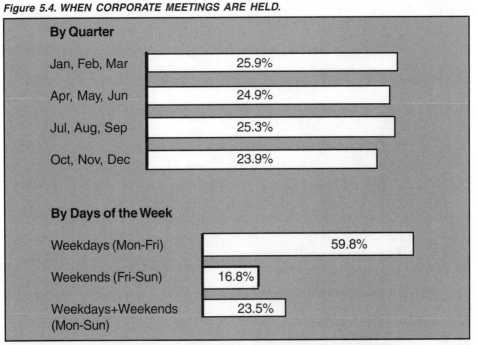

By Quarter

Jan, Feb, Mar	25.9%
Apr, May, Jun	24.9%
Jul, Aug, Sep	25.3%
Oct, Nov, Dec	23.9%

By Days of the Week

Weekdays (Mon-Fri)	59.8%
Weekends (Fri-Sun)	16.8%
Weekdays+Weekends (Mon-Sun)	23.5%

Source: 2005 State of the Industry Report by Successful Meetings magazine.

months to a year in advance, and, in the case of great numbers, the time may stretch to two years. But that is still much shorter than the lead time of associations.

The annual sales meeting is usually planned eight to twelve months prior to convening. Corporate structure in this decision making is simple. Some middle-level person, or perhaps two, will suggest, investigate and screen properties and pass along the recommendation to one executive who generally makes the final decision. In some companies, one person does it all, which certainly can shorten lead time. There are many variations, of course.

Most other company meetings have a very short lead time -- less than three months is becoming typical. Due to changes in the economy, the introduction of new products and companies, mergers and acquisitions, and breakups or expansions, businesspeople meet more often on short notice (see box titled "Shrinking Lead Times"). Short lead times are especially prevalent in the technology and pharmaceutical industries due to product breakthroughs. Nearly every company meeting planner can recall instances when it seemed like the meeting was needed for the next day. There is one kind of company meeting that we refer to as a *crisis* meeting. That follows when someone says, "Let's get everyone together as soon as possible and talk this thing out!"

It is too late to start selling your property at that point. If you had been in there selling, or had enjoyed some business from that company before, you might get a chance at this business. Certainly, there is no time for anyone to shop around. The situation calls for fast action and the meeting generally goes to a place the company has used before or to some wide-awake salesperson who had been in there pitching at the time.

It is such types of corporate business that must fill the gap when the convention function book is less than filled. The unexpected sales meeting, the crisis that calls for facing dealers or distributors, the new modification for which service personnel must be trained — all these bring opportunities for business meetings. These are meetings executives don't discuss when you talk to them. You must sell them on the idea of using your

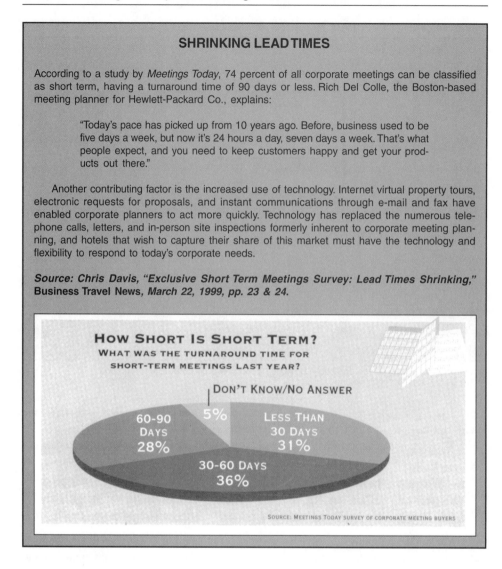

SHRINKING LEAD TIMES

According to a study by *Meetings Today*, 74 percent of all corporate meetings can be classified as short term, having a turnaround time of 90 days or less. Rich Del Colle, the Boston-based meeting planner for Hewlett-Packard Co., explains:

> "Today's pace has picked up from 10 years ago. Before, business used to be five days a week, but now it's 24 hours a day, seven days a week. That's what people expect, and you need to keep customers happy and get your products out there."

Another contributing factor is the increased use of technology. Internet virtual property tours, electronic requests for proposals, and instant communications through e-mail and fax have enabled corporate planners to act more quickly. Technology has replaced the numerous telephone calls, letters, and in-person site inspections formerly inherent to corporate meeting planning, and hotels that wish to capture their share of this market must have the technology and flexibility to respond to today's corporate needs.

Source: Chris Davis, "Exclusive Short Term Meetings Survey: Lead Times Shrinking," Business Travel News, March 22, 1999, pp. 23 & 24.

HOW SHORT IS SHORT TERM?
WHAT WAS THE TURNAROUND TIME FOR
SHORT-TERM MEETINGS LAST YEAR?

DON'T KNOW/NO ANSWER
5%

60-90 DAYS 28%

LESS THAN 30 DAYS 31%

30-60 DAYS 36%

SOURCE: MEETINGS TODAY SURVEY OF CORPORATE MEETING BUYERS

facility when the need next arises, and hope you made enough of an impression that they'll remember.

Geographical Patterns

There is no general geographic pattern for company business. To begin with, there is often no reason to vary sites to attract attendance, as in the case of associations. When the vice-president of sales calls a meeting in Chicago or Montreal at the first of the month, it is not surprising to find the sales staff in Chicago or Montreal at that time.

There is also no reason not to go back to the same hotel if it performed satisfactorily. The main reason for another selection may very well be mere boredom on the part of the meeting planner or his or her boss. It really depends on the kind of meeting. The annual meeting, with much hoopla and singing of the company song, may call for a variety of sites from year to year, but the hastily organized meeting doesn't. In fact, a strong case can be built for repeating at a hotel proven dependable by the last meeting, or at least for some hotel that had been pushing for the business.

Training directors, in particular, prefer to deal with the same hotel on a consistent basis. Some feel that with only small meetings to offer, they reach the status of *important customer* only through the promise of repeat business. Most training directors feel the need for distraction-free, classroom-type isolation, with a good supply of audiovisual equipment and service. Once having worked out such an arrangement with a suitable facility, they are understandably loathe to change.

There is some geographic factor involved, but it is the most obvious one. An Atlanta hotel obviously will have a better chance at getting a regional sales meeting for a staff covering the southeastern states than will a hotel in Boston or St. Louis. Time, the cost of transportation and convenience are all factors affecting the geographic location.

Imagine the assignment given to the company meeting planner to arrange for a series of regional meetings for an international sales staff. He or she might plan to use hotels in New York, Chicago, Seattle, Los Angeles, Atlanta and Toronto. If you have a hotel in any of these general areas, geography will work for you and give you a chance at the business in your sector. But the planner is also free to meet in Ottawa instead of Toronto, in St. Louis or Milwaukee instead of Chicago, in Boston or Philadelphia instead of New York.

This is where selling comes in. The hotel sales staffer must present the hotel positively and turn what might be a liability into an asset. If Kansas City is less glamourous than New York, it is more centrally located. If your property is not downtown, it offers fewer distractions, easier access by automobile and free parking. If it is downtown, it offers more opportunities for entertainment. A salesperson should concentrate on the property's positive factors, instead of being haunted by its shortcomings.

Company meetings, unlike many association meetings, rarely have regulations against meeting anywhere. The company president or board may favor some types of sites and frown on others in keeping with the image they want to project, but that's not the same as restrictions written into a constitution or bylaws.

Kinds of Sites

What kind of hotel does a company prefer? The answer has as many variations as there are companies and kinds of meetings (see Figure 5.5). A meeting planner should select a site to benefit from its locale and the hotel's attractions. The hotel that would be good for an incentive trip or annual dealer meeting may not be the wisest choice for that crisis meeting or training session.

For a successful sales and marketing career, help your customer achieve the kind of meeting he or she wants. Try to get those meetings that go well in your establishment. Let the ones that get away be those that really should be held in some other type of hotel.

Give careful thought to the kind of meetings most suitable for your hotel. Is yours a downtown hotel? Then stress its convenient location, especially when some people participate in only part of the program. Comfortable and familiar, the downtown hotel is a frequent choice.

Is yours a suburban hotel/motel? It offers easy access by auto and free parking. Stress its informal atmosphere. Will the meeting be the only one in the house? That is considered by many corporate planners to be so important that it may be the very factor that swings the business to you.

Airport location? The obvious advantage is convenience when air transportation is used, plus all the features of the suburban hotel. Once small properties, airport hotels come in all sizes today.

Figure 5.5. TYPES OF FACILITIES USED BY CORPORATE MEETING PLANNERS.

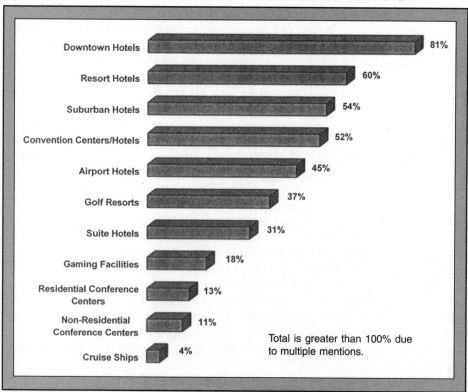

Meeting planners, who typically pay an average daily room rate of $151.00, prefer downtown hotels, followed by resort hotels and suburban hotels. The key selection criteria is generally the purpose of the meeting.

Source: The 2004 Meetings Market Report conducted by **Meetings & Conventions** *magazine.*

Resort? This is the obvious choice for incentive meetings, but is also often chosen to get away from the distractions of the city. Resorts in the off-season offer excellent rates, charm, exclusivity, industrial security, physical beauty and a good image.

Conference center? As mentioned in Chapter 1, conference centers are growing in popularity with corporate meeting planners, and many major hotel companies, including Marriott, Hilton, and Sheraton have noticed this shift and are becoming key players in the conference center segment. While the few conference centers of past decades had a "going back to school" stigma, today's state of the art facilities are often the choice of corporate planners looking for high-tech presentation equipment and locations that minimize distractions.

These are but a few benefits and characteristics of each type of property. You should be able to add others and to present your property positively as the one that best fits the meeting planner's event.

Attendance

One characteristic of corporate meetings that makes them popular with hotel people is the predictable attendance. Whether attendees come alone or with their spouses, attendance is nearly always mandatory. A rooming list submitted before the event is usually accurate. Barring mishap or illness, no-shows are minimal. Nancy Holder, RJR/Nabisco's conference planner says,

> "In corporate planning, if you book 200 rooms, you're going to use 200 rooms, unless there's an emergency. In other areas of planning (associations), you have to convince people to come. In the corporate world, if the CEO tells you to show up, you're going to show up."[3]

While attendance at corporate meetings is mandatory, one problem associated with corporate meetings is the risk of cancellation of the entire event. Poor financial returns or unexpected delays may result in a corporate official changing or cancelling the meeting. For this reason, most hotels now require nonrefundable deposits and have included stringent cancellation clauses in their contracts with corporate groups (cancellation clauses are explained and illustrated in Chapter 9).

Care should be taken to get a VIP list. It can be embarrassing to everyone to have the fledgling sales trainee assigned to the fine corner room and the vice-president of sales in a minimum single. If no VIP list is submitted, bring up the subject yourself and help your customer create one. If no need exists for him or her, fine. But check it out and at least flag a few names for preferred treatment. Those executives' comments may determine whether you get the group again.

Duration

Most corporate meetings are short. Some are limited to a single day and others may run as long as five days, but three days are about the most common. Arrival on the previous evening is popular so that the meeting can start early the next morning. Cocktail receptions and/or brisk action at the hotel bars add to the profits to be derived from corporate business.

Take care to coordinate the final day meeting program with your policy on check-out time. Plan ahead. If you can't gracefully extend the normal check-out time, perhaps you can arrange to check all the luggage with the bell captain or arrange for all luggage to be placed in just a few rooms before the check-out deadline. If you don't look ahead and decide how you will cope with the many requests at the last minute (or even with the entire group checking out late without even discussing it with you), your staff will be forced to improvise. And they may not always handle it as you would like.

Bring the matter up with the meeting organizer even if he or she doesn't. State your policy and suggest how to arrange matters. You can arrive at an agreed-upon arrangement. At the very least, you have alerted the planner to a potential problem.

Exhibits

The exhibit is a trademark of the association for the most part. Corporate meetings, however, frequently have exhibits too. It is not uncommon, for example, for such meetings to display new products or to use live presentations on a grand scale. Thus you can expect requests for stage facilities and exhibit space when servicing corporate events.

The most recent *Meetings & Conventions* Meetings Market Report found that roughly 60 percent of corporate meeting planners plan trade shows for their companies. While the average number of attendees (406) is less than the number of attendees at association trade shows, the average duration of the show is similar (about three days). Therefore, meeting groups that hold trade shows in conjunction with their meetings are potentially very profitable for your hotel.

Meeting Room Requirements

There is a need for large and small meeting rooms, varying from event to event. Some meetings call for small committee-type rooms. In many training set-ups, the main group breaks into units of as few as ten people who meet separately for awhile, then reconvene in the main meeting room. Most meeting organizers prefer such *breakout* rooms to be right at hand.

If your hotel has such rooms in the same wing of the building, you have an edge when you solicit such business. It leaves something to be desired if the group has to huddle around a few tables in different parts of the main meeting room. It certainly is difficult to attract such a group under those circumstances if the competition can offer more suitable arrangements.

With corporate meetings, there is little likelihood that meeting rooms will have to be changed at the last minute. Association meetings, on the other hand, have higher attendance and the program often features concurrent meetings (several topics covered at the same time in various meeting rooms). The more popular topics may draw a larger audience than anticipated, requiring the meeting room set up staff to bring in extra chairs or make other arrangements (which may include moving the meeting to a larger room).

One Meeting, One Check

It is nice for a hotel to have most group business paid for with one check. That's one appeal of corporate business. Many companies pay all the expenses for their employees; others have different guidelines. Discuss with the meeting planner what he or she will approve for payment on the master account and what the individual must pay for upon checkout. Your front desk must be informed. Your credit manager may want to do some homework on the customer-corporation and may propose a schedule of payments, beginning with a deposit. As a general rule, corporate business is paid for en masse.

Multiple-Booking Potential

Hosting company meetings offers the opportunity to promote other business. Each person attending the meeting has sampled your hotel. If the impression is favorable, you may become the first choice whenever that person stops in your city on business trips. Or you may benefit from recommendations to others both in and out of the organization. Remember that most association boards include businesspeople who hold their own organizational meetings.

Help to execute a smoothly functioning meeting and you can pick up future business from the company as well. What appears to be a single meeting may be repeated in several parts of the country. This is a great situation for hotel chains. One person may order meetings in a number of locations, and that person may handle the logistics of all those meetings.There is often enough flexibility in the designation of the cities to be used that a chain may sell dates in a number of different properties (see Figure 5.6).

Figure 5.6. HILTON NATIONAL SALES OFFICE MAXIMIZES MULTI-BOOKING POTENTIAL.

In an effort to market its chain, Hilton's national sales office offers Hilton Direct U.S.A. This chain-wide meeting site search is offered to meeting planners at no charge. The meeting planner's specifications are matched against more than 2,000 Hilton hotels and its new brands, and information on availability and prices is provided to the planner within 24 hours. This service is just one example of how chains are turning to national sales offices to market properties to meeting planners.

The appeal to the meeting planner is achieving the status of a more important customer and he or she has only to explain his or her needs once and have them duplicated in different hotels.

Surprisingly, however, chain loyalty is not a trademark of corporate meetings. A survey of corporate meeting planners conducted by *Meeting & Conventions* magazine determined that only 25 percent of corporate meeting planners used the same hotel chain for the majority of their meetings.

What does this mean to a single-location hotel? In order to compete with a chain effort, the individual hotel must present a good case for being the best choice in the city. Ideally, that image would be so strong that a meeting planner normally using a chain for the entire group of meetings would break that pattern when it comes to your city.

Many wise hotel salespeople cooperate with their counterparts in independent hotels in other cities. They try to get the meeting planner to buy from independents as often as possible, and make it easy for that to happen by recommendations and the passing of the sales lead to each other. Independent hotels in different cities recognize that they function as true allies in the sales competition with chains. This concept has helped in the development of the hotel representative who, with a stable of independent hotels, can offer the same kind of "one-stop shopping" as the chains.

Corporate Meeting Decision Makers

No sales effort succeeds unless it is directed at the person or persons with the authority to make the decision. The convention sales picture is no different. Your story may be a good one, but it will be to no avail unless it is told to the right person.

Who is the *right* person? Not only does it vary from company to company, but it may vary from year to year within the same company. But some titles do keep coming up and they certainly represent a starting point for sales penetration (see Figure 5.7).

To find the decision maker, you have to ask the right questions. "Who coordinates your meetings?" is not a good question; the person who coordinates the details of a meeting may not be the actual decision maker. It is far better to ask, "Who is responsible for deciding which hotels your company uses for meetings?" With this approach, you will be able to make immediate contact with the decision maker or recommender rather than having to deal with one or more "go-betweens," saving valuable time and effort.

Another approach, which may require slightly more time and effort, but which may also prove profitable, is to start at the top of the company and work downward. While speaking with the president of a company may not result in an immediate booking, this

Figure 5.7. MEETING PLANNERS CORPORATE POSITIONS.

Job Title or Position	Corporate Planners
Corporate Executive Management	20 %
Meeting Planning/Convention Management	38
Sales/Marketing	16
General/Other Management/Administration	24
Other	2

Many corporations do not have professional meeting planners. Therefore, in prospecting for business, it is wise to know the common job titles for corporate decision makers. These are summarized above.
Source: The 2004 Meetings Market Report conducted by Meetings & Conventions magazine.

contact can prove valuable in two ways: you won't be referred to someone below the decision making or recommending level and a referral "from above" is a great door opener.

Once the key contact is determined, you should pay attention to tomorrow's decision makers. As the account is worked and information is secured on the organizational structure, "star performers" should be identified and relationships with them cultivated. Knowing the people who are likely to succeed present decision makers can pay dividends in the future.

Full-Time Meeting Planner

When companies have centralized meeting planning activity, you deal with a full-time meeting planner. Hopefully, this should make your job easier because you deal with an experienced, knowledgeable pro who knows what he or she wants and how to go about getting it.

It is easier to deal with someone who knows what he or she wants. It can protect you from overlooking something in the arrangements. Both parties want the same thing — a smoothly run meeting — and it helps if both parties are expert. Build a reputation for competence and fair dealing and you are on your way to a successful sales career in the convention field.

There are several organizations of active corporate meeting planners, including the Society of Corporate Meeting Professionals and Meeting Professionals International. SCMP is a small group, but its membership, which are all full-time planners, boasts larger companies, including Dow Chemical, 3M Companies, and State Farm Insurance. Membership in MPI is much larger, but members are mostly part-time planners.

Company President

Smaller companies seldom have enough meeting activity to warrant a full-time meeting planning employee. In many such companies, the decision maker is the president or some counterpart, such as a partner or chairman. It is understandable that the president of a large corporation such as General Motors will not be involved in such decisions, but the president of a company employing several hundred people might get involved in the national sales or dealer meeting. Never worry about making contacts too high up the corporate ladder. If he or she isn't involved personally, a president is seldom hesitant about naming the right person. And the recommendation of the president does you no harm when you deal with subordinates.

Profile of Corporate Meeting Planners

- 77% are female; average age is 44.

- Spend an average of 55% of their professional time on meeting planning activities.

- Have been arranging meetings for nine years.

- Plan most of their meetings (53%) for 50 or fewer people.

- Duties include: selecting hotels (92%), selecting locations (85%), planning entertainment (82%), setting budgets (71%), planning meeting agendas (55%), arranging for transportation (air, 54%; rental cars, 42%) and trade show/exhibit planning (54%).

- Only 12% are Certified Meeting Professionals (and only 2% are Certified Meeting Managers), but 25% are members of Meeting Professionals International (MPI)

Source: The 2004 Meetings Market Report conducted by Meetings & Conventions magazine.

Marketing and Sales Executives

Marketing and sales executives are key people. The exact title may be *vice president, sales* or *marketing director* or *manager* or *product manager.* They may operate on a national, international or even a regional basis. The bulk of corporate meetings involves the important areas of sales and marketing, so it makes sense to zero in on these people.

Such executives don't join meeting planning societies. They don't think of themselves as meeting or convention planners. But they do plan many of them, or, more accurately, are involved with them. They call the meetings, control the kind of meetings they want, and most often have the most important voice as to where and when they will take place. That makes them very important people for you to contact.

Advertising and Sales Promotion Managers

One step down the corporate ladder is the *advertising* or *sales promotion manager.* One person may carry both titles because the work is interrelated. In addition to usual duties, such middle executives frequently handle meeting planning functions. There is no relationship in such assignment to the size or type of company. If the company does not have a full-time meeting planner, the task is assigned to some departmental or divisional manager, and since it involves marketing activity, the advertising or sales promotion manager is often selected.

At the very least, such middle managers get involved in the initial screening of a site and the planning and execution of a meeting. They could be your first hurdle. You need them to recommend your property. In some cases, that is sufficient; in others, the final selection is made by their boss — the vice president, director or manager of sales and marketing. Some people freely admit when their authority is limited, but some find it too painful to do so.

It helps you to know who the final decision maker is, but you have to pay attention to the level that screens, too, or you may never get to the final selection stage. Make sure that your presentation summarizes your strong points very clearly so that they may be passed along in discussion with others.

Other Corporate Executives

Not all meetings stem from marketing divisions. Other executives get involved with staging meetings and therefore site selections. They carry titles such as *manager of corporate relations, public relations, industrial relations,* or *communications.* Such personnel may very well be active in sales and marketing, too. Corporate organization charts seldom indicate anyone as meeting specialists, yet many executives are. The executive in charge of meetings may have that assignment for a period of time and then it may pass on to another. The role of meeting planner is often a part of the career path for upward bound middle management.

Passenger Traffic/Corporate Travel Managers

Many companies maintain a travel desk, which handles arrangements for employee business travel. When plane or hotel reservations are needed, they are requisitioned through the passenger traffic personnel. Traditionally, these corporate travel planners were responsible for booking hotel rooms and travel for individual corporate executives, and commonly negotiated with hotels and travel providers for a *commercial rate*, a lower rate guaranteed to their personnel.

Increasingly, however, because of consolidation of the meetings and travel departments at a number of corporations, the responsibilities of corporate travel planners have expanded to include planning meetings. These personnel, therefore, not only negotiate for rates for guestrooms but also for meetings space and food and beverage functions.

Membership in the National Business Travel Association (NBTA), an organization of corporate travel managers, once consisted of corporate travel planners who dealt primarily with individual travel for their personnel. Today, 94 percent of NBTA members are involved in planning meetings for their corporations. In order to better assist corporate travel planners, especially those new to the meeting planning area, the NBTA offers training classes and, in 2005, joined the Convention Industry Council (CIC) to provide additional opportunities for the education of their membership.

The NBTA also sponsors an annual trade show in August, and another organization for corporate travel planners, the Association of Corporate Travel Executives (ACTE) holds its meeting in February. Both are good shows and well attended by hotels seeking to build corporate group travel business, especially since the position of corporate travel manager is expected to grow in scope.

Procurement (Purchasing) Managers

Another answer for companies who wish to cut costs by consolidating their meeting and travel departments is to structure meeting planning within the procurement (purchasing) department. The involvement of the procurement department in meeting planning is changing the nature of planner/hotel relationships. While hotels traditionally have dealt directly with the meeting planner (who answered to his or her company or organization regarding the meeting budget), the procurement department is increasingly involved in the decision-making process – from selecting hotel sites to approving menus and costs for food functions.

While meeting planners generally have some knowledge of the nuances of meeting costs, such as paying more for guestrooms or food functions to enable them to receive free meeting space, for example, procurement managers often look at buying hotel rooms and services in much the same way that they look at purchasing other commodities; in other words, they want to get the best price possible. And this doesn't mean strictly in terms of rooms or meeting space; procurement managers also look for the best values in such products and services as audiovisual equipment, decorators and so on, which can result in decreased revenues for the hotel.

This trend has not only resulted in increased competitiveness among hotels, but has also affected the way in which salespeople do business. The decision-maker for a corporate meeting may now be the procurement manager, and the salesperson dealing with this decision-maker has to be able to prove the value of what his or her hotel has to offer. This can include explaining everything from the quality of the hotel's food to its reputation for high service standards to something as intangible (but important) as the experience of the attendees.

Fred Shea, vice president of sales for Hyatt Hotels Corp., says:

"Our sales managers have to show price value, but not just price, because dates and rates are all online, right there for the customer to see. We are training our people how to do a better job of making that procurement customer understand the value that goes back to them, both in service and actual attendee experience."[6]

Training Director

Training directors use a wide variety of hotel types. Airport and other suburban locations are popular because of ease of access and parking. Small resorts are used in the off-season, especially when executive development programs call for more prestigious sites. With lower budgets, training directors make good use of secondary hotels, off-season rate breaks and all-cost packages.

Training departments usually handle their own meetings, even in cases where the company already has a setup for sales meetings. You may sell the sales department for their meetings but still have to sell another group for training sessions.

Training directors' requirements do not differ from those of most small meetings, but they are less likely to be permissive about such things as audiovisual equipment, permanent dividing walls, low-hanging chandeliers and nearby distractions in the hotel. Actually, these specifications are similar to those that any good meeting planner would want (see Figure 5.8).

Figure 5.8. ADVERTISING TO PLANNERS OF SMALL MEETINGS.

This ad for The Hotel Monteleone in New Orleans promotes its commitment to servicing small meetings. The ad focuses on how the hotel works hard to make a meeting a success, and adds to its credibility by featuring a testimonial from a meeting planner who typically holds small meetings of 20-25 persons.

Meeting Specialists/Third-Party Planners

Just a few years ago, nearly all corporate meetings were planned by in-house departments. Due to downsizing, many companies, like associations, are looking outside their own organizations for meeting planning services. Some of these **third-party meeting planners** only get involved in larger meetings. Others select hotels, airlines, destination management companies and other meeting services. They conduct site searches, negotiate rates on behalf of the companies and associations they represent, and assist in conducting meetings and conventions. Travel organizations are called in at times, especially for incentive programs. These organizations are important sources of business.

As mentioned in the opening chapter, companies such as Carlson Marketing Group, Conferon, Helms Briscoe and Maritz McGettigan have become prominent sources of meetings business. And, other independent meeting planning companies will likely grow in size as hotel chains continue to consolidate. Hotel chains now focus their efforts on deriving their business from the biggest clients and have justified this approach based on the rationale that 80 percent of group business comes from 20 percent of their clients. Therefore, third-party leads will grow in importance.

Steve Armitage, vice president of sales and managing director of Hilton Hotels, says:

> "We want to increase our market share with key accounts, and the more business we get from an organization, the better positioned we can be to partner with them on the rates they need for an event to be successful."[4]

Third-party companies make their money by charging a management fee to the meeting groups they represent or by charging the hotel a commission on the room rate. Obviously, hotels would prefer that these third-party planners secure their fee from the groups they represent, but, recognizing the volume of business provided by third-party planners, many hotels are willing to pay commissions.

Many smaller associations and corporations have limited bargaining power when negotiating with hotels. But when they outsource their meetings to a large third-party planner they often realize the advantage of volume savings. To get more personal attention -- and perhaps greater concessions from hotels -- it is likely that more planners will turn to third-party meeting management companies to locate and negotiate facilities for their meetings.

Sources for Finding Corporate Business and Decision Makers

It's a great big business world out there, and while you may be eager to just get out there and knock on doors, that isn't the recommended use of time. Tom McCarthy, a veteran of hotel sales, believes prospecting should be more calculated:

> "A salesperson might have a territory that includes 35,000 companies. If a salesperson can qualify 20 new prospects a week, it doesn't take much figuring to determine that the salesperson can qualify about 1,000 accounts a year.
>
> "Wouldn't it make more sense to work with a list broker and pick 1,000 companies in advance that would be assigned the salesperson (based on proximity, size, and type of business), rather than just telling the person

to 'hit the bricks'? Do we think the person will call on the best 1,000 out of the 35,000 by chance?

"Here we are working with computers and sophisticated software and still living in the 19th century when it comes to the most basic principles of prospecting."[5]

In today's competitive environment, prospecting for new business is essential, but going up and down the street knocking on doors is not the way. Once you know the kind of corporate executives you want, there are a number of ways for you to reach them effectively.

Special Meetings and Business Publications

The corporate meetings business is served by several publications that have literally done your job of sorting out those executives interested in meetings. It is hardly a surprise, therefore, to find that advertising appearing in these publications seems to be an industry rundown of the leading convention hotels. These magazines also offer advertisers sales lead services, providing the names of and data about likely prospects.

Leading publications include *Corporate & Incentive Travel*, *Corporate Meetings & Incentives*, *Meetings & Conventions*, *Meeting News*, *The Meeting Professional*, *Smart Meetings* and *Successful Meetings*. Most of their circulation is to readers in the corporate area, and all have Internet sites for instant access. A list of trade magazines and their addresses is given in Appendix I.

There are other publications of interest to hotel marketing people, although they do not specialize in conventions; they either deal with related editorial subjects or reach the executives likely to make meeting decisions. Most relevant is *Sales and Marketing Management*. As its name implies, the publication is directed to sales and marketing executives who are frequently involved with meetings.

General business publications can be considered as well. Although these publications are not directed specifically to executives who are involved with meeting decisions, their circulations reflect profiles similar to those of meeting planners. Hotels with adequate advertising budgets can promote their meeting facilities in such publications as *The Wall Street Journal*, *Business Week*, and *Fortune*.

Trade Directories and Publications

It is possible to develop sales leads by working your way through a specific industry. If your records indicate meetings of similar companies, it may be that industry is a fertile field for more business. The insurance industry, for example, is a prolific meeting group. There is even an association of meeting planners solely within that field. Other individual trades and industries may offer names of companies similar to those that have met in your hotel.

Dun and Bradstreet's Million Dollar Directory lists the nation's largest businesses and their officers. It is published by Dun and Bradstreet, 99 Church Street, New York, NY 10007.

Standard and Poor's Register of Directors and Executives is a similar publication. The *Register* alphabetically lists over 60,000 companies and provides addresses and basic information on numbers of employees, revenues and key personnel. The address for this publication is Standard and Poor's, 25 Broadway, New York, NY 10004.

Meeting Professionals International Membership Directory is available to members and allied members of Meeting Professionals International (MPI), 1950 Stemmons Freeway, Dallas, TX 75207. To obtain a copy of this guide — the best-known source of corporate meeting planners — hotel people must join the organization along with a meeting planner.

Scientific and Technical Societies in the U.S. and Canada is published by Canadian Business Magazine, 300 St. Sacrament Street, Montreal, Quebec, Canada.

The *National Associations of Businesspersons* is published by the U.S. Department of Commerce. Listed are the names, addresses and chief executives of associations of business firms. The publication is available from the Superintendent of Documents, U.S. Government Printing Office, Washington, DC 20401.

Best Insurance Reports, published by A.M. Best Company, Ambest Rd, Oldwick, NJ 08858, lists some ten thousand executives of insurance firms.

The *Directory of Corporate Meeting Planners* lists 12,000 meeting planners, with address, phone number, number of meetings, and when and where meetings are held. It is available from Douglas Publications, Richmond, VA (1-800-223-1797).

Trade Associations

If you feel that specific industries might be worth following, call on the executive directors of their trade associations. *You should be calling on them anyway for their own association business*, but they can also be a prime source of leads. They can pinpoint the larger companies in the trade and those in your part of the country. Their trade directories could be a good source of leads and a good addition to your mailing list.

Many meetings are held in the principal locale of the sponsoring company. It makes sense, therefore, to study directories of businesses within your city, state or area of the country. Chambers of commerce could also supply such lists.

The local library, chamber of commerce, and state industrial commission are also excellent sources for local leads. Most offer publications that list businesses according to Standard Industrial Classification (SIC), developed by the federal government. In many cases, your property may already have a breakdown of businesses booked by SIC code; this makes it particularly easy to target other businesses from the same category.

Don't neglect to solicit the local branches of national organizations. You may be told that meeting decisions are made at the national headquarters, but don't ignore the local firms. It is common for a corporate meeting planner to ask a local district manager about a suitable hotel in the area. The order may come from corporate headquarters, but the important input could come from your own area.

In addition, local branches often hold meetings of their own, albeit smaller ones. Local dealer meetings, training sessions and regional sales meetings are often within the responsibility of the regional sales manager. Going after the regular commercial business of a branch sales office may give you a chance at some group business as well.

Internet Sites

Another effective way to find meeting planners is to visit Internet sites that provide membership information and search services. One of the largest is MPIWeb, the Web site of Dallas-based Meeting Professionals International. MPI has more than 58 chapters in 51 countries, including 30 in North America, and you can click on MPI Chapters to find chapters in specific geographical areas. The site offers a free search service (a hotel salesperson does not have to be a member or associate member of MPI to use the search feature) that allows you to select such items as "Meeting Consultant/Independent Planner." By entering a specific city and state, you will be provided with a list of updated names and contact information.

This is just one of the many sites available on the Internet. Online corporate directories, such as Hoovers Online (www.hoovers.com), can also be very helpful (some services offered require a subscription). A hotel salesperson can search for companies by name, access financial data and find key executives through financially-oriented sites, and access vendors that serve the conventions and meetings industry for leads without leaving the comfort of the sales office.

Steve Tremewan, director of marketing at the Radisson Resort and Spa Scottsdale (Arizona), says:

> "We used to do research at the library and subscribe to all the local newspapers in our target markets. But now we are able to do most of our research on the Internet."[6]

He still reads local newspapers in his property's major target areas, but their online versions rather than printed publications, to determine if new businesses may be coming to town as well as what conferences and meetings are scheduled to be held. He also uses these and other online sources to find contacts in market segments that his property wishes to target.

Convention and Visitors Bureaus

Many hotel salespeople are also finding that working with their city's convention and visitors' bureau can be an excellent way to build corporate business. While CVBs formerly dealt with associations business, many are now targeting smaller corporate markets and can provide leads for your property.

Just a few years ago, the International Association of Convention and Visitor Bureaus held its first Destinations Showcase event in New York City to promote CVB services to corporate planners. While many corporate decision makers had not previously used CVBs, interest in using them as "one-stop shopping" venues has increased. If a corporate meeting planner is interested in booking space in Orlando, for example, he or she need make only one call to the CVB; the CVB will respond with information on only those hotels that meet the planner's needs.

And, properties can also find additional leads by participating in the destination marketing efforts of CVBs. Many of them participate in trade shows promoting their destination city, and participating properties may either send salespeople to meet with show visitors or make promotional materials available at the CVBs booth (selling with CVBs is explained in detail in Chapter 7).

Lateral Referral and Account Penetration

Many hotel people are content when they get meetings business from a large corporation. But hosting company meetings offers the opportunity to promote even more business. Just help to execute a smoothly functioning meeting and your hotel will have an edge on the competition when it comes to additional business from the firm.

Some companies are so large that employees in one division have little or nothing to do with those in other sectors. If your meetings business comes from a product manager in one division, give serious thought to following up with everyone who has the title of product manager in that and other divisions of the company.

The operating structure of the company may be uniform throughout, and if the product manager in one instance has the meetings responsibility, it is likely that others would too. If not, the manager will likely be able to point you to a decision maker. Your case is stronger if you can get a recommendation from your original product manager customer. Even if he or she doesn't know the others personally, an endorsement from someone within the firm should open some doors.

Such lateral referrals and complete **account penetration** of all sectors of a large firm is the sign of a successful hotel sales manager. Think of the large companies in your area as a multi-divisional entity simply loaded with business potential.

This will also help your prospects for business in other companies. You will gain an insight into corporate structure that will help you analyze other companies in the same industry. The structures are generally similar. It certainly provides you with a good starting point by knowing the titles you are seeking. Understanding the corporate setup and who most likely has the meetings chore gives you a big leg up to penetrating and selling corporate business.

Other opportunities await at the property level. Local suppliers, such as your produce wholesaler, dairy operator, insurance agent and other suppliers of products and/or services are potential sources of meetings business. Even if a property's suppliers do not require meeting space for themselves, many belong to trade, professional or civic organizations or social or religious groups. The property's suppliers, then, could very well be in a position to recommend the property as a meeting site for future meetings of their respective organizations.

Employees of a property are also good sources of meetings business. Many employees belong to organizations (bowling teams, garden clubs, the P.T.A., religious groups, etc.) that meet regularly or have need of function space for special occasions such as installation dinners, awards nights and other events. Property employees could very well influence the choice of "their" property for those events.

Summary

In this chapter, we have taken an indepth look at the corporate meetings segment, which is typically viewed as the most profitable group market segment. Not only does this segment often pay higher rates for rooms (despite meetings held during slow seasons), but it also can add to the hotel's bottom line with food and beverage, audiovisual and recreation revenues. We have discussed the kinds of meetings held by corporations and the characteristics of the various company meetings. We have determined who the key corporate decision makers are likely to be and how to find them. This lucrative market segment is becoming increasingly important to hotels, and hotel salespeople who understand the requirements of corporations and can match these requirements to their properties can successfully target the corporate market. In the next chapter, we will take a look at the third segment of the group meetings market, the varied nonprofit groups.

Endnotes:

1. Terence Baker, "Coffee With...Mark Beaupre," *Meetings & Conventions*, May 2004, p. 12.
2. Marshall Krantz, "Combo Meetings: Seeking Efficiencies," *Meeting News*, October 11, 2004, p. 1.
3. Michael Adams, "Career Jumping," *Successful Meetings*.
4. "Hilton Makes Fast Progress Absorbing Promus," *Meetings News*, March 20, 2000, p. 53.
5. Tom McCarthy, "Get Your Sales Management Ready for the 21st Century," *Hotel and Resort Industry*.
6. Cheryl-Anne Sturken, "Making Inroads," *Meetings & Conventions*, April 2005, p. 44.

Additional References:

*   Meetings, Expositions, Events, and Conventions: An Introduction to the Industry, George G. Fenich, Prentice Hall, 2005.

*   Chris Davis, "Meetings Today," *Business Travel News*.

*   Cindy Estis Green, "The Information Revolution in Hospitality: A Guide to Intelligent Marketing 2000-2020," *The HSMAI Foundation Research Review*. www.hamai.org

Internet Sites:

For more information, visit the following Internet sites. Internet addresses can change without notice. If a site is no longer available at the address listed below, a search engine can be used to find the new address or additional, related sites.

Association for Corporate Travel Executives (ACTE) - www.acte.org
Carlson Marketing Group – www.carlsonmarketinggroup.com
Conferon – www.conferon.com
Corporate & Incentive Travel – www.corporate-inc-travel.com
Corporate Meetings & Incentives – www.cmi.meetingsnet.com
Helms Briscoe – www.helmsbriscoe.com
Hoovers Online – www.hoovers.com
Maritz McGettigan – www.maritzmcgettigan.com
Meeting Broker - www.MeetingBroker.com
Meetings & Conventions magazine - www.meetings-conventions.com

Meeting News magazine - www.meetingnews.com
Meeting Professionals International (MPI) - www.mpiweb.org
National Business Travel Association (NBTA) - www.nbta.org
Smart Meetings – www.smartmtgs.com
Successful Meetings magazine - www.successmtgs.com

 ## Study Questions:

1. There are many similarities between association meetings and corporate meetings, but there are also clear distinctions. Contrast the two considering lead time, attendance, and kind of site required.
2. Company meetings come in many sizes and shapes. If you were the sales manager of a small property with limited meeting facilities, what types of company meetings would you target?
3. Discuss the multi-booking potential of corporate meetings.
4. As with associations, finding the key decision maker is of utmost importance. Why is this problem so acute in the corporate meetings market? List probable decision makers within the corporate structure.
5. What role do local chapters or business offices play in the determination of meeting sites?
6. Discuss how hotels are upgrading guestrooms with extra services and "perks" to meet specific business traveler needs.
7. List the six major sources for finding corporate meetings and tell how each is used to develop a client base.

 ## Key Terms:

Account penetration. The process of determining new sources of business within an organization.

Dealer meetings. Meetings held on a regional and national basis for dealers and distributors. Usually held to introduce new sales and advertising campaigns and new products.

Incentive meetings. Meetings held during incentive trips given to employees, distributors and dealers as a reward for top performance.

Management meetings. Relatively small meetings consisting of top management. Often request upgraded accommodations and services.

Professional/technical meetings. Meetings held in order to update the company's technical personnel. Usually take the form of seminars/workshops.

Sales meeting. Often a meeting dealing with such company objectives as product introduction, sales policies, company goals, discussion of sales techniques, or to boost morale.

Stockholder/public meetings. Meetings for non-employees.

Third-party meeting planners. Outside individuals or firms who handle meeting planning for companies. Services may include site selection, negotiations, and assisting in all phases of staging the meeting.

Training meetings. Meetings held to update personnel in new company policies, methods or procedures. Usually fairly small in size.

Learning Objectives:

This portion of your text introduces you to the third major source for meetings business, nonprofit organizations. While this segment is smaller than the associations and corporate markets, it is equally important to hotels wishing to fill space during typically slow periods. Also included in this chapter is a discussion of incentive meetings, insurance meetings, and medical meetings. While these groups are not nonprofit, they merit special attention as a source for meetings business. When you have studied this chapter, you will:

- Be able to identify the types of nonprofit organizations that provide extensive meetings business.

- Be able to describe the types of meetings held by each and the factors that influence site decisions.

- Know who makes the decisions for these meetings and how to best reach the decision makers for these groups.

Outline

Nonprofit Organizations

The SMERF Groups
- Social Groups
- Military and Other Reunions
- Educational Meetings
- Religious Meetings
- Fraternal Meetings

Government Agencies

Labor Unions

Incentive Meetings

Insurance Meetings

Medical Meetings

Summary

Successfully Targeting SMERF Groups

Lyn Matthew, CHSE
Director of Sales and Marketing
Embassy Suites Resort, Scottsdale, AZ

"The remaining group market segments, commonly referred to as SMERF (Social, Military, Educational, Religious and Fraternal) as well as government, union, medical, insurance and incentive markets are by far the most diverse and challenging...Research is critical in determining which groups can best be served by the property... Since a property can be perceived in many different ways by targeted prospects, it is important to communicate the benefits that highlight the planner's needs and wants...Meeting needs vary widely...The astute sales executive must carefully match property capabilities with the needs of the conference planner. By selling the benefits of the property relative to the conference needs and wants, the sales executive has the opportunity to become a top producer while at the same time satisfying the needs of the meeting planner and paving the way for future bookings."

174

6   Selling Other Markets

While many properties place their emphasis on selling to associations and corporations, there are several other sources of meeting business that can prove profitable to properties that seek them out (see box titled "Convention Income Survey"). While the structures of these organizations can be similar to those of associations and corporations, they possess unique characteristics and are worth special mention.

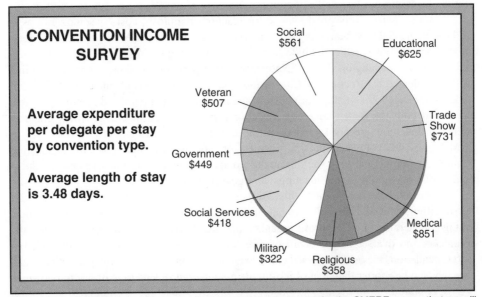

CONVENTION INCOME SURVEY

Average expenditure per delegate per stay by convention type.

Average length of stay is 3.48 days.

Social $561
Educational $625
Veteran $507
Trade Show $731
Government $449
Social Services $418
Medical $851
Military $322
Religious $358

This chart illustrates the average expenditure per delegate per stay for the SMERF groups that we will discuss in this chapter. Medical groups and trade shows have the highest average expenditures, while military and religious groups are the most price-conscious and spend the least money. While most of the SMERF groups fall below corporations and associations in terms of convention expenditures, these groups typically meet during months in which corporations and associations are not holding group meetings and conventions, making them a very attractive source of business for hotels.

The "Market at a Glance" boxes in this chapter give a "snapshot" of these groups. They identify each segment's key characteristics, including location requirements, facilities commonly used, price range, services needed, typical decision makers, and the best ways to reach each market. This will enable you to identify the group(s) best suited to your property and develop strategies to capture their business (a list of the major associations to which planners in these categories may belong is also listed at the end of the chapter).

Nonprofit Organizations

Although many organizations cannot be termed associations, they are structured in similar fashion. They have members, are nonprofit and were created to accomplish some common purpose. Some, such as the Red Cross and the Boy Scouts and the Girl Scouts, promote charitable causes. In addition to meetings business, these types of organizations, which exist through fund-raising, may be excellent sources of business for your banquet department. Others of this category include political clubs and parties, which need hotel meeting accommodations for their regular conventions and frequent meetings. Still others include social, military, educational, religious and fraternal (SMERF) groups and government agencies, labor unions and medical groups, which will be discussed in greater detail in this chapter.

Selling to these organizations is much the same as selling to trade associations, although it is difficult to find a central source that identifies these organizations since they are so varied. The records of a convention or tourist bureau may be of some help, and there are also directories from which a list of nonprofit meeting groups can be compiled. The *Guide to American Directories,* published by the Klein Company in New York City may provide leads in your targeted categories.

Another particularly good avenue for reaching nonprofit, cost-conscious groups is the Hospitality Sales & Marketing Association International's (HSMAI) Affordable Meetings® series of shows, which include Mid-America (Chicago), West (San Jose, California) and National (Washington, D.C.). Named the most popular meetings event in an online survey conducted by *Meetings & Conventions* magazine, these events include a 650-booth trade show as well as seminars for planners and hospitality suppliers, and meeting planners can attend both the trade show and educational program free of charge. Most planners attending this show are not members of traditional planners associations such as MPI or PCMA; they are volunteer meeting planners or those whose titles don't imply meeting planning. These people plan such events as hobby conventions, military reunions, educational, religious and fraternal meetings, and government meetings.

Once you have determined which of these groups you can best service, you can start by soliciting local chapters of national groups (always stay alert for autonomous local groups). Generally, most nonprofit organizations are staffed by permanent employees and volunteers and overseen by a board of directors. Site selection processes will vary, but recommendations are usually passed along to a board of directors for a final selection. Lead time tends to be shorter than that of most trade associations; a lead time of one to two years is most common.

Since most local committees are made up of volunteers, it is a good policy to assure them of your aid should they succeed in getting the national organization to schedule its event at your property. If you offer to extend help for the chores associated with being the host chapter, this may encourage them to push for consideration of your locale as a meeting site.

As a further selling point, don't be reluctant to point out the many economic benefits to the community when a convention is held there. Research has indicated that delegates to regional and state conventions account for expenditures of about $145 a day for three or four days.

Once you are past the local chapters and have penetrated the national organization, you will usually find that there are experienced meeting planners on the staff. Some of these national organizations do a great deal of convention work. They will work with you in the manner of association staffs, especially if you have been successful in getting the local chapter to request the position of host chapter.

The SMERF Groups

One of the most important subsegments in the nonprofit organizations market are the **SMERF groups** (see box titled "The SMERF Market at a Glance"). This acronym repre-

The SMERF Market at a Glance

- Many SMERF meeting planners work part-time or are volunteers.

- 32% plan one to three off-site meetings a year; 27% hold up to 10 off-site meetings annually.

- 70% of SMERF meeting planners report attendance of less than 500 persons; 50% reported that attendance at their largest event was less than 500.

- 43% have meeting budgets of less than $100,000.

- A little over half of SMERF annual events include a trade show or exhibition.

Types of Facilities Used by the SMERF Market:

Urban/Midtown Hotels	65%	Convention Centers	29%
Suburban Hotels	44%	University Facilities	20%
Conference Centers	36%	Arenas/Stadiums	7%
Resorts	32%		

Source: Howard Feiertag, "SMERF Business Ideal to Help Fill Weekend Room Nights," Hotel & Motel Management, *July 19, 2004.*

sents the collective group of social, military, educational, religious and fraternal groups. These groups, though typically price-conscious, are economically viable to properties (large and small) both because of their sheer numbers and their ability to fill "soft spots" as most meet during the typically slow summer months (see box titled "Typical Monthly Meeting Patterns").

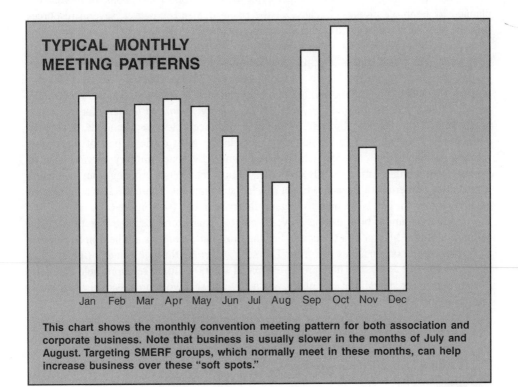

TYPICAL MONTHLY MEETING PATTERNS

Jan Feb Mar Apr May Jun Jul Aug Sep Oct Nov Dec

This chart shows the monthly convention meeting pattern for both association and corporate business. Note that business is usually slower in the months of July and August. Targeting SMERF groups, which normally meet in these months, can help increase business over these "soft spots."

Social Groups

People are avid "joiners," and there are groups for almost every interest. Just looking through the "Groups and Organizations" listing in a local telephone directory may yield such prospects as chess clubs, ethnic groups (Italian-American clubs, etc.), garden clubs and bowling leagues. These organizations may be local, or they may be part of a regional or national organization. No matter what their size, these social groups should not be over-looked as potential sources of business. Since most SMERF meetings are not driven by business needs, but rather by social and personal ties, they are generally more recession-proof than other types of meetings. Even a small local group may require meeting space or can generate meals business, while large groups can be an excellent source of banquet and convention business. Many social clubs hold awards banquets or fund-raising functions or can be a source of business for annual events such as Christmas parties and installation ceremonies. Groups such as garden and craft clubs often host local shows or fairs, which not only result in meeting space sales, but may bring in out-of-town business and generate publicity for your property.

Military and Other Reunions

The reunions market, which consists of family, class and military reunions, is a rapidly growing market segment. This segment is an excellent source of flexible weekend business.

In recent years, military reunions in particular have paved the way for an entire new industry that assists in planning these nostalgic events. Bob Brooks, president of THE Reunion Network, Inc., estimates the military reunion market to be worth $15 billion a year in air travel, hotels, food, drink and entertainment.

In the past, military reunions, which typically draw 100 to 300 people or more, were planned by nonprofessionals. Because of the rising demand, however, several resources were developed to assist inexperienced meeting planners.

THE Reunion Network, established to provide assistance and training, publishes a newsletter, *TRN News,* that offers tips for planning a successful reunion and provides additional services to planners, such as offering lists of "reunion friendly" hotels. Military reunion planners can also look to other publications, such as *Reunions Magazine, Military Reunion News,* and *The Reunion Handbook: A Guide for Reunion Planners,* for assistance in planning their meeting. In addition to these resources, Service Reunions, a registry listing over 9,000 military units, helps planners in the most difficult part of their jobs: locating members. This service, which lists planners by state, military service, size of meeting, and month of meeting, also provides telemarketing lists, making it an invaluable resource for properties that wish to target this lucrative market. There are also a number of other resources for hotels wishing to target military reunions (see Figure 6.1).

Military reunion business has several notable characteristics (see box titled "The Military Reunion Market at a Glance"). For the most part, reunions are held in September and October, and occupancies run from Thursday or Friday through Sunday (the average length of stay is 4.6 days). There are an estimated 15,000 military reunions held annually. Most groups meet annually or biennially, and many will seek your professional expertise in setting up their meeting.

Most military reunion programs include a Saturday night banquet, a memorial service, and a short business meeting. Also critical to military reunion groups is an adequate hospitality room in which attendees can share stories and consume drinks. Ted Dey, president of Armed Forces Reunions, Inc., says:

Figure 6.1. SOURCES FOR FINDING REUNIONS BUSINESS.

Properties wishing to target the lucrative reunions market can utilize a number of sources to find leads:

Publications

Reunions Magazine
P.O. Box 11727
Milwaukee, WI 53211-0727
800-373-7933
www.reunionsmag.com

Reunion Research
40609 Auberry Road
Auberry, GA 93602
www.reunited.com/tomstips

Reunion Research
Publisher of:
Family Reunion Handbook
Reunion Handbook:
*A Guide for School &
Military Reunions*

Reunion Planning

THE Reunion Network
5688 Washington St.
Hollywood, FL 33020
800-225-5044

Books on Reunions

Reunions: Step By Step
TRN 5688 Washington St.
Hollywood, Fl 33020
800-225-5044

Reunions for Fun-
Loving Families
by Nancy Funke Bagley
Brighton Publications
P.O. Box 120706
St. Paul, MN 55112
800-536-2665

Let's Have a Reunion:
A How-To-Do-It Guide
by Philip A. Hannema

In addition, hotels can join such organizations as THE Reunion Network. This group publishes *TRN News*, a free newsletter for reunion planners, and offers help — including lists of "reunion friendly" properties — to inexperienced meeting planners. In addition to being included on THE Reunion Network's list of contact properties, your hotel can advertise to meeting planners in the newsletter.

> "The hospitality room is the reunion. That's where it happens. The ideal hospitality room would be one that's large enough to accommodate tables of memorabilia and where attendees are allowed to bring their own liquor."[1]

Room occupancy is usually 75 to 150 per night, although this can go higher for larger reunions. Since many are on fixed incomes, paying their own way, they are extremely price-conscious. Attendees often share rooms with spouses or friends.

Hotels with planned spouse programs have a competitive edge in attracting this market. Attendees are typically male, but spouses have a strong voice in the decision to attend. One meeting reunion planner states:

> "All of the men have something in common, but almost none of the women do. If you do the job right, the wives will send the check in the day the registration notice arrives."[2]

Military towns also have an edge as veterans like to visit their old haunts and tour bases, ships and museums. The Pensacola, FL Convention and Visitors Center, for example, touts its history as "The Cradle of Naval Aviation." The Montgomery, AL Chamber of

```
┌─────────────────────────────────────────────────────────────────────┐
│                The Military Reunion Market at a Glance                │
│                                                                       │
│  Location:   Family and/or military-oriented destinations that can offer a combined vacation/reunion. │
│              Past destinations have included San Diego, California, Daytona Beach, Florida, │
│              Branson, Missouri, San Antonio, Texas and Norfolk, Virginia. Almost any city with │
│              popular local attractions or a good climate, however, can compete for this market. │
│                                                                       │
│  Facilities: Programs usually consist of a short business meeting, a memorial service, and a │
│              Saturday night banquet. Requirements include limited audiovisual equipment, but │
│              there must be enough banquet space to seat the entire group and their spouses at │
│              one time. A hospitality room is usually required.        │
│                                                                       │
│  Price:      Since many attendees are on fixed incomes, this group is very cost-conscious. │
│              Properties that offer low rates, free or low-cost meeting space or discounts to local │
│              attractions are especially inviting.                     │
│                                                                       │
│  Services:   Properties targeting this group can expect to assist with the planning of functions, as │
│              many military reunions are planned by nonprofessionals. Some groups will also │
│              require special meal menus.                              │
│                                                                       │
│  Decision    Contact must be made with individual military unit or group to determine the decision │
│  Makers:     maker.                                                   │
│                                                                       │
│  Best Ways   Join THE Reunion Network, and advertise in THE Reunion Network News. Other │
│  To Reach    advertising opportunities include Reunions, the Magazine and Military Reunion News. │
│  Market:     Find contacts through the Military Reunion Handbook, and purchase lists or labels │
│              from Service Reunions National Registry. Attend military reunion training conferences │
│              and organize fam trips for military reunion planners.    │
└─────────────────────────────────────────────────────────────────────┘
```

Commerce estimates that military reunions have a $10 million annual impact on the local area economy because the Air Force keeps its historical records at a base there. Or, a site may be chosen for its uniqueness. The Hangar Hotel in Fredericksburg, Texas, for example, is reminiscent of a World War II hangar and offers a number of nostalgic touches, including a 1940s style diner with a menu that generates déjà vu for military reunion attendees.[3]

In order to assist planners in selecting venues for military reunions, THE Reunion Network, the organization of military reunion planners, is now planning and organizing familiarization trips for their members. These fam trips are sponsored by the THE Reunion Network and the convention and visitors bureaus of military reunion friendly destinations.

Class and family reunions differ from military reunions in terms of size, meeting frequency, and types of programs. Recreational amenities are considered very important, and there may be several food and social functions but little in the way of meeting space needed. Like military groups, however, these groups pay their own way, and usually provide a good number of double occupancy rooms.

Class reunions are the largest in terms of numbers of events and number of attendees. However, attendees stay an average of just one night in a hotel. Family and military reunions, on the other hand, draw fewer people but the attendees stay for a longer period of time -- an average of two nights in the case of family reunions and 2.5 nights at military reunions.

Although most family reunions are hosted by nonprofessionals, there are a growing number of trained class reunion meeting planners. The National Association of Reunion Planners (NARP) is an organization that offers meeting planning training and networking. In addition, exhibiting at the African-American Family Reunion Conference, held annually at Temple University in Philadelphia, is an excellent way to reach potential customers. According to the National Coalition of Black Meeting Planners (NCBMP), African-Americans are an excellent source of reunions business, especially if your city can offer points of interest relative to the black heritage (museums, entertainment, etc.) and your property is sensitive to African-American issues.

Other ways to target the class and family reunions market are to advertise in *Reunions Magazine*, a Milwaukee-based monthly publication, and to work closely with your local convention and visitors bureau or chamber of commerce. These organizations are often contacted by individuals or groups wanting information about "reunion friendly" hotels (see Figure 6.2).

Educational Meetings

The educational meetings market is an excellent market segment for filling rooms during slow summer occupancy periods. Elementary, high school and college teachers and others affiliated with academic programs are prime sources of convention business. They hold a number of meetings, and every state has a teachers' association of some sort as well. In addition, most states have continuing education requirements that necessitate periodic seminars and classes for teachers.

Most educational meetings are relatively short (sometimes lasting only a day), and meeting planners look for accessibility and value. Since most attendees come at their own expense, they are extremely price sensitive. Properties that are located close to major transportation arteries or an educational center (college, university, etc.) and can offer reduced room rates are especially attractive.

Since this market is so diverse, there are many potential contact persons. Cooperative extension services often sponsor seminars, and the state director is the decision maker (a county agent's directory is an excellent source of contact names). Alumni offices and divisions of continuing education at local colleges and univer-

Figure 6.2. REUNION-FRIENDLY HOTELS.

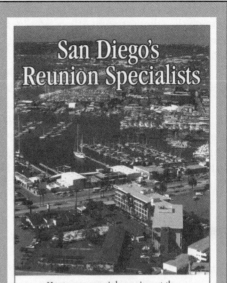

This ad for the Holiday Inn, San Diego Bayside, promotes an experienced staff who can assist the planner in organizing a "perfect event" as well as special reunion amenities, such as special reunion rates, a complimentary hospitality suite and a welcome letter and gift of chocolates in each room.

sities are sources of leads for meetings business, and admissions offices can provide transient business from visiting parents and prospective students. Other leads can be obtained through the administrative offices at a local educational institution or board of education. Personal contacts and referrals are often available from college professors and teachers who belong to professional associations.

A pamphlet specifically keyed to the educational meetings market is *Educational Associations and Directories.* Providing the names and addresses of educational offices, it can be obtained from the Superintendent of Documents, U.S. Printing Office, Washington, DC 20401. The *National Directory of College Athletics* identifies personnel in the athletic departments of universities and colleges throughout the United States. This directory can be secured by writing the Collegiate Directories Inc., P.O. Box 450640, Cleveland, OH 44145. Or, you may wish to utilize the Blue Book of College Athletics, published by Athletic Publishing Company, P.O. Box 931, Montgomery, AL 36101.

Religious Meetings

Religious groups are an excellent source of business for gatherings both small (board meetings, committee meetings, seminars and workshops) and large (area and regional meetings and conventions). Large conventions of 10,000 to 45,000 attendees are a common annual occurrence, and a property that understands the unique needs of religious groups can take advantage of this opportunity to fill "soft spots" — most groups meet over a three-day to two-week period during the summer months (see box titled "Religious Meetings at a Glance").

Most large religious meetings are "family affairs," and meeting planners tend to choose locations that are family oriented (Orlando, Anaheim, Dallas, Indianapolis). Since most attendees pay their own way, they are price-sensitive, usually opting for double occupancy rooms.

Religious meeting attendees often make up for their lack of alcohol consumption in food consumption. D'Wayne Leatherland, meeting planner for the Church of the Nazarene, states:

> "Our meetings history supports the claim that our group likes the 'f' in
> food and beverage."[5]

He suggests that hotels convert bars into ice cream parlors or coffee shops during his group's meetings, turning lost alcohol revenue into food revenue.

One reason that religious meetings can be profitable to a hotel is that they do not displace corporate or association business. Because these groups are value conscious, religious meeting planners negotiate lower rates by booking on holidays and weekends and seeking shoulder or valley periods. Vaughn Hall, director of convention sales and marketing for the Santa Clara, CA Chamber of Commerce/Convention and Visitors Bureau, says, "We've targeted the religious market because our weekends are slow and it's a good filler market for us."

There is another very good reason to target this market. Many religious groups do community service projects when they visit a city. In Indianapolis, for example, 2,000 meeting attendees helped local neighborhood associations rehabilitate ten houses and clean up city parks. Other groups work at soup kitchens or run blood drives. The Jehovah's Witnesses even have built a clause into their contract with convention centers saying that *they* will clean the center at the convention's end.

Religious Meetings at a Glance

Attendance: Consists of hundreds of organizations from dozens of denominations throughout the United States and the world; may range in size from small board meetings to mega-conventions of up to 75,000 (see photo). May consist of clergy, lay people, or both; are often family affairs.

Location: Favor family-oriented cities such as Orlando, Anaheim, and Atlanta. Also prefer second and third tier cities, generally in the South or Midwest, such as Birmingham, Indianapolis, and St. Louis. Mark McCulley, CMP, festival administration manager for the Worldwide Church of God, evaluates each city for facility size and quality; affordability of hotel and convention facilities; area attractions and amusements; friendliness of the city; and, overall entertainment value of the region.

Facilities: Need a wide selection of meeting and convention space — small meeting rooms for seminars, workshops, and meetings; large convention halls to hold large crowds. Often require numerous breakout rooms and have many, often simultaneous meal functions.

Services: Restaurant availability is a high priority. According to April McWilliams, V.P. of Sales for the Greater Birmingham CVB, "Whenever people finish up with a meeting, they're always hungry. They want a place to eat, so it's important that hotels or centers have restaurants open for them, even if it's just for pie or coffee." Some religious groups will require special menus as well (i.e., Jewish Kosher foods).

Price: Middle- to low-budget hotels are preferred since most pay their own way. Double occupancy is the norm. Property offered discounts and complimentary transportation are valued.

Decision Makers: Most national events are planned by professional meeting planners. Local and regional events planned by a committee or the leader of the organization.

Best Ways To Reach Market: The RCMA (Religious Conference Management Association) is a national organization representing over 250 denominations and religious organizations. They publish a quarterly magazine, *Highlights*, and a membership directory.

Religious groups, such as the Promise Keepers, a men-only ministry based in Boulder, CO, generate over 7,200 conventions and meetings internationally and represent 30 million nights of hotel accommodations annually.

Many of the larger religious meetings are planned by professional meeting planners, many of whom belong to the Religious Conference Management Association (RCMA). This group was founded in 1972 and has approximately 800 meeting planner members and 2,100 associate members that represent hotels, convention bureaus, and other suppliers. RCMA members are responsible for over 2,000 meetings a year, and represent more than 250 denominations and religious organizations.

RCMA's Annual Conference and Exposition is an ideal arena for direct sales to this market. The group also publishes a quarterly magazine, *Highlights,* and a membership directory. Properties seeking the religious market would find associate membership in the organization to be an excellent investment.

Fraternal Meetings

Fraternal organizations can be broken down into two categories: "The Greeks," which are the familiar college campus societies, and fraternal and service groups, such as the Benevolent Protective Order of Elks, the Fraternal Order of Eagles, the Lions Club, and the American Legion, to name a few.

National fraternities and sororities, which number 55 and 26 respectively on college campuses across the country, typically meet during the summer months at events planned by a paid executive. The activities of this vast market are coordinated by three major groups: the National Interfraternity Conference (NIC), which represents 48 fraternities; the Panhellenic Conference, the female counterpart of the NIC; and the Fraternity Executives Association (FEA), whose membership is made up of paid executive officers from a number of fraternities (see box titled "Sources for Reaching the Fraternal Market").

The size of most general membership meetings, held during the months of June through August, ranges from approximately 150 to 800 or more. Multiple occupancy rates are high, since spouses or fellow students often share rooms. Meeting agendas typically include a banquet lunch, so properties wishing to service this market must have ample facilities to seat the entire delegation at one time. Lead time is typically two to three years.

Sources for Reaching the Fraternal Market

Fraternal Executives Association

Attendee Profile: College fraternity executives (executive directors and national presidents) from the top college fraternal organizations in America.
Program: Fraternity-related suppliers from the hospitality industry can socialize with executives and participate in a trade show.
Contact: Fraternity Executives Association, www.fea-inc.org

National Panhellenic Conference

Attendee Profile: College sorority executives (executive directors and national presidents) from the top women's fraternal organizations in America.
Program: Geared mainly toward hospitality industry suppliers, the best opportunity for business development occurs during the trade portion of the event.
Contact: National Panhellenic Conference, P.O. Box 90264, Indianapolis, IN 46268 (313) 872-3185

National Interfraternity Conference

Attendee Profile: National fraternity executives and college fraternity advisors from throughout the country.
Program: Mainly fraternity related; the trade show portion of the event offers the best opportunity for business development.
Contact: National Interfraternity Conference, Inc. 3901 West 86th Street, Suite 390, Indianapolis, IN 40268-1791 (317) 872-1112

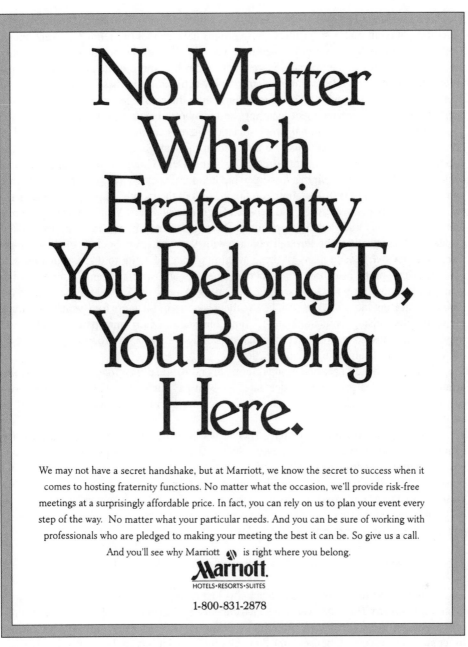
In addition to general meetings, sororities and fraternities hold educational retreats and leadership training institutes, which are usually held during the school year to train newly elected officers. While some of these meetings are held on college campus for cost-effectiveness, properties that can offer discounted rates may be able to capture some of this business.

Other possibilities for business include national board or council meetings, which usually consist of the governing boards of sororities and fraternities. Since group size is small, ranging from six to 125 people, and meetings are shorter, these meetings are often held on weekends (usually during the months of October and February). Airport facilities and properties close to the campus can often draw this type of business.

A subsegment for special consideration is African-American fraternal organizations. Consisting of eight major fraternities, these groups have annual or biennial conventions of 2,000 to 20,000 people. Besides generating high attendance, the advantage of servicing this market is that the membership is generally older and more affluent than the typical collegiate fraternity member. Alumni chapters play active roles in these organizations, and attendees tend to have more disposable income than their college counterparts — which translates to higher entertainment, catering, and alcoholic beverage revenue for hotels.

In addition to the traditional Greek societies, there is another group of professional or honorary societies that should also be included in this category. Some examples include Alpha Omega, a professional dental fraternity, Sigma Delta Chi, a professional journalism society, and Delta Epsilon Sigma, a scholarship honorary society. Some of these host large conventions, meeting on an 18-month rotational basis in the months of August and December. The December conventions, held between Christmas and New Years Day, are an excellent way to fill this traditionally slack time. These groups can be reached through related professional associations or through contact with the American Society of Association Executives (ASAE), since many of these meeting planners belong to that association.

Service groups also hold a number of meetings and special events throughout the year. While many of these (such as the Elks and the American Legion, for example) have their own meeting facilities, they can be excellent sources of business for special occasions, including fund-raising events and annual functions such as Christmas parties. This group may also play host to regional and national conventions or generate rooms business from out-of-town guests attending local functions.

Both fraternal and service groups' regional and national meetings are usually family affairs and are often presented to delegates — who pay their own way —as a vacation-convention combination. Planners, therefore, look for recreational amenities as well as value.

Some service organizations have special needs. The Lions Club International, for example, strives to serve people with sight challenges, and above five percent of the attendees at the group's annual meeting are blind. That means that meeting planner Renee Aubin must look for a destination that doesn't require a lot of walking yet has enticing activities close by for the group's multi-national attendees. She found that "Montréal excels as an easy multilingual destination with a compact downtown and tantalizing pre- and post-convention tourist opportunities." She adds:

"It was one of the best cities, with its housing package and diversity."[6]

There are a number of ways to reach this lucrative market segment. *Leland's Annual Fraternity-Sorority Directory* is issued each January by Leland Publishers, Inc. It lists the officers of national sororities and fraternities. Sororities and fraternities can also be reached by contacting college campuses and their alumni associations or by contacting the national governing groups mentioned in this section. Service groups may be found in local telephone directories or through chamber of commerce listings.

To solicit this market on a larger scale, you may wish to consider participating in three events held by major fraternities and sororities. The Fraternal Executives Association (FEA) holds a meeting and vendor trade show during the first two weeks of July, while the National Interfraternity Conference (NIC) holds a larger event during the first week of December. While this event also includes a trade show, it is less hotel specific than FEA's. The National Panhellenic Conference (NPC), which is held in October, also features a trade show and gives vendors the opportunity to meet with the executives and staff members of 25 attending sororities.

Government Agencies

Another frequently overlooked — but potentially lucrative — nonprofit market segment is government meetings business (see box titled "The Government Meetings Market at a Glance"). This market segment can be an excellent source of conventions business, especially when agencies deal with business groups. The Department of Agriculture and the International Food Organization of the United Nations are two examples of this type of agency.

The Government Meetings Market at a Glance

Location: Preferred locations are those that are easily accessible. Cities to which airlines offer direct flights and discounted fares are given priority. Government planners must be sensitive to the public appearance of booking a resort or elegant location.

Facilities: Preferred facilities offer double-double guest rooms and reasonably priced restaurants. Most meetings involve training, so quality meeting rooms and audiovisual support are prime concerns.

Price: Generally are cost conscious. Planners must deal with a strict bid process and sparse per diems. Hotels bidding must know how to fit within government per diem guidelines; rates quoted must include taxes.

Services: All "low-cost" or "no-cost" services that the property can provide are solicited by planners, i.e. free shuttle van from airport, complimentary coffee breaks, and waived meeting room rental. Require flexible payment schedules as the government is often slow in paying.

Decision Makers: Meetings are planned at the local, state and federal levels. Key contacts include the agency director, training officer, contract specialist and procurement officer.

Best Ways To Reach Market: Join the Society of Government Meeting Professionals. SGMP's monthly chapter meetings, national newsletter, directory, and annual conference are excellent for identifying and contacting prospects. List your property in the *Official Airline Guide Government Edition* and subscribe to the *Commerce Business Daily*, a publication listing requests for meeting proposals.

It is difficult to generalize about the kind of business that comes from government agencies. It varies a great deal, as does interest in different parts of the country. We are strong believers in "fishing expeditions." Go into any local government office and ask the supervisor about meetings held by his department or any emanating from the national or state office. This takes patience and hard work, but you may be able to add a number of prospects to your lists. And don't overlook chambers of commerce. Some are funded by local governments while others are independent membership organizations; in either case, local chambers can be excellent sources of meeting business.

If the people expected to attend meetings are government employees, it would help if you learned what the current **per diem** allowance, the fixed amount of money allowed for government employees for each day of travel away from the office, is for your city. It is seldom a generous sum, and employees often add to it out of their own pockets. If you can offer a meeting package of lodging and meals that is covered by the per diem allowance, you will be more likely to attract this market segment.

When going after government business, you will find that it is not too different from dealing with corporations. You deal with the strata of executives. When you get to the person of authority, you can close the deal. You can expect many small meetings, on short notice, just as you do in corporate business.

The majority of government meetings are held for training purposes, and there are several key needs that must be met in order to attract this business. First, accessibility is important; direct flights at discounted rates are a major factor in the choice of locations. Second, most agencies look for free meeting space; a property that hopes to secure government business must make this concession in exchange for room business. Third, government meetings are on a tightly controlled per diem basis; a property that can offer a rate within government guidelines has a distinct advantage in attracting this market. Government agencies are also often slow in paying (it can take as long as 45 days to receive payment); a property must be able to work within government payment schedules. Since lead time is short (less than one year), government agencies often keep files on properties that meet their requirements and can book meetings on short notice.

Since most meetings are training meetings, the meeting planner is often a training officer, contract specialist or procurement officer. Although properties will usually work with one of these people in regard to meeting details, site selection is often based on two distinct types of price submission: Invitation for Bids (IFB) and Request for Proposals (RFP).

The IFB procedure uses sealed bids that are mailed or hand-delivered to the requesting government office in sealed envelopes until a preset bid opening date. All prices are announced during the bid opening. The RFP is a confidential method of selection. The government is free to negotiate with a supplier who meets government standards. Once a final selection is made, the property must prove that it can provide the contracted services (physically and financially).

There are several sources for locating government business (see Figure 6.3). Local legislators can also be invaluable contacts; often, the suggestions of a legislative committee will result in a booking. Direct mail contact may also be made with various government agencies and officials. A direct mail package might include a government rate sheet, third-party endorsements from government groups that have met at your property, and an offer for a member of the agency to visit your hotel. Advertising is another option frequently used to reach the government market.

The Internet can also be used to reach this market. Allmeetings.com, an online meeting planning site that matches planners with hotels, now has a special area for government planners. Planners input their meeting specifications (number of attendees, budget constraints, etc.) and allmeetings returns only the hotels that meet the strict requirements of government travel policies and per diems. And, two key organizations can assist a property in obtaining business from this lucrative market: the Society of Government Meeting Professionals and the Society of Travel Agents in Government.

Labor Unions

The labor union meetings market has become so important that many properties employ sales personnel to specifically target this category. There are over 150 unions in the United States, and most hold meetings fairly regularly. In addition, most unions stay with a property with which they have been satisfied, providing an excellent opportunity for repeat business.

Figure 6.3. SOURCES FOR LOCATING GOVERNMENT TRAVEL BUSINESS.

Information Publications

Official Airline Guide - Government Edition
    Reed Travel Group
    Secaucus, NJ 07096
    (201) 902-1988
    Fax: (201) 319-1761

Features include contract air and car listings, all qualifying noncontract hotels, per diems by location, policies, procedures and other information needed by a government employee for travel.

United States Government Manual
    Superintendent of Documents
    U.S. Government Printing Office
    Washington, DC 20402
    (202) 783-3238
    Stock #69-000-00015-1

Includes listing of executive agencies and department functions, guide to boards, commissions and committees, complete explanation of government structure by branch, unilateral organizations, federal region map, independent establishments and government corporations, and commonly used abbreviations and acronyms.

Commerce Business Daily
    c/o Superintendent of Documents
    U.S. Government Printing Office
    Washington, DC 20402
    (202) 783-3238

Features on-line database service, lists all government contract opportunities over $25,000, and lists the names and locations of federal agencies buying products or services, description of requirements, contract supervisor and ordering process. On subscription basis.

Government Services Administration Traffic and Travel Zone Offices:

EASTERN ZONE
Federal Supply Service Bureau
75 Spring Street S.W.
Atlanta, GA 30303
(404) 331-5121

CENTRAL ZONE
Federal Supply Service Bureau
1500 East Bannister Road
Kansas City, MO 64131-3088
(816) 523-6029

SOUTHWEST ZONE
Federal Supply Service Bureau
819 Taylor Street
Ft. Worth, TX 76102
(817) 334-2737

WESTERN ZONE
Federal Supply Service Bureau
525 Market Street
San Francisco, CA 94015
(415) 974-9292

NATIONAL CAPITAL ZONE
Federal Supply Service Bureau
7th and D Streets SW
Washington, DC 20407
(202) 472-2003

Media

Government Executive
    1730 M Street NW
    Washington, DC 20036
    Edited to help top government managers perform their jobs.
Governing
    2300 N Street NW Suite 760
    Washington, DC 20037
    Edited for state and local government executive, providing "how-to" information.

Organizations

Society of Government Meeting Professionals
    908 King St
    Alexandria, VA 22314
    (703) 549 - 0892
    www.sgmp.org

Society of Travel Agents in Government
    6935 Wisconsin Circle NW
    Washington, DC 20815
    (301) 654-8995

Union meetings, which are usually held only at hotels that are unionized, fall into three general categories: national conventions; regional conferences; and executive and committee meetings.

National conventions are usually held every two years, with site locations shifting between the eastern and western regions of the United States. National conventions typically generate:

- high spouse attendance
- high per person expenditures
- a number of social programs
- several sponsored functions, providing good food
  and beverage revenue

Because of their size, national conventions are held at larger properties that can provide the rooms and meeting space needed to accommodate the delegates and their spouses. The general session, which typically takes on a political atmosphere, is the focal point of the convention and is usually attended by all of the delegates. Sophisticated audiovisual equipment is often required, as is media accessibility, since prominent political speakers are often part of the program.

In addition to the large amount of space needed for the general session, sufficient space is needed for the various social functions in the program. These may range from banquets for the entire contingent to breakfast meetings for key leaders to a number of hospitality suites.

Regional conferences are usually held in central locations. Meetings typically last two to three days and draw attendances of 200 to 500 delegates. As in the case of national conventions, meeting planners seek out properties that can accommodate all of their delegates and offer sophisticated audiovisual equipment.

Executive and committee meetings, which number as many as four a year, are usually held in the union's headquarters city. Since participants are key union people, attendance is smaller (15 to 20 people). These meetings are important to a property, however, as the success of a small meeting may lead to the booking of larger meetings and conventions.

Contact persons for union business include the general secretary of a union for national conventions and the secretary-treasurer for executive and committee meetings. Meeting planners are professional and well-disciplined, and the selling process must include a sense of trust based on personal relationships and the ability to meet the meeting planner's needs.

Incentive Meetings

While incentive travel is a part of the corporate meetings market, this important market segment is sufficiently different to deserve special mention, especially due to its growing impact and importance to resort properties.

What is **incentive travel**? It is a travel award — often a deluxe tour package — offered as motivation to employees and customers to put forth extra effort and meet criteria established by the program sponsors. Since the trip is a reward for selling (or buying), incentive meeting planners seek first-class accommodations and service, and look for locations that offer good weather, sight-seeing, recreational facilities, entertainment and a choice of restaurants (see Figure 6.4).

The economic environment has a great impact on the degree of incentive travel. When times are tough, it becomes critical to motivate employees and customers. Incentives have been proven to increase employee and distributor participation in moving products and services. Travel incentives, which are recognized as effective motivators, have been

Figure 6.4. *FACTORS IMPORTANT TO INCENTIVE TRAVEL PLANNERS WHEN SELECTING GROUP DESTINATIONS.*

Factors Considered "Very Important"	Incentive Trips
Availability of recreational facilities, such as golf, tennis, swimming, etc.	75%
Climate	74
Sightseeing, cultural, or other extracurricular attractions	73
Safety and security of destination	72
Affordability of destination	64
Glamorous or popular image of location	61
Availability of hotels or other facilities suitable for meetings	57
Clean and unspoiled environment of destination	54
Ease of transporting attendees to and from location	54
Transportation costs	50
Distance traveled by individual attendees	46
	Total is greater than 100% due to multiple mentions

Since incentive travel is largely motivational — a "reward" for a job well done — incentive travel planners have different requirements than general corporate meeting planners. Interestingly, while the availability of recreational facilities, such as golf, swimming, tennis, etc., is ranked number one on the list, the safety and security of the destination is now also a top concern.
Source: The 2004 Meetings Market Report conducted by Meetings & Conventions magazine.

used to improve morale, reduce turnover and achieve special sales targets. They have also been used to get dealers to concentrate on specific brands and to increase purchases.

Travel award programs are frequently established for automobile dealers, appliance distributors, insurance salespersons, and other employee and customer groups. The insurance, auto parts and electronics industries are the heaviest users of incentive travel (see Figure 6.5).

Most incentive trips last five days to a week (occasionally longer), and have an average attendance of approximately 105 people to ensure that everyone involved gets special attention. While most incentive trips have typically been group affairs, *individual incentive travel* is a trend that has been gaining momentum. Many qualifiers prefer to take an individual trip with a significant other. Approximately 35 percent of all incentive trips are individual rather than group trips.

Why is incentive travel so important to hotels? Typical per person costs for a group incentive trip average about $2,500. Also of importance is that many incentive travel trips include spouses. The presence of spouses not only contributes to increases in the double occupancy figures of a property (which, in itself, has a favorable effect on operating results), but is also a factor in increased spending. The award winners will often spend their own money on "extras," such as gift items, recreation, and entertainment options not included in the award package.

Figure 6.5. THE TOP 10 USERS OF INCENTIVE TRAVEL.

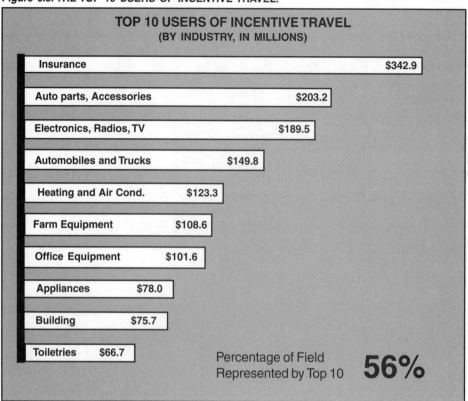

TOP 10 USERS OF INCENTIVE TRAVEL
(BY INDUSTRY, IN MILLIONS)

Insurance	$342.9
Auto parts, Accessories	$203.2
Electronics, Radios, TV	$189.5
Automobiles and Trucks	$149.8
Heating and Air Cond.	$123.3
Farm Equipment	$108.6
Office Equipment	$101.6
Appliances	$78.0
Building	$75.7
Toiletries	$66.7

Percentage of Field Represented by Top 10 **56%**

This graph shows the industries that rely most on incentive travel to motivate their staffs and promote sales and gives an idea of the scope of this lucrative market segment. Properties wishing to target these groups may wish to invest in the Directory of Premium, Incentive and Travel Buyers. *This directory, available from the Salesman's Guide, Inc., is organized by industry and contains a list of corporate buyers along with buyer profiles to help qualify them.*
Source: Society of Incentive Travel Executives.

Obviously, incentive trips call for a desirable vacation setting. All the tourist attractions come into play here — be it a natural attraction, an ideal climate, excitement or even some tie-in with the industry or company. The experienced incentive planner will analyze his or her people carefully to decide what type of site and program will draw the greatest number of people. It may be a big-city trip, a trip abroad, a cruise or an exciting visit to a playground such as Las Vegas or Hawaii. At the Hilton Waikoloa, for example, the lobby of the hotel features a lagoon populated by dolphins, and guests are transported to their rooms by boat. This type of "fantasy resort" is extremely popular among incentive meeting planners. A Pocono resort, a ski lodge in Colorado or a country club with a famous golf course may be just the thing for a smaller group. In addition, 32 percent of American corporate planners sponsored incentive programs outside the United States. The sidebar titled "Top Factors When Selecting Hotels for Incentive Trips" details what incentive planners look for when selecting a particular hotel for their events.

Much less is called for in the way of meeting facilities for incentive groups than for a convention or conference as the meeting business that is conducted is much less complex. Usually a general assembly hall and banquet facilities will suffice. The accent is on the vacation activities, and the business connection is definitely of the soft sell variety. Almost any resort property should be able to handle this type of business.

If your property could be considered a candidate for incentive travel, you would greatly benefit by developing a marketing strategy to reach incentive travel planners.

There are a number of ways to reach this market segment. Contacts and leads can be developed through the Society of Incentive Travel Executives (SITE). SITE publishes an annual directory of incentive travel executives and also sponsors an annual trade show called the Incentive Travel and Meeting Executives Show, where incentive travel suppliers such as hotels, attractions and airlines can exhibit their products.

Top Factors When Selecting Hotels for Incentive Trips	
Quality of food service	88%
Number, size, and quality of sleeping rooms	84
Negotiable food, beverage and room rates	74
Number, size and quality of suites	67
Cost of hotel or meeting facility	66
Efficiency of billing procedures	63

Source: The 2004 Meetings Market Report conducted by Meetings & Conventions *magazine.*

The international marketplace (primarily Europe, Asia and Canada) has also become an attractive area. Convention bureaus and hotels can attend key international shows such as the Canadian Travel Expo (held in Toronto), the Asian Business and Incentive Show (in Singapore) and the European Incentive Business Travel Meetings Expo (staged in Barcelona, Spain).

Still another option is dealing with **incentive travel houses** (see box titled "Incentive Travel Houses"). While repeat business from groups is rare because destinations are varied each year, incentive travel houses, which represent several different companies, can provide repeat potential; they often will return different groups to a property that they have successfully dealt with in the past.

Advertising is yet another way to reach this market. Unlike ads to corporate meeting planners, which stress a property's professionalism in handling meetings, incentive travel ads must stress the desirability of your location and the recreational and entertainment amenities available (see Figure 6.6). The two principal trade publications for reaching incentive planners are *Corporate Meetings & Incentives* and *Corporate & Incentive Travel* (see Appendix I for addresses).

Insurance Meetings

While the insurance companies fall into the corporate market category, they deserve special attention because they spend more money — roughly $4 billion annually – on meetings than any other industry (75% of insurance companies' meeting budgets are spent on incentive meetings; the other 25% is spent on sales and training meetings).[7] In addition, insurance meeting planners anticipate an across the board increase in incentive, sales and training meetings in the future as insurance companies are consolidating and merging at a significant pace. A recent study reports that one in three have acquired another company within the last two years. These mergers mean more meetings as field forces and home offices must learn each others' culture and practices.

There are over 6,000 insurance companies in the United States, and each holds about 20 meetings a year, ranging in size from 20 attendees at small workshops, to conferences of 200, and major conventions of 3,000 or more. These national conventions are the largest, held annually for three to five days and planned a minimum of a year in advance.

INCENTIVE TRAVEL HOUSES

E. F. MacDonald is generally regarded as the innovator in incentive travel. Working as a stock boy in a luggage factory, he observed an NCR representative picking up merchandise. He learned the luggage was intended as incentive prizes for dealers. He conjectured that if luggage could be used as an incentive, so could travel. From this was born the specialized incentive travel agent. E. F. MacDonald (now Carlson) was soon joined by other firms. S and H Travel Awards, Maritz, Business Incentives and others have moved in to capture a share of this growing market. At one time incentive travel was planned exclusively by the company, but the tremendous growth in incentive travel created a demand for full-time professional incentive travel companies (houses). These organizations fall into three basic categories.

1. *Full-service incentive houses* — These organizations offer clients a wide range of services from program planning and development to implementation. This type of firm handles both travel and merchandise fulfillment, and offers specific measurement criteria, promotional materials and sales campaigns based on each company's goals.

2. *Travel fulfillment companies* — These organizations handle the travel planning while the corporate clients design and operate their own incentive programs.

3. *The travel agency with an incentive division* — This type of firm does not offer marketing services, but has personnel that specialize in incentive trips.

These companies see to the details of the incentive program. They negotiate with airlines and hotels and then package the transportation, lodging and meeting accommodations, meals, tours and entertainment. They often prepare the promotional literature and may even get involved in setting the goals of the program. Before the group arrives, the agent visits the site and reviews with the hotel the arrangements for servicing the group. The agent sees the group through its stay, serving as the liaison between the group and the hotel. In essence, then, the agent serves as a bona fide meeting planner, seeing to the needs of the group he or she represents. Minneapolis, Chicago and St. Louis are the locales of the top incentive travel companies in the country. Large hotel chains and convention bureaus often schedule an "incentive house blitz" to these cities to solicit these companies.

Regional meetings are smaller and held more frequently than national meetings, and tend to be sales oriented. While expenditures per person are typically less, resorts are considered for this type of meeting. Convenience and accessibility, however, are the important factors in site selection, and lead times average six to nine months.

Local meetings are usually held in hotels, and are primarily training seminars and board meetings. Local meetings may have a lead time of as short as two weeks, and proximity to the home office is a prime consideration in site selection, as is quality of service and facilities.

Although the insurance industry sells two basic types of insurance, life insurance and casualty insurance, most business comes from the life insurance segment. Life insurance companies employ large sales forces with regular training meetings and conferences. This segment also holds a large number of incentive meetings to keep its sales staff motivated.

Whether large or small meetings are planned, this group is not overly price conscious, and the availability of recreational amenities often plays a role in site selection. The agenda of a small meeting usually calls for business meetings in the morning and afternoon and scheduled recreational or social activities in the evening. At larger meetings, business sessions are held in the morning, recreational activities are offered in the afternoon, and social functions figure prominently in the evening. Since spouses are usually invited to larger regional and national meetings, the availability of spouses' and guests' programs is an added plus when attempting to solicit insurance company business.

194

Figure 6.6. SAMPLE INCENTIVE TRAVEL AD.

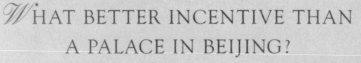

What Better Incentive Than a Palace in Beijing?

Within the ancient imperial boundaries of Beijing, a short stroll from the Forbidden City and the main shopping district, stands the magnificent Palace Hotel. Part of the renowned Peninsula Group, it is famous for incomparable levels of service–making it the perfect reward for excellence.

All 530 rooms and suites are superbly appointed and offer all modern conveniences, including satellite television.

A wide range of recreational facilities are at your disposal, including a well-equipped health club and swimming pool, plus a variety of world-class restaurants featuring international cuisine and regional Chinese delicacies.

For a memorable banquet, The Palace offers a selection of exciting ballroom theme parties and spectacular outdoor catering events at the Great Wall, Prince Gong Mansion and many other unique venues.

And because every detail is carefully planned by the hotel's highly experienced staff, the success of your event is assured–leaving you and your top performers feeling like emperors.

Circle #311 on Free Information Card

王府飯店
THE PALACE HOTEL
Beijing

Managed by THE PENINSULA GROUP

8 Goldfish Lane, Wangfujing, Beijing 100006, P.R.C. Tel: (86-10) 6512 8899 Fax: (86-10) 6512 9050
The Peninsula Group Regional Sales Office in U.S.A.: Los Angeles, Tel: (310) 278 8777 Fax: (310) 278 2777;
Chicago, Tel: (312) 263 6069 Fax: (312) 263 3744; New York, Tel: (212) 489 9568 Fax: (212) 397 0380
The Peninsula: Hong Kong • Manila • New York • Beverly Hills • Quail Lodge Resort & Golf Club Carmel • The Palace Hotel Beijing • The Kowloon Hotel Hong Kong
E-mail: tph@peninsula.com Website: www.peninsula.com or CONTACT YOUR TRAVEL PROFESSIONAL

This ad, targeting the lucrative incentive travel market, focuses on giving top performers a break to reward them. Unlike ads directed to meeting planners looking for value, this ad features the resort's exotic location and luxurious atmosphere.

To solicit this lucrative market, you should start at the company's home office. There may be a number of decision makers within the company (see box titled "Insurance Company Decision Makers"). Many large insurance companies have their own travel departments, often staffed by five to seven meeting planners. When selling to this market segment, it is important to remember that even the persons responsible for meeting planning of

---

Insurance Company Decision Makers

A recent survey by *Insurance Conference Planner* magazine determined the principal job titles for insurance company decision makers were:

Job Title	Insurance Planners
Vice President	28%
Director of Meetings	26%
Marketing/Administrative Executive	25%
Meeting Planner	16%
President	5%
	100%

Statistics from the survey also revealed that:
- 80 percent were female;
- their average age was 44;
- planners had an average of ten years of experience;
- there were approximately five persons in their department.

---

smaller companies are highly skilled professionals who are good negotiators who demand the same quality in their suppliers.

Because insurance companies plan numerous similar training and sales meetings over a large geographic area, they often look to hotel chains for one-stop shopping for meeting sites. Sharon Chapman, CMP, CMM, of Berkshire Life Insurance Co., says:

> "Hotel chain national sales offices are a real time saver. I can go through one contact rather than call each individual property, and the national sales offices understand my business. They can tell me if a property I'm thinking about will fit my needs, make other recommendations, and find the best value."[8]

As in other meeting market segments, third party planners are increasingly being used by the insurance industry. Approximately one-third use incentive travel houses and/or meeting management companies to assist in site selection and program planning.

When targeting insurance meeting planners, a professional, well-prepared, and sincere approach is the best, whether you are reaching them through advertising or direct sales. They typically conduct their own site inspections, and detailed letters of agreement are important to them. The better you understand their needs for each meeting and demonstrate how your property can meet the high standards of the meeting planner, the better chance you will have in securing their business.

Most insurance executives and meeting planners belong to trade associations, the two most well-known being Meeting Professionals International (MPI) and Insurance Conference Planners Association (ICPA). The Life Insurance Marketing Research Association (LIMRA) is also a key life insurance trade organization (its members write more than 90 percent of all life insurance). Allied membership is available in most associations serving this market, and this would be a worthwhile investment in gaining insurance groups meetings business.

According to a recent survey, insurance meetings planners are also turning to technology to search potential sites. Some 88 percent said that they researched hotel chains' Web sites while conducting an online search, while such online resources as Allmeetings,

EventSource, PlanSoft, and StarCite were also used.[9] Establishing a Web presence, then, can greatly enhance your chances of tapping into this lucrative market.

Medical Meetings

Last, but certainly not least, is the medical meetings market. While this market segment may be part of the associations market, this dynamic and rapidly growing segment merits additional attention (see box titled "Medical Meetings at a Glance").

Medical Meetings at a Glance

Location: Meetings are normally attended by an average of 200 people. They require a large meeting room and a number of smaller breakout rooms. The nature of the meetings is best suited by a quiet location in close proximity to a medical facility. Most meetings travel from city to city, other meetings are sponsored by associations. National association meetings are usually held in a vacation location to draw the most delegates.

Facilities: Medical meetings usually involve the use of audiovisual equipment during demonstrations. Most association meetings require exhibit space as well as meeting rooms and banquet facilities.

Price: This group is not overly price conscious, but as they join managed care organizations they are given a budget. Professionals in the medical field need these meetings in order to gain certifications and stay current in their practices.

Services: Many require faxes, voice mail, photocopiers and computers. A health club is an excellent selling point.

Decision Makers: The decision makers are experienced professionals in associations. The newer meetings are coordinated by hospitals and managed health care organizations. The managed health care facilities are also requiring doctors to attend certain seminars in order to stay abreast of the latest medical developments.

Best Ways to Reach: Many medical meeting planners are members of PCMA and receive *Convene* magazine. HSMAI has a national convention every year and INCOMM RESEARCH is a medical meeting industry leader. Healthcare Convention and Exhibitors Association and the National Pharmaceutical Council sponsor many conventions, as do hospitals.

Today's ever-changing technology and healthcare reforms make it mandatory for medical professionals to keep abreast of how the latest trends impact their profession. It is estimated that medical and healthcare groups currently hold over 35,000 meetings annually, and this number is expected to grow dramatically for a number of reasons:

- Medical professionals must stay current on new treatments, potential cures and the latest surgical procedures and medical techniques.
- Modern advances such as lasers, ultrasound and electrodiagnostic machines are changing the way medicine is practiced. Trade show exhibitors and product demonstrations provide opportunities to introduce medical professionals to the latest technology.
- Doctors and other healthcare professionals must earn Continuing Medical Education (CME) credits to maintain certifications. The most popular

places to earn CME credits are forums sponsored by medical societies, associations, universities, and private providers.

- The constant emergence of new medical specialties (and subspecialities) has spawned a number of new medical organizations. This trend will create additional continuing education needs.
- Globalization has also impacted the medical profession. Record numbers of international attendees have been reported at the medical meetings held in the United States, and more American medical professionals are attending meetings abroad.

Most medical meetings are small (the majority have 200 or less in attendance) and are usually held in sites close to major medical facilities. While most meet during peak periods (fall and spring), some groups also meet during traditional "soft spots" (summer and winter months). And, since many medical groups plan several meetings a month, there is a great potential for repeat business.

Medical meetings require a high level of presentation. Technical presentations, in which demonstrators can interact with the audience and take questions from all over the world, are sometimes done via satellite. One medical meeting planner explains:

> "We show live surgeries on a big screen...our camera work allows for close-ups and instant replays...busy physicians are drawn to medical meetings with new techniques and new knowledge."[10]

Requirements for medical meetings also include several breakout rooms for small group discussion and good message service. For larger medical meetings, exhibit space with adequate electrical outlets will be needed. The Center for Exhibition Industry Research reports that nearly 25 percent of all exhibitions are medical or healthcare shows. Since most meetings are technical meetings, most medical groups prefer to meet in a quiet location; a meeting booked near rooms used for a college reunion or a bowling league will lose future business.

One difficulty with medical meetings is that the amount of function space they require is incredibly high relative to the number of guestrooms typically used. Therefore, they are sometimes not a good piece of business for a hotel, particularly during high demand periods. Meeting planners have responded to this dilemma with a space-saving technique that is becoming increasingly used for medical and scientific group meetings: **poster sessions** rather than formal verbal presentations. Using horizontal corkboards, presenters can post a visual summary of their findings, experiences, or opinions instead of giving an oral presentation from a platform.

It is fairly simple to reach this lucrative and growing market segment. The typical medical meeting planner is an experienced professional; most belong to the Professional Convention Management Association (PCMA), a trade association originally formed for medical meeting planners and now open to all association planners. This association holds an annual meeting in January, and is an opportunity for hotel salespeople to interact with planners. You can also place print ads in the numerous medical periodicals and journals published for doctors, dentists, and the scientific community.

Summary

In this chapter, we have detailed the types of meetings held by nonprofit organizations and specialized segments of the corporate meetings market. We have seen how nonprofits, though largely price sensitive, can add to a property's bottom line by filling typically slow periods and providing potential repeat business (a chart listing these organizations, number and composition of members, membership restrictions, major meetings and publications to reach them is included at the end of this chapter). And we have seen how other segments, such as labor unions and incentive travel, can be lucrative for specific types of hotels. In this chapter, as in the two previous chapters, we have determined:

- Each segment's characteristics and needs.
- The kind of meetings they hold.
- What they look for when selecting a property.
- The decision maker for each market segment.
- How to locate key sources of potential business (a chart listing these organizations, number and composition of members, membership restrictions, major meetings and publications to reach them is included at the end of this chapter).

These crucial factors are essential in determining what type(s) of group business your property can handle. In the next two chapters, we will see how these factors also play a key role in determining the most effective ways to sell and advertise to each segment of the meetings market.

Endnotes:

1. Larry Keltto, "Tailor-Made Meetings," *Association Meetings*, April 2005, p. 32.
2. Fred Gebhart, "Reunion Meetings," *Meeting News*, April 12, 1999, p. 10.
3. "Front Words," *Reunions*, February/March 2005, p. 4.
4. Larry Keltto, "Tailor-Made Meetings," *Association Meetings*, April 2005, p. 31.
5. June Norman, "Moving Toward the Mainstream," *The Meeting Manager*.
6. Larry Keltto, "Tailor-Made Meetings," *Association Meetings*, April 2005, p. 29.
7. Regina Barban, "Insight 2005," *Insurance Conference Planner*, January 2005, pp. 22-24.
8. Ibid.
9. Allison Hall, "Meetings Made Us," *ICP* (www.meetingsnet.com), January/February 2001, p. 49.
10. Joseph Dabrian, "The Changing Pulse of Medical Meetings," *The Meeting Professional*, July 1999, p. 69.

Internet Sites:

For more information, visit the following Internet sites. Internet addresses can change without notice. If a site is no longer available at the address listed below, a search engine can be used to find the new address or additional, related sites.
African-American Fraternities/Sororities: The Natl. Pan-Hellenic Council - www.nphc.org
Collegiate Directories, Inc. – www. collegiatedirectories.com
Fraternity Executives Association - www.fea-inc.org
Insurance Conference Planners Association - www.icpa.org
National Association of Reunion Managers – www.reunions.com
National Interfraternity Conference - www.greeklife.org/nic
National Panhellenic Conference - www.greeklife.org/npc
Professional Convention Management Association - www.pcma.org
Religious Conference Management Association - www.rcmaweb.com
Reunion Planners – www.classmates.com
World Wide Travel – www.wwts.com

Study Questions:

1. What are SMERF groups? Why are they an important market segment? What SMERF market segments show the most potential for future growth?
2. How does dealing with government agencies differ from dealing with other meetings groups? What types of hotels are best suited for the various types of government meetings?
3. What types of meetings do labor unions typically hold? What factors are important to planners booking labor union meetings?
4. What makes the incentive market different from the corporate market in general? What types of properties are best suited to handling this market segment? What types of amenities would you stress if you were trying to attract the incentive market?
5. What are the characteristics of insurance meetings? What types of hotels might be most attractive to this type of business?
6. Cite several reasons why the medical meetings market segment is likely to grow.
7. Who are the key decision makers for each of the segments discussed in this chapter? How can each type of meeting planner most effectively be reached?

Key Terms:

Fraternal organizations. Groups in which membership is based on common personal interests rather than on common work or career responsibilities.

Incentive travel. Travel financed by businesses as an employee or dealer reward for outstanding performance.

Incentive travel houses. Full-time professional travel companies that make arrangements for companies that wish to offer incentive trips. Usually represent several different firms.

Per diem (means per day). The fixed amount of money given to government representatives for each day of travel away from home. Government employees have a fixed amount of money that they can spend per day on food, beverage and lodging.

Poster session. Display of reports and papers, usually scientific, accompanied by their authors or researchers. Can also refer to a session dedicated to the discussion of posters shown inside the meeting area. When this discussion is not held in a special session, it can take place directly between the person presenting the poster and interested delegates.

SMERF groups. An acronym for the nonprofit organization market segment made up of social, military, educational, religious and fraternal groups.

Summary of Sources for Reaching Meeting Planners

Meeting Planning Associations	Number of Members	Composition of Members
American Society of Association Executives www.asaenet.org	25000	84% association executives 16% suppliers (hotels, convention bureaus)
Insurance Conference Planners Association www.icpanet.com	470	All insurance planners, full or part ime. Suppliers cannot become members but can attend meetings
International Association for Exhibition Management www.iaem.org	3600	54% trade show managers 46% suppliers. Suppliers may join as associates
Meeting Professionals International www.mpiweb.org	18000 in 42 countries	50% meeting planners (45% corporate, 19% assoc., 19% independent, 8% other), 50% suppliers
National Business Travel Association www.nbta.org	2500	Corporate travel managers and travel service providers
National Coalition of Black Meeting Planners www.mcbmp.com	1500	Professional meeting planners, suppliers and contractors
Professional Convention Management Association www.pcma.org	5000	60% suppliers, 40% meeting planners
Religious Conference Management Association www.meetingsnet.com	3300	Meeting planners, contractors, suppliers of religious organizations or denominations
Society of Government Meeting Professionals www.sgmp.org	3500	51% suppliers contractors, 49% meeting planners
Society of Incentive Travel Executives www.site-intl.org	2000	Hotels, airlines, cruise lines, tour operators, travel agents, official tourist organizations as well as supporting organizations

Membership Restrictions	Convention	Publications
Active members must be executives of non-profit associations. Suppliers may be associate members	Annual meeting and exposition in August	*Association Management* magazine
Must be employed by an insurance company or insurance association	Two: Annual in November, summer forum in June	*Insurance Conference Planner* newsletter
Trade show managers. Suppliers may join as associates	Two: Mid-year in June, annual meeting and expo in December	Weekly newsletter
Open to all meeting executives. The number of supplier members must be matched by the number of planners	Two: Trade shows in July, education conference in January	*The Meeting Professional* magazine, newsletter to chapter leaders, newsletters from Special Interest Groups
Suppliers may join as allied members	Annual meeting in August	Daily news brief
Only professional meeting planners with at least one year experience	2 annual meetings: one in spring, the other in fall	*The NCBMP Newsletter*
Members responsible for meetings of nonprofit associations. Affiliate members may be vendors or independent planers	Annual convention held in January	*Convene* magazine and *PCMA Perspectives*
Restricted to religious organizations	Annual meeting held in January or February	*Religious Conference Manager* magazine
Restricted to government meeting planners, suppliers and contractors	Annual meeting in May	*The Society Page* newsletter plus the *Membership Directory*
Application needs approval, letter of recommendation	Annual meeting held in November	Monthly newsletter as well as *Insite* magazine

Learning Objectives:

This portion of your text discusses direct selling to meeting planners. In the chapter, we will cover personal sales calls, telephone sales calls, and the other most commonly used methods of selling to planners. When you have studied this chapter, you will:

- Be able to describe the six steps of a personal sales call and be able to explain why each is important.

- Know how to most effectively use the telephone to sell to planners, handle inquiries, and follow up on your accounts.

- Be able to detail other methods of direct selling, including sales blitz selling, trade show selling, selling with convention bureaus, site inspection selling and familiarization tour selling, and know the advantages and disadvantages of each.

Outline

Personal Sales Calls – Mastering Consultive Sales
- Pre-call Planning
- Opening the Sales Call
- Getting Prospect Involvement
- Presenting Your Property
- Handling Objections
- Closing and Follow-up

Customer Service and the Telephone
- Telephone Techniques
- Screening Prospects
- Setting Appointments by Phone
- Telephone Sales Call Follow-up
- Handling Inquiries
- Telemarketing

Sales Blitz Selling

Trade Show Selling

Selling With Convention Bureaus

Site Inspection Selling and Familiarization Tours

Summary

Common Sense Strategies for Convention Sales

Charlotte St. Martin
Executive Vice President Operations and Marketing
Loews Hotels

"Salespeople close sales...They do their research; they follow-up; they are consistent and persistent; they do what they say they will do and they deliver what they say they will deliver...I firmly believe that establishing that relationship [with a customer] is the single most important thing a salesperson can do to make a sale... Research and planning are critical to any discipline in the sales process... whether it be personal sales calls, sales blitzes, booth selling at industry trade shows, site inspections, or telephone sales."

7 Selling to the Meetings Market

T he size and diversity of the meetings market makes it a viable target market for all types and sizes of hospitality properties. However, reaching meeting planners and securing meetings business is too important to be done haphazardly. Capturing a share of the meetings market requires carefully planned strategies that fall within the guidelines of the property's marketing plan while meeting the needs of meeting planners.

There are two basic ways to reach this lucrative market: *selling* and *advertising*. Advertising techniques will be discussed in Chapter 8. In this chapter, we will take a look at some of the most effective direct sales tools used by properties today:

- Personal sales calls
- Telephone selling
- Sales blitz selling
- Trade show selling
- Site inspection selling and familiarization tours

While it is impossible to cover each of these areas in great depth in this book (volumes have been written on personal sales calls, for example), we have covered the essentials, giving an overview that will demonstrate the importance of direct selling to meeting planners.

Personal Sales Calls – Mastering Consultive Sales –

The most effective tool in convention sales, or any other kind of sales, is the personal sales call. This type of face-to-face selling works well with both professional and non-professional meeting planners. The personal sales call offers the opportunity to present your case in a detailed manner, to answer questions immediately, and to read the reaction of the prospect so you can gain a better understanding — and take remedial action if necessary.

In today's competitive environment, salespeople have to do more than simply sell meeting space and guestrooms; they must become *consultants* who determine customers' needs and provide solutions by adopting selling methods tailored to potential meeting customers. Although consultive selling is a low-pressure form of personal selling, it is a highly effective sales strategy (even though it involves considerable time, effort, and attention to details) and well suited to hospitality sales.

The personal sales call consists of six essential steps (see Figure 7.1). Each of these steps is vitally important in presenting your property effectively to the meeting planner, and we will cover each of them in the following sections.

Step #1: Pre-call Planning

While getting out there and selling is the best way to ensure that you will generate meetings business for your property, there is another — quite logical — step that should always precede the selling process: *pre-call planning*. While this planning (and the research inher-

Figure 7.1. THE SIX STEPS OF A SALES CALL.

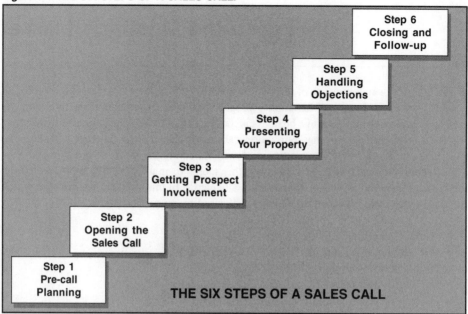

The sales process is a systematic series of actions that directs the meeting decision maker toward a buying commitment.

ent to it) may seem time-consuming and tedious, knowing your property, knowing your competition, and knowing your prospect are the keys to effective selling.

Knowing your property can help your sales effort in two ways. First, you will know exactly what you have to sell. You will know your property's strengths and weaknesses — and how to showcase or downplay them as needed. Second, and just as important, knowing basic facts about your property will give you the confidence you need for making a sales call. You won't have to worry about what questions a prospect will ask — you will already have the answers to most of his or her concerns (how many rooms are available, the size and capabilities of meeting rooms, audiovisual equipment available, etc.).

William Tiefel, vice chairman, Marriott International, and chairman emeritus, the Ritz Carlton Hotel Company, advises salespeople to:

> "Learn as much as you can about the business through a variety of jobs. It's a mistake to go right into sales and then try to learn by osmosis, or by working a week here and there and think you really know the hotel. The best-prepared salespeople are those who have product knowledge. I don't think you get as much from a training program as you do when you experience something long-term. We (Marriott) have a myriad of sales schools and activities for people at different levels in the organization, which is great. But I still think the basic concept of knowing the product is important."[1]

Since it is virtually impossible to memorize every detail about your property, many hotels prepare a **property fact book** (see Figure 7.2) to assist their salespeople (old and new) to know enough about the property to properly present it. This information can be updated as necessary and serves as an excellent tool for the selling process.

Knowing your competition can also help you to better sell your property. If you know a competitor's rates are slightly lower than yours, for example, you may expect a prospect

Step 1. Pre-Call Planning

In order to best sell your property, you must know what your property has to offer and how to best present it to interest a potential client. Conducting a property analysis, competition analysis, and prospect analysis, then, should always precede your sales presentations. Good pre-call planning also includes making sure you have the materials you will need for each sales call, managing your sales calls to ensure the best use of your time (combining an appointment call with a cold call in the same area, for example), and ensuring that you are projecting a professional image.

Step 2. Opening the Sales Call

Prepare an introduction, a statement regarding the purpose of the call, benefit statement (what the prospect can expect to gain), and bridge statement (asking for permission for the salesperson to continue) that will be interesting and appealing enough for the prospect to want to hear more about your property.

Step 3. Getting Prospect Involvement

Build rapport and get the client to discuss his or her needs and concerns. This involves projecting a professional image, using — and interpreting — body language, and listening skills. This step may make or break your sales presentation — if you can't develop rapport or get the prospect involved, he or she will have little interest in your presentation; on the other hand, a prospect who likes and trusts you will be far more open to what you have to say.

Step 4. Presenting Your Property

The "meat" of the sales presentation, this step explains the property's facilities and services — and should always be structured to show how the property's *features* can *benefit* the client. The presentation itself may include visual aids and collateral materials, but if the client sees little benefit to his or her organization, it will be difficult to close a sale.

Step 5. Handling Objections

This step gives the salesperson an opportunity to answer the concerns of the prospects — and can actually be instrumental in making the sale...if the salesperson is seen as a problem-solver concerned with the needs of the organization. You should always anticipate objections (most are over price or some aspect of your product) and be prepared to offer solutions that will satisfy the client's needs.

Step 6. Closing and Follow-up

A successful close is the ultimate objective of a sales call, but, incredibly, some salespeople don't even ask for the sale! Trial closes can be used during various stages of the presentation, but it is essential that you ask for a sale before leaving your prospect's office. Once a sale has been made, it is important to followup immediately. Follow-up demonstrates your property's commitment to service, and is an essential part of building rapport — as well as future repeat business and possible word of mouth referrals from the meeting planner.

to raise an objection — and you can be prepared to justify your additional cost by pointing out your property's special amenities, free parking space or some other feature that the meeting planner may perceive as well worth the rate difference.

Fred Shea, vice president of sales at Hyatt, says:

> "Our hotels always want you to know what they're up against because, hopefully, they know the strengths and weaknesses of hotels in their competitive set and can sell against that. If, as a hotelier, I'm bidding in a vacuum, I'll give what I think is our best bid, but if I knew that a competitor had more services to offer, it may compel me to do different things."[2]

Figure 7.2. OUTLINE FOR PROPERTY FACT BOOK.

GUESTROOM INFORMATION	RESTAURANTS & LOUNGES	MEETING AND BANQUET FACILITIES
Priority I Number of rooms Number of singles/doubles/suites Size of rooms — square footage Number of floors Phones in rooms Fire alarms/detectors in rooms Handicapped rooms Non-smoking rooms Amenities in rooms	**Priority I** Seating capacity Number of tables and types Atmosphere/interior design Non-smoking sections Dress requirements Pricing by restaurant Restaurant positioning	**Priority I** Location of meeting rooms Square footage/seating capacity Utilities available Exhibit space Meeting room rental rates
Priority II Room rates Check-in/check-out times	**Priority II** Menu style/theme Types of food by restaurant	**Priority II** Function room furniture Audiovisual capabilities
Priority III Customer mix Average occupancy by day of week Average length of stay by segment Sales budget Profitability by segment Group check-in/check-out procedures Front desk staffing	**Priority III** Entertainment Reservation policy Cocktails available Wine cellar/list Food served in lounge Special promotions Opening/closing times	**Priority III** Banquet seating capacities Banquet menu Theme parties Outside services Types of banquet specialties Beverage service Banquet staffing levels

New salespeople cannot learn everything about a property in their first week. To help them gain knowledge in a logical order, questions about each area (guestrooms, restaurants and lounges, meeting and banquet facilities, etc.) should be arranged by priorities. At the end of week one, a salesperson should master all Priority I questions; and each week, master another priority level. The Director of Sales should assign the responsibility of updating and maintaining the property fact book to one specific person in the sales department.

The third phase of pre-call planning, *knowing your prospect,* is essential for tailoring presentations to meet the needs of meeting planners. David Scypinski, vice chairman of development and senior vice president, industry relations of the Starwood Hotels and Resorts, believes that hotel salespeople must know the customer as never before:

> "It's not enough to know your customers' products, services and objectives. You have to know everything about their business and industry. Hotel salespeople should understand how the organization they are trying to book makes money and how large their budget is...there's no substitute for knowing your customers' organization, business needs, and objectives."[3]

Many properties — even those that utilize mailing lists to develop new sales leads — send out surveys or make telephone calls to gather information about potential prospects (see Figure 7.3). And, don't forget the benefit of obtaining information right under your own roof; talk to meeting planners currently using your property and ask them about potential leads (and their requirements).

Once you decide that a prospect is indeed a valid one, you must make contact to try to sell. Sales calls in which you initiate the contact without any degree of interest indicated by the prospects are called **cold calls**. The anticipated percentage of success in these cases is understandably lower than when you are dealing with past customers or recommendations. It is often a problem just getting in to see the right person.

While the primary purpose of cold calls is to find the name of the decision maker and to determine prospect needs, these types of calls are often not well-received by meeting

Figure 7.3. SAMPLE SALES PROSPECT CARD.

Date of Contact ______________________ Trace Date ______

Name of Contact ______________ New Prospect ☐ Yes ☐ No

Company Name ______________ Type of Business __________

Address ______________________ Telephone __________

______________________ Fax __________

Prospect's estimated sales potential:

Room nights ______________

Meetings/Banquets ______________

Dollars ______________

Facilities/services needed:

____

____

____

Background information on prospect and company:

____

____

____

Salesperson's Name ______________________

To make the most of a sales call, it is helpful to have some basic information about the needs of a prospect. A sales prospect card can help the salesperson to determine how to best structure his or her presentation to appeal to the needs of the client.

Source: Used with permission of the Grand Traverse Resort, Traverse City, Michigan.

planners. Harlan Didrickson, operations and events manager at Skidmore, Owings & Merrill, a Chicago-based architectural firm, says:

> "I work in an almost constant state of chaos, so cold calls are very irritating. They're a waste of my time, and I find them rude."[4]

Didrickson's opinion is shared by 51 percent of 235 meeting planners surveyed by *Meeting News*. Receiving cold calls was the top complaint among respondents, who say that salespeople should do their homework before making cold calls. It is a waste of both the planner's and the salesperson's time, for example, if a small hotel calls a planner who books only with large hotel chains.

You can increase the efficiency of such efforts if you precede your visit with some sort of preliminary campaign. You might send your convention facilities brochure to the contact person, along with a personal letter. Follow up with another letter if you hear nothing within a few weeks. Then call for an appointment. If you fail to get an appointment, try again.

Your most effective calls will likely be **appointment calls**, where you have prearranged a visit with the prospect, but don't completely rule out calling without an appointment. When you are already in the area for another appointment, a cold call is worth a try. Cross index your prospect list geographically. Mixing cold calls with your appointments will increase your number of sales calls. Cold calls sometimes work, but even if you cannot get in to see the right person at that time, you stand to lose little except a few minutes time. Sales success, to use an analogy from baseball, is accomplished not so much from achieving a high "batting average" as from your total number of hits. More "turns at bat" (sales calls) mean the chance for more "hits" (sales).

Once you have completed the research phase of your pre-call planning, assemble the materials needed to make an effective presentation. A well-organized and professional **presentation book** should include only that information pertinent to each prospect's needs. Fumbling through too many materials in a sales kit may result in a loss of presentation momentum. Most sales kits contain basic information such as a general property information sheet, a meeting and banquet room information sheet, a convention brochure and other visual aids, including color photographs, a map of the property, etc. Many properties also include **third-party endorsement letters**, also called *testimonials*, which are letters of recommendation from meeting planners who have used their facilities. If these are used, however, they should be relevant to your prospects. A letter from an association meeting planner praising your theme party, for example, would have little significance for a corporate meeting planner wishing to hold a training session.

If your property targets a number of market segments, you should consider preparing a presentation book tailored to each of those segments. While incentive and tour groups can be adequately served with glossy brochures and information on local attractions, meeting planners require "working documents." Your presentation book for meeting planners should include meeting space layouts on white, uncoated paper to allow the planner to easily make notes during a site inspection. These diagrams (ideally one per page) should include all specifics for meeting rooms, including anything that impacts the usable square footage of the room, and you may also want to include specifications for alternative room setups.

Additional "must haves" in a presentation book for meeting planners include large, detailed area maps with clear driving directions (these should be designed to enable the planner to fax or otherwise duplicate them), audiovisual price lists, parking information, transportation information (such as airport shuttles, hotel shuttles to nearby destinations and so on), dining outlets (including types of cuisine, hours of operation), detailed summaries of guestroom types and amenities and business center information.[5]

Step #2: Opening the Sales Call

Selling is essentially helping someone to buy. Open your sales call in such a way that it puts the customer at ease so that he or she can build rapport with you. Your opening should consist of an introduction, a statement of the purpose of your call (and its benefit to the prospect), and a bridge statement that leads into the actual presentation. You can start by introducing yourself and your property ("Good afternoon, Mr. Jones. I'm John Doe from the Golden Gate Resort in San Diego, California."), while offering a brief but firm handshake. You may also wish to add a few words at this time to show your interest in the prospect. For example, "I've heard so much about what your firm has been doing in the area of microcomputers, and I'm looking forward to hearing more about your innovative uses of microchips." But take care not to get so immersed in discussion about the company that you neglect your objective.

As soon as possible after the introduction, state the purpose of your call. Can you offer the prospect additional meeting space or are you there to try to win back former business? After stating your purpose, you should present a benefit or two that will give the prospect a reason to listen to you. Once you have stated your property's benefits, lead into the body of the sales presentation with a bridge statement. This statement basically asks the prospect for permission to continue, and is usually in the form of a question: "Would you be interested in learning how other associations used one of our theme parties to increase attendance?" or "May I show you just a few examples of our state-of-the-art audiovisual system?" If the prospect gives a positive response, you have the green light to continue. If the prospect is not interested, thank him or her for their time and ask for an appointment in the future.

Step #3: Getting Prospect Involvement

Involve the prospect in the sales process to determine his or her needs. Do it by asking questions, and always ask *before* making your presentation. Two types of questions are generally used: closed-ended questions and open-ended questions.

Close-ended questions require a specific reply. These include such queries as "How many training meetings do you stage each month?" or "What is your average attendance at your annual convention?" **Open-ended questions**, on the other hand, give the prospect an opportunity to express his or her feelings. Open-ended questions such as "Why do you think last year's meeting was so successful?" or "What factors are most important to you in selecting a resort?" will provide clues into what is important to the prospect and can help you to adjust your sales presentation to meet those concerns.

Effective questioning is among the more critical aspects of selling. Decide what information you need from the prospect in advance, and use it as a checklist for asking questions during your sales call.

Don't forget that the most important skill in gaining client involvement is *listening* to the client's responses. Sal Dickinson, president of Dickinson Associates, a consulting firm to hotel sales executives, stresses that successful salespeople are active listeners who relate to the prospect's needs and desires. He says,

"Get to know your prospects' needs better than the competition by being a better listener. Do your due diligence and research well. Knowledge is power, and the more you know the more effective you'll be...Come armed with solutions, not features, and spell out how what you have will be valuable and make life easier."[6]

Step #4: Presenting Your Property

While every salesperson should have a prepared and rehearsed sales presentation that addresses the needs of each market segment, you increase your chances of a sale if you custom-tailor this general presentation for specific clients. Most clients are really interested only if what you offer will benefit them. Rather than being a product-seller, become a problem-solver; always present your property's features as benefits to the client (see Figure 7.4).

Your presentation should directly address the client's needs — and should include visual aids, such as pictures, charts and graphs, to enable the planner to envision how your property will work for his or her meeting. Many salespeople today use more sophisticated visual aids — slide presentations or video brochures (see Chapter 8) — but the important factor is how these presentations relate to the client.

Figure 7.4. TURNING FEATURES INTO BENEFITS.

Feature		Benefit
All of our breakout rooms are adjacent to the room where your general session will be held	SO THAT	no time will be wasted between sessions and you will be able to keep your meeting on schedule.
We offer 24-hour room service	SO THAT	those attendees who must check-in late may still enjoy a late meal in the comfort of their room.
Every room has a desk	SO THAT	your meeting attendees will have plenty of room to review and work on handouts they receive during the daily meeting sessions.
We have a health club and spa	SO THAT	your trainees can relax and unwind after a day of intensive educational meetings.

Benefit		Feature
Those attendees who check-in late may still enjoy a late meal in the comfort of their room	BECAUSE	we offer 24-hour room service.

Salespeople who present only features rely on their prospects to interpret how those features can benefit them. Instead, salespeople should try to influence the interpretation by always linking features with benefits and explaining to prospects how the features will benefit them and enhance their meetings. To assist you in thinking "benefits," the words "so that" can be used to tie the two. The selling sentence can also be reversed, using the word "because" to link the benefit to the feature.

Tom McCarthy, CHME, CHA, past president of Hospitality Sales & Marketing Association International, suggests that each hotel create several five- to six-minute introductory presentations (with pictures) to be used at a prospect's office, a one-minute presentation to introduce your hotel over the telephone, a presentation to use on a tour of the hotel and presentations to overcome the most frequently raised objections. Salespeople should then rehearse these presentations before actually giving them to prospects.[7]

When presenting, use testimonial letters and publicity reprints to increase your credibility. Prospects are more likely to believe the good things their peers and unbiased reviewers have to say about your property than what a salesperson might say. Third-party endorsements from meeting decision makers in the same segment as your prospect are best; use association-related letters when selling to association meeting planners, corporate letters when presenting to corporate decision makers, and so on.

Once your presentation is completed, make a transition statement (which can be as simple as asking "Do you have any questions?) that may lead to a close — or to what is often the next phase of the sales call, overcoming objections.

Step #5: Handling Objections

It is a rare meeting planner who will not have some questions or objections. It is important, therefore, to anticipate the most likely areas of concern and to be able to respond immediately.

The most common objections involve concerns over price or product, or simply a lack of interest. *Price* objections ("Your competitor has cheaper rates") can often be overcome by pointing out a compensatory benefit ("Perhaps. But our meeting package includes free meeting and function space as well as free golf and tennis facilities."). Whenever possible, try to get the focus off price ("Putting price aside for the moment, do you have any other concerns?"). This tactic may work if you can demonstrate how your property meets the client's needs so well; then, price diminishes in importance.

Product objections ("Your property may not be as attractive to our attendees as the new resort in your area") may be handled in a number of ways. Try restating the objection and offer a positive response: "I gather that you don't feel our property is modern enough. Although we are an older property, our rooms and meeting space have been completely renovated and we offer all amenities found at new properties in our area. Clients tell us our property has a great deal of character and charm."

Lack of interest objections ("We are happy with our present hotel") can be overcome by finding out why the client is satisfied and offering comparable —and additional — benefits. Or, you may point out that a change of site may prove to be stimulating to the attendees. Then a change in site could then be considered acceptable to the planner; by you having offered an alternative without the implication that the selection of the previous property was wanting in any way. If nothing changes the client's mind at that time, it is still a good practice to ask to be considered for a meeting or function in the future. There are many factors that may come into play at some future date that may open the door for you.

When handling objections, it is vital that you *never* knock your competition. At best, this is unprofessional; at worst, the meeting planner may feel that your words reflect on his or her judgment — and you may lose any possibility of booking a sale at that time or in the future.

Step #6: Closing and Follow-up

While many salespeople enjoy presenting their product, some hesitate when it comes to asking for the sale! The skill of closing, however, can be learned, and can be more comfortable when salespeople realize that clients *expect* to be asked to book at the property.

There are two types of closes: trial closes and major closes. **Trial closes** are used to elicit responses from the client, and are generally used to build an "agreement staircase." In other words, the salesperson periodically asks for positive client response ("Don't you agree that our audiovisual equipment will greatly enhance your training sessions?" or "Don't you think our ballroom would make an elegant setting for your awards banquet?" or "Don't you find our golf course to be one of the finest in the state?"). Positive responses, repetition of benefits by a client, and positive nonverbal signs (frequent smiles, the client leaning forward, etc.) are excellent indicators that the salesperson can proceed with his or her major close.

The **major close** is the question or statement that asks for the sale. It should be attempted as soon as the client has reached a peak of excitement, and should elicit a commitment. This close should be as direct as possible ("May I reserve space on a definite basis?"), and after making it, you should stop talking and give the client a chance to respond. Avoid the temptation to keep talking — you may inadvertently say something that brings up concerns the client had not previously considered!

Once your call is completed, leave as soon as is politely possible. And, whether you have made a sale or not, always follow up your sales call promptly with a "thank you" letter. This gesture shows your commitment to customer service and may result in future sales.

If a commitment has been made, follow-up is even more important. You will want to service your client with frequent post-sale contacts, including keeping him or her informed on the progress of preparations for the function. It is also important to check with the planner during the function. Arlene Sheff, CMP, a planner for Boeing Company, recently held a meeting and said she:

> "...never saw the salesperson once on site. I spoke to him on the phone
> several times before the meeting, but while the meeting was going on, he
> never came by even once to see how things were going. If a hotel sales-
> person wants my repeat business, they need to track me down and check
> on my meeting. It's all about building a relationship with me." [8]

Contacting the client after the function to ensure that all went according to plan is also essential. This type of commitment leads to customer rebookings and word-of-mouth referrals for additional business.

Customer Service and the Telephone

One of the problems with personal calls is that they are getting increasingly expensive. Many properties are cutting down on the expense of personal calls by stepping up their use of the telephone, especially as a tool to screen prospects and to set appointments with clients.

Although telephone calls should not be a substitute for as many personal visits as you can manage, you should become proficient in using the telephone as a means to increase customer contact, screen prospects to make personal calls more effective, and offer immediate assistance to clients in the event of urgent situations.

Telephone Techniques

Since using the telephone is much more impersonal than talking face-to-face with a prospect, it is important that you and your salespeople develop techniques to make the most efficient use of this sales tool. As with a personal sales call, *preparation* is the key. Before making a call, you should have an outline of what you are going to cover. A clearly typed topical outline will help you maintain control of your thoughts and maintain a logical flow in your conversation. You can even use a prepared presentation — as long as it doesn't sound "canned." Along with your outline or presentation, you also want to keep pertinent backup information — room rates, function room sizes and capacities, availability, and so on —at hand so that you never have to fumble while searching for it. Also, keep paper and pencil handy to jot down notes or to remind yourself of information requested by the client.

It is easy to dismiss a voice on an impersonal electronic instrument so you will want to make your telephone time as productive as possible. Set aside times when you will not be interrupted; a prospect is likely to be annoyed if you put him or her on hold. At many properties, salespeople are given specific blocks of telephone time in which to make their calls.

Using the telephone involves the mastery of several simple techniques. Always hold the receiver slightly away from your mouth and speak slowly and distinctly. Immediately identify yourself and your property. Put your personality into the call — be cheerful yet professional — and always be willing to listen to the prospect's view. Don't be reluctant to ask the prospect to spell his or her name if it isn't clear. No one minds repeating or spelling their name.

Screening Prospects

The telephone makes it easy to prequalify prospects before making appointments for personal calls. Many properties use sales lead services, often referred to as *tip sheets* (see Figure 7.5), to analyze information about frequent convention and meeting planners. All of these names will not be high-priority prospects; they must be scanned to determine those who best fit into your marketing plan. But, since other hotels are receiving the same tip sheet, you must take quick action after an initial screening. Since you already have basic information about each lead, you can tailor your telephone calls to these prospects.

Other prospects can be interviewed directly by salespeople, who will enter information that could be helpful in a sales presentation on a **call report** (see Figure 7.6). This form can help the salesperson to determine the needs of the prospect — if the prospect represents viable business. In some cases, marketing surveys are conducted by members of the property's clerical staff, while large properties and chains may have an entire department that surveys potential prospects (see the telemarketing section in this chapter). Training clerical staff specifically in telephone techniques pays dividends.

Setting Appointments by Phone

Since cold-calling is less effective than calling on prospects who are already interested in what the property has to offer, the telephone is a useful tool for setting appointments for sales presentations.

One of the most challenging tasks in using the telephone to set appointments is getting by the intermediaries — the receptionist, secretary, administrative assistant, etc. —

Figure 7.5. SAMPLE "TIP SHEET."

SM DATABANK
Division of **SM**/SUCCESSFUL MEETINGS

10/26
CONFIDENTIAL REPORT

FILE NO. BUGYP00021

GYP
H R | **SAMPLE REPORT** | ANNUAL MTG
201
WAS

SCOPE: INTERNATIONAL EXHIBITS: 50 BOOTHS FREQUENCY: EVERY YR. NO. MTGS: 1

SITE DECISION: 2 YRS IN ADVANCE BY EXEC DIR IN FALL
PREFERRED AREA: METRO OR RESORT
MEETING ROOMS: 16 NEEDED LARGEST FOR 200
FOOD FUNCTIONS: 3 HELD LARGEST FOR 900
SLEEPING ROOMS: 40 SINGLES, 400 DOUBLES, 60 SUITES, FOR 900 6 NIGHTS (SUN-THU)
SPORTS: TENNIS, GOLF
PRE/POST CONV: MONTEGO BAY
NO. TRNG/EDUC SEMINARS: 6

** HISTORY **

DATE	SITE	HEADQUARTERS	ATTENDANCE
95 FEB 26-MAR 3	SAN FRANCISCO, CA	SHTN-PALACE	400
96 MAR 10-15	MIAMI BEACH, FL	DEAUVILLE	400
97 MAR 10-14	LOS ANGELES, CA	INTERNATIONAL	500
98 MAR 9-12	WASHINGTON, DC	MAYFLOWER	750
99 MAR 22-25	NEW ORLEANS, LA	JUNG	750
00 MAR 6-9	LAS VEGAS, NV	LV HILTON	1,000
01 MAR 5-8	ATLANTA, GA	HYATT REGENCY	1,000
02 MAR 17-20 (T)	LAS VEGAS, NV	LV HILTON	1,000
03 MAR			
IS CONSIDERING: LONDON ENGLAND, DUBLIN IRELAND, NEW YORK CITY, NY, FL, UT			1,000
04 MAR			
IS CONSIDERING: SAN FRANCISCO CA, SD			1,000
05 MAR			
IS CONSIDERING: HOUSTON TX			1,000
06 MAR			
IS CONSIDERING: FL			1,000
07 MAR			
IS CONSIDERING: CA			1,000
08 MAR			
IS CONSIDERING: DALLAS TX			1,000

BY PERMISSION OF *SUCCESSFUL MEETINGS* MAGAZINE

Tip sheets allow you to "do your homework" before making a sales call. Perhaps the most common complaint planners voice about hotel salespeople is their failure to take time to research a prospect's business. Planners resent the waste of their time when given a sales pitch by a salesperson from a property wholly unsuited to their requirements. Tip sheets can be used to screen prospects and then follow up with a telephone call or letter asking for an appointment. They are also an invaluable tool for customizing a telephone appointment call and the actual sales presentation.

to reach the decision maker. The intermediary is often your contact person in determining who makes the decision for holding meetings and can be your best friend — or worst enemy; his or her response and level of assistance can make the difference between whether you get an appointment or not! These people can be an added source of information, too. It is important, then, to build rapport with these support people. They should always be treated with respect, and, for best results, should be told the objective of your call — and how it will benefit their boss.

Figure 7.6. SAMPLE CALL REPORT.

RED LION HOTELS

CALL REPORT

FIRST CALL
REPEAT CALL
FILE NO.

COMPANY / ORGANIZATION:

STREET ADDRESS

CITY   STATE   ZIP

CONTACT: PHONE:

DOES YOUR COMPANY HAVE MEETINGS?   ☐ NO   ☐ YES   HOW OFTEN?

SIZE   CONTACT

WHEN IS YOUR NEXT MEETING?   WHERE

DO YOU NEED GUEST ROOMS?   ☐ NO   ☐ YES   HOW MANY

WHO MAKES THE RESERVATIONS?

DO YOU NEED OUT OF TOWN RESERVATIONS?   ☐ NO ☐ YES   WHERE?

DO YOU HAVE SUCH THINGS AS:

- CHRISTMAS PARTIES
- AWARDS BANQUETS
- OTHER

ARE YOU OR ANYONE ELSE IN YOUR COMPANY AFFILIATED WITH AN ASSOCIATION?

COMMENTS:

SALESPERSON   DATE

FORM NO. 001-S47 (4/88)

Call reports are used by salespeople to survey the needs of a potential contact and to trace the follow-up on each account. At some properties, surveys are taken by support staff and the names of qualified prospects are passed on to the salespeople for follow-up.

Meeting planners are usually busy, and their time is scarce, so you should remember that the objective of your call is to simply set an appointment — not to make a sale. Once you have reached the decision maker, the telephone appointment call involves three steps: opening the call, the presentation, and setting the appointment (see box titled "Sample Script for a Telephone Appointment Call").

Be careful that your telephone effort to make an appointment doesn't turn into such a detailed telephone "visit" that the prospect feels he or she has received enough information to withhold the appointment. It is better to be there in person. Stress that you have material, such as an audiovisual presentation, that must be shown.

Telephone Sales Call Follow-up

It is just as important to follow up on your telephone calls as it is on your personal calls, especially since a telephone call does not leave as lasting an impression as a personal visit. Since you are either looking for information or an appointment when you make telephone contact, you should take the time to write a friendly note thanking the prospect for his or her time or confirming an appointment date.

Use this further contact as an additional pre-sale tool. Along with a professionally typed letter, include requested information (room rate sheet, menus, etc.) or some hotel brochures to familiarize the prospect with your property before you arrive. Then, a few days later, you can call the prospect to verify that they received your materials.

This type of follow-up not only keeps you in the prospect's mind, but also demonstrates your property's commitment to customer service. Meeting planners, especially those who are nonprofessionals or those with limited experience, are more likely to choose a property that has demonstrated its willingness to work closely with its clients.

Handling Inquiries

In today's high tech world, many meeting planners prefer doing business via e-mail, and sales departments without e-mail will find themselves left behind. Today, the Hilton chain equips its salespeople with BlackBerry hand-held wireless units to enable them to read and respond to email communications as timing is critical for clients with short-term meetings and the hotel that responds first often gets the business. Larry Luteran, vice president of industry relations for the chain, says:

> "Speed to market is critical now. A good response time used to be two
> days, then it was 24 hours, and now it's a few hours."[9]

Inquiries about your property also come via requests for proposals on the Internet or your hotel's web site, by fax, telephone calls or mail and from walk-ins. Walk-ins should always be immediately referred to a hotel salesperson; other inquiries require an immediate follow-up by telephone (see Figure 7.7).

A large number of properties use voice mail systems. While these systems are convenient, many planners are put off by them. They want a timely response, so sales department phones should be answered by a live person. Not only does this show that a property is interested in the planner's business, it provides the opportunity for the salesperson to determine the prospect's needs.

SAMPLE SCRIPT FOR A TELEPHONE APPOINTMENT CALL

There are three steps in making a telephone appointment call once you have reached the decision-maker: opening the call; the presentation; and setting the appointment. Sample statements include:

Opening the Call

"Hello, Mr. Stubbs. My name is Diane Street, sales manager of the Oakbrook Hotel, the new hotel just down the street from your offices. Since we are neighbors and so convenient, I thought you would be interested in hearing about our hotel and the affordable meeting package we have just designed for local businesses."

The Presentation

"Mr. Stubbs, from my research, I've learned that you schedule intensive training meetings lasting two or three days with several evening working sessions. We have developed a 24-hour meeting program for companies with needs such as yours. The program reserves your meeting rooms on a 24-hour basis so that you will not be inconvenienced with removing training materials each evening and resetting equipment the next morning. In addition, our copying equipment is available to you 24 hours a day for any timely additions or changes in your handout materials."

Setting the Appointment

"I know you'll be impressed with our state-of-the-art meeting rooms and our convention service staff who will assist you in staging successful training meetings. When could we meet for lunch to discuss your upcoming employee development seminars?
"Would you prefer the beginning or later part of the week? Is 11:30 or 12:00 most convenient for you?
"Great. I'll see you Thursday at 12 noon at our concierge desk. I'll have my name tag on so you can recognize me.
"Thank you for your time, Mr. Stubbs. I'm looking forward to meeting with you personally. Have a good day."

Note that the salesperson clearly identified herself and her hotel, stated the purpose of her call and how the prospect would benefit from an appointment, appealing to his need for convenient meeting facilities. Note that in setting the appointment, she asked forced-choice questions, giving the planner a choice between two positive alternatives.

Inquiry calls should be handled like sales calls, and all inquries -- no matter what their source -- should be followed up by a phone call. Salespeople are not simply order takers. During the call, the salesperson should ask enough questions to be able to present the property effectively. By getting to know the prospect and his or her needs, even if the property cannot handle the business at that time, a relationship has been built and there is a greater potential for future business.

Telemarketing

Besides individual telephone calls, the hospitality industry is making extensive use of **telemarketing** — large-scale telephone qualifying and research — to identify potential prospects. While the larger chains have used telemarketing for some time, the practice has become more widespread. Smaller properties have found that telemarketing can be an invaluable tool to reach prospects before sending salespeople out on expensive sales calls.

Telemarketing falls primarily into two basic categories: qualifying and market research. When a property simply wishes to obtain information, smaller properties can utilize additional staff — secretaries, front desk personnel, etc. — to assist in a telephone effort. It

Figure 7.7. CROWNE PLAZA'S GUARANTEED RESPONSE TO INQUIRIES.

In today's competitive marketplace, it is essential that hotels make immediate responses to inquiries. This ad for the Crowne Plaza Hotels & Resorts promotes the chain's 2-Hour Response Guarantee, which promises to respond to a Request for Proposal within two hours or the chain will take 5% off the group's master account.

should be noted, however, that this type of "telephone blitz" is not true telemarketing — which is a specialized program backed by technology which offers instant access to information.

For large-scale efforts, a professional telemarketing staff is trained to work from prepared scripts. Using such a script, an experienced telemarketer may reach 50 or more prospects a day, either to obtain information or to present the property and close a sale. Reduced sales budgets have caused many properties to increase telemarketing efforts through to final sales. This is especially true when dealing with prospects in distant areas that you cannot get to economically.

A good telemarketing script must be short enough to keep the prospect on the line, but long enough to get the desired information or sale. It should also be specific, with benefits to the client spelled out early. It should be structured to draw the prospect into the conversation and offer the opportunity for him or her to become involved by expressing views and needs. When pressing for an actual sale, follow the same steps as you would in a personal sales call.

Telemarketing is also used for market research, to determine exactly what meeting planners are looking for. Such information is used to upgrade facilities and services, making it easier for salespeople to present the property as meeting the needs of meeting planners.

No matter what type of telemarketing program is implemented, is it essential that it be as disciplined as any other form of selling. The staff should be thoroughly trained, and there should be clear-cut goals and follow-up to ensure that goals are being met.

Sales Blitz Selling

A **sales blitz** focuses on contacting potential clients in a concentrated area over a brief period of time (usually three days), and is an effective tool for both reaching and qualifying new business (see Best Practice box titled "Hyatt's CRUNCH Time Maximizes Sales Blitz Success"). A sales blitz may consist of simply "cold calling" on businesses and associations in an area, but unannounced, random sales calls on meeting planners are usually not a good idea. Planners often feel such calls are intrusive and discourteous. Instead, hotels should carefully plan and identify prospects prior to a sales blitz -- and, ideally, send prospective clients a letter advising them of the coming visit.

Other sales blitzes may be more elaborate. A new property, for example, may wish to use the sales blitz technique to introduce itself to the community; the blitz would serve as a way to invite potential clients to attend a special property presentation. If a sales blitz is used to introduce a new property or to promote a special property presentation, however, extensive planning is needed. The program may include audiovisual presentations, property tours, and food and beverage functions. In many cases, notables such as local or national celebrities or political figures are invited to stimulate interest and lend credibility to the property. No matter what type of program is planned, however, its ultimate purpose should be to demonstrate a property's ability to handle meetings business. It is of obvious importance, therefore, to get as many of the prospects to attend the event and receive the special presentation.

Still other properties join up with their local convention and visitors bureau to conduct a sales blitz. In this case, several entities are involved (the CVB, area hotels, destination management companies, and area attractions) in a coordinated sales effort to attract a specific market.

Best Practices

HYATT
HOTELS & RESORTS ®

Hyatt's CRUNCH Time Maximizes Sales Blitz Success

When the Hyatt chain sought to jump-start its sales efforts, it organized a program called CRUNCH TIME, which stands for: Close tentative business; Refer new business; Unite our forces; Network our clients; Clean up data base; and Have fun. The program translated into a massive 12-day sales blitz that involved more than 600 corporate and property salespeople targeting 40,000 potential customers.

The program, which included incentive prizes for top performers in a number of categories (number of calls made, revenue, referrals and so on), was kicked off when corporate headquarters sent lists of clients to be called on to individual hotels and regional offices. The lists were generated to minimize possible overlaps, and were followed up by electronic CRUNCH Grams to stimulate interest in the program and keep salespeople up to date on the campaign's progress (salespeople sent in their results every three days).

CRUNCH Time resulted in a total of 36,219 contacts made by 566 employees. Nearly 2,200 of these calls led to business closings, generating $30 million in bookings, including a single $600,000 piece of business and several bookings of approximately $500,000 each. In addition, some 1,250 referrals were sent property to property, which would likely result in additional business.

Not only did the program generate sales and sales leads, it also led to camaraderie in the sales force, and CRUNCH Time was deemed so successful that the chain planned to repeat it at least annually and expand the program to targeted segments with Catering CRUNCH and Corporate Traveler CRUNCH.

Source: Harvey Chipkin, "Success Stories That Inspire," HSMAI Marketing Review, Spring 2002, p. 10.

Whether a sales blitz will lead to a property presentation or will be used simply to survey potential clients, most properties begin planning several weeks in advance. Sales letters are often sent out to prospective clients to advise them of the coming visit. This strategy leads to "warm calls" — contacts with planners who have some idea of what the property can offer. Proper preparation is important as it will result in the sales blitz participant getting in to see more prospects and create an atmosphere conducive to selling.

When planning a sales blitz, a city directory is used to map out specific target areas. Providing each participant with a list of prospects in a concentrated area greatly reduces the traveling time involved, enabling a sales blitz participant to make 75 to 90 calls over a three-day period.

In most cases, the sales blitz is used simply to collect information, qualify prospects, or invite prospects to that special property presentation, so it is not always necessary to tie up the property's sales staff in a sales blitz effort. Some properties hire a temporary sales blitz staff or utilize sales-oriented college students for blitzes over break periods.

Each person involved should clearly understand the purpose of the blitz, including how many calls he or she is expected to make and what questions he or she can answer (if using an outside blitz team, participants are usually instructed to refer contacts to a member of the property's sales staff). Sales blitz participants should be given an adequate supply of survey sheets (see Figure 7.8) and collateral materials, such as property business cards, convention brochures, and low-cost specialty items imprinted with the property's name and telephone number to keep the property's name in front of the prospect.

A great deal of effort is put into a sales blitz, so proper follow-up is important to maximize results. It is wisest to evaluate the results of a sales blitz on a daily basis. This

Figure 7.8. SAMPLE SALES BLITZ SURVEY SHEET.

Sales Blitz Survey Sheet

Organization_____

Address_____

_____Zip_____Phone_____

Contact_____Title_____

Contact_____Title_____

1. How many meetings do you have a year?_____ When?_____
   Size_____ Who plans them?_____

Contact_____Title_____

When is your next meeting? _____

Where are meetings usually held? _____

2. Do you have incoming visitors that require sleeping accommodations?

   Yes_____ No_____ How many per month?_____

   If yes, where are they housed?_____

   Do you reserve the room? Yes_____ No_____ (If not, who does?)

Contact_____Title_____

3. Does your organization plan such things as:

   ___Christmas Parties?   ___Retirement Dinners?
   ___Award Dinners?   ___Other Social Events?

   Are you the organizer, or is there a social chairman?
       Yes____ No____ Contact_____

4. Are you, or any of your associates, affiliated with any other organizations or associations that might have need for meeting or banquet space? Yes____ No____

Name_____Contact_____

Comments:

Taken by: _____Date Taken_____

Source: Howard Feiertag, "Blitzes and Sales Calls: Indispenable Selling Tools," *HSMAI Marketing Review.*

During a sales blitz, survey sheets are used to record prospect information. Once qualified, the prospects with the highest potential for business will merit additional contact. Besides this vital information, additional questions might include: "Who else is involved in decision making?" and "How are meeting sites selected?"

enables the sales manager to determine if there are any leads that should be followed up immediately, to make any changes in strategy (if, for example, there seems to be considerable interest in one geographical area, some participants can be redirected to that location) and, in cases where incentives are offered, reward the day's most successful participant (thereby motivating the other participants).

Trade Show Selling

Trade shows provide an opportunity for a property to reach meeting planners (see Figure 7.9). One of the advantages of trade show participation is that you will meet people who are buying. Anne Marie Spatharakis, senior account executive for the Renaissance Hotel in Washington, D.C., extols the advantages of trade shows:

> "Trade shows are great places for big sales to happen. Calling on customers individually takes a lot of time and effort, but at shows you have everyone either buying or selling, so there is a collaborative spirit where quality matches are made."[10]

Another advantage is the relatively low cost. While trade show participation requires effort and expense, it can be cost-effective. According to the Center for Exhibition Industry Research, the average dollar amount to close a sale from a trade show lead is $625, while it costs $1,117 to close a personal sales call. And, if your convention bureau is exhibiting in a trade show, it may be posible for your property to share booth space and expenses with them. In addition to these benefits, trade shows also provide excellent opportunities to see what your competition is doing!

There are also some disadvantages to selling through trade shows. First, there is the initial cost and transportation of a property's display; these expenses are especially prohibitive for small properties that must compete with the elaborate displays of larger com-

Figure 7.9. TRADE SHOWS FOR REACHING THE MEETINGS MARKET.

Exhibit Shows	Number of years	Number of exhibitors	Usual attendance
1. American Society of Association Executives Annual Meeting & Expo	49	800	5,000
2. Incentive Travel & Meetings Exec Show (The Motivation Show)	35	963	14,319
3. Religious Conference Management Association Annual Conference	31	688	1,250
4. Meeting Professionals International Annual Meeting	21	350	1,700
5. Health Care Convention & Exhibitors Association Annual Meeting	46	130	600
6. International Association for Exhibition Management	10	125	1,000
7. HSMAI's Affordable Meetings	15	550	1,800
8. IACVB's Destination Showcase	19	300	1,150
9. IMEX Incentive Meetings Show	3	3000	7,000

Thirty years ago, the only major industry trade show was the American Society of Association Executives Expo. Today, there are a number of shows aimed at different segments of the meetings industry. Above is a brief listing of national and regional exhibit shows, the number of years each show has been held, and recent attendance figures. When selecting a show at which to exhibit, keep in mind your primary target markets and plan your trade show strategy specifically for these markets.

petitors. Secondly, your competition is likely to be participating in the same show and wooing the same target markets you are trying to attract. And, lastly, your booth time may be taken up by a number of meeting planners who will not generate business for your property.

To make the most of trade show selling, planning is again the key (see Figure 7.10). A pre-show action plan identifying potential clients and a strategy for contact and follow-up is an excellent way to ensure that the maximum benefit is derived from trade show participation. Strong potential business should be targeted, and your representatives should find out where these planners are staying; this enables your reps to see planners that don't make it to the property's booth. It is best, therefore, to allow at least two days to make calls before the show opens and to allow at least one day after the show to follow up on new local contacts made through the show.

Both your booth and personnel should adequately reflect your property's image and professionalism. Personnel should always be friendly, courteous and informative, and the

Figure 7.10. EXHIBITING AT TRADE SHOWS.

Exhibiting at Trade Shows

Before

- When choosing trade shows, ask show management for a rating ratio of meeting planners to salespeople.
- Contact previous exhibitors; ask about attendance and quality of prospective buyers. Set measurable sales and qualified lead goals.
- Use pre-show promotions. Target important prospects by mail or phone. Arrive early to make sales calls in the area prior to the show.
- Be prepared with meeting planner kits for distribution at the booth.
- Meet with the sales team to clarify team objectives, set individual goals. Train salespeople with written sales scripts. Role play different sales situations — using a sales brochure, qualifying prospects and securing information from prospects.
- Design a custom lead form to qualify your prospects.

During

- Set up the booth in advance and assign salespeople to no more than three hour shifts before a break.
- Ask quick, qualifying questions to help determine interest. Be courteous and friendly but discontinue discussion when the visitor is not a prospect.
- Smile; act and look knowledgeable; stand, don't sit; don't smoke, eat or drink in the booth.
- Use prospect's business card to take notes of specific needs for follow-up.
- Schedule sales team meetings before and after each day of the show to discuss problems and solutions and to coach the sales team.

And After the Show

- The sixty days after the show are most critical. Assign responsibility for following up on leads and appointments; establish deadlines for follow-ups.
- Review exhibit objectives to see if goals were attained. Each dollar invested should return ten dollars in sales.
- Use the telephone, mail and email to follow up. Make sure all your leads are followed up within 48 hours after the show and your results will soar.

Used with permission of Howard Feiertag, CHSE, CMP.

To make the most of trade show exhibiting, the above list details what to do before, during, and after a trade show.

booth should be arranged in a manner that involves the prospects. Rather than setting tables across the booth, it is more effective to place tables along the sides and back to draw people into the display. Giveaway materials should be kept to a minimum; it is a mistake to offer too many giveaways. Most meeting planners prefer to "travel light" and do not wish to be overwhelmed by too many materials. It is far better to show a video brochure and/or give live presentations at scheduled times. These can be enhanced by one or two pieces of concise, informative material accompanied by your business card.

No matter how simple or elaborate your display, it is important to always remember your purpose: selling. It is important to qualify prospects. If your property is a resort, for example, it would have little appeal for a meeting planner seeking airport hotels at which to hold training meetings. While you shouldn't discount these prospects entirely — they may have contacts who can use your property or may have use for your property at a later date — it is important to deal primarily with meeting planners who offer a high potential for business for your property. In other words, you must quickly qualify prospects to determine how much time you should spend with them. A survey sheet or questionnaire is an excellent way to determine if a booth's visitor is a good prospect. If he or she is unlikely to have a need for your property, be polite but brief and move on to a better qualified prospect as soon as possible.

Trade show selling is not complicated if you have set clear-cut goals for before and during the show and have established guidelines for follow-up. The contacts made at a trade show should be followed up as quickly as possible after the show to keep your property fresh in the contact's mind. This interest and demonstration of your property's commitment can result in both business from your trade show contacts and referral business in the future.

Selling with Convention Bureaus

Even if you represent a large property with extensive convention facilities, a local convention bureau can be an invaluable partner in selling to the meetings market, even serving as an extension of your property's sales staff. Bill Snyder, past president of the Anaheim Convention and Visitors Bureau states:

> "A Bureau's function is to bring conventions, trade shows and tourists to its respective area. A secondary objective is, of course, to offer those services which necessarily follow the attraction of conventions, trade shows and tourists.
>
> "A Bureau should be the nucleus for the sales effort in the visitor industry for that community and should also represent the point of "one stop shopping" for any prospect or client contemplating holding a convention or trade show in that city. A Bureau must be impartial in its representation of its facilities if it is to be successful."[11]

Convention bureaus are structured in different ways. Some are membership organizations to which hotels, transportation companies, restaurants, and local merchants turn to organize efforts to bring in convention business. Others are funded through **room taxes** and work to promote general tourism (see Figure 7.11). In some cases, they operate exhibition halls that were built with public funds.

The convention bureau's sales office is set up similarly to a hotel sales office, but on a larger scale. Its job, sometimes called **destination marketing**, is to sell the city, bring

Figure 7.11. FUNDING OF CONVENTION AND VISITORS BUREAUS.

Bed Taxes in Selected Trade Show Cities

City	Bed Tax
Houston	15%
Chicago	14.9%
Los Angeles	14%
New York City	13.25% + $2.00 per night
Atlanta	13%
Anaheim	11%
Las Vegas	9%

Las Vegas boasts far and away the largest bureau budget, double that of Hawaii, which in turn is nearly double that of Reno.

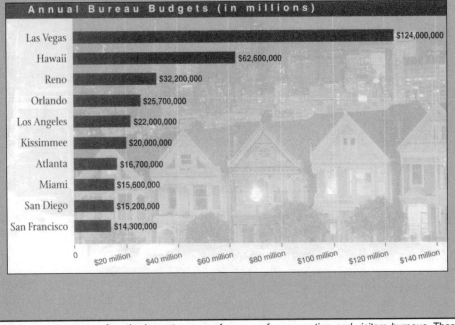

Annual Bureau Budgets (in millions)

Las Vegas	$124,000,000
Hawaii	$62,600,000
Reno	$32,200,000
Orlando	$25,700,000
Los Angeles	$22,000,000
Kissimmee	$20,000,000
Atlanta	$16,700,000
Miami	$15,600,000
San Diego	$15,200,000
San Francisco	$14,300,000

Hotel room taxes are often the largest source of revenue for convention and visitors bureaus. These taxes, also known as bed or pillow taxes, are levied on a percentage basis of room rate, and nationally account for over 60 percent of the typical convention and visitors bureaus' budgets. These taxes sometimes generate controversy, however, as they are not always used to promote the city as a convention, group meeting, and vacation destination. In some cities, these taxes are instead diverted to fund community programs.

conventions to the area and to make the group's stay productive and enjoyable (see box titled "Destination Marketing"). When a bureau receives a letter or phone call from a meeting group saying the city has been selected for its convention, the bureau sends out a **convention lead form** to local hotels (see Figure 7.12). Many bureaus now distribute this information electronically, sending leads to selected hotels via the Internet. The hotel may then contact the group.

In addition to providing leads to area hotels and convention support firms, the bureau also assists in executing conventions, often supplying registration clerks, guides, spouses' program personnel, and so on. Most important for hotels, most convention bureaus also provide a housing bureau for placing delegates in the city's hotels when large conventions are booked.

Figure 7.12. SAMPLE CONVENTION LEAD FORM.

SAN FRANCISCO
CONVENTION & VISITORS BUREAU
1390 MARKET STREET, SAN FRANCISCO, CALIFORNIA 94102

CONVENTION LEAD FORM

Date ___xxx___

TO _____ All major hotels

FROM _____ Matt Miller

GROUP _____ XYZ CORPORATION

CONTACT _____ Mr. John Jones   TITLE _____ Convention Manager

ADDRESS _____ 6000 K Street N.W.

CITY _____ Washington, DC 20097   PHONE _____ (202) 123-4567

ATTENDANCE _____ 500   NO OF ROOMS _____ 350

EXHIBIT SPACE NET SQ FT _____ 4000

REQUESTED DATES _____ February 3-6, February 10-13, 2004
arrivals 2/2 or 2/9; departures 2/7 or 2/14

MEETING REQUIREMENTS

2/2 or 2/9	6 p.m. reception for 300 people
2/3 or 2/10	8 a.m. breakfast for 150
	12 noon lunch for 500
	9:00-5:00 general session for 500 theatre style
2/4 or 2/11	9:00-12 noon 5 workshops for 100 each theatre style; afternoon free
2/5 or 2/12	9:00-12 noon general session for 500 theatre style
	12 noon reception & lunch for 500
	2:00-5:00 5 workshops for 100 each
2/6 or 2/13	9:00-12 noon general session for 500 theatre style
	7 p.m. reception & dinner dance for 500 people

San Francisco is definite; hotel selection within three months

Please copy the Bureau on all your correspondance

History

2001	New Orleans	476	registered; 327 rooms used
2002	Las Vegas	498	registered; 319 rooms used

This is an example of a form sent by the San Francisco Convention & Visitors Bureau to hotels in the city advising them of an upcoming convention. Note that the form includes the group's requirements (number of rooms, types of functions that will be held, room space requirements, etc.) to enable hotels to decide if they can realistically service the business.

If your area has a convention bureau, it most likely is a member of the IACVB, the International Association of Convention and Visitors Bureaus (the name of the organization was changed to Destination Marketing Association International –DMAI – on August 2, 2005). If so, you are fortunate, because the IACVB offers a wealth of detailed, confiden-

DESTINATION MARKETING

Over a century ago, in 1895, Detroit hotelier Milton J. Carmichael presented an idea of promoting the city as a whole to help build individual hotel business. The concept proved to be so successful that the Detroit hoteliers created the nation's first convention bureau. Before long, the idea spread to other cities, and today hundreds of such bureaus exist around the world.

The convention bureaus' primary objective is *destination marketing* — promoting their respective areas as a whole to attract meetings and convention business. To do so, convention bureaus engage in advertising campaigns, participate in trade shows, and offer a number of services to meeting planners, including general destination information, centralized housing of convention delegates, and registration services.

Once given a meeting's requirements — dates, rates and space — bureaus go to work for planners. The bureau usually arranges site inspection visits. After a group is booked, the bureau's focus shifts from marketing to service.

While the scope of services offered by bureaus depends largely on staff size and budget, some bureaus have become very innovative. The Chicago Convention and Tourism Bureau utilizes its in-house telemarketing department to help planners build attendance at conventions. Using a prepared script and a database of the convening group's members, the bureau's staff makes up to 2,500 calls free of charge. This service is credited with increasing convention attendance in the Windy City by as much as 16 percent. With each additional attendee representing an average of $800 in spending, such effort benefits both planners and local businesses.

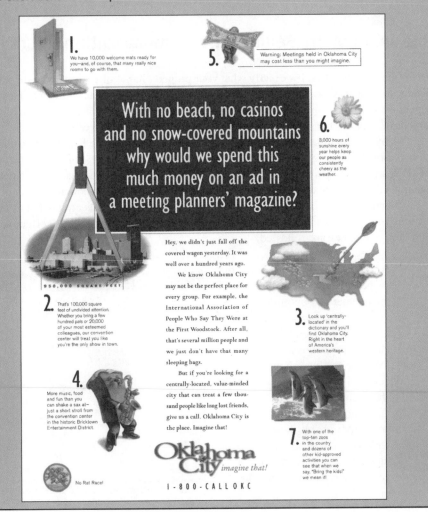

tial information to assist you in your selling efforts. Each IACVB member receives and files reports dealing with convention performances and characteristics of all associations that convened within the member's city. This data includes promised attendance and actual attendance figures, prices paid, concessions granted, and almost everything else you would want to know about a prospect. When you track a convention over a period of five years, a pattern emerges that enables you to decide whether or not you have a good chance to get such business — and how to go after it.

In addition to maintaining records on major associations and corporations, bureaus also subscribe to key association and corporate publications, such as the <u>Encyclopedia of Associations</u> and <u>The Directory of Corporate Meeting Planners</u>, and make them available to local hotels for research. These publications, among others, are invaluable in securing the meetings market, but are often too expensive for individual properties to purchase.

The most important facet of working with convention bureaus, however, is the advantage of pooled resources. The convention bureau serves as a coordinator when the size of an event makes it mandatory to present the sales proposal as a group and to house the delegates in a number of hotels. And, since the convention bureau's function is to promote the area as a whole, its efforts — exhibitions at trade shows, print advertising and direct mail efforts — will directly benefit your property and serve as an additional marketing resource in helping you to obtain a share of business.

Site Inspection Selling and Familiarization Tours

One of the best ways to show exactly what your property has to offer is to invite the meeting planner to visit it personally. This can be done in two ways: on an individual basis *(site inspection selling)* or in a structured group setting *(familiarization tours)*, which offer a number of planners the chance to experience what the hotel has to offer.

Many meeting planners will not book a site unless they have had the opportunity to see it personally. In a recent survey conducted by *Meetings & Conventions* magazine and NTM Research, 90 percent of all planners reported that they personally visit potential meeting sites before making a final decision (see sidebar titled: "Shopping Around").[12]

Therefore, a **site inspection tour**, at which prospective clients are invited to personally tour your hotel, is an ideal sales situation. Site inspection selling is most effective if the following guidelines are followed:

- Always schedule a visit when the property is busy. This will give the planner an opportunity to see your efficient service in action — and will give credibility to your claims of excellence.
- Don't be too busy, however, to devote time to the planner. He or she should be greeted like a guest, and should have the opportunity to meet those people with whom he or she will be dealing (the catering manager, convention services manager, and so on).

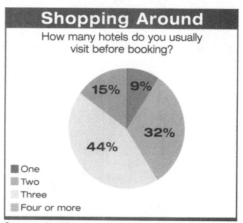

Shopping Around

How many hotels do you usually visit before booking?

9%
15%
32%
44%

■ One
■ Two
■ Three
■ Four or more

Source: Art Pfenning, "Site Visits Still Key," *Meetings & Conventions*, April 2004, p. 24.

- Alert the staff of the impending site inspection. If possible, post a photograph of the meeting planner and provide pertinent information to enable employees to greet the planner by name.
- A welcoming note from the general manager upon the planner's arrival and a brief visit with the general manager sometime during the visit are good gestures. Many planners indicate they can tell a lot about how a hotel is run by meeting the general manager.
- Feature only those items of interest to the planner. Don't waste everyone's time showing your state-of-the-art audiovisual equipment to a planner whose focus will be social functions or recreational activities.
- Train a number of staff personnel to serve as "tour guides" in the event a salesperson is away. These staff members should be able to answer questions — and sell features as benefits. It is also helpful if they can offer supplemental material, such as photographs of past successful events, third-party endorsements, and so on, to capture the planner's interest.
- Remember the purpose of suggesting a site inspection: selling. Knowing your property, competition, and prospect are keys. Follow the six steps of personal selling discussed in the opening of this chapter. Laura Anevedo, meeting planner for Alder Droz, Inc. says:

> "My favorite part about site inspections is being able to visualize my next meeting taking place at the prospective property. Usually the salesperson is putting his/her best foot forward in order to capture the busines and is really excited about showing off the property. If the salesperson has done homework on my past programs, he/she can really be influential in my ultimate decision to book a program at that property."[13]

Many of today's meeting planners, especially those who plan a number of small meetings, do not have time to personally tour every hotel that can potentially stage their meetings. Hotels are responding by offering *virtual site tours*. While some hotels already offer photographs and moving images of their guestrooms and their meeting facilities on their websites, it is much more effective for a hotel to combine this sales tool with an actual telephone call with a salesperson. In this way, the salesperson can determine the planner's needs and steer him or her to specific features of interest as well as answer any questions that might arise.

If a hotel targets several market segments, it should consider tailoring virtual tours to individual segment needs. Some hotels create a "bank" of digital photographs to enable them to present features most important to a potential client. Whether these photographs are presented online or emailed to the client, you will capture far more business if a "live" representative from the property walks the prospect through the presentation.

Familiarization (fam) tours require more planning than individual site inspection visits, and, since they can be expensive for the property, involve qualifying prospective visitors. Michael Smith, Director of Convention Sales for the Portland (OR) Visitors' Association, states:

> "We do not invite people just because they happen to plan meetings. Unless they are seriously thinking of meeting in Portland, they are not invited. Our members need to know that the people we are bringing in are legitimate and the trip is an investment."[14]

Qualified meeting planners may be contacted either by mail or telephone, and should be given a reasonable lead time to make plans (four to six weeks is the norm). If a group tour, planners invited should have similar professional needs. One planner stated:

> "I hate to go on fams where everyone is an association planner and I'm the only corporate planner. They show you everything from an association standpoint, and there's a big difference."

The property should let attendees know exactly what the fam tour involves: its duration; what is included (meals, transportation, etc.); and whom the invitation includes (spouse, other members of the selection committee, etc.). When the meeting planners arrive for the tour, they should be greeted individually and given a schedule of events. Events should be planned to show prospects exactly what the property can offer (see "Best Practices" box that follows). Staff members usually handle property tours, although an outside person (a member of the local Convention and Visitors Bureau, for example) may conduct off-property tours of the area's leisure and cultural activities.

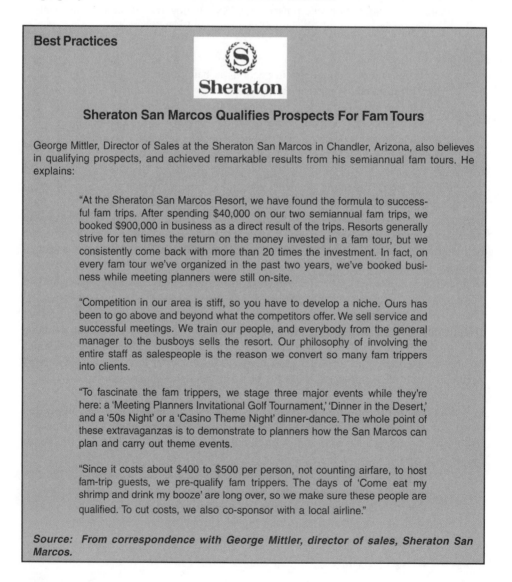

Best Practices

Sheraton San Marcos Qualifies Prospects For Fam Tours

George Mittler, Director of Sales at the Sheraton San Marcos in Chandler, Arizona, also believes in qualifying prospects, and achieved remarkable results from his semiannual fam tours. He explains:

"At the Sheraton San Marcos Resort, we have found the formula to successful fam trips. After spending $40,000 on our two semiannual fam trips, we booked $900,000 in business as a direct result of the trips. Resorts generally strive for ten times the return on the money invested in a fam tour, but we consistently come back with more than 20 times the investment. In fact, on every fam tour we've organized in the past two years, we've booked business while meeting planners were still on-site.

"Competition in our area is stiff, so you have to develop a niche. Ours has been to go above and beyond what the competitors offer. We sell service and successful meetings. We train our people, and everybody from the general manager to the busboys sells the resort. Our philosophy of involving the entire staff as salespeople is the reason we convert so many fam trippers into clients.

"To fascinate the fam trippers, we stage three major events while they're here: a 'Meeting Planners Invitational Golf Tournament,' 'Dinner in the Desert,' and a '50s Night' or a 'Casino Theme Night' dinner-dance. The whole point of these extravaganzas is to demonstrate to planners how the San Marcos can plan and carry out theme events.

"Since it costs about $400 to $500 per person, not counting airfare, to host fam-trip guests, we pre-qualify fam trippers. The days of 'Come eat my shrimp and drink my booze' are long over, so we make sure these people are qualified. To cut costs, we also co-sponsor with a local airline."

Source: From correspondence with George Mittler, director of sales, Sheraton San Marcos.

As with individual site-inspection selling, property salespeople should try to get a meeting commitment before the guests leave the property. If this is not possible (in some cases, for example, the planner must report back to the site selection committee), the fam tour should be followed up as soon as possible. Many properties include a questionnaire in their follow up letter, asking what the participants liked and disliked. This type of questionnaire not only can assist the property to plan better fam tours, but can also be used to provide insights into the needs, likes and dislikes of the individual participants.

Fam tours not only bring business from the participants, but can influence their peers as well. Today, a number of properties are using technology to make their fam tours available to a wide audience of meeting planners. A fam tour, marketed to a specific segment of planners, is videotaped and is made available on tape and on the property's web site. This not only enhances the experience for the participants but also provides a "virtual tour" of the property -- and feedback from the attendees -- to other meeting planners.

Chapter Summary

As you can see, personal selling — whether it be an individual effort, such as a face-to-face sales call or telephone call, or a strategy to sell to groups at a trade show — plays a key role in booking meetings. But direct selling is not the only way to introduce your property to meeting planners. In the next chapter, we will see how *advertising* can supplement your sales efforts. We will take a look at how this sales tool can work hand-in-hand with personal selling to help generate lucrative meetings market business for your property.

 Endnotes:

1. "Interviews With Marketing Leaders," *HSMAI Marketing Review*, Spring 2002, p. 35.
2. Rayna Katz, "Planners as Honest as Relationships Dictate," *Meeting News*, May 3, 2004, p. 1.
3. "A New Approach to Selling," *The Meeting Professional*, February and April 2000, pp. 43 & 46.
4. Rayna Katz, "Planners, Sales Reps Often Out of Sync," *Meeting News*, March 15, 2004, p. 10.
5. Joan Barker, "Stand Out in the Crowd," *HSMAI Marketing Review*, Fall 2002, p. 17.
6. Robert Gilbert, "Mastering the Basics," *Lodging*, October 2003, p. 33.
7. Tom McCarthy, "Don't Forget to Rehearse," *Lodging Hospitality*, January 2005, p. 22.
8. Becky Cumming and Melina Legos, "Squaring Off," *Successful Meetings*, June 1999, p. 37.
9. Rayna Katz, "Hilton Eases Buying Process Via Package of Web Enhancements," *Meeting News*, January 31, 2005.
10. Ruth Hill, "Lost and Found," *HSMAI Marketing Review*, Spring 2003, p. 47.
11. From correspondence with Bill Snyder, past president, Anaheim Convention and Visitors Bureau.
12. Art Pfenning, "Site Visits Still Key," *Meetings & Conventions*, April 2004, p. 24.

13. "In the Trenches," *Meetings in the West*, July 2000, p. 6.
14. Suzanne Miller and Ross Weiland, "Planners Want Better Fam Trips," *Meeting News*.

Additional References:

- <u>Conferences and Conventions: A Global Industry</u>, Tony Rogers, published by Elsevier Butterworth Heinemann, 2003.

- <u>Convention Tourism: International Research and Industry Perspectives</u>, Karin Weber, MSc and Kye-Sung Chon, PhD, Editors, The Haworth Hospitality Press, 2002.

- <u>Current Issues in Convention and Exhibition Facility Development</u>, Robert R. Nelson, PhD, Editor, The Haworth Hospitality Press, 2004.

- <u>Destination Marketing</u>, Richard Cartrell, Kendall Hunt Publishing, Dubuque, Iowa.

- <u>Hospitality Sales: A Marketing Approach</u>, Margaret Shaw and Susan Morris, John Wiley and Sons, 2000.
www.hospitality@wiley.com

- <u>Hospitality Sales and Marketing, Fourth Edition</u>, James Abbey, Educational Insitute, AHLA, 2003.
www.ei-ahla.org

- <u>Hospitality Sales: Selling Smarter</u>, Judy Signaw and David Bojanic, Thomson Learning, 2005.

Internet Sites:

For more information, visit the following Internet sites. Internet addresses can change without notice. If a site is no longer available at the address listed below, a search engine can be used to find the new address or additional, related sites.

Chicago Convention and Tourism Bureau - www.chicagoil.org
Educational Institute of the American Hotel & Lodging Association –
www.ei-ahla.org
Hospitality Sales & Marketing Association International (HSMAI) – www.hsmai.org
International Association of Convention and Visitor Bureaus (IACVB) –
www.iacvb.org
Sales & Marketing Executives (SME) International – www.smei.org

Study Questions:

1. Identify the steps in making a personal sales call. Why is each important?
2. List the steps in making a telephone appointment call. Why is follow-up especially important after making telephone contact? What kind of follow-up can be done?
3. In what other ways is the telephone used to sell to and service customers?
4. What is a sales blitz? Why can a sales blitz be a cost-effective sales tool?
5. What is a trade show? How can a property make the most of its trade show exhibit?
6. What are the advantages of working with a convention bureau to secure business?
7. What is a "fam" tour? What steps should a property take to ensure that a "fam" tour is successful?

Key Terms:

Appointment call. A prearranged appointment with a prospect to introduce the features and benefits offered by a property. During this visit, the salesperson may or may not attempt to close the sale.

Call report. A document, usually resulting from some personal contact, that provides general information about an account (address, contact person, etc.) as well as remarks on the needs of the group and any action steps that can be taken to sell the hotel's products and services to the group.

Close-ended question. A question requiring a specific answer that often can be given in just a few words.

Cold call. A fact-finding call on a prospect with whom there has been little or no previous contact; often made without a definite appointment. Sometimes referred to as **canvassing**.

Convention lead form. Information sheet used by convention and visitors bureaus to circulate announcements about meetings to hotels, destination management companies and other potential suppliers.

Destination marketing. Promotion of a particular location as a meeting site and/or tourist attraction.

Familiarization (fam) tour. Free or reduced-rate trip given to meeting planners, travel agents, travel writers and other sources of potential business to acquaint them with a property or destination, and to stimulate the booking of an event.

Major close. A question or statement at the end of a sales presentation that asks for a definite commitment on the prospect's part.

Open-ended question. A question that gives a prospect the opportunity to express his or her feelings and knowledge.

Room tax. Tax placed on hotel/motel room rentals. Generally all or part of the revenues generated from these taxes are used to finance the operation of convention facilities. Also called a **bed tax** or **occupancy tax**.

Presentation book. Sometimes called a **sales kit**, this sales tool provides detailed information on a property's facilities and services. Materials should include floor plans, photographs of rooms and creative banquets, sample menus, complimentary letters from satisfied guests and favorable press comments. In some cases, special presentation books are prepared as handouts for meeting planners visiting the property on fam tours.

Property fact book. A summary of what a lodging property has to offer, including: numbers and types of guestrooms; room rates; booking policies; food service available, including menus, seating capacities and hours of operation; descriptions, layouts and capacities of meeting and banquet facilities; recreational facilities and area amenities. The property fact book is used as a tool for salespeople, enabling them to translate the property's features into benefits.

Sales blitz. Concentrated canvassing by several sales representatives of a selected geographic area over a specific time period in order to gather information on potential leads.

Site inspection tour. Prospective customers visit the property and are given a tour that showcases such features as guestrooms, meeting facilities, food and beverage facilities, recreational amenities and other property services, such as valet parking, shuttle service and other services that may give the property an edge in the site selection process.

Telemarketing. The systematic use of the telephone for marketing or sales purposes.

Trial close. A statement or question posed by the salesperson during a sales presentation that seeks to evoke a positive response from the client.

Learning Objectives:

In this chapter, we will discuss the types of advertising most commonly used to reach the meetings market. We will focus on print ads, collateral materials, direct mail, and the newest medium for business-to-business marketers, the Internet. In addition, we'll look at how to plan an advertising strategy and discuss how public relations and publicity can be used to project an image that will attract meeting planners to your property. When you have studied this chapter, you will:

- Be able to describe the various types of media used to advertise to meeting planners.

- Know what factors are involved in developing an effective advertising strategy.

- Be able to explain the difference between public relations and publicity and tell how each is used to project the desired image for your property.

Outline

Print Advertising
- Trade Magazines
- Hotel Directories

Using Technology for Advertising
- The Internet
- E-mail Advertising
- Fax Transmissions

Collateral Materials
- Brochures
  - Convention Brochures
  - Video Brochures
  - CD-ROMs
- Other Collateral Materials
- Specialty Items

Direct Mail Advertising

Planning an Advertising Strategy
- Reach, Frequency, Timing, and Consistency
- Exchange Trade Advertising
- Cooperative Advertising and Strategic Partnerships
- Advertising Agencies

Public Relations and Publicity

Summary

The Planners' Perspective on Advertising

Ed Griffin, Jr., CAE
President/CEO
Florida Hotel and Motel Association
Orlando, Florida

"Advertising wins when the meeting planner understands both the benefits and the unique qualities of a product or service. The hotel must explain how the product will satisfy the planner's needs. In order to do that, the advertiser must know what's important to the planner. Planners want to know about such things as room capacities, pricing, guarantees, restrictions and value seasons. Advertisers increasingly compete for the planner's time vs. the planner's wastepaper basket...it is essential for messages to be direct, simple and concise. The ad copy must be directed specifically at the planner, with a view to planner benefits rather than product features."

8 Advertising to the Meeting Planner

A dvertising can play a key role in your sales effort since its primary function is to generate interest in your property. Advertising supplements your sales effort. It is an invaluable tool for targeting meeting planners who have not previously been reached and offers additional information to those who are aware of your facilities.

When a property advertises, its message is seen by a vast audience, generating potential leads that can be followed up by the sales staff. Marketing efforts, then, should be supported by an advertising and promotional strategy that is carefully planned and executed.

One of the benefits of advertising is that it, like sales presentations, can be "tailored" to meet the needs of potential customers. For example, properties can target the corporate segment, whose meetings are often staged by inexperienced planners, with one type of ad and target the association segment, which looks for a desirable location as well as meeting planning assistance to increase attendance, with an ad promoting those benefits (see Figure 8.1).

While there are a number of media available, including newspapers, trade magazines, travel guides, direct mail, collateral material, outdoor advertising, radio, television, and the Internet, not all are used to reach meeting planners. You will have to make very specific choices based on your target customers, marketing goals, and budget.

Print Advertising

One of the most effective ways to reach meeting planners is through **print advertising**. Most meeting planners look for information. Advertising in printed media most likely to be seen by meeting planners can increase your property's chances of generating meetings business.

While some properties advertise in such newspapers as the *Wall Street Journal* and magazines including *Fortune* and *Time*, which are often read by meeting planners, the most promising media in which to advertise is **trade magazines**, especially the specialized meetings publications that we discussed in Chapters 4, 5, and 6.

Trade Magazines

Magazine advertising offers several advantages. First, ads can be printed in color and photographs reproduced with good quality. Second, many magazines have a long reading life. Back issues of some magazines are kept and reread, often passed on to others, giving ads a longer life. Third, and most important, magazine advertising gives the hotel an opportunity to key its convention promotion efforts to a select group of readers.

Once you have opted to use print advertising, you will need to develop effective print ads. Good print ads don't just happen. They are carefully thought out and targeted toward a specific audience (see Figure 8.2).

The most effective ads follow the AIDA principle, which focuses on *attention, interest, desire,* and *action.* To attract *attention*, your ad must stand out from the rest. In most

Figure 8.1. TAILORING ADVERTISING TO THE NEEDS OF THE MEETINGS MARKET.

The needs of corporate and association planners often differ greatly. Corporate meeting planners, especially those inexperienced in planning events, want assurance that they will have help in staging a successful meeting. Association meeting planners have an additional concern — selecting a site that will appeal to the greatest number of members as attendance is largely voluntary. These print ads are tailored to address the needs of each segment. The San Francisco Hilton ad promotes the property's experience in successfully handling all details for the meeting planner. The ad developed by the Hawaii Visitors Bureau Meetings & Conventions Department promotes Hawaii as a popular destination site for meetings, both corporate and association.

cases, this is done through the use of a **headline** or eye-catching illustration. If an illustration is used, it must tie in with the copy of the ad. Whenever possible, use *color* to attract attention. If your budget prohibits using full-color ads, even a property with limited funds can use black plus one other color to draw attention to key points.

To keep the reader *interested*, your **body copy** should be specific and to the point. Don't be reluctant to use plenty of white space and large or bold type for easy readability. Use bulleted lists for key points. Keep the copy simple, using short sentences and words that are easy to understand. Make your ad quick to read and easy to comprehend.

To build *desire*, the text should present your features as benefits and tell the reader why your property is different. If you offer special services to the meeting planner, tell them so — and offer this as a benefit to them. You may also want to include photographs of your expertise in action. But don't make the mistake of including a photograph of an empty room — nothing looks more sterile; portray action by including people in your meeting or function room photographs.

Last, but certainly not least, you will want to create an ad that stimulates *action* on the part of the reader. Since the primary purpose of your ad is to generate a response, offer a way to do so. In many cases, ads are accompanied by a reply card or include a coupon (or, at the very least, an address) to enable the respondent to request additional information. Today, most properties offer toll-free numbers, fax numbers, web addresses, and e-mail addresses to encourage prompt responses (see Figure 8.3). Peter Warren, past president of

Figure 8.2. SAMPLE PRINT AD.

I **want** someone to make me look good with my board, attendees and exhibitors.

Ask about
Wyndham Meeting Rewards

Earn up to 25,000 miles
$500 event credit
Palm™ m515 and more

WHAT'S YOUR REQUEST?[SM] Do you want enough coffee to keep 300 people on the edge of their seats? Or someone to take care of the things you haven't even thought of yet? We'd like to hear about it. Tell the meeting managers at Wyndham your idea of the perfect meeting and they'll make it happen – and give you a special reward when it's over.
Call us or visit our website. **1.888.WYNDHAM www.wyndham.com**

WYNDHAM PHOENIX 602-333-0000
50 East Adams Street • Phoenix, Arizona 85004
one block west of Phoenix Civic Plaza Convention Center

WYNDHAM PHOENIX

This print ad for the Wyndham Phoenix appeals to the personal needs of meeting planners. It offers a skilled professional to ensure that the meeting planner stages a successful event as well as special rewards for booking a meeting at the hotel.

the Hotel Sales & Marketing Association International and owner of one of the leading hospitality advertising firms, says:

> "The purpose of your ad should be to begin the process of 'awareness, interest, desire, then action.' A mistake made by some clients is to expect the ad to do everything, so they try to make their ads into brochures. Because a one page ad cannot tell the whole story, entice them to visit your website where they can find a more compelling story, or call an 800 number for more information."[1]

Always be sure your ad includes your property's name, address and your **logo**. It is highly effective to have ads that are readily identifiable, and, since your logo is distinctly yours, it should be used in all media efforts (it generally appears toward the bottom of the ad).

Figure 8.3. ADVERTISING CONTACT NUMBER.

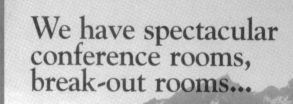

Most properties now promote their fax numbers, e-mail address(es) and their web sites address in addition to the toll-free numbers common in ads of the past. Note that the e-mail address goes directly to the sales department. This type of response mechanism connects the planner directly to a department that deals with meetings as well as enabling the planner to respond to an ad quickly.

Once you have developed the components of your ad, you will have to decide on how you want it positioned in the magazine. Magazine space is sold in a variety of sizes (see Figure 8.4). You will have to determine which size and placement will work best for your ad.

The positioning of your ad is important. Studies have shown that the reader's eye is drawn initially to the upper part of the right hand page. For an ad smaller than a full page, the position on the upper right hand page might mean more readership. It is even more preferable to have your ad positioned in the editorial section of the magazine and, when possible, ask that your ad be the only hotel ad on the page. The magazine's placement of your small ad next to competing ads may reduce its efficiency. Sometimes you can negotiate to avoid such circumstances; sometimes an additional fee will guarantee it. Good position, facing editorial copy, will help your ad do the job.

The size and frequency of your ad is largely dependent on your budget (see box titled "Magazine Advertising Rates"). While some properties can afford full-page color ads, other properties have to opt for smaller ads if they are to place them frequently. Ads are like sales calls; frequency is important. Your prospects may require several exposures to your advertising before they respond. Advertising gurus advise you to run ads at least every other month throughout the year. If, in your eyes, a publication doesn't warrant six ads a year,

Figure 8.4. MAGAZINE SPACE OPTIONS.

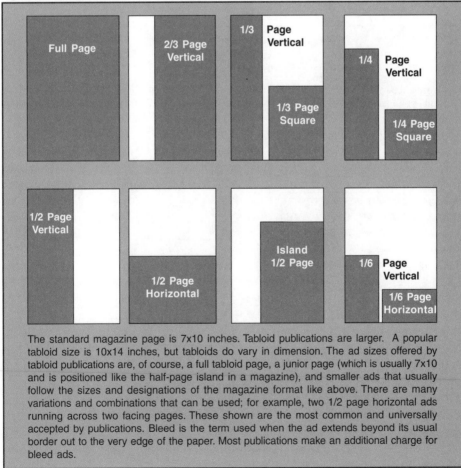

The standard magazine page is 7x10 inches. Tabloid publications are larger. A popular tabloid size is 10x14 inches, but tabloids do vary in dimension. The ad sizes offered by tabloid publications are, of course, a full tabloid page, a junior page (which is usually 7x10 and is positioned like the half-page island in a magazine), and smaller ads that usually follow the sizes and designations of the magazine format like above. There are many variations and combinations that can be used; for example, two 1/2 page horizontal ads running across two facing pages. These shown are the most common and universally accepted by publications. Bleed is the term used when the ad extends beyond its usual border out to the very edge of the paper. Most publications make an additional charge for bleed ads.

Magazine ad space is sold by the page or fraction of a page, and ads can be positioned in standard layouts in a variety of ways. These are some of the sizes and placements most commonly used.

perhaps you ought to rethink your decision to advertise in it at all. Frequency is important for effective advertising.

Hotel Directories

In addition to trade magazines, hotel directories (especially those directed to meeting planners) and other business directories are excellent media for reaching meeting planners. These directories list property information in a standard format (see Figure 8.5). The meeting planner has the opportunity to "comparison shop" various factors such as location, facilities, transportation, and price. And while your property is presented exactly as all others in these editorial listings, most directories offer advertising space for your property's print ad.

Other directories to consider are those for meeting planners, executives in business and industry, and any other publications for your specific target markets (education, military reunions, etc.). While these directories primarily list information for and about their members, most offer display advertising space through which you can directly target your market.

It is important to note, however, that advertising in these types of directories will differ from your standard advertising. You do not have the continuity that comes with a

---

Magazine Advertising Rates

Listed below is a sampling of *Meetings & Conventions* magazine's advertising rates. Costs for print advertising vary depending on a number of factors. For example, the use of color is more expensive, but color ads have a greater "stopping power" than black and white advertising. The position of an ad is also a factor; the inside and back covers are the most expensive placements because of their higher exposure. Hotels also have the option of using special inserts for a higher rate. While rates will vary from publication to publication, most magazines offer discounts to frequent advertisers.

A. Black & White

	1x	4x	7x	13x	26x
One Page	$17,015	$16,955	$16,310	$14,955	$14,390
2/3 Page	12,290	12,205	11,780	10,790	10,465
1/2 Page*	9,655	9,570	9,220	8,435	8,195
1/3 Page	6,745	6,725	6,445	5,920	5,790

*Island 1/2 Page plus: $655

B. Color

2-Color: B/W earned rate plus	$1,935
Match Color: B&W earned rate plus	2,545
Match Color Spread: B&W earned rate plus	4,425
4-Color: B&W earned rate plus	5,095
4-Color Spread: B&W earned rate plus	8,895
5-Color: B&W earned rate plus	7,385

C. Covers

	1x	7x	13x
Inside: 2-Color	$24,870	$23,200	$21,095
4-Color	27,955	26,330	24,300
Back: 4-Color	29,340	27,655	25,540

D. Inserts

	1x	7x	13x
2 pages	$16,940	$16,280	$14,960
4 pages	30,495	29,305	26,930
6 pages	41,170	39,565	36,355
8 pages	49,405	47,480	43,630

E. Commission and Credit Policy

15% to recognized agencies. Net 30 days. It is understood that all orders are accepted for space subject to our credit requirements. There are no additional discounts for cash payments.

Figure 8.5. HOTEL DIRECTORIES.

OFFICIAL MEETING FACILITIES GUIDE

Planning meetings is complicated enough without worrying about where to find the right facilities with the best accommodations and support services. That's why you need OMFG— the comprehensive directory of more than 1,500 convention centers, hotels, and resorts in the US, Canada, and the world. OMFG's five big sections are chock-full of information on site location . . . accommodations and current rates . . . dining, entertainment, and recreational facilities . . . meeting rooms, ballrooms and exhibit space . . . conference equipment and support services . . . access to airports and transportation . . . even the facts on local climate, attractions, and shopping.

Packed in OMFG's 1,100 information-filled pages, you'll find just about everything you need to help you choose the right facility at the best price. So your chances of having a flawless meeting are greatly enhanced—every time.

Published semiannually, OMFG is the complete source meeting planners turn to first.

OFFICIAL MEETING FACILITIES GUIDE EUROPE

Created especially for the European meeting planner, with complete descriptions of over 300 premier meeting sites throughout Europe and around the world. A complimentary subscription is available to qualified meeting planners in Europe.

THE ESSENTIAL GUIDEBOOK
FOR TRAVEL, MEETING,
AND CONVENTION PLANNERS

Hotel directories provide detailed information that meeting planners need to screen properties. Using directory information, planners can compare properties with regard to location, meeting facilities, amenities, recreational activities, and costs. In addition to the Official Meetings Facilities Guide, *other directories commonly used by meeting planners include* Meetings & Conventions *magazine's* Gavel, Successful Meetings' SourceBook, *and* The Hotel Guide.

series of ads in a periodical. You have just the one time ad in which to make your sales pitch. Readers of directories turn to them for *facts.* Take a leaf from their book and load your ad with details. Your ad should supply all the information necessary to generate an inquiry — and a means for the meeting planner to respond, doubly so if the publication does not have a built-in ad inquiry reader service card system.

Using Technology for Advertising

Over the past few years, a number of new technologies have made a difference in how hotels market themselves to the meetings market. While print advertising is still an important way to get a property's message out, these new technologies make it even easier for a property to reach new and existing customers and to interact with them in exciting new ways.

The Internet

The Internet (also known as the "Net") is becoming an increasingly powerful tool in marketing to meeting planners and other sources of group and transient business. Today, meeting planners and other decision makers can directly access a variety of travel services over the Internet, and they are finding it indispensible for comparing properties and services. According to the 2004 Meetings Market Report, some 94 percent of association planners used the computer to help plan meetings (this includes the use of e-mail).

Meeting planners cite a number of benefits to using the Internet, including 24-hour availability, a wealth of up-to-date information on potential meeting sites not only locally but around the world, and the ability to "interact" on most sites (see box titled "Rating of Web Site Elements Used to Help Plan Meetings"). Using the Internet can save time and money and make the planner's job easier. Cathy Shurety, meetings and events coordinator at Aluma Systems in Concord, Ontario, Canada, says:

> "The Internet definitely makes it easier for me to do my job. Now when a department comes to me with a meeting request, I can come up with a list of potential venues based on their criteria within half a day. Before the Internet, we mostly looked at local venues. Now I can easily inspect properties anywhere in the world."[2]

Rating of Web Site Elements Used to Help Plan Meetings

Web site elements considered "very useful"	Association Planners	Corporate Planners
Floor plans	74	68
Meeting space specifications	66	52
Facility search	62	65
Maps/directions	56	58
Photographs	55	49
Destination information	50	48
Virtual tours	36	42
Special dates/rates	26	34
Meeting management tools	17	27
Video	14	18

This chart ranks what is important to both association and corporate meeting planners who access a convention hotel's web site.
Source: *2004 Meetings Market Report* conducted by Meetings & Conventions *magazine.*

Meetings related magazines have made the planner's job easier by featuring popular hospitality and planning sites and giving tips on how to use the Web. Loews Hotels jumped on the "information bandwagon" by developing a 44-page "Meeting Planners' Guide to Using the Web" advertising supplement that appeared in *Meeting News*. The guide featured tips on using search engines and listed top industry sites in addition to promoting the chain's own site and properties.

Property web site. There are basically two ways in which properties can use the Internet to reach prospects. The first is for a property to set up its own Web site, allowing meeting planners and other clients to directly access a chain's site or information on specific properties. According to the 2004 Meetings Market Report, 17 percent of association planners accessed individual hotel sites to make a meeting decision. The Internet enables hotels to create high-quality presences via computer. No longer does a property have to rely on constantly updating its color brochure or getting the word out about a new product or service — using the Internet, it can create a graphic presentation featuring full-color images with sound and video and even offer a "virtual" tour of the property.

Hotels using the Internet to market their properties to meeting planners can instanteously provide them with the following:

- A listing of meeting facilities and floor plan diagrams
  (some hotel web sites have floor plans and photos of function rooms with full
  360-degree panoramas)
- The name and telephone number of a contact person
- A form to fill out about their upcoming meetings that can be faxed
  or e-mailed to the property with the click of a button
- A reservations system that lets the planner guarantee rooms by using a
  credit card

Features also include interactive electronic brochures, enabling planners to "tour" the facilities or talk to the chef and then tap into the hotel's computer to book function space for banquets and meetings as well as book their guestrooms. Most hotels now have an interactive request for proposal, and it is now possible for meeting planners to do virtually all their meeting business with a property on-line.

To promote a property, a hotel must first set up its "web site," which includes its own "address." These sites will vary significantly, depending on the property and the services it promotes, but all start with a "home page" or directory to subsequent pages or "web pages." The home page typically includes the property's name, logo, and a "menu" of information from which to select. If a chain services a number of market segments, it is best to provide links to information of specific interest. Sheraton, for example, offers a "Meeting Facilities" section, Hilton has a "Meetings & Groups" link, Marriott features a "Meeting Planning" section, and InterContinental Hotels Group offers information for both the professional and occasional meeting planner (see illustration).

The best, most effective home pages are visually attractive and should project the company's image or positioning. As with other advertising, the first step is to attract attention, and the home page should also feature navigational links (text, an icon, an image or some combination) to direct planners to site content that showcases your meeting facilities and other items of interest. Links should include other features and tools that will assist planners, including meeting guides, special offers and promotions, and, most importantly, a way to communicate with your hotel, including Request for Proposal (RFP forms) and links to direct e-mail contacts with key hotel personnel, such as the convention service manager, food and beverage manager, and so on. Subsequent Web pages should be designed to be as interactive, informative, and convenient to the user as possible. The Web pages should include all pertinent information required by a user (room rates, square footage of meeting space, a biography of your chef, etc.), interesting graphics (photos, charts and graphs, etc.), and up-to-date information.

Marriott, for example, uses its web site (www.marriott.com) to offer greater value to meeting planners. The site's meetings section contains a comprehensive suite of tools, including event space calculators, a budget calculator, a planning timeline, publicity and promotion tools, and a food and beverage planner. It also provides a link from which planners can order a free printed meeting planner's brochure. The Hilton chain (www.hilton.com) also offers support to planners with its free meeting planning software (developed with software maker Newmarket) that can be downloaded via the Groups & Meetings section of the web site. Planners can use this software to create a custom layout (including seating arrangements, tables, exhibit displays, and other elements) of a meeting room at a specific Hilton hotel or resort.[3]

Most sites now offer the opportunity for planners to search for specific meeting criteria. The planner enters specifics and the computer will search for a "match" for his or her requirements within the chain. And, as we have said earlier, RFPs are usually available. But sites should also include a direct link to the property sales office or reservation system

This website for InterContinental Hotels Group provides information of interest to both professional and occasional meeting planners. Note the links to customer service, featured offers, and a meeting and event guide in addition to a search feature that enables planners to find potential meeting sites in the chain by city, state, and country.
Source: Courtesy of InterContinental Hotels Group.

as well as pertinent e-mail addresses and your property's toll-free and fax telephone numbers.

Links to Meeting Related Websites. The second way to reach meeting planners is to "*link*" your property to other meetings-related sites, such as a CVB site (used by 13 percent of association meeting planners), city site (cited as being used by five percent of meeting planners), meeting planner services, or the sites of other firms to which planners turn for information. *Convene* magazine publishes an annual "Web Site Directory" that provides the addresses of national and international Convention and Visitors Bureaus, conference and convention centers, hotel chains, hotels and resorts, convention services, and airlines and car rental agencies. By linking with one of these entities, you are likely to reach prospects looking specifically for meeting services.

You can also link to meeting site services, including StarCite, PlanSoft Network, and a host of others, which compile lists of databases of properties interested in hosting meetings and group business. These services help planners to narrow down choices by filtering such aspects as location and size and facilities and then provide electronic RFP forms to send to hotels identified as meeting their requirements. Robert Bennett, vice president of marketing solutions for StarCite, whose technology is used by HelmsBriscoe, says:

> "The number of inquiries and leads distributed from our sites has increased 428 percent in the last two years."[4]

A property may also choose to *advertise* on other sites likely to be visited by its targeted segments. One of the most popular choices is a "banner ad" that appears when a site is accessed. Linking and advertising costs vary widely, so it is a good idea to determine the overall benefit. One disadvantage is that many of your competitors may also be linked to the same site, so you will want to promote a unique benefit if you choose to link with other sites or buy space on sites that feature other hotel advertising.

E-mail Advertising

According to the 2004 Meetings Market Report, 89 percent of meeting planners use **e-mail** for planning purposes. Over half use e-mail for facility search/site selection, while 48 percent negotiate with vendors by e-mail. Hoteliers who want to get the word out about their products and services are finding e-mail an inexpensive and effective way to advertise. Compared to traditional direct mail advertising, e-mail is highly economical and almost instantaneous. Buggsi Patel, President and CEO of Buggsi Hospitality Group, says:

> "We still do direct mail, but we're finding e-mail to be an extremely effective use of our time and money. The Internet is changing the way properties go to market. It's the medium that everyone who is looking ahead is looking to leverage."[5]

As with other advertising, however, planning is needed before sending out e-mail messages. First, using e-mail requires building a database of qualified prospects. Second, content must be developed that will appeal to your various targeted segments. And, last but certainly not least, e-mail must be welcomed by your prospects.

Time and privacy are important to planners, and sending "spam" -- the electronic equivalent of unsolicited "junk mail" -- may drive potential customers away. Today's successful e-mail marketers are using **permission marketing** to ensure that their messages make a favorable impression. This strategy involves asking a planner's permission before sending an e-mail about your property. You can create an *opt-in form* on your website to enable meeting planners to enter their e-mail addresses if they wish for you to send updates on your property. Most planners would welcome information to help make their jobs easier, and your property could structure its e-mail campaign to alert the planner of seasonal rate changes, special offers, or other items of interest that may make a meeting decision easier (the expansion of your meeting rooms, the addition of a gourmet chef, etc.). When meeting planners share their e-mail addresses with you, they are giving you permission to contact them in the future. Since 80 percent of your meetings business generally comes from 20 percent of the meeting planners with whom you communicate, it is critical to send regular (but pertinent) e-mails to planners who have expressed a willingness to hear from you.

E-mail advertising typically yields responses up to 15 times greater than those generated from direct mail and also has the advantage of doubling as a lead qualifying tool.

Hoteliers are also seeing the value of e-mail as a new way to communicate on a regular basis. E-mail is seen as an effective way to nurture customer relations by demonstrating the hotelier's commitment to staying in touch and serving the planner's future needs.

Fax Transmissions

Fax (facsimile) transmissions are useful to provide meeting planners with up-to-date information on new products and services. Faxes provide a copy of the original document — a letter, proposal, advertisement, special announcement, etc. — and are advantageous in that they are instantaneous and that meeting planners make them a priority to read. There are two ways in which fax transmissions are commonly used: fax-on-demand and broadcast fax.

Fax-on-demand offers the latest in property information directly to a meeting planner via a special fax number. This information can be accessed at any time, even when the sales office is closed, and can be updated as required to supply the latest information.

Broadcast fax provides simultaneous transmission of information to a database of interested or qualified prospects. Special announcements, changes in services offered, or other information can be sent to a number of planners at once.

Will technological developments, such as the Internet, e-mail, and fax transmissions (as well as the CD-ROMs we will discuss in the next section), replace personal site visits or diminish the role of the hotel salesperson? A recent study by Meeting Professionals International (MPI) and PlanSoft Corporation found that while technology is a useful tool for initial screening, it cannot replace in-person visits to investigate space for meetings. The large majority of respondents to the survey say that personal contact and building relationships are still essential to the meetings process.[6]

Collateral Materials

Collateral material is supplementary advertising pieces used along with direct mail, magazine advertising, and other promotional efforts. This includes a vast array of promotional materials such as convention and rack brochures, newsletters, postcards, menus, tent cards, matchbooks, and many other items.

The greatest distinction between collateral material and other advertising devices is the directness of collateral pieces. Newspaper advertising takes a shotgun approach; collateral material is more specific and is often directed right to the decision maker.

Brochures

Perhaps one of the most familiar collateral materials is the brochure. Most convention hotels use two brochures: a standard *rack brochure,* which is directed to the leisure market, and a *convention brochure.* As with other advertising, the focus of these brochures will differ widely. The rack brochure usually promotes rooms, restaurants, and recreational amenities and is targeted to leisure travelers and travel agents. The convention brochure, on the other hand, provides detailed information regarding function space, food and beverage service, and convention services and is targeted to meeting planners.

Convention Brochures. The convention brochure may be prepared in a number of ways. It can be a standard three or four-fold type, loose-leaf pages bound in an attractive cover, or presented in booklet style. Whatever style you choose, remember that it should fit in with your property's overall advertising and project your property's image. In addition, no matter what type is used, it should always contain pertinent information.

When planning your brochure, start with the assumption that your prospect has never seen or even heard of your hotel, and certainly has never been informed of its convention capability. Image yourself as a meeting organizer looking for a suitable hotel for your next event. The information you would want should be presented clearly and concisely. A common complaint from planners is the lack of good, accurate descriptive material from hotels.

A brochure will give the planner enough basic data for preliminary planning (see box titled "Basic Convention Brochure Information").

The larger meeting rooms should be diagrammed, if possible, or at least described adequately. "Large" is not a very accurate phrase. How many people will the grand ballroom accommodate? In what sort of setup (auditorium-style offers greater capacity than seating at round tables, for example)? A good brochure will give enough information so it can be used as a tool by meeting planners to narrow down a field of contestants for meeting functions.

One of the primary sources for ideas for preparing a convention brochure is, of course, existing pieces. Begin collecting brochures. There are some excellent ones in the field. Start a reference file of brochures you admire for one reason or another. They'll give you many ideas you may want to incorporate into your own brochure.

The best brochures show scaled outlines (blueprints) of all major rooms. One meeting planner stated,

---

BASIC CONVENTION BROCHURE INFORMATION

Your property's convention brochure should provide all the information a meeting planner needs to make a decision on a meeting site. Effective convention brochures should include most — if not all — of the following information:

- Your property's name
- Your property's address and, when possible, an area location map detailing proximity to airports, major highways, and area attractions.
- Your property's telephone number (a toll-free number encourages responses) and name of contact person, if applicable (convention services manager, convention coordinator, etc.)
- Your fax number and pertinent e-mail addresses
- Photographs, diagrams, or *complete* descriptions of exhibit space (dimensions, scaled drawings, floor load, ceiling height)
- Audiovisual equipment available
- Other meeting services available (teleconferences, fax service, personal computers, clerical and/or registration help, business center)
- Special services and facilities (photographic services, flowers, entertainment)
- Banquet and beverage arrangements
- Theme party arrangements
- Guestroom information (descriptions, floor plans, room block policy, reservations, rates, arrival/departure information)
- Special procedures (billing procedures, shipping and receiving procedures, signs and notices policy, etc.)
- Recreation and amenities (hotel attractions, spouse entertainment, area attractions)
- Transportation (parking facilities, shuttle service, tours, taxis, public transportation)
- Other general information (climate, dress, gratuities, the availability of room service, etc.)
- References from past conventions
- Checklists and planning guides for the meeting planner

This checklist may also be used for an electronic brochure on the Internet. A website is an ever-evolving marketing tool on which electronic brochures can be updated whenever the need arises.

"I like to receive a meeting planner's kit, not general information about the hotel. I need to see a floor plan with specific seating capacities. It takes time and it's expensive for a hotelier to send out information; it should be useful."

The brochure need not be so utilitarian that it fails to present your property in a good light. A facility is not chosen merely for its ability to house the event. The beauty of the structure and surroundings, the convenience of the location, and the expertise of the staff are all important. But such data should not be included at the expense of basic facilities information. Always include your usual hotel brochure along with your convention brochure.

Design your material to enable your contact to present your case completely and favorably. Good brochures will work for you in sales presentations, mailings, and trade shows, and through intermediaries such as convention bureaus, airlines, and convention specialists.

Video Brochures. In addition to printed brochures, many properties produce video or DVD (digital video disc) brochures. Video is both inexpensive and versatile, and a videotape can show a property's selling points in a way that no printed piece can (see Figure 8.6).

A video brochure can show the property at various times of the year, and is an excellent resource for the meeting planner who is unable to visit the property in person. Video brochures can show a property at its best, in a variety of setups (both meeting rooms and banquet facilities), and can also show other important selling points, such as seasonal attractions.

Most video brochures are fairly short, running four to six minutes in length, and must present the property's best points in that short time. Many properties, therefore, enlist the services of a firm that specializes in hotel video brochures before attempting to shoot one on their own. This may cost slightly more, but the benefits of the expertise of the professional firm (and high quality shooting techniques) are worth the additional time and expense. The brochure is presenting your property just when the potential buyer is researching it and therefore calls for professional expertise.

CD-ROMs and Electronic Brochures. Like the video brochure, **CD-ROMs**, computer discs that can store a great amount of data (including text, pictures and sound), can be used to give meeting planners a "tour" of the property. Often used in conjunction with Internet advertising, CD-ROMs can be sent to meeting planners for use on their own personal computers for a "virtual" look at a property or area. According to the 2004 Meetings Market Report, over one-fourth of meeting planners used a CD-ROM for meeting planning purposes.

CD-ROMs offer several advantages over video brochures. First is their format: CD-ROMs typically offer 650 million characters — or approximately 160,000 pages of text); they are durable (with a shelf life of approximately 100 years); cannot be erased by magnetic fields; and they can be easily and inexpensively reproduced and mailed. In addition, a growing number of meeting planners utilize personal computers, and most of these computers are equipped to use CD-ROMs.

In many cases, CD-ROM presentations are duplicates of those on Internet web sites, greatly reducing the cost of production. And, CD-ROMs can be used on a personal computer even if a meeting planner does not have access to the Internet.

CD-ROMs are currently in use by a number of properties and Convention and Visitors Bureaus, including those in San Antonio, TX, and Santa Clara, CA (see Figure 8.7). Radisson Hotels distributed CD-ROMs that include a directory of Radisson properties, including floor plans of all the chain's hotels, to meeting planners in addition to its Internet

Figure 8.6. SAMPLE HOTEL VIDEO BROCHURE.

Hotels such as the Saddlebrook directly advertise and distribute their videos to potential meeting clients. Video brochures are also used for in-house presentations to meeting planners and at trade shows and conventions. Video brochures directed to meeting planners often combine live action with animated graphics of meeting room configurations.

directory. And, Sheraton is adapting its Meeting Facilities Guide to CD-ROM. According to Kay Heder, director of corporate sales, North America, "It will allow the user to virtually go into a hotel and browse" (eliminating any concern over the location of ballroom pillars, etc.).

As with other types of advertising, CD-ROM presentations should project the desired image for your property and should meet the needs of meeting planners by offering perti-

Figure 8.7. "VIRTUAL" SANTA CLARA ON CD-ROM.

One of the first on-line site inspections designed for meeting planners, Destination Santa Clara is available on the Web and on CD-ROM. The virtual presentation was developed by the Santa Clara (CA) Convention & Visitors Bureau to provide meeting planners with interactive information on the city's meeting facilities. The CD-ROM version is available in three formats: fact sheets (electronic brochures complete with pictures), overviews presented in two-minute "infomercials," and a "virtual walk-through." Vaughn Ball, director of sales and marketing for the CVB, says: "Because we are located in Silicon Valley and making an effort to target high-tech groups, it's essential that we use technology to reach our market both nationally and internationally."

nent information. The detailed floorplans mentioned above are an excellent selling point, as are interviews with key convention services personnel, a "tour" of the property (preferably when there are groups in-house), testimonials by satisfied clients, and so on. Many properties opt for professional assistance when creating their first CD-ROM, especially if it will be used in conjunction with an Internet marketing program.

Many of today's Internet marketing programs include *electronic brochures*, which are offered on the property's website. Online brochures, like CD-ROMs, usually feature "virtual tours" of a property and its facilities, but they also offer several other benefits. First, they can be updated whenever needed, such as for special offers, changes to facilities, and so on. Second, they don't have to be mailed by properties or stored by meeting planners. All a meeting planner has to do is access the hotel's website and view or download the online brochure on an "as needed" basis. And last, but certainly not least, electronic brochures are far less expensive than printing full-color collateral materials or preparing a CD-ROM.

As with CD-ROMs, however, the information offered should be pertinent for meeting planners. The guidelines in the box titled "Basic Convention Brochure Information" should be applied to convention brochures developed in every format.

Other Collateral Materials

In addition to brochures, collateral materials may include such diverse pieces as postcards, fliers, maps, menus, tent cards, and newsletters (see Figure 8.8). These materials not only serve to keep your property's name and its features in the prospects' minds, but also can be used by salespeople to enhance their sales presentations.

As with brochures, all pieces used should be carefully planned and integrated into the property's overall marketing and advertising strategy. All pieces should be attractively designed and, as in print advertising, list the benefits offered by your property as well as its features. And, most importantly, printed collateral materials should be targeted to the conventions market (separate newsletters should be developed for the meetings market and the leisure travel segment, for example).

Specialty Items

Collateral materials also include **specialty items** (sometimes called **premiums**) that are marked with the property's name and toll-free number. These may include such inexpensive items as matchbooks or keychains, or "signature" items, such as glassware, plush toys, or sportswear featuring the property's logo.

Chain properties have the advantage of ordering specialty items from the chain's catalog at greatly discounted rates. But even small properties can take advantage of this advertising tool — which, according to the Specialty Advertising Association (SAA), boasts a recall factor of up to 40 percent even after six months. It is fairly easy to find suppliers of specialty items, and costs can be kept down by ordering in quantity and staying with the same imprint.

Select items that reflect the image of your property, not necessarily the cheapest. It is far more cost-effective to choose items that a meeting planner will probably use (keeping your property's name constantly in his or her mind), such as a desk calendar or a coffee mug.

Direct Mail Advertising

Another popular tool in the promotion person's kit is **direct mail advertising**. Direct mail can be used to screen prospects (see Figure 8.9), to follow up on advertising leads, and to make a printed sales presentation in great detail to many prospects at once — at far less a cost than for print or broadcast advertising. Direct mail preselects the client and reaches him or her personally and privately. No other media can do this as effectively.

Unfortunately, there are also disadvantages to direct mail. The cost of direct mail efforts has increased over the years, especially due to increasing postal rates. Another

Figure 8.8. SAMPLE PROPERTY NEWSLETTER.

The newsletter is an excellent — and relatively inexpensive — way to convey property information to meeting planners. Newsletters may be produced at the property level or as part of a chain's effort to introduce its properties to meeting planners. Newsletters typically contain such features as property statistics, articles and/or photographs of successfully staged events, personnel profiles, special offers, and general meeting information. Newsletters are typically used in convention kits, enclosed with sales letters, used in direct mail campaigns, or may be accessed on a hotel's website.

disadvantage of direct mail is that pieces frequently end up in the wastebasket. An efficient program that will overcome these difficulties, however, can be produced at almost any budget level.

One factor in the success or failure of direct mail is ensuring that you are advertising directly to your target market. Whom are you trying to reach? If your objective is to

Figure 8.9. SAMPLE DIRECT MAIL SURVEY.

```
                                                    FREE DIRECT LINES
                                              New York City: 212-966-7210
                                                            212-226-0841
                                              Philadelphia Area: 215-561-5850

mount airy lodge                              DIRECT TOLL FREE NUMBERS
                                              From Eastern Pa. (Area Codes 215 & 717)
                                                            1-800-532-8271
Mount Pocono, Pennsylvania 18344              From N.Y., N.J., Md., Del.
Telephone: 717-839-8811                                     1-800-233-8116
```

GROUP & CONVENTION FORM

In order that we may up date our files and supply you with accurate
information, we would appreciate your completing this form and returning it in the self addressed envelope. Thank you.

1. Name of Organization:_____._____

    Your Name:_____Phone Number_____

    Address:_____City:_____State:_____Zip:_____

2. Are you planning any function? ( ) yes   ( )no

3. Would you be interested in Mount Airy Lodge? ( ) yes ( ) no

4. If yes, for what function: ( ) Convention   ( ) Seminar

                               ( ) Incentive Program   ( ) Social Outing

                               ( ) Board Meeting   ( ) Conference

Month:_____Days of Week:_____Year:_____Any Specific Dates:_____

Number of Persons:_____Number of Rooms:_____

5. Have you ever held a function in the Poconos? ( ) yes ( ) no

6. Are there any reasons why you cannot hold a function in the Poconos?

    ( ) yes   ( ) no If yes, please state reason_____

7. Do you have a copy of our full color 24 page convention brochure?

    ( ) yes ( ) no If no, would you like one? ( ) yes ( ) no

8. What do you look for in a convention site?_____
    _____

9. What convention publications do you read?_____
    _____

10. If you can supply any additional information regarding your

    requirements, it would be greatly appreciated:_____
    _____
    _____

In addition to promoting a property, direct mail can be used to solicit information and qualify leads. Surveys such as this one are an invaluable resource for obtaining "hot leads" — prospects with a definite interest in the property — and provide salespeople with client information that can be used in a follow-up letter or sales call.

increase your convention market share by 10 percent, then direct mail should be directed to meeting planners, not travel agents. Therefore, a direct mail campaign is only as good as the **mailing list** used. If your hotel does not have a mailing list, start one immediately. Begin by compiling a list of people who have met in your hotel in the past. Keep in mind that we are a mobile business society and lists must be updated frequently. Expect many returns and changes of names and addresses after each mailing, and remember to budget for postage due on returned pieces. It is vital to delete the undeliverables and note the changes of addresses on your list so that expensive printing and postage are not wasted in subsequent mailings.

As we have discussed, there are also several directories and a number of publications that supply the names, addresses, and phone numbers of most association, corporation, incentive, fraternal, and other meeting planners. It is also possible to rent names from the circulation lists of suitable magazines.

Convention bureau notices from past years can also be a source of prospects for your mailing list, since major city-wide conventions are channeled through the bureau. Groups that have met in years past may hold smaller meetings that you may be able to attract. The convention bureau list might also show some groups have a repeat pattern for the city. These groups should be given a high priority in your sales campaign.

It is a good policy to develop two lists: a *general* one of all prospects you feel reasonably sure are relevant and a *preferred* list of screened prospects and past customers. You will probably mail more frequently to the second list than to the first.

Before sending any mailings, you should also decide on a follow-up method. Ideally, your direct mail efforts will give you a list of "hot" leads to follow up. The list of new leads generated through direct mail will be wasted if these prospects are not attended to promptly. You may wish to have follow up literature readily available, or forward responses directly to your salespeople for an immediate personal contact.

Direct mail, only one part of a hotel's total advertising effort, should be carefully planned for maximum results. The direct mail campaign must be integrated into the hotel's overall sales objectives, and mail pieces should blend with the property's other media advertising.

Some of the most commonly used direct mail pieces include sales letters, surveys, and postcards, but more creative and elaborate visual aids may also be used (see Figure 8.10). When deciding what types of materials would be most effective to use, several factors must be considered such as the purpose of the mailing, its scope, and the costs involved.

Writing Better Sales Letters. *Sales letters* are the meat of any direct mailing. Their function is to convince and to sell. Time does not permit a salesperson to make personal calls on every prospect, so the message must be communicated through the written word.

It is effective to use well-written personal letters, with convention brochures as enclosures. Seemingly personal, individually typed letters can be produced using your in-house word processing system or local letter shop services. If you want to create more ambitious direct mail programs, use your advertising agency or local creative services to produce the mailing pieces. But don't underestimate the power of personal letters addressed to a person by name. The high cost of brochures and postage make it advisable to polish your techniques (see box titled "Writing Effective Sales Letters").

Many properties find that a number of mailings must be used to achieve best results. A one-time mailing is not too effective unless it is a birthday or holiday greeting or an answer to an inquiry. Direct mail *campaigns*, then, should be a part of your direct mail efforts.

When using more than one mailing, the frequency, as well as the content, is important. There is no hard and fast rule, but the maximum interval between mailings is considered to be about two months. Obviously, multiple mailings must never be the same. The first letter must be an attention-getter. Its content must be appealing and retain the reader's interest. Future mailings should be built around the theme presented in the first one, but the information and point of the letters should be different. In some cases, you may want to build on each letter sent. The point of your message may be the same, but the content should be stated differently and creatively or the reader's interest is sure to wane (see Figure 8.11).

Figure 8.10. DIRECT MAIL "NOVELTIES".

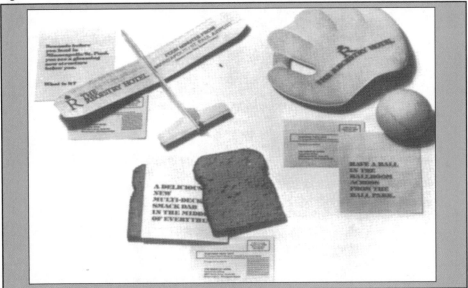

Direct mail sometimes includes novelties or gifts to stimulate interest. A series of three novelty mailings were used to introduce the Registry Hotel at the Minneapolis/St. Paul airport. The items — a rubber sandwich, a baseball and glove, and a balsa wood airplane — were keyed to fliers stressing the hotel's proximity to the airport and a sports center. The campaign won a first-place award in the HSMAI's annual advertising contest.

Planning an Advertising Strategy

As you can see, there are a number of ways to reach meeting planners, and you must develop a strategy that will work best for your property (see box titled "Selling Sheratons to the Meetings Market"). Developing such a strategy, of course, means working within the marketing plan — and budget — established for your property, and structuring your efforts accordingly.

Some of the factors you will want to consider in devising your strategy include whom you wish to target, what media you will use, and how much money you can spend. Many

---

WRITING EFFECTIVE SALES LETTERS

Effective letter writing is a skill than can be developed. Here are a few fundamental techniques that should be used:

- Use the correct titles of hotel personnel and the person with whom you are dealing.
- Be informative but brief. Stick to the facts.
- Be yourself; write like you speak. Write as if the client were with you in the office.
- Emphasize key points by underlining them or using bold-faced lettering.
- Avoid using computer-generated form letters that do not address specific needs.
- *Always ask for the sale* — and provide a means for the client to respond (a reply card, toll-free number, etc.)

Keep in mind that you should always write in the client's language; avoid the use of hotel terms that may confuse or mislead. Don't give the sales copy second billing in direct mail pieces. Be specific, and make your correspondence meaningful and convincing.

Figure 8.11. SAMPLE DIRECT MAIL SERIES.

The Bloomington Convention & Visitors Bureau in Bloomington, Minnesota, developed a series of mailings to introduce its Executive Director, Bonnie Carlson, and her staff to meeting planners. Each mailing in the series featured people who would actually help planners in staging their functions, creating an atmosphere of familiarity and trust long before the function was held. Each three-fold mailing had an illustration, a copy panel and a tear-off reply card. This type of series mailing reinforces your property's message in the minds of meeting planners. If done correctly, planners will actually look forward to additional mailings.

SELLING SHERATONS TO THE MEETINGS MARKET

When the Sheraton Corporation sought to position itself to attract meeting planners, it went directly to the source, conducting extensive research with clients to learn what was important to them and what was needed to help make their job easier. The result was the Sheraton Master Plan for Meeting Planners, which responded to the meeting planners' requests for more information to ensure professionalism in the industry.

The Sheraton/PCMA Showcase I is a program for new meeting planners (and serves as a refresher course for full-time professionals). These workshops cover the basics of meeting planning, including site selection, working with properties, room setup, food and beverage planning, etc.

The Sheraton/PCMA Showcase II is more comprehensive, exploring new trends in the industry, and offers in-depth information on subjects such as negotiations, contracts and liability, meeting specification preparation, and program design, among others. Like Showcase I, it is offered free to meeting planners, along with a complimentary continental breakfast and lunch.

Our New Workbook is Used.

Our new Sheraton workbook is already being used by over 100,000 meeting planners and travel planners all over the world.

Created by experienced meeting planners and Sheraton's Convention Service Professionals, this is more than just a workbook; it's a real working tool for planning meetings. It covers everything from budgets to food and beverage, from meeting room set-ups to site selection. It even includes detailed worksheets.

Let Sheraton help you plan your client's next meeting. Order your free *Sheraton Meeting and Conference Workbook* today. It will be new when it arrives, but it will be used right away.

For your FREE Workbook, call 1-800-325-1847 in the U.S. For information or to book a meeting call G.R.A.B. 1-800-343-6520.

Sheraton
ITT

In addition to these workshops, Sheraton developed a comprehensive free meeting planning manual. The manual plays an important part in the chain's advertising, showing its willingness to assist meeting planners and its commitment to successful meetings.

To further enhance its professionalism, Sheraton also launched the industry's most comprehensive training program for its own Convention and Conference Services Managers — a strategy that has generated tremendous interest within the industry and adds credibility to the chain's advertising, which positions the Sheratons as both dedicated to maintaining high standards of professionalism and being "meeting planner friendly."

properties prepare a media chart (see Figure 8.12) to plan advertising placement and expenditures over the course of a year. Annual planning is much more effective than last-minute, haphazard efforts. When you plan on an annual basis, keep in mind that you can schedule your advertising expenditures to match your property's fiscal or budget year. Publications compute frequency discounts on a consecutive twelve month period. You can, if it suits your purpose, schedule your advertising from March 2006 through February 2007, for example. Also, it is helpful, if you can manage it, to set aside a sum for special situations that crop up during the year.

Reach, Frequency, Timing, and Consistency

When planning your advertising strategy, four key factors should be taken into consideration: reach, frequency, timing, and consistency.

Reach refers to the number of different individuals who are exposed to your message during a specific period. This, of course, is determined by the media you select. When

Figure 8.12. SAMPLE HOTEL MEDIA CHART.

Client number: BM100-3   MEDIA SCHEDULE 01/01/_ THRU 12/31/_
Media: MEETINGS

Publications	January	February	March	April	May
Association Management Pub Number Issued Circulation AS700-6A Monthly 21,120 96 Rates 15th of 2nd Month Publication Total $8,372.50				Page 4/C $4,186.00 Or Pg 4C	
Business Travel News Pub Number Issued Circulation BTN15-8A Bi-Weekly 51,046 Jr Pg or 1/2SPD 3 Weeks Prior Publication Total $34,000.00			Jr Pg 4/C $6,800.00 Mtgs Today 22 +BRC	Jr Pg 4/C $6,800.00 Mtgs Tday 19	Jr P4\C $6,800.00 Mtgs Tday 10 +BRC
Corporate & Incentive Travel Pub Number Issued Circulation C0605-6A Monthly 49,698 One Month Prior Publication Total $4,764.00		Page 4/C $4,764.00 DSTNTN Colorado			
Executive Memo **Colorado Soc. Of Assn Executives** Pub Number Issued Circulation COSAE-6A Monthly 250 One Month Publication Total $12,605.50				Page BW $500.00	
Executive Update - GWSAE Pub Number Issued Circulation EU478-6A Monthly 9,000 33% DSCNT Publication Total $12,605.50					Page 4/C $3,740.00 SPGNTME PK
Forum (CSAE) Pub Number Issued Circulation For 10-9 11X/Yr ½ SPD or Pg 6 weeks Prior Publication Total $6,262.37				Page 4/C $1,789.25	
Incentive Pub Number Issued Circulation IN150-6A Monthly 40,281 15th, 2 Months Prior Publication Total $39,467.80				Page 4/C $4,911.30 +BRC	Page 4/C $4,911.30
Insurance Conference Planner Pub Number Issued Circulation IN500-6A Bi-Monthly 7,451 1st of Month Preceding					Page 4/C $2,622.25 Incentive

All listed rates are based on applicable rate card as of the date of preparation and are subject to change.

In order to plan an effective advertising strategy, many properties prepare an annual media chart that lists such data as name and type of publication to be used, size of ad (or length of spot), and advertising expenditures, both for production and space costs. This approach provides an at-a-glance overview of the property's advertising, controls budget commitment, and can also be used to measure the effectiveness of advertising. This sample shows data from January- May; a complete chart would extend through December.

Direct Mail Marketing

Carolyn Hamilton-Proctor
President
Graphic Communications, Las Vegas NV

"Direct mail is a powerful weapon in your sales arsenal. Studies show repeatedly that the direct mail package outpulls any other printed format. Properly used, direct marketing will make your marketing plan more targeted — and more profitable.

Direct mail makes advertising accountable. Direct mail to meeting planners does not replace journal or directory advertising, rather it complements them. Proper integration of general advertising and direct mail will have a synergistic effect on your profits.

A solid list of names and current addresses of your guests is worth its weight in gold. Direct mail requires the maintenance of a guest database which includes both demographic and psychographic profiles of your guests. The more specific the guest profile in your database, the more successful your direct mail campaigns can be. Compiled lists that match your guest profile, rented from outside sources, will yield respondents who also can be added to your existing database. Increasing and updating your in-house guest database is an ongoing process."

targeting the conventions market, for example, you are focusing on a smaller number of specific prospects than if you were targeting the transient market. You should select the media that will be most effective in reaching them (a specialized trade journal, for example) rather than opting for indiscriminate media (a television spot). You are interested in how many potential customers you can reach for each dollar spent.

Frequency refers to the number of times your target audience sees or hears your message. As with sales calls, advertising is rarely effective on a "one-shot" basis; it is usually necessary to expose your prospects to your message on a frequent basis — and often in a number of ways, such as the combination of trade journal advertisements and direct mail efforts. It is beneficial to expose your prospect to your message a number of times.

Timing, then, is an important factor. Some properties prefer to advertise or send out mailings on a *continuing* basis, timing their advertising to appear once a month, for example. There are times, however, when you can take advantage of a *pulsing* approach. Pulsing is used to promote business over slow periods. A property, for example, may wish to offer special rates during its valley periods of early fall and mid-winter, and would advertise over a predetermined time prior to these periods. Similarly, *flighting* (advertising only when managers feel it necessary, with no regular pattern) can be used when it is necessary to promote special packages or events. Perhaps the area will be host to a local festival or special event; advertising can promote the property's participation or proximity to the action.

Most convention publications run special editorial sections throughout the year dealing with meetings in certain geographic areas, such as a city or state, or specific types of properties, including golf resorts, airport hotels, conference centers, etc. Editors and publishers will usually supply the schedule of such features for the full year. When you plan your advertising, you might be able to take advantage of such targeted sections by placing your ad in them while still maintaining your objectives in timing and frequency. There are additional advantages to appearing in editorial sections describing your specific area.

No matter what approach is used for timing, **consistency** in advertising is vital. Your advertising must develop distinguishing characteristics — a logo, special colors or design, etc. —to stand out from the rest. Your prospects should be able to identify your property's ad at first glance.

Not only should your advertising have distinguishing characteristics, but it should also be consistent with and supportive of other elements in your marketing plan. This approach, called **integrated marketing**, ensures that your advertising and marketing activities have a common focus for both your marketplace in general and specific market segments in particular.

Since the purpose of your advertising is to become known and patronized, your advertising strategy should also include a program of follow up and monitoring and evaluation. *Follow up* is extremely important, especially in the conventions and meetings market. Most planners are "comparison shopping" and if they have responded to your ad or mailing it is likely they have responded to others. Your prompt handling of an inquiry will demonstrate your commitment to provide efficient service.

At the very least, inquiries should be followed up with a personal letter and information that was requested. Whenever possible, especially if the respondent has included his or her telephone number, make a personal call of thanks and request an appointment. This can lead to an immediate sale.

To develop the most cost-effective program, however, you must carefully *monitor and evaluate* your program periodically. Determine which ads or direct mail pieces seem to attract the most interest; check to see which publications are generating the most leads; and monitor the number of conversions from inquiries. And, take steps to determine the actual cost per conversion from each type of inquiry. If your ad series is costing $35,000, for example, but you have only generated $15,000 in business, take another look at your ad program.

Exchange Trade Advertising

To cut advertising costs, many properties have looked for alternatives, such as trading out goods and services or sharing advertising expenditures. **Exchange trade advertising** is an arrangement in which the hotel exchanges its services (rooms, food, beverage, use of recreational amenities, etc.) for advertising (newspaper, magazine, outdoor space, radio and television spots). Such arrangements are also referred to as *reciprocal advertising, barter advertising* and *trade-out advertising,* and can be very worthwhile as long as the hotel fully understands the procedure. It is important to realize that exchange trade advertising is not free; there is a cost to the hotel, and this cost must be budgeted, just as print advertising costs are. And, whether you are paying cash or exchanging services, your hotel's advertising efforts must be directed to your target markets. If you are trying to build group meeting business, for example, a trade exchange with a billboard specialist would not be the wisest use of your money.

Exchange trade advertising does offer some real advantages to a convention hotel, and its possibilities should be investigated. As with any advertising strategy, there are factors that should be considered and guidelines to follow in order to utilize this type of arrangement for your maximum benefit (see box titled "Making the Most of Exchange Trade Advertising").

MAKING THE MOST OF EXCHANGE TRADE ADVERTISING

Exchange trade advertising can be a viable advertising tool if it is used properly. Bob Stein, a senior vice-president of an advertising agency and author of <u>Marketing in Action for Hotels/ Motels/Restaurants</u>, offers these recommendations for negotiating exchange trade agreements:

1. Consider some variations on the "one-for-one" arrangement, especially when the publication or station approaches you. You could receive $1.50 or $2.00 of advertising for every dollar of hotel facilities, especially if food and/or beverage are included in the arrangement. When such is the case, point out that food and beverage represent an out-of-pocket cost to you, whereas available publication space or radio and TV time ordinarily do not.
2. Consider these limitations, all of which mean money in your pocket: For commercial hotels and motels, (a) rooms only, and then only during periods when you don't expect to be at capacity, or (b) food only, rather than food and beverage. For A.P. (American Plan) or M.A.P. (Modified American Plan) resorts, the room portion only.
3. Bring your advertising agency into the picture and require the publication or station to pay the customary 15 percent commission. Your ad agency will undoubtedly handle the placement of the advertising, and if it receives the commission, you will not be required to pay it.
4. Include as a condition of your reciprocal deal that your facilities are limited to use by certain individuals (publisher, station manager, key executives, employees), and secure in advance a list of those persons.

Reprinted courtesy of *Lodging Hospitality Magazine*, a Penton/IPC publication.

The use of exchange trade advertising does require increased record keeping, but it also affords yet another benefit — the opportunity to build relationships with media firms. A friend in the media can be a real asset when it comes to editorials and publicity about your hotel (and, the hotel is in a position to extend extra courtesies to the media's important clients). In the final analysis, exchange trade advertising can be mutually beneficial if a fair arrangement is negotiated.

Cooperative Advertising and Strategic Partnerships

Cooperative advertising also provides an additional way to save on advertising costs. In a cooperative arrangement, several properties — or a property and several related entities, such as a convention and visitors bureau, an airline or car rental company or local area attractions — advertise together to both save on costs and maximize results.

Cooperative advertising can be used as either a "one shot" promotion, or, as is done more commonly, in an advertising campaign that promotes the services and attractions available in an area. This type of advertising provides meeting planners with more information and options, and can also prove beneficial to your property. If your property has limited meeting facilities, for example, you can advertise with a full service meeting hotel, offering your rooms to accommodate meeting overflow.

Strategic partnerships are another form of cooperative agreement. These alliances are relationships between independent parties or chains that agree to cooperate in advertising but still maintain their separate identities. A common example is several hotels combining forces with each other (and often the city's CVB and/or other attractions) to offer a "one-stop shopping" alternative to compete with larger cities (see Figure Figure 8.13 and the "Best Practices" box titled "Hilton Hotels & Sheraton Hotels Form a Strategic Partnership to Capture Meetings Business in New York City").

Susan Henrique is director of sales and marketing for Coastal Fairfield County, Connecticut, which is located near New York City. Her CVB as well as those in Arlington,

Figure 8.13. SAMPLE COOPERATIVE ADVERTISING.

MEET. THEN RETREAT.

The 10 Hotels At Knoxville's Airport are ideal for any meeting, convention or conference. We offer a wide array of options, including facilities to accommodate up to 350 people at cost-effective prices.

And when you're done, we're right next door to just about everything. An hour from Gatlinburg/ Pigeon Forge. Half an hour from the Great Smoky Mountains National Park. Fifteen minutes from downtown Knoxville. Close to shopping, cultural activities, live entertainment and the great outdoors.

The Hotels At Knoxville's Airport. Perfect for work. Perfect for play.

THE HOTELS AT KNOXVILLE'S AIRPORT
We're Right Next Door

Smoky Mountain Visitors Bureau
Blount Partnership

CALL GINA CAPPELLETTI AT 1-800-525-6834 OR 423-984-2657.

gcappelletti@chamber.blount.tn.us   www.smokymountains.org
201 S. Washington Street • Maryville, Tennessee 37804

Cooperative advertising provides the opportunity for two or more properties and/or related services to share advertising space and costs. In this example, ten hotels at Knoxville's airport and the Smoky Mountain Visitors Bureau have teamed up to promote a number of features, including their ability to host meetings and their convenience to area transportation and attractions, from shopping to the Great Smoky Mountains National Park.

Virginia (near Washington, DC), Prospect Heights, Illinois (near Chicago), and Irving, Texas (near Dallas), formed an "Edge City Alliance" to promote themselves to meeting planners. She says:

> "In an ever-changing economy, meeting planners seek affordable alternatives for their meetings. The program illustrates that there are alternatives, which include accessibility and benefits of the larger destination cities without the bigger price tag. We all need help for weekend occupancy and have similar budgets for meetings marketing. The real key is that we are all on the outside looking at a first-tier city."[7]

Members of the alliance see their consolidated efforts as a way to bring their resources to the notice of meeting planners who might not have considered alternatives just

Best Practices

"Hilton Hotels & Sheraton Hotels Form a Strategic Partnership to Capture Meetings Business in New York City"

Hilton New York, Sheraton New York and the Sheraton Manhattan, which are about 150 feet from one another in mid-town Manhattan, have 100 meeting rooms, more than 225,000 square feet of meeting space, and a combined total of 5,000 guestrooms. They can also accommodate up to 425 exhibits. Although they are competitors, the three hotels took advantage of an opportunity to market their combined facilities to appeal to meeting planners.

The three hotels created NY 5000, a partnership geared to a joint sales and marketing effort. Christopher Perry, director of sales and marketing for Hilton New York, said:

> "We wanted to offer an alternative for conventions that need 1,400 rooms or more on a peak night. We are ideal for events that want to come to New York, would like to stay with two or three hotels, and prefer not to use the convention center. It saves them money on transportation and creates better networking opportunities. We also have a consistency of product and service, including food and beverage."

Although meetings customers negotiate independently with each hotel in order to protect any proprietary information, the hotels have developed a presentation, designed collateral materials, and developed a web site, and salespeople regularly meet and make pitches for NY 5000 business when appropriate.

While the three hotels had previously been averaging about eight large meetings jointly, they added four additional large group bookings in the first year of the formation of NY 5000.
Source: Harvey Chipkin, "Success Stories That Inspire," HSMAI Marketing Review, *Winter 2003/2004, p. 10.*

across big-city borders. Their strategic partnership also allows individual participants to stretch their advertising dollars; with their participation in the "Edge City Alliance," each property and CVB can get maximum exposure at less cost, enabling them to save money for their own promotional efforts to their other targeted market segments.

Advertising Agencies

A hotel that has its own advertising department should make special efforts to develop material and advertising dealing solely with the convention market. In smaller properties, the sales manager may be his or her own advertising manager. At larger properties, a full creative and production department may be employed.

Such efforts may be supplemented by an outside advertising agency. A properly selected — and properly utilized — agency adds skilled specialists to the work force of any advertising department. Even smaller hotels can afford an arrangement with smaller ad agencies (it is difficult to work without one, in fact). Advertising agencies are not a substitute for your own sales efforts, but they have the skills and the resources to back up the sales department with the required promotional material.

What services can you expect from an agency? That depends on the type of agency. *Full-service agencies* are appropriately named; they provide a full range of services, from creative design to the production of materials to the media placement of completed ads and spots. Many also offer research and assistance in planning campaigns — and offer the benefit of having branch offices across the country. The agency's commission — 15 percent — is usually paid by the media in which the ad or spot is placed; the property pays for print space or air time and production costs.

A la carte agencies, also called *modular services* and *creative shops*, are usually smaller in scope than full-service agencies and work on a negotiated fee basis. These agencies are often used for one-time advertising assignments, such as an ad or brochure production or in the placement of an advertisement. Payment, therefore, is on a per-job basis.

Media-buying services buy space for submitted promotional materials. These services do not usually produce materials, but can be helpful in placing advertising created by the property's in-house advertising department.

Many convention hotels have found it advantageous to use advertising agencies, but it is extremely important that when a hotel uses an advertising agency both are in agreement as to the direction of the advertising campaign. Naturally, a hotel is more familiar with its strengths than the outside agency. The hotel must communicate its positioning and goals to its agency representative to ensure that the advertising creates the image a property wishes to project and is aimed at its target market(s). To ensure that the property and the agency can work well together, it is important to select an agency carefully (see box titled "Selecting an Advertising Agency"). A properly functioning agency offers you an experienced and objective view of your property's promotional efforts. One advertising executive says:

> "We're concerned not just about creating and placing [clients'] advertising, but helping them with their in-house promotions in all of their market segments; developing new segments; motivating their salespeople; building their collateral; redesigning Web sites; and managing direct mail promotions...We truly want to become the client's marketing partner, and not just its [ad] studio."[8]

SELECTING AN ADVERTISING AGENCY

Before you select an advertising agency, you should evaluate your property's needs. Will you need full services or just assistance in placing your own promotional material? How would an advertising agency be utilized — as a supplement to your in-house advertising department, occasionally as needed for research or production, as an extension of your advertising and sales effort? How much can you afford to spend on outside services?

Once you have established guidelines, informal meetings should be held with representatives of agencies of interest to you. Each representative should provide the answers to the following questions:

1. How long has the agency been in business? Does it have a proven track record in the hospitality industry?
2. Does the agency represent competitors? If so, how will this affect the handling of your account?
3. What services can the agency provide? Does it offer full creative services? market research? media placement?
4. Who will be assigned to your account? How much time can he or she spend learning about your property and its needs? In the event "your" account person is not available, who will be assigned to handle your account?
5. How will costs be handled? Is the agency willing to work within the property's budget?

Public Relations and Publicity

While advertising is a powerful method of reaching target markets, you can do more to keep your hotel's name before your potential customers. Advertising coupled with public relations and publicity can form a stronger combination to reach planners.

Public relations is a broad term that encompasses a number of methods of communicating favorable information about a property. Its purpose is to create a positive image about the property. Loews Hotels, for example, began a model program -- and won an award -- with its Good Neighbor Policy. This community outreach program seeks to address a number of concerns, such as homelessness, illiteracy, and environmental preservation, and mobilizes not only the chain's properties but meeting planners as well. The hotel's contracts include an offer for meeting planners to donate surplus products and materials to a local charity. Donations have ranged from clothing to items from food shows to basic supplies (poster board, masking tape, etc.) that are donated to area preschools.

As with advertising, a good public relations plan must be developed — and people trained to implement it. While every employee — from general manager to front desk personnel to a valet attendant — plays a role in developing and maintaining a positive image for the property, it is essential that a professional public relations person or staff be employed to oversee the property's efforts in this important area. Small properties may employ one person or work with an outside public relations firm. Large properties may also utilize an outside public relations firm or engage a multi-talented public relations staff. In either case, public relations people or firms will be called upon to perform a variety of duties: acting as the property's spokesperson, contacting the media about the property, maintaining contacts with past guests, and so on.

One of the public relations staff's most important responsibilities is dealing with the media to obtain favorable publicity for the property. **Publicity** is the gratuitous mention of your hotel in newspapers, magazines, and over the airwaves. When you advertise, you pay for space or air time and control what is said about your hotel and its services. Many readers or listeners may be apprehensive about whether you can or will deliver on your promises. Publicity, however, which comes from an impartial third party, lends credibility to a property.

In the hospitality industry, there are many opportunities to generate good news that is of interest to meeting planners. Some of it just happens — a celebrity stays at the property, the property wins a prestigious award, a trade magazine does a story on a particular area, and so on. Much of it, however, is created — the hotel sponsors a festival or creates innovative theme parties. Or, the property can get its name in the news through its expansion and renovation programs or the involvement of its staff members in community affairs.

Meetings magazines — one of your best resources for reaching meeting planners — are always interested in stories of interest to meeting planners. Innovative meeting techniques, reports on new methods used to service successful meetings, renovations programs that will impact the meetings industry (the opening of additional facilities, etc.), and personnel changes are all of interest. "Meeting Calendars" listing hotels that are hosting major meetings are also published; these are excellent vehicles for a free listing for your property. Make a strong effort to get photographs of meetings in progress at your property. Meetings magazines are always looking for such illustrations. In addition, the organization sponsoring the meeting may use your photographs in their own publicity efforts, giving you additional exposure at the same time. It is not by accident that hotel lecterns carry the hotel's logo prominently across the front panel so that all photos of the speaker show the logo as well.

Trade magazines, such as those listed in earlier chapters, are spearheaded by an editor who makes the decisions about the subjects of articles and when they will run. They also have a managing editor who coordinates the makeup of the magazine. These people should be on your mailing list to receive publicity materials (press releases, newsletters, personal letters and invitations, etc.), as should editors of major newspapers in your property's target markets. The news generated about your property must meet their requirements of editorial interest, timeliness, and accuracy to be considered for publication.

There are two basic ways to communicate your property information to the media: finished pieces and press releases. Some properties employ staff writers to write articles and features for submission to trade magazines and newspapers. If you want to improve your chances of having such articles accepted for publication, you should study the publication to emulate their editorial style. Also, an editor is more inclined to accept a story if the thrust of the story is on the meeting that was held, with the property getting its publicity with some subtlety through photographs and mentions of the meeting site.

Almost all properties send out **press releases** about events of importance (see Figure 8.14). Press releases are usually printed on stationery with the property's logo and name, address and telephone number, and include basic information (time, place and other pertinent details) and the name of a property contact person. Press releases should always be sent well in advance of a deadline, but it is important to note that there is no guarantee that your material will be featured — or that it will be presented as written. You are not paying for space and you have no control over editorial content or its presentation.

It is important, then, to plan your press releases to ensure the maximum coverage possible. Since your press releases will be aimed at meeting planners, consider those events and personnel changes most likely to get them thinking about your property. The development of a state-of-the-art audiovisual system, for example, is of interest and is likely to make it to trade magazines. As is news of expansions (again, think how you can best word your release to appeal to the meeting planner — present a benefit in your copy), personnel changes (especially if the staff member is well-known in the meetings field), and special events held by your property — your innovative execution of an elaborate function will appeal to other meeting planners.

Since your submissions will result in additional interest — and require a prompt response — it is advisable to have follow up information readily available. In addition to promotional material to send to respondents, most properties with a planned public relations and publicity strategy prepare a **press kit** to both introduce the property to the news media and to provide back-up information. Press kits generally feature a property information sheet, the property's brochures, biographies of key personnel, and, when available, previous press clippings. Press kits should be updated as necessary and targeted for your property's market segments; a press kit for meetings magazines, for example, would contain different material than a press kit directed to travel writers.

In today's high-tech world, the computer is also being used to get the word out about a property. The Walt Disney World Swan and Dolphin hotels, for example, have a "media only" website to provide journalists with immediate access to press releases, photographs, logos, hotel specifications, dining and entertainment options, and other information online. Information is continually updated, and the site is "user friendly," enabling writers to cut and paste a press release (or a portion of it) directly into the writer's document. Other methods of contacting the press include "breaking news" features; e-mails sent to a database of journalists that have requested to be contacted in the event of a newsworthy event. These options are usually less expensive than sending traditional press releases and preparing press kits, but can be just as effective if the effort is carefully planned and targeted.

A good public relations and publicity plan does not just seek to get your property's name in the media. To be effective, *the plan should be integrated into the overall hotel marketing strategy, targeted toward specific market segments and scheduled to coincide with the property's slow periods.*

Figure 8.14. HOW TO WRITE A PRESS RELEASE.

1. Use hotel's letterhead for releases

RAMADA© NEWS
P.O.Box 590 · PHOENIX, AZ 85001 · (602) 273-4000

2. Always give a release date

FOR IMMEDIATE RELEASE

3. Always give a contact name who can answer a reporter's questions.

CONTACT: John J. Doe
(602) 123-4567

4. The headline tells the editor what the release is all about.

WEAVER FAMILY SINGERS TO APPEAR AT RAMADA EAST

5. Location of the hotel and the date the release is given out.

PHOENIX, AZ — January 23, 20__ — The Weavers, one of the oldest family folk and gospel singing groups in America, will begin a three week engagement at the Ramada East Resort in Phoenix on January 30.

6. Always double space lines.

The world famous singing family just completed an extended stay at the Century Hotel in Los Angeles. The group is comprised of five members of the Weaver family, including Joe Weaver, the 73-year old grandfather of Mike Weaver, who, at 20, is the youngest member of the group. Others include Mary Weaver, Sally Weaver and Bill Weaver. The younger Weavers are brothers and sisters.

The group will be appearing in the hotel's newly remodeled East Room, which was specially redecorated and modified to handle name entertainment, according to John J. Doe, the hotel's general manager.

The group will be appearing nightly except Sunday and Monday through February 15.

###

7. ### indicates the end of the release. Use "more" at the bottom if the release is longer than one page. Very few releases are longer than two pages. Never print on both sides of the page.

8. Always double space. Always indent paragraphs. For releases that run more than one page, always end each page with a complete paragraph or sentence. Never continue a sentence to the next page.

Press releases are used to inform the media of special events, property and personnel changes, and property involvement in community affairs. The press release should always be double-spaced and contain pertinent, newsworthy information. Today, press releases commonly include the fax number and e-mail address of the property's contact person in addition to his or her telephone number.

Summary

As you can see, a good advertising strategy coupled with a carefully planned public relations and publicity plan can greatly enhance the sales effort and actually "pre-sell" the property by creating awareness and a positive image in the meeting planner's mind. These tools can help the salesperson to close a sale and begin the second phase of his or her job — helping to coordinate the meeting planner's function. In the next chapter, we will take a look at what happens after a meeting planner commits to a property. We will discuss how negotiating skills and contracts can help to forge long-term business relations in the lucrative meetings market segment.

Endnotes:

1. "Ad Agencies Are Your Marketing Partners," *HSMAI Marketing Review*, Winter 2003, p. 36.
2. Anne Dimon, "Are You E-Planning Savvy?," *Meetings & Incentives*, June 2000, p. 24.
3. Donald E. Bender, "Marketing Your Property to Meeting Planners Online," *HSMAI Marketing Review*, Summer 2004, p. 11.
4. "StarCite, PlanSoft Give Planners Faster Response from Hotels," www.hotel-online.com, April 2004.
5. Marty Whitford, "You've Got Mail," *Hotel & Motel Management*, August 14, 2000, p. 34.
6. Lauren Shababb, "In-Person Inspections, Please," *Successful Meetings*, August 2000, p. 14.
7. Ruth A. Hill, "A United Front," *Lodging*, December 1999, pp. 27-28.
8. "Ad Agencies Are Your Marketing Partners," *HSMAI Marketing Review*, Winter 2003, p. 37.

Additional References:

• E-Commerce and Tourism Technology in Hospitality and Tourism, Zongqing Zhou, Thomson Delmar Learning, 2003.

• Event Web Newsletter, Doug Fox, Publisher and Editor
www.eventweb.com

• Hospitality Sales and Marketing, Fourth Edition, James R. Abbey, Educational Institute, AHLA, 2003.
www.ei-ahla.org

• Marketing in the Hospitality Industry, Fourth Edition, Ron A. Nykiel, Educational Institute, AHLA, 2004.

• Passport to Internet Success – The Hotelier's Guide to Internet Marketing.
www.blizzardinternet.com

Internet Sites:

For more information, visit the following Internet sites. Internet addresses can change without notice. If a site is no longer available at the address listed below, a search engine can be used to find the new address or additional, related sites.

Allmeetings – www.allmeetings.com
American Hotel & Lodging Association – www.ahla.com
EventSource – www.eventsource.com
Hilton Hotels – www.hilton.com
(site offers online hotel directory that features floor plans and group value dates)
Hotel Marketing – www.hotelmarketing.com
Hot Dates Hot Rates - www.hotdateshotrates.com
Hotelier – www.ehotelier.com
Hyatt's Meeting Planner Index – www.hyatt.com
(site contains a facilities guide and meeting services and planning information)
Marriott – www.marriott.com
(site offers a hotel search of Marriott convention hotels)
Meeting Path – www.meetingpath.com
Official Meeting and Facilities Guide – www.omfg.com
PlanSoft - www.plansoft.com
Public Relations magazine – prweek.com
StarCite – www.starcite.com

Study Questions:

1. What is print advertising? What elements should always be included in print ads? Where can print ads be placed to effectively reach meeting planners?
2. Why is the convention brochure an important sales tool for the meetings market? What information should be included in a convention brochure?
3. Why is direct mail an effective tool for reaching meeting planners? What are the elements involved in an effective direct mail campaign?
4. Why is it necessary to plan an advertising strategy? What factors should be considered?
5. What are exchange trade and cooperative advertising? What are the advantages and disadvantages of each?
6. Why do some properties use advertising agencies? What types of advertising agencies are available and what services does each offer? What factors should a property consider when selecting an advertising agency?
7. What is the difference between public relations and publicity? How can each be used to enhance the property's advertising efforts?

Key Terms:

Body copy. The main text of an ad.

Broadcast fax. A function that transmits fax messages to a large number of pre-selected recipients.

Collateral material. Supplementary advertising materials, including brochures, tent cards, key rings, matchbooks, postcards, and video brochures.

Cooperative advertising. A pooling of marketing dollars by several tourism businesses for promotional purposes in order to increase market impact and/or reduce costs.

Consistency. In advertising, refers to the design of advertising messages for a similar look or sound to enhance audience recognition and greater cumulative impact.

CD-ROM. A read-only-memory compact disk used to hold data, including printed text and graphic images. Can hold many times the data on a traditional floppy disk.

Direct mail advertising. Advertising sent via mail to prospects' residences or places of business. Contains copy to motivate the reader to purchase a product or utilize a service and usually includes a means to respond.

E-mail. Electronic mail messages sent via computer.

Exchange trade advertising. An arrangement in which the hotel exchanges rooms, meals, recreational amenities, etc. for advertising space or time. Also called **reciprocal advertising**, **barter advertising** and **trade-out advertising**.

Fax-on-demand. A function that provides an immediate response to information requests via fax transmission. In most cases, information is requested through a toll-free number.

Frequency. The number of times advertising appears in print or on the air.

Headline. The most prominent part of a print advertisement. Used to get attention, it usually promotes a promise or benefit.

Integrated marketing. Marketing activities with a common focus on the marketplace or a specific customer segment. The execution of each individual component is consistent with, and supportive of, each of the other elements in the marketing plan.

Logo. A unique trademark, name, symbol, signature or device used to identify a company or other organization. Used in advertising, for promotion and for image building.

Mailing list. A collection of names and addresses of past and potential customers to which mailings are directed. Generally maintained on a computer.

Permission marketing. An e-mail marketing campaign in which messages are sent only to those who have requested (opted-in) to receive specific types of information.

Press kit. News releases, fact sheets, photographs, news clippings, and other materials, often attractively packaged, designed to give the news media background information about a property.

Press release. A prepared statement, usually one or two pages, released to the news media regarding a hotel, one of its products or services, an individual, or a special event. Designed to be newsworthy, can be "For immediate release" or prepared to be released at a specified time or date. Also called a **news release**.

Print advertising. Advertising appearing in print in such media as newspapers, magazines, and directories.

Public relations. The systematic effort of a company to create a favorable image in the minds of various segments of the population.

Publicity. One facet of public relations, it comprises the gratuitous mention or exposure a company receives from announcements, events, and press releases.

Reach. The percentage of different people or locations exposed to a media message at least once during a specified period of time.

Specialty items. Supplementary advertising items, such as coffee cups, t-shirts, beach towels, and so on, that bear the name of the business and other advertising and contact information. Also called **premiums**.

Strategic partnerships. Relationships between independent parties that agree to advertise cooperatively but sill retain their separate identities.

Timing. In advertising, refers to the scheduling of ads.

Trade magazine. A publication, such as *Insurance Conference Planner*, that targets a specific industry or profession.

Negotiations and Contracts

David C. Scypinski
Senior Vice President of Industry Relations
Starwood Hotels

"The most successful salespeople take a long-term approach to negotiating contracts by looking to develop an agreement that benefits both the hotel and the customer. A one-sided contract may bring in much-needed revenue in the short-term, but may make it impossible to re-book the business. And in this business, as in any other, the key to profitability is repeat business...This is not to say you shouldn't seek to negotiate the most profitable contract possible; but you should be professionally aggressive in your negotiations, looking to balance the financial goals of your hotel and the customer's objectives."

9   Negotiations and Contracts

In today's competitive "sellers' market," hotels largely book business based on its maximum profitability. With the growth of individual business and leisure markets, which tend to pay higher rates than the group meeting segment, properties have become stricter in terms of room rates and contract negotiations for meetings business. But wise hoteliers know that their relationship with planners is equally if not more important. Charging exorbitant rates simply because demand is high may produce revenue in the short-term, but may adversely affect future business -- both from the planner and from potential word-of-mouth referrals.

Today's hoteliers must negotiate contracts that provide optimum benefits to both the property and the planner. In this chapter, we will see how contracts are negotiated, the areas of concern taken into consideration and included in the contract to ensure the successful execution of a function, and detail how hotels use specific clauses to protect themselves financially. This process begins with negotiations.

Negotiations

Negotiations involve two or more parties coming together to reach an agreement for their mutual benefit. This process should be viewed as a friendly, problem-solving partnership, not as a fearful or uncomfortable situation. Negotiating can result in a win-win situation for both your property and the meeting planner when handled properly.

The first step involves preparation by gathering information. Knowledge is power and good negotiation skills begin by researching three key areas: your product, your competition, and the prospect.

Product knowledge begins by studying the *property fact book*. It is nearly impossible to effectively sell features and benefits or to demonstrate how your property is best equipped to meet the prospect's needs without thorough knowledge of your property (see Chapter 7).

In addition to knowing your property's features, you must also understand *when* your property needs group business, the optimum guest mix, and the average daily rate for each market segment. The bargaining position of meeting planners will vary depending on your hotel's level of business, which can be divided into three categories:

- *Peak* — this is the period when demand for a property and its services is highest and the highest prices can be charged. Also called "high season."
- *Valley* — this period, also known as the "value season" or "low season," characterizes times when demand is lowest. Reduced prices are offered to meeting planners during valley periods to attract business.
- *Shoulder* — this period falls between a peak and a valley. Rooms are available and a mid to high rate can be charged. The shoulder period is the time when many properties concentrate their sales and marketing efforts.

You must know as much about your competitor's product as your own in order to successfully sell against them. When negotiating, emphasize the strengths of your property where you know the competition is weak (this information is available from the property's Competitive Analysis Charts, which we discussed in Chapter 2).

Being a good negotiator means learning as much as possible about the buyer. There are several factors to consider when evaluating your prospect's position:

- **Budget.** Knowledge of the meeting planner's past and present budget gives you an indication of how much they may be willing to spend on similar events and if price is a major concern.
- **Purpose of the meeting.** Every property has its appeal. If a meeting is for training, a small suburban property can offer the group the option of being the only meeting in the house, which pleases some planners.
- **Dates.** When is the meeting scheduled? How flexible is the group? Do your competitors have the preferred dates open? You are negotiating from a position of strength when you know your competitors don't have the desired dates open.
- **Hot buttons.** What are the meeting planner's key concerns and what are the most important buying factors? Is it the availability of special services, such as express check-in/check-out, extra staffing at the front desk, or special meals? Key concerns tell you what to emphasize and also give clues to the importance of price. Obviously, planners who mention VIP service and extra amenities as crucial to their meeting are going to be less price resistant.
- **Past problems.** Did the planner experience problems with another property? If poor food service is mentioned more than once, then price may not be as important a consideration as quality food at next year's event.
- **Group history.** Find out what properties the group has previously used to enable you to compare what you have with what other properties offered. Determine the arrival and departure patterns to see how well the group will fit in with business you have already booked. What has been their spending history at previous hotels with regard to various profit centers (food and beverage, shops, recreation, and so on)?
- **Decision deadline.** Your hotel's negotiating position will be affected by how quickly a decision must be made. Your negotiating strategy will be different when dealing with a planner who must make a decision immediately versus a planner who does not have to decide on a site until sometime in the future.

When negotiating, it is essential to look at the **customer's lifetime value**. Would offering concessions for a minor function for the client today result in additional, long-term lucrative business tomorrow? Sometimes, hotels will under price to gain new customers or be generous to existing customers in order to retain them over the long term. Trade-offs are a part of negotiating, but you should sell value and offer concessions only when absolutely necessary. Successful negotiating is a give and take process — the end result is that both parties are satisfied. The planner can look forward to a successful meeting within budget, while your hotel benefits from a profitable piece of business and from the positive relationship that may lead to additional business in the future.

Letter of Agreement/Contract

While contracts are now the norm, the word *contract* frightens many people — people who readily enter into an agreement made formal by a letter. Most businesspeople would not dream of drawing up a contract without legal counsel, but will sign a letter that lists the terms of an agreement. For all practical purposes, a letter of agreement and a contract function the same way, the difference being one of semantics.

Much has to be discussed when a meeting planner indicates a willingness to consider a hotel for a particular event. The essential elements of a contract are (a) an agreement (an offer by one party and an acceptance by the other), (b) an obligation on the part of one or more of the parties, and (c) consideration (usually expressed in monetary terms, but could be expressed as mutual promises).

A **letter of agreement/contract** should include, in simple language, all arrangements that have been negotiated and agreed to. This protects the client and the hotel, but it also does something else of extreme importance. By itemizing all matters to be covered, the letter of agreement is essentially a clearly stated checklist of what is expected of either party. This is vital because most misunderstandings reflect a lack of communication and a lack of experience by either the hotel executive or the client or both.

The letter of agreement should cover each point clearly in a separate paragraph. Each point should be documented. Nothing should be left to verbal agreement. The parties that negotiated the deal may no longer be employed by the hotel or the client when the convention actually takes place. In any case, memory is decidedly fallible. Everything should be included *in writing*. This will eliminate many misunderstandings when the time comes to settle up the accounts, and even prevent malfunctions during the meeting itself.

It is also sound practice to contact a hotel that was previously used as a convention site by the group. This contact can be made by using an **inquiry questionnaire**, which asks a group's former hosts to critique the group for the benefit of a prospective host property (see Figure 9.1). This information is helpful intelligence data to use during negotiations.

Cooperation of this kind is commonplace among hotels. Such inter-hotel conversations will not only make you aware of possible pitfalls with a group, but can also keep you abreast of current practices and trends throughout the hotel industry. Some discretion should be exercised not to make inquiries from a hotel — or a hotel within a chain — that is in a position to make a last minute bid to book the business. But with some care, past sites of the group could be valuable sources of helpful data.

Before offering a letter of agreement, many hotels send a **proposal letter** to the meeting planner. This proposal letter should spell out exactly what the customer will receive at the hotel. Proposal letters usually follow a standard format, including much of the same information included in the letter of agreement/contract, but they are usually not as detailed. Remember, your written proposal is a selling document and should present your key features and benefits. Include convention brochures, fact sheets, complimentary letters from past groups, and other promotional materials with your proposal letter. The conclusion to your proposal letter should always ask the prospect to take action -- to do business with you. Be sure to establish a trace date to follow up every proposal letter.

A proposal letter is normally initiated from a site inspection or a **request for proposal (RFP)** from a meeting planner (see Figure 9.2). A written RFP from a planner includes the group's desired dates, guestroom and meeting space requirements, and the group's meetings history. Since planners often send out a RFP to several hotels at the same time, your response should be timely. Planners expect to receive information on availability and pricing within a day or two of their request.

Should the group accept your proposal, you should send a letter of agreement along with a note of thanks. It is customary for this letter to be sent in triplicate, and to request that it be countersigned by a responsible person from the association (or other sponsoring organization) and returned. As we explained, this constitutes a legal contract whereby both parties have agreed to the terms and arrangements. An alternative to the triplicate-copy method might be a letter from the meeting planner stating that the letter of agreement is correct and accepted.

Figure 9.1. INQUIRY QUESTIONNAIRE.

U.S. Grant HOTEL

AN ATLAS HOTEL

Post Office Box 80098
San Diego, California 92138
(619) 232-3121

Dear Colleague:

The U.S. Grant Hotel is working with:

We understand this group met with you. At your convenience we would sincerely appreciate receiving the following information:

1.

Date								
Original Room Block								
Actually Used								

Meeting Requirements (Program if available):

2.

	Persons	Set-up
General Session	_____	_____
Breakouts	_____	_____

Catered Functions:

3.

	No. of Functions	Persons
Breakfast	_____	_____
Lunch	_____	_____
Dinner	_____	_____
Receptions	_____	_____

4. Comments: _____

_____

Thank you in advance for your cooperation. We will be happy to reciprocate at any time.

Sincerely,

_____
Signature

It is sound practice to track the historical performance of meeting groups. A questionnaire such as this one requests a post-convention critique from hotels used by the meeting group in the past. This information is extremely valuable in negotiations as it gives the hotel an early sense of whether the group meets its commitments. While it is acceptable practice for competitor hotels to exchange basic information on groups (such as rooms blocked, actual pickup, percentage of double occupancy, number of food functions and the like), it is a violation of antitrust law and a criminal offense to exchange pricing information (such as room rates or banquet charges).

Figure 9.2. SAMPLE REQUEST FOR PROPOSAL.

Date: 3/1/20__

REQUEST FOR PROPOSAL

2004 Plastic Surgery Senior Residents Conference
Sponsored by the Plastic Surgery Educational Foundation
Galveston, TX

Only possible dates:
April 14-18, 20__
April 21-25, 20__
May 5-9, 20__

EVENT PROFILE:

This meeting provides a forum for third-year residents to present their papers and helps to prepare them for medical practice.

ORGANIZATION PROFILE:

The PSEF is the educational arm of the American Society of Plastic and Reconstructive Surgeons, which is a 6,000 member national medical association representing 97% of all plastic surgeons in the U.S. The ASPRS/PSEF sponsors approximately 40 meetings/year throughout the U.S. and abroad.

ATTENDEE PROFILE: Third-year medical residents; average age early 30's
                      From all over U.S.
                      70% male, 30% female
                      15% traveling with spouse

PROPERTY TYPE NEEDED: City location close to restaurants and nightlife.

GUEST ROOM REQUIREMENTS:

Arrival	Tuesday night	5 rooms
	Wednesday night	120 rooms
	Thursday night	130 rooms
	Friday night	130 rooms; 2 suites
	Saturday night	110 rooms; 2 suites
Depart	Sunday	5 rooms

Notes: Need flat single/double rate. 85% sgl, 15% dbl. 85% non-smoking. Rate-sensitive group.

Concessions: 2 1BR suite upgrades for Assn. Presidents
                 1/50 comp
                 2 reduced rate staff rooms.

MEETING SPACE REQUIREMENTS:

Day	Time	Function	Attendance	Budget
Wednesday	3:00pm-7:00pm	Registration	2 6' tables	
	6:30pm-7:30pm	Reception	200 people	$30/p
	7:00pm-24 hrs	Exhibit Setup	25 6'tables plus	
			20 double-sided posters	

The RFP provides general information about the requesting organization and event, including specifics about the group's space requirements, a history of the group, and its decision date. The RFP may be mailed, faxed, e-mailed, or, as is becoming increasingly common, sent via the Internet to hotels. In most cases, meeting planners not only request proposals from hotels, but from a number of other suppliers as well, such as service contractors (companies that set up exhibits), security companies, audiovisual suppliers, tour shuttle firms, florists, and housing companies if the event is outsourced. This particular RFP includes three sheets; only the first is shown. Page two lists daily functions, meeting room requirements, the group's meeting history, and a space hold request; page three provides special requirements, a response date, information on the group's decision date, and the name and contact numbers of the meeting planner. The CIC has created a standardized RFP that can be downloaded at www.conventionindustry.org.

When sending out contracts or letters of agreement, it is important that the salesperson or other hotel contact not sign them before the meeting planner does. If someone at your property is the first to sign, you do not have the chance to correct anything or change your mind about a point once the buyer has signed (the signatures of both parties constitute a binding legal document). The best policy is to send three originals, asking the buyer to sign two and return them to you and keep the third for his or her files. Then, once the signed originals are received, you can sign both originals and send one back to the meeting planner.[1]

Do not be in a rush to sign the returned contracts. You will want to carefully look them over and initial any changes that may have been made. The customer will also have to initial those changes for them to be binding.

It is worth repeating that a soundly written letter of agreement helps both parties execute a successful meeting and prevents misunderstandings by stating exactly what is to be done, by whom, and at what price. Be sure that there are no "surprises" – each aspect should be reviewed with customers in order to protect your business relationship.

Since nothing is part of the agreement that is not included in the contract or letter of agreement, it is essential that certain information be recorded. Details on essential information and commonly negotiated points will be covered in the following paragraphs.

Names of Organization and Hotel

Name both parties to the agreement, and addresses and contact information for both parties should be listed. Both the organization and the hotel should be clearly indicated, along with the intent to select the hotel as the site for the meeting. The meeting should be identified by name or any other designation.

Official Dates

It sounds basic, but make sure the exact dates of the event are listed. They are often referred to as the *official dates*. It is wise to indicate the dates for moving in and moving out as well.

Not only the date, but also the hour of beginning and ending should be specified. This protects the hotel against the meeting tying up a room beyond the cutoff time. You don't want a breakfast ending too late to set up the room for a luncheon or training session later in the day.

Number and Kinds of Rooms

Specify the number of guestrooms to be held, spelling out the number of suites, single, double and twin rooms. Sometimes a client will want the location of the rooms specified, as in the case of a multi-room structure. If you agree to it, specify the number of rooms in Building A and the number in Building B.

Many hotels present the sleeping room block in a table format, such as the one illustrated on the following page. This table shows the dates and days of the week, the specific breakdown of room-suite types, rates, and the number of rooms contracted for each night.

Also include a reservation **cutoff date.** Attendees who make their reservations after the cutoff date are not guaranteed a room or the negotiated convention rate. If this is the

ROOM TYPE(S)	ROH	RCST	EXEC	STAFF	Contract
ROOM RATE	$260	1500	260	165	
Monday, 10/20				7	7
Tuesday, 10/21				7	7
Wednesday, 10/22	3			7	10
Thursday, 10/23	46	1	5	7	60
Friday, 10/26	46	1	5	7	60
Saturday 10/27	46	1	5	7	60
Sunday, 10/28				7	7
(2) Executive suites will be at $425					

Key: ROH – Run of House
RCST – Ritz-Carlton Suite
Exec – Executive Room

case, attendees must pay the "market rate" for available rooms. A typical clause might read: "*A cutoff date of thirty days prior to the opening of the convention is established. This cutoff date is May 1, 20__. After this date, any of your unused room commitment will be released to the general public. After the cutoff date, we will continue to accept your group's reservations on a space-available basis.*"

Specify the method by which room reservations will be made: by mail using a pre-printed reservation reply card; by rooming list; through the Housing Bureau of the Convention and Visitors Bureau; to the hotel directly or to an "800" number. Also specify who is to handle the receipt of the reservations – the hotel, the convening group, or a third-party housing company.

Rates

Specify clearly the rates for each type of accommodation. If a range is agreed to, list rates from the lowest to the highest. If a flat rate is negotiated, state it clearly. If rooms are to be priced differently in different sections of the hotel, it may be wise to list such rates separately. And when listing rates for suites, be sure to note that the suite includes a parlor and a number of guestrooms, such as a parlor and one bedroom or a parlor and two bedrooms.

Many large conventions are planned well in advance, and most hotels will not quote firm room rates more than a year out. In this case, a formula for establishing future rates will need to be negotiated. Often, a "percentage off rack rate" is used to establish a future rate. For example, if the hotel's current rack rate is $150 per night and the current convention rate is 20 percent less ($120), this percentage would be used to determine room rates at the time of the meeting (attendees would get 20 percent off the rack rate in effect at the time of the meeting). Other formulas used to establish future rates might be to specify a maximum percentage increase from current rates or to tie the future rates to the Consumer Price Index.

Applicable taxes should also be spelled out. In most cases, attendees will be required to pay the state sales tax and any applicable room taxes. If service charges and gratuities are also assessed, these, too, should be listed to avoid any unpleasant surprises.

Arrival/Departure Pattern

It is important that you know the group's **arrival/departure pattern** – the dates and times that meeting attendees will arrive and depart. If 400 rooms are being held, it is unlikely that all 400 room occupants will arrive on the same day. You should develop a **flow chart** to reserve rooms in accordance with the agreement. The agreement, for example, might call for 100 rooms for arrival on Monday, January 10, 200 rooms for arrival on Tuesday, January 11, and the remaining 100 rooms on Wednesday, January 12. It is also wise to indicate the breakdown of the rooms into singles, doubles, twins and suites. You may find arrival dates easier to secure than check-out dates, but these too are of great importance to you.

Public Space

The experienced convention planner will want you to hold all your public rooms until he or she has firmed up the program and the resultant traffic flow pattern. If the event is far in the future and if it will not occupy the entire hotel, this may be difficult. You need public space to sell other meetings. Keep in mind that while eye-catching events are the big ones, most meetings do not fill the hotel; usually there are several in the house at once. The second or third meeting in the hotel at the time, albeit smaller ones, represent important income, as well as opportunities to serve repeat customers.

How much of your public space to hold is a point to be negotiated, but it is reasonable to hold all rooms that might possibly be used for the event. A date must be set by which the program will be completed to the point that unused public space can be released. If you agree to hold rooms without setting an option or **release date**, you may find yourself unable to use them to solicit other meetings or banquets.

Many meeting planners prefer specific meeting rooms to be named in the contract. This limits your flexibility. If possible, avoid naming the specific function rooms and include a clause to indicate how and when meeting space may be released. For example:

We have reserved function space based on the requirements described to us. The meeting group will provide the final program to the hotel nine months before the meeting. At that time, all space not being used will be released back to the hotel. The specific names of the function rooms will be furnished to you when you are ready to print your program. This allows time for attendance figures to be well established.

Another consideration is the guestroom to public space ratio. Groups and transients are both part of the hotel's overall room demand. Groups book well in advance, so hotels can generally offer them lower rates for a guaranteed block of rooms. The booking cycle for transients is much shorter (a week or two) and they pay higher rates. Depending on demand, a hotel's group room allotment differs daily throughout the year.

Consider a 400-room hotel with a **group ceiling** (targeted number of group rooms) of 300 rooms over a given period and an expected transient demand of 100 rooms. The property is effectively a 300-room group hotel. Revenue is lost if the hotel assigns all its public space to a 200-room group as that leaves no meeting space for the remaining 100 group rooms.

Complimentary and Reduced Rate Rooms

It is commonplace in the convention industry for hotels to supply some complimentary rooms, but the number varies a great deal. A hotel may be more generous if the meeting is scheduled during an off-time of the week or season. A more successful hotel may be tougher when it comes to concessions. A very common rule of thumb is one complimentary guestroom for every fifty rooms used. No matter what formula is used for complimentary rooms, it should be clearly spelled out. If charges are to be made for meeting rooms, the rooms and the rates should be specified. Such charges are usually made in the event that few guestrooms are used.

A hotel and a client may also agree to a number of reduced rate rooms. This is done for staff members, speakers and performers. This is subject to negotiation, of course, and should not be taken for granted. A contract clause on complimentary rooms might read:

We will be pleased to furnish one complimentary guestroom for every fifty room nights utilized. The complimentary commitment will be provided on a cumulative basis for the length of the meeting. The hotel offers a choice of accounting procedures for complimentary rooms. A bottom line dollar credit on the Master Account will value each unit at the daily average guestroom rate generated by the group, or guestrooms/suites can be reserved on a complimentary basis prior to arrival.

The above clause specifies how comps are calculated (on a cumulative rather than on a per night basis) and explains how they can be credited to the master account. Some hotel contracts state that comp rooms are only awarded if the group's room pickup is 80 percent of their room block. If this is your policy, specify what happens if the pickup is less than 80 percent.

Prior Visits

A hotel often will not charge for guestrooms used by the meeting organizer and his or her staff during visits to the hotel before the event to make preliminary arrangements. This is often done on a *space-available* basis. It is wise to set a specific limit on the number of rooms made available for this purpose.

Working Space

Offices, press rooms and similar working space should be discussed. If a charge is to be made for them, specify the rates. If no charge is to be made, specify this clearly, but also spell out the maximum number of rooms to be used for this purpose. Many meeting planners insist upon indicating the location of such rooms to make sure the locations are convenient to the meeting sessions.

Registration Control

In the case of association conventions, hotels usually agree to clear all requests for accommodation from people of that particular industry with the convention organizer. You need to do this in order to credit the association with the total number of rooms used in conjunction with the convention. All such rooms should be applied against the guaranteed number of rooms. In addition, a convention organizer often wants to control the use of suites as hospitality centers or even as setups which circumvent the exhibit itself and its booth space and decorating costs.

Exhibit Space

If a charge is to be made for the exhibit hall, say so clearly and state what is to be included in the charge. Items to be considered are hours the exhibit is to be open, electricity, air conditioning or heat, carpeting, and the number of tables and chairs. List what the hotel is to furnish and what must be contracted for with a show decorator.

Secure exact dates for the exhibition from the meeting planner, including beginning and ending times that include an allowance for the move-in and move-out of the exhibits. Many hotels provide forms for the meeting planner to verify dates and times for both the exhibit and exhibitor move-in and move-out.

Some hotels charge on the basis of the number of booths sold by the association. The charge is usually a per booth rate by day for the duration of the convention including move-in and move-out days. However, this ties the hotel's rental income to the show manager's ability to attract exhibitors; hotels, therefore, normally levy a flat charge. A fee of one to two dollars per square foot for each exhibit day is quite common.

Food Functions

Meeting planners will not expect you to establish menu prices today for a meeting three years in the future. Most realize that, because of rising costs and daily fluctuations in market prices, catering managers usually won't quote firm menu prices until six months out. But a meeting planner has to make budget projections, so expect experienced planners to negotiate a fixed percentage off the printed menu prices in effect at the time of the meeting or to attach a current banquet menu to the contract and negotiate that prices won't increase by more than a certain percentage each year.

Specify how much notice you require for guarantees on food functions. Most common is 48 hours advance notice, but many hotels have increased their guarantees to 72 hours. If you need more time, and you may over weekends, negotiate it and include it in your letter of agreement. Menus have to be priced and approved. Most hotels will agree to set tables for a percentage above the number guaranteed in order to accommodate additional guests. Many set for an additional five percent, others hold it to three percent, and still others base the percent on the number of persons to be served. For example, a typical contract might include points such as the following:

A 48-hour guarantee is required on all meal functions. Your catering manager must be notified of the exact number of attendees for whom you will guarantee payment. For functions scheduled on Sunday or Monday, the guarantee must be received by noon on the preceding Friday.

The hotel will set up as follows:

20-100 persons set	*5% over guarantee*
101-1000 persons set	*3% over guarantee*
1001 persons and over	*1% over guarantee*

In the event a guarantee is not received, the original estimated attendance count will be prepared and billed.

When a salesperson quotes food and beverage prices, he or she will note a "price, plus, plus." The price is the price per person and the **plus, plus** represents taxes and service charges added to the per person charge. The actual percentages will vary depending on state sales taxes and property services charges. For example, a Carmel Valley, California hotel might quote a per person rate for a reception as $20.00 ++. The total price would then be $25.45 — $20.00 plus $1.45 (7.25 percent sales tax) plus $4.00 (a 20 percent service charge).

Refreshment Breaks

It is amazing how many arguments stem from refreshment break arrangements. Many meeting organizers think in terms of coffee shop standards. They do not understand the conditions under which the hotel operates. As a result, much resentment is evidenced, and it is important to explain all that is involved when the hotel supplies refreshment breaks. Spell out the costs and labor required for all refreshment breaks. Include prices for cakes, soft drinks and juice, too. It is important to the hotel that its clients have faith that the hotel charges are fair.

Liquor

Spell out the hotel's policy on liquor service. Most hotels prohibit meeting planners from bringing in food or liquor from outside the property. State your policy on this matter clearly so that no misunderstandings arise during the meeting. A typical contract clause might state:

No food or beverages of any kind will be permitted to be brought into the hotel from the outside without the written permission of the hotel. The hotel reserves the right to assess a service charge for any food and beverages brought into the facility in violation thereof. If any alcoholic beverages are to be served on the premises (and/or elsewhere under the hotel's alcoholic beverage license) the hotel will require these beverages to be dispensed by hotel servers and bartenders. The hotel's alcoholic beverage license requires the hotel to (1) request proper identification (Photo ID) of any person of questionable age and refuse alcoholic beverage service if the person is either under age or proper identification cannot be produced and (2) refuse alcoholic beverage service to any person who, in the hotel's judgment, appears intoxicated.

If you charge by the bottle, an arrangement should be made for inventory control and credit given for unopened bottles after the convention. It is important both for the hotel and the client to identify the person authorized to tally the inventory with your staff. The credit could be issued at that time.

Audiovisual Equipment

Some hotels supply audiovisual equipment from their own inventories; others use local dealers. In either case, it is important to show the rate structure for equipment and services, or to indicate that it is the convention staff's responsibility to make its own arrangements. You may prefer to supply the names of local service companies that deal directly with and bill to the client. Some hotels will accept the local dealer's bills and rebill the convention. It is important, then, that there be a clear understanding as to who has the responsibility to provide the necessary equipment so that the client receives the service needed.

THE CONVENTION INDUSTRY COUNCIL

The best customers are the ones who really know their business. And they like to do business with vendors who know theirs. It is amazing how rapidly and steadily the convention business grew, with very little done to expand areas of knowledge and expertise. Fortunately, leaders of four associations met in 1949 to come to grips with the situation. This group —including both vendors and buyers — formed a council to establish a set of commonly accepted trade standards.

The Convention Industry Council, as it is now known, adopted four basic objectives:
1. to bring about a sympathetic understanding and acceptance among these organizations of the responsibility of each to the other.
2. to create a sound and consistent basis for handling convention procedures and practices through a program of study and education.
3. to conduct educational and activities of mutual interest to participating organizations.
4. to acquaint the public with the fact that conventions are essential to industry and to the economy of the community and nation.

The four original organizations were the American Hotel and Motel Association, the American Society of Association Executives, the Hospitality Sales Marketing Association International, and the International Association of Convention & Visitor Bureaus.

Today, 31 organizations comprise the Council, about half representing seller groups and half representing buyer organizations.

Through the years the Council has been the educational leader for the industry. It created the Certified Meeting Professional (CMP) program. In 1961 it published the *Convention Industry Council Manual*. This manual presented detailed responsibilities of each of the three groups involved in a convention — the sponsoring organization, the hotel and the convention bureau — and how they were interrelated. This manual, now in its seventh revised edition, contains useful checklists, forms and an industry glossary. The CIC published an economic-impact study of the meetings industry and recently initiated APEX, the development of accepted practices for the industry.

31 ORGANIZATIONS COMPRISING THE CONVENTION INDUSTRY COUNCIL

Air Transport Association of America
Alliance of Meeting Management Companies
American Hotel and Lodging Association
American Society of Association Executives
Association for Conventions Operations Management
Association of Destination Management Companies
Center for Exhibition Industry Research
Council of Engineering
Exhibit Designer and Producers Association
Exposition Service Contractors Association
Healthcare Convention and Exhibitors Association
Hospitality Sales and Marketing Association Int'l
Insurance Conference Planners Association
International Association for Exhibition Management
International Association of Assembly Managers
International Association of Association Management Companies
International Association of Conference Centers
International Association of Convention & Visitors Bureaus
International Association of Speakers Bureaus
International Special Events Society
Meeting Professionals International
National Association of Catering Executives
National Business Travel Association
National Coalition of Black Meeting Planners
National Speakers Association
Professional Convention Management Association
Religious Conference Management Association
Society of Government Meeting Professionals
Society of Incentive Travel Executives
Trade Show Exhibitors Association

Union Regulations

Convention organizers are accustomed to union help and regulations, but you should list the basic workday, rates and overtime charges. You should also state any out-of-the-ordinary union requirements in your labor contract. Making your client aware of them eliminates much aggravation.

Many astute meeting planners will not sign confirmations or agreements without first checking out union conditions. The hotel has a responsibility to alert the meeting planner to the possibility of local labor contracts terminating before the meeting, any likely labor rate increases, or possible labor disputes.

Master Account and Credit Procedures

The meeting planner will have a master billing account. He or she must furnish the hotel with a list of people authorized to sign for charges that are to be placed on the **master account**. The client must also indicate which charges the convention organizer will pick up for such people as speakers and performers. The client may choose to pay room rate only and let the individuals pay all incidental charges. In the case of a corporate meeting, the arrangement may have to be clarified for each attendee. Make it clear that the master account will have to be verified and initialed before the client leaves after the meeting.

Before extending credit to a corporate group or an association, hotel sales executives frequently request a completed credit application (see Figure 9.3). Calls also may be made to colleagues at properties where the group has met previously. These references combined with Dun and Bradstreet credit checks are used to determine the credit limit extended to the meeting group.

Method of Payment

Specify how the group's bill is to be paid. If you want a deposit, say so and give the date that it is due. Also negotiate any additional sum to be paid, as well as the final payment.

Most convention organizers prefer to go over the master account before they leave the hotel, but some hotels cannot have it ready that quickly. It is a common practice to leave some portion of the account unpaid, should there be some items that require negotiations or that aren't ready for final accounting. But most hotels do insist that the master account be approved by the client before leaving, while all matters are fresh in the mind and the staff is available for consultation. A statement such as the following might be included:

The hotel will be expending money immediately in labor and services to ensure the most successful meeting for you. Therefore, it is our policy to ask for 75 percent of the master account to be paid prior to your departure from the hotel. The remaining 25 percent will be direct billed.

Termination/Cancellation Clauses

A **termination clause**, sometimes termed a force majeure or Act of God clause, should be included in the agreement for cases when either party might cancel because of circumstances beyond its control. Termination means that both parties are excused from performance without liability. For example, the hotel should not be held responsible for nonperformance in the event of a strike, lockout, fire or failure of heat, light, power or natural disasters. Planners might terminate if there is a change in ownership, hotel chain affiliation, management company or bankruptcy proceedings by the hotel. Other forces beyond the control of the group or the facility that would apply include weather events, large-scale disasters or civil unrest.

Figure 9.3. APPLICATION FOR DIRECT BILLING.

---MARRIOTT'S---

Camelback Inn

---RESORT GOLF CLUB & SPA---

P.O. BOX 70 · SCOTTSDALE, AZ 85252 · (602) 948-1700

CREDIT APPLICATION

Direct billing privileges are not automatically extended. To apply for direct billing privileges, please complete and return this application to the hotel. Should you have any questions regarding the status of your application, please call the Credit Manager at (602) 948-1700, ext. 7715 or your Sales Representative.

Name of Group: _____

Address: _____

City: _____ State: _____ Zip: _____

Telephone: _____ Date(s) of Event: _____

References:
Hotel Reference: _____ Contact: _____

Address: _____ Phone: _____

Date(s) of Event: _____ Amount Billed: _____

Hotel Reference: _____ Contact: _____

Address: _____ Phone: _____

Date(s) of Event: _____ Amount Billed: _____

Bank Reference: _____ Officer: _____

Address: _____

Telephone: _____ Account #: _____
(please indicate the acct. # from which payment will be drawn)

Items to be Billed: (Please check)
All Room Charges ( )
Some Room Charges ( ) please specify
Restaurant Charges ( ) please specify
Banquet Charges ( )
Recreational Facilities ( )
Other ( ) please specify
Other ( ) please specify

Estimated Value _____

I have completed this application in behalf of this group and believe all information contained to be correct. I understand that the extension of direct billing privilege is conditional upon our agreement to pay our account in full within thirty days of receipt of the hotel's statement.

Signed: _____ Date: _____

Title: _____

Accounting Department Approval _____

Many hotels do not automatically issue credit to new clients. Meeting groups that do not have a credit history with the hotel must fill out a credit application form. Note that both hotel and bank references are requested on this form.

The next paragraph after the termination clause should be the **cancellation clause**. Cancellation means that one party elects not to perform, which ordinarily requires the payment of damages. Many conventions are planned a number of years in advance, so occasions do arise that call for a cancellation of the event. The cancellation clause should spell out what it will cost the hotel and/or the group if either party should cancel for reasons not identified in the termination clause. Cancellation clauses in hotel contracts often establish cancellation fees on a sliding scale with the amount increasing the closer the cancellation is to the anticipated date (see Figure 9.4). Planned food and beverage functions might also be factored into the scale. Since cancellation fees are based on lost profits, not lost revenues, the percentage of revenue received by the hotel cannot exceed its profit margin (generally 70-80 percent for sleeping rooms and 30-40 percent for food).

Recently, the Hyatt chain implemented a new standardized contract, which was most notably changed in the area of cancellations. Hyatt now uses a graduated formula for cancellation damages; the closer to the group's scheduled arrival date a meeting is cancelled, the more the group's damages increase. In the event of a cancellation between the

Figure 9.4. SAMPLE CANCELLATION POLICIES OF FOUR HOTELS.

Anatole Hotel Cancellation Policy
In the event that you have to cancel your meeting within ____of the actual date, you will be asked to pay a cancellation fee of half the anticipated room revenue. This fee will be used to recuperate loss of revenue which cannot be replaced. In the event we are able to resell all or part of your block, an adjustment will be made.

In the event of a national emergency or an act of God, where you had no control over the circumstances, the above paragraph is null and void. If you are able to rebook the meeting or one with similar requirements within one year of the cancellation date, we will be pleased to apply the cancellation fee to this meeting.

Any controversy or claim arising out of, or relating to the cancellation of the contract or the breach thereof, shall be settled by arbitration in accordance with the rules of the American Arbitration Association, and judgment upon the award rendered by the Arbitrator(s) may be entered in any court having jurisdiction thereof.

South Seas Plantation Cancellation Policy

Cancellation Notice Received	*Cancellation Charge*
0-60 days prior to scheduled arrival date	Full payment on rooms for the duration of the dates agreed upon
60-90 days prior to scheduled arrival date	75% of above
90-120 days prior to scheduled arrival date	50% of above
120-180 days prior to scheduled arrival date	Forfeit deposit

NOTE: Same cancellation policy applies in the event the agreed upon length of stay of days is reduced.

It is further provided there shall be no right of termination on your part for the sole purpose of holding the same meeting in another city or facility. Neither does South Seas Plantation have the right to cancel your room block if another larger group requests the same space and dates.

Opryland Hotel Cancellation Policy
In the event that it become necessary for you to cancel your conference with us, we would be in a difficult position to try to resell your room nights and the cancellation would, no doubt, result in additional lost revenue for our Hotel. We will, however, attempt to resell the room nights that were reserved for you and would only assess a cancellation fee for those room nights not resold over the initially agreed upon dates. This fee would be based upon the unsold room nights multiplied by your established group rate for that period.

Hotel Del Coronado Cancellation Policy
In the unfortunate event that the Group cancels the meeting due to extraordinary and unforeseeable circumstances, the Group agrees (1) to pay one night's rent for the number of rooms confirmed if the cancellation occurs within one year of the scheduled dates, the night paid for being the night the largest number of rooms had been confirmed, and (2) to pay for the entire number of rooms confirmed if the cancellation occurs less than three months prior to the scheduled dates of the meeting.

(Used with permission of the Anatole Hotel, Opryland Hotel, South Seas Plantation Resort and Hotel Del Coronado Legal Department, Timothy R. Binder, General Counsel)

time the contract is signed and two years before the meeting date, the charge is 40 percent of rooms revenue and 15 percent of food and beverage and meeting room minimums. Meetings cancelled within six months of the meeting date carry the heaviest charges: 80 percent for rooms; 40 percent for food and beverage and meeting room rentals. If it is the hotel that cancels, it pays the same fee to the group. Because Hyatt either owns or manages under contract all its 120-plus properties, it has little trouble applying the new contract (with its penalties) uniformly.

Damage Clause: Liquidated or Mitigated Damages

To protect themselves in the event of cancellation, most hotel contracts include either a **liquidated damage clause** or a **mitigation of damage clause**. A liquidated damage provision is an agreement by both planner and hotel in advance as to the penalty for cancellation. Damages are collected upon cancellation. With a mitigation of damages clause, the penalty is not predetermined — the hotel must wait until the convention dates actually pass and then prove its loss. Tracking and reporting the use of space following a cancellation is inconvenient, difficult, and requires waiting much longer to recover damages, so most hotels prefer a liquidated damage clause.

A liquidated damage clause allows the parties to agree in advance as to the amount and method for calculating damages that might be paid in the event of cancellation. The amount of liquidated damages is less than what a hotel might have received from mitigating damages, but it is a "sum certain." The liquidated damage clause sets the limits of damages well in advance of the meeting. If the hotel resells some of its rooms, there is no reimbursement to the meeting group.

LIQUIDATED DAMAGES	MITIGATED DAMAGES
Amount agreeed upon in advance of breach	Actual damages proven after breach
• Predetermined	• Must wait until dates pass
• Risk on hotel	• Risk on group
• No proof problems	• Hard to prove/calculate

Liquidated damages are a compromise that reduces risks to both parties. The hotel is not required to prove its actual loss and no proof of mitigation is required.

A liquidated damage clause is generally stated in a sliding scale tied to a percentage of anticipated profits and/or to a specific dollar amount. The amount would be low for cancellations two or three years out and higher for cancellations closer to the meeting date. For example:

Under the terms of this Agreement, the Hotel is reserving for your use the room block and public space requirements described herein. In the event these reserved facilities and related services are not used, the Hotel will experience significant monetary losses.

Notwithstanding any other provision of the Agreement, you shall have the right to cancel this Agreement without cause upon written notice to the Hotel at any time prior to the event and upon payment of an amount based on the following scale:

Notice and payment received on or before 12/15/06 - $183,060
(15 percent of total anticipated profit)

*Notice and payment received on or before 11/15/08 - $366,120
(30 percent of total anticipated profit)
Notice and payment received on or before 11/05/09 - $854,280
(70 percent of total anticipated profit)
Notice and payment received after 11/05/09 - $1,220,400*

Carolyn Colton, assistant general counsel for Marriott International, cautions that in calculating a liquidated damage amount the hotel should consider other profit centers beyond sleeping rooms. She says:

> "When a group cancels an event, the hotel also experiences substantial damages in lost food and beverage/banquet sales and/or lost fees for use of function space. In addition, the hotel suffers losses in other aspects of its business, such as lost restaurant and gift shop sales, movie purchases, and room service."[2]

Most meeting planners will favor a mitigation of damage clause. Such a clause requires the hotel to try to minimize its damages by working to find business to replace the business lost by cancellation. Hotels that agree to mitigate damages must wait until after the meeting dates have come and gone before determining damages and then are faced with the difficulty of computing damages.

Computing Damages

The difference between liquidated damages and mitigated damages is that mitigated damages are *actual* charges and liquidated damages, while predetermined, are less than actual damages. For example, assume a hotel books a group needing 200 room nights at $100 per night; the estimated room revenue for the group would be $20,000.

Group Rooms Blocked:	200 Room nights
Group's Average Rate:	$100
Profit Margin for Guestrooms:	70 percent

What happens if the group cancels? With a *mitigated (actual) damage clause*, the hotel would be entitled to 70 percent ($14,000) of the lost revenues. The hotel collects only 70% of lost revenues because damages are based on *lost profits*, not on lost revenue. Lost profit is defined as gross revenue minus variable expenses.

Hotels track profit separately for each revenue-producing department. The industry average profit margin for guestrooms is 70 percent. Catered food has an average profit margin of 35 percent, while alcohol has an average profit margin of 80 percent.

If the cancellation clause spelled out *liquidated damages*, both the meeting planner and the hotel might agree to a penalty of 20 percent of lost profits if the group were to cancel. In the above case, the damages would total $2,800.

Mitigated (Actual)	Liquidated
$20,000 x 70% = $14,000	$20,000 x 70% = $14,000
	$14,000 x 20% = $ 2,800

With a mitigated damage clause, if the hotel is able to resell 50 of the cancelled rooms, it would credit $3,500 back to the meeting group:

50 rooms resold @ 50 x $100 x 70% = $3,500	$14,000-3,500 = $10,500

It is common for meeting planners to request that a combination of both clauses be included in the contract. David Scypinski, senior vice president of Starwood Hotels, warns against this. He says:

> **"Include a liquidated damages clause...or a mitigation clause... but never both.** Mitigation is the process of reselling your hotel's loss brought about by a cancellation or through attrition. Mitigated damages can only be collected *after* the dates of the cancelled event. Liquidated damages, on the other hand, are damages collected immediately upon cancellation. Obviously, the best cancellation clause includes a liquidated damages proviso, which is what you should negotiate. Sometimes a customer will insist on a mitigation clause. *Reason:* Both the liquidated and the mitigated clauses discount the amount of revenue you'll be able to recover; if you include both clauses, you'll be penalizing your hotel twice."[3]

Gratuities and Service Charges

Gratuities and service charges should be discussed in advance of the meeting and should be spelled out in the letter of agreement. Most meeting planners view gratuities as part of convention costs, and even though a touchy area, no problems should arise if guidelines are clearly established at the outset. For example, a gratuity clause might read:

Bellperson gratuities of $3.00 per person round trip are mandatory on group arrivals. Maid gratuities of $1.00 per room, per night, are optional, but suggested.

A service charge statement might read:

All catered food, beverage and related service charges will be subject to the current sales tax. Each catered function will automatically reflect a service charge of 17 percent.

Note that the above clause specifies that the service charge is taxable. Taxes on service charges may vary from city to city, and the amount of tax (if any) on the service charge should clearly be spelled out in the contract.

Attrition Clause

An attrition clause (also called a slippage or under performance clause) is relatively new and may be unfamiliar to some meeting planners. Until recently, it was industry practice for hotels to accept the risk of low pickup by agreeing to hold a block of rooms for a group until a specific cutoff date (generally 30 days). After that date, the unused rooms reverted to the hotel for resale with no additional liability to the group.

Although some hotels still adhere to this practice, most, especially in periods of high demand, have altered their contracts to include attrition clauses. An attrition clause allows the hotel to collect damages if the actual sleeping rooms used are significantly fewer than the group's **block**, the number of rooms originally reserved for the meeting. Guestrooms that are used are referred to as **pick-up**; unused rooms are known as **slippage.**

Attrition clauses protect hotels from excessive losses due to slippage. John Foster, an attorney specializing in meeting law, states:

> "Slippage clauses are making planners a little sharper in their forecasting. You're better off in today's climate to underbook your convention

than overbook. It's always easier to go back to the hotel and ask for more rooms than to decrease your block."[4]

The number of rooms for which a planner must pay attrition is negotiable. Kristy Sartorious, Director of Sales for Wyndham Hotels in Dallas, says that they allow a group twenty percent attrition off their room block before penalties are assessed. In contrast, Westin Hotels adjusts the percentage from city to city and by type of property: resort versus downtown.

For example, the Westin St. Francis in downtown San Francisco allows a ten percent slippage while the Westin La Paloma Resort in Tucson allows only five percent. The reason for the difference is that downtown properties can more easily resell rooms to business travelers while the resort hotels primarily rely on vacationers.

Attrition fees are generally based on a sliding scale: the fewer the rooms occupied, the greater the penalty. Attrition fees are best negotiated as an exact dollar amount, and should provide several option dates to review the room block with an agreed-upon percentage of reduction. For example:

From one year to nine months prior to arrival, the group will be allowed to reduce their room block by twenty percent without penalty. For reduction over twenty percent, a fee of ___ dollars per room will be assessed. From six months to three months prior to arrival, the group will be allowed to reduce their room bock by ten percent without penalty. For reduction over ten percent, a fee of ___ dollars will be assessed.

In addition to attrition fees for sleeping rooms, some hotels are requiring planners to pay penalties for meeting space and food and beverage that are not picked up because the group did not meet its guestroom commitment. A food and beverage attrition clause might read:

The number of catered food and beverage functions and the attendance figures for such functions have been taken into consideration in establishing the room rates for this convention. Should any food and beverage functions be cancelled, the Group will be responsible for 50 percent of the estimated food and beverage revenue lost, based on the minimum catering prices in effect at the times of the meeting times the number of scheduled attendees.

A meeting room (function space) rental attrition clause might read:

The hotel is currently holding function space based on the attached Schedule of Events. Should it be necessary for you to cancel or reduce the estimated attendance by more than 25% of any of the major functions listed on the Schedule of Events, the hotel will be entitled to liquidated damages based on the following scale:

More than 60 days to 120 days prior to the scheduled date: An amount equal to one-half (1/2) of the estimated food & beverage profit based on the minimum estimate of the total cost of the function.

Less than 60 days prior to arrival date: An amount equal to 75% of the estimated food & beverage profit based on the minimum estimate of the total cost of the function.

These attrition clauses clearly spell out what is required of the group and the specific penalties that will be levied should the group fail to live up to its contract. Many meeting planners are vocal against these clauses, claiming that attritition clauses force them to look into a crystal ball. Richard Granger, meeting planner for Allmerica Financial, explains:

"Five years ago you didn't see attrition clauses. Now you're lucky to be permitted ten to fifteen percent shrinkage. Attrition clauses are not only tougher, but broader. They used to cover only room slippage, but now include food and beverage costs too."[5]

Hotels, citing their need to be financially accountable, feel that such clauses are justified and prevent the unethical practice of meeting planners overestimating room counts to obtain additional concessions.

Arbitration

Arbitration clauses are often used because **arbitration** provides an efficient, timely, and relatively inexpensive alternative to litigation. An arbitration rather than a court action is usually in the best interests of both the hotel and the meeting planner. A typical arbitration clause might read:

Any controversy or claim arising out of or relating to this agreement, or the breach thereof, shall be settled by arbitration in accordance with the Rules of the American Arbitration Association, and judgment upon the award rendered by the Arbitrator may be entered by any court having jurisdiction thereof.

The Convention Industry Council created the Alternative Dispute Resolution (ADR) as an alternative to lawsuits and arbitration. This program is designed to provide a streamlined, but nonbinding, means to resolve disagreements. The ADR program is designed to allow hotels and meeting planners to submit a written statement of claims and to present their case at an oral hearing before a three member panel composed of individuals from within the industry. Contracts must include a provision that the ADR program will be used if a dispute arises. Each party must agree to submit its dispute to the Convention Industry Council.

The following paragraph is typical of the language that may be used in a contract between the hotel and the meeting planner:

Any unresolved dispute related to this contractual agreement shall be initially submitted for review to the Convention Industry Council Alternative Dispute Resolution Program in Washington, DC. By signing this contract, both parties agree that they are voluntarily submitting all of their disputes that arise under this contract to the Convention Industry Council Alternative Dispute Resolution Program.

A hearing is held within thirty days after the statements are filed. Each party has three hours in which to present its case and is limited to three witnesses, who may be cross-examined. Lawyers may not be present at the hearing, but may assist in drafting complaints and preparing answers. All rulings by the panel are nonbinding, unless the parties to the dispute agree otherwise.

Warranty of Authority

The principles of agency law specify that if both parties are authorized to sign a contract for a meeting, the contract is still binding on both the hotel and the meeting group if one or both of the signers is no longer with their employer. A warranty of authority clause states that the signers have been granted authority by their respective organizations to enter into an agreement. Such a clause is especially relevant given the turnover of both hotel salespeople and meeting planners and in light of the considerable time frame between the signing of the agreement and the execution of the event.

A warranty of authority clause might read:

The Group Name and the person signing this Agreement on its behalf represent and warrant that the undersigned person is an authorized and appointed agent of the Group Name, fully empowered to bind the Group Name to all provisions contained in the agreement, and that no further action is required on the Group Name's part to enter into this agreement.

This agreement shall be binding upon the Group Name and its successors and assigns.

Insurance/Indemnification

Many hotels stipulate that the meeting group must agree to carry adequate liability insurance that protects the hotel against claims arising from the group's activities conducted in the hotel during the convention. In doing business with associations and trade shows, a hotel incurs specific liability in its relationship with trade show exhibitors. Although exhibitors sublease hotel space from the association or trade show, the hotel should require the exhibitor to sign a "hold harmless" or liability agreement that confirms that the hotel is not responsible for damages or theft of material or equipment. Some hotels extend this to deny accountability for accidents occuring in public areas that are not the result of negligence by the hotel.

Convention hotels also request that a copy of the meeting group's exhibitor contract be submitted to the convention services department prior to its printing and distribution. The reason for this is to ensure the meeting group and the hotel are protected.

An insurance clause might read:

The group acknowledges that the hotel and its owners do not maintain insurance covering property brought into the hotel by exhibitors and that it is the sole responsibility of the exhibitor to obtain insurance covering such losses. The group shall give written notice of such to any exhibitors. The group is responsible for submitting to the hotel an executed release of liability from each exhibitor.

Indemnification is a word found in many meeting contracts. To indemnify means to protect. An **indemnification clause** provides mutual protection. The hotel and the meeting group indemnify each other. A typical indemnification clause might read:

Each party agrees to indemnify and hold harmless the other from any and all loss, damage, or expense (including attorneys' fees) arising from the negligence or willful misconduct of the indemnifying party, its agents and employees in the performance of its duties and responsibilities under this agreement.

This clause states that each party will be responsible for its own negligence and that each party agrees to hold the other party harmless if the actions of one party cause the other party to be sued or suffer loss.

If doing business by letter of agreement/contract seems complex and detailed, think of this format as a checklist or order form. Arranging for a convention requires more than ordering a certain number of guestrooms. Your letter of agreement shows you, the hotelier, what the client expects and also shows the client his or her responsibility. It works out well when thought and time are given to each detail.

The first letter of agreement/contract may be the hardest to write. After you get it polished, save it as a sample. It will save much work if that polished letter and its various clauses are individually stored in a word processor file so that they may be used when you are formulating new contracts or letters of agreement.

It will help you also if you list details in such a manner that they can be transposed directly onto function setup sheets. That makes the meeting easier to service and errors less likely to occur. Do keep in mind that some details just cannot be supplied when the letter of agreement is signed, so provision may have to be made to add a supplementary agreement later on.

Contract Standardization

To facilitate the formerly time-consuming process of contract negotiation and to meet the requests of meeting planners for more consistency when dealing with properties, the industry has responded with an important trend: the standardization of contracts and other meetings-related paperwork. Following the introduction of the Marriott Meetings Network (see Figure 9.5), a number of chains have developed their own standardized forms and services (see box titled "Contract Standardization").

Standardized contracts, which are most prevalent in the area of small meetings due to their short lead time, essentially provide a heightened degree of communication by standardizing language and covering all relevant issues, and most meeting planners are very receptive to them. Blanca Diaz, manager of corporate event planning at McGraw-Hill in New York, says:

> "If I receive a contract that is not that customer friendly, I have to run it by
> the legal department and it delays the signing of the contract. In the past,
> it was nightmarish. Now I'll approve some of the contracts on sight."[6]

There are drawbacks, of course. Some meeting planners, especially independent ones, prefer to use their own forms. Their point of view is that every event is unique and no

---

Contract Standardization

Hilton: A leader in standardization, with development of a standardized group resume 20 years ago, the chain now offers standardized contracts and general meeting forms at 52 corporate-owned and managed properties.

Hyatt: Developed Meeting Connection program featuring standardized contract for groups of fewer than 100; now, 104 properties have standardized contracts for larger groups as part of The Standard. Also mail out their standardized resume on microsoft disks, enabling planners to enter meeting specs into the program and mail or e-mail documents back.

Marriott: Led the industry in meeting paperwork standardization with the Marriott Meetings Network, a computerized network system providing standardized contracts, master billing forms, group resumes, and post-convention reports (see ad). Thirty-six of the chain's properties in the United States, Mexico, and Canada offer this service.

Ritz-Carlton: All meeting-related paperwork — contracts, group resumes, banquet event orders, billing formats, and post-convention reports — are standardized at 30 Ritz-Carlton properties.

Sheraton: Developed ITT Sheraton Connections, providing standardized contracts, banquet event order forms, and billing formats, at 27 domestic convention properties.

Renaissance: Offers standardized meeting paperwork (contracts, billing formats, group resumes, and post-convention reports) at 49 Renaissance properties in the United States.

Westin: Provides standardized forms and offers Grouplink, a computerized system that enables planners to enter group rooming lists themselves.

Figure 9.5. STANDARDIZED SERVICES FOR THE MEETINGS INDUSTRY.

In response to meeting planners' needs for consistency when negotiating with hotels within its chain, Marriott developed the Marriott Meetings Network after two years of intensive customer research. This computerized system enables properties within the chain to standardize contracts and eliminates the need for meeting planners to update contracts. Since a group's paperwork is stored in the chain's computer system, it can be easily retrieved and previous histories can be checked to ensure that the group's requirements are met.

one form can handle all individual group needs. But their perspective is being overshadowed by the sea of planners who welcome not only standardized contracts, but other standardized forms and services as well — event resumes, banquet event orders (BEOs), and billing procedures and computerized access to such areas as rooming lists. Diana Johnson, conference administrator for 28 events in different cities across the nation, says:

> "Once you've read the standard BEO you know the format. You know right where to look to find the same things; meeting setups, guarantee policies, set menus. You don't have to scrutinize it as much."[7]

The standardization of these previously time-consuming pre-convention documents and procedures enables both the meeting planner and the convention staff at individual properties to concentrate on servicing the event and offers yet another benefit besides saving time and money — meetings clout. Jack Breisacher, vice president of group sales for Renaissance Hotels and Resorts, explains:

> "After all, the customer is often spending a few hundred thousand dollars with us, and all they want to know is how much money was spent in each area. Then they'll take that information to a property next year and say, 'Here's what we did, and based on that here's what we need at this time.' It becomes a solid negotiating tool."[8]

Multiple-Meeting Contracts

Negotiating multiple-meeting contracts is becoming commonplace in the hospitality industry. These contracts, which schedule business over a period of one to several years, have grown in popularity -- especially with corporate meeting planners, who laud them as time- and cost-saving. A planner from a healthcare organization, for example, says she signs a multiple-meeting contract with a major hotel chain for her group's 200 educational seminars held every year around the country. The contract guarantees a price that is a percentage off the rack rate at each hotel and saves time, eliminating the need to negotiate separate contracts.

Another advantage for the meeting planner is meeting clout; a hotel is usually more open to making concessions for a planner who schedules a great deal of business. Judi McLaughlin, CMP, of Martiz McGettigan, one of the largest meeting management firms in the world, states:

> "In many companies, meeting planning is fragmented and decentralized. One of our clients found that it used 29 different properties in Chicago in one year for some 70 meetings. Through consolidated planning, the company has named ten preferred hotels in that city.
>
> "The benefits to the company are guaranteed discounts in pricing, overall agreement to standard contracting terms and conditions, increased efficiencies throughout the planning process, and better quality meetings. And the preferred properties are certain to see a dramatic increase in their market share of the company's business."[9]

Best Practices

Marriott Contracts with MetLife for 15 Incentive Meetings Over a Two-Year Period

In 2004, MetLife, a large insurance company that previously held its meetings in a number of different hotels, signed a deal with Marriott International to book 15 incentive meetings into the chain's Marriott, J.W. Marriott, and Ritz-Carlton properties across the country over a two-year period. The deal, which represents 15,000 room nights, came about because MetLife's recognition programs represent some of the company's biggest meetings, and the company's management felt that these meetings were too important for a "cookie cutter" approach.

In addition to the benefits of a meetings consolidation plan that would both save money and create consistency, MetLife gained major clout as a potential client when it put all 15,000 of its room nights on the table to potential hotel companies. Bob Pizzute, AVP, conference planning and event services at MetLife in New York, says:

> "When we took an enterprise approach to meeting planning, where all of our distribution channels come to one source for meetings, we became a much larger player in the market."

After looking at hotel companies (and hotels within those companies) that best matched MetLife's goals and strategy, the company's conference planning team and the procurement department at MetLife worked together, meeting with national sales contacts on the hotel side (these contacts included Mark Friscone, director of national accounts, Marriott International, and Pam Ferguson, director of insurance sales, The Ritz-Carlton Hotel Co., both of whom had extensive experience in the insurance market).

Negotiations for the actual terms of the contract took months, as there were hundreds of details to be worked out, including space, rates, and concessions. Jeff Calmus, CMP, director, conference planning and event services for MetLife, says:

> "Rates were different based on the time of the year and availability, but we had developed concessions that every hotel agreed to."

The successful deal benefited both parties, as MetLife got as good a deal for a 3,800-room-night program as for a 220-room-night program and Marriott not only benefited from the large piece of business but may see additional income as Pizzute says he will go to hotel chains with future RFPs. The win/win negotiation between the parties on their first multiple meetings deal (and Marriott's successful execution of the meetings for which it contracted) will likely result in the chain being a strong contender for MetLife's future business.

Source: Alison Hall, "Big Deal," Insurance Conference Planner, September/October 2004, pp. 26-29.

There are of, course, some disadvantages for meeting planners, including the difficulty of accurately predicting meeting attendance (unless attendance is mandatory), future developments, such as company downsizing or mergers, or being "locked in" by contracts. In the last instance, the meeting planner is bound by the previously negotiated multi-meeting contract and cannot take advantage of opportunities that arise when other properties can provide the same services at a lower rate.

For hotels, multiple-meetings contracts offer the advantage of guaranteed business, but there is also a major disadvantage: perhaps another group comes along that would generate more rooms or food and beverage revenue for the property. If the space is tied up, the property has no recourse but to let the new business go. It is imperative, therefore, that hotels consider multiple-meeting contracts carefully, weighing the proposed multiple-meetings business while maintaining a degree of flexibility in these contracts, especially those that are a year or more out. Other factors, such as the history and stability of the group or possible business developments on either the part of the group (a possible merger in the group's future, for example) or the property (perhaps the obtaining of new, more lucrative business) should also be considered before entering into multiple-meetings contracts.

Summary

As you can see, the hotel industry is working hard to deal with meeting planners on a highly professional basis and to make the process of securing profitable meetings business easier through the development of "win-win" contracts and the standardization of meetings-related services. In the next section of this book, we will take a look at the various areas involved in actually executing the meetings and conventions secured through excellent salesmanship and effective negotiating.

Endnotes:

1. Howard Feiertag, "We're Into a Seller's Market Again, So Watch Those Contracts," *Hotel & Motel Management*, June 21, 2004, p. 12.
2. Carolyn Cotton, "Liquidated Damage Provision Reflects Compromise on Hotel's Part," *Convene*.
3. Correspondence with David C. Scypinski, senior vice president of industry relations, Starwood Hotels.
4. Mary Ann McNulty, "Be Prepared for a Slippage Clause," *Meeting News*.
5. Melinda Legis, "Killer Contracts," *Successful Meetings*," May 1999, p. 50.
6. Kenneth Hein, "Standardization Efforts Paying Off," *Meeting News*.
7. Ibid.
8. Ibid.
9. Alison Hall, "Fewer Suppliers, Better Deals," *Corporate Meetings & Incentives*, July 2004, pps. 16-20.

Additional References:

• <u>Hospitality Law</u>, Steven Barth, John Wiley and Sons, 2001.
  www.hospitality@wiley.com

• <u>Meeting Manager Standards and Meeting Coordinator Standards</u> by the Meeting Professionals International Canadian Council and the Government of Canada, The Department of Human Resources Development
  www.mpiweb.org

• "Resolving Disputes in the Global Marketplace", Arbitration Seminar, American Bar Association
  www.abanet.org

Internet Sites:

For more information, visit the following Internet sites. Internet addresses can change without notice. If a site is no longer available at the address listed below, a search engine can be used to find the new address or additional, related sites.

American Bar Association Alternative Dispute Resolution Section - www.abanet.org/dispute/drlinks.html
Convention Industry Council - www.conventionindustry.org
Hospitality Sales and Marketing International (HSMAI) - www.hsmai.org
PCMA Toolbox (Model Contracts) - www.pcma.org/toolbox
Project Attrition Final Report 2004 – www.conventionindustry.org/resources/ project_attrition_report11204.pdf

Study Questions:

1. Distinguish between a proposal letter and a letter of agreement (contract).
2. What elements should be considered when developing a contract?
3. What is the master account? In what ways is this account billed?
4. What is a damage clause? An attrition clause? What is the difference between a termination clause and a cancellation clause? How extensively are each of these clauses used?
5. What is the Convention Industry Council? What groups make up its membership and what is their role in the convention industry?
6. What are standardized contracts? What types of properties typically use them? What are the pros and cons of using standardized contracts?
7. What are the advantages and disadvantages of negotiating multiple-meetings contracts?

Key Terms:

Arbitration. The settling of a disagreement by the review and decision of an arbitrator rather than using the courts.
Attrition clause. Allows the hotel to impose a penalty if the actual guestrooms used are significantly less than the rooms blocked. Can also apply to food and beverage and meeting room rental.
Arrival/departure pattern. Anticipated date and times of the arrival and departure of a meeting group's members.
Block. The number of guestrooms reserved for a group.
Cancellation clause. Provision in the contract that specifies damages that apply for both parties should either party terminate the agreement. A cancellation is a breach

of the contract.

Customer lifetime value. The value of profits expected from a customer's future purchases. A corporation or association meeting planner who is satisfied and books several meetings with your property over his or her buying lifetime is more valuable than a one-time purchaser. If the satisfied customer refers other meeting planners, the value would be even greater.

Cutoff date. The designated date when the buyer (upon request) must release or add to their function room or guestroom commitment.

Flow chart. Indicates the arrival and departure pattern of the meeting participants.

Group ceiling. The maximum number of guestrooms that can be allocated to groups on a particular day. Sometimes referred to as the hotel's **group room allotment**.

Indemnification clause. Contract clause that specifies compensation for injury, loss or damage. Also referred to as a **hold harmless clause**.

Inquiry questionnaire. Questionnaire requesting a post-convention critique from hotels used in the past by specific meeting groups.

Letter of agreement/contract. Letter from the buyer accepting the proposal. No legal agreement/contract exists unless both parties have accepted the proposal.

Liquidated damage clause. A contract clause that specifies in advance the exact amount of money parties agree to pay in the event of breach of contract.

Master account. One folio for the group on which all charges are accumulated. Also called the **master folio**.

Mitigation of damage clause. A contract clause that requires parties to determine damages after the dates of the canceled event. Mitigated damages are actual damages.

Pick-up. Number of guest rooms actually used out of a room block.

Plus, plus. Addition of taxes and service charges to the standard prices charged for food and beverage. Designated on a catering contract and a BEO by the notation "++."

Proposal letter. A letter sent by the hotel before the letter of agreement or contract that spells out exactly what the customer will receive.

Request for proposal (RFP). Action initiated by the meeting planner for an offer or bid for hotel services.

Release date. The date beyond which the hotel is free to rent the unused function space to other groups.

Slippage. The number of guestrooms not used from the original reserved block.

Termination clause. Contract clause that limits liability should the convention be prevented due to circumstances beyond either party's control. Sometimes referred to as an **Act of God clause** or a **force majeure clause**. When a contract is terminated, neither party is considered in breach of the contract.

Convention Sales and Services

Part II

Convention Services

Learning Objectives:

This portion of your text looks at the role of the convention service manager and his or her staff in ensuring that the property delivers all that was promised to the meeting planner. When you have studied this chapter, you will:

- Be able to describe the role of a convention service manager at a number of types of properties.

- Know how the convention service staff helps to ensure a smooth meeting.

- Be able to describe how group business is turned over to the convention service department from the salesperson and the different ways in which sales-people are involved after the sale.

Outline

Service Is the Key

Who Services?
- Convention Service Manager
- Increased Recognition
- Convention Service Staff

The Transition

An Overview of the Service Function

Summary

The Role of Convention Service Professionals

Devon Walter, CMP
Convention Services Manager
Sheraton El Conquistador
Tucson, Arizona

"Convention service professionals have only one job, and that is to give the meeting professional the best meeting ever... The keys to producing a great meeting are communication and planning...The convention services and meeting professional become a team, and communication between team members is critical...Pre-planning is so important to the success of the meeting. There will always be some little glitch when the meeting is on-site, and that is so much easier to deal with when everything else is running smoothly — because it has been PLANNED...A convention services professional can expect to spend over 40 hours a week at the facility when there is a group in house... Depending on a group's evening activities, the convention service manager may be at the facility quite late checking on a reception, dinner, or dance... But when the meeting professional and you sit down to conduct the post-convention evaluation and the former says it was the best one ever, that is tremendously rewarding...For those who enjoy working with new people daily, learning about new organizations, working hard, multi-tasking, delegating, administering, coordinating, juggling, creating, and working with details, this is the PERFECT job!"

10

The Service Function

S ecuring a convention is only the beginning; once business has been booked, you must deliver what was promised. How a convention goes out of a hotel is equally -- or even more -- important as obtaining the group's business. A hotel salesperson does not sell just guestrooms, meeting space and complicated audiovisual equipment -- his or her most important product is reassurance; reassurance that the hotel is capable of handling the group's business. To a great extent, the meeting planner's job depends on how well the hotel does its job.

Hard work and many dollars are invested in advertising and promotional material in an effort to recruit group business. Yet, satisfied meeting planners and delegates are the best and most economical advertising medium. If the hotel performs well, the meeting planner will likely return to the property. Delegates are well traveled today and expect more from hotels. If your hotel has made a favorable impression, planners may recommend it to their peers and delegates may stay with you on return visits -- and recommend that their business associates and friends do the same.

Since nothing attracts another piece of group business more than a satisfied convention, it is crucial that all promises made in the selling process be fulfilled. An indelible impression will be made when the hotel provides service that is above and beyond the preconvention promises.

Service Is the Key

Sometimes, the service follow-through is regarded as an afterthought to the heavy emphasis placed on selling a convention or meeting. But failure in the essential service phase can be costly. A meeting planner evaluates the success of his or her convention on the extent to which the hotel's commitments were kept. Lack of communication, poorly trained or indifferent employees, failure to heed details and rude responses to requests are all detriments that may result in lost future business.

How might the hotel better serve the convention group? Most important is a well trained and courteous staff with a service attitude. The hotel industry is essentially a people business and it is important to communicate the property's willingness to assist the meeting planner during both the selling and servicing process (see box titled "Selling and Servicing Small Meetings"). Hotel staff members should be made aware of the importance of convention delegates and should be trained to understand that nothing short of top performance is expected.

You can build good will in other ways — make arrangements with labor if exhibits are used, obtain any official permissions that are required by local government departments, such as police or fire, and assist with transportation needs. Help convention delegates schedule their time and keep them informed about the facilities in the hotel. Book special entertainment, arrange tours to points of interest and provide the highest quality food and beverage service possible. In short, give convention delegates every reason for staying at your property -- and returning in the future.

SELLING AND SERVICING SMALL MEETINGS

A single hotel contact person and easy accessibility to a source of assistance are of prime importance to planners of small meetings. The Marriott Corporation addressed this need with the introduction of a new position, the Executive Meeting Manager. This person, who is responsible for booking and servicing small meetings and catering functions, is viewed as a one-stop shopping source to simplify planning for the small group client.

Other chains followed suit, either designating individuals to work one-on-one with meeting planners or developing programs designed to help planners of small meetings. Hyatt, for example, introduced the "Hyatt Meeting Connection," which offers a toll-free number, a fax number and a web address to enable a meeting planner to get in touch with the hotel quickly. After providing pertinent details on the date and size of the meeting, the planner is contacted by a Hyatt Meeting Connection Manager who assists with meeting details.

Hilton's program, "Hilton Direct," is targeted to inexperienced meeting planners, as is Sheraton's "One Stop" program. These sources simplify planning to set the stage for suggestive selling and creative presentations, which, in turn, build repeat business and revenues.

With Renaissance Hotels and Resorts' "Meetings Express" service, a sales manager handles meeting details for planners, including guestrooms, function rooms, and audiovisual services. Other programs include Westin's "Westin One Call," Omni's "Omni Express," and Wyndham Hotels' "Wyndham One."

Radisson's "Meeting Solutions" provides on-line requests for proposals, a toll-free meetings desk help line, and faxing of guestroom confirmations to meeting planners. Fairmont Hotels guarantees small groups a 24-hour turnaround of availability and rate confirmations, and each hotel has a "one-stop" shopping salesperson.

Stuck Planning A Small Meeting?

HYATT**MEETING CONNECTION**
Making Small Meetings A Big Success
1-800-543-1818
or fax your meeting requirements to (402)593-4030
or visit our Web site at www.hyatt.com.
HYATT
HOTELS & RESORTS

Just attach this sticker to your Rolodex.
Then call Hyatt Meeting Connection and leave the details to us (see inside).

History of Convention Services

1960s — *Beginning of the convention service position, but with limited authority.* Salespeople were now confronted with the problem of spending a considerable amount of their time servicing groups. Feeling the need to concentrate more time on the selling of the hotel and its facilities, many sales managers turned servicing over to either the sales secretary or the lowest level salesperson.

1970s — *Role of convention service manager increased in importance.* As the number and complexity of the meetings held grew annually, so did the importance of the convention service manager. This increased recognition was advanced by the Society of Corporate Meeting Professionals, which opened its membership ranks to convention service managers.

1980s — *Gained industry respect.* Convention service managers formed their own association (seven hundred strong) called the Association of Convention Operations Management (ACOM). Meeting planners came to rely on the dedication, knowledge and hard work of the convention service department.

1990s — *Elevated to the Hotel's Executive Committee.* Now most of the major hotel chains have a corporate level position for convention services. Within the hotel, convention service managers generally report to marketing, occasionally to food and beverage or catering, and now increasingly directly to the general manager. In hotels that look to conventions for a major portion of their room nights, the Director of Convention Services is part of the hotel's executive committee.

2000s — *Serve as Meeting Consultants.* The role of the convention service manager has expanded beyond delivering meetings service. Increasingly, meeting planners look for partners who can consult and present customized solutions to their problems. Most hotel chains have raised the bar, requiring their convention service managers to become certified with the same education and training as the customer.

Regardless of how smoothly a program is planned, snags and slipups inevitably occur. If your hotel helps meeting planners solve these problems, future business is nearly always assured. It may be necessary to shuffle meeting rooms around, help find a last-minute substitute speaker or prepare a special entree for the wife of the chairman of the board. The attitude with which you accept these common occurences will, to a great extent, determine the location of next year's convention. The professionalism your staff demonstrates is the hotel's best promotion for future business from the convention organizer and it increases the likelihood of business referrals. If you conquer any crisis that threatens the flow of the meeting, the parting handshake may well be accompanied by the meeting planner's promise, "We'll see you next year."

Who Services?

One of the frequently discussed issues in convention management is the extent to which the salesperson should be involved in the servicing process. The structure of the hotel staff is based on how this issue is resolved.

Some hotels say that a salesperson is just that, and that he or she shouldn't become involved in servicing the client. They claim that the service function is a specialty, distinct from selling, and that there is a more efficient use of staff and a higher rebooking percentage when salespeople spend 100 percent of their time selling. Howard Feiertag, a veteran hotel salesperson, says:

> "In my opinion, the person who books the business is not the best person to follow through on the details. Large hotels should pass the booking to a convention services manager. Small hotels should pass the food and beverage details to catering and the rooms details to a rooms division manager or front office manager. Although sales people often do not like to let go of a piece of business, they should turn over the minutiae of the group to the operations staff, remove themselves from the details and use their skills to book more business."[1]

Others hold that the convention salesperson should handle the sales and servicing completely. They suggest that the sales representative should follow up all hotel visits, write up the actual bookings and coordinate the servicing of the group during its stay at the hotel. These are diametrically opposed points of view. Which should you follow?

Resort Management, a lodging and foodservice publication, asked the managers at three hotels how they handled sales and servicing. Their comments on how they handle this controversial issue are presented in Figure 10.1. Judging from this discussion, there seems to be basically three approaches to the question: "Who services?"

The Tamarron's position is that the sales manager should sell, arrange and work with the meeting from beginning to end. They feel that the salesperson who does not get involved in servicing may be concerned only with putting business on the books, thus perhaps making hasty promises that are impossible to keep.

Opposed to this view is the Kingsmill, with the opinion that once the sale is made the salesperson should step aside in favor of the in-house conference coordinator, who then documents the client's needs, draws up the letter of agreement and follows through to the end of the meeting.

A third, middle-of-the-road, approach is practiced at Jug End. There, the salesperson meets the group as it arrives, but then steps out of the picture until the function is nearly completed. He or she then returns on closing day to attempt to sell upcoming meetings.

Which approach should you practice? Our experience says "the best approach is the one that works." No one procedure is best for all situations. If the size of the hotel justifies an in-house convention service manager, we support separation of sales and service.

The Convention Service Manager

Throughout the text, we have taken the position that the servicing responsibility is handled by the convention service manager. Such a practice assures the association or corporate executive that whatever his or her requirements — reservations, banquet, meet-

Figure 10.1. VIEWPOINTS ON WHO SHOULD SERVICE MEETINGS.

TAMARRON

Located in the Rocky Mountains about thirty miles from Durango, Colorado, the Tamarron is a resort owned by Golf Hosts International. It offers 415 guest rooms and 7,000 square feet of meeting space.

I find that both direct sales and service selling have very valid points. However, I feel that the points in service selling far exceed those in direct sales. The advantages of direct sales do give the opportunity to the sales staff to concentrate their total effort in the booking business, and do not tie them up in the laborious task of accumulating the multitude of details that it always takes to conduct a successful conference. But when you have a sales department whose only responsibility is getting meetings on the books, they seem to lose contact with the other departments and see their responsibilities as only that of putting business on the books.

Salesperson Services

I am a strong believer in service selling with modifications. I believe there is a definite need for a conference coordinator to assist in the many details that are involved in successful conferences. However, conference coordinators should never eliminate any of the responsibilities of the salesperson who actually sells the group.

I think the salesperson who is instrumental in booking business has got to be kept involved from beginning to end. By doing this, it builds the association executive's confidence in the hotel, makes the salesperson more aware of the strong and weak points of his people and, consequently, makes the salesperson better in booking other groups and puts him or her in an excellent position to rebook meetings. It also helps the salesperson tremendously in building his or her own reputation with the meeting planners because they understand the promises and assurances that were made when the booking was made, and the planners see that he is always available and visible during the conference to see that these promises are carried out.

KINGSMILL

The Kingsmill Resort is a part of a large development program undertaken by Anheuser-Busch, Inc. just outside of Williamsburg, Virginia. It houses a large convention center and has more meeting square footage than either of the other two properties discussed.

There is so much more to this question concerning service selling vs direct sales than meets the eye that I can only classify the subject as an "explosive issue."

The subject is not just "How is the salesperson best employed?" or "How can management keep salespeople happy?" or "How to reduce costs?," but perhaps should be defined as "Complete client satisfaction ensures rebooking without sales costs." Meeting planners are not sheep, but they need a shepherd to turn to at all times.

Salesperson Sells, Then Turns Over To a Convention Service Manager

Let us, therefore, trace sales procedures, starting with a given company name only, coupled with a reasonable belief that this company would possibly hold meetings.

Sales Step 1: Having been given a cold lead by the sales manager, a sales telephonist is employed to determine the company's meeting plan profile. The information to obtain is broadly as follows:

A. Meeting frequency
B. Time(s) of the year
C. Length of meeting — arrival date and departure date

    D.   Number of attendees
    E.   Type of property preferred and why
    F.   Type of meeting
    G.   Purchase center and responsible individual
    H.   Any other attendant information which will help the account executive

Sales Step 2: Having qualified the prospect, the information obtained is then turned over in a written report to the area account executive who then telephones for an appointment, or, if feasible, arranges for the conference planner to participate in a house visit. Sales literature is normally not passed until personal face-to-face contact is made with the potential client.

Sales Step 3: When the verbal sale is made, the client is turned over to the property's conference coordinator, who is responsible for all of the client's needs, preparing the sales contract or letter of agreement, and following through every step of the way to the end of the meeting.

While the conference coordinator has the full responsibility for the smooth running of the client's meeting, and for informing by conference specification sheet, the various department heads concerned, the conference coordinator will, where practical, introduce the client and sit in on discussions with the various department heads (such as food and beverage director, front desk supervisor, conference setup manager, etc.). The client receives a copy of the internal conference specification plan in order that he or she may check that all arrangements have been made in accordance with his or her instructions. The points to be learned by this process are:

    A..   The salesperson does not waste his or her time soliciting prospects who would not be suitable for the particular property.
    B.   The salesperson can devote 100% of his or her time "selling" to live prospects.
    C.   After the verbal sale has been made, the client is assured that there is a responsible person who will look after his or her needs and who will always be available on the spot, and is, therefore, not "out of town," "will call back later," etc.
    D.   Management can reduce their number of salespeople needed because the sales people can spend 100% of their time selling to prospects instead of 30% of their time checking internally, 30% making introductions to department heads, and other time setting up meeting rooms.
    E.   Service promises concerning actual meeting room availability, function areas and times, audiovisual equipment availability, etc. are kept because the service manager will be in the house at the time. How often, in poorly coordinated properties, is a client anguished when he finds a particular meeting room, a function site or a particular piece of equipment promised by the salesperson is not available because it has been committed elsewhere.
    F.   Furthermore, and equally important, a strong conference coordinator will control the flow of traffic into the main dining room by staggering the times groups break from cocktail parties, banquets and recreational activities. Such planning minimizes the burdens on the chef, the head bartender, and setup people, and provides the client with the type of service anticipated.

In other words, efficient service and attention to small details throughout the length of the meeting is of paramount importance, and, when given, assures that the client will rebook.

JUG END

The Jug End in the Berkshires is a 180-room resort in Massachusetts with about 6,000 square feet in its largest meeting room. It, like the Tamarron, is a mountain resort with winter skiing and summer golf facilities.

In many cases, the servicing of group business depends on the size of the house. If the property has 50 rooms or less, many times the owner/manager can sell and service the property himself (or with the help of his wife)...but when the property is larger than that, I prefer that specialists handle the servicing.

Salesperson Sells; Responsibility for Group Based on Size

Let the salespeople do the selling...get the business "in the house." The reputation of the hotel (and the food service) is mostly dependent on the in-house servicing. With larger groups, the salesperson should be on hand to welcome them, and then, the servicing should be handled by others, preferably by the food staff, since the food staff is so made up that, should one member be unavailable, the whole service operation does not fall apart. I have seen sad situations develop where details have not been properly attended to by the salesperson, and such lack of attention or mishandling reflects poorly on the whole operation.

Should the group planner prefer to deal with the owner/principal of the hotel, we don't object. We will do everything he wants to make him feel at ease. The big thing is not to have a meeting planner come in and feel uneasy...be fearful that the meeting might "bomb out" and so jeopardize his own future in his company. It is also important to let meeting planners know that you recognize their authority and attendant responsibilities and to assure them that you are not going to let them down.

At our property, I always make it a point to meet the head of each group. He has done a great deal of planning for the meeting, has spent thousands of dollars in organizing the meeting, considerable money on transportation, etc., plus what he will spend at our hotel. Consequently, I feel that the head of the hotel has an obligation to the convention group to let them know that the entire staff, from the top right down to the bottom, is interested in making their meeting a success.

ing room setup — there is one individual with complete authority and responsibility for his or her meeting.

The title *convention service manager* has not been adopted by all hotels. Many use such other titles as conference or convention or service coordinator, convention manager, and, at many smaller properties, banquet or catering manager. (Chapter 14 offers a thorough discussion of the role of the banquet manager as practiced at most small properties.)

Regardless of the title, the position carries a lot of prestige and a hefty amount of responsibility (see box titled "The Perfect Convention Service Manager"). If any one person can make or break a conference, it is the convention service manager, often referred to as "the person who makes things happen." He or she is the meeting planner's contact person, and so should be readily available to handle all of the convening group's on-the-spot needs. Quite simply, he or she is the single communication link between the meeting planner and the hotel.

The convention service manager should not be satisfied with just selling rooms and food. He or she must be a problem solver and an excellent communicator. The convention service manager should request full and detailed information so the hotel can better serve the group. Likewise, the hotel should communicate accurate data to the client.

Horst Schulze, the former president of Ritz-Carlton Hotels, says:

"Hoteliers must understand that a meeting planner has put his job on the line by selecting their hotel. The convention service manager (CSM) must build a quality product around that one customer, specifically and individually. The CSM must see himself as a true partner and loyal assistant to that planner. To supply a defect-free meeting, there must be communication between the planner and the hotelier. This communication helps the hotelier understand the planner's desired outcome for the meeting."[2]

The role of convention service manager has grown beyond service to meeting consultant at some hotels (see Figure 10.2). David Kassel, CMP, senior convention service manager, Walt Disney World Dolphin Hotel, states,

> "I try to educate the planner on how to do events with a little more creativity. A lot of my expertise is anticipating needs — having the forethought to put myself in the planner's place. It also means that I find alternatives to save them dollars."[3]

Ideally, the convention service manager has the authority to get the job done and to get it done fast. The Loews Hotel chain, for example, has increased the stature of the chain's convention service managers, promoting them to the executive committees of their respective hotels (the executive committee is made up of senior-level hotel managers who report directly to the general manager, and may include the director of food and beverage, the controller, the resident manager, the director of marketing and the director of convention services). Jonathan M. Tisch, the President and CEO of Loews hotels, said the change came about because *he listened to meeting planners*. Meeting planners are able to rest much easier when they have the assurance that their liaison has authority within the hotel as well as the responsibility to fulfill their needs.

Leroy Smith, association executive of the National Automobile Association, has suggested that the convention service department should report directly to the hotel's general manager, not to the director of sales.[4] He suggests that hotels should have an organizational structure that gives the convention service manager line control over the functions of the front desk, housekeeping, banquet, and food and beverage departments as related to conventions.

The working hours of the person in charge of service are often very long. Bill Tobin says of the time he was convention service manager at Caesars Palace in Las Vegas, "I wanted to give the meeting planner the impression that I never went home." One hour before every function, he checked out the facilities with the group's coordinator. This is a commendable policy, but convention managers typically work on three to five meetings simultaneously, each in different stages of completion. This work schedule underscores the need for convention service managers to possess the abilities to organize and multitask, but, no matter how skilled they may be, convention service managers often find they have little time for themselves. Cutting still further into time off are the preconvention and postconvention meetings often scheduled for weekends.

But there are rewards for these long hours. In addition to the salary paid by the hotel, the convention service manager may receive compensation for long hours in the form of gifts and tips from the meeting planner. Association and corporate executives have been known to be extremely generous in saying thanks for a job well done. Further remuneration is sometimes received from the hotel. The Sheraton Waikiki, recognizing the importance of the convention service manager, has given this individual a suite in the hotel. Sheraton Hotels, like a growing number of chains, has also established advisory boards made up of meeting planners to help the chain respond to the needs and concerns of meeting planners. One of these concerns centers around the role of the convention service manager; in many cases, the advisory boards recommend giving convention service managers more authority to ensure that meeting details can be worked out through a single contact person. Brian Stevens, former Vice President, Sales, Hilton Hotels, agrees,

> "Today, more than ever, hotels need to make sure their customers work with the most experienced, most highly trained convention service managers possible — or there simply won't be any customers after a while."[5]

Figure 10.2. CONVENTION SERVICE MANAGERS AS EVENT PLANNERS.

Today's convention service managers do not just sell function space and food and beverage functions. Hotels have recognized the importance assisting meeting planners with both large and small events, and most CSMs today take an active part in the planning and execution of events. This ad for The Scottsdale Plaza Resort in Scottsdale, Arizona, promotes its Plaza Planner program, which offers a trained hotel professional to assist planners in making their events stress-free and successful.
Source: Courtesy of The Scottsdale Plaza Resort.

How does one become a convention service manager? Most have advanced through either the banquet or front office departments, where they were exposed to the problems frequently encountered in group business. Then some alert sponsor placed him or her over the department. Often the next step up the corporate rung is to convention sales. The salesperson who has had experience in group servicing knows what can be promised and

TRAINING CONVENTION SERVICES PERSONNEL

Many hotel chains have recognized the importance of the service function, and have introduced training programs for their convention service managers and other key convention personnel. This increased knowledge and meeting planning expertise helps build the confidence of meeting planners, and is an important selling point in today's highly competitive meetings market.

what can be delivered, and thus is a most valued employee. However, many are not sure this move to sales is a promotion, and more and more managers are staying with convention services.

Another career move for some is promotion to resident manager. This is not surprising since the convention service manager interacts with virtually all other hotel departments. In a recent speech, Joyce Inderbitzin of Hilton's Corporate Convention Services estimated that 70 percent of Hilton's general managers were convention service managers at one time in their careers.

Increased Recognition

The convention service manager's position has steadily been elevated in status in hotel organizations. The Society of Corporate Meeting Professionals has invited convention service managers to join their ranks and *Successful Meetings* instituted an annual Convention Service Manager of the Year award.

Convention service managers also have their own organization, the Association for Convention Operations Management (ACOM). Membership includes convention service

---

THE PERFECT CONVENTION SERVICE MANAGER

The Convention Industry Council advises meeting planners that the "perfect" convention service manager is one who: begins working with you as soon as the meeting is booked; knows his or her property and has the respect of people in other departments; has the authority to get things done; anticipates problems and has solutions at hand; offers creative suggestions for set-ups, programs, meals and entertainment; considers himself or herself an extension of your staff; stays in contact with you throughout the planning process to check on your needs; covers your meeting 24 hours a day, personally and through his or her staff; is flexible and honest enough not to over-promise or to under-commit; balances the needs of professionals with the needs of his/her own organization; treats all meeting planners with equal respect. (Source: The Convention Liaison Manual, 6th Edition, p. 66.)

Many CSMs think that this description is "too good to be true," especially in regard to working 24 hours a day, although the vast majority of CSMs put in long hours and have little free time. Therefore, it is not uncommon for hotel CSMs to become meeting planners (conversely, it is less likely that a meeting planner will join the hotel industry because of the long, demanding hours).

While meeting planners work long hours as well, especially in the planning stages and during a function, the hours are generally predictable. It is easier to schedule free time when the planner knows exactly when he or she will be tied up with events and when the work load will be relatively light. A hotel CSM, on the other hand, has a more unpredictable schedule – he or she may be needed to solve a crisis or handle the details for an unexpected piece of business.

Hotel CSMs that become meeting planners bring a wealth of knowledge to their new positions. They know how hotels operate and they understand hotel industry jargon. They are also familiar with the issues that are the most important in terms of meeting and event planning, and they know which issues can and cannot be negotiated in contracts.

directors, managers and coordinators from hotels, and event service managers from convention centers and convention bureaus. Hotel convention service managers can also join the Professional Convention Management Association (PCMA). This organization serves the convention industry with educational resources, networking, and an annual meeting that offers nearly 100 educational sessions to meeting planners.

Marketing gurus tell us that the best future customer is the one you've already got, and hotels are placing a heavy emphasis on the convention service manager's role in rebooking. Increasing the authority and responsibility of this department has been used by hotels to show commitment to the meeting business and convention service personnel.

A profile of ACOM's membership supports this contention. The average tenure is five years in their positions, with less than 10 percent going into sales and marketing. Also, a number report directly to the general manager and are members of their hotel's executive committee, along with the directors of marketing, food and beverage, operations and the controller. A number of hotel chains have standardized the position of convention service manager and bring them together annually for networking and idea exchange. Hilton, Hyatt, Marriott and Sheraton have established corporate directors of convention services.

Several chains have made major commitments to training their convention service managers and other convention support staff to better assist meeting planners (see box titled "Training Convention Services Personnel"). As part of its recently introduced "Network Plan," the Marriott chain has committed to staffing each of its convention properties with a minimum of two Certified Meeting Professionals (CMPs). The CMP exam, given by the Convention Industry Council, also figures prominently in the Hyatt chain's "Learning Environment Specialist" (LES) program (passing the CMP exam is a pre-requisite for this advanced training). Developed in association with the Professional Convention Management Association (PCMA), this six-day program offers instruction to help enhance all phases of meeting planning. And, the Hilton Hotel chain has developed its own program, Customer-Focused Convention Service Skills (CFCSS), to sharpen the skills of its convention service managers.

Figure 10.3 ORGANIZATIONAL STRUCTURE OF A CONVENTION SERVICE DEPARTMENT IN A LARGE HOTEL.

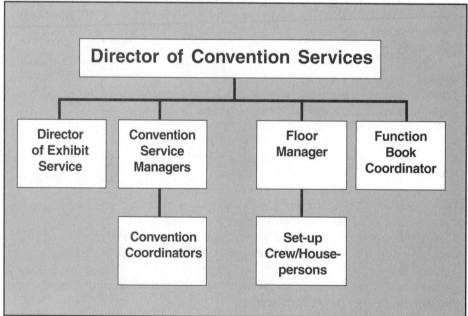

INTRODUCING THE CONFERENCE CONCIERGE

As the convention industry has grown, the time commitment of the convention service manager has increased. Hotels that once realized 25 percent of their occupancy from meeting groups now look to capture 40-50 percent of their room nights from meetings, which would stretch even the most capable of convention managers too thin to adequately service business.

In response, Starwood Hotels (owner of the Sheraton and Westin brands, Four Points Hotels, the Luxury Collection and the new W hotels) is just one of the chains (Hyatt is another) that has introduced a new position: the *conference concierge.* The conference concierge's responsibilities begin when the group arrives. The concierge stays in constant communication with the planner, improving the level of attention and service planners receive. Typical tasks for the concierge might include getting copies made for the planner at the last minute or assisting with package shipment. With the addition of this position, planners now have two people on site to assist them, and the level of attention is greatly improved.

The new position also frees up the convention service manger to spend more time with advance planning with groups whose meetings may be months in the future. And, the position offers an opportunity for those wishing to break into convention services.

David Dvorak, convention services vice president for Starwood, says:

"The new title creates a great entry-level position because the concierge sees room setups, how to deal with emergencies and meeting planners, and how to multi-task."

Source: Christopher Hasford, "Starwood Takes Scientific Path to Serving Meetings,"Meetings News, September 15, 2003, p. 62.

Convention Service Staff

How the convention service department is staffed depends on the size of the hotel, the percentage of occupancy accounted for by convention groups, the size of the groups using the hotel, and the number and size of the property's meeting rooms. Figure 10.3 illustrates a sample organization chart of a convention service department.

Some properties have expanded their convention service departments, creating new positions to better serve meeting planners (see box titled "Introducing the Conference Concierge"). Following are position titles and brief descriptions of the responsibilities of individuals who might work in the convention service department of a large convention oriented property.

Director of Convention Services — oversees, trains and assists the convention staff in all phases of managing meeting accounts. Assigns meeting accounts to convention service managers, keeping the workload evenly distributed among staff. Generally reports to the director of sales/marketing, but at large properties may report directly to the general manager.

Convention Service Manager(s) — services meeting groups as assigned by director of convention services and is the primary contact for assigned groups. There are usually several convention service managers in a large hotel. A sample job description for this position is given in Figure 10.4.

Convention Coordinator(s) — entry-level position in convention service department. Primary responsibility is to service small meeting groups and to assist convention service managers.

Floor Manager — responsible for servicing and setup of all meeting room and food and beverage functions. Oversees housepersons to ensure instructions from the specification and function sheets are carried out. At some properties, particularly smaller hotels, this position may be given the title of *Banquet Set-up Manager*.

Set-up Crew (sometimes called *Housepersons*) — responsible for the physical setup of all meeting and banquet rooms.

Director of Exhibit Service — works closely with the meeting group's trade show manager when the hotel's exhibition facilities are utilized. This position is only present in hotels with substantial dedicated exhibit space.

Function Book Coordinator — the single person who records entries from the function book reservation forms, responsible for ensuring the accuracy of the function book. This individual works closely with the sales staff, catering, and the convention service manager(s).

Convention Service Secretary(ies) — performs secretarial duties, including typing of correspondence, specification sheets and function sheets for the convention service department.

The Transition

A frequent debate in convention management is, "How and when should meeting planners be turned over to the individual within the hotel who will have charge of coordinating their conference?" Timing depends greatly on the meeting planner, the size and type of the meeting, and how far in advance the meeting has been booked. Four commonly used times for this transition include:

1. *During the site inspection* —The hotel salesperson is the key contact when booking the event, but some planners try to meet the convention service manager during the site inspection visit, saying there is a "reassurance factor" in making early contact with the person who will be handling the details of their meetings.
2. *Right before signing the contract* — Some meeting planners ask for an interview with convention services before signing the contract. This step helps ensure that promises made regarding space, set-ups and meeting services can be met. One meeting planner has stated,
   "Before signing a contract, I want to meet the convention service manager and let him or her know who I'm bringing in and what my meeting is all about. The salesperson may wine and dine me, but the convention service manager makes it happen. That's the person I'm married to for three days."
3. *Immediately after the point of sale* — If the convention is large and complex, some planners start working with convention services as soon as the contract is signed.

Figure 10.4. SAMPLE JOB DESCRIPTION FOR CONVENTION SERVICE MANAGER.

Job Title: Convention and Conference Service Manager
Reports to: Director of Convention and Conference Service
Department: Convention and Conference Service

Summary of Position

Services all convention and conference groups as assigned by the Director of Convention Service. Plans and coordinates all arrangements, (i.e., golf bookings, audiovisual needs, etc.) related to assigned groups to ensure the success of the convention and to promote repeat business.

Scope

This position is responsible for identifying and communicating the needs of the customer to the hotel departments to ensure proper service throughout the hotel operation for assigned groups.

Objectives/ Responsibilities

A. Plans and executes conventions and conferences as the primary customer contact for assigned groups.   *25% of time*

B. Coordinates and distributes all interdepartmental paperwork necessary for the successful implementation of assigned groups.
               25% of time

C. Oversees activities of assigned groups and functions as the onsite contact for the Meeting Planner.   *15% of time*

D. Assists with training of Convention and Conference Coordinator as assigned by the Director of Convention and Conference Service.
               15% of time

E. Attends daily and/or weekly meetings as assigned by the Director as well as arranges and conducts Pre-Convention and Conference meetings for assigned convention groups.   *15% of time*

F. Assists in preparation of forecasts and budgets.   *3% of time*

G. Performs additional tasks as assigned by Director.   *2% of time*

Supervision Exercised

Directly supervises: Assigned Clerical Staff
Indirectly supervises: Convention and Conference Coordinator
                          Floor Manager
                          Support Staff
                          Function Book Coordinator

Supervision Received

Responsible to the Director of Convention and Conference Service

Responsibility/ Authority

Employee Relations:
Responsible for communicating and following through with hotel management to ensure that the sales commitment is being fulfilled. Distribute written communications (resumes, event orders) detailing the needs of the customer and the sales commitment. Maintains effective relationship with Sales and Service Staff as well as all department heads.

Materials or Products:
Maintains up-to-date group files to ensure proper coordination of sales commitment as well as customer needs. Maintains trace system for these files.

Equipment:
Assists in proper use and adequate inventory of meeting equipment to properly service all functions.

	Financial: Responsible for maximizing revenues associated with meetings for assigned group files as well as maximizing function space usage. **Business Contacts:** Maintains proper communications between groups, outside vendors and hotel staff. Also responsible for establishing customer relationships that will encourage repeat business.
Preferred Knowledge/ Qualifications	**Equivalent Education Level:** College degree (or equivilent Convention and Conference Service experience) required. **Experience:** A minimum of two years in Convention and Conference Coordination with exposure to office procedures and experience in function room setups and service with strong interpersonal skills and organizational skills. **Knowledge Required:** Function space configuration, room setups, maximizing space, art of negotiating and selling. General knowledge of hotel management, operations and facilities.

4. *One year before the meeting* — Many planners feel no need to involve convention services before one year in advance to begin the formal planning process. This procedure will not work in the case of short-term bookings that will require immediate contact between the meeting planner and the convention service manager.

It is difficult to divorce the salesperson entirely from the service function. The salesperson who simply dismisses a client after the sale, assuming that the convention service manager will shoulder the burden, will probably not get a rebooking. Jim Hill, Director of Sales at the Inverness Hotel and Golf Club in Englewood, CO, uses a unique approach to ensure that both the salesperson and the convention service manager are known and trusted by the meeting planner:

> "What we've introduced is a buddy system. Each sales associate is working with a conference service manager, and they actually work through the sales process together. From day one, we introduce the conference services manager, who the sales associate knows and has been working with throughout the year."[6]

Repeatedly partnering the convention service manager with a specific salesperson creates strong bonds and efficient teamwork. If the sales staff is deployed by market segments, partnering benefits convention service managers by concentrating their work with similar types of groups. For example, working with a salesperson dedicated to medical groups allows the convention service manager to gain an indepth understanding of how to service these types of meetings.

The transition from the salesperson to the convention service manager must be handled smoothly. Frequently the client has dealt exclusively with the salesperson for two or three years and has complete trust in the sales staff. The salesperson's exit can be traumatic if the planner has not been reassured of the service manager's competence.

We recommend that once the sale is made the salesperson step aside and turn the meeting over to the service people. We don't believe, however, that the client should be abandoned by the salesperson. We suggest that the salesperson greet the planner, if pos-

Best Practices

Crowne Plaza Hotel and Resorts' "The Place to Meet" Program

In order to better meet the needs of meeting planners, Crowne Plaza Hotels and Resorts, a brand of the InterContinental Hotel Group (which also includes Holiday Inns), offers the "Place to Meet" program, which includes a two-hour response to a request for proposal, *the services of a Crowne meetings director* (CMD) and daily on-site meeting de-briefings.

Kevin Kowalski, Crowne's vice president of brand management, North America, says the chain's advisory board told hotel management that "meeting planners want an experienced go-to person at the hotel; someone to partner with throughout their event." Therefore, the chain has taken steps to ensure that their convention service managers are a cut above the norm. Tina Lyle, manager of marketing operations, says:

"We want them (CMDs) to have the authority and empowerment to make something right, no matter what the service issue might be...When we started discussing what would enable a partnership between CMDs and buyers, we started looking at certifications, and we saw that the CMP would make our staff focus on the information meeting planners need, instead of just on what the hotel needs. It raises them to a level where they can speak to planners intelligently."

Crowne meetings directors (CMDs) must have at least eight years of meeting experience and must either hold or be working toward holding CMP credentials. To enable their staff to become CMPs, the chain launched a rigorous training program that includes a walk-through of the CMP application and an action plan for those who wish to take the CMP exam.

CMDs are also part of their properties' executive committees, meaning that they are included in weekly management meetings. This enables CMDs to learn about changes at the hotel, report in detail on incoming and departed group business and work with other hotel departments, from housekeeping to engineering, to address a group's needs. At many properties, CMDs also report to the general manager rather than the director of sales or director of catering.

Several of the chain's top-performing CMDs also serve on an advisory board to serve as problem solvers and mentors to less-experienced CSMs. The advisory board not only assists newer CMDs in becoming CMPs, but members also serve as consultants to hotels when needed.

The program, which is promoted in advertisements and in literature that includes the illustration shown, has lived up to its name as meeting planners find a comfort level working with experienced hotel CMDs. Kowalski says, "The bottom line is that planners have enough challenges and stresses and stress factors these days. If we can help eliminate some of these issues, they will be more likely to look at us first."

Sources: "Crowne Courts Meetings: Chain's On-Site Experts Woo Planners," Meetings & Conventions, *April 2004, p. 20; Rayna Katz, "Crowne Plaza Putting Teeth Into CSM Position,"* MeetingNews, *September 15, 2003, p. 6; "Crowne Plaza Creates Board to Advise Conference Services Managers,"* MeetingNews, September 20, 2004, p. 4.

Crowne Meetings Director: another way we set the standard.

Noluna Ceballos, Crowne Meetings Director, Crowne Plaza Redondo Beach

Figure 10.5. SAMPLE LETTER OF INTRODUCTION AND TIMELINE SHEET.

February 6, 20__

Ray Harper, President
Harper and Pritchard Construction
611 S. Bridge Street
Columbus, OH 48850

Dear Mr. Harper:

I would like to take this opportunity to introduce myself as your Convention Service Manager for your upcoming meeting which will take place at the Las Vegas Hilton during the dates of September 1-4, 20__. I will be responsible for all aspects of your meeting with the exception of food and beverage arrangements, which will be handled by Gus Moser in our Catering Department.

Below I have noted a few of the key items relating to your meeting. Please bring any discrepances to my attention as soon as possible so the appropriate changes may be made internally.

Room Block — 125 king rooms and 4 suites in the North Tower
Room Rate — $110 guest rooms, $150 suites
Method of Reservations — Rooming list
Billing — Master Account

Additionally, please find enclosed a time line for required information which will assist both of us in planning your upcoming convention. This schedule ensures that your program receives the attention and service that it deserves. Please review the schedule and advise me if any dates seem unattainable.

If you will be shipping any packages to the hotel in conjunction with your meeting, please insure they are addressed to my attention in care of the Las Vegas Hilton Convention Service Department along with your organization's name and date of your function. However, due to storage requirements, we ask that these items be sent as close to the convention as possible.

Sincerely,

Cindy O'Keefe
Executive Director of Convention S

cc: Sean Steward, Sales Manager
     Gus Moser, Catering Manager

TIME LINE

GROUP: Harper and Pritchard Construction
CONTACT: Ray Harper, President
MEETING DATES: September 1-4, 20__

Listed below are areas of concern with review dates that will assist us both to ensure a successful meeting.

ITEM	DUE DATE
Preliminary meeting program	April 1
Final meeting program	May 1
Credit application finalized	July 1
Cut off date	August 1
Meeting & audiovisual requirements	July 15
Food & beverage menus finalized	July 15

Please make any changes as necessary then sign and return the form to me. If these dates seem practical as listed above, I would appreciate your signing and returning this form to me. Thank you.

Ray Harper, President	Cindy O'Keefe
Harper and Pritchard Construction	Executive Director of Convention Services

The convention service manager and meeting planner should communicate often —and in writing — from the time the business is turned over to the convention service department. Today, the convention service manager and the meeting planner also exchange e-mail addresses early in the planning stage. Establishing a written timetable with the customer for pre-planning and communicating the group's requirements is essential to effectively service meeting groups. Most convention service managers tell us that their biggest problems in servicing groups stem from not getting enough information from their planners in a timely manner. A timeline such as this one alleviates that problem by setting dates when specific information is needed.

sible, when the meeting comes to the hotel and reassure him or her that the meeting is in good hands. Further, the salesperson should keep in touch and reenter as the meeting closes to suggest a rebooking. It just makes good sense for a salesperson to maintain contact with a client who has bought the property as a meeting site, and could, of course, buy again in the future.

An Overview of the Service Function

Thus far, we've talked about the importance of service, the role of the convention service manager, and his or her position in the hotels' organizational structure. In subsequent chapters, we will cover in detail every facet of this person's job and how he or she works with other departments within the hotel. To assist you in understanding the service process, an overview of the convention service manager's role follows. Additional information on each of these steps can be found in the Convention Service Checklist detailed in the chapter Appendix.

Step No. 1 — Once a group is booked, the convention service manager reviews all correspondence to find out what information has been documented and what information is still required. Many times he or she will review **account files** from two or three years before the date of the convention. A **sales to service turnover data sheet** is now used by many hotels to quickly bring the CSM up to date on the group. This short form summarizes specifics negotiated by the salesperson, including guestroom block, preliminary meeting program, cut-off dates, and so on. With this information, the CSM begins to assemble the **working file** needed for servicing the group. (Refer to Appendix, items 1-5)

Step No. 2 — The booking is listed in the function book, and contact is made with the meeting planner through a **letter of introduction** (see Figure 10.5). This letter specifies that the group will be dealing the the convention service manager while in the hotel. At this point, the salesperson goes behind the scenes and the convention service manager begins to get answers to the three basics: *reservations, program and billing.* (Refer to Appendix, items 6-10)

Step No. 3 — **Tracing** — using follow-up letters, telephone calls and personal contact with the meeting executive — is initiated to build a relationship of trust and cooperation between the two parties. Correspondence is made as clear as possible, and includes lots of detail. Technology has made tracing easier, more efficient, and faster. In the past, convention service managers relied on telephones and letters; today, e-mail and faxes are used to speed up the tracing process. (Refer to Appendix, items 11-27)

Step No. 4 — Details of the program are formulated in a *personal interview* with the meeting planner at least six months before the event. Reservation requests are also mailed to the delegates at about this time in an effort to determine the number of guestrooms (see Chapter 11 for additional information). (Refer to Appendix, items 28-42)

Step No. 5 — A monthly preconvention meeting is held with all department heads to review upcoming groups (see Chapter 12). All convention *resumes* and *banquet event orders* are discussed in detail. (Refer to Appendix, items 43-50)

Step No.6 — Two or three days before the conference opens, a preconvention meeting is held with the front office manager (see Chapter 12), the supervisor in charge of room setup (see Chapter 13), the catering manager (see Chapter 14), and the meeting planner. The entire program is reviewed, the menus are reaffirmed, and the meeting setups are verified.

Step No. 7 — During the event, the convention service manager is on hand as much as possible. He or she will be at each meeting location one hour ahead of time to view the setup, check the audiovisual equipment (see Chapter 15), exhibit setup and check security (these are discussed in Chapters 16 and 17). (Refer to Appendix, items 51-62)

Step No. 8 — A post-convention meeting is held at the end of the event (see Chapter 18). All charges to the master account are verified and initialed a second time by the client. The post-convention meeting is a review of the event by those persons in attendance at the preconvention meeting. At this time, the salesperson steps in to sell the group on a repeat convention. When the service department does its job, a rebooking percentage of 70 percent is not uncommon. (Refer to Appendix, items 63-70)

Summary

Your attitude and professionalism in serving your guests will be what sets you and your property apart from the rest. And the foundation of your professionalism begins with knowledge. You must know what tangible products and services are required by meeting planners and how to deliver the successful meetings and functions that they demand (see "Best Practices" box).

In this chapter, we have presented an overview of the convention services structure and the importance of meeting with the planner to ensure that his or her requirements will be met. In the next chapter, we will discuss how to get the meeting or convention off to a good start by discussing the most efficient way to register guests. In subsequent chapters in this section, we will provide a foundation in other elements of service. Armed with this knowledge, you will have the confidence to embark on the most important aspect of your job: building the trust and rapport that results in satisfied customers and repeat business for your property.

Endnotes:

1. "Five Tips to Help the Sales Staff Perform at Their Best!", *The Rooms Chronicle*, Volume 8, Number 5, p. 6.
2. "Building Loyalty," *Convene*, April 2003, p. 17.
3. Robert Carey, "Leaders of the Pack," *Successful Meetings*.
4. Speech given at a Hospitality Sales and Marketing Association International (HAMAI) meeting in Las Vegas, Nevada.
5. Brian Stevens, "A New Commitment to Convention Service," *Convene*.
6. Connie Goldstein, "Productive Meetings," *Corporate Meetings & Incentives*.

Additional References:

- <u>Hospitality Marketing Management, Third Edition</u>, Robert Reid and David Bojanic, John Wiley 2001.

- <u>Marketing for Hospitality and Tourism, Fourth Edition</u>, Philip Kottler, John Bowen, James Makens, Prentice Hall 2006.

Internet Sites:

For more information, visit the following Internet sites. Internet addresses can change without notice. If a site is no longer available at the address listed below, a search engine can be used to find the new address or additional, related sites.

Four Seasons Regent Hotels and Resorts - www.fshr.com
Hilton Hotels - www.hilton.com
Hyatt Hotels and Resorts - www.hyatt.com
Loews Hotels - www.loewshotels.com
Marriott International - www.marriott.com
Professional Convention Management Association (PCMA) - www.pcma.org
Society of Corporate Meeting Professionals (SCMP) - www.scmp.org
Successful Meetings magazine - www.successmtgs.com

Study Questions:

1. Should sales department personnel become involved with group servicing? Discuss the three approaches used by the Tamarron Resort, the Kingsmill and the Jug End.
2. Where does the convention service manager fit into the hotel organizational structure?
3. What types of programs are available to train convention service managers and their staffs to better assist meeting planners?
4. Describe the titles and duties of the members of the convention services staff.
5. What is meant by the transition? At what four times can transitions take place?
6. What is tracing and how is it used to build a relationship with the meeting planner?
7. Briefly define the eight steps inherent to servicing a group's meeting.

Key Terms:

Account file. A file that includes all correspondence, call reports and information used in selling the group. Prepared by the sales department, additional information, such as the contract, the meeting agenda, room block data and so on are added to the group's file if business is booked.

Letter of introduction. Letter sent by the convention service manager to the meeting planner. Specifies whom the group will be dealing with while in the hotel.

Sales to service turnover data sheet. Prepared by the salesperson, this sheet summarizes key information from the account file (room block, meeting program, cut-off dates and so on) and is given to the convention service manager to assist in preparation of the working file.

Tracing. Building a relationship with the client by using follow-up letters, telephone calls and personal contacts.

Working file. A file set up by the convention service manager after a booking is definite. This file initially contains information from the account file. As the service manager works with the meeting planner, additional information, such as the group's resume and banquet event orders, is added. At the conclusion of the event, the working file is broken down and appropriate materials are re-filed in the group's account file for future reference.

CHAPTER APPENDIX

CONVENTION SERVICE CHECKLIST

Detailed checklists serve as planning guides and often prevent the overlooking of important items in staging a successful convention. Numerous checklists exist for helping the meeting planner avoid oversights, but few are available specifically for the convention service manager. This is the format used by the Penta Hotels and is the best checklist of its type that we have seen in the industry.

Penta Hotels
CONVENTION SERVICE CHECKLIST

NAME OF GROUP _____

DATES OF MEETING _____

MEETING PLANNER _____

MASTER ACCOUNT ADDRESS _____

_____

TELEPHONE NUMBER _____

SALES MANAGER _____

BANQUET MANAGER _____

	Completion Date
TWELVE (12) MONTHS AWAY FROM MEETING DUE DATE	

1. Sales manager to turn account file over to Convention Service with a copy of the signed contract, a copy of the approved booking notice, a copy of the approved room block, a copy of the credit form (if credit has not been determined, trace three days and follow-up), and a past history on pick-up for the last two (2) years. _____

2. Review account file _____

3. Verify definite program, confirm diary space, meeting room rental, exhibit rental, set-up charges, and date all space hold to be released (if applicable). _____

4. Confirm room commitments with Front Office and Group Rooms Control for accuracy, based on past history, block VIP suites. Determine when room rate will be established, and trace if not already established. _____

5. Determine if all exhibit information is complete in contract and remind account of need for floor plans to be approved, exhibitor's contract to be approved, hold harmless clause signed, insurance certificate for $250,000.00. _____

6. Initial contact and letter of introduction — obtain names of other key meeting personnel. _____

   a) Request most recent convention history. _____

   b) Review credit procedures and billing address. _____

   c) Review reservation procedures, when mailing will go out, clarify need for approval of reservation form if they act as housing bureau. _____

6. d) Check need for hospitality suites, who will use them, their names and addresses, and previous suite number if annual. _____

   e) Ask about public relations opportunities, famous people, unusual events, and newsworthy issues. _____

   f) Inquire if account is tax exempt; ask for tax exempt form. _____

7. Discuss their needs and requirements for outside security per corporate policy. _____

8. Send Penta meeting planner fact book. _____

9. Send Penta convention kit. _____

10. Order reservation cards (if the salesperson has already done so, obtain a copy of this form.) _____

SIX (6) MONTHS AWAY FROM THE MEETING DUE DATE

11. Contact public relations for coordination of publicity. Place director of Public Relations in contact with the meeting planner. (If this is applicable.) _____

12. Accentuate the need for the accounts to provide detailed instructions at an early date so that proper service may be administered. _____

13. Explain convention resume procedure. _____

14. Reconfirm staff and VIP housing requirements; double check suites blocked. _____

15. Determine audiovisual needs. Discuss how extensive set-ups are. Sell in-house audiovisual company. _____

16. Discuss registration personnel and procedures. Penta needs to maintain integrity of our property. All signs must be professionally printed; no signs allowed on walls. No signs allowed in the main lobby, except by management approval. _____

17. Coordinate contact with banquet representative, give name, telephone number, have banquet representative call account. _____

18. Review account's needs in regard to office equipment, i.e., typewriters, telephones, need for decorations or decorators, florist. _____

19. Request name of drayage company. Review needs of union labor. This is a union house. _____

20. Inquire into anticipated companion programs, anticipated bus tours. Coordinate information regarding bus tour loadings and unloadings. _____

21. Request finalized meeting and exhibit floor plans for approval. _____

22. Review final meeting schedule and check diary. _____

THREE (3) MONTHS AWAY FROM MEETING DUE DATE

23. Reconfirm required suites and staff requirements with guest and Front Office. _____

24. Review billing arrangements, identify all master accounts and authorized signatures. _____

25. Remind client of cut-off date for rooms. _____

26. If rooms do not materialize, a rental may have to be implemented (if there is not a rental or sliding scale in the contract) by the salesperson. _____

27. Request official printed program. Compare published program to space requirements in regard to time, set-up times, coffee services, etc. _____

SIX (6) WEEKS AWAY FROM MEETING DUE DATE

28. Process letter for VIPs. _____

29. Verify attendance at all functions, establish rental based on contractual agreement and establish master account and billing instructions along with authorized signatures. _____

30. Secure deposit if required, due 30 days prior to arrival date, unless we have devised a payment schedule. _____

31. Review file on the departmental basis to alert key people of heavy or unusual requirements. _____

32. Review microphone requirements. _____

33. Review lighting requirements and any production set-up needs. _____

34. Review room block against pick-up and cut-off date with the convention service manager. _____

35. Review complimentary rooms. If pick-up is below what the client anticipated, causing a comp room assignment problem, confer with Sales Manager and Convention Service Manager to explore best means of satisfying customer. _____

36. Request complete set-up information. _____

37. Review room registration, check-in arrangements. _____

38. Review special housekeeping requirements, if applicable. _____

39. Obtain a copy of authorized signatures for the master account. _____

40. Review cash advance needs. _____

41. Review safe deposit needs. _____

42. Review shipping arrangements of materials. _____

THREE (3) WEEKS AWAY FROM MEETING DUE DATE

43. Forward resume (specification sheet) and check with Catering on menu progress. _____

44. Distribute resume to hotel departments and include affiliated activities. _____

45. Establish date and time for a pre-convention meeting, process in-house memo. _____

46. Inquire if client wishes to guarantee rooms not picked up. _____

TWO (2) WEEKS AWAY FROM MEETING DUE DATE

47. Order limousine if applicable. _____

48. Re-check program with diary for possible quick meeting room turn-over and enter proper times for all events. _____

49. Review complimentary room arrangements. _____

50. Request posting instructions. _____

FORTY-EIGHT (48) HOURS AWAY FROM MEETING DUE DATE

51. Check hospitality and complimentary orders and VIP reservations. _____

52. Reconfirm pre-con meeting. _____

DURING MEETING

53. Check setting of meeting rooms (a.m., afternoon, p.m.). _____

54. Public Space Mgr. or Asst. to complete checklist for each function room. _____

55. Assist with restaurant reservations for VIPs. _____

56. Review shipping arrangements for post convention materials. _____

57. Review complimentary room arrangements. _____

58. Compare room pick-up to complimentary list, make necessary adjustments. _____

59. Set up post-convention meeting. _____

60. Verify booth and exhibit hall by walk through with customer. _____

61. Determine exhibit rental charge if determined by booth. _____

62. Determine repeat booking potential and advise Sales Manager. _____

63. Review master account with account credit department at a predetermined meeting. This should be completed each day. _____

IMMEDIATELY AFTER MEETING

64. Conduct post-convention meeting. _____

65. Call account and send thank you letter. _____

66. Complete report of convention and profit and loss statement and distribute. _____

67. Determine report on abnormal circumstances in the post convention memo. _____

68. Post-convention report to include under "comments" section an objective evaluation of the hotel's performance. _____

69. Turn file over to Convention Service Manager for review. _____

ONE (1) MONTH AFTER MEETING DUE DATE

70. Breakdown working file and return appropriate correspondence to account file. _____

Learning Objectives:

This portion of your text introduces you to the various systems used to make reservations for meeting and convention attendees. We will also take a look at how the room blocks for group meetings are managed, and see how the computer has changed the way in which group reservations are processed. When you have studied this chapter, you will:

- Know the methods commonly used to make reservations and the advantages and disadvantages of each.

- Be able to detail the factors that affect room assignments and identify factors that hotel staff take into consideration when managing room blocks.

- Be able to describe how the computer has changed reservations, registration and room assignments procedures and is being used to facilitate check-in and check-out and billing for convention groups.

A Planner's Perspective on Room Reservations

Sara R. Torrence, CMP
Chief, Special Activities
National Institute of Standards and Technology

"The meetings for which I have been responsible have used a variety of reservations systems — ranging from rooming lists to postal reply cards to call-in reservations, to housing bureaus. We have even used a combination of services, and once created our own housing bureau, through a travel agent, because we were using four hotels for a relatively small international conference (800 attendees — too small to use the CVB housing bureau for the host city)...One of the MOST important points about any reservation system is that the Hotel Sales Manager MUST get the details of the convention to the Reservations Department as soon as the contract is signed, and these details must be entered into the computerized reservations system as soon as possible. I cannot tell you how many times I have had attendees call a hotel for a reservation only to find that the Reservations Department has no record of the conference...."

11

Guestrooms

T he letter of agreement has been signed and countersigned. The dates are firm. The room block is specified in the contract. At this point, many departments and organizations become involved as the service process branches out into different areas. One area is assigning guestrooms through the front desk. Through cooperation between the convention's housing staff and your own front office and reservations departments, this area plays a strong supportive role in the success of a convention.

Reservation Systems

Guestroom reservation information is sent to the group's membership three to six months before the event. The systems that are primarily used today include:

- postal or fax reply cards.
- toll-free numbers.
- making reservations on the hotel's Internet site.
- rooming lists.
- convention center housing bureaus.
- third-party housing companies.

In addition, the use of other technologies (such as e-mail, which is growing in popularity) is making it easier for meeting attendees and other guests to make their reservations. Making reservations using such technology as fax reply cards and hotel web sites is especially attractive to meeting attendees because of the convenience and speed of making the reservation and the capability for almost instant confirmation (or notification if there is a problem).

Postal Reply/Fax Response Cards

The usual agreement calls for the meeting planner to mail reservation forms to his or her membership along with promotional material about the meeting. These **reply cards**, which are printed by the hotel and sent in bulk to the convention group's headquarters, may be self addressed postal reply cards (see Figure 11.1) or similar information cards that can be faxed back to the hotel. Whatever the format used, a cover letter from the hotel, providing information and instructions, is enclosed with the reply cards.

The convention headquarters then sends its promotional material and the cards to its membership from its mailing list. While postal reply cards have long been used by convention attendees, cards that can be faxed are increasing in popularity with both hotels and attendees. Attendees appreciate the ease of faxing, while hotels are more likely to get an immediate response; there is no need to wait for the mail.

To facilitate this reservations process, an effective form is essential. This form will be used in-house and to confirm reservations for guests, and may be required for coordination with a housing bureau. If you have to develop a form or revise one, look at our sample or start from scratch, keeping the following factors in mind:

Clarity.
- Be concise.
- Ask guests to print or type. Allow enough space for hand printing.
- Use standard-sized forms for easy handling and storage.

Pertinent information.
- Include spaces for responses for all the the information you will need to process the reservation.
- Arrival and departure date.
- Arrival and departure times.
- Rate requests (unless flat rates are part of the agreements).
- Kind(s) of room(s) requested.
- Number in the party.
- Indicate how long rooms will be held.
- Indicate if and how the room may be held past that time (guarantee or deposit).
- Indicate if deposit is required for all reservations.
- Use self-addressed forms or specify where reservation is to be sent.

Keep the form simple.
- Use terms in common usage. Indicate number of bedrooms in suites.
- Don't ask for unnecessary data.

If the group uses its own housing form, the hotel must approve the reservation card to ensure that all information is communicated to attendees to minimize misunderstandings. The reservation card policy of the Chicago Hilton reads as follows:

> *"The Chicago Hilton and Towers will supply your organization, at no charge, a reasonable amount of self addressed reservation cards imprinted with the name of your association and the dates of your convention.*
>
> *In the event that your company or association plans to use its own housing form or you intend to use the Chicago Convention and Tourism Bureau for housing, the Chicago Hilton and Towers must approve the copy in writing prior to its being printed in its final form and sent to your members or the Bureau to ensure that all information listed on the form pertaining to the Chicago Hilton and Towers is correct and complete, thus eliminating any discrepancies in room rate when your members receive their confirmations."*

Toll-Free Telephone Numbers

Many convention delegates opt to use the property's toll-free numbers to make their reservations. If this is the case, they should be notified beforehand that they must indicate that they are attending the convention when making their reservations. Another alternative is for the hotel to offer a special toll-free number for the group's use (especially if the group is a large one or if several groups are meeting at the same time) or to have the group's delegates ask for a specific operator when making a reservation.

These measures eliminate several potential problems. Since the hotel and meeting planner agreed to reserve a specific block of rooms, the commitment becomes overesti-

Figure 11.1. SAMPLE POSTAL RESERVATION REPLY CARD.

Front of the reply card.

IIII

NO POSTAGE
NECESSARY
IF MAILED
IN THE
UNITED STATES

BUSINESS REPLY MAIL
FIRST CLASS   PERMIT NO 5216   ORLANDO, FLA

POSTAGE WILL BE PAID BY ADDRESSEE

ORLANDO **Marriott**®

8001 International Drive
Orlando, Florida 32819

ATTENTION:
Reservations Manager

THE ORLANDO MARRIOTT WELCOMES

ARRIVAL DATE: _____ DEPARTURE DATE: _____
ARRIVAL TIME: _____ FLIGHT NO.: _____
NUMBER OF ROOMS _____ NUMBER IN PARTY: _____
ADULTS _____ CHILDREN & AGES: _____
SPECIAL REQUEST _____
_____
NAME _____
ADDRESS _____
CITY _____ STATE: _____ ZIP: _____
TELE # _____
For those who wish to arrive early and/or extend their stay, the
above mentioned special group rates will apply to three nights
before and/or after the dates indicated above - rooms subject to
availability.

DAILY ROOM RATES   SINGLE $ _____ DOUBLE $ _____
SUITE $ _____
CHILDREN STAYING IN THE SAME ROOM WITH THEIR PARENTS
NO EXTRA CHARGE
ALL RATES ARE SUBJECT TO 8% STATE TAX
MAXIMUM NUMBER OF PEOPLE IN ROOM - FIVE (5)
RESERVATIONS ARE TENTATIVELY HELD PENDING RECEIPT OF
DEPOSIT OR AMERICAN EXPRESS OR DINERS CLUB CARD
NUMBER _____. EXPIRE DATE _____
Special request for location, connecting room, etc., will be noted
but cannot be guaranteed. Suites are space available at rates
above and will be confirmed by RESERVATIONS MANAGER

AFTER
CHECK IN: _4:00 P.M._ CHECK OUT: _11:00 AM_

Baggage **must** be checked with the Bell Captain if departure time
is later than 11:00 A.M.

THIS IS A **RESERVATION REQUEST** AND MUST BE ACCOMPANIED BY ONE(1) NIGHTS ROOM DEPOSIT. A WRITTEN CONFIRMATION WILL
BE SENT TO YOU AFTER RECEIPT OF DEPOSIT. ALL REQUESTS MUST BE RECEIVED BY _____. AFTER SUCH DATE, THEY WILL BE
ACCEPTED ON A SPACE AVAILABLE BASIS.

Back of the reply card.

This is a self-addressed postal reply card that is filled out by delegates and returned to the hotel. Other forms of reply cards may include printed return envelopes (usually used when a deposit is required) or a card that may be faxed to the hotel. Whatever form is used, reply cards include such pertinent information as the name and dates of the meeting and room rates. Many associations include such reply cards with their general mailing detailing the convention program, activities, and costs.
Source: Courtesy of the Orlando Marriott.

mated if individual reservations are not credited to the group. The hotel may be stuck with unfilled guest rooms and the association will not get credit for the number of complimentary rooms to which it is entitled.

Hotel Internet Site Reservations

Today, the Internet has become the prominent way for convention groups to make hotel reservations. A recent study by *Convene* magazine showed that just a few years ago most planners selected reservation cards, forms or faxes over the Internet as their preferred reservation method. Today, however, the Internet wins by a mile as shown in the sidebar titled, "What's Your Preferred Reservation Method?" On-line hotel reservations were ushered in by The Hotel Industry Switch Company (THISCO), offering a TravelWeb site that enabled guests to make reservations with five major chains (Hilton, Hyatt, Marriott, InterContinental and Starwood) using computer terminals. Current screens include only the rates found in properties' central reservation system — not the group's negotiated rates.

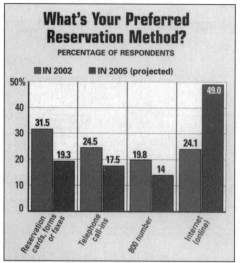

What's Your Preferred Reservation Method?

PERCENTAGE OF RESPONDENTS

■ IN 2002   ■ IN 2005 (projected)

Source: Maxine Golding, "Convention Housing," Convene, February 2003, p. 33.

However, most major chains and a number of independent properties have created individual web sites that provide specific convention information and group rates.

Hilton Hotels Corporation, for example, now offers group reservations on its HiltonNet website. A planner who has reserved a room block at a Hilton property can link his or her organization to a special page on Hilton's site. This site not only provides details about the meeting, but attendees are also given a passcode to access the group reservations module. There, they can book a room at the group's designated rates during a specified time. Hilton's system tracks these reservations and planners can view pickup data via a password protected area of the site. The chain also provides a hard copy of room pickup upon request.

While this technology is still in its infancy, Hilton is reporting good results, and other chains, including Sheraton, are testing the concept. Sheraton is also partnering with software companies that will allow for interactive bookings for city-wide conventions.

Rooming Lists

Many hotels prefer to get a consolidated **rooming list** from the planner (see Figure 11.2). When rooming lists are used, reservations are not made with the hotel, but with the housing staff at the planner's headquarters. The meeting planner prepares the rooming list from the reservations received and sends it to the hotel prior to the **cutoff date**. When the hotel receives the list, the front office assigns attendees rooms from the block that is committed to the group and preregisters attendees.

It is extremely important that the front office knows whether a group's reservations are coming individually or through a list. It is standard operating procedure that the trace file on any group for which a rooming list is expected be brought up in sufficient time to remind the customer that the list is expected.

Rooming lists are most commonly used by corporate accounts and incentive travel groups as their meetings are usually small, attendance is predictable (it is sometimes mandatory) and the organizer is generally picking up the room charges. The convention service manager should encourage the use of rooming lists, when possible, because it reduces the load on the hotel's reservation department.

Convention Center Housing Bureaus

When several hotels are used, the convention is commonly called **city-wide** and the reservations are handled by a convention center **housing bureau** (see box titled "Case Study: City Housing Bureau").

Case Study:

City Housing Bureau

When several hotels are used, the convention is commonly called city-wide and the reservations are handled by a city housing bureau. We will illustrate this more complicated reservation system with the hypothetical National Popcorn Association case study.

National Popcorn Association

The NPA has an active membership of 3,550 delegates. The association executive and the site selection committee have narrowed down their selection for the upcoming annual convention to Chicago, Miami and Las Vegas. It will be necessary for such a large group to use a number of hotels so the planners have been in touch with the convention bureau of each city.

The NPA staff makes personal visits to each site and picks hotels. It then prepares a list of the desired hotels in each city and asks the convention bureau to request room commitments from each property.

The **bid sheet** used by the Las Vegas Convention and Visitors Authority is shown in Figure 11.3. Upon receiving it, the hotel sales department checks room availability for the dates designated. It then specifies the number of singles, doubles and suites the hotel has available and gives a price range for each. Note that the hotel stipulates a cutoff date by which time the NPA must send a written acceptance of the hotel's offer. The completed form is then mailed back to the convention bureau. The bureau forwards or personally presents the proposal sheets to the association's site selection committee for analysis and a decision.

On the basis of price, location and service, the NPA chooses Las Vegas as the site for the convention. It also selects a headquarters hotel and designates four others as overflow hotels.

Approximately eight months before the convention the NPA association executive requests assistance from the Las Vegas Housing Bureau in setting up a reservation system. The association, in conjunction with the housing bureau, prepares a reservation form (Figure 11.4) to be sent to each member, who in turn completes it, writes out a deposit check, and returns it to the housing bureau. The members each indicated their first, second, third and fourth preferences in hotels, and they have also specified the type of room desired. The housing bureau sorts through the forms and approves reservations on a first-come, first-served basis. As each reservation is approved, the form is returned to the sender specifying which hotel he or she is to stay in during the convention. If none of the choices are available, the form is returned to the member with a note of explanation and a request for new choices.

As each batch of new reservations is approved, it is sent to the respective hotel and processed there by the reservation department. Each week before the convention, a **reservation housing report** (see Figure 11.5) prepared by the housing bureau is sent to the hotels and to the association to indicate the reservation status of the hotel's room blocks. This report is extremely important to the hotel. If a room block is not filling up as expected, the hotel will probably contact the association and ask for an update on its room commitment. Although the housing bureau specifies a thirty-day cutoff, if only half of the 3,550 rooms commited are reserved, the five hotels might have difficulty in booking the remaining guestrooms.

The handling of the deposit checks by the housing bureau can be avoided if the NPA collects the deposits itself and pays each hotel its respective amount. This procedure is almost the only method some groups use and it is definitely preferred by the hotel.

Once NPA reservations begin to come in, the hotels start convention reservation records and master accounts for the group. Usually a rooming list (Figure 11.2) is developed and each delegate is assigned a room and sub-account under the master. If and when checks are received by the hotel, a credit is added to the sub-account.

Many meeting planners, however, cite several problems with city housing bureaus. Many are understaffed, especially when it comes to handling large conventions. Meeting planners tell "horror stories" of constantly busy phone lines, long delays when calls finally get through, and delayed reservation confirmations. While some CVBs are now offering their housing systems on-line to eliminate some of these problems, a growing number of meeting planners are turning to other outside sources for their housing needs.

The most recent PCMA Housing Report showed that meeting planners are moving away from using convention bureau housing services and relying more on third-party providers for their housing needs (see sidebar titled "What is Your Preferred Method for Handling Citywide Housing?"). We will take an in-depth look at these third-party housing companies and their impact on the meetings industry in the next section.

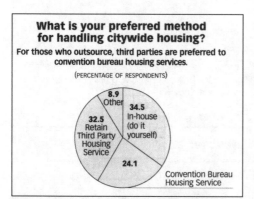

What is your preferred method for handling citywide housing?

For those who outsource, third parties are preferred to convention bureau housing services.

(PERCENTAGE OF RESPONDENTS)

- 8.9 Other
- 34.5 In-house (do it yourself)
- 32.5 Retain Third Party Housing Service
- 24.1 Convention Bureau Housing Service

While a large number of associations handle citywide housing in-house, planners still rely on outside sources, such as convention bureau housing services and, increasingly, third-party providers.
Source: Convene's Annual Meetings Market Report, March 2005, p. 32.

Figure 11.2. SAMPLE ROOMING LIST.

THE
HERSHEY
LODGE & CONVENTION CENTER
ROOMING LIST

Group Name: _____   Send to attention of:

Date: _____

Group Number: _____   _____
(For Lodge use only)   Convention Coordinator

To guarantee your room block, this list must be received 30 days prior to arrival.

ARRIVAL DATE	DEP. DATE	ROOM TYPE	NAME (Last Name First)	SHARING WITH Please also list sharer's data on next line	NUMBER OF PEOPLE OCCUPYING RM	NUMBER OF CHILDREN	COMMENTS

Rooming lists are generally used for small corporate meetings for which the corporation will pay room charges and attendees will be responsible for their incidental charges. Some associations, however, also use them rather than having individual delegates contact the hotel for reservations directly. After the meeting planner obtains room information from delegates, he or she prepares a list to be sent to the hotel by an agreed upon date. Information typically includes the names of attendees, the type of room desired (and how many will occupy a room), and arrival and departure dates.
Source: Courtesy of The Hershey Lodge and Convention Center.

Figure 11.3. SAMPLE BID SHEET

LAS VEGAS CONVENTION BUREAU
CONVENTION CENTER · PARADISE ROAD
P.O. BOX 14006
LAS VEGAS, NEVADA 89114

Date: May 15, 20__

FROM: Adam James Stubbs, Convention Sales

SUBJECT: REQUEST FOR ROOM COMMITMENT

THE ___National Popcorn Association___ HAS REQUESTED US TO OBTAIN TENTATIVE / FIRM ROOM COMMITMENTS FOR THEIR CONVENTION IN LAS VEGAS, NEVADA. FOR MEETING DATES OF ___Oct. 18, 20___ THROUGH ___Oct. 21, 20___. THE ___Abbey Hotel___ AGREES TO RESERVE THE FOLLOWING NUMBER OF SLEEPING ROOMS AT THE RATES SHOWN BELOW: PROVIDING A WRITTEN ACCEPTANCE BY THE CONVENING ORGANIZATION IS RECEIVED BY THE HOTEL OR MOTEL PRIOR TO ___Sept. 15, 20___.
DATE

NUMBER OF:

SINGLES ___100___ RATE ___$75-85___

DOUBLES ___475___ RATE ___$85-95___

TWINS _____ RATE _____

SUITES ___25___ RATE ___$110 --170___

GRAND TOTAL ROOMS ___600___

ROOM DEPOSIT (IS) (NOT) REQUIRED. (IF REQUIRED, STATE AMOUNT) $75.00

SIGNED BY:

___Chantal Puepke___   ___Abbey Hotel___
NAME   HOTEL OR MOTEL

___Sales Manager___   ___May 20___
TITLE   DATE

* * * * *

PUBLIC SPACE AVAILABLE ___yes___   ___negotiable___
                                       RATE OR GRATIS

PUBLIC SPACE DESCRIBED ON ATTACHMENT (NOTE TO HOTEL: IF APPLICABLE PLEASE ENCLOSE BROCHURE)

RESERVATIONS FOR PUBLIC SPACE TO BE REQUESTED AND CONFIRMED BY LETTER.

* * * * *

NOTE: TO BE COMPLETED IN TRIPLICATE. MAIL TWO (2) COPIES TO THE LAS VEGAS CONVENTION BUREAU. HOTEL OR MOTEL TO RETAIN ONE (1) COPY.

When a number of hotels must be used for large conventions, a bid sheet is filled out by individual properties and returned to the city convention bureau. In this case, the form is filled out in triplicate. The hotel keeps one copy, the bureau keeps another, and the third is incorporated into a summary of local hotel rates that is sent to the organization.
Source: Courtesy of the Las Vegas Convention and Visitors Authority.

Figure 11.4. TYPICAL RESERVATION REPLY FORM.

APPLICATION FOR HOTEL ACCOMMODATIONS

MAIL COLORED COPY TO:
NPA Housing Bureau
Las Vegas Convention/Tourist Authority
P.O. Box 14006
Las Vegas, Nevada 89114

October 19-21, 20__
Las Vegas Convention Center
Industry Day
October 18th 20__

NPA

COMMITTEE

Send Confirmation to:

Company Name _____

Attention _____

Street Address or P.O. Box _____

City _____ State _____ Zip Code _____

Hotel Preference:

1. _____   3. _____

2. _____   4. _____

Please Reserve The Following Accommodations: (See reverse side for Rates and Map Locations)

...... Singles(s) for .... persons(s)   Rate Preferred $ .... per room

...... Double(s) for .... person(s)   Rate Preferred $ .... per room

...... Parlor Suite(s) with .... Bedroom(s) for person(s)   Rate Preferred $ .... per suite

REMARKS: ....

....

If Rate Requested Not Available, Next Higher will be Assigned.

List each type of room, its occupants and their arrivals and departures.

Type of Room	Names of Occupants	Arrival & Departure Dates & Hours
1.		
2.		
3.		
4.		
5.		
6.		

Please Attach List of Additional Names, if necessary.

CONFIRMATION OF THE ABOVE REQUEST WILL BE SENT BY THE HOTEL.
PLEASE MAKE ALL RESERVATION CHANGES DIRECTLY THROUGH THE CONFIRMING HOTEL.

A form such as this one is used when a city housing bureau handles hotel room assignments. The delegate fills out the form and returns it to the housing bureau. Maps (such as the one shown on the next page) and hotel rates are included to assist delegates in determining their choice of hotels. Note that this particular form gives delegates four options when it comes to the choice of a hotel. This practice can be a major factor in hotel overbooking, which is discussed in detail later in this chapter. **Source: Courtesy of the Las Vegas Convention and Visitors Authority.**

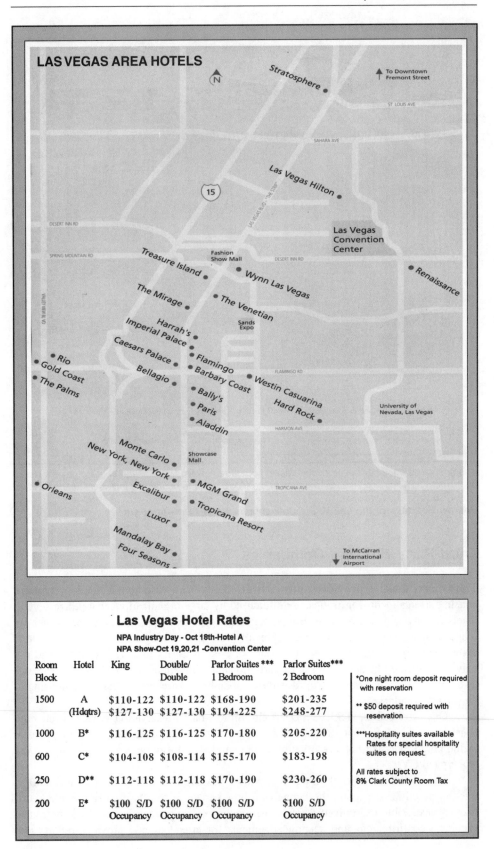

LAS VEGAS AREA HOTELS

Las Vegas Hotel Rates

NPA Industry Day - Oct 18th-Hotel A
NPA Show-Oct 19,20,21 -Convention Center

Room Block	Hotel	King	Double/ Double	Parlor Suites *** 1 Bedroom	Parlor Suites*** 2 Bedroom	
1500	A	$110-122	$110-122	$168-190	$201-235	*One night room deposit required with reservation
	(Hdqtrs)	$127-130	$127-130	$194-225	$248-277	
1000	B*	$116-125	$116-125	$170-180	$205-220	** $50 deposit required with reservation
600	C*	$104-108	$108-114	$155-170	$183-198	***Hospitality suites available Rates for special hospitality suites on request.
250	D**	$112-118	$112-118	$170-190	$230-260	All rates subject to 8% Clark County Room Tax
200	E*	$100 S/D Occupancy	$100 S/D Occupancy	$100 S/D Occupancy	$100 S/D Occupancy	

Figure 11.5. RESERVATION HOUSING REPORT.

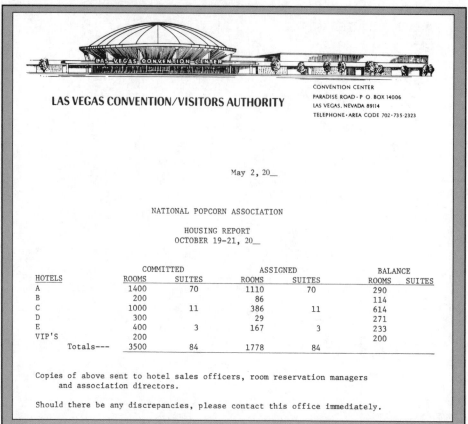

A form such as this one is used by the housing bureau to inform hotels of the meeting group's pickup on its room commitment. Reports are sent on a periodic basis to enable the individual hotels to adjust their reservations information.
Source: Courtesy of the Las Vegas Convention and Visitors Authority.

Third-Party Housing Companies

Third-party housing providers, private firms that typically use high technology to make housing arrangements for groups, are often used by large organizations that utilize several hotels for city-wide conventions. But associations, who need consistency as they generally rotate their annual conventions geographically, are also turning to third-party providers, citing the inconsistency of housing services offered in CVBs in different cities. And not only are meeting planners using third-party housing companies, many CVBs have recognized the cost savings of using third-party companies and are now outsourcing housing to third-party vendors.

One private firm, ITS Inc., a Deerfield, Illinois-based reservation service, offers both consistency and sufficient staffing. ITS President Steve Martin employs 135 employees, including 55 that take hotel reservations, compared to a dozen dedicated housing staffers at a typical CVB.

The growth of other third-party providers has been fueled by Internet technology. Internet-based Passkey.com, the largest and best known of the third-party providers, utilizes an accessible centralized database to process housing transactions. Its system also generates confirmations and acknowledgements for attendees and provides reports that enable meeting planners to manage their room blocks. Passkey is now utilized by 85 percent of the major convention cities, including those in Atlanta, Boston, Detroit and Orlando. The system is also marketed to other third-party housing vendors and to tradeshow organizers and meeting planners who formerly made housing arrangements internally. In addition, both the Hyatt and Marriott chains have signed licensing agreements with Passkey, enabling them to pass along the technology to meeting planners at no additional charge. Omni Hotels, Hershey Entertainment and Resorts Company and the Hotel Monteleone in New Orleans also offer Passkey.[2]

Planners now have over two dozen third-party housing firms from which to choose, and the competition has resulted in innovation and better service to the planners that use these services. In many cases, meeting attendees still fax or mail in their housing reservations, but the Internet is expected to account for the majority of reservations received by housing companies in the near future. No matter how reservations are received, these third-party providers prepare a rooming list for the hotel.

Third-party housing firms are the "preferred providers" for large conventions and a growing number of smaller meetings, and it is estimated that about 50 percent of all multi-hotel events are handled by third-party firms. There is a downside, however. Private firms, unlike convention and visitors bureau housing services, charge a fee, often as much as ten percent of the room rate. A CVB will pay this fee when outsourcing its housing, but meeting planners, especially those who have used no-cost CVB housing services, must find a way to pay for housing assistance. In some cases, the meeting planner will negotiate with the hotel to pay the fee of a third-party provider, passing the cost along to the attendees in the form of higher room rates. Some hotels balk at this arrangement and insist that the service be paid for separately, either by the planner or the attendee, to eliminate artificially raised room rates. Some third-party planners negotiate with the hotel to have their fee paid, much as travel agents are compensated.

Tally Sheets

No matter how reservations are made, a breakdown of the precise types of rooms needed must be made and kept current. **Tally sheets** such as the one shown in Figure 11.6 give the hotel a clear picture of each day's convention reservations and group movements and provide an arrival and departure flow study for each group.

From the tally sheet, the hotel's reservation department sends out **reservation confirmations** (see Figure 11.7). If a housing bureau is handling reservations, a confirmation form by the hotel is a must. Confirmations should be made in any case, but it is particularly crucial when a number of hotels are pressed into use.

Room Assignment

The front desk carries off most convention and trade show room assignments without incident. Problems do arise, however, and must be handled smoothly.

Prior to the meeting, the convention service manager should review and confirm with the customer:

- the rate structure by category of room.
- the room block, including the types of rooms needed by the group.

- complimentary room assignments.
- guest room priorities for VIPs and speakers.
- the arrival and departure pattern for the group.
- the group's history in regard to guestroom pickup, no-shows and cancellations.

Figure 11.6. SAMPLE TALLY SHEET.

HOUSING COUNT TALLY

Name of Organization or Convention ______________________

Convention Official ______________________

Address ______________________ **Tel. No.** ______________

Convention Dates: ______________________

Number of Rooms Allotted: ______________

Breakdown:

Singles ________

Doubles ________

Twins ________

Suites ________

Total ________

Arrival and Departure / Day Date															TOTAL ROOMS USED
	Arr.	Dep.	Arr.	Dep.	Arr.	Dep.	Arr.	Dep.	Arr.	Dep.	Arr.	Dep.	Arr.	Dep.	
Singles															
Doubles															
Twins															
Suites															
Parlors															
Complimentary															
Makeup Suites															
Total Res. per Day		X		X		X		X		X		X		X	
Total Dep. per Day	X		X		X		X		X		X		X		X

A form such as this one provides a hotel with a summary of convention reservations and pickup of the group's rooms. Note that the form is broken down into room type and that arrival and departure times are noted to ensure smooth front desk staffing.

Source: Reprinted with permission from The Convention Liaison Manual, published by the Convention Industry Council.

Rate Structures

Rates are extremely important to the planner. If the rates negotiated are beyond the budget of some attendees, they may book sleeping rooms elsewhere (outside the designated room block). This could significantly impact rental agreements for meeting rooms and could result in attrition fees.

Because most large scale conventions are planned well in advance, the hotel will not commit itself to any firm rates. This policy is usually made clear during initial negotiations. It is also included in the final contract.

One of the preliminary decisions to be made in booking a convention is what rates to charge for delegates' rooms. Naturally the rates will vary between hotels and even within the hotel itself. Rates are determined according to a number of factors, including season (busy or slow), days of the week, size of the group, length of stay, type of room, number of persons in the room, and the known attendance and difficulty with the group's past conventions. Of course, the interpretation of these factors is up to the individual property. A resort hotel, for example, fills up with social guests on weekends, so it is not likely to offer

Figure 11.7. RESERVATION CONFIRMATION FORM.

Name_____ Pr._____
_____
_____
                                                                    (Convention)
Address _____

Type Room _____ Rate $_____ to $_____
Time of _____ A.M.
Arrival: _____ P.M. Date_____ Departing Date _____
Confirmed by_____ Hotel
Signature _____
    Title _____ Date_____

ATTEN: HOTEL MGR. 1. Signature and date to appear legibly on all copies. 2. Separate by holding top and bottom of paper and snap off at perforation. 3. (a) Mail Guest Copy to applicant. (b) Retain two hotel copies. (c) Return Blue & Pink copies to:

HOUSING BUREAU, CONVENTION CENTER, PARADISE ROAD, LAS VEGAS, NEVADA.

GUESTS: PLEASE NOTIFY YOUR HOTEL OF LATE ARRIVALS AND ANY OTHER CHANGES OR CANCELLATIONS. SEND A COPY to the Housing Bureau, Las Vegas Convention/ Visitors Authority, P.O. Box 14006, Las Vegas, Nev. 89114.

PRESENT THIS CONFIRMATION WHEN YOU CHECK INTO YOUR HOTEL.

GUEST COPY   THANK YOU
HOTEL COPY
    PRESENT THIS CONFIRMATION...
HOUSING BUREAU COPY

Forms such as these are sent by the housing bureau to the hotel. The guest, the hotel, and the housing bureau retain copies.
Source: Courtesy of the Las Vegas Convention and Visitors Authority.

discounted rates to a meeting group, while a downtown hotel that realizes the majority of its business during the middle of the week is more likely to offer discounted rates on the weekends.

Many hotels work within the limits of certain rate scales determined by management. The main ones are:

Rack rate. All rates remain as posted, with no discounts or concessions. This is generally preferred by the hotels for easy bookkeeping, but rack rates are rarely used because convention groups are able to negotiate a group rate lower than rack rates.

Run-of-the-house rate. All similar rooms except suites are priced at the average between minimum and maximum rates, despite level or location. All guests pay the same rate. This is also called a *flat-rate arrangement.*

Split rate. Rates are offered to a group based on the room type. For example, regular guestrooms would be offered at a different rate than tower club rooms.

Discounted rate. This type, also called *spread rates,* is used primarily when the result will bring preferred return business, encourage current business, or attract business from the hotel's competition for preferred groups.

It is important to remember that many conventions are planned years in advance, and that rates could vary a great deal over that time. This makes it essential to "peg" a rate of increase to determine the rates that the group will pay in the future.

In most cases, the hotel's rack room rate is used to find the "peg rate." If, for example, the current rack rate is $150 per night and the group rate is $120 per night, the percentage below the "peg rate" is 20 percent. This percentage would be used to determine room rates at the time of the meeting (attendees would get 20 percent off the rack rate in effect at the time of the function). Other planners insist on more specific room rate guarantees; one planner, for example, specifies the following clause be included in the contract:

"The Hotel guarantees that room rates extended to the Symposium shall not exceed 85 percent of the rack rate and the present applicable rate shall not increase more than 5 percent per year. The final rate shall be established 12 months in advance of the Symposium."

Small groups tend toward the use of flat rates, while large conventions find split or discount rates more to their liking. Rack rates are seldom used for conventions unless the group is small or the hotel is running at high occupancy.

Discounts typically range up to 30 percent of the rack rate. Naturally, the hotel's objective is to ensure that it gets business, but at the highest possible rate. Questions often asked about the group to determine the amount of discount include:

- How much can they be expected to spend? Will they have cocktail parties? Banquets? Requests for meeting and exhibit space?
- What are the opportunities for future business with the group?
- Is the group willing to put down a firm financial hold on its room block?

Regardless of the rate decided upon, it is important to make the rate arrangements clear. If there is a range of rates, the reservation form should indicate the range and serve notice that rooms in the next higher category will be supplied if those at the requested rate are no longer available. Even if the contract calls for rack rates, it is best to indicate those on the reservation form.

Sometimes the association requests that the hotel charge the delegate more than the agreed upon room rate and to refund the excess to the association. Hotels generally decline such requests for obvious ethical reasons, particularly if the convention attendee is unaware of the arrangement.

Complimentary Arrangements

Most hotels offer concessions to get group business. It is common practice to extend one complimentary guestroom (**comp room**) for every 50 rooms used, or one suite for every 100 guestrooms.

A rooming list supplied by the meeting planner should specify who will occupy these rooms. To avoid heated arguments at the cashier's window, it is the planner's responsibility to spell out the extent of the complimentary arrangements to the guest and provide a copy to the hotel.

The meeting planner should tell his or her people, especially if complimentary rooms will be used by speakers and program members, what they must pay for themselves and what may be applied to the master account. It is easiest to use complimentary rooms for staff, but that is at the option of the meeting planner. It doesn't matter so long as everyone knows what is expected of him or her.

Additional concessions are sometimes granted. Some hotels provide a complimentary cocktail party upon arrival, free travel to and from the airport and free meeting space. There is no general guideline. A hotel must use sound judgment and integrity.

Priorities

It is important that the convention planner supply a list of VIPs to the hotel. It is necessary to codify certain types of guests and the accomodations indicated for them. This is certainly important when you have accommodations in different buildings of the hotel. Association officials such as officers, board members and staff usually get special treatment. Exhibitors, speakers and entertainers may also require special attention.

It is important to block rooms so that oceanfront rooms and suites in resort hotels and the "best rooms available" in commercial properties are assigned to VIPs without question, regardless of the occupancy of the house. It is often the responsibility of the convention service manager to see that these reservations are in order. He or she should set up a procedure to check the day before arrival on what type of accommodations are blocked for VIPs and also on the day of arrival to make sure that these accommodations are delivered. In addition, the service manager might find out the VIPs' arrival times.

It is the policy of some hotels to have the sales office see that the VIPs get the proper attention. The feeling is that the salesperson's self-preservation is determined by his or her impression on the association's decision makers, and the decision makers are usually found on the priority list.

The VIP list should also be coded to include the possible supply of fruit, liquor and/ or flowers. The allocation of suites is also important, especially if the hotel has a limited number. Discuss this with the convention planner. Some associations have a rule that non-exhibitors cannot maintain hospitality suites.

Take care to hold a small number of rooms in a prime area of the hotel for late priority listings; they inevitably appear late in the game.

Room Types

You must know the number and kinds of rooms to be held. Most agreements with convention planners call for a guarantee of a total *number* of rooms to be used. This may be fine at the negotiating table, but as the event approaches you need to know how many of these are singles, doubles, twins or suites. Don't forget that there is much confusion about suite designation. Some hotels go so far as to indicate suites as having "one bedroom for two people" or "two bedrooms for four people." In addition, people confuse twins and doubles. This can be clarified by indicating "one bed for two people" or "two beds for two people." The box titled "Room Types" provides definitions that are common throughout the industry.

Release and Confirmation Dates

Since many conventions are booked far in advance, the number of rooms blocked out is an estimate, based on past conventions. Communication between hotel and planner is vital.

The letter of agreement, as we said in Chapter 9, should indicate a date by which the organization will either confirm or release the rooms. Reservations received after the cutoff date, usually about thirty days, are accepted on a **space available basis** only and often the convention rate is not available to reservations received after the cutoff date. In all cases, the reservations should be confirmed individually, with a copy sent to the meeting planner.

The hotel and association should re-examine the room commitment on several intermediate dates and readjust the number if necessary. Most convention center bureaus and

Room Types

Single:	A room assigned to one person. May have one or more beds.
Double:	A room assigned to two people. May have one or more beds.
Queen:	A room with a queen-size bed. May be occupied by one or more people.
King:	A room with a king-size bed. May be occupied by one or more people.
Twin:	A room with two twin beds. May be occupied by one or more people.
Double-double:	A room with two double (or sometimes queen) beds. May be occupied by one or more persons.
Mini-suite or junior suite:	A single room with a bed and a sitting area. Sometimes the sleeping area is in a bedroom separate from the parlor or living room.
Suite:	A parlor or living room connected to one or more bedrooms.
Connecting rooms:	Rooms with individual entrance doors from the outside and a connecting door between. Guests can move between rooms without going through the hallway.
Adjoining rooms:	Rooms with a common wall but no connecting door.
Adjacent rooms:	Rooms close to each other, perhaps across the hall.

hotels provide weekly room pick-up reports showing the inventory status of the room blocks to meeting planners. Mutual reassurance will reduce the chances of double booking by delegates and overbooking by hotels.

The convention planner must be alert for early signals that might affect meeting attendance. These could be an unusual circumstance, such as the 50th anniversary of the association, an unusually good or bad year, the selection of a prime resort site, or an unusual number of members recruited that year. The smart planners will communicate their apprehensions and revelations to their hotel counterparts so that all attendees may be housed conveniently.

You should not bury your head in the sand and go blithely about your business if you don't receive periodic communiques from your client. D-Day will come and you may face a milling mob around the registration desk or a multitude of unfilled rooms. You cannot afford just to wait hopefully if you don't hear from your client. Keep constant tabs on the reservations being received and interpret how the flow affects the total number of rooms being held.

Constant communication between both parties leads comfortably to the day when the organization executive confirms or releases the number of rooms held. (This is vital to resorts that have little or no business off the street, especially during off-season periods).

The planner and hotel person who keep in touch constantly and adjust room allotments along the way seem to continue to do business together. They execute meetings together without the shock of housing problems at the outset of the event.

Arrival/Departure Pattern

In assigning rooms you need an overall pattern that will indicate when people will arrive and depart. The convention planner may have some idea from previous years, but you will have to finalize detailed patterns when you get the reservations from the guests. Even for corporate meetings, where the meeting planner has greater control, attendees frequently arrive a day or two early because of transportation difficulties, personal travel plans or the attraction of local tourist or recreational facilities.

For example, typical arrivals for a 400 room convention beginning on Monday and concluding on Thursday might look something like this:

Day	Number of Rooms	Flow of Attendance
Friday	20	meeting planner and staff
Saturday	150	early arrivals
Sunday	360	opening of convention
Monday	400	peak convention attendance
Tuesday	400	peak convention attendance
Wednesday	350	early departures
Thursday	30	post convention meetings and extended days

It is also wise to indicate the breakdown of the group's rooms into singles, doubles, twins and suites. Arrival dates are easier to secure than check-out dates, but these too are important to you.

Be especially careful if you designate the availability of a *specific* suite. That extra-special VIP suite may be earmarked for the chairman of the board, who may very well decide to test your golf course and arrive a day or two before the meeting or stay in it several days after the event. Impress on your client that you must have advance notice of such plans to make sure the room is available and that there is no conflict with another group.

You will also need to determine the **major arrival/major departure** pattern of incoming convention guests. That is, the dates and times at which large numbers of attendees can be expected to check-in at the hotel and when large numbers of delegates will be checking out. The group's resume should provide this information, which is vital for planning staffing – you will need to have enough desk clerks and bellpersons available for a large influx of guests at particular times. The typical ratio is one bellperson and one front desk receptionist/cashier for every 75 guests arriving or departing. If a group is to arrive or depart en masse, however, one staff person for every 50 guests may be required.

Should the check-in for the group be early afternoon, the hotel may need to set up a hospitality area where attendees can wait until vacated rooms are readied by housekeeping. This is a problem for European hotels because most large planes arrive from the United States in the early morning but check-out time for departing guests is not until noon or so.

Other Hotels

As we mentioned earlier in this chapter, sometimes a number of hotels are to be used for a large convention. In such instances, a competitor becomes a friend. It is nice to have a nearby hotel bail you out with a number of rooms when you may have overbooked. It is just as nice to receive guests from the other hotel when you have a number of rooms available — and to have the favors returned on other occasions. It pays to work together.

Similarly, you may be unable to supply a function room for the convention or for a local customer's banquet. Show the customer that you are interested in his welfare even when you are full by helping him to book the event at another hotel. The other hotel may appreciate the recommendation and reciprocate; your customer appreciates the help and the fact that you didn't turn your back on him when you didn't need the business. Always look to the future. The key to success in the hotel business is a good reputation for expertise and *caring*.

A variation may involve only the use of hotel facilities, such as golf courses or tennis courts. An inter-hotel billing arrangement also must be worked out in the case of multi-hotel involvements, which may bring local bus companies into the act.

Managing Room Blocks

Hotels that cater to group meetings and conventions face potential difficulties when it comes to their rooms inventory. While it is important to ensure that enough rooms are booked to house all meeting and convention attendees there may be cases in which the group's block is not fully occupied, resulting in lost revenue for the hotel. Meeting planners, naturally, want to ensure that there are enough rooms set aside for their attendees – and the number of rooms blocked can play a key role in negotiations for such perks as free meeting space and complimentary rooms. Hoteliers, of course, want to properly house the group, but the hotel's potential profitability can suffer if room blocks are overestimated or rooms otherwise go unfilled (not only do hotels lose money on unsold rooms, but projected revenue from such areas as food and beverage, recreational amenities, transportation and other services may be far less than projected).

In this section, we will discuss some of the factors involved in managing room blocks. We will take a look at some of the most common potential problems that may arise when trying to manage room blocks and detail how hotels, meeting planners and housing providers can work together to ensure that these problems can be avoided or minimized.

No-Shows/Overbooking

When hotels book blocks of rooms for groups, they allow for some **slippage**, the difference between the contracted room block and the guestrooms actually utilized by the group. Slippage (which is also called the "wash factor") might occur for a number of reasons. Sometimes, a planner may inflate the group room block to achieve a better negotiating position. Usually, however, convention attendees are responsible for the difference between projected room usage and the actual amount of rooms picked up.

Attendees who fail to check into the hotel despite having a reservation are termed **no-shows**. No-shows may either be guests who fail to attend the convention, whether or not they cancel their reservations, or guests who attend the event but do not use the rooms booked in the group's block. When attendees bypass the group's housing service and book rooms at hotels other than those specified by the meeting planner, the hotel doesn't attribute those reservations to the group's block. This practice, called **booking outside the block**, is becoming more common, especially with easy access to hotel information on the Internet and the increasing use of third-party providers.

In some cases, especially when a large convention requires housing the delegates in a number of hotels, delegates may make multiple reservations because they fear they won't get a room at their first-choice hotel. And, attendees frequently use the Internet to find travel "deals" (Hotels.com, Expedia and Travelocity represent 75 percent of online sales).[3] It has become increasingly common to find that between 20-30 percent of a group's attendees book their rooms online, whether at the host hotel or at other properties in the convention city.[4]

Attendees who use the Internet may find cheaper rates at the host hotel and book rooms not designated in the group's contract. In other cases, convention guests book into a hotel in which they are members of a loyalty program. Whatever the reason, the group's block is adversely affected, impacting both the meeting planner, who may lose free meeting space and other perks and possibly face penalty fees (discussed later in this section), and the hotel, which can lose financially when rooms go unused.

In addition to no-shows, a hotel's profitability can be affected by guests who check out early. An **early departure** is a guest who leaves the hotel before the end of the contracted rooms. Although this is less of a problem for city and airport hotels, which get a certain amount of **walk-in** business after five o'clock to fill in no-show vacancies, the early departure can be devastating on resort hotels, which usually don't have the advantage of capturing transient business.

Early departures, like no-shows, can result in a significant loss of room revenue, as well as food and beverage, incidental and recreational income. Scott Boone, vice president of sales for InterContinental Hotels and Resorts, says,

> "We've noticed an increase in early departures over the past three to four years, especially with convention attendees. Attendees usually book rooms months ahead for the whole conference, then adjust their schedules and neglect to notify the hotel...We just want guests to focus on their departure date so that we in turn will have inventory to offer."[5]

The increasing problem of no-shows and early departures has resulted in hotels taking additional measures to minimize losses. The Hospitality Sales Marketing Association International strongly recommends the use of deposits as a solution to no-shows. With a **deposit reservation**, the hotel receives payment for at least the first night's lodging prior to the guest's arrival and is obligated to hold the room regardless of the guest's arrival time. A hotel that is going to take deposits must consider the necessary control and record keeping involved and the possibility of refunds.

Another solution offered is the use of *guaranteed reservations*. **A guaranteed reservation** is a room being held without a deposit, but for which payment is guaranteed; in the case of a no-show, billing takes place in the usual manner. But many hotels cite difficulties collecting such payments. The term is often misinterpreted; guests do not always understand that they are agreeing to guarantee payment regardless of whether or not the room is used.

Because the no-show problem is more significant at high-demand resorts than at city and airport properties, resorts have been the leaders in instituting stricter cancellation policies. In an effort to eliminate no-shows and control rooms inventory, some convention hotels have pushed their cancellation deadline to 72 hours before expected check-in.

Attrition. While the above measures generally apply to attendees, a great many hotels are protecting themselves by inserting *attrition clauses* (such as those discussed in Chapter 9) into contracts. Attrition fees, which are charged to the group, not the individual attendees, apply when the meeting group contracts for a specific number of rooms but the total amount of rooms used is below the original contracted block. Many meeting planners balk at such fees, and some fight the problem by reducing their room block. This practice, however, can cause a different set of problems; booking fewer rooms weakens a planner's negotiating position, perhaps adversely impacting meeting space or reducing the group's number of complimentary rooms.

Attrition has become such a large problem in such a short time that the Convention Industry Council launched Project Attrition, a nine-month study of the problem. The final report was published in February 2004 and can be viewed online at www.convention industry.org/resources/project_attrition_report11204.pdf.

While the CIC was developing guidelines that could be used industry-wide, many hotels and convention centers had already taken steps to help meeting planners minimize attrition. Hotels are not in the business of collecting fees; they want to fill rooms. Group guests spend more time in the hotel than other types of guests and therefore spend more money at the property, so it is important for hotels to find solutions to help a group to manage its block. Joel Pyser, vice president of field sales for Marriott, says:

> "Attrition is the number one issue our customers talk about, and we want our customers to see us as providing them solutions."[6]

Rather than rely on attrition damages, which rarely make up a hotel's entire loss, many hotels are "partnering" with meeting planners — offering services and suggestions to help planners to manage and promote their room blocks to avoid attrition fees. Three chains have adopted online attendee management applications that they offer to planners at no charge. Marriott International and Hyatt Hotels are using RegLink (Passkey's housing management application) and Wyndham International is using the event registration module of PlanSoft's qReg system in conjunction with their own room reservations system.

Still other properties have created event websites with registration and room reservations capabilities. These sites promote the value of staying at the headquarters hotel, including the proximity to events and opportunities for networking. And, to compete with possible lower Internet rates, some hotels, such as the Hilton chain, fix a price for guestrooms — no matter what the source of booking (including the Internet, travel agents, the hotel's own reservations system and so on).

Hotels can also help meeting planners to fill their designated blocks by suggesting that planners "bundle" registration; that is, charge delegates one fee for the entire event (including registration, room, event attendance and other services, such as transportation). Delegates who book outside the block would be required to pay a higher registration fee or be charged additional fees for specific events, such as an evening banquet. Planners can also discourage booking outside the block by including the reasons for the group's block in promotional materials. Delegates tempted to book outside the block might be persuaded to change their minds when they realize that such benefits as free meeting space, complimentary receptions, audiovisual equipment and other services are based on filling a guaranteed number of rooms.

Underdeparture. Rising attrition is not the only challenge facing hoteliers in managing group room blocks. At the other end of the spectrum, problems may also arise if the guest decides to stay another day; this is called **underdeparture**. The hotel may have set aside a block of 250 rooms and if 20 attendees decide to stay on there may not be enough rooms available for other booked business (this can be especially critical if the group was booked at one rate but the hotel can get a higher rate for the rooms once they are vacated by the group).

Many hotels require a guest to initial the registration card indicating the day of departure; this institutes a contract between the hotel and the guest. The hotel meets its obligation by providing the room through that date. Once the date has passed, the guest may be considered a "trespasser." The hotel has two options: it can enter a new contract at

Effective Guestrooms Management

Kristine K. Gagliardi
Corporate Director of Convention Services
Hilton Hotels Corporation

"During the past several years, I have had the opportunity to develop and implement standardized quality assurance programs for Hilton Hotels Convention Service Departments corporate-wide...During the initial research phase, all existing hotel-wide guestroom block procedures were examined...Aware that Hilton's system-wide computerized reservation/front office system would jointly benefit the group/hotel alliance by means of technical support, it was our intent to offer meeting groups an effective, accurate guestroom system during every stage of the meeting — pre-planning, on site, and beyond, to post-meeting information.

"Also important to our research was the initial booking process by sales. Was a group's historical data properly checked? Did this information correlate with the current booking? Was the pattern of arrival and departures in line with the group's meeting program? Did the proposed reservation method work to benefit the group and hotel? Did the group's cut-off date give the group and hotel enough time to react to casualty?

"In order to monitor reservations closely, a convention service file activity checklist was developed to systematically track group pick-up and other pertinent group arrangements. By use of this checklist, the convention service managers could trace group block activity and, if warranted, have subsequent discussion with the meeting planner regarding pick-up information...One week prior to the cut-off, the group was contacted again to re-verify all room-related issues...the checklist once again was to be utilized as a primary tool to initiate action ten days before the group's arrival.

"Equipped with valuable customer information regarding check-in/check-out expectations, the hotel could then prepare a strategy to ensure a smooth arrival. Arrival patterns, transportation methods, and peak check-in times are closely reviewed...The pre-registration of rooms, suites, and VIP accommodations would also be accomplished in preparation of the group's arrival...At the conclusion of the meeting, this information would be compiled into a 'meeting report.' Sent directly to the meeting planner, and routed throughout the Hilton system, this report was to cover all aspects of the meeting, including guestroom particulars: reservation method, sequence of hotel reservation pick-up, arrival/departure patterns, final pick-up data, casualty and no-show percentages, suite usage, etc."

a different rate (the hotel is not obligated to extend the convention rate); or, the hotel may evict the guest (the problem is that in the vast majority of states the hotel has to take the overstaying guest to court, which obviously is costly and time-consuming).

Overbooking. In some cases, hotels that have experienced a great number of no-shows (and especially those who cannot rely on transient business to fill unused rooms) try to cover projected losses by booking more rooms than they actually have available. This practice is known as **overbooking**.

SOME ASSOCIATION HOUSING POLICIES CONTRIBUTE
TO HOTEL OVERBOOKING

In a perfect world no hotel would ever overbook guest rooms. But hotels can't stop taking reservations when all their rooms "appear" to be sold. Because of "early departures" and "no-shows," hotels that do not confirm more than 100 percent of their rooms run the risk of going 10 percent to 15 percent unsold.

The system is broken, and no one is fixing it. Consider the scenario for city-wide conventions. Attendees return a form indicating which hotel(s) they prefer to be in. Registrants are asked to select their top three to six choices, in case the first choice is sold out.

The housing organization attempts to assign the attendees to their desired hotel. If the No. 1 or No. 2 choice is available, there is a high probability the attendee will use the reservation. However, that likelihood decreases the further down the list you go. When all of an attendee's preferred hotels are sold out, most housing authorities will arbitrarily assign a hotel.

This is where the real trouble begins.

Hotels get notification of reservations from the housing organization without knowing if their hotel was a primary request or if it was an "assigned" reservation. (This information would be helpful because there is traditionally a larger "no-show" factor among attendees who are "assigned" rooms.) Many of these "assigned" attendees do not bother to call the hotel to cancel their reservations. Even advanced deposits made by credit card do not deter this practice because most travelers know that if they challenge a charge, most credit card companies will not pay the deposit to a canceled hotel.

The net result: Hotels that don't overbook during a citywide convention have absolutely no hope of selling out their available rooms.

Another reason for overbooking is when booking many years out, planners tend to be overly optimistic, resulting in hundreds (or even thousands) of excess room nights requested.

If past history doesn't support the block, hotels are caught in a bind. If the group doesn't pick up, many rooms will go unsold. One strategy many hotels employ, whether they admit it or not, is to disregard the contractual block and instead protect a smaller block for the group. This enables the hotel to sell the remaining rooms to any interested buyers, be it other groups or individuals. Ideally, when the cut-off date arrives, the group will be under its contracted block by the same number of rooms that the hotel oversold.

Unfortunately, this is not an ideal world. Walks result when a group picks up beyond its history...or when a hotel sells too deeply into its block. This creates the overbooked situation where some attendees have to be "walked" to a different hotel.

The solution here is to establish realistic room blocks based on past performance. After each year's convention, future room blocks would be adjusted to reflect actual growth (or decline) in attendance. This would create a situation in which, at 12 months out, the room block would be within 3 percent to 4 percent of the previous year's pickup.

This adjustment would give hotels a much tighter comfort level. And, instead of 10 percent to 15 percent, overbooking could drop to 5 percent or less.

Source: Bruce Harris, president of Conferon, the nation's largest independent meeting planning company.

If a hotel overbooks, a convention guest who arrives late may find that there are no rooms available. This constitutes a breach of contract by the hotel, which now owes the latecomer damages. These guests are termed **walked customers**, as the hotel is responsible for finding other accommodations for them. This situation has led many meeting planners to specify that a *relocation clause* be included in the group's contract. This clause provides for specific actions by the hotel in the event of overbooking, and may include such points as a complimentary room at a different hotel for each night that the attendee cannot be accommodated at the original hotel, a complimentary telephone call to allow the attendee to inform others of the change, complimentary transportation (or payment of the cost of transportation) to the new hotel, upgraded accommodations if the delegate returns to the original hotel, an in-room amenity upon the guest's return and a letter of apology to the guest in which the hotel accepts responsibility for the overbooking situation.

Hotels can minimize potential problems from overbooking by contacting properties previously used by the group to determine the group's no-show history. If a group typically fills its room block, the hotel will see less reason to overbook (the property may still oversell to a lesser degree to guard against any slippage). Conversely, it is a smart meeting planner who checks among his or her peers for a hotel's overbooking pattern. Wise planners also inform their members of the practice of hotels to hold reservations only until a certain hour, such as 5:00 p.m. They urge their members to arrive earlier than the hold deadline or to guarantee or pre-pay to make sure they get their rooms.

Historical Performance

Whenever possible, find out where the group met in previous years. It may be best to do this after the contract is signed in order to maintain business security. Don't hesitate at that point to call the sales manager of the hotels used in the past. They will gladly cooperate because they will want to call you sometime for the same reason. See Figure 9.1 in chapter 9 for an example of an inquiry questionnaire

The historical pattern of a convention tells you a great deal. It can inform you early that this group seldom meets its commitments, or that it always does. You may learn that more attendees show up each year than are expected, or that early departures are common. You may find out that the no-show situation is an ever present problem, or just an odd one or two that is not of major significance.

If nothing else, these calls will give you insight into the meeting planners and let you know whether you are dealing with well-organized pros who can be relied on to control

---

Best Practices

Westin's Creative Approach to Tracking a Group's Historical Performance

The Westin chain uses three interrelated procedures in an effort to assess the accuracy of a convention's commitment by observing its past performance. First, a standard letter of inquiry is sent, along with a questionnaire, to the last two hotels in which the group met. The letter states that the group has booked with a Westin property and asks the hotels to make a post-convention critique of the group. The critiques then are matched with the requirements that have been requested. If there is an indication that the group has exaggerated its needs, the hotel goes back to the customer to clarify the discrepancy.

Westin's second procedure is to question a meeting planner who books a year or more in advance about his or her schedule of upcoming meetings. Through the use of the tickler system, the hotel brings up the file two weeks before the group's next meeting and two weeks after it.

On the first date, the hotel wishes the meeting planner the best with the scheduled meeting and advises the planner of an evaluation questionnaire to be sent in four weeks. The planner usually is impressed with the hotel's meticulous approach to detail, and the hotel can be alerted to any change or trends that might alter the number of guest rooms or function space it is holding for the group.

The third technique used by Westin might be called "preparticipation." When convention groups with complicated programs or unusual requirements are booked, the hotel salesperson and the convention service manager might request to be admitted as observers to the group's next meeting. By observing the meeting process and requirements, the convention service manager is better able to service the group at its forthcoming convention in his or her hotel. And, again, the client is reassured that he or she is in good hands.

When the convention planner and the hotel executive have mutual confidence in each other, they can work things out so that all delegates are housed and no one gets hurt by variations in expectations.

their conventions or planners who lack expertise or experience. The more you learn about your customers, the better equipped you are in handling them.

If you do learn that a convention generally fails to fill its quota, don't duck the issue. Call the convention executive and indicate that you know they had problems in previous years and ask him or her to reconsider the number of rooms to be held. Don't just release rooms without telling him because the planner may have good reason to believe it will not reoccur. Corrective steps may have been taken or something may have happened to stimulate attendance. At the very least, you may hasten the room release data and get a more realistic appraisal.

Check-in/Check-out

A hotel should determine in advance when the heaviest influx of delegates can be expected so it can staff accordingly at the front desk. It would be foolhardy to step off on the wrong foot in the beginning. A delegate who is forced to wait in long lines becomes disgruntled and is a likely complainer throughout the stay.

Check-in Procedure

Arrival lines can be noticeably shortened if a distinction is made between guests with and without reservations. By the process of **pre-registration**, rooms are assigned in advance according to the rooming list provided by the group or developed by the reservation clerk based on reservation requests.

Pre-registration of all guests is being done more frequently. Special receiving desks, and even special lobbies, are being used by some hotels that service extensive group business. Many conventions set up a **housing assistance desk** near the registration area where the meeting planner and members of the housing staff can greet and assist delegates. This desk services attendees who encounter reservation problems. These arrangements minimize lobby confusion, long lines and slow check-in procedures. Whether individual or group check-in is used, the convention service manager should ask that the meeting planner be present at check-in time.

Check-out Procedure

A poor check-out procedure can destroy an otherwise perfectly organized convention. The group may have had a smooth meeting for three or four days, with excellent food and beverage service, but when the delegate arrives at the cashier's window to check-out, he or she is greeted by a long line, or worse, a sharp remark from the cashier. That delegate is very likely to leave with a bad taste, and three or four days of good meetings are out of the window. Group check-out procedure may be one of the little elements of a convention, but it really counts, particularly if it is not handled expeditiously.

Hotels often establish a **check-out time** of noon or 1:00 PM. If the wrap-up meeting is a luncheon, late check-out service allows the attendees to attend the conference climax. But if guest arrival patterns prohibit late check-outs, guests should be told to sign out before the luncheon session. Their bills should be ready so that the entire group can be processed quickly and their baggage checked in a convenient storage place until departure time.

The Computer Influence

One of the most important trends for the lodging industry is the increased use of computers. In this section, we will briefly consider how computers have influenced the servicing of groups, from reservations to check-out and billing.

Reservations

Of all front office operations, reservations are most associated with computers. Computer assisted reservations systems require fewer labor hours and provide higher accuracy than manual systems, allowing reservation clerks to enter, retrieve, modify and question reservations in seconds. Reservation clerks can check availability from meeting room blocks and print confirmations and registration cards on high-speed printers. In addition, various summary reports, including reservation tally sheets that track room pickup against the block, can be generated to assist managers in scheduling and forecasting.

When the reservation department receives a reply form from a delegate, all the information about the guest is typed into the computer and stored. Once the information is entered, there is no need to duplicate the data. The same information is used for confirmation and deposit receipt notices, pre-registration, check-out and billing procedures.

This eliminates the onerous task of keeping a tally sheet on each convention.

Best Practices

GAYLORD PALMS
RESORT & CONVENTION CENTER

Gaylord Hotels: Using Technology to Better Service Large Groups

Gaylord Hotels, which operates the 2,881-room Gaylord Opryland Resort & Convention Center in Nashville, Tennessee, the 1,406-room Gaylord Palms Resort & Convention Center in Kissimmee, Florida and the 1,511-room Gaylord Opryland Texas Resort & Convention Center in Grapevine, Texas, is using technology to successfully host large groups and provide convention attendees with comprehensive information on their event online. Computers are used to manage group business from centrally managing and distributing sales leads to automated check-in and check-out.

Craig Ratterman, director of strategic systems, says:

"Gaylord Hotels set up group-specific Web sites for attendees, and can accept rooming lists from any group that sends them in electronic format. They also use wireless terminals at check-in to give maximum flexibility, and give each attendee an individually customized map with directions to their room and to their conference's registration and location information...With the new Gaylor iConnect technology, convention goers can also see their group members' phone extensions and check their convention schedule. They can also view a welcome message and other e-mails from their group, check property maps to find their specific events, visit the layout of the exhibit hall and find out where the booths are – all online."

Source: "Gaylord Gets Groups", Hospitality Upgrade, Spring 2003, p. 13.

Registration and Room Assignment

The computer saves considerable time in the preparation of rooming lists and room assignments. Pre-registration of convention attendees, particularly corporate groups, begins the night before the guest arrives; the required rooms are blocked off, registration cards are pretyped for each guest (Figure 11.8), and room keys are sorted. Delegates are listed alphabetically within each convention group and assigned rooms according to the type of accommodation and rate range requested. When delegates arrive, they are given preprinted registration cards, prepared by the computer, which they inspect and sign if all is in order. Some hotels set up separate counters away from the main desk to reduce traffic congestion for pre-registered guests.

To speed check-ins, sophisticated systems are emerging, following the lead of Hyatt Hotels' Touch and Go Instant Check-in Machine. Used much like an ATM machine, these **self check-in, check-out terminals**, which are located in hotel lobbies, have been promoted as "line busting technology" as they eliminate long lines at the front desk by allowing guests with reservations to swipe their credit cards to receive their room keys and printed room number and other information in less than 90 seconds.

Hilton Hotels Corp., which installed its first 15 kiosks in a "pilot program" at four hotels, has high expectations for the technology. Tim Harvey, Hilton senior vice president/ chief information officer, says:

> "We've found usage of these kiosks to be exceeding our early expectations, what with some 10% to 12% of our guests [on average] using them, and, in some instances, as high as 35%."[7]

While kiosks can eliminate long waits and may save on labor costs, they do have their drawbacks. First, they are expensive, costing between $10,000-$18,000 each. Second, although customers are becoming more used to self-service terminals, such as ATM machines and airline kiosks, many are hesitant to use the machines, preferring instead to speak to a front desk clerk. Hotels are responding to this concern by reassigning front desk personnel to assist guests using the kiosks.

For those guests preferring to make accommodation arrangements in the privacy of their home or office, another innovative service that uses today's technology is Radisson Hotel's "Express Yourself[SM]". This program allows guests to check in at their own convenience over the Web. First, guests reserve a room via any Radisson booking process (Web site, call center, hotel direct or through a travel agent). Seven days prior to the visit, guests receive an e-mail inviting him or her to "express" themselves by checking in at the Radisson Web site (www.radisson.com). There, guests enter such information and requests as specific room location, preferred amenities (such as high-speed internet access) and other special service requests. Upon arrival, guests need only identify themselves at the front desk, where they will promptly receive their room key and hotel packet.

The Hilton Hotels Corp. is eliminating long lines at the front desk by offering free-standing automated check-in/ check-out kiosks at its properties.

Figure 11.8. COMPUTER PREPARED ROOMING ENVELOPE FOR A PRE-REGISTERED GUEST.

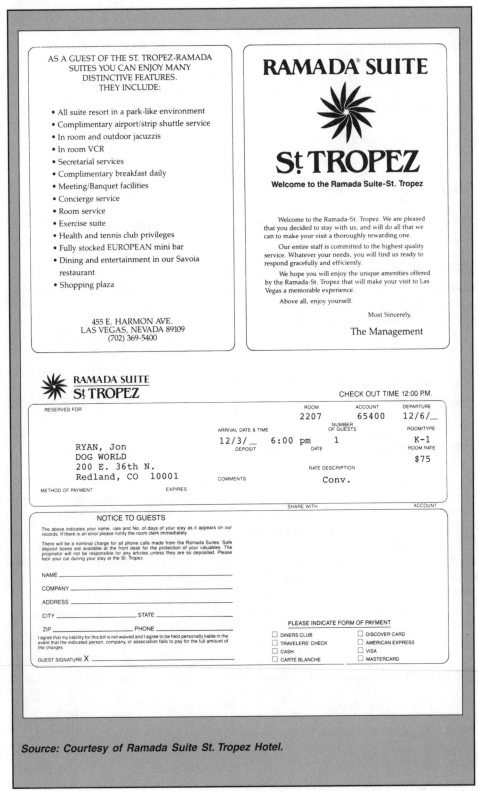

AS A GUEST OF THE ST. TROPEZ-RAMADA SUITES YOU CAN ENJOY MANY DISTINCTIVE FEATURES. THEY INCLUDE:

- All suite resort in a park-like environment
- Complimentary airport/strip shuttle service
- In room and outdoor jacuzzis
- In room VCR
- Secretarial services
- Complimentary breakfast daily
- Meeting/Banquet facilities
- Concierge service
- Room service
- Exercise suite
- Health and tennis club privileges
- Fully stocked EUROPEAN mini bar
- Dining and entertainment in our Savoia restaurant
- Shopping plaza

455 E. HARMON AVE.
LAS VEGAS, NEVADA 89109
(702) 369-5400

RAMADA® SUITE

St. TROPEZ

Welcome to the Ramada Suite-St. Tropez

Welcome to the Ramada-St. Tropez. We are pleased that you decided to stay with us, and will do all that we can to make your visit a thoroughly rewarding one.

Our entire staff is committed to the highest quality service. Whatever your needs, you will find us ready to respond gracefully and efficiently.

We hope you will enjoy the unique amenities offered by the Ramada-St. Tropez that will make your visit to Las Vegas a memorable experience.

Above all, enjoy yourself.

Most Sincerely,

The Management

RAMADA SUITE
St. TROPEZ

CHECK OUT TIME 12:00 P.M.

RESERVED FOR		ROOM	ACCOUNT	DEPARTURE
		2207	65400	12/6/__
	ARRIVAL DATE & TIME	NUMBER OF GUESTS		ROOM/TYPE
	12/3/__ 6:00 pm	1		K-1
RYAN, Jon	DEPOSIT	DATE		ROOM RATE
DOG WORLD				$75
200 E. 36th N.		RATE DESCRIPTION		
Redland, CO 10001	COMMENTS	Conv.		
METHOD OF PAYMENT	EXPIRES			

SHARE WITH   ACCOUNT

NOTICE TO GUESTS

The above indicates your name, rate and No. of days of your stay as it appears on our records. If there is an error please notify the room clerk immediately.

There will be a nominal charge for all phone calls made from the Ramada Suites. Safe deposit boxes are available at the front desk for the protection of your valuables. The proprietor will not be responsible for any articles unless they are so deposited. Please lock your car during your stay at the St. Tropez.

NAME _____

COMPANY _____

ADDRESS _____

CITY _____ STATE _____

ZIP _____ PHONE _____

I agree that my liability for this bill is not waived and I agree to be held personally liable in the event that the indicated person, company, or association fails to pay for the full amount of the charges.

GUEST SIGNATURE X _____

PLEASE INDICATE FORM OF PAYMENT

- ☐ DINERS CLUB
- ☐ TRAVELERS' CHECK
- ☐ CASH
- ☐ CARTE BLANCHE
- ☐ DISCOVER CARD
- ☐ AMERICAN EXPRESS
- ☐ VISA
- ☐ MASTERCARD

Source: Courtesy of Ramada Suite St. Tropez Hotel.

Bjorn Gullaksen, Carlson Hotels Worldwide executive vice president and brand leader, says:

> "Radisson is taking a bold step to transform what consumer research has consistently shown as the least desirable experience in the hotel stay – standing in line for a slow check-in or slow check-out. We will never replace the human element of a friendly front-desk person, but 'Express Yourself' will eliminate the paper work that has traditionally been the main focus of today's check-in process. By freeing our staff from these procedural restraints, they can now concentrate on welcoming the guest and getting them quickly to their room."[8]

Check-out and Billing

Throughout the delegate's stay, charges are posted to an electronic folio, either at the front desk or at several *points-of-sale*. Point-of-sale terminals are located in profit centers throughout the hotel and are linked to the central computer, so guest charges are entered directly to the electronic folio instantaneously. Because vouchers do not have to be physically carried from the points-of-sales to the desk for posting, time delay and possible revenue loss are significantly reduced. Folios are often preprinted for convention attendees expected to depart on a given day. As delegates arrive at the cashier's window for departure, the clerk quickly scans the folio on the screen for late charges, prints a new folio only for those needing updating and presents the printed folio. When the guest is ready to check out, he or she is given a running account of the transactions. Computer systems also maintain master accounts for the meeting staff and can separate all charges by specific service location.

Reports and Analysis Applications

The applications of the computer to the front desk operation are not the only benefits that are obtained from such a system. Management information, such as marketing reports and control features are additional advantages of an in-house computer. An automated sales office can quickly generate lists and reports that would take hours to produce manually. For example, the *Booking Report* shown in Figure 11.9, allows the sales and rooms departments to select and summarize important marketing criteria such as booking status, arrival dates, room night totals and booking patterns. These statistics are a vital tool to help management plan sales strategies and to give insight into targeting promotional efforts.

The computer frees personnel from laborious bookkeeping and paper shuffling, allowing them to provide convention groups with more prompt service.

Summary

A smooth reservations procedure sets the stage for a successful function. Both the hotel and the meeting planner should ensure that communication regarding this crucial area begins at an early stage and that the progress of reservations is monitored on a regular basis to ensure that adjustments can be made. Proper room arrangements and efficient check-in and

Figure 11.9. COMPUTER GENERATED BOOKING REPORT.

The Durham Resort
Bookings Report Short Form
For Bookings Arriving Between February 1 to February 7, 20__

Arrival Date	Days	Account Name / (Total RN) Pattern	Booked By	Stat	Funct Space	Average Rate	Total Contribution
2/ 1- 2/ 3/94	Tue Thu	Adams Point Landing (104) 2 102	LMS Post As: Adams Point Landing	D	Y	100.67	10756.00
2/ 1- 2/ 5/94	Tue Sat	Automobile Travelers Association (119) 20 47 44 5 3	LS Post As: Automobile Travelers Assoc.	D	N	95.00	8131.27
2/ 1- 2/ 4/94	Tue Fri	Grant Retirement Party (70) 1 19 42 8	LS Post As: Grant Retirement Party	D	N	79.00	3663.10
2/ 6- 2/ 7/94	Sun Mon	Wed City Anniversary Celebration (45) 20 25	LS Post As: Wed City Anniversary Celeb	D	Y	95.00	3174.85
2/ 6- 2/11/94	Sun Fri	Society Of Technical Writers (905) 8 103 294 272 218 10	AJ Post As: Society Of Technical Writers	T	N	68.62	37964.75
2/ 7- 2/ 7/94	Sat Sat	New England Conservatory (9) 9	LMS Post As: New England Conservatory	D	Y	98.00	641.97

The Durham Resort
Bookings Report Summary by Market Segment
For Bookings Arriving Between February 1 to February 7, 20__

Market Segment	# of Bookings	# of Rm Nights	Guestroom Revenue	Food Revenue	Beverage Revenue	Rooms Rental	Resource Rental	Other Revenue	Total Revenue
National Association	3	180	21600	5400	1345	600	1200	800	30945
Regional Association	2	1024	112640	28160	4525	500	500	800	147125
State Association	3	0	0	5850	890	1500	250	500	8990
National Corporation	1	0	0	2450	580	250	500	400	4180
Local Corporation	2	70	8750	2580	1200	600	600	400	14130
Tour & Travel	7	347	38864	9716	2500	700	660	1200	53640
TOTAL	18	1621	181854	54156	11040	4150	3710	4100	261010

Data entered into the computer system is often used to generate reports such as booking activity by market segment. Producing such reports manually would require hours of labor.
Source: Delphi Reports Sampler, Newmarket Software Systems, Inc., 44 Market Rd., Durham, NH 03824.

check-out procedures also add to a delegates favorable impression of the property -- and may result in future business from the meeting planner.

Getting the delegates into the hotel smoothly is just one segment of the servicing process, however. They are coming for a meeting or a function and their expectations are high. In the next chapter, we will see how the convention service manager communicates the numerous details required for the service staff to execute a successful meeting.

Endnotes:

1. Maxine Golding, "Convention Housing," *Convene*, February 2003, p. 30.
2. "Passkey Penetrates Hotel Market," *Corporate Meetings & Incentives* May 2004, p. 23.
3. Mary Ann McNulty, "Pandora's Box," *pcma convene*, September 2003, p. 42.
4. Susan Hatch, "Online Booking Blues," *Corporate Meetings & Incentives*, September 2002, p. 80.
5. Linda Humphrey, "Early Check-Out Fees Gaining Momentum, "*Business Travel News*.
6. *Meeting News*, November 17, 2003, p. 35.
7. ehotelier.com, November 4, 2004.
8. Michael Billig, "Technology Snapshot," *HotelBusiness*, August 2004, p. 16A.

Additional References:

<u>Managing Front Office Operations, Sixth Edition</u>, Michael L. Kasavana and Richard M. Brooks, Educational Institute, AHLA, 2001.

Internet Sites:

For more information, visit the following Internet sites. Internet addresses can change without notice. If a site is no longer available at the address listed below, a search engine can be used to find the new address or additional, related sites.

Convention Industry Council, Hotel Best Practices for Managing Room Blocks – www.conventionindustry.org/projects/hotel_BP.htm.
Four Seasons Hotels and Resorts – www.fourseasons.com
Greenbrier Hotel - www.greenbrier.com
The Hospitality Sales Marketing Association International (HSMAI) - www.hsmai.org
Hyatt Hotels and Resorts - wwwhyatt.com
International Association of Convention and Visitors Bureaus (IACVB) -

www.iacvb.org
Passkey - www.passkey.com
Project Attrition Final Report – www.conventionindustry.org/resources/
project_attrition_report11204.pdf.
Sheraton Hotels - www.sheraton.com
Starwood Hotels & Resorts – www.starwood.com
THISCO (The Hotel Industry Switch Company) – www.thisco.com

Study Questions:

1. Describe in detail the types of reservations systems used to handle group bookings.
2. Trace the procedures used to service a city-wide convention. Describe the forms used and tell why individual properties make use of a tally sheet to track their reservations.
3. Distinguish between rack rates, run-of-the house rates, spread rates, and split rates.
4. What three procedures are used by the Westin chain to assess the accuracy of a group's commitment?
5. What is the relationship between no-shows, under departures, and overbooking?
6. What factors are taken into consideration to ensure the smooth check-in and check-out of a convention group?
7. Assess the present-day application of the computer in servicing convention business and project technology's likely role in the future.

Key Terms:

Bid sheet. Form used by local convention bureaus to obtain room commitments and prices from local hotels. The list is later forwarded to the meeting planner or site selection committee.

Booking outside the block. Meeting attendees book rooms at hotels other than those specified by the meeting planner or book rooms within the specified hotels but not as part of the conventions group's block of rooms.

Check-out time. The time (set by the hotel) at which guests are expected to vacate their rooms.

City-wide. A convention which, because of its size or special requirements, requires accommodations at several hotels for its delegates.

Comp rooms. Complimentary rooms; rooms that the hotel offers to a group at no charge in ratio to the number of rooms occupied by the group. The standard is one comp room per fifty rooms occupied.

Cutoff date. The deadline for holding the number of guestrooms booked by a group (the last day a meeting attendee can buy a guestroom from the room block reserved for the meeting). Generally, hotels specify a date (also called a **reservation review date**) 30 days before the first day of the meeting for the group to either guarantee, add to or release the guestrooms booked for the convention.

Reservation requests made after the cutoff date may be accepted on a space-available basis, but late bookers may not be entitled to the group room rate.

Deposit reservation. Payment to the hotel for the first night's lodging prior to arrival. The hotel is obligated to hold the room regardless of the arrival time of the guest.

Discounted rate. The practice of marking down normal rates by a percentage or dollar amount as a concession to the group. Usually aimed at a specific type of client or offered at a particular time of the year. Also called a **spread rate**.

Early departure. An attendee who checks out of the hotel earlier than scheduled. A fee may be charged by the hotel to make up for lost business. Also called an **understay** or an **early out**.

Guaranteed reservation. A reservation that assures the guest that a room will be held until check out time of the following day of arrival. The guest guarantees payment for the room, even if it is not used, unless the reservation is properly cancelled.

Housing assistance desk. An area used to provide service to convention attendees who have concerns about their reservations.

Housing bureau. Provided by a city's convention bureau, housing bureaus help place delegates into the city's hotels when large conventions are booked.

Major arrival/major departure. The expected dates and times of arrivals and departures of large numbers of event attendees. Usually obtained from the group's resume, this information aids in staffing adequate front desk and bell staff.

No-shows. Customers who have made reservations but have not cancelled them before the hotel's cancellation deadline.

Overbooking. The hotel has committed more rooms that what are actually available for use (usually due to anticipated no-shows).

Pre-registration. Often used for group business, the hotel assigns the attendee a room that will be available upon the attendee's arrival.

Rack rate. The standard rate established by a property for a particular category of room. May vary depending on the season.

Reply card. A pre-printed, self-addressed card used for reservations for large conventions. Information on the card includes the name of the group, dates of meeting and room rates.

Reservation confirmation. Written agreement by a facility to accept a request for accommodations. To be binding, the agreement must state the intent of the parties – the particular date, the type of accommodations and the number to be accommodated. Normally requires a credit card number.

Reservation housing report. A report indicating the group's pickup of its room commitment. Send by a housing bureau to both the hotel and the group.

Room block. An agreed-upon number of rooms set aside for members of a group planning to stay at a hotel.

Rooming list. A list of the names of attendees who will occupy the previously reserved accommodations. Submitted by the meeting planner, it is also called a **housing list**.

Run-of-the house rate. An agreed upon rate for all available rooms except suites. Generally priced at an average figure for group accommodations. Also called a **flat rate**.

Self check-in, check-out terminal. A computerized kiosk system, usually located in the hotel lobby, that allows guests to review their registration information and receive their room keys at check-in. At check-out, they can review their folios and settle their accounts to the credit card used at check-in.

Slippage. The number of guestrooms not used from the original room block.

Space available basis. Reservations that have no claim against the block of convention rooms because the request arrived after the official cutoff date.

Split rate. The pricing of group guestrooms based on different room types, such as regular guestrooms versus tower rooms.

Tally sheets. A breakdown of each day's convention reservation and group movements. Also provides an arrival and departure flow schedule for each group. Also called a **housing report**.

Third-party housing provider. A private company that is contracted to manage the housing of convention delegates.

Underdeparture. Occurs when a guest scheduled to leave decides to stay longer. Also called an **overstay**.

Walk-in. A guest who does not have a reservation but requests accommodations at a hotel. Also called **transient business**.

Walked customers. Guests holding confirmed reservations who are sent to another facility because of overbooking. If a hotel accepts a reservation but can't provide a room, the hotel has breached the contract and the injured guest is owed damages. The usual term is for the guest to be compensated for the first night to stay at the second hotel (reimbursement for transportation between the two hotels is usually also included).

Learning Objectives:

In this chapter, we will discuss the specifics of a pre-convention meeting and detail the forms used by the hotel to ensure that departments servicing the event execute it to the planner's specifications. When you have studied this chapter, you will:

- Know the importance of the pre-convention meeting, and its key players

- Be able to distinguish between a resume and a banquet event order and tell how each is used.

- Recognize the importance of communication in the execution of an event and be able to describe how the computer is used to communicate meeting details.

Outline

Pre-convention Meeting
- Key Personnel Roster

Resume (Specification Sheet)

Banquet Event Order (Function Sheet)

The Importance of Communication

Communicating Details Electronically

The Importance of Follow-up

Summary

The Pre-Con: The Most Critical Meeting on the Program's Agenda

Marilyn McIver
Director of Convention Services
Marriott Desert Springs Resort, Palm Desert

"The Pre-Con meeting is possibly the most critical meeting on the program's agenda!...Executive support is of paramount importance for any event, and General Manager attendance at Pre-Cons is a real plus! After introducing the planner and allowing him/her an opportunity to give a brief of the program, our staff introduces themselves and their departments' roles during the convention...Don't make the mistake of confusing 'pre-con' with 'pre-planning'...By the time you've gathered the 'players' together, the majority of the work has been done via function sheets...I cannot stress enough the importance of detailed function sheets sent by the group, well in advance of the actual event. These sheets are usually transferred to a property format, so both parties should review function sheets to ensure accurate translation...Detailed function sheets, an accurate group resume with a timely distribution and finally a well-run pre-con are all tools we can use to make our joint venture a success."

12 Preparing for the Event

A fter a letter of agreement has been signed by both parties and the reservation cards sent, the event must be planned in great detail. Some conventions are planned a number of years in advance; others, a year or two. Some member of the organization's staff will be the primary coordinator for the group. It may be the executive director for a small or medium-sized association or a convention coordinator for a large organization. It could be a professional convention coordinator who is paid a fee by the association to run the event.

For the hotel, logistics are controlled by the convention service manager. As we discussed, the convention service manager is a most vital person on the hotel staff. He or she is the liaison person with the client and the control person within the hotel. It is not an exaggeration to consider the convention service manager as the key to the success or failure of an event. He or she is responsible for seeing that the event is properly planned and for taking quick, positive action should things go wrong during the event.

In many small hotels, the catering manager may serve as the convention service manager. It is not unusual in such a case for the catering manager also to be active in soliciting banquet business. If this is the case, communication with the sales department and use of the function book must be diligently controlled. This is doubly true when many promises are verbal, and not documented in correspondence or the letter of agreement.

Pre-convention Meeting

A **pre-convention meeting (pre-con)** is essential and goes a long way toward eliminating problems that may surface during conventions. A smart hotel sales executive will arrange for a pre-conference meeting to introduce the hotel's convention service personnel, the organization's people and all outside contractors involved in serving the group (see box titled "Pre-Con Meeting Agenda"). Hotels should make it a firm practice to bring the entire convention staff together for an unhurried pre-convention session with the meeting planner and contractors for goods and services. This get-together gives all parties an opportunity to review the convention agenda item by item to ensure that everyone fully understands what is to take place and to finalize any last minute details.

Westin's Larry Stephan, former director of sales at the Detroit Plaza, says that his chain services meetings with "Operation Excell." This program begins with a pre-convention meeting held a day or two before the arrival of the group's main delegation (many convention service personnel feel that the ideal time to hold a pre-con is two days prior to the group's meeting or event. The hotel's CSM should determine the best time to schedule the meeting; morning meetings are commonly held, but an afternoon pre-con may enable the hotel's staff from two different shifts to attend). At this time, the meeting planner and his or her staff meet with the convention service manager and all the hotel's department heads who are involved in the direct servicing of the group. The upcoming program is thoroughly reviewed.

Attendees at the meeting vary. For simple or one-day meetings, the pre-con may include only the meeting planner and the convention service manager. For a large convention with a number of banquets, meetings and complex setups, the following individuals are likely to be in attendance:

Pre-Con Meeting Agenda

It is important that pre-cons be carefully planned for maximum effect. Pre-cons are typically held 24 hours prior to the group's first event and should include all personnel involved in the successful execution of the event. Attendees typically include the CSM and members of departments that will be servicing the group (front desk, catering, housekeeping, engineering and so on), outside contractors (such as decorators, for example) and key group personnel, including the meeting planner and other group decision-makers, such as an association executive or CEO.

The pre-con is held to reconfirm all written and verbal details of the event, discuss arrangements and answer any questions relating to the program, but it should also serve as a relationship-building tool. Relationship building begins with the hotel's staff. Staff members should dress professionally and wear name tags to help meeting planners identify and remember key personnel. Hotel staff also should stand and greet clients as they enter, and the meeting should focus on the client (this means that pagers, beepers or walkie-talkies should not be allowed).

The pre-con meeting room should be set up to facilitate conversation between participants (a U-shape set up is typically used, with the client seated at the head of the "U"). And, most pre-cons also include food and beverages (staff members should limit themselves to beverages only).

To ensure that the meeting flows smoothly and all details are covered, a pre-con agenda should be established. Most pre-con briefings include a chronological review of the group's events, but the agenda may be modified as necessary. An agenda typically includes:

- Introduction of the planner (by the CSM).
- Brief review of the purpose of the meeting and agenda items.
- Introduction of attendees (by the meeting planner).
- Introduction of hotel staff, including a brief description of the job functions of each (by the CSM).

Meeting details to be discussed can include (but are not limited to):

- Review of meeting resume.
- Updated room pick-up report.
- Review of banquet event orders for each event.
- Review of master account, including authorized signers and billing instructions.
- Other pertinent group details, such as VIP and special considerations, business center requirements, recreational activities and so on.
- Review of any items specific to the event (if the program includes a trade show, for example, union procedures should be covered).
- Review of the facility's fire, safety and emergency procedures.
- Distribution of lists of contact names and contact numbers.

Remember that the pre-con is a confirmation of details, not the time for the planner to make drastic changes in the program. A continuing dialogue with the meeting planner as plans progressed prevents last-minute problems.

- Meeting planner and his or her staff.
- Director of convention services and the convention service manager responsible for servicing the group.
- Salesperson who secured the group and perhaps the director of sales.
- Food and beverage manager, catering/banquet manager and the chef.
- Hotel's general manager and perhaps the comptroller or credit manager.
- Director of exhibit service, floor manager, and a convention service secretary.
- Representatives from the following departments:
  - front office
  - security
  - reservations
  - uniform services
  - publicity/public relations
  - housekeeping

- telephone   - recreational facilities   - concierge
- room service   - audiovisual
- garage/valet   - spa director

- Outside vendors who will play a significant role, such as third-party housing companies, destination management companies or audiovisual firms.
- For large programs, a representative of the Convention and Visitors Bureau may be invited.

Some astute hotel convention service managers suggest to the meeting planner that they invite a higher-up, such as the company president or association executive, to at least drop in at the introductions portion of the pre-con meeting. This helps the hotel's staff to recognize them as VIPs, gives the executives a clearer understanding of the complexities of managing meetings and helps to strengthen the relationship between the hotel and the meeting group.

A small ceremony takes place at the end of the pre-convention meeting. The meeting planner and his or her key personnel are given VIP pins, which serve two functions. First, they give distinction to the meeting planner and staff, recognizing that the hotel is aware of their positions and the importance of the meeting. Second, they help the hotel staff single out members who are in charge should there be any last minute changes or requests.

This concept works well for Stephan, who offers a step-by-step review of his chain's "Operation Excell" program used to facilitate the servicing of convention groups in the "Best Practices" case at the end of this chapter. The procedure is not put into operation at every convention, nor is it always necessary for all department heads to be present; the convention program determines which department heads will attend. Major conventions and smaller ones with complicated requirements, however, are preceded by such a meeting.

Regardless of who attends the pre-con, from that meeting on, it should be the service manager, not the salesperson, who deals with both the client and the hotel staff. If a hotel wants to suceed with convention business, it must develop good salespeople to bring in the right kind of business, and good convention service people, functioning in-house, to guide that business through to successful completion. In larger convention facilities, a convention service manager would have an assistant and possibly other specialists.

Key Personnel Roster

Meeting planners often request a **key personnel roster** from the convention service manager so they have someone to contact should trouble arise. This roster would list the names and telephone numbers of hotel department heads and other specialists (such as the in-house audiovisual contact). Many convention service managers, however, are hesitant to provide such a list, prefering to have all requests channeled through them. We feel that the wisest course lies between these two positions.

If the convention service manager will *always* be on the scene and available to the meeting planner, it is possible for him or her to receive every request. But if this is not feasible, an assistant should be designated to act in such instances. If this is not practical, department heads should be trained to inform the convention service manager of all requests.

During a convention, a meeting planner will often refuse to wait until the manager can be located before taking action in what he or she deems a crisis. In any case, prompt action on the part of the hotel staff is crucial; communication between key personnel and the convention service manager is obviously essential.

Minita Wescott, past president of both the Chicago Trade Association Executives Forum and the American Trade Association Executives, suggests:

> "One person on the hotel staff should be assigned to the convention for the duration of the meeting. This person should be readily available to handle all on-the-spot needs. It makes for a smoother meeting if the executive of the association can meet and get acquainted with all top members of the hotel staff with whom this executive and his staff will have to work."[1]

The Marriott chain has responded to such meeting planners' requests for hotel contact people to act on last-minute needs and further expanded on it with the introduction of its Red Coat service. A number of property convention staff personnel, easily identified by their red jackets, are both trained and empowered to handle last-minute details and crises. This program helps free up the property's convention service manager while still ensuring that immediate help is available to meeting planners who need it. The visibility and accessibility of these trained professionals helps to boost the confidence of even the least experienced meeting planner and demonstrates the chain's commitment to service.

Crowne Plaza Hotels & Resorts offers the innovative The HotPhone Service[SM] program, which provides a "hot phone" to meeting planners to enable them to keep in constant contact with the property's Crowne Plaza Conference Concierge® assigned to the group. The service, which is complimentary, features a digital two-line cell phone that not only lets the planner call for assistance with the touch of a button, but also provides communication with the "outside world" (the planner is free to make local and long-distance calls while on property).

In the pressure cooker of an ongoing convention, meeting planners are most appreciative of reassurance that last minute problems will be dealt with, and promptly. Gestures of such reassurance go a long way towards making a property a favorite of convention planners.

In summary, we feel it a positive action to furnish a roster of key hotel personnel to the client (see Figure 12.1), along with the request that all action be taken through the convention service manager, *whenever possible.*

Resume (Specification Sheet)

The convention service manager is responsible for writing a detailed schedule for each convention. The title for this schedule may vary. It may be known as the master prospectus, the bible, the summary, the specification sheet or the resume. We will use the latter term as it is most commonly used in the industry today.

Do not confuse the *resume* with the *banquet event order (function sheet)*, which is explained in the next section. The **resume** provides a comprehensive overview of the entire program in a chronological narrative, from pre-convention to post-convention, to the hotel staff. The banquet event order details only a single event.

Although they are titled differently, all convention hotels use similarly constructed resumes when servicing groups that meet for more than one day. Resumes set forth activities day by day and hour by hour, covering meetings, meals, refreshment breaks, cocktails, reservation procedures, billing, exhibit instructions, special events, guest programs, recreational activities, and anything else that needs the hotel staff's attention. It is undoubtedly

Figure 12.1. HOTEL KEY PERSONNEL ROSTER.

HOTEL PERSONNEL

Hotel staff personnel contact for over-all service during the convention of _____

Period	Hours	Name	Title	Phone Extension
Early morning	___a.m. to ___p.m.	_____	_____	_____
Daytime	___a.m. to ___p.m.	_____	_____	_____
Evening	___a.m. to ___p.m.	_____	_____	_____
Saturdays	___a.m. to ___p.m.	_____	_____	_____
Sundays	___a.m. to ___p.m.	_____	_____	_____
Holidays	___a.m. to ___p.m.	_____	_____	_____

Hotel key staff by departments
Check marks on the hotel staff list given below indicate the departmental key personnel with whom the organization will come in contact during the servicing of the convention.

Check	Department	Name	Title	Phone Extension
___	_____	_____	_____	_____
___	_____	_____	_____	_____
___	_____	_____	_____	_____
___	_____	_____	_____	_____

The meeting planner should have a principal contact on the hotel staff at all times during the day. In addition to key personnel rosters, some planners insist on being supplied with a two-way radio, beeper, pager or cellular phone to ensure immediate contact with the hotel staff.
Source: Reprinted with permission from the Convention Liaison Manual, **published by the Convention Industry Council.**

the single most important element of the convention servicing process, providing a tool for planning and communication between hotel departments.

The resume is prepared by the convention service manager in conjunction with the meeting planner. Much of the information is extracted from correspondence and discussion with the convention group and from **event specification guides** prepared by the meeting planner (see box titled "Industry-Wide Event Specification Guides"). For larger groups (such as associations that meet annually), the convention service manager may request a copy of the group's previous year's resume. The group's information is then put in the hotel's format and the resume is distributed to everyone involved with servicing the convention. This must be done far enough in advance to ensure that departments will have time to staff and prepare appropriately (in most cases, at least a week before the group arrives).

The length of the resume varies, of course, with the size, number of days, and details required for each convention. We have seen some group resumes that were more than 40 pages long. Most, however, run eight to 12 pages for a three-day session. Simply put, a resume should be long enough to include all the details (some hotels use legal size sheets to cut down on the number of pages).

The importance of putting every detail in writing cannot be overstated. And the more detailed the better. "Nobody told me," is heard too often in hotels. Putting everything in writing lessens the chance of this occuring.

Industry-Wide Event Specification Guides

Event Specification Guides (ESGs), prepared by meeting planners, differ from the resumes prepared for events by hotel personnel. To ensure that the details compiled by the meeting planner could be effectively incorporated into hotel resumes, APEX (the Accepted Practices Exchange), an initiation of the Convention Industry Council, developed a template that could be readily used for this important function.

As a result of the efforts of its Resumes & Work Orders Panel, APEX developed standardized Event Specifications Guides that could be used by planners to convey necessary information to venues and suppliers:

"The term Event Specifications Guide or ESG (acronym) should be the industry's official term for the document used by an event organizer to convey information clearly and accurately to appropriate venue(s) and/or suppliers regarding all requirements for an event. This is a four-part document which includes:

- Part I   The Narrative – general overview of the event.
- Part II   Function Schedule – timetable outlining all functions that compose the overall event.
- Part IIIa Function Set-up Order – specifications for each function that is part of the overall event (each function of the event will have its own Function Set-up Order)
- Part IIIb Function Set-up Order (Exhibitor Version) – specifications for each booth/stand that is part of an exhibition."

The template, a 22-page document that was approved as an "accepted practice" on September 30, 2004, is essentially a staging guide (such as the one depicted in Figure 12.5). It can be accessed online at www.conventionindustry.org/apex/acceptedpractice/eventspecifications.htm.

The new ESGs have been praised by planners and hotel personnel alike. Vicky Betzig, CMP, vice president of JR Daggett and Associates, says:

"The amount of time a planner spends putting together event specifications is enormous. The template includes all of the specs most often required by hoteliers. I will be one of the first to use it."

ESGs are also extremely helpful to a CSM preparing the group's resume. The CSM can take required information from the ESG, prepare a resume and banquet event orders in the hotel's format and return them to the planner for approval. Richard Green, vice president of industry relations and association sales for Marriott International, states:

"Standardized events specifications will help planners to focus their requirements around the information that hotels and convention centers need to deliver a zero defect meeting."

Sources: The APEX Event Specifications Guide Template, ©2004, Convention Industry Council; quotes from an October 14, 2004 APEX day audioconference (Betzig and Green were among the speakers), published in pcma convene, December 2004.

Figure 12.2 illustrates an abbreviated resume written for a ficticious convention, the Architectural Draftsmen International. Note that the specification sheet opens with a pre-convention setup and closes with a post-convention meeting. The resume begins with a general description of the group and a brief statement informing the hotel staff of the basic purpose and objectives of the meeting. Note that a list of the individuals and departments that receive this information is listed on the left-hand side of the first page. The first page also includes such information as complimentary accommodations, arrival and departure schedules, the reservation procedure, and billing to both master and individual accounts.

Figure 12.2. SAMPLE GROUP RESUME.

```
* * * * * * * * * * * * * *
        GROUP RESUME
* * * * * * * * * * * * * *
```

General Manager	**SUBJECT:** Architectural Draftsmen International Attendees are the world's leading architects. The focus of the meeting is on customer service. The theme of the meeting is, "Building Better Relationships with Clients."

General Manager
Food/Bev. Dir.
Front Office
Showroom
Exec. Chef
Beverage Mgr. (2)
Coffee Shop
Room Service
Group Billing
Hotel Manager
Asst. Hotel Mgrs. (2)
Food Checker
Reservations
Publicity
Security
Housekeeping
Head Houseman
Head Banquet Waiter
Sales (2)
Food & Bev. Control
Linen Control
Doorman
Benihana Manager
Stage & Sound (2)
Public Porters
Steward
Catering Director
Group Services (4)
Uniform Room
Purchasing

SUBJECT: Architectural Draftsmen International Attendees are the world's leading architects. The focus of the meeting is on customer service. The theme of the meeting is, "Building Better Relationships with Clients."

DATES: February 16-20, 20___

CONTACT: Jay Bryan
Master Draftsman
206 Clark - Suite 307
Lakeview, Michigan 48850

HOTEL SALESPERSON: Larry Kingsbury, National Sales Manager

ARRIVAL/DEPARTURE PATTERN:
ROOM RES. MANAGER
ASSISTANT MANAGERS
FRONT DESK
HOTEL CASHIER
300 rooms have been committed to this group. Most are arriving late Sunday, February 16 and departing Thursday, February 20, 20___. Arriving individually - Preregister

RATES - European Plan
$95.00 Single or Double occupancy, plus 6% County room tax, net, non-commissionable.

SUITE RATES - One Bedroom
$100.00 - Petite Suite
$120.00 - Deluxe Suite
$180.00 - Royal Suite

LOCATION: DESERT VIEW, FOUNTAIN VIEW, POOLSIDE HEXAGON, CENTRAL TOWER

COMPLIMENTARY ACCOMMODATIONS: A King Bedroom (North Tower) for Marney Vartanian, Associate Convention Manager
ARR: February 15, 20___
DEP: February 20, 20___

Additional complimentary units to be assigned based upon 1 complimentary unit for every 50 rooms actually occupied. (Names forthcoming)

HOSPITALITY REQUEST FOR: Ms. Marney Vartanian
Dewars Scotch w/setups
ARR: February 15, 20___

RESERVATION ACCEPTANCE PROCEDURE: This group utilized our return reservation cards.

MASTER ACCOUNT: All Group functions should be billed to the master account. Ms. Marney Vartanian will be the authorized signer.

INDIVIDUAL ACCOUNT: Room, tax, and incidentals to be paid by individuals.

(continued)

This form for a fictitious convention is similar to those used by hotels to provide an overview of a group's event. At the left is a list of the people and departments that will receive this sheet. In addition, the convention service manager usually sends the resume to the meeting planner well in advance of the pre-convention meeting to ensure that details are correct and that nothing has been overlooked. This saves time during the pre-convention meeting as the major points have already been negotiated and accepted by both parties.

```
*  *  *  *  *  *  *  *  *  *
        SCHEDULED FUNCTIONS
*  *  *  *  *  *  *  *  *  *
```

Saturday, February 15, 20___

  3:00 P.M.   ADI/HOTEL STAFF PRECONVENTION MEETING   Board Room

                              15 persons

  Attn: Set-up Crew   "U" shape

  Attn: Banquet Wtr.   Complimentary coffee, soft drinks, sweet rolls

Sunday, February 16, 20___

  6:00 - 8:00 P.M.   ARCHITECTURAL DRAFTSMEN INTERNATIONAL   Sec. F
                              COCKTAIL RECEPTION
                              Approximately 30 persons. All are convention officials
                              and board members

  Attn: Set-up Crew   Cabaret style

  Attn: Banquet Wtr.,
        Bar Manager   Call brand liquor to include: Beefeater, Johnny Walker Black,
                              Dewars, Smirnoff, Jack Daniels Black, Old Grand Dad, CC,
                              Bristol Cream Sherry @ $26.00 ++ and $30.00 ++. Two bottles
                              Chablis and Pinot Noir @ $7.00 per bottle ++. Beer @ $1.00 ++.

  Attn: Banquet Wtr.,
        Exec. Chef   Following hors d'oeuvres: 5 orders Polynesian Pu-Pus @ $7.50++,
                              5 orders Selection #3 @ $6.75 ++, 10 orders Selection #4 @ $6.75 ++
                              10 orders hot seafood @ $8.00 ++, 10 orders cold seafood @ $8.50 ++,
                              and one shrimp bowl @ $100.00 ++. Hors d'oeuvre table to be
                              decorated with two gold candelabra and 6 silver chafing dishes, white tapers.
                              Cold hors d'oeuvres to be passed by waiters.

  Attn: Accounting   Bill to Texas Instruments - Exhibits Master Account.

Sunday, February 16, 20___

  3:00 - 6:00 P.M.   REGISTRATION   Foyer

  Attn: Set-up Crew   6' draped table rear of registration desk.
                              2 house phones. 1 directory board. Ice water
                              stand. Bb/c/e. (blackboard/chalk/eraser)

Monday, February 17, 20___

  9:00 A.M. - NOON   GENERAL BUSINESS SESSION   Sec. F

                              500 Persons

  Attn: Set-up Crew   Theatre style with stage 12' x 40' x 24'
                              twenty feet out from kitchen wall. Projection platform
                              will be required against kitchen wall for rear screen projection.
                              Size to be determined. Head table for 8 on stage. American
                              Flag stage right. 1 35mm Carousel slide projector. 1 Lantern slide
                              projector. 1 electric pointer. 2 center aisle mikes. Central dimmer
                              to be located at projection platform. 1 projectionist.

  9:30 A.M. - NOON   EXHIBIT HALL SETUP   Exhibit Hall

  Attn: Hall Supervisor   20 - 8' x 10' exhibit booth to be set up by
                              Scott Stubbs Service Company.

                                                                        (continued)

The next two pages provide an indication of the detail required in a specification sheet. Every scheduled event is documented and thorough instructions provided regarding room setup and food and beverage arrangements. While reading through the sheet, keep in mind the importance of the meticulous recording required in the preparation of this form.

12:15 P.M.	LUNCHEON	Sec. B
	500 Persons	
Attn: Set-up Crew	Rounds of 10 with raised head tables on 32" dais for 12 centered in south wall.	
	Lighted table podium mike center of head table.	
Attn: Banquet Wtr. Exec. Chef	Tickets to be collected except at head table. Linen will probably be alternated on this function. This is to be advised.	
Attn: Banquet Wtr.	Serve our Group Luncheon Menu #7 with tomato juice appetizer @ $6.10 ++.	
Attn: Accounting	Bill to ADI Master Account.	

Thursday, February 20, 19

3:00 - 5:00 P.M.	ADI/HOTEL STAFF POST-CONVENTION MEETING	Board Room
	Same setup as on Saturday	

As you can see, a large volume of information must be entered -- and often changed -- which is not only time-consuming, but may also result in costly errors.

In order to standardize resume data, and to minimize error, technology is being developed with financial backing from the Hyatt, Marriott, and Sheraton chains, along with the ASAE and MPI. The venture, called PlanSoft Ajenis Limited Partnership, uses the Ajenis software to speed up the entry (and any subsequent changing) of meeting data and to eliminate communications problems during meeting planning. The system, which will provide a "one-stop" planning service, will use a database from which planners can choose properties, "view" meeting rooms and call up specifications, and enter and change their meeting specs. A planner using the same property for a subsequent meeting can simply modify such details as dates and attendance.

Banquet Event Order (Function Sheet)

When the program is finalized, each function should receive individual attention. Such attention to detail translates into service efficiency. This is done by means of a **banquet event order (BEO)**, such as the one illustrated in Figure 12.3. This banquet event order for a cocktail party shows the relationship between a resume and a banquet event order – the resume provides an overview of the event while the banquet event order breaks the event down into minute details.

The banquet event order, like the resume, has been tagged with a variety of names: event form, worksheet, function sheet and so on (as with the resume, we are using banquet event order as that is the term most commonly used today). Banquet event orders can also vary from hotel to hotel in the amount of detail required. Individual banquet event orders, however, are generally prepared from the resume and are the working form for hourly employees (in Figure 12.3, for example, details are given regarding the staffing of a bartender, set-up crew and cooks).

Ideally, the resume and any banquet event orders should be completed and two copies sent to the meeting planner two to three weeks in advance of the meeting and prior to distribution to the hotel staff. These materials should be accompanied by a letter asking

Figure 12.3. BANQUET EVENT ORDER (FUNCTION SHEET).

FUNCTION ORDER - FOOD AND BEVERAGE

EVENT DATE February 16, 20__	DAY Sunday	ORDER NO 126

ORGANIZATION
Architectural Draftsman International

FILE NO   N-614

POST AS
Architectural Draftsman International Cocktail Reception

BILLING ADDRESS
Bill to Master Account Texas Instruments, 120AK, Lakeview, MI 48851

CONTACT Deanne Pritchard	ON SITE CONTACT Robert Olson		BUS PHONE NO 363-1906	RES PHONE NO
EXPECTED 30	GUARANTEED 30	SET UP 33	BOOKED BY Amber S.	DATE TYPED 2/1

TIME	SETUP REQUIREMENTS	LOCATION	TIME	MENU	LOCATION

SETUP REQUIREMENTS:

6:00 PM - 8:00 PM Cocktail   Sec. F

Cabaret Style Set-Up
Draped Cocktail Rounds with ashtrays,
no chairs

MENU:

5 orders Polynesion Pu-Pus @ $22.50++,
5 orders selection #3 @ $20.25++,
10 orders selection #4 @ $20.25++,
10 orders hot seafood @ $25.50++,
10 orders cold seafood @ $25.50++,
1 shrimp bowl @ $300.00 ++

Hors d'oeuvre table to be decorated
with two gold candlabra and 6 silver
chafing dishes. White tapers.
Cold hors d'oeuvres to be passed by
waiters

Food @ $ 20.25+T+T
Seafood @ $ 25.50+T+T
Shrimp bowl @ $ 300.00 +T+T

HOTEL TO ORDER

_X_ Decorations
3 Tropical Florals
Charge to Master
___ Entertainment

REFRESHMENT BREAK

AUDIO VISUAL

Time   Location:

SPECIAL NOTES

BEVERAGE REQUIREMENTS

RECEPTION

Call Brand Liquor to include: Beefeater,
Johnny Walker Black, Dewars, Smirnoff,
Jack Daniels Black, Old Grand Dad, CC,
Bristol Cream Sherry @ $78.00 ++, $ 84.00 ++
and $ 90.00 ++. Two bottles Chablis &
WINE SELECTION   Pinot Noir @ $21.00 ++ per
bottle. Beer @ $3.00 ++.

SUMMARY OF CHARGES

FOOD   See Menu
BEVERAGE   See Beverage Requirements
RENT
LABOR
PARKING
DEPOSIT RECEIVED
METHOD OF PAYMENT
BALANCE DUE DATE

TIME   LOCATION

WE NEED YOUR ASSISTANCE IN MAKING YOUR BANQUET A SUCCESS PLEASE CONFIRM YOUR ATTENDANCE AT LEAST
BUSINESS DAYS IN ADVANCE IF WE ARE NOT CONTACTED WITHIN THE SPECIFIED TIME, YOUR EXPECTED ATTENDANCE WILL
SERVE AS YOUR GUARANTEE THIS WILL BE CONSIDERED YOUR MINIMUM GUARANTEE WE WILL ADD THE CUSTOMARY 17
SERVICE CHARGE AND SALES TAX FOR GROUPS SERVED UNDER 25 THERE WILL BE A $50 LABOR CHARGE
I HAVE READ AND I UNDERSTAND THE REVERSE SIDE OF THIS DOCUMENT
IF IN AGREEMENT, PLEASE SIGN ONE COPY AND RETURN X _____

Las Vegas Hilton

This form is used to detail each convention function listed on the specification sheet.

the planner to review the copies, note any changes and sign and return one copy to the hotel at least a week prior to the meeting. An example of this type of letter is shown in Figure 12.4.

Figure 12.4. TRANSFER OF RESUME AND BANQUET EVENT ORDERS TO CLIENT.

MARRIOTT INTERNATIONAL, INC.
Hawaii Area Sales Office

92-1001 Olani Street
Kapolei, Oahu, Hawaii 96707
Phone: 808/440-2356
Fax: 808/679-0293

February 28, 2005

Ms Colleen Abee
The Meetings Group
Meeting Planner
1605 Iron Ridge Drive
Las Vegas, NV 89117

Dear Ms. Abee:

Enclosed for your review are two copies of your group resume and two copies of each Banquet Event Order. Please look them over carefully and note any changes. Please sign and return one copy of each BEO prior to your meeting.

Please notify our office of the exact number of guests attending each banquet function no later than 10 days prior to the event. As is our standard policy, the hotel will set and prepare for 5% over this guarantee. Once this number is received, you will be charged for the guarantee even if fewer attend of if you cancel over that time. Should your attendance go over that guarantee, you will be charged for the actual numbers served or for any higher subsequent guarantee that you submit to us.

Please feel free to contact me at any time should you have further questions or needs. I look forward to receiving your signed copies – and assisting you in staging a most successful event.

Warmest aloha,

Christopher Blunt
Director of National Accounts
Marriott International - Hawaiian Islands Hotels & Resort

Hotels generally send copies of the group's resume to the meeting planner two to three weeks prior to the event for approval before distributing the resume and any accompanying banquet event orders to departments involved in servicing the event. This sample letter not only provides the meeting planner with these materials, but also requests attendance figures and reiterates the hotel's guarantee policy.

Whether the function is a general session or a small committee meeting, document it. The basic seating layout, decorations, visual aids, and any other special services required should be detailed on the function sheet. Most hotels assign a specific number to each banquet event order for easy reference. Copies of each function sheet, as with the specification sheet, should be distributed to hotel department heads at least a week prior to the event. There may be times when changes need to be made to banquet event orders. The most efficient way to communicate these changes is with a BEO addendum, commonly referred to as a banquet change order or banquet change sheet. These change orders contain the identification number and any other pertinent identifying information from the original banquet event order, and includes, very specifically, the changes to be made. In many cases, hotels use a color-coded system to immediately identify banquet event order status – the original BEO is printed on a white sheet, revisions can be printed on canary paper and pink paper can be used for guarantees, for example. Other hotels reduce paper flow and instantly communicate changes via their computer systems.

It is essential that *each program segment* have its own banquet event order (function sheet) to ensure that all details will be handled. Document the head table, platform, basic seating layout and all other arrangements. But also have a checklist for small but needed items, such as water glasses, pads and pencils, audiovisual equipment, sound systems, floral arrangements, and so on.

You may find that many well-organized association and corporate meeting planners make their own checklists of what is needed. As we mentioned earlier in this chapter, some meeting planners will even provide you with a complete **event specifications guide (ESG)**, also known as a **staging guide** or **specifications guidebook**, which is a concise document detailing how the meeting will proceed (see Figure 12.5). ESGs include activities (by day, time, room, setup and requirements), complimentary room assignments, signature authority and other details authorized by the meeting planner. You can use these guides to prepare your own group resumes, incorporating the itemized requests contained in the ESGs. One convention service manager shared with us,

> "Most people think that all the convention service manager does is handle the group while it's in-house, but 90 percent of our work is the extraction of details one to two years prior to arrival. My job is to direct, produce and extract information from the meeting planner and in turn pass this information on to various department heads through specification and function sheets."

A master schedule should be made. This will assist you in determining the number of pieces of anything needed anywhere at any particular time. You may have specified on a number of function sheets that a digital slide projector is needed, but the master schedule would indicate how many such projectors are needed at the same time.

Many hotel people feel that such details are truly the responsibility of the meeting planner. However, it is the hotel staff that will be called upon under crisis conditions to rectify any oversights. You could avoid those last-minute panics by being well organized; develop your own checklists and suggest that the meeting planner do the same.

If planners are inexperienced and fail to anticipate their needs correctly, they may say you gave them insufficient notice and you may end up as the victim. Given a choice between blaming you and accepting the blame themselves, they may find it all too easy to blame you.

Not only is it important to plan defensively, but your suggestions and organization also will establish your reputation. Clients will retain the memory that meetings at your hotel always run smoothly. That memory is the one you want to leave with clients.

The Importance of Communication

Problems during meetings can be largely eliminated if a "pipeline" of communication has been established from the very beginning. It has been said that "the job of servicing meet-

Figure 12.5. **EVENT SPECIFICATIONS GUIDES (STAGING GUIDES).**

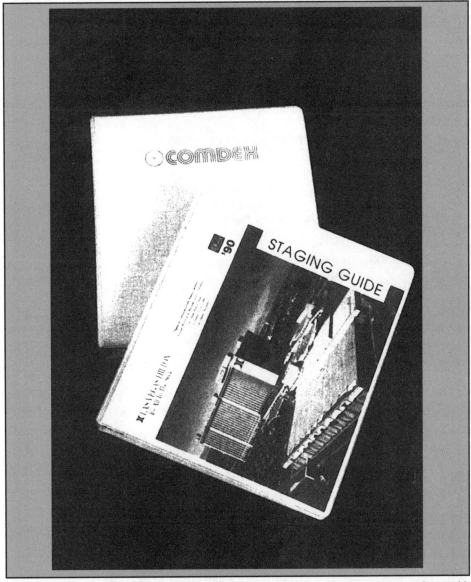

The overriding factor in the success of a meeting is communication. Meeting managers who provide event specification guides (ESGs), detailed instructions for each event or setup in a loose-leaf notebook, facilitate the convention service manager's task of preparing the resume.

ings is 95 percent communication and 5 percent service." Securing detailed information and expectations from the meeting planner is one of the most important tasks of the convention service manager.

Letters, telephone calls, emails, and personal on-site visits are normally used to get initial information. Another excellent tool to initiate the communication process is to send a **resume questionnaire** (see Chapter Appendix) to the meeting planner. This form consolidates a list of important questions and reduces the frequent telephone calls and exchanges of correspondence on individual items. Other ways to improve communication are for the convention service manager to provide the meeting planner with a formal and mutually agreed upon timetable for communication of meeting details. And, some convention service managers ask to be put on the meeting planner's mailing list, while others will send the meeting planners a sample specification sheet to inform the planner of the format used by the hotel.

Figure 12.6. BANQUET EVENT ORDER (FUNCTION SHEET).

The Durham Resort
44 Newmarket Road
Durham, New Hampshire 038244
(603) 868-1500

GROUP NAME: Automobile Travelers Association
POST AS: Annual Meeting
IN CHARGE: Mr. Harry McArthur   **FUNCTION ORDER NO: 104**

DAY	DATE	TIME	FUNCTION	ROOM	PEOPLE	RENT
Tue	10/12	8:00 AM - 5:00 PM	Lunch Meeting	Cherry Room	75	$250

BEVERAGES

Service: 17.5%   Tax: 9.5%
Bartender Fee: $65.00 each

ARRANGEMENTS

In charge of service: Banquet Service

Chairs (18")
16mm Movie Projector
6' Round Dinner Table for Rounds of 10
Slide Projector with remote control
   capabilities
Rear Screen Projection (10' x 10')

FOOD

Stuffed Pork Chop from 8:00 AM to 5:00 PM
Room: Cherry Room   Attendance: 75

Tender Pork Chop Filled with a Special
   Sausage Stuffing in a Mushroom Sauce
Whipped Potatoes
Vegetable du Jour
Tossed Garden Salad, Choice of Dressing
Assorted Rolls
Coffee, Tea & Decaf
Charge: $18.00 Per Person

Billing: Master Account
Address: 1234 Albany Drive
              Atlanta, GA 01234
Phone: (404) 555-2141

Client Signature:_____ Date:_____
Prepared By: Kathy McDonald_____ Date: June 14, 20_

The contents of the above meet with my approval. I consider our agreement definite and confirmed.
Guarantees must be sumbitted 48 hours in advance of all functions (Monday functions, 72 hours).
Prices are subject to 17.5% gratuity and 9.5% sales tax (where applicable).

This function sheet, generated in an automated sales office, merges important account information and relative booking information on one display screen. This report retrieves the information from the hotel's meetings database.

Communicating Details Electronically

Computer technology has altered the way specification and function sheet information is created. Figure 12.6 illustrates a computer generated banquet event order (function sheet). Automated sales systems can build a function sheet as information is gathered and input by the salesperson into the client's file. Also, a computerized system allows the creation of a number of forms that can be tailored to specific servicing needs. For example, you can create a form that contains just menu information for your chef, or a form containing just setup information for your service staff.

Database management programs also allow meeting information stored in the computer to be isolated, manipulated or sorted to answer specific requests. With just a few keystrokes, the meetings can be sorted by location, time, date, size, and so on. For example, you may wish to ask the computer to list all meetings scheduled in the convention area that require overhead projectors on Monday between 7:00 A.M. and 7:00 P.M. or which rooms require classroom setup this week. This information is available instantly on a computerized data management program and would not require searching through numerous typed resumes. Additionally, changes and deletions are made simply by calling up the meeting in question and revising the individual fields or deleting the record.

In addition, new technology processes driven by the Internet and e-commerce will alter the way in which specification and function sheet information is communicated. In the future, this information will be transmitted electronically via a direct Internet link between the meeting planner and the hotel's convention service manager. Each will have all the details on-screen and will be able to make corrections online, eliminating the mailing of large amounts of paperwork.

Once approved by the meeting planner, the resume and banquet event orders will be distributed electronically to departments within the hotel rather than having sheets (even computer generated ones) copied and distributed. With the click of a mouse, the exacting details of the meeting will be distributed to all involved with servicing the group.

The Importance of Follow-up

Follow-up is an important part of showing your commitment to servicing a group's meeting. Follow-up, of course, should begin after initial contact with the client, as discussed in the communications section in this chapter. Checking details increases the likelihood that there will be fewer problems during the event.

During the meeting, frequent contact with the meeting planner and/or his or her staff is also important. Checking to ensure that all is going well reassures the meeting planner of your commitment to his or her group.

After an event, a **post-convention meeting** should be held. The same people who met for the pre-convention meeting should meet for an after-the-fact review of the convention. This meeting is an opportunity for both the planner and the hotel staff to assess the success of the event and to address any problems (and determine ways to solve them in the future).

Summary

In this chapter, we have seen the necessity of working closely with the planner in the days leading up to a meeting or convention and the necessity of informing all hotel departments

---

Best Practices

WESTIN

Westin's "Operation Excell"

It is important for meeting planners and a property to get off to a proper start. A well-organized pre-convention procedure such as Westin's "Operation Excell" eliminates many of the unforseen crises inherent to group meetings and could well mean the difference between a successful convention and one that is plagued by disorganization. The following, a step-by-step review of the "Operation Excell" checklist, is a concept for servicing meetings that can be used by any size property, whether resort, commercial hotel or motel.

1.   A pre-convention date and time is agreed upon by the hotel and the meeting planner. A reminder is sent to all departments involved, with a notation that all department heads are to be there ten minutes before the meeting begins. This is to give the convention service manager a chance to prepare the staff for any unusual characteristics or demands of the convention group. All the normal procedures used in setting up meeting rooms should be applied in planing an Operation Excell meeting. Taking care of details such as proper seating setup, the right sized meeting room, and comfortable chairs gives the client the impression that the hotel will service his or her meeting as well as it runs its own. Coffee, soft drinks and sweet rolls should be provided so there is an atmosphere of informality. To instill confidence that the hotel knows how to service meetings, the convention service manager should check the room an hour ahead of time for those little things, such as lighting, pads and pencils, and comfortable temperature, that make for a pleasant, attractive meeting setup.

2.   An inventory of nameplates of all department heads should be maintained so that the client may relate in the meeting to the key people on the hotel's staff. VIP identification pins are presented to the meeting planner and his or her staff.

3.   The meeting format gives department heads a chance to ask questions about matters that relate directly to their roles in servicing the group. The convention service manager then goes over the program event by event. A sample agenda might include:

- review of the specification sheet and function sheets
- review of the master account
- an updated room pick-up report

If there are areas of misunderstanding or changes are needed, the client has an opportunity to inject input. A secretary should be on hand to take note of these changes. These last-minute changes are typed up after the meeting and distributed to all involved.

4.   A specification sheet (resume), which covers the entire convention program and is the hotel's in-house communication medium, should be distributed not only to those at the Operation Excell meeting but to every department in the hotel. Each department needs to be kept informed so it can forecast staffing needs. For example, if no luncheons or dinners are scheduled on a particular day, the people in charge of staffing the hotel's coffee shop and restaurants should be alerted to the possibility of extra volume. Likewise, if a late evening activity is scheduled outside the hotel, security personnel should be informed to take extra precautions.

---

of their roles in the event. Pre-convention meetings, detailed resumes and banquet event orders, and communication with both the planner and hotel staff will ensure the success of a meeting and will leave a good impression of the property's commitment to service.

The banquet event orders discussed in this chapter cover the requirements discussed by the planner and the property to set the tone for and properly execute the planner's event. These details include food and beverge requirements and room setups. In the next chapter, we will take a detailed look at the types of set-ups commonly used for meetings and other functions.

Endnotes:

1. HSMAI Sales Manual.

Additional References:

- Meetings and Conventions: A Planning Guide, Don MacLaurin and Ted Wykes, Meetings Professionals International. www.mpiweb.org

Internet Sites:

For more information, visit the following Internet sites. Internet addresses can change without notice. If a site is no longer available at the address listed below, a search engine can be used to find the new address or additional, related sites.

Convene - www.pcma.org
Convention Industry Council (CIC) Accepted Practices: Event Specifications – www.conventionindustry.org/apex/acceptedpractices/eventspecifications.htm.
Delphi-Newmarket Software - www.newsoft.com
Marriott International - www.marriott.com
Meeting News - www.meetingnews.com
Meetings & Conventions - www.meetings-conventions.com
Westin Hotels - www.westin.com

Study Questions:

1. What is the purpose of the pre-convention meeting? Who should attend?
2. What are the positions of the meeting planner and the convention service manager regarding a key personnel roster? What have some hotels done to compromise?
3. What key information is provided on a resume?
4. How does the the banquet event order differ from the resume?
5. How is the computer used to facilitate the communication of meeting details?
6. Why is follow-up so important? Describe three key times when hotel personnel commonly follow-up on a meeting.
7. Describe Westin's "Operation Excell." Outline the four stages of this program and discuss why each is important.

Key Terms:

Banquet Event Order (BEO). A form that provides a detailed breakdown of a single event. The banquet event order generally serves as a contract for the client and as a work order for the hotel's departments. Also called a **function sheet**.

Event Specifications Guide (ESG). A concise document, prepared and authorized by the meeting planner, detailing the specifics of a meeting or other event. ESGs include activities (by day, time, room, setup and special requirements), complimentary room assignments, signature authority and other important details. The ESG, which encompasses the full operation of the event, is shared with all key individuals. Also called a **staging guide** or a **specifications guidebook**.

Key personnel roster. A list of hotel personnel who are available to the meeting planner to help service the event.

Post-convention meeting (post-con). A meeting held after the completion of a meeting or convention to evaluate the forecasting and planning that preceded the convention and the hotel's performance during the event.

Pre-convention meeting (pre-con). A meeting held before the convention or event to review the entire program to ensure that the planner and hotel understand each other's requirements and expectations. This meeting is attended by the planner and key hotel personnel who will be involved in servicing the event to eliminate any misunderstandings and ensure a smooth event.

Resume. Form providing a comprehensive overview of the entire convention program. Sent to the various hotel departments involved in the event, it provides specific instructions to the staff for servicing the event. Resumes include a summary of all group activities, billing instructions, key attendees, arrival and departure patterns and other relevant information. Also called a **specification sheet**.

Resume questionnaire. Form on which meeting planners answer questions relating to the upcoming event. Having detailed information readily available reduces the need for frequent contact with the meeting planner and assists hotels in preparing for both the pre-convention meeting and the event itself.

CHAPTER APPENDIX

RESUME (SPECIFICATION SHEET) QUESTIONNAIRE
Resume questionnaire to be completed by the meeting planner.
(By permission, Penta Hotels)

NAME OF ORGANIZATION _____ Page _____

PROGRAM AND SET-UP INSTRUCTIONS

DAY/DATE	FUNCTION	LOCATION	TIME	SET-UP INSTRUCTIONS
Monday, 12/13	Registration	Georgian Foyer	8am-5pm	3 - 6' x 30" tables with 2 chairs each. 2 easels, a corkboard, a wastepaper basket.
	General Session	Georgian Ballroom	9am-5pm	Theater style for 200pp facing a head table for 6pp on a 1' high platform. Provide a table lectern.
				Audio: Provide a lectern mike.
				Audiovisual: Provide a Carousel projector with remote control with long cord and screen.
	Refreshment service	Georgian Foyer	10:30am-11am	Please discuss with Banquet Manager.
	Luncheon	Gold Ballroom	12N-1pm	Please discuss with Banquet Manager.
	Refreshment service	Georgian Foyer	3pm-3:30pm	Please discuss with Banquet Manager.
Tuesday, 12/14	Registration	Georgian Foyer	8am-5pm	Set-up: Same as the previous day.
	General Session	Georgian Ballroom	9am-5pm	Set-up: Same as the previous day.
	Refreshment Service	Georgian Foyer	10:30am-11am	Please discuss with Banquet Manager.
	Luncheon	Gold Ballroom	12N-1pm	Please discuss with Banquet Manager.
	Refreshment Service	Georgian Foyer	3pm-3:30pm	Please discuss with Banquet Manager.
etc.				

Penta Hotel

RESUME GUIDELINES

1. EVENT TO BE POSTED AS FOLLOWS:

_____

_____

2. OFFICIAL OFFICERS:

     NAME   TITLE

_____

_____

_____

3. AUTHORIZED SIGNATURES:

     NAME   SIGNATURES   TITLE

_____

_____

_____

4. MASTER BILLING ADDRESS, TELEPHONE NUMBER AND TO WHOM'S ATTENTION IT SHOULD BE LISTED.
   (Upon approval of credit manager)

          _____

          _____

          _____

5. NEW YORK STATE TAX EXEMPT: ____YES ____NO

        (If your organization is tax exempt, please forward a copy of the certificate to the Convention Service Department.)

6. CONVENTION HEADQUARTERS HOTEL : _____

   OTHER HOTELS USED: _____

                  _____   _____

7. EXPECTED CONVENTION REGISTRATION: _____ADVANCE _____ON-SITE

8. WILL THERE BE A NECESSITY FOR HOTEL SAFETY BOXES FOR THE CONVENTION OFFICERS? ____YES ____NO
   (If yes): HOW MANY? ____ AND WHAT NAMES SHOULD THEY BE LISTED UNDER:

_____

_____

_____

-2-

9. MONEY EXCHANGE: Will there be a necessity for the officers to exchange large bills during the conference? _____YES _____NO
(If yes, in what denominations?)

PENNIES _____   NICKELS _____   DIMES _____   QUARTERS _____

$1 BILLS _____ $5 BILLS _____ $10 BILLS _____ $20 BILLS _____

10. RESERVATIONS: _____ HOTEL FORM   _____ OWN FORM   _____ HOUSING BUREAU

_____ ROOMING LIST   _____ PHONE IN

11. ARRIVALS: Will most of your arrivals be arriving by:

_____AUTOMOBILE   _____TRAIN   _____COMMERCIAL AIRLINE   _____CHARTERED BUS
Note: For bus arrivals, please have the person(s) and/or organization contact our Reservation Manager directly.

12. HOSPITALITY SUITES: Please have the companies who will be sponsoring Hospitality Suites contact our Room Service Manager directly for their food and beverage needs. Also, our Reservation Manager and Credit Manager should be contacted to expedite their reservation and billing needs.

13. BUS DEPARTURES: Have you contracted for buses for tours, trips, etc. _____YES _____NO
If yes, please advise us of your schedule in the program and setup instructions.

14. CELEBRITIES: Will any of your speakers attract media attention? _____YES _____NO
If yes, please list their names and speaking date/time below:

_____

_____

_____

15. SECURITY SPEECH: Do you require our Security Department to give a short speech on security tips on this city and the hotel?

_____ YES   _____NO   If yes, it will be conducted at your first General Session.

16. OFFICERS, SPEAKERS AND VIP RESERVATIONS:

NAME: _____   Double - 1 bed

ADDRESS: _____   Twin - 2 single beds

_____

TELEPHONE #: _____

ARRIVAL DATE:_____   ESTIMATED TIME: _____

DEPARTURE DATE:_____   ESTIMATED TIME:_____

ROOM TYPE: _____ SINGLE   _____DOUBLE   _____TWIN

_____ 1 BEDROOM SUITE   _____2 BEDROOM SUITE

(Sharing with: _____)

Arrival: _____ Departure_____

BILLING INSTRUCTIONS: _____ Pays own room, tax and incidental charges

_____ Room and tax to the Master Account

_____ Room, tax and incidentals to the Master Account

SPECIAL REQUIREMENTS: _____

389

-3-

17. REGISTRATION: (Speakers - Exhibitors - Registrants)

      DAY   DATE   TIME   LOCATIONS

_____

_____

18. ADMISSION: _____

19. EXHIBITS: DAY/DATE   TIME   LOCATION(S)

    Drayage setup: _____

_____

    Exhibitors Setup: _____

_____

    Show Opens: _____

_____

    Exhibitors Dismantle: _____

_____

    Drayage Dismantle: _____

_____

20. NUMBER OF EXHIBITORS: _____ TYPE OF BOOTHS:_____
    Forward the exhibitors contract to the Convention Service department.

21. HOTEL HOLD HARMLESS CLAUSE: Please sign and return.

22. CONTRACTORS: (Contact, address and telephone number)

    DRAYAGE CONTRACTOR   SECURITY CONTRACTOR

    _____   _____

    _____   _____

    _____   _____

    AUDIOVISUAL CONTRACTOR   TYPEWRITER CONTRACTOR

    _____   _____

    _____   _____

    _____   _____

    SIGN CONTRACTOR   COPY MACHINE/OFFICE EQUIP CONTRACTOR

    _____   _____

    _____   _____

    _____   _____

-4-

SOUND/LIGHTING CONTRACTOR   OTHER CONTRACTORS

_____   _____

_____   _____

_____   _____

23. CONVENTION BUREAU PERSONNEL USED: ____ YES ____NO

_____

_____

24. ROOM SERVICE/RESTAURANTS/BARS: L=Light, M=Moderate, H=Heavy

	BREAKFAST	LUNCH	DINNER	COCKTAILS
Room Service	_L _M _H	_L _M _H	_L _M _H	_L _M _H
Restaurants	_L _M _H	_L _M _H	_L _M _H	_L _M _H
Bars	_L _M _H	_L _M _H	_L _M _H	_L _M _H

25. TELEPHONE INSTRUCTIONS:

Will there be a need for outgoing calls? ____YES ____NO

If yes: ____LOCAL ____LONG DISTANCE ____BOTH

The special code word for all outgoing calls will be: _____

26. CHECKROOM FACILITIES:

The hotel does have a Main Checkroom located in the lobby. Will you require a second checkroom? ____YES ____NO

(If yes, our checkroom manager will contact you directly for charges incurred.)

27. PACKAGE ROOM:

Will you be shipping boxes to the hotel Package Room? ____YES ____NO

If yes, approximately how many? _____Basic Size _____Basic Weight

28. PROGRAM AND SET-UP INSTRUCTIONS:

On the following page, please find an example of the format followed for the Convention Service resume. We suggest this format for simpler communications and easy understanding. For more detailed set-ups, we suggest attaching a diagram.

This information will be included in the hotel's convention resume, which is distributed to all departments in the hotel.

Learning Objectives:

This portion of your text introduces you to the various types of function rooms and setups used for meetings and food functions. We will also discuss how to manage function room space to best serve the group while maintaining maximum profitability for the hotel. When you have studied this chapter, you will:

- Be able to identify factors that convention service managers consider before assigning function space to meeting planners.

- Be able to describe various meeting room setups and tell when each is commonly used.

- Be able to detail how to monitor function room usage and make the most of function space.

Outline

Function Rooms
- Types of Function Rooms
- Function Room Size and Layout
- Meeting Room Plans
- Timetable for Setup and Breakdown

Managing Function Rooms
- Sales Restrictions on Function Space
- Function Room Charges
- Function and Meeting Room Revenue Management
- Release Dates
- Several Meetings Simultaneously
- Use of Meeting Rooms by Others
- Employee Procedure Manuals

Meeting Setups
- Function Room Furniture
- Basic Meeting Setups
- Setups with Tables

Breakdown of Function Rooms
Meeting Rooms of the Future
Monitoring Function Room Usage
Summary

How to Assign Meeting Rooms and Determine Meeting Room Setups

David Scherbarth, CMP
Director of Banquets and Convention Service
Sheraton Bal Harbour Beach Resort

"The convention service department is an extension of the sales department and must work closely with the sales manager to maximize function space while providing the group with a comfortable environment to achieve the goals of the meeting...Working closely with the meeting planner on the agenda will allow you to select proper function space so that the space is not too large or small for their meeting...The type of setup and the number expected to attend has a direct impact on how much space you need...You must know the various setups and what the capacity seating of each setup is for every function room in your facility...Other items that need to be considered when assigning function space are: noise conflicts with other meetings or banquets; traffic patterns of associated public space; lighting needs; ceiling heights; decor; electrical needs; competitive groups."

13

Function Rooms and Meeting Setups

Any hotel can supply guestrooms. A convention hotel is one that has a sufficient number of function rooms and the trained staff needed to handle the many different kinds of meetings and conventions.

Function Rooms

When the hotel sales representative originally solicited the convention, he or she presented the client with information about the hotel's meeting rooms. Most larger convention hotels have a number of suitable meeting rooms and often more than are needed for an event. In the case of a smaller meeting, the hotel needs to obtain the release of unneeded meeting rooms as early as possible to enable its staff to sell another event.

Often a convention planner will request that all the convention facilities be held for his or her event, at least until the program is roughed out and it is obvious what facilities are needed. This is rarely possible. Unless the convention is large and virtually sells out the house, the hotel management cannot lock up a precious commodity like meeting rooms for any longer than absolutely necessary.

It is urgent, therefore, for you to get together with the meeting planner to place a hold on the rooms thought to be needed and to urge that planning be done to determine realistically the needs of the event. There is no pressure if you have no other meetings scheduled for those dates, but most sizable hotels handle a number of smaller meetings simultaneously.

Types of Function Rooms

Before assigning rooms, the convention service manager must be aware of what the hotel has to offer. A common mistake is to assume you have only those rooms specifically designed as function rooms. Actually, all public space may be function area depending on the group and its needs.

Some of the most common **function rooms** depicted in the hotel's convention brochure are exhibit halls, ballrooms for banquets, and conference rooms for meetings.

Unless meeting planners are advised otherwise, these are the rooms with which they will work as they lay out their schedules. Foyers and hallways outside the meeting rooms, however, can be used as **pre-function space**. These areas are often ideal for morning and afternoon refreshment breaks and as cocktail areas prior to evening banquets. Other possiblilities include use of the foyer, the parking lot and swimming pool areas for cocktail parties; upper-floor suites equipped with conference tables for small, intimate meetings; and the garden area behind the hotel for an evening party. The possibilities are limited only by the imagination of the convention service manager. The unusual is often what makes a hotel unique, so it is important to keep in mind that all public areas may be used as function space.

Breakout rooms are used when a session divides into small groups for discussion and feedback. The trend toward breakout configurations as a method of training has be-

One Seal You *KNOW* You Can Count On

Another Seal You Will Grow to Count On

CERTIFIED MEETING SPACE

Responding to the need to provide meeting planners with the actual dimensions of meeting rooms and their capacities under a wide variety of setups, the Professional Convention Management Association (PCMA) began a program to certify the dimensions of meeting rooms at hospitality properties. Properties that take advantage of this program are given detailed computer printouts of their meeting space and permission to use the PCMA certification seal on promotional literature.

The Hilton chain is among a growing number of properties that offer certified meeting space specifications to meeting planners. In addition to bearing the PCMA certification seal, this ad promotes the Hilton's adherence to Convention Industry Council guidelines to assure meeting planners that they will get the meeting space promised in the chain's promotional materials.

When you book your meeting **Make Sure Your** or convention at a certified Hilton, it always comes out according **Meeting Is A** to plan. Because Hilton's quotes for capacity are 100% **Certified Success.** accurate. Only Hilton performs a formal inspection, making certain we follow Convention Liaison Council Guidelines like no one else. So don't trust your meeting to chance. Go with Hilton's 75 years of expertise. And you'll know what to expect before you arrive. Call your Hilton National Sales Office or Hilton Direct at 1-800-321-3232.

HILTON. SO NICE TO COME HOME TO.

come increasingly popular, so many hotels are making suites available near the main conference room. Others have provided rooms that can be subdivided with movable **air walls** to accommodate these setups.

Function Room Size and Layout

Many factors come into play when discussing meeting room size. First and foremost, of course, is the number expected to attend. Then you must consider the room setup desired and the number and type of audiovisual equipment needed. Additional space may be required for clothes racks, props, or tables to distribute literature. And you must allow more space if refreshment breaks are scheduled.

The basic layout indicates the style of seating. It is wasteful of labor to set each room to utmost capacity, but you obviously must provide enough seating. This is the time to examine the kind of sessions that will go on just before and just after this specific program to make sure the setup is the same or enough time is allotted to make the change. Hotels are frequently able to put similar meetings back to back and thus keep manpower and equipment change-over time to a minimum.

The meeting planner will also have to confer with you about the style and size of the head table. Pads, pencils, folders and printed material may all be placed on chairs and tables. And water glasses and pitchers may be put at a number of tables or stations if tables are not used. Each session has its own requirements; some, for example, call for name signs. Attention to details is the key to service.

Meeting Room Plans

It is important to include meeting room plans on resources used by meeting planners, including the hotel's convention brochure, websites, and directory advertising. For years, convention brochures gave general — often approximate — dimensions of meeting rooms, and meeting planners were often dismayed to find that there was not enough room to stage their functions. To eliminate this problem, the Professional Convention Management Association (PCMA) developed a program to help both properties and meeting planners by actually measuring the dimensions and capacities of meeting rooms. After the rooms are measured with sophisticated laser powered equipment, computer software is used to accurately map out the room and determine room setup capacities. The detailed computer printouts generated are given to the property to be used in presentations. Properties that have had their space certified are provided with gummed seals that can be affixed to current promotional materials, and are given permission to use the PCMA seal in advertising to assure planners that they are getting the space promised (see box titled "Certified Meeting Space"). Recently, the PCMA partnered with Meeting Maker software to offer a diskette containing floor plans of their meeting rooms to properties that have been space verified. Meeting planners can download, at no charge, a companion version of the software from the PCMA website. The PCMA and Meeting Maker now advertise that "The combination of these software packages enables properties and meeting managers to send meeting room sets back and forth via the Internet, a whole new way of doing business."

In addition to the dimensions of rooms, meeting planners need to know the capacity of each under a variety of setups (see Figure 13.1). While planners are made aware of the kinds of rooms available to them during a sales presentation, the convention service manager should be available to help planners decide which function would work best in each

Figure 13.1. MEETING ROOM CAPACITIES AND DIMENSIONS.

CAPACITIES AND DIMENSIONS*

ROOM	CAPACITIES						EXHIBITS		DIMENSIONS		
	THEATRE	SCHOOL ROOM	BANQUET	RECEPTION	U-SHAPE	HOLLOW SQUARE	8x10	10x10	SQUARE FEET	DIMENSIONS	CEILING HEIGHT
GRAND SALON	–	–	640	1,373	–	–	28	28	9,612	178'x54'	12'
GRAND BALLROOM	4,556	1,008	3,340	4,556	–	–	307	254	50,112	270'x150'	22'-16'
ADELPHI ROOM	1,896	1,008	1,020	1,929	–	–	85	74	13,500	150'x90'	22'-16'
BROADWAY ROOM	1,120	735	650	1,286	–	–	52	52	9,000	150'x60'	22'-16'
CAPITOL ROOM	1,120	735	660	1,286	–	–	52	52	9,000	150'x60'	22'-16'
RIALTO ROOM	1,120	735	600	1,286	–	–	52	52	9,000	150'x60'	22'-16'
RIALTO 1	150	84	120	264	52	65	–	–	1,850	45'x37'	22'-16'
RIALTO 2	150	84	120	264	52	65	–	–	1,850	45'x37'	22'-16'
RIALTO 3	150	84	120	264	52	65	–	–	1,850	45'x37'	22'-16'
RIALTO 4	150	84	120	264	52	65	–	–	1,850	45'x37'	22'-16'
REGISTRATION OFFICE	–	–	–	–	–	–	–	–	350	14'x25'	10'
GOLDWYN BALLROOM	5,000	3,400	3,400	5,200	–	–	291	237	44,600	180'x240'	10'-23'6"
GOLDWYN OFFICE	–	–	–	–	–	–	–	–	1,221	37'x33'	10'
GOLDWYN FOYER	–	–	–	–	–	–	–	–	1,232	22'x56'	12'
PALACE ROOM**	–	–	340	462	–	–	24	24	5,082	–	10'
PALACE 1	65	40	40	113	22	34	–	–	792	22'x36'	10'
PALACE 2	96	63	50	113	32	40	–	–	792	22'x36'	10'
PALACE 3	280	154	170	280	70	85	–	–	2,112	32'x66'	10'
PALACE 4	76	54	50	99	32	40	–	–	693	21'x33'	10'
PALACE 5	76	54	50	99	32	40	–	–	693	21'x33'	10'
PALACE 6	84	45	50	102	32	40	–	–	713	23'x31'	10'
PALACE 7	84	45	50	102	32	40	–	–	713	23'x31'	10'
DIRECTOR'S ROOM	Permanent Conference Table Seats 22								1,189	41'x29'	12'-10'
GROUP INFORMATION BOOTH	–	–	–	–	–	–	–	–	196	14'x14'	9'
ASSN. OFFICE 1, 2, 3, 4	–	–	–	–	–	–	–	–	108	9'x12'	9'
CELEBRITY ROOM	Permanent Seating for 1,499								2,640 (Stage Dimensions Only)	60'x44'	26'
ZIEGFELD ROOM	Permanent Seating for 1,096								5,016 (Stage Dimensions Only)	88'x57'	30'

Most hotels, conference centers and city convention facilities offer charts such as the one above to meeting planners. This is a particularly good example as it includes seating capacities in a variety of seating arrangements as well as detailed information on square footage, room dimensions, exhibit capacities and ceiling heights. These statistics, coupled with the computerized scaled drawings now available, help meeting planners to assess the ability of properties to meet their requirements for various types of meetings and functions.

Source: Courtesy of Bally's Casino Resort, Las Vegas, NV.

room. We will discuss the setups commonly used and how capacity is affected by various setups later in this chapter.

Convention service managers should also be aware of the impact of the **Americans With Disabilities Act (ADA)** in regard to their property's function space. While there are still a number of "gray areas" in terms of responsibilities of the property, certain physical requirements must be met by properties offering convention space. These include (but are not limited to) adequate handicapped parking, easy accessibility (ramps, wide doorways, etc.), adapted restroom facilities, and assistive devices for the hearing and visually impaired.

Not only must hotels be **barrier-free** (free of obstacles that prevent handicapped persons from moving freely to all public areas), but meeting planners may also have special requirements for accommodating their handicapped attendees. Wider aisles and increased space for seating arrangements may be needed to allow wheelchair access or a signer may be required for hearing impaired attendees. In some cases, it is not difficult for a property to make the necessary adjustments; in others, it will be up to the property and the meeting planner to determine who is responsible for providing the additional services needed.

Scaled Drawings. If a hotel does not present its meeting rooms in complete detail, it will be necessary to prepare other material. Most properties prepare scaled drawings of each room (see Figure 13.2). These should indicate doors, windows, pillars, elevators, electrical outlets and any obstructions that might affect the setup of the meeting. Meeting planners will probably ask for scaled drawings of each room, so you should have accurately scaled drawings of each function room for your own use and for distribution to customers.

These drawings should be accurate enough to be used to designate meeting or exhibit layouts. If you indicate capacity on the drawings, keep in mind that different setups accommodate widely differing numbers of people. Some properties have simplified room arrangement planning by the use of a magnetic planning board. The setup for a particular room is worked out in advance by using scaled metallic pieces to represent various sizes of furniture. The meeting planner using such a technique is able to get a better feel for the setup suggested by the convention service manager.

In addition, meeting planners also like to visualize the flow of their attendees. Figure 13.3 shows an overall schematic of a facility. While this plan does not provide the detail inherent to scaled drawings of the meeting rooms itself, it may prove helpful to the planner in planning his or her program.

Scaled drawings of function rooms and overall schematics are important to meeting planners, and they are also used to ensure a safe event. For large events, detailed scaled drawings of the function are required by local fire marshals. These scaled drawings, unlike the scaled drawings provided to the meeting planner by the hotel, must include both the room's schematics and the proposed room setup. In most cases, this finalized scaled drawing is the responsibility of the meeting planner and should be a part of a hotel's contractual terms with the meeting planner. The Las Vegas Hilton, for example, advises:

"Your Company or Association is responsible for scaled diagrams for events with attendance of 300 guests or more. These must be approved by the Clark County Fire Marshal. The Las Vegas Hilton cannot guarantee these diagrams will be approved if submitted less than 30 days prior to your function. The Las Vegas Hilton can assist in providing a scaled diagram of your event."

Using Computer Technology to Assist Meeting Planners. Many properties are taking advantage of today's computer technology to assist meeting planners in determining the optimum room setups. Using computer programs is far quicker than manually drawing floorplans (often to find that the space does not accommodate the function), and offers the advantage of flexibility (features of a room — pillars, curved spaces, etc. can be considered when determining the best layouts — and a number of room setups can be compared). Additionally, they can show a number of options that the meeting planner (and the convention services staff) may not have previously considered, they enable meeting planners to see at a glance how various setups will work in terms of traffic flow as well as capacity, and they can be stored to enable them to be used for future functions.

Many properties, such as the Marriott (which utilizes its own software to offer computerized room drawings to meeting planners as part of its Network Plan) are finding this technology to be an invaluable tool for the varied needs of meeting planners. This technology is expected to be increasingly used by both properties and meeting planners themselves and should be considered as part of your property's program to assist meeting planners with staging a successful function.

We have already mentioned the PCMA computer printouts that provide room capacities for varied setups, but still other software is available, such as MeetingMatrix and Room Viewer, which also "draw" room setups (see box titled "Using Computer Technology to Assist Meeting Planners"). The MeetingMatrix is one software program used to enable meeting planners to see which setups will work best for their functions. After entering such basic information as room dimensions, number of attendees and special requirements (size or shape of tables, space needed for exhibits, etc.), the program "draws" one or more pos-

Figure 13.2. DETAILED MEETING ROOM PLANS.

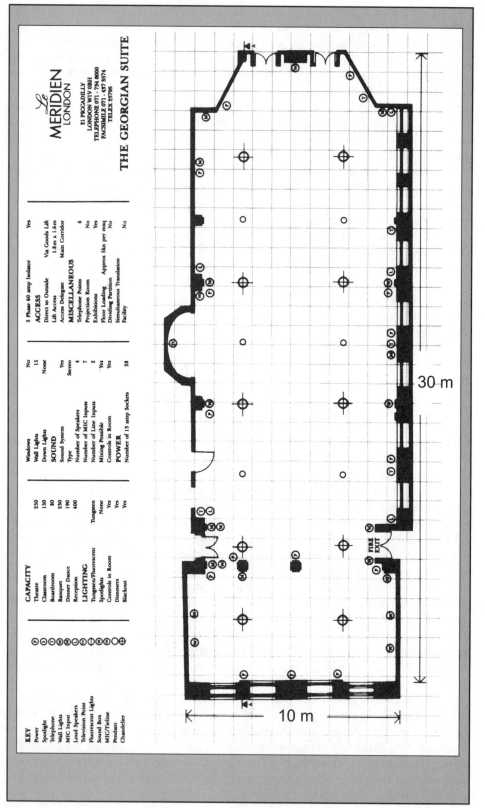

Figure 13.3. AN OVERALL FACILITY SCHEMATIC AS A SALES TOOL.

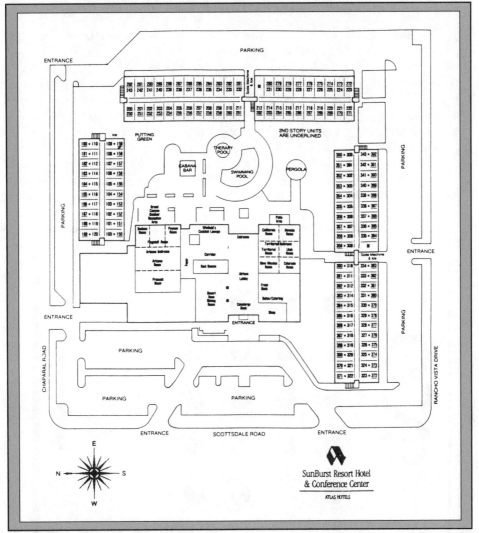

Using a plan as illustrated here, a salesperson can help the meeting planner visualize the attendees'
flow from guestrooms to function rooms.
Source: Courtesy of SunBurst Resort Hotel and Conference Center.

sible room configurations, enabling the meeting planner to see which one will be best —
and providing the convention services department with a list of function room furniture
and equipment needed for the setup chosen.

Jim Barr, catering/convention service manager at the Sheraton Chicago Hotel and
Towers, states:

> "MeetingMatrix diagrams are complete and easy to modify and read and
> that helps us both with sales and operations. From a sales perspective,
> clients are more confident about their buying decision when we use
> MeetingMatrix to show how their function will work in our space. On
> the operations side, using the diagrams during final event preparations
> keep questions, miscommunications and re-sets to a minimum."[1]

Using Computer Technology to Assist Meeting Planners

MeetingMatrix is one software program used to enable meeting planners to see which setups will work best for their functions. After entering such basic information as room dimensions, number of attendees and special requirements (size or shape of tables, space needed for exhibits, etc.), the program "draws" one or more possible room configurations, enabling the meeting planner to see which one will be best — and providing the convention services department with a list of function room furniture and equipment needed for the setup chosen.

Sample Banquet Setup

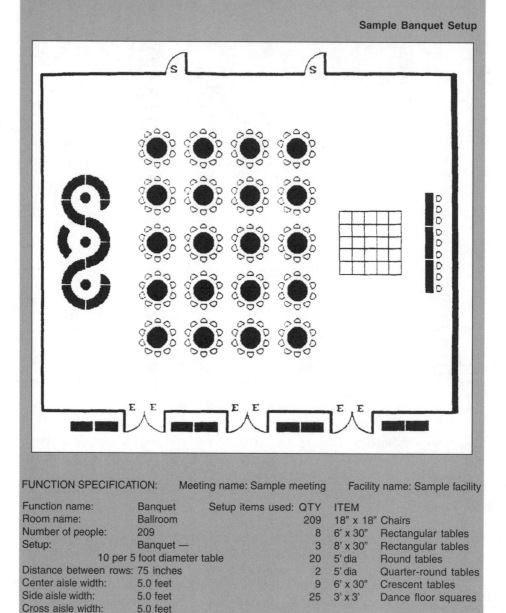

FUNCTION SPECIFICATION: Meeting name: Sample meeting   Facility name: Sample facility

Function name:	Banquet	Setup items used:	QTY	ITEM	
Room name:	Ballroom		209	18" x 18"	Chairs
Number of people:	209		8	6' x 30"	Rectangular tables
Setup:	Banquet —		3	8' x 30"	Rectangular tables
	10 per 5 foot diameter table		20	5' dia	Round tables
Distance between rows:	75 inches		2	5' dia	Quarter-round tables
Center aisle width:	5.0 feet		9	6' x 30"	Crescent tables
Side aisle width:	5.0 feet		25	3' x 3'	Dance floor squares
Cross aisle width:	5.0 feet				

MEETINGMATRIX is a trademark of SCLM, Inc. Used with permission.

FACTORS TO BE CONSIDERED WHEN ASSIGNING FUNCTION SPACE

David Scherbath, CMP, director of banquets and convention service at the Sheraton Bal Harbour Beach Resort, says that details are important when deciding how to effectively manage function rooms and meeting setups. Factors that should be considered include:

- Day(s) of meeting. If more than one day, try to keep the meeting in the same room. This minimizes labor and gives the group consistency.
- Beginning and ending times. Accurate times allow the room to be utilized more than once a day — sometimes for as many as three or four times for different functions.
- Setup style and attendance. The type of setup and number expected to attend has a direct impact on how much space is needed.
- Audiovisual & staging requirements. These two items can dramatically alter the size of space needed. A 24-hour hold may be necessary for extensive audiovisual and/or staging requirements.

Working closely with the meeting planner on the agenda will allow you to select proper function space so that the space is not too large or small for their meeting. This is important because the comfort of a meeting room can have an affect on the environment and on the focus of the meeting. This also allows the sales team every opportunity to maximize function space and guestrooms with additional bookings. Releasing space unneeded by one group may allow your sales team to book another group in the hotel, increasing your occupancy and revenues.

Monica Cheeks, director of convention services at the Hyatt Newporter in Newport Beach, California, is equally enthusiastic about the Room Viewer technology:

> "We use it every day. Previously, we were sketching out meeting setups by hand, which is obviously neither precise nor very fast. Now with Room Viewer, I can plot out a planner's request very quickly and accurately, print it out and give copies back to the planner, as well as to our catering manager. Our sales team uses it in proposals, and it's helped to close deals. It even has six different aisle sizes, so it can conform to our complicated fire codes."[2]

MeetingMatrix is available from SCLM Software Inc., 6 South Main, Stewartstown, Pennsylvania 17363. Room Viewer information can be obtained from TimeSaver Software, 10884 Kimball, Tustin, California 92680. Free room layout software demos can also be downloaded from both MeetingMatrix (www.meetingmatrix.com) and Room Viewer (www.timesaversoftware.com).

Timetable for Setup and Breakdown

Most hotel brochures do an adequate job of presenting the basic contours of each meeting room, and many are designed to show how a room is used in a variety of ways. Few, however, tell the convention organizer how much time is required for room setup and breakdown. But there is a great need to communicate that information.

It is very important to know exactly how long it takes a crew to set up each room under the many seating arrangements. Many a meeting program has failed because those planning it did not take into account the time it takes to set up and break down and the program was designed much too tightly to permit good service. The planner would have developed the program more realistically if he or she had some idea of the time needed to perform these services.

Too often, the hotel bears the stigma of failing to perform well, give good service, or show much expertise, so the hotel staff should make the meeting planner aware of its **function room turnover time** – the amount of time needed to tear down and reset a function room. Most meeting planners would gladly loosen up their timetables if they knew what was involved to assure that their shows ran smoothly and on time.

We strongly recommend that convention service managers have charts made up indicating such requirements. These charts should list the time it takes to set up each room for maximum capacity under each seating arrangement. They should give the time it takes to break them down, plus union regulations regarding workday, hours, overtime charges and any unusual characteristics that may affect costs and time. Specify the number of people needed. Time may be saved by using a larger crew but this will cost more; at times a meeting planner might choose such an option.

Managing Function Rooms

Your hotel function space is a precious asset, and your goal as a convention service manager is to maximize its utilization (see box titled "Factors to be Considered When Assigning Function Space"). Empty rooms, whether guestrooms or function rooms, are a perishable product.

The convention service manager is the person most qualified to assign rooms for specific events. This should be done in communication with the meeting planner. The service manager knows the hotel's facilities; the planner knows the event's characteristics.

In assigning a room, its size, its capacity under a specific layout, the type of event, and the presentation style should be considered. The room size should "match" the expected attendance. Too much space or too many empty seats can create the wrong psychological setting. These fundamental requirements probably were hashed out during the sales presentations, but other factors must be considered, too.

Consider the room's location within the hotel in regard to traffic in corridors, elevators, escalators, parking arrangements and coat check rooms. All program segments must be definitely allocated to specific locations about sixty days before the event, at the latest. This is especially important if a group wishes to reserve their space on a 24-hour basis. According to Maria Dempsey, director of sales and marketing North America for Pan Pacific Hotels and Resorts, this can pose a problem for the hotel:

> "The request for access to public meeting space on a 24-hour basis means
> no other groups may use those rooms, even if the room is not occupied
> overnight."[3]

A number of groups, however, wish to reserve their rooms for the duration of their meeting, especially if functions involve exhibits or extensive staging or if there is the possibility that a meeting will not end on schedule. David Kilman, CMP, past president of MPI, offers this perspective:

"There is a tug-of-war between planners and suppliers regarding 24-hour space holds. It all comes down to the total value of the meeting. If a planner expects, or demands, the luxury of a round-the-clock hold on space, there must be an appropriate financial return to the supplier...Once the economic impact of a meeting is resolved, it should be easy to determine if a 24-hour hold is a reasonable request."[4]

When considering a 24-hour hold, therefore, it is vital to analyze the economic impact of the meeting, including the value of the meeting itself and subsequent business from the group, and the time of year. If, for example, the group wishes to book during the Christmas holidays, when you can expect to generate a large volume of lucrative catering business, it may not be a sound business decision to reserve function rooms on a 24-hour basis (see Sales Restrictions section in this chapter). If you decide to reserve the rooms around the clock, a clause should be included in the group's contract guaranteeing the 24-hour hold and any restrictions put upon it by the hotel.

You should get a list from the client of all the people on his or her staff who are authorized to move an event to a different location, should the need arise. Just before the

Figure 13.4. GUIDE TO FUNCTION SPACE CHARGES.

SHERATON FUNCTION SPACE CHARGES

The Sheraton Waikiki charges for function space under the following circumstances:

1. All Exhibits.
2. All function rooms that are held on a 24-hour block.
3. All function space for groups that have meetings only and are holding no sleeping rooms at the Sheraton Waikiki Hotel.
4. All function space when unusual or costly setups are required.
5. All function space when the sleeping rooms decrease proportionately from the original commitment.

FUNCTION SPACE VS. SLEEPING ROOM CONSUMPTION (PROPORTINATE SLIDING SCALE)

Percent of Decrease From Original Block	Amount of Meeting Room Charges
Up to 40% decrease	No charge
41%-60% decrease	50% charge for meeting rooms as listed on "meeting room charge sheet."
61%-80% decrease	75% charge for meeting rooms as listed on "meeting room charge sheet."
81%-100% decrease	100% charge for meeting rooms as listed on "meeting room charge sheet."

In addition to the above "sliding scale,"...the hotel will also take into consideration your definite food and beverage events when determining your meeting room charges.

The Sheraton Waikiki provides meeting planners with the following space pricing policy. Note the charges increase if sleeping rooms slip from the original room block commitment. In determining meeting room charges, many hotels consider "slippage" — when guestroom pickup decreases significantly, the charge for the group's function space increases. Meeting room rental at this 1,900-room property totals over $250,000 annually.

event, and especially during it, it is absolutely essential to know the channels of authority within the convention staff. Time may be too short and the need for action too great to let you double-check any instructions. Cancellations of sessions, changes in timetables and the like may be made at the last minute.

Such a list should be in writing, of course. And the degree of authority should be specified. What can these staff members order? Changes in layout or location can be costly in terms of time and labor.

The list you get from the convention organizer should be similar to the list of your department heads that you give to the organizer. The key people of both the hotel and convention group staffs should attend the preconvention meetings. Let them get acquainted before the pressure begins. Discuss possible changes. This is the time to indicate what the hotel staff will need in the way of time and labor to bring about such program alterations.

Because association conventions must cope with optional attendance at both the convention and individual programs, it is often necessary to move workshops and meetings from one room to another to accommodate smaller or larger groups. Airing such possibilities in advance allows your staff and the client's staff to understand such conditions and to react more quickly and constructively in crisis situations.

Sales Restrictions on Function Space

Both the hotel sales staff and the catering department are involved in selling function space. The sales department is responsible for selling space that is used by convention groups requiring sleeping rooms. The catering department is responsible for selling function space to local groups. Since hotels are primarily interested in filling sleeping accommodations because of the high profit margin, the hotel sales department should have preference in booking the available function space.

Therefore, most hotels have local catering sales restrictions. For example, during its peak convention season, a hotel may limit local catering to a short booking cycle. That is, the catering department may only sell function space to local groups after the hotel is assured that the needs of groups needing sleeping rooms have been met. Once the hotel sales staff sells their group room allotment on a given day, any function space still available may be sold by catering.

The further out this commitment is made by convention groups, the greater the opportunity for catering to sell the unused space. This period of time is frequently referred to as the **open sale period**. Holidays are often designated as open sales periods as group guestroom business is traditionally slow around Christmas, Thanksgiving, and the Fourth of July. Any hotel business booked by catering during those times is not likely to displace conventions needing meeting space.

Function Room Charges

How do you determine what to charge for meeting space? Brochures list rates for guestrooms but rarely for meeting rooms. The latter situation is most flexible; it depends on the meeting group, the time, and the space required. If a group uses enough guestrooms, there is often no charge for meeting rooms. In the case of food functions, the cost per person often covers the use of the room.

Properties with unique function space may be able to charge more for their room rental. Function space characteristics that might command a premium include:

- large ballrooms that are free of pillars or other obstructions.
- high ceilings with retractable chandeliers.
- tiered theater-style auditoriums.
- advanced audiovisual equipped rooms.
- meeting rooms that are convenient to guestrooms.

It is important that the meeting planner understands your property's policy regarding function room charges. Many hotels include a clause similar to the one below to eliminate potential misunderstandings:

"Meeting and function space is assigned based on the type of setup and the number of people in attendance. Should advance setup and late teardown or an abnormal amount of meeting space be required, a charge may be incurred. Specified meeting rooms cannot be guaranteed and are subject to change. If the final attendance figures are less than the original estimate, an adjustment to the meeting and function space will become necessary. Any changes requested in your agenda after receipt of this contract are based upon space availability at the time of your request. Any cancellation of food and beverage functions after acceptance of this agreement will result in the organization being charged the full dollar value of that function based on either the actual menu price or an average menu price. Should the hotel be able to resell a function of similar value in the originally scheduled room, there will be no charge assessed."

There may well be circumstances in which the hotel management prefers to charge for a function room. A hotel that hosts a catering event where no guestroom nights are used, for example, may specify a *minimum sales amount* on the room. That is, the hotel could require that a group not using sleeping rooms spend a specific amount, such as $20,000, to secure a large ballroom without incurring a function room rental charge for their event. You should consider having a listed price for each room; after all, it looks great when you waive the fee. When you do charge for a function room, a list of charges should be available. Function room rental rates should be determined for each meeting room by time of day. Some properties will list specific rates for morning, afternoon, evening, full-day, and 24-hour weekday hold, and weekend rates.

You might outline a sliding scale arrangement, tying the meeting room fees to the number of guestrooms used for the convention (see Figure 13.4). For example, if the group picks up 200 room nights or more, the $1000 fee for the ballroom could be waived; if 100-199 room nights are used, the cost would be $500; and, if the group uses fewer than 100 room nights, the cost would be $750.

There is a trend today to charge for space. A hotel that handles a number of small meetings would be wise to consider a fee, particularly if the group plans to meet in one room, hold a food function in another, and conduct breakout meetings in another three to five rooms.

In such situations, room charges should be stipulated if the guestroom commitment is not enough to cover the labor costs of setting up, servicing, cleaning and tearing down. After all, a hotel is in business to make a profit.

You might also want to charge for meeting rooms when companies participating in a trade show take the opportunity to hold dealer or sales meetings. The people attending may already be registered for the trade show, and the requirements of the trade show would place great strain on the allocation of meeting rooms. Of course, if the food functions of such additional meetings mount up, it may justify not charging for the use of the room. But a room charge may be justified if the food function is only a refreshment break. In final analysis, there is no hard and fast rule on charging for meeting space. A hotel needs to look at the food, at the room, at all the profit areas to determine its rate structure.

Function and Meeting Room Revenue Management

Increasingly, hotels are applying traditional guestroom yield management methods to meeting and function rooms. Yield management sets prices based on the forecasted demand for function space. Rental rates are increased or decreased from the established rates depending on the time and date of the meeting and on the total revenue the event brings to the property. Several Hiltons, for example, have begun to determine intricate yield management formulas for pricing their function space. Steve Armitage, senior vice president of sales at Hilton Hotels Corporation states:

> "The meeting buyer can expect to see meeting room yield management become more widespread as technology advances."[5]

The use of yield management techniques can be beneficial to both hotels and meeting planners. Setting prices according to predicted demand levels not only helps hotels to manage their revenues but also provides the opportunity for price-sensitive customers who are willing to purchase at off-peak times to do so at favorable rates. It is necessary, however, to identify and communicate high and low demand periods and to be able to justify the different rates available to different clients at different times of the year. And, any fee increases should be made incrementally to avoid alienating corporate buyers.

Fred Shea, vice president of sales operations for Hyatt Hotels Corp., says:

> "We do not want to have huge swings where we charge $3,000 one day and nothing the next. We want to slowly move the margins up or down. We don't want there to be a big culture shock. It's a matter of degrees."[6]

When establishing your yield management strategy, you will want to consider a number of factors, including the performance of each of your function rooms (a large ballroom, for example, may actually yield a lower occupancy rate than a smaller meeting room that is used several times a day), physical "rate fences" (such as amenities offered, location, and so on, that can justify a higher charge) and non-physical "rate fences", such as customer characteristics (a property can justify lower rates to a potential customer likely to use other hotel facilities, such as sleeping rooms, restaurants and so on).

Once these factors have been determined, you will want to develop a strategy that can be easily implemented. One simple approach is to color code demand periods on a calendar or table. High-demand periods, for example, can be coded in red for instant recognition as a "hot" period, moderately high-demand periods can be coded in yellow to signify "warm" periods and low-demand periods can be coded in blue. Each of the demand levels (colors) should have a different set of prices associated with it, and those prices should be communicated to all staff members involved in selling meeting space or catering functions. It is also important to communicate when qualified discounts can be offered to meeting planners or groups (usually in low-demand periods).[7]

Release Dates

When a convention buys out the house, a request to **hold all function space** seems reasonable. *All space blocks* requests are typical from large groups who are booking two to three years out. But a request to "hold all function space" is difficult for a hotel, especially in periods of high demand. Groups requesting an all space block on your function space should be closely monitored, and all space blocks should be negotiated with reasonable release date increments, such as one year, nine months or six months, to allow your property to sell the space with some lead time should the large group not materialize as anticipated.

Release dates should be set in every letter of agreement. At some early date when a rough program is available, the room assignments can be tentatively made. At this point, *some* function rooms can be released if there seems to be more than enough. The convention in the house should have a priority for meeting rooms, but you may get other calls. Here again, it is obvious why there is a need to have just one function book, under one person's control.

At a somewhat later date, when a detailed program is worked out, try to get unneeded rooms released. Planners often to try to hold onto every room indefinitely, to have a reserve for some occasion that may come up. But the practice can inhibit your other sales efforts.

Many properties specify their release date policies in meeting contracts. The following clause spells out one property's policy:

"In order to ensure that adequate space is available for your meeting, please provide the Convention Service Department with a tentative function schedule six months prior to your meeting/convention, or as soon as possible. A final program is required no later than 90 days prior to the start of your convention. Space not assigned at 90 days will be released to the hotel for scheduling of other functions, as required."

Several Meetings Simultaneously

Most meetings are small. More than 75 percent of all corporate meetings have fewer than 100 in attendance. To do much business in meetings, you must be able to house more than one simultaneously. Naturally, this is not the case when you virtually sell out the house, but most often the function book fills up with a number of more modest events.

Handling several smaller meetings calls for careful planning. You cannot negotiate with all groups at the same time, so you must take care not to commit all your public space to one group, leaving you with no facilities for the other. Most hotels want the option of moving groups around to maximize usage, especially when groups are not using guestrooms, and often include a function room assignment clause in their contracts. A typical clause might read:

"The function room assignments listed in this contract are tentative. Final function and meeting rooms will be assigned by the Hotel three months prior to the meeting dates. The Hotel reserves the right to reassign function rooms to accommodate both Group and all other groups or parties using the Hotel's facilities during Group's meeting."

Some meeting planners, who feel that they have negotiated for a specific room or rooms that will meet the objective(s) of their function, object to such a clause and try to negotiate it out of the contract. A hotel can address the concerns of the meeting planner by pointing out the reasonable time frame (most groups do not publish a program with specific room names more than three months before the function) and assuring him or her that the hotel will meet specific requirements if another room is substituted. The hotel should then follow through on its promises, ensuring that basic requirements (such as square footage and other needs, such as hard walls to minimize noise) are met.

Traffic patterns must be carefully planned to avoid confusion and congestion. Give thought, too, to the proximity of different kinds of groups. Don't forget to find out what will be going on in the room next door. Holding a training session next door to a college reunion is asking for trouble; a rock band next door to a speech could be disastrous. And even a seemingly ordinary meeting can become quite noisy merely by adding a sound film.

You may find it extremely profitable to go after smaller meetings. To begin with, there are more of them. And smaller meeting organizers are generally not as demanding of price and concessions, often can offer much repeat business, and tax your staff less in serving them. It is tempting to hit that home run by bagging a full house convention. But a steady stream of good base hits in the form of modest size meetings often wins the ball game by providing what every hotel wants — profitable business.

Use of Meeting Rooms by Others

Some organizations ask, or demand, that all requests by other groups for meeting facilities in the hotel at the time of their event be cleared with them. They are trying to control the entire environment of their event and they don't want rival organizations meeting at the same time under the same roof. Apprehensions of industrial security cannot be dismissed lightly.

The hotel must be careful about this. Imagine an IBM research seminar in the house at the same time as Control Data or Honeywell meetings! When a competitive organization appears on the scene, the usually easygoing meeting planner gets quite uptight. And you may find yourself needing strict security systems for a relatively easy, small seminar.

And should you be concerned about only the exact date of the meeting, or must you worry, too, about the days immediately before and after the event?

Small properties that can handle only one average-sized group at a time can use such situations to sell themselves. In the off season the small resort can claim that walk-in business from competitive personnel is highly unlikely. The meeting organizer is assured of receiving all your facility and attention and need not worry about traffic pattern and unwanted guests.

The convention organizer may want to veto a meeting held in the hotel during his or her dates. Many companies hold dealer meetings at trade shows. Most association executives have no objections, and many feel that it adds importance to their event. But many worry that the timing of such meetings may pull delegates away from the main sessions or events.

It is safe to say that you can expect meeting planners to be interested in who and what is scheduled in the hotel during *their* time.

Employee Procedure Manuals

Convention service managers, as we have said, are the in-house coordinators of the convention. They work with virtually every department in the hotel. Their authority in dealing with these departments is to a great extent determined by their character and the respect they have earned from those with whom they work. In many hotels, convention service managers do not have direct line authority over rooms or food and beverage departments. This often necessitates that they use tact and discretion in getting the job done.

However, they do have line authority within their own department and must function as managers there. Serving under them are three to ten housepersons who set up the function rooms. Each of these people should be trained in the various types of meeting setups. Our experience shows this is best accomplished with the use of an **employee procedure manual**.

A procedure manual is not a job description. A procedure manual tells the employee how to do the job, whereas the job description is prepared primarily for management and states the job's responsibility and authority. Ideally, the procedure manual should include illustrations or drawings. For example, setup illustrations similar to those used in this chapter should be included. The manual also should include a step-by-step outline of the houseperson's job.

The procedure manual will have the same importance for employees in the convention service department as the master recipe card does for a cook. Successful restaurants are largely successful because of consistency; the same should be true for convention servicing. A procedure manual will help ensure that setups will not be done in a slightly different way each day.

It is often difficult for employees to recall each procedure in a setup and all the required supplies. The manual eliminates the exclusion of certain setups, as well as serving as a valuable training tool for new employees. Manuals might also include rules and regulations that apply to the setup houseperson.

Efforts should be made to personalize the manual. It should be published in a small booklet form that can easily fit into a shirt pocket for quick reference.

No such manual is permanent. On the contrary, new tables, chairs and operating techniques will necessitate updating. Hopefully, the employees themselves may suggest ways to perform certain aspects of the job better.

Meeting Setups

The physical arrangement of chairs and tables plays an important role in meetings. Convention planners know that the atmosphere of a meeting can be enhanced or destroyed by the size of the room and the manner in which it is arranged. Thus it is essential that you have an orderly presentation for each of your facility's meeting rooms, giving its dimensions and its capacities under a variety of layout designs.

Function Room Furniture

Hotel function rooms get heavy use. Often a number of functions are scheduled on one day for a single room, with only an hour or two between events. These events are usually quite different, and housepersons must work quickly to set up a variety of functions — business meetings, lectures, training sessions, fashion shows, banquets and others. The only flexibility the room can provide is through the use of air walls or folding division doors. The major change must be provided by the equipment and setup.

Function room furniture is the term coined for equipment used in meeting and banquet rooms. Jacob Felsenstein of King Arthur Incorporated, a leading supplier of such furniture to the hotel industry, has suggested four general features to look for in function room furniture.

Strength and durability. Watch for the weakest link such as mechanical folding devices which are easily broken, or strong components which may depend on a weak hinge or spring. Safety of guests is a foremost consideration. There are simple and effective folding devices that minimize the possibility of failure. Keep in mind, frequency of use means frequency of cleaning. Parts in contact with the floor must be made to withstand and facilitate frequent scrubbing, waxings and vacuuming.

Ease of handling. All folding or knock-down equipment should be simple to set up. Equipment that is light in weight may not be the most durable. There are a wide variety of carriers, such as dollies and trucks, which are designed to aid in handling.

Ease of storage. Equipment should be able to be stacked so that one piece does not mar the next, and in a manner that prevents vulnerable parts from protruding. In choosing dollies or trucks, check to see that they are designed to handle the particular piece of equipment in your particular setting.

Flexibility. It may be advisable to buy function room furniture that serves two or more purposes in order to avoid extra handling or storage. For example, a Knockdown Cabaret Table allows for different sized tops to be used interchangeably with one column and base, enabling it to fill many different needs; one Dual Height Folding Platform serves two different levels, many different purposes, can save up to 50 percent on initial outlay and an additional 50 percent on handling costs and storage space.[8]

Chairs and Tables. Meeting room chairs and tables vary a great deal, but there are certain types and sizes that are used most frequently. We will use these basic types when we present layouts and schematics for setups. Your capacity figures should be based on such equipment, and will vary when you use other than the standard. Most variations are used in small meeting setups, such as board room facsimiles; we have relaxed during many such meetings in posh swivel chairs. Conference centers frequently boast ergonomic chairs, which are bigger than a regular chair, upholstered in leather, come with a cushion seat and swivel and are said to be comfortable for 18 hours at a stretch.

Most chairs used for meetings are 18 inches wide by 18 inches deep by 17 inches high. Stacking armchairs (not the deluxe type mentioned in the previous paragraph) are slightly larger, such as 20 by 20 by 17. Most folding chairs are smaller and not as comfortable, and are generally used for last-minute overflow accommodations. Planners want their attendees comfortable so they can concentrate on the program.

Kevin Shanley, director of sales and marketing at The Kalahari Waterpark Resort & Convention Center in Wisconsin Dells, Wisconsin, says:

> "You don't want people thinking about how uncomfortable they are or how much they want to get up and stretch [instead of paying attention to the presentation]."[9]

Rigid chairs are recommended for food functions. They are more comfortable than folding chairs, which are smaller and lower. Folding chairs should only be used for emergency backup or for outdoor events.

The standard height for tables is 30 inches; the standard depth, either 30 or 18 inches. When people are to be seated opposite each other, the 30-inch table is required. When people sit on only one side of the table, as we shall discuss in *schoolroom* setups, the 18-inch depth is sufficient and saves much space. There is a growing use of 15-inch tables to save even more space. The 30-inch-deep rectangular table, however, is used most frequently for head tables, even when people are seated on only one side. This deeper table is also used as display tables, exhibit stands and other purposes. It is most versatile and comes in lengths of four, six and eight feet so that a variety of total lengths may be achieved easily.

Round tables are used for many food functions and also for some kinds of meeting sessions. They most often are five, five and one-half, or six feet in diameter. Comfortable seating calls for a five-foot round table for six to eight people; a five and one-half foot table for eight to ten guests; and a six-foot table for ten to 12. A **cocktail round** of about three feet in diameter is used for receptions, and can accommodate up to four people comfortably.

An almost infinite number of variations can be created by using half-rounds and quarter-rounds. The more imaginative curved serpentine tables are commonly used for buffets. You are restricted only by your imagination in developing unique buffet arrangements.

Tablecloths, mitered on the corners, are used on tables because most banquet and meeting room tables are damaged and unsightly from continual breakdown and storage. When ordering tablecloths, you will have to specify the exact measurements needed. Tablecloths for round tables should be approximately 18 inches wider than the table diameter to allow for a nine-inch drape over the sides (a 90-inch round tablecloth should be used for a 72-inch diameter table, for example). Since the standard table measures 30 inches from the floor and the average chair seat is 17 inches from the floor, the nine-inch drape will not touch the chair seats or interfere with the guests' comfort. Floor length tablecloths are sometimes used at formal functions, however.

Several companies have begun to market folding tables that are attractive and not easily damaged, and they can be used without tablecloths, saving on laundry and labor costs. Such tables, however, are expensive and fail to provide the warmth and color of tablecloths.

Head tables, as well as display and buffet tables, stages and platforms, require special drapery. Traditionally, T-pins and tacks have been used to attach floor-length linens for such setups, but **velcro** is now being used by many hotels.

Snap-drape skirting is also available. Plastic clips are fitted along the top edge of platforms and tables, and grippers sewn into the upper pleat of the skirting are snapped into place quickly. Snap-drape skirting is made of permanent-crease polyester and fiberglass, making it easy to clean and wrinkle-free.

Platforms and Staging. Folding platforms are used in many ways; they elevate head tables for banquets and speakers. They come in different sizes, with different names: platform, riser, stage, **dais**, podium or rostrum. You must construct them to size. Check local safety regulations carefully. The usual heights are six, eight, 12, 16 and 24 inches, plus a 32-inch high *riser*. Lengths may be four, six or eight feet, or any combination of these. Widths vary from four to six feet. If you maintain adequate stocks, a variety of combinations can be created. If the platforms are old and unsightly, put pleated skirting around the bottom and perhaps carpeting on top.

Staging height is determined by the room length. In general, divide the room length by 50 to determine the stage height. For example, a room that is 100 feet in length would require a 24-inch (two foot high) stage or platform.

Lecterns. Lecterns are reading desks used to hold the speaker's papers and come in two basic types. The smaller *table lecterns* are placed on tables, while full-size *floor lecterns* are set on the floor. Both sizes should feature built-in light fixtures and enough connecting wire to reach wall outlets.

Many a room becomes difficult to set up because the wall outlets are on the same circuits as the overhead lights and are controlled by a common switch. Make sure the lectern's light unit is connected to a wall outlet that will not be cut off with the overhead lights. House lights are often dimmed for effect or for greater visibility of audiovisual presentations. Check each setup carefully; smart meeting planners will double-check such items themselves.

Lecterns (and head tables) should not be located near an entrance or other high-traffic area to ensure that speakers and their audiences are not distracted by people moving about. If a video or power point presentation is planned, the room should be set up so that any doors are off to the side so latecomers will not have to walk in front of the projector.

Permanent stages allow you to develop more sophisticated lecterns with full audiovisual controls. Such units don't lend themselves to the temporary setups of most meeting rooms, but they are received most enthusiastically by program members. Consider these units whenever a permanent installation is possible. A must item that is most versatile for temporary setups is a portable lectern with a built-in sound system that plugs into an ordinary outlet.

Basic Meeting Setups

A number of basic seating arrangements have evolved. Be sure that your customer is using the terminology correctly. Layout or schematic sheets will help in this area.

Auditorium or Theater Style. One of the most common seating arrangements, termed the **auditorium/theater style**, calls for chairs to be set up in rows facing the speaker, stage or head table. Good for lecture sessions with limited note taking (see Figure 13.5), it is used in both large and small meetings.

To set auditorium style, place two chairs first to position the aisle. Two inches, called the *space*, must be left between chairs side by side. The *distance* is the dimension from a chair to the one in front of it. Minimum distance is 36 inches from chair center to center.

When chairs have been positioned to indicate the aisles, the bulk of the chairs can be placed. One-square-foot carpet patterns is the most popular with hotel people because it helps to align setups. If there is no carpeting, the lines in hardwood floors might guide you.

Aisle sizes and numbers are regulated by local fire departments. If you have any doubts, get the specifications from the fire department. Most regulations call for aisles to be six feet wide if 400 or more people are involved; aisles of four or five feet are sufficient for smaller groups. Double aisles are preferred if the meeting format calls for questions from the floor or anything that will result in back-and-forth movement of people or passing of objects such as microphones.

The first row of chairs should be about six feet from the front edge of the head table or platform. The most popular auditorium style uses a center aisle but many experienced planners avoid a middle aisle because the presenter is facing an empty space. Many planners prefer to divide the seating area into three sections with two aisles of four feet. In larger halls, fire departments may require aisles across the front and back of the room and an additional horizontal aisle halfway down. It pays to check and to keep a record of local fire regulations.

Keep in mind the number of chairs in a row. It is extremely uncomfortable for an attendee to have to make his or her way across fifteen people to find a seat in the middle of the row. Many planners opt for a "mini row" of no more than seven seats. There are variations, but they require more room. One is *auditorium style, semicircular, center aisle.* You need at least 12 feet from the head table or platform to the front row of chairs. Set the outside chair where you want it. Use a piece of string tied loosely between the two ends of the curved row. Line up the rest of the rows measured from the first one.

Figure 13.5. VARIATIONS OF THE AUDITORIUM STYLE SEATING ARRANGEMENT.

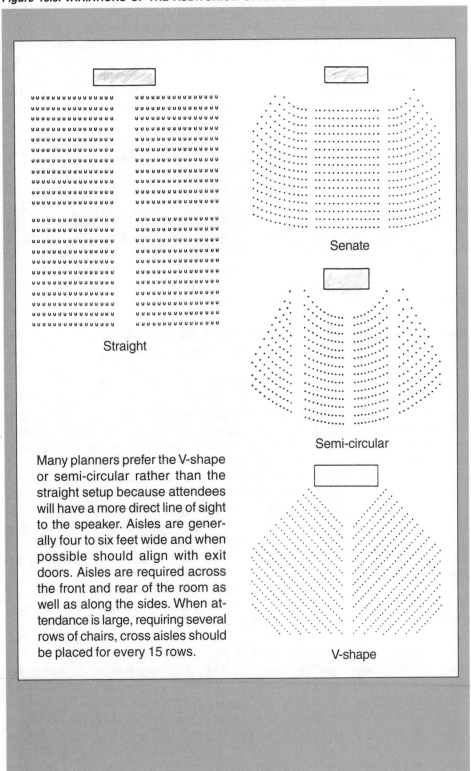

Straight

Senate

Semi-circular

Many planners prefer the V-shape or semi-circular rather than the straight setup because attendees will have a more direct line of sight to the speaker. Aisles are generally four to six feet wide and when possible should align with exit doors. Aisles are required across the front and rear of the room as well as along the sides. When attendance is large, requiring several rows of chairs, cross aisles should be placed for every 15 rows.

V-shape

Source: Reprinted with permission from <u>Function Room Set-Up Manual</u> *by Gerhard M. Peter; published by the Hospitality Sales and Marketing Association International.*

Auditorium, V-shape (sometimes referred to as *chevron*) sets up similarly; the side sections form an angle to the center aisle. This is an ideal setup if space isn't an issue, as, by offsetting each row, attendees are not sitting directly behind one another.

Space and distance vary from the norm when armchairs with writing arms are used. Because of the bigger dimensions of these chairs, use three-inch spacing and a 40-inch distance from chair center to center.

When on a dais, regardless of the floor arrangement, make sure that the head tables are draped down to the floor. Place water and glasses at the lectern and on the head table. Use one water carafe for every two people seated on the stage.

Quick Calculation - Theater Style

Allow 12 square feet per person for groups of less than 60 people
11 square feet per person for groups of 60-300 people
(the most common size for a breakout session)
10 square feet per person for groups of more than 300 people

Setups with Tables

A great many meetings and most food functions require tables as well as chairs. In this section, we will take a look at some of the most commonly used setups and their variations.

Schoolroom Style. One of the most popular setups among both large and small groups is the **schoolroom/classroom style** (see Figure 13.6). This is the best setup for meetings in which most of the talking will be done by a presenter and attendees will take notes, refer to information in binders or work on computer equipment, such as laptops. It is also the most comfortable design for very long sessions. This setup, however, is not the preferred setup for encouraging conversation among attendees, although it can be used for small group interaction – participants at every other table can turn to face those behind them. In the most common arrangement, people sit on just one side of the table. In such cases, use the 18-inch-deep rectangular tables and, most of the time, allow for a center aisle. Allow about 24 inches of space for each person. However, if attendees will be using binders or laptop computers, allow 2.5-three feet per person. While this means that a six-foot table will seat only two people, it is better than seating three people uncomfortably (both physically and psychologically).

Schoolroom tables are either six or eight feet in length. Six-foot tables can seat two or three persons per table; eight foot tables seat three or four. For groups requiring space to spread out, the smaller number should be set for each table.

The 30-inch-deep tables are usually too wasteful to use in schoolroom setups because people are seated on only one side. But there are instances when you do have to use them, especially if a great deal of paperwork is to be done. In such cases, allow 60 inches from center of table to center of table. The length of each row depends on the room size and attendance.

The tables should be draped. Place pads and pencils at each setting, plus water pitchers for every 16 persons. You can put a glass at each setting or provide a tray with ten or 12 glasses for every 16 persons. A variation is *schoolroom, perpendicular style*. In this arrangement, the rows of tables are perpendicular to the speaker's table. The 30-inch-deep tables are used because people will be seated on both sides. It is necessary to allow additional room for each person because the seats must be turned somewhat to face the speaker.

Figure 13.6. THE SCHOOLROOM STYLE ARRANGEMENT AND VARIATIONS.

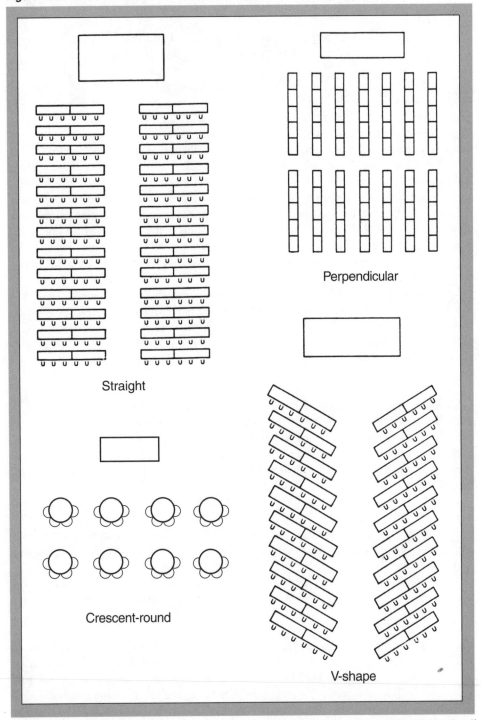

Perpendicular

Straight

Crescent-round

V-shape

The V-shape schoolroom allows the best sight-lines between attendees and towards the speaker. If attendees are expected to use laptops, 30-inch wide tables are preferred rather than the standard 18-inch wide tables. The crescent-round setup is often used when a planner wishes to follow a meal function with a presentation and desires to keep participants in the same room. Once the meal is finished and tables are cleared, attendees are seated on one side of the round, facing the speaker.
***Source: Reprinted with permission from* <u>Function Room Set-Up Manual</u>.**

Quick Calculation - Schoolroom Style

Allow 22 square feet per person for groups of less than 60 people
20 square feet per person for groups of 60-300 people
(the most common size breakout session)
17 square feet per person for groups of more than 300 people

Allow 30 inches of table space per person instead of 24 for the wide table and 60 inches from center of table to center of table. Tables should be six feet from the head table, with six-foot aisles on both sides of the room and a four-foot horizontal aisle in the center.

Schoolroom setups may also be *V-shape*, off a center aisle. Angled seating improves sight lines and gives attendees a sense of being closer together. Angling the rows to form a herringbone or chevron pattern brings attendees at the outside ends of the rows closer to the speaker. Schoolrom styles may also be set up using round tables. The **crescent-round** setup uses either 60, 66 or 72-inch diameter rounds. Seating is used on only one side so all attendees can face the speaker. This setup works well when the same room will be used for meals and an educational session and for general sessions in which in attendees break into small discussion groups in the same room.

Many groups schedule a break if a meeting is longer than two hours. The break should be programmed so that your staff can take the opportunity to **refresh the meeting room**. When the meeting breaks, housepersons should refill ice water pitchers, replace dirty glasses with clean ones, replace soiled or wet linen, straighten all chairs and pick up all obvious trash on the tables and floor. Such procedures help project a positive image of the hotel.

U-Shape. Some smaller meetings require a more face-to-face arrangement, making the U-shape setup popular (see Figure 13.7). This setup is often used for board of directors meetings, committee meetings and breakout sessions with audiovisual presentations, as all attendees can see the presentation when it is placed at the open end of the U (for optimal learning, group size should be limited to 20-24 people). The U-shape can also be used for banquets, with seating on all sides of the U.

Use 30-inch rectangular tables if people will be seated on both sides. Eighteen-inch deep tables can be used if only the outsides will be used, but most planners prefer 30-inch deep tables. The usual per-person allowance is 24 inches, but training and technical groups may need more space (2.5-three feet per person) if attendees will be using training materials or computer equipment.

Drape the front part of the U all the way to the floor. When the tables are draped, make sure that the crease is straight; it should run continuously along the center of the table.

Horseshoe. The **horseshoe setup** is just like the U-shape except the head table is connected to both legs with serpentine sections to soften the corners (see Figure 13.8). The U-shape and horseshoe arrangements are good for board meetings and idea exchange and lend themselves well to audiovisual presentations. The horseshoe and U-shape setups are ideal for training meetings in which the speaker needs access to the participants. These setups

Quick Calculation - U-Shape and Horseshoe

Allow 35 square feet per person

Figure 13.7. THE U-SHAPE SEATING
ARRANGEMENT.

Figure 13.8. THE HORSESHOE
ARRANGEMENT.

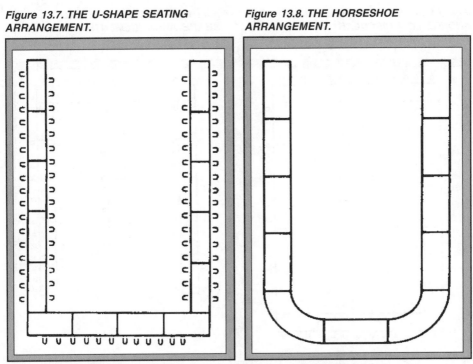

Source: Reprinted with permission from <u>Function Room Set-Up Manual</u>.

allow all participants to see and hear each other, but the size of the group is limited to approximately 24 persons.

Hollow Square and Hollow Circular. The **hollow square setup** and the **hollow circular setup** are preferred by meeting planners who want to do away with the head table concept (see Figure 13.9). This setup, which makes efficient use of space in a room, works best for small groups (up to 30 people) for which there is a facilitator leading the discussion or decision-making or problem-solving sessions as there are good sight lines and the setup is conducive to eye contact between participants. There is also no sense of preferential seating, so there is a sense of equality among participants. This type of setup, however, does not work well for sessions requiring audiovisuals.

These setups are formed like the U-shape (using 30-inch wide tables) except that the open end is filled in. Naturally, chairs are placed only on the outside. The hollow square and the hollow circular are popular for small meetings. Both arrangements should be skirted on the inside and are usually constructed to accommodate up to 30 persons.

Quick Calculation - Hollow Square and Conference

Allow 30 square feet per person

Variations. The **E-shape setup style** is a variation of the U-shape (see Figure 13.10). You need about four feet between the backs of the chairs to facilitate traffic. The *T-shape setup* has a head table 30 inches deep. A single leg extends from the center of the head table for as long as is needed. The leg is often set with double tables to make a 60-inch solid rectangular unit.

Figure 13.9. THE HOLLOW SQUARE AND HOLLOW CIRCULAR ARRANGEMENTS.

Figure 13.10. THE E-SHAPE AND T-SHAPE ARRANGEMENTS.

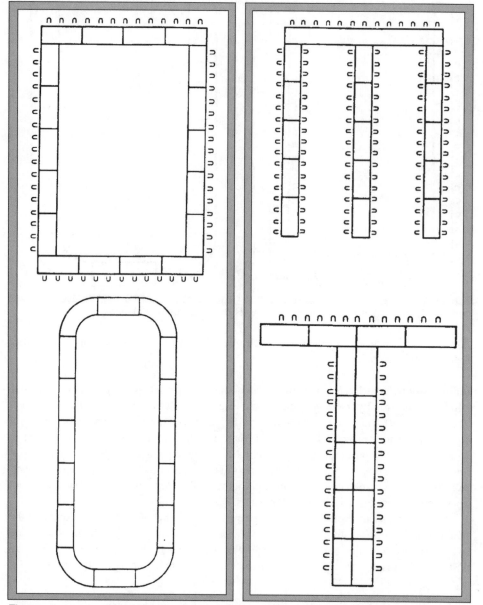

These setups are used for groups that do not want a head table concept. The T-shape arrangement shown here uses a row of two tables for the base of the "T"; the T-shape is also commonly seen with a row of single tables forming the base.

Source: Reprinted with permission from Function Room Set-Up Manual.

Figure 13.11. THE BOARD OF DIRECTORS SETUP.

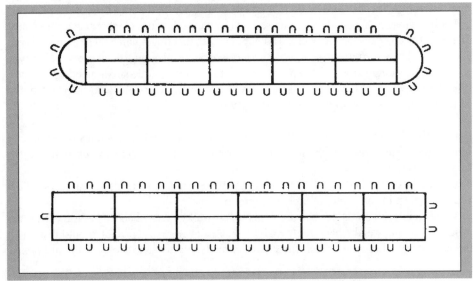

Popular seating arrangement for small meetings shown with its oval variation.
Source: Reprinted with permission from <u>Function Room Set-Up Manual</u>.

Figure 13.12. ROUND TABLE ARRANGEMENTS.

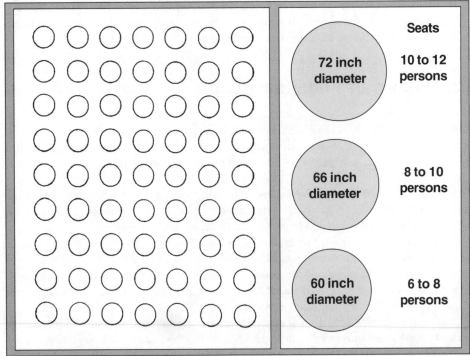

Rounds can be used for food functions and for meetings that break up into smaller discussion groups. Seventy-two inch rounds seat ten to 12 people. Sixty-inch rounds seat six to eight persons. There are also 66-inch rounds, that seat eight to ten. For greatest comfort, the lesser number of seats is preferred. When spacing tables, it is important to remember that 60-inch rounds require nine linear feet center to center. This takes into account the amount of space needed for both seated guests and the aisles between tables to facilitate seating and service.
Source: Reprinted with permission from <u>Function Room Set-Up Manual</u>.

Board of Directors. The **board of directors/conference setup** is a popular arrangement for small meetings. It calls for a single column of double tables making a draped table of 60 inches by as long as necessary (see Figure 13.11). Allow 24 inches of table space per person. The board of directors arrangement is so popular with meeting planners that many convention hotels have permanent setups with fine wooden tables and deluxe executive-type chairs. Suites equipped with such permanent fixtures are versatile small meeting rooms.

The *board of directors oval setup* is simply the board setup with a 60-inch half-round table at each end of the long table. Chairs may be set at the curved end.

Round Tables. *Round tables* (see Figure 13.12) can be used when meetings break up into smaller discussion groups without leaving the room. Round tables are also used most often for food functions.

Use the design in the carpet or lines in the floor to align the tables in neat rows. Allow at least nine feet from center of table to center of table.

Waiters need 36 inches between chairs and walls. Place chairs near the tables and position after the waiters have set the tables. The front edge of the chair should just touch the tablecloth. Afterwards, stack the chairs immediately to facilitate cleanup and breakdown.

Circular Buffet Table. The *circular buffet table*, most useful at food functions, is made by using four serpentines and four 30-inch deep four foot tables (see Figure 13.13). This makes up a 20-by-20-foot buffet table. A round center table can be used for flowers or a display. Tier arrangements can be made with risers.

Many variations can be made by using tables of various shapes. You are limited only by imagination, time and space.[10] If you design one you particularly like, draw a schematic of it. You can show this to a prospective client and use it for future reference.

Breakdown of Function Rooms

After a meeting or party is completed, housepersons should break down the room and clean it. The reason for this is obvious. Business could be lost, or a poor impression given, if a prospective customer saw an untidy meeting room while walking through the convention area.

Chairs and tables need to be stacked. Function chairs probably receive more damage than any other furnishings in a hotel. Housepersons who display more speed than caution in setup and dismantling should be instructed to avoid such carelessness.

If the meeting room isn't scheduled for immediate use, tables and chairs may need to be stored. Storage is a common headache to convention servicing. Hotels unfortunately often do not allot adequate and accessible storage space for function room equipment. Space that is too small or is too difficult to maneuver in shortens the life of the equipment. Furniture that is "forced" into storage is often damaged.

Some properties keep formal control over the location and storage of their equipment. In large convention hotels where the volume justifies it, a requisition system is used for issuing equipment and supplies. An inventory is taken periodically and all articles are locked up when not in use.

Figure 13.13. THE CIRCULAR BUFFET TABLE ARRANGEMENT AND VARIATIONS.

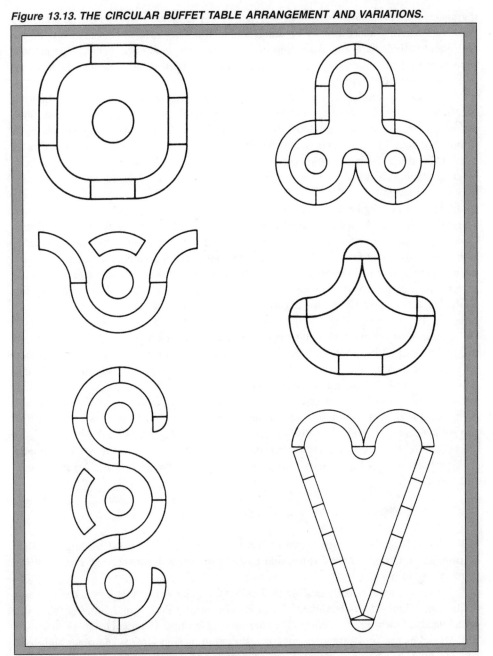

Source: Reprinted with permission from Function Room Set-Up Manual.

Meeting Rooms of the Future

As we entered the 21st century, dramatic changes were already taking place in how meeting rooms were designed and equipped. The Hyatt Hotels, for example, replaced drywall construction with open-structured ceilings in their ballrooms, providing greater versatility as well as faster set up time. In its meeting rooms, the chain installed infrared lighting controls, giving the speaker the ability to make instant adjustments to the lighting system. Distracting noises were eliminated by adding light and sound vestibules between public areas and the actual meeting space and by creating double walls between the subdivisions of the ballroom to eliminate noises from adjacent meetings. The chain also installed permanent state-of-the-art communications systems featuring fiber-optic cable, Category 5 data cable and ample telephone wiring.[11]

A growing number of properties are also providing wireless, high-speed Internet access in their meeting rooms – and throughout the hotel (including lobbies, guestrooms, business centers and even food and beverage areas). While Internet service has been offered for some time, the wireless technology has made accessing such information as exhibit directories, seminar schedules and other data easier than ever before, and both meeting planners and attendees have come to expect the technology to make their meetings more productive.

Another development for meeting rooms of the future is the use of plasma screens. These three-inch thick, self-contained units will not only change the way in which presentations are made, but will also change the shape of meeting rooms. As plasma screens become the dominant feature in meeting rooms, lighting requirements will change -- and the sizes of the rooms themselves will have to be adjusted to accommodate the new wide screens. Acording to Martin Dempsey, director of the media and business center at the Scottsdale Conference Center in Arizona, "Ambient light is not an issue with the plasma screen."[12] There is no need to dim lights to see the image.

Other changes cited by architects in the field include changes in table shapes, room decor, and simplifying controls used for presentations. Tomorrow's tables, although they will have the look of heavy wooden tables, will be hollow, light and easily moved. Rooms will be white or light colored to provide for better contrast when video cameras are used, while rooms in which plasma screens are dominant can be painted in lively hues. While high technology will continue to play a major part in presentations, it is expected that control panels will become less visible (concealed yet readily accessible).

Despite these exciting innovations, there is, conversely, a trend toward a traditional look for boardroom setups. Cindy Carney, an interior designer with Debra Myers Associates, says,

"Five years ago, everyone wanted laminates and a techy look."[13]

Now, clients want a more conservative, throwback style. Wood paneling, leather seating, and traditional light fixtures add to the trend toward a masculine, conservative, "clubby" atmosphere.

Whatever trends finally emerge as dominant, it is important that hotels keep abreast of the latest innovations but make decisions concerning design and function with the actual needs of the meeting planners they are serving in mind. If a hotel caters primarily to SMERF segments, for example, a large investment in plasma screens and other high-tech gadgets would be a waste of money. Corporate groups, however, would demand the latest in technology.

Monitoring Function Room Usage

It is important to understand the dollar value of function room space. One chain calculated that meeting space cost $.08 per square foot per day when it was not being utilized. In other words, a 10,000 square foot ballroom costs $800 per day just sitting vacant. To get a handle on function space utilization, it is useful to track and monitor the following:

- Function room occupancy by meal period
- Types of functions
- Use of guestrooms by function groups
- Popularity of individual banquet menu items
- Sales revenue per square foot of function space
- Average banquet check by type of function
- Pattern of unused times and days
- Average number of persons by type of function

Reporting function room statistics can be revealing. While the hotel's function rooms may seem very busy, during certain times of the year only one function per day is often booked in each of the meeting rooms. The data gathered with help you to develop an effective strategy for yield management, which was discussed earlier in this chapter.

Summary

In this chapter, we have taken a look at the various types of function rooms and the setups that are commonly used when servicing convention groups. We have discussed the importance of assigning function rooms for maximum efficiency and revenue and detailed the factors that should be considered when assigning function room space. We have also seen that the use of function rooms must be monitored to ensure maximum profitablilty for your hotel. In the next chapter, we will take a look at how some of the function room setups we have discussed are used when servicing one part of the convention business: food functions.

PUTTING IT ALL TOGETHER

This time, *you* will be using the information that you have learned in this chapter to demonstrate how a property's meeting space can be utilized to its maximum potential. You have been named convention service manager of a hotel with fairly limited meeting space (see diagram). It is your job to fill this space as effectively as possible, so you have booked a number of functions. On Thursday of next week, your property will be hosting:

1. A morning (9:00 a.m.-12:00 p.m.) training seminar for 50 distributors of a multilevel marketing company. The distributors will need to check in and will receive packets of information before entering the training room. A refreshment break will be taken at 10:30 a.m.
2. An afternoon (1:00 p.m.) press conference for a local official announcing her candidacy for Congress. Attendance is projected to include approximately 20 news reporters, three television crews, and the candidate's key staff of nine people. In addition, the candidate has requested the provision of additional seating in the event the public wishes to attend. She has also requested the availability of floor microphones for a question and answer session.

3. A two-hour afternoon (2:00 p.m. - 4:00 p.m.) meeting of twelve directors of the board of the community's hospital.
4. A local charity's evening fund-raising dinner. A cocktail reception will be held from 6:00 p.m.- 6:30 p.m., with dinner following at 7:00 p.m. Dancing will follow from 8:30 p.m. until midnight. Expected attendance is 300 people. Special requirements include a head table for 20 VIPs and the availability of an area for ticket collection and the viewing of prizes that will be raffled throughout the evening.

The following morning, another training session will be held from 9:00 a.m.-12:00 p.m., and you will want the room set up before the staff goes on overtime at 1:00 p.m.

1. Which room(s) would be most suitable for each meeting? What factors did you take into consideration in making your decision?
2. What style of seating would you choose for each meeting? Draw up a sample floorplan for each function.
3. Develop sample function sheets that detail the special needs for each function and how these requirements will be met.

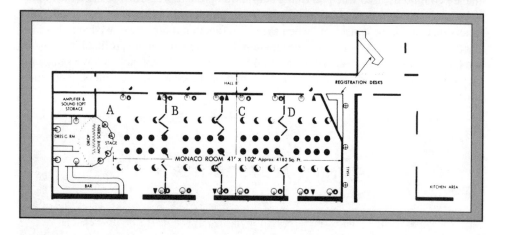

Endnotes:

1. Jim Barr, Catering/Convention Service Manager, Sheraton Chicago Hotel and Towers, MeetingMatrix advertising brochure.
2. Bryant Rousseau, "Low-Cost Software for Room Layouts," *Meeting News*.
3. M. Jill Wien, "Holiday Holds," *The Meeting Manager*.
4. Ibid.
5. Chris Davis, *Business Travel News*, May 15, 2000, p. 39.
6. Chris Davis, "Room Rental Rising: Hotels Revisiting Mtg. Room Yield Mgmt.", *Business Travel News*, April 26, 2004, p. 37.
7. Information in this section adapted from Sheryl L. Kimes and Kelly A. McGuire, "Function-space Revenue Management: A Case Study from Singapore", *Cornell Hotel and Restaurant Administration Quarterly*, December 2001, pp. 43-44.

8. Guide to Function-Room Furniture, Jacob Felsenstein; King Arthur Incorporated, Pennsauken, NJ.
9. Elaine Yetzer Simon, "Comfort, ease of use help determine seating selection", *Hotel &Motel Management*, April 7, 2003, p. 30.
10. "Quick Calculations" charts in this section were developed by David Lutz, then executive vice president and now president of Conferon. From the CONFERON Guide published by *Convene* magazine. Used with permission.
11. Doug Fox, "Hyatt's Improvements Upgrade Presentations," *Convene*, February 1999, p. 57.
12. Justin Henderson, "21st Century Box," *Successful Meetings*, January 2000, p. 20.
13. Ibid, p. 21.

Additional References:

* The Americans with Disabilities Act: A Review Course for Meetings and Conventions Industry Professionals, by Ciritta Park, CAE, Professional Convention Management Association. Available online in the PCMA Publications Library www.pcma.org/publications

* The Convention Industry Council Manual, 7th Edition, Susan Krug, Executive Director, 2000 – www.conventionindustry.org

* Pocket Guide to ADA, Revised Edition, by Evan Terry Associates, P.C. www.mpiweb.org

Internet Sites:

For more information, visit the following Internet sites. Internet addresses can change without notice. If a site is no longer available at the address listed below, a search engine can be used to find the new address or additional, related sites.

Event Sketch – www.timesaver.com
Meeting Matrix International – www.meetingmatrix.com
Optimum Settings – www.optimumsettings.com
Professional Convention Management Association – www.pcma.org
3D Event Designer – www.eventsoft.com
TimeSaver Software – Room Viewer – www.timesaversoftware.com

Study Questions:

1. What is a function room? List the basic types of function rooms.

2. What is mean by the statement: "All public space may be function area depending on the group and its needs." What other areas can be used to host functions?
3. What factors must be considered in charging a group for meeting space? For assigning meeting rooms?
4. List the basic styles of meeting room setups and tell when each is used. What styles are commonly used for food functions?
5. What is "function room furniture"? What features should you look for when selecting function room furniture?
6. How will meeting rooms of the future differ from today's meeting space?
7. What methods are used to monitor function room space?

Key Terms:

Air walls. Moveable barriers that partition large areas into smaller ones. Not necessarily soundproof.

Americans With Disabilities Act. U.S. legislation that requires public buildings (offices, hotels, restaurants, etc.) to make adjustments to meet minimum standards to make their facilities accessible to individuals with physical disabilities.

Barrier-free. Absence of obstacles preventing handicapped persons from moving freely to all public areas within a building.

Auditorium/theater style. Chairs set up in rows facing head table, stage or speaker. Number of aisles may vary. Some variations are V-set up and semicircular.

Board of directors/conference setup. One wide table or series of tables set up in a rectangular shape with chairs on both sides and at the end. Some hotels have permanent board setups featuring expensive furniture and executive chairs. Oval setup is also used.

Breakout rooms. Smaller meeting rooms used when larger sessions divide into smaller groups for discussions and group work. Usually planners request that these rooms be located near the main meeting facilities.

Cocktail round. Small round table, available in 18-, 24-, 30- or 36-inch diameters, used for cocktail-type parties. Also called **Cabaret table**. For sit down service, use 30-inch height; use bar height for stand-up service.

Crescent-round. Seating arrangement in which 60-, 66- or 72-inch diameter rounds have seats on two-thirds to three-quarters of the table and no seats with their backs to the speaker. Also called the **Half-Moon** setup, it is often used for banquet-to-meeting or meeting-to-banquet quick setups.

Dais. Raised platform on which the head table is placed.

Employee procedure manual. Instructions for employees to do specific jobs.. Often includes illustrations or drawings. Helps ensure consistent setups.

E-shape setup style. Tables set in the shape of an E with chairs on the outside of the closed ends and on both sides of each leg.

Function room turnover time. The amount of time needed to tear down and reset a function room.

Function rooms. Rooms specifically designed to house meetings or social gatherings.

Hold all function space. A blanket hold on all available space (without specific meeting or function room names) in a facility.

Hollow circular setup. Same as horseshoe setup except both ends are closed; chairs placed on the outside.

Hollow square setup. Tables set in a square with a hollow middle; chairs placed only on the outside.

Horseshoe setup. Similar to U-shape style; set in shape of a horseshoe. Chairs can be placed around both the inside and outside.

Lectern. A reading desk used to hold the speaker's papers. Either rests on the floor (full size) or on the table.

Pre-function space. Area adjacent to the main event room; used to assemble attendees prior to a function. Often used for receptions prior to a meal or for refreshment breaks during an event.

Open sale period. Period of time during which catering is free to sell function space due to projected slow convention business (catered events would not be likely to displace convention groups needing meeting space).

Refresh the meeting room. Clean a room after or between meetings (refilling water pitchers, changing glassware and other general housekeeping).

Schoolroom/classroom style. Tables six feet by 18 inches are lined up in rows on each side of a good sized center aisle. Usually six chairs to two tables. All tables and chairs face the head table. Variations are the V-shape and perpendicular style.

U-shape setup. Tables set up in the shape of the block letter U; usually used for smaller meetings. Chairs are placed on the outside of the closed end and on both sides of each leg.

Velcro. Brand-name special tape with loops and fabric that is used to adhere table drapery.

Learning Objectives:

This portion of your text introduces you to the various types of food and beverage functions typically held at a convention hotel. When you have studied this chapter, you will:

- Know the different types of banquet food service and understand both the service and control issues related to banquet food functions.

- Be able to describe several types of beverage service and explain how beverage service is billed.

- Be able to describe service and control issues related to beverage functions.

- Be able to describe post-function activities for food and beverage functions and understand in-house coordination at both large and small properties.

Outline

Food Service
- Types of Food Functions
- Themed and Special Events
- Off-Premises Catering
- Changing Tastes
- Types of Service
- Pricing Food Functions
- Attendance
- Attrition
- Function Rooms
- Control Procedures
- Staffing
- Uniserve or Duoserve

Beverage Service
- Types of Setups
- Hospitality Suites
- Brands
- Pricing Methods
- Beverage Control

Post-Function Actions
In-House Coordination: Large vs. Small Properties
- Role of the Catering Manager
- Servicing and Selling
- Communication and Cooperation

Summary

Planning Food Functions

Gene Meoni
Director of Food and Beverage
Grand Traverse Resort and Spa, Michigan

"The catering or conventions services department is the most profitable division of any hotel food and beverage operation provided the proper planning, controls, service and creativity are utilized for an event, be it a refreshment break for 20 or a five course gala dinner for 1,000...When planning meetings, conventions or catered events, you must utilize the controls planned to guarantee service to your guests and the profitability of your operation. Function sheets for food and beverage products and services must be detailed and specific...When setting up for a convention, meeting or catered event, organization and pre-planning are necessary for a successful execution...The plans, controls and teamwork involved in food and beverage service are immense. But, if effective, will lead to operational success, which I define as exceeding guest expectations, motivated employees who take pride in their accomplishments, and exceeding budgeted bottom line profits."

14   Food and Beverage Service

Food and beverage functions have always played an important part in meeting and convention programs, but the "traditional" food and beverage options of past years, such as the choice between one chicken and one beef entree at a banquet or simply providing an urn of coffee and hot water for tea for meeting delegates, have been replaced with new choices that add variety and excitement to meetings and conventions.

These changes have resulted from the public becoming more knowledgeable about food and beverages and meal presentation. Robert Briggs, associate director of continuing education at the Culinary Institute of America in Hyde Park, New York, says:

> "People are reading culinary magazines, watching the Food Network, taking cooking classes, traveling, and becoming much more food savvy in recent years."[1]

The result is that attendees have higher expectations regarding the food and beverages served at their meetings or conventions, they are more willing to experiment with new foods, and they expect attractive presentations. Hotels are responding to their demands with creative menus, including incorporating local specialties into meals and staging themed functions, and offering alternate food and beverage options.

The Hyatt Hotels, for example, has led the way in several service trends. George Vizer, vice president of food and beverage, says:

> "We are trying to create a restaurant-quality dining experience in a banquet setting. Having a banquet doesn't have to mean that you have servers in a banquet setting with large service trays, distributing food in an institutional manner. Instead, servers come to the table and introduce themselves to the guests. They recite the menu. They announce what wine they're pouring. So that there's interaction with the guests, just as you find in a restaurant setting."[2]

Steve Enselein, assistant vice president of catering and convention services for the chain, adds:

> "We're also offering guests a choice of entree selection at dinner, which creates more of a restaurant feel than a banquet feel...it's been well received by groups. It may not be practical for 1,200 people, but it's not a challenge for 200, 300, or even 400. Anytime you give people an opportunity to choose, you increase their satisfaction."[3]

Increased attendee satisfaction means more attendees at an organization's next function – and repeat and word-of-mouth business for a hotel that makes food and beverage functions memorable. In this chapter, we will discuss the various types of food functions typically staged for meetings and conventions and detail how creativity and communication play important roles in successful functions ranging from simple refreshment breaks to elaborate themed events.

Food Service

Banquets, parties, and other business or social functions involving food and beverage can produce additional, often high, revenues for your hotel. Bill Carlin, managing editor of *Nation's Restaurant News*, states,

> "Banquets are the most profitable area of hotel food and beverage operations."[4]

Successful banquets can contribute greatly to the overall profitability because the profit margin on sales for banquets often runs 35-40 percent, as opposed to 10-15 percent for hotel restaurants. There are several reasons for this difference.

- In convention oriented hotels, banquet sales volume often exceeds restaurant volume by as much as two to one.
- Banquets allow flexibility in pricing. A New York steak dinner priced at $30 on the restaurant menu may bring $45 on the banquet menu. The justification for this difference is the cost of setting up and tearing down the banquet area and also the short time allowed for serving a large number of people in one seating.
- Food costs are lower due to volume preparation and no large inventory is needed since ordering can be done as needed and all attendees normally receive identical meals.
- Beverage profits are high because beverage costs are easily controlled and revenues are greater because of pricing flexibility.
- Labor costs are significantly lower because banquet servers and bartenders are often part-time employees used on an as-needed basis. The cost of restaurant employees, in contrast, is largely fixed because a regular staff must be maintained even during slow periods.
- Employee productivity is high since staffing levels can be set for a predetermined, guaranteed attendance.

Types of Food Functions

Meetings may call for breakfasts, luncheons, dinners, dinners with entertainment and/or dancing, refreshment breaks, bars, receptions, buffets and continuous hospitality setups in suites, meeting rooms or exhibit halls. Gene Meoni, Director of Food and Beverage at the Grand Traverse Resort and Spa, says that banquet menus should be varied in selection and price range to meet your market segments. Menus should include regional specialties, property specialties and upgraded menus that have been executed during past events.

Group menus come in a variety of forms and sizes. For convenience, we recommend a small bound booklet, such as used by the Radisson Hotels (see Figure 14.1). The Radisson booklet gives both sit-down and buffet suggestions for breakfast, lunch and dinner.

These Radisson menus are effective because of their descriptions of the various items offered and the use of graphics to showcase menu choices. Many hotel banquet menus, however, simply list the foods and beverages offered; there are no detailed descriptions or illustrations.

In designing your own group menus, your presentation is just as important as the choices you offer. Begin by collecting sample menus from other properties to glean ideas you may want to incorporate into your own design. If your budget is limited and you can't

Figure 14.1. SAMPLE MENUS FROM THE GROUP MENU BOOKLET USED BY THE RADISSON HOTEL.

Breakfasts

The aroma of freshly brewed coffee. Fresh juices, pastries, muffins and breads warm from the oven.

Launch a successful day at the Radisson Hotel St. Paul with breakfast full of homemade American goodness.

Chef's Breakfast Recommendations

The French Connection $6.75
Grapefruit Juice or Orange Juice, Egg Dipped French Toast Topped with Apples, Bananas, Pecans and Maple Whipped Butter. Canadian Bacon or Sausage. Freshly Ground and Brewed Guatemalan Antigua Coffee or Colombian Supremo Decaffeinated Coffee. Granola Bars and Assortment of Whole Fresh Fruit Basket.

Midwestern Sunrise $6.95
Vegetable Juice or Cherry Cider. Scrambled Eggs with Wisconsin Cojack Cheese, Fresh Chives, Canadian Bacon or Smoked Ham Steak and Sautéed Red Potatoes. Blueberry Muffin Basket. Freshly Ground and Brewed Guatemalan Antigua Coffee or Colombian Supremo Decaffeinated Coffee.

The All American $6.50
Grapefruit Juice or Orange Juice, Scrambled Eggs, Bacon, Hash Brown Potatoes, Assorted Breakfast-Bakeries, Butter, Jams and Marmalades, Freshly Ground and Brewed Guatemalan Antigua Coffee or Colombian Supremo Decaffeinated Coffee, Assorted Herbal and Premium Teas

Breakfast Buffets (minimum 50 people)

Sunrise Buffet $7.95
Orange Juice, Grapefruit Juice, Fresh Fruit Medley, Scrambled Eggs, Home Fried Potatoes, Bacon and Sausage, Assorted Muffins and Pastries, Beverage

Northwoods Buffet $11.50
Apple Cider, Orange and Vegetable Juice. Country Style Eggs Scrambled. Display of Seasonal Fruits and Berries. Homemade Granola, Smoked Fish and Cheese Platters, Hickory Smoked Ham. Flapjacks with Blueberry Compote, Grilled Homefried Potatoes. Assorted Muffins and Pastries, Beverage.

Omelette Bar (maximum 75 people) $11.95
Orange Juice, Apple Juice, Fresh Fruit Medley, Omelettes or Eggs cooked to order, Home Fried Potatoes, Hickory Smoked Ham, Yogurts, Granolas and Muffins.

*Low Cholesterol Eggs Available

A la Carte Breakfasts

FRUITS AND JUICES   (Choice of One)
Half Grapefruit, Grapefruit Juice or Orange Juice, Fresh Fruit Medley, Chilled Melon

COMBINATIONS
Served with Basket of Muffins and Breads, Butter, Jams, Marmalades and Beverage

Scrambled Eggs, Sausage or Bacon Strips $6.50
Home Fried Potatoes

Scrambled Eggs, Ham or Canadian Bacon $6.90
Home Fried Potatoes

Ham and Cheese Egg Croissant $7.50
Home Fried Potatoes

Roast Beef Hash with Poached Eggs $7.50
Home Fried Potatoes

Grilled Tenderloin Steak with Scrambled Eggs $9.95
Home Fried Potatoes

---

afford expensive graphics, you can still get your point across with mouth-watering word images (words such as "melt in your mouth," "piping hot," "savory," "flaky," and so on create a word picture – and a desire to purchase).

Be sure that your menu conveys your image – and generates sales – by following basic design elements, such as an attractive cover, an appealing design format and an easy-to-read layout. Menus should always be printed on a good quality paper stock. Dark ink on ivory or cream paper stock gives a more "cultured" look. Pages should not look cluttered – always allow plenty of white space between items and columns. And don't forget contact information – always include your property's logo, name, address and telephone numbers and e-mail addresses. An original copy (not a photocopy) should always be presented to

Figure 14.1. SAMPLE MENUS FROM THE GROUP MENU BOOKLET USED BY THE RADISSON HOTEL.

Lunch

Take a memorable mid-day break. Introduce the occasion with our Chef's creative soups of the day or a picture-perfect salad. Select one of our savory main courses. Then top off the meal with a dessert guaranteed to set your guests to talking.

Chef's Luncheon Recommendations

Chicken Salad Plate with Fresh Fruit $9.95
Soup of the Day, Breadsticks, Beverage

Roasted Top Sirloin of Beef $10.50
Mushroom Sauce, Tossed Green Salad, Fresh Vegetable, Potato, Rolls and Butter, Beverage

Grilled Breast of Chicken $10.95
Basil Cream Sauce, Fresh Fruit Salad, Fresh Vegetable, Three Rice Blend, Rolls and Butter, Beverage

Deli Platter $9.95
Soup of the Day, Roast Beef, Turkey, Ham and Salami, Assorted Cheeses, Relishes, Potato Salad, Assorted Breads in a Basket, Beverage

Tuna Salad, Canteloupe $9.95
Soup of the Day, Hard Boiled Egg, Cottage Cheese, Relishes, Rolls and Butter, Beverage

Roast Breast of Turkey $9.95
Gravy and Dressing, Apple, Orange Waldorf Salad, Fresh Vegetable, Whipped Potatoes, Rolls and Butter, Beverage

Baked Chicken Breast $11.95
Mustard Sauce, Filled with Spinach Wild Rice and Jarlsburg Cheese, Fresh Vegetables, Rolls and Butter, Tossed Green Salad, Beverage.

Grilled Chicken & Shrimp Stirfry $10.95
Florentine Rice, Peapods and Carrots, Luncheon Salad, Rolls and Butter, Beverage

Broiled Orange Roughy $10.50
Fresh Dill Sauce, Danish Cucumber Tomato Salad, Three Blend Rice, Fresh Vegetables, Rolls and Butter, Beverage

Grilled Salmon Filet $11.50
Dilled Salsa Verde, Butter Lettuce Salad, Three Rice Blend, Steamed Broccoli, Rolls and Butter, Beverage

Desserts A La Carte $1.75
Chocolate Fudge Cake, Vanilla Ice Cream with Berries in Season, Chocolate Rum Mousse, Carrot Cake, Apple Pie, Cheesecake, Pound Cake Compote

Hearty Deli Box Lunches $9.50
Choice of One in Each Category:
Mustard Glazed Ham, Roasted Turkey Breast, or Lean Roast Beef
Cheddar, Smoked Gouda or Swiss
Onion Bun, Whole Wheat Bun or Pumpernickel Bread
Marinated Vegetable Salad, Pasta Salad or Dill Potato Salad
Granola Bar, Chocolate Chip Cookie, Peanut Butter Brownie, Banana or Apple
Soda or Spring Water

LUNCHEON BUFFETS

New York Deli $12.50
Soup of the Day, Roast Beef, Turkey, Ham and Salami, Assorted Cheeses, A Variety of Breads, Condiments, Salads, Relish Platter, Cheesecake, Beverage

Picnic Time (minimum 25 people) $10.95
Sliced Tomatoes, Sliced Cucumbers, Potato Salad, Southern Style Fried Chicken, Rolls and Butter, Apple Pie, Beverage

Boulevard Buffet $15.00 (minimum 75 people)

Tossed Green Salad, Fresh Fruit Medley, Soup of the Day, Sliced Tomatoes, Sliced Cucumbers, Relish Platter, Potato Salad, Salad Dressings, Breads and Butter, Assorted Cold Cuts, Assorted Cheeses
Select Any Two:
Fish and Chips, Grilled Chopped Sirloin, Roast Top Sirloin, Fried Chicken, Baked Ham, Roast Half Chicken
Chef's Select Fresh Vegetable, Potato,
Carrot Cake, Apple Pie, Chocolate Rum Mousse, Beverage

meeting planners (the only exception to this rule is sending menu information to a meeting planner via fax).

Two other types of food functions held in conjunction with beverage service are **refreshment breaks** and cocktail **receptions**. Refreshment breaks, which take place between meeting sessions, should ideally be set up in a room adjacent to the meeting room. If this is not possible, beverages and/or food items can be set up in the hallway or lobby outside the meeting room (you will want to ensure that any set up required will not disturb the meeting program) or brought to the meeting room itself. Serving carts or portable tables can be used outside the meeting room or the items can be carted outside the meeting room

Figure 14.1. SAMPLE MENUS FROM THE GROUP MENU BOOKLET USED BY THE RADISSON HOTEL.

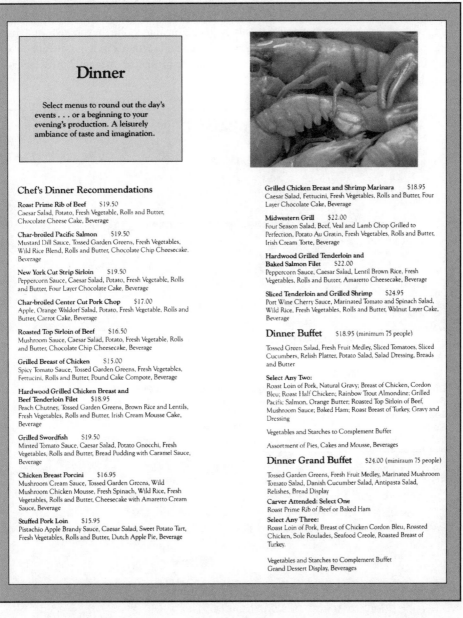

Dinner

Select menus to round out the day's events . . . or a beginning to your evening's production. A leisurely ambiance of taste and imagination.

Chef's Dinner Recommendations

Roast Prime Rib of Beef $19.50
Caesar Salad, Potato, Fresh Vegetable, Rolls and Butter, Chocolate Cheese Cake, Beverage

Char-broiled Pacific Salmon $19.50
Mustard Dill Sauce, Tossed Garden Greens, Fresh Vegetables, Wild Rice Blend, Rolls and Butter, Chocolate Chip Cheesecake, Beverage

New York Cut Strip Sirloin $19.50
Peppercorn Sauce, Caesar Salad, Potato, Fresh Vegetable, Rolls and Butter, Four Layer Chocolate Cake, Beverage

Char-broiled Center Cut Pork Chop $17.00
Apple, Orange Waldorf Salad, Potato, Fresh Vegetable, Rolls and Butter, Carrot Cake, Beverage

Roasted Top Sirloin of Beef $16.50
Mushroom Sauce, Caesar Salad, Potato, Fresh Vegetable, Rolls and Butter, Chocolate Chip Cheesecake, Beverage

Grilled Breast of Chicken $15.00
Spicy Tomato Sauce, Tossed Garden Greens, Fresh Vegetables, Fettucini, Rolls and Butter, Pound Cake Compote, Beverage

Hardwood Grilled Chicken Breast and Beef Tenderloin Filet $18.95
Peach Chutney, Tossed Garden Greens, Brown Rice and Lentils, Fresh Vegetables, Rolls and Butter, Irish Cream Mousse Cake, Beverage

Grilled Swordfish $19.50
Minted Tomato Sauce, Caesar Salad, Potato Gnocchi, Fresh Vegetables, Rolls and Butter, Bread Pudding with Caramel Sauce, Beverage

Chicken Breast Porcini $16.95
Mushroom Cream Sauce, Tossed Garden Greens, Wild Mushroom Chicken Mousse, Fresh Spinach, Wild Rice, Fresh Vegetables, Rolls and Butter, Cheesecake with Amaretto Cream Sauce, Beverage

Stuffed Pork Loin $15.95
Pistachio Apple Brandy Sauce, Caesar Salad, Sweet Potato Tart, Fresh Vegetables, Rolls and Butter, Dutch Apple Pie, Beverage

Grilled Chicken Breast and Shrimp Marinara $18.95
Caesar Salad, Fettucini, Fresh Vegetables, Rolls and Butter, Four Layer Chocolate Cake, Beverage

Midwestern Grill $22.00
Four Season Salad, Beef, Veal and Lamb Chop Grilled to Perfection, Potato Au Gratin, Fresh Vegetables, Rolls and Butter, Irish Cream Torte, Beverage

Hardwood Grilled Tenderloin and Baked Salmon Filet $22.00
Peppercorn Sauce, Caesar Salad, Lentil Brown Rice, Fresh Vegetables, Rolls and Butter, Amaretto Cheesecake, Beverage

Sliced Tenderloin and Grilled Shrimp $24.95
Port Wine Cherry Sauce, Marinated Tomato and Spinach Salad, Wild Rice, Fresh Vegetables, Rolls and Butter, Walnut Layer Cake, Beverage

Dinner Buffet $18.95 (minimum 75 people)

Tossed Green Salad, Fresh Fruit Medley, Sliced Tomatoes, Sliced Cucumbers, Relish Platter, Potato Salad, Salad Dressing, Breads and Butter

Select Any Two:
Roast Loin of Pork, Natural Gravy; Breast of Chicken, Cordon Bleu; Roast Half Chicken; Rainbow Trout Almondine; Grilled Pacific Salmon, Orange Butter; Roasted Top Sirloin of Beef, Mushroom Sauce; Baked Ham; Roast Breast of Turkey, Gravy and Dressing

Vegetables and Starches to Complement Buffet

Assortment of Pies, Cakes and Mousse, Beverages

Dinner Grand Buffet $24.00 (minimum 75 people)

Tossed Garden Greens, Fresh Fruit Medley, Marinated Mushroom Tomato Salad, Danish Cucumber Salad, Antipasta Salad, Relishes, Bread Display

Carver Attended: Select One
Roast Prime Rib of Beef or Baked Ham

Select Any Three:
Roast Loin of Pork, Breast of Chicken Cordon Bleu, Roasted Chicken, Sole Roulades, Seafood Creole, Roasted Breast of Turkey.

Vegetables and Starches to Complement Buffet
Grand Dessert Display, Beverages

and wheeled in when the person in charge of the group gives a signal for the food service staff to enter (see box titled "Refreshment Break Guidelines").

Refreshment breaks generally include such beverages as coffee, tea, soft drinks and bottled water and usually feature various light food items. A break between morning sessions, for example, may include muffins, low-fat yogurt and fruit in addition to beverages. Serving heavy, sugar-laden foods may lead to attendee sluggishness, especially between afternoon sessions.

Receptions are usually stand-up social functions that bring attendees together to socialize, and they may be held at various times during a meeting program. Sometimes, there are welcoming receptions for attendees, other receptions precede a meal function (this ensures that all guests are in the same place before a sit-down dinner), or receptions may be held to enable attendees to socialize with outside participants, such as vendors, outside sales representatives and so on.

At most receptions, beverages, usually including alcoholic beverages, and light foods, often **hors d'oeuvres** (hot or cold finger foods) and **canapés** (hot or cold appetizers with a bread or cracker base), are served. Foods may be presented on small buffet tables or passed by servers.

Refreshment Break Guidelines

1. Breaks normally last 15 to 30 minutes.

2. Space stations so bottlenecks are kept to a minimum.

3. Open stations farthest from the main entrance first to draw people into the room.

4. Separate coffee and soda stations

5. Identify each hot beverage with a sign.

REFRESHMENT BREAK ESTIMATES FOR 200 PEOPLE

	A.M.		P.M.
Coffee	65% x 200 = 130 cups = 6.5 gals	Coffee	35% x 200 = 70 cups = 3.5 gals
Decaf	30% x 200 = 60 cups = 3 gals	Decaf	20% x 200 = 40 cups = 2 gals
Tea	10% x 200 = 20 cups = 1 gal	Tea	10% x 200 = 20 cups = 1 gal
Soda/		Soda/	
Water	25% x 200 = 50 drinks = 50 sodas	Water	70% x 200 = 140 drinks = 140 sodas

6. Lay out stations for quick service: coffee cups, followed by regular coffee, decaf, tea bags and hot water. Accessories, cream, sugar, sweetener and spoons should be available on a separate table a short distance from the beverage station.

7. Set one beverage station per 75 to 100 attendees.

8. Staff one server per 100 people for refreshment breaks; one server per 50 people at receptions and buffets.

9. Figure 20 six-ounce cups of coffee in a gallon.

10. "Marry" (combine) coffee stations toward the end of the break.

When presenting foods in a buffet style, keep in mind that easy access to food results in greater consumption. Figure 14.2 details how different types of buffet setups affect the amount of food that would be required for a reception. If a planner has a limited budget or simply wants to ensure that the food he or she has ordered lasts through the event, you should suggest the round buffet or 180-degree buffet arrangements.

Figure 14.2. SAMPLE RECEPTION BUFFET SET UPS.

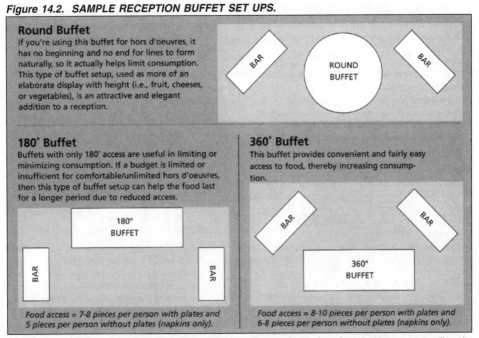

Round Buffet
If you're using this buffet for hors d'oeuvres, it has no beginning and no end for lines to form naturally, so it actually helps limit consumption. This type of buffet setup, used as more of an elaborate display with height (i.e., fruit, cheeses, or vegetables), is an attractive and elegant addition to a reception.

180° Buffet
Buffets with only 180° access are useful in limiting or minimizing consumption. If a budget is limited or insufficient for comfortable/unlimited hors d'oeuvres, then this type of buffet setup can help the food last for a longer period due to reduced access.

360° Buffet
This buffet provides convenient and fairly easy access to food, thereby increasing consumption.

Food access = 7-8 pieces per person with plates and 5 pieces per person without plates (napkins only).

Food access = 8-10 pieces per person with plates and 6-8 pieces per person without plates (napkins only).

The physical layout of a reception buffet controls access to food, therefore limiting or expanding the amount of time that food lasts. This chart details how much food can be expected to be consumed per person using the three most common reception buffet set ups, enabling you to assist a meeting planner in deciding which setup to use and how much food to order for the event.

Source: Developed by David Lutz, then executive vice president and now president of Conferon. From the <u>Conferon Guide</u> published by Convene magazine. Used with permission.

The cocktail reception with hors d'oeuvres should create a carnival atmosphere, so many receptions include music, dancing and entertainment. There should also be plenty of room to allow attendees to socialize. Not only do these activities put attendees in a good frame of mind, they also serve as distractions that will cut down on reception food consumption (this not only ensures that attendees will have room for dinner if the reception precedes a meal, but also helps the meeting planner's budget).

To assist meeting planners in ordering food for receptions, the following guidelines have been developed:

Dry snacks	1 ounce per person
Anchor foods (cheese, vegetables, fruits)	enough for 1/3 of attendees
Action stations (carving station, pasta station)	enough for 1/2 to 2/3 of attendees
Passed hors d'oeuvres	1 of each for all attendees
Dessert and coffee	enough for 1/3 to1/2 of attendees

Source: Developed by David Lutz, then executive vice president and now president of Conferon. From the <u>Conferon Guide</u> published by Convene magazine. Used with permission.

Keep in mind that many guests at receptions enjoy sampling every item. Therefore, encourage meeting planners to order at least one piece of every item for each attendee. For a reception for 500, for example, it is wiser to order 500 pieces of three types of hors d'oeuvres rather than 250 pieces of six different types. If the planner wants more variety, the menu can be supplemented with less expensive items, such as cheese and crackers, chips and dip and vegetable and fruit trays.

Two basic methods are used in charging for hors d'oeuvres and finger food: by the person per hour and by the bowl or tray. Figure 14.3 shows these two methods.

Each function should be dealt with separately to make sure of details. A banquet event order should be filled out for each event, listing all the information needed for smooth execution.

Figure 14.3. PRICING CATERED ITEMS.

Canapés and Hors D'Oeuvres

No.1: $6.50 per person	**No. 2:**

Hot   Grilled Cocktail Franks, Mustard Sauce
      Swedish Savory Meatballs
      Knishes
      Chinese Egg Rolls
      Butterfly Shrimp, Cocktail Sauce
	Cold Canapes
	Large Tray...$68.50
	(Serves approximately 25 persons)
	Medium Tray...$46.00
	(Serves approximately 15 persons)

Cold   Canapes
      Savory Cheese Spread, Pimento
      Cornets of Imported Genoa Salami
      Smoked Nova Scotia Salmon
      Deviled Eggs with Anchovies
	Selection: A variety of Assorted Cold
	Canapes including Stuffed Eggs
	Moscovite

This hors d'oeuvres menu shows two methods of pricing: by the person per hour and by the tray or bowl. While the eating habits of groups may vary, the industry standard for a two-hour reception is eight pieces per person for the first hour and four per person during the second hour.

Themed and Special Events

Every meeting planner tries to do something different at each event. Most conventions have a high percentage of people who repeatedly attend, so the planners want to "add a new twist" to the program, from adding flair to the cocktail party to staging a themed banquet.

Experienced meeting planners disguise the same old cocktail party by introducing a different theme each year. **Themed events**, both large and small, are very popular and are remembered by the attendees. In addition, themed events do much to enhance the reputation of the hotel. The focal point of any such function is the menu, and hotels that offer several different types of themed menus are a step ahead of the competition. There are many themes that can be effectively executed even if the meeting planner has a limited budget. An "Old Mexico" theme, for example can offer taco bars, a chili bar, an interactive fajita bar and chips with salsa and guacamole. Not only are most of these menu items inexpensive, but it also takes time for guests to assemble a taco, which greatly cuts down on the amount of food consumed. Other low-cost themes include a State Fair or Fourth of July theme (traditional, but low-cost foods such as hot dogs, hamburgers and so on) or a Western theme (beef stew served from a "chuck wagon" or typical barbecued foods).

If you are in a locale that offers unique cuisine, consider featuring a locally grown themed menu. In Calgary, for example, themed "local" menus might include Alberta beef, caribou, lamb, salmon, halibut or goat cheese. Amy Johnson, director of catering and convention services at the Hyatt Regency Calgary says,

"One of our biggest sellers right now for banquets is venison."[5]

At a recent event, Johnson served Alberta venison and wild mushroom soup in an acorn squash, veal wrapped in an Alberta potato and a Canadian cheese platter. These menu items were an excellent way to introduce delegates to the "flavor" of the destination.

The menu should be served in creative ways that will enhance the theme. **Action stations** featuring costumed chefs, for example, are more memorable than having a guest simply choose from pre-prepared dishes on a buffet table. A chef wearing colorful garb as he or she makes fajitas at an Old Mexico event or dressed as a cowboy while preparing cooked-to-order steaks for a Western-themed party are just two examples. Costumes for servers can also add to the atmosphere, as can creative decorations and entertainment. Incorporate the theme into your table and serving ware; use clay dishes and colorfully decorated serving platters and bowls for a Mexican theme, tin plates and cups at a barbecue and so on. The theme should also be reflected in table and wall decorations and lighting (paper lanterns for an Oriental theme, torches for a Hawaiian luau, for example).

Many decorations and other enhancements, such as bubble machines, fog machines and other "effects," are inexpensive and can be easily stored for future functions. Themed props may also be obtained at low (or even no cost) from such sources as vendors (most beverage vendors can supply "game themed" props, such as Super Bowl decorations or NASCAR posters), travel agencies or airlines (good sources for travel posters). If you have requests for unusually themed events, it can be cost-effective to work with outside sources and rent props needed for special functions.

When you have developed functions that work well, these can easily be promoted to other groups. Some properties and chains, such as Fairmont Hotels and Resorts, offer brochures promoting their popular themed events. Brochure pages detail the setting and decorations for the event, the food and beverages that will be served, entertainment provided as part of the function and "extras," such as a fireworks show to end the evening. Themes range from a Mexican party (complete with a performance of the Mexican Folkloric ballet) to a Bohemia Party to a Las Vegas Night.

This type of promotional material (as well as photographs taken during past events) is a great help in selling other business. If you have successfully staged themed events, clients will likely respond to your suggestions. This is especially true if you can offer not only the expertise but also the other elements needed to stage such an event. While planners usually love themed events, many have budget constraints or need help with stimulating their thinking. When you help meeting planners stage events that guests remember long after the meeting or convention, everyone benefits. The guests have a memorable experience and meeting planners have the confidence level to book more, bigger and better events with the hotel, which can look forward to both future repeat business and word-of-mouth bookings resulting from satisfied planners and guests.

Off-Premises Catering

In addition to servicing functions in-house (known as **on-premises catering**), a great many hotels and restaurants are turning to **off-premises catering**, preparing food and/or beverages for events away from the hotel, to boost food and beverage revenues. While some events are held on the grounds of a property or restaurant, these are still serviced directly by the hotel's on-premises kitchen(s). With off-premises catering, food must be either partially or fully prepared in the hotel's kitchen and then transported to the site of the function or fully prepared at the event site.

Off-premises events can be held at a local attraction (in Dallas, some events are held at the Southfork Ranch, where the TV show, Dallas, was filmed, for example), or at other venues, such as a fund-raising dinner at a museum or an opening reception at an art gallery, or at outdoor locations. The location of the event will be an important factor in determining both the menu and the method of food preparation.

Before a hotel or restaurant gets into the off-premises catering business, it is important to determine the feasibility of such an operation. Off-premises catering can be an expensive proposition. Mobile kitchen equipment and other equipment, such as portable furniture and decorations, may have to be purchased. Since off-premises catering may be seasonal in some locales, storage would have to be arranged for equipment not being used on a regular basis.

Some hotels opt to partner with local venues or work with destination management companies to get the maximum value from off-premises catering. In some cities, hotels can partner with unique local venues, such as the Liberace Mansion in Las Vegas, for example, or a reception facility (such a facility usually stocks its own furniture and props, all the

---

Best Practices

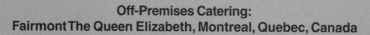

Off-Premises Catering:
Fairmont The Queen Elizabeth, Montreal, Quebec, Canada

The 1,039-room Fairmont The Queen Elizabeth in Montreal generates $1.6 to $1.9 million annually with its off-site catering department, which brings in almost 18 percent of the hotel's total food and beverage revenues. The service, which began when the hotel began catering meals to one nearby office building in 1976, now handles some 300 events a year, which translates into 130,000 to 140,000 covers.

Headed by Armando Arruda, director of outside catering for the hotel, the department prepares a variety of cuisine, including Canadian, continental and French dishes. Most of the food for the off-site events, which range from continental breakfasts to high-end gala dinners, is prepared in the hotel's kitchen, which is manned by 80 chefs. For some events, the food is finished in off-site kitchens. Although outside help, including wait staff, is sometimes hired for large events, the hotel maintains quality control by employing its own chefs.

In addition to providing food for corporate events, the Fairmont also caters a number of off-premises functions, such as fund-raising or award dinners, for hospitals, art organizations and other groups. A major event for the Fairmont's off-site catering team is the Canadian Cancer Society's Daffodil Ball. The 2004 event took place at Windsor Station, a function site housed in a former railroad station. Some 660 people were served at the prestigious and exclusive event.

Other Fairmont hotels, such as the Fairmont Pallister in Calgary, Alberta, and the Fairmont San Jose in California, also offer off-premises catering at venues that range from large barbecues at Calgary's rodeo grounds to intimate dinners on private jets.

Source: Cathy Urell, "Outside Catering Service Boosts Revenues for Fairmont's F&B Department," Hotel Business, November 7-20, 2004.

hotel or restaurant would have to do is provide the food and/or beverages). Destination management companies can help with such off-site arrangements as equipment, decorations, entertainment and other services.

Revenue potential can also be maximized by preparing menus that are both cost-effective and easily prepared and transportable. A barbecue menu can easily be executed at local parks or other facilities, for example, or a property may opt for catering only one or two types of events, such as receptions or buffet breakfasts, off-site.

Changing Tastes

Banquet menus should reflect meeting attendees' desire for a more healthful diet. People are increasingly conscious that the food they eat and the way it is prepared has an impact on their overall health. Hotels have responded by offering lighter, low-cholesterol items and providing alternative menus for attendees with dietary or religious restrictions. These menus may offer vegetarian, gluten-free and lactose-intolerant substitutes, and offer choices that reflect the latest dietary trends, such as the low-carb Atkins and South Beach diets.

Ruth Butler, CMP, CMM, manager of event operations at Conferon's northeast regional office in Norwood, Massachusetts, says:

> "The low-carb craze has really hit in the past four months – since people started dieting in the New Year. All the meeting and event managers in our office are dealing with it."[6]

The Sheraton chain has responded to the low-carb trend by introducing Lo-Carb Lifestyle, the most extensive line of low-carb food offerings in the hotel industry. In the spring of 2004, four senior chefs from Hilton Hotels Corporation attended an extensive three-day nutrition course at Johnson and Wales University. Upon their return, they created a roster of recipes geared toward low-carb dieters and people with diabetes.[7] And, New York-based Loews Hotels responded to the trend with its "No Carb-tails" drink menu, which includes such libations as diet-friendly daiquiris and vodka-infused green tea.[8]

The biggest change in eating habits has occurred at breakfast. Meagan Kiessling, the association conference manager for Alcoholism and Substance Abuse Providers of New York State in Albany, New York, says:

> "Low-carb and protein are definitely playing a larger role in menu planning, particularly with breakfast. There is almost no point to adding a continental breakfast for your group without at least two low-carb options."[9]

Eggs, potatoes, bacon and sausage have given way to a variety of lighter, health-conscious offerings such as whole grain muffins and rolls, low calorie yogurt, fresh fruits and low-fat dairy products. Hot oatmeal, cooked wheat cereal and shredded wheat are very popular alternatives to the traditional fare. Lunches and dinners have also become less formal. Diet-conscious attendees appreciate extensive salad bars featuring fresh vegetables and low-calorie dressings. Poultry, fish, veal and lean pork entrees, grilled rather than fried, are popular with fitness conscious attendees. Heavy meals promote sleepiness, so offer moderate portions and food groups that are high in protein.

Today, new technology is being used to assist planners in making their decisions — and to improve the quality and variety of food and beverages offered to meeting and function guests. Sheraton's "Sheraton Cuisine," the umbrella name for the chain's hotel kitchen software, provides colored pictures of the 365 dishes offered in its "Cuisine of the Americas" menu, along with the recipes and a breakdown of the nutritional content of each entrée. Scott Geraghty, director of culinary services for the Sheraton New York Hotel Complex, is enthusiastic about this program and its next phase, which calculates nutritional content after substitutions have been made. He states:

> "A catering manager will be able to sit down with a meeting planner, call up a color picture of what a plated dish would look like, and make substitutions like: 'What would this dish look like with carrots instead of zucchini?'"[10]

Refreshment breaks no longer require doughnuts, Danish and other surgary bakery items. Health conscious participants know that simple sugars provide few nutrients and play havoc with the waistline. Fruit juices, flavored mineral waters, yogurt, muffins, fresh fruits such as pineapple, melon and strawberries plus decaffeinated coffee and hot tea are popular items.

Types of Service

An important planning decision is the type of service to be used at food functions. The kind of banquet service selected influences pricing, staffing and the overall effect of the function.

American/plated service is the most common form of banquet service. The food is assembled in the kitchen and waiters deliver plates to the tables. Cold food may be plated ahead of time and stored in refrigerators. Hot food is plated just prior to delivery and is sometimes served from a number of stations set up in the kitchen. Guests are served food from the left and beverages from the right. All items are picked up from the right at the end of the course. Plate service requires the least skill on the part of the service personnel.

With **Russian service**, all food is fully prepared in the kitchen and courses are served to the guests directly from soup tureens, platters or an escoffier dish by waiters working as teams. While Russian service, also called *platter service*, requires more space between tables to enable waiters to move freely and a larger, skilled labor force, it is an efficient way to control portions, as waiters place a pre-determined amount of food into the bowls or on the plates of guests.

French service, also called *cart or tableside service,* is generally used only for small groups, but also requires sufficient space between tables for waiters to move about freely. More experienced waiters are required for this type of service as much of the food is prepared tableside on a gueridon (rolling cart).

Pre-set service is frequently used for luncheons where faster service is needed. The first course of soup, salad or appetizer is set on the table prior to the guests' arrival; occasionally the dessert may also be pre-set. While pre-set service works well when the schedule is tight, pre-set food is rarely as attractive as food delivered in courses during the meal.

English/family-style service is similar to Russian service as food is brought to the table on a platter or tray. In most cases, the food is presented to the host, who either cuts the main course himself or herself or chooses to have it done by the server away from the table.

Vegetables and other accompaniments are placed in bowls or other serving dishes on the table, allowing the guests to serve themselves.

Buffet service is a presentation of several food items from which the attendee makes a selection. Buffet service is efficient because a large number of people can be served in a short period of time with a small serving staff. Since buffets can be more expensive to serve than plated meals because there is no portion control and surplus food must be ordered to ensure adequate amounts of offerings, hotels may suggest several alternatives to the "traditional" unlimited buffet. These choices can include *attended buffets*, in which guests are served by chefs or attendants (this not only offers better portion control, but is also more elegant), *combination buffets*, in which inexpensive items, such as salads, are presented buffet style and expensive items, such as meats, are served by an attendant for portion control and *plated buffets*, at which a selection of pre-plated foods are set on the buffet table.

Butler service is sometimes used at receptions or upscale dinners. At receptions, servers circulate with trays, from which guests help themselves. At formal dinners, food is presented on silver trays and serving utensils are offered to allow guests to help themselves from the tray.

Another trend in food functions is **a la carte catering**, which offers more options to both planners and diners. Under the a la carte system, catering departments develop menus offering two or three items from which guests can choose or unique combinations of entrées to suit more palates (a *combination* of meat and seafood or creative vegetarian entrées, for example).

The Marriott chain has made extensive use of a la carte catering, even offering seated guests a menu to give more of a sense of fine dining. The Peabody Orlando, which has offered a choice between beef and chicken for some time, has extended its a la carte service to include duo and trio entrée choices in its regionally-oriented banquet dishes (such as jerk chicken and Caribbean-style pork). Karl Edlbauer, executive chef of the hotel explains:

> "The clientele is looking for more upscale menus that are daring, but with a classical presentation."[11]

In order to enable planners to sample banquet dishes so they'll know in advance how the food will look and taste, many hotels offer a "tasting dinner", also called a **chef's tasting**. A chef's tasting is especially important to meeting planners who are staging larger, unusual events or one that is extremely important, such as a board dinner.

Chef Gordon Marr of the Hilton Washington in Washington, DC recommends that the tasting meal be an exact replica of the banquet meal and that it should approximate meal service. Figure 14.4 shows a sample tasting given by the Grand Hyatt New York.

Chef's tastings can take place at two crucial times during the meeting planning process. Some planners opt for a tasting shortly after they have selected the menu. This gives them the opportunity to talk with the chef to let him or her know what they hope to achieve with the banquet. Chefs can then come up with other inventive ideas to enhance the experience for attendees. Planners may also schedule tastings one or two weeks before the function to enable them to experience seasonal foods that may be on the menu.

Hotels do not charge for chef's tastings, but properties sometimes limit the number of attendees. To be fair to the venue, attendees should be directly involved in the function. Therefore, attendees would include the meeting planner and such executives as the executive director of an association or the program chairman of a group event. Some hotels also allow one or two guests to attend, but it is more cost-effective if these guests will have direct

Figure 14.4. CHEF'S TASTINGS.

The elements of a tasting firsthand at the Grand Hyatt New York by Convene staff members Jamie Roberts and Michelle Russell. They were joined by Grand Hyatt staff James Dale, senior director of catering; Chef Arbeeny; Jerry Perez, executive sous chef; Ricardo Morales, banquet captain; and Chris Reed sous chef. Terry Dale, formerly of NYC & Co., sits next to PCMA's Peter Shure.
Source: Reprinted with permission of Convene, the magazine of the Professional Convention Management Association, www.pcma.org ©2005. Photo courtesy of Grand Hyatt, New York.

input into the meeting (a board member who will be attending a function, an actual attendee, and so on).

Pricing Food Functions

Many convention planners prefer to complete all negotiations in detail before signing the letter of agreement. Some even want to go so far as to select menus and agree on prices. A planner would prefer this because it makes budget projections so much easier. But with conventions planned years in advance, it is not possible for a hotel to make accurate quotations.

Most hotels will gladly say what they charge for menus currently in use, feeling that this is a sufficient guide for meeting planners. There is obvious danger in pricing a menu so far in advance. Most meeting planners with any experience at all realize that any such agreements may have to be modified because of rising costs. If you examine the currency values of the past fifty years, you see constant inflation. When the spiral goes up sharply, everyone recognizes the inflation, but in reality there has been a steady curve upwards over the years.

You must be very careful when you have to make price guarantees for dates several years ahead. Most hotels have adopted a policy of quoting room rates not more than one year in advance and firm menu prices not more than six months before the event. Some hotels even quote a more restricted policy. For example, the Orlando Marriott contract reads:

Menu prices cannot be confirmed more than 60 days prior to the function due to the daily fluctuation of market prices. The organization grants the hotel the right to make reasonable substitutions on the menu to meet increased market prices or commodity shortages.

You cannot avoid such a policy unless you have no need to be competitive and can build in a fat reserve in your quotations. But few of us have such prerogatives. To be competitive, you figure prices closely and cannot absorb inflationary additions to cost.

You will find some exceptions, but most meeting planners understand such limitations and are concerned about unduly squeezing a hotel. After all, each event is a custom production and the planners are concerned with the quality of what they will receive. If they *are* obliged to set an early price on tickets, they understand that a flexible attitude on the menu can enable them to carry out the meal function while allowing the hotel a fair profit. Some astute meeting planners attach a copy of the hotel's current menu to the contract and specify that prices cannot be raised "more than X percent per year" over current prices.

All agreements on menus, prices and terms must be made in writing and signed by both parties. This eliminates misunderstandings.

Attendance

The planner initially will estimate attendance at a food function. This is vital as it indicates the scope of the event. The figure is only for preliminary preparations, and must be reviewed.

The convention planner owes it to the facility to keep it informed of the closest possible estimates of attendance at each food event. The planner may not know for sure, but a time will be set by which a firm guarantee must be given in order to prepare for the event.

The convention service manager can assist the planner in determining banquet attendance figures by suggesting that there be a **ticket exchange** and reserved seating for the *final* banquet, which is usually the most cost- and labor-intensive function. A ticket exchange is a control procedure that requires attendees to exchange a coupon from their registration packet for an actual event ticket and a reserved seating arrangement for the final gala banquet. Using this method, the planner can set a reservation deadline that falls during the meeting but still within the hotel's deadline for a head count.

Properties doing banquet business face the problem of determining a fair and workable **guarantee** policy. A typical guarantee clause might read:

In order to best serve your guests, a final confirmation of attendance or 'guarantee' is required by NOON, three (3) business days prior to your meal event. The guarantee is not subject to reduction after the 72-hour deadline. If no guarantee is received, the hotel will charge for the expected number of guests indicated on the Banquet Event Order (BEO) or the original contract, whichever amount is greater. The hotel will set 5% over the guarantee for all food functions with less than 500 attendees and 3% for all groups exceeding 500 guests. Guests arriving over and above the guaranteed number may be served an alternate menu.

No one policy is applicable to all hotels or all situations. However, the Hospitality Sales Marketing Association International surveyed a number of hotels and found that most adhere strictly to their guarantee policies. Those surveyed stressed the importance of explaining the guarantee and working with the planner to set a realistic attendance figure.

Most hotels require a guarantee either 48 or 72 hours before a food function. The meeting planner then agrees to pay for the guaranteed number of people whether or not that many appear. If 200 people are guaranteed for luncheon at a per-head charge and only 185 show up, the organization will pay for all 200. It is a touchy situation, but the obligation is clear-cut.

What happens when more show up? The experienced planner will ask that places be set for more than the guaranteed number; an **overset safety margin** of three to five percent is common. It is to the advantage of both the hotel and the convening group to avoid last minute scrambling with chairs, tables, and place settings.

Often the guarantee is included in the function sheet and is signed by both the hotel and a convention representative. Any agreement between the hotel and client is binding. If the guarantee calls for 200 and the hotel agrees to set for 5 percent over, the hotel sets tables and chairs for 210. If 210 show up, all is in readiness and the bill indicates 210. If 230 show up, the hotel is allowed to substitute 20 meals of a quickly prepared item.

Another guarantee method suggested by meeting planners, but seldom used, is to guarantee only labor. If only 185 of the guaranteed 200 showed up, the association would pay for only the cost of one waiter and not the extra fifteen meals prepared. Obviously, a hotel should never consent to this unless the extra meals can be used somewhere else.

The organization must designate, in writing, who is authorized to make changes in attendance estimates, menus and prices. A guarantee sheet (see Figure 14.5) summarizing the functions and the guarantees for each day is printed daily and distributed to appropriate staff.

Attrition

Food and beverage attrition clauses have become increasingly common in recent years. Attrition is the difference between the actual number of food and beverage covers consumed and the number agreed to in the contract between the meeting planner and the hotel. When hotels book a piece of business, they often base the room rate quoted to the group on the amount of food and beverage and the meeting room rental anticipated. Typically, hotels look at the type and size of functions planned for the convention, put a dollar value on each one, add up the numbers and then allow about 20 percent of that number for attrition (slippage). The resulting number is the minimum amount the group is expected to spend on food and beverage and meeting room rental. If the group fails to spend this amount because of poor attendance or the need to cancel banquets, the attrition clause in the contract allows the hotel to collect damages for lost profits.

Function Rooms

The type of function room to be used for a food event depends on the nature of the session, its location in relation to other functions and the hotel traffic flow, and the kind of seating arrangement desired. Pay attention, too, to the decor, lighting and other decoration requested. And, thought must be given to heating and cooling controls.

All these factors must be considered when the convention service manager sits down with his or her counterpart in the convention organization to select a room for the function. Priorities may dictate that the most suitable room go to another event, but any room used for a food function must be able to provide satisfactory results. Figure 14.6 shows how the

Figure 14.5. GUARANTEE SHEET.

The Durham Resort
Guarantee Sheet
For February 8, 20_

Time	BEO #	Room	Func.	GTD	Set	Sources	Post As
4:00A-4:00A	121	Madison	EXHB	25	28	DJ/AO/JH/CH	Kopykat Sales
7:00A-9:00A	378	Monroe	BMTG	150	165	AO/AO/JH/JH	Auto Travelers Assn
7:00A-9:00A	127	Grant	BMTG	100	110	DJ/DJ/AO/AO	Auto Travelers Assn
7:00-11:00A	382	Ballroom J	RECP	200	220	KZ/KZ/JH/JH	Kopykat Sales
7:30A-8:00A	352	Ballroom J	CONT	50	55	AO/AO/JH/JH	Kopykat Sales
8:00A-4:00P	482	Ballroom A	EXHB	20	22	ML/ML/MW/MW	Auto Travelers Assn
8:00A-6:00P	482	Ballroom A	EXHB	20	22	DJ/DJ/AO/AO	Auto Travelers Assn
8:00A-6:00P	371	Webster	EXHB	20	22	AO/AO/JH/JH	Auto Travelers Assn
8:00A-12:00P	487	Coolidge	REG	20	22	AO/AO/JH/JH	Auto Travelers Assn
8:00A-5:00P	877	Washington	GS	80	88	DJ/DJ/AO/AO	Kopykat Sales
10:30A-4:30P	472	Jackson	MTG	75	85	JH/JH/DJ/DJ	Kopykat Sales

This computer printout lists all food functions on a particular day. Copies of the form are generally distributed to the executive chef, banquet chef, executive steward, food and beverage control, function book coordinator, banquet manager and convention service manager.

Adam's Mark Dallas promotes its commitment to serving food "hot and fast" to meeting attendees by offering fully equipped, fully staffed kitchens adjacent to every ballroom.

A reminder is in order here to note the time it takes to set up the food function room and clean it up afterwards. It is important to know whether the cleanup noises will disturb the meeting session going on next door. It may not be possible to avoid such proximity, but it shouldn't come about because no one thought about it. The clash of silver and china can be most distracting at a serious meeting and can reflect on the hotel's image.

On one occasion, the Salvation Army had a meeting scheduled next door to a luncheon for the governor of Hawaii. As the governor was presenting his opening remarks, the Salvation Army opened its meeting in the traditional way with a song to the resounding beat of the bass drum. Needless to say, the hotel's convention service manager gave greater consideration to a group's program after this incident.

Figure 14.6. AD PROMOTING THE PROXIMITY OF THE KITCHEN TO MEETING SPACE.

Control Procedures

Most food functions are charged on a per-head basis. Every hotel should devise a **head count** procedure to determine the actual number of **covers** (meals) served. Guesswork has no place in banquet billing. The charges should be agreed to in writing, and the menu selection should be indicated.

Many meeting planners prefer to use coupons or tickets. The delegate at registration is issued a coupon book with tear-out tickets for each function. There is need for caution if this system is suggested. Here are the two most common methods of ticket collection:

At the door — A table should be set up with a representative from the association and one from the hotel there to collect tickets.

At the banquet table — In this case, the waiter collects the tickets. This can be a touchy area if delegates do not have their tickets. A common delegate response is, "I left my ticket in my room." This is a difficult situation to police; if the hotel is paid for only the tickets collected, the waiter is forced to refuse service. Hotel personnel should be instructed what to do if a conferee shows up without the proper ticket.

Counting the dishes expected to be used in advance is another method of determining the number of covers served. The chef or convention service manager then counts the number of dishes that were not used and subtracts this from the first figure. Perhaps the best system is to totally count the people seated. The convention service manager and the meeting planner should both take counts. This should be done immediately after the entree has been served.

Some food functions, such as refreshment breaks and hospitality centers, obviously cannot be charged in this way. Spell out clearly the formula used. You may charge for coffee by the cup or by the gallon, fruit juice by the gallon, Danish pastry by the piece or by the tray.

Some canny sales managers will give away hors d'oeuvres or favors. In such cases, it enables them to close the deal at higher rates for rooms or meals. Psychologically, the practice may make for a better presentation; economically it may represent less than the price advantage. In addition, the higher rate will bring in a further dividend should more people attend. The buffet and hors d'oeuvres are fixed costs on your part, while the higher rate for additional guests adds to your profit.

Small food functions are often tagged with additional charges. If the function is not large enough to cover labor and setup costs, hotels frequently add on to the bill. Figure 14.7 provides an example of banquet labor and miscellaneous charges.

Figure 14.7. MISCELLANEOUS FUNCTION CHARGES.

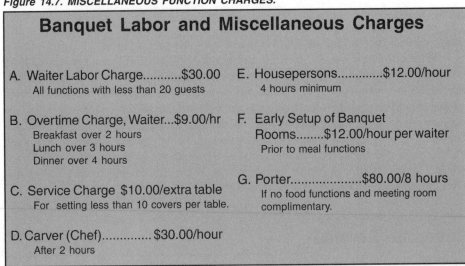

Banquet Labor and Miscellaneous Charges

A. Waiter Labor Charge..........$30.00
   All functions with less than 20 guests

B. Overtime Charge, Waiter...$9.00/hr
   Breakfast over 2 hours
   Lunch over 3 hours
   Dinner over 4 hours

C. Service Charge $10.00/extra table
   For setting less than 10 covers per table.

D. Carver (Chef)..............$30.00/hour
   After 2 hours

E. Housepersons.............$12.00/hour
   4 hours minimum

F. Early Setup of Banquet
   Rooms........$12.00/hour per waiter
   Prior to meal functions

G. Porter...................$80.00/8 hours
   If no food functions and meeting room complimentary.

Hotels frequently add on to the bill if the food function is not large enough to cover labor and set up costs. In addition to the charges listed above, it is common for properties to apply a flat service charge to food and beverage functions under a certain size (typically 25 people or less). In some cases, labor and charges are waived entirely or based on the total dollar amount spent on the function. Any specifics negotiated should be clearly spelled out in the contract.

Staffing

Hotels generally provide more waiters per guest as the price per cover increases. The minimum wait service for standard plated dinners is one waiter per 20 guests (at rounds of ten, one waiter per two tables; at rounds of eight, two waiters per five tables). French and Russian service generally require one server for every ten guests. For buffet meals, the standard is one wait staff to 40 persons for breakfast and one wait staff for 30 persons at lunch and dinner. The minimum bus staff is one for every three waiters. If the menu calls for wine service poured by wait staff, the minimum is one waiter per 16 guests.

Pre-meal briefings should be conducted before all large banquets by the **banquet captains** (one banquet captain should be staffed for every ten to 12 servers). Menus, special service requirements, station assignments and other pertinent items should be reviewed. The setup and service of the head table should be assigned to the captains. Special attention is paid to silverware, glasses and proper arrangement of place settings.

Finally, the times for serving must be carefully controlled. The salad course typically takes about 20 to 30 minutes, the entrée about 30 to 50 minutes (from serving to the removal of plates) and desserts can usually be handled in 20 to 30 minutes. Normally, complete service takes about 1¼-hours for luncheon and about two hours for a dinner event. Keep in mind, however, that a more elaborate function will take additional time so staff accordingly.

It is necessary to adhere closely to scheduled meal times, so extension of cocktail parties should be kept to a minimum. Meal functions should also run on schedule. Not only are some attendees reluctant to attend a catered event that will run over two hours, but an overly long event may also give the impression that there is something wrong with the catering department.

Uniserve or Duoserve

The food and beverage service is generally handled in one of two ways by hotels. In a **uniserve** system, the meeting planner makes all arrangements for both function space and food and beverage through one service contact, the convention service manager. In this system the banquet/catering department reports to convention services.

With a **duoserve** system, the food and beverage responsibilities are separated from the scheduling of function space. In this case, meeting planners must work with the banquet/catering department for their food and beverage requests and with the convention services department for their function room needs. When the duoserve approach is used the banquet/catering personnel generally report to the food and beverage director. As we indicated earlier, most meeting planners want to deal with only one contact person at a hotel. The assistant director of convention services at the Sheraton Tucson El Conquistador makes a strong case for the uniserve system (see box titled "Should Hotel Catering and Convention Services Departments Be Combined?").

Beverage Service

More discontent has been voiced over beverage service and charges than over most factors of a convention. Of all the price policies at a convention, the liquor arrangement brings the loudest and most frequent outcry.

Should Hotel Catering and Convention Services Departments Be Combined?

by Nora May, assistant director convention services, Sheraton Tucson El Conquistador

"UNISERVE" — the word used by the Sheraton Tucson El Conquistador to define a manager who specializes in catering AND convention services.

When it was announced that our hotel would be switching to the Uniserve concept, there was a definite concern that arose in my mind on how a person could "do it all!" After all, in my experience as assistant catering director, catering alone took all of my time, including my personal family time, and now they want to add to my responsibilities? It seemed almost impossible.

Several years have passed since the Uniserve concept was put into action, and there is no doubt in my mind that this is THE BEST way to run the business. The positive aspects of this concept outweigh the negative aspects. As a matter of fact, I can't think of a negative aspect. These are the positives.

1. **Efficiency!** The meeting planner benefits from working with just one person. It simplifies the job. Plus it saves on communication time for the meeting planner and the Uniserve convention service manager. When working the split method, often times I would get little notes on my desk from convention services that said something like, "Spoke with ABC Company on the phone. They want to add a continental breakfast to the meeting on Monday." It is incredible how much time it takes to find out exactly what this message means. Which meeting? There are three breakouts and a board meeting scheduled. How many people? First you go the the convention services person to obtain more details, and usually you have to call the client to confirm. Uniserve eliminates this type of time waste.

2. **Control!** As a sole person handling all of the group's conference requirements, one has a grasp of the whole picture. The Uniserve CSM is responsible for every detail of the conference.

3. **Rewarding!** Opportunities and challenges continuously arise prior to a group's conference and during the conference. There is no getting around the problem-solving issues that tend to keep our blood flowing in the hospitality industry. That is what makes our jobs so interesting, exciting and sometimes exhausting. In Uniserve, when the group departs and the guests are grinning from ear-to-ear, sending compliments in every direction and the meeting planner re-books for the following year on the condition that YOU are assigned to work their file... rewarding? You bet!

4. **Free Time!** It's the best part of Uniserve! Prior to Uniserve, I literally spent 90% of my time at work. Family life barely existed. And although this type of job can be addicting, everyone has a right to a personal life. Uniserve permits a personal life. I say this with caution as this is dependent on a number of things.

(continued)

A. Adequate staffing is necessary in the Uniserve department. The Sheraton El Conquistador convention services department consists of four Uniserve people who handle the convention groups, one local catering manager, and a one-stop-shop manager who blocks, contracts and caters to groups of 20 sleeping rooms and under. Of course, staffing varies from hotel to hotel and is dependent on the type of market the hotel pulls.

B. The convention files must be assigned strategically between managers to allow adequate days for paperwork between groups and allowing for *days off.*

C. The banquet manager, banquet captains and conference floor manager *must* be trained to handle problem solving situations effectively and with confidence. The same captain should handle as many of the group's meal functions as possible so that the meeting planner can feel comfortable with familiar faces. It is the Uniserve convention services manager's responsibility to introduce the client to the banquet manager, captain and conference floor manager prior to the function. After introductions are made and the banquet room is checked for details, the Uniserve CSM can depart if the banquet manager/captain/client are comfortable. If a client seems uncomfortable, or you personally know of a problem that might arise, the Uniserve CSM MUST be in attendance.

D. A daily meeting with the hotel staff to include the chef, banquet manager, conference floor manager and Uniserve CSMs is a MUST! The purpose of the daily meeting is to cover all functions in the hotel for the upcoming three days. Any questions about group's meetings and banquet functions should be brought up at this meeting and solved so that there are no questions as to room setups or service. This system prevents the necessity of constantly putting out fires prior to or during functions. With this type of detailing, the Uniserve CSM can feel confident when turning the functions over to the banquet manager, captain and conference floor manager.

I cannot claim that the Uniserve system will work for all hotels. However, I believe there are many hotels who could use this system and it would relieve many of those catering and convention service managers who are "burned out."

Unfortunately, meeting planners or the hosts at hospitality suites usually specify their favorite brands of liquor, and they are familiar with package store prices. Many planners and hosts resent what they consider to be unfair markups on name-brand liquor by the hotel. Some hotels have taken to charging the same prices as local liquor stores, but most have a much higher rate — two, three or even four times the cost. This is a management decision. The additional revenue gained by marking up must be weighed against the frequent ill will engendered.

Types of Setups

A number of beverage arrangements are used in catering to private parties. We will discuss the four most common procedures specified by meeting planners:

The **host bar**, also called an *open bar* or *sponsored bar*, is used most frequently by corporate meeting planners. At a host bar, guests drink freely of the beverages offered and the host pays the bill at the end of the function. This type of bar is stocked to prepare for all types of drinks and is staffed by a bartender. A purchase amount is almost always guaranteed. If, for example, at least $300 worth of beverage is not consumed, the host will pay for what was consumed, plus an additional amount to cover labor. Figure 14.8 shows typical labor costs for beverage service.

Figure 14.8. TYPICAL LABOR COSTS FOR BEVERAGE SERVICE.

Beverage Labor and Miscellaneous Charges

A. Bartender Charge —
   If less than $150 sales, labor charge
   ....$70.00

B. Bar Supplies — If group supplies liquor
   Cocktail Napkins
   Stir Sticks $1.00/person
   Assorted Bar Fruit
   Mix - Sodas $2.50/quart
   Bloody Mary Mix, Orange Juice
   and Sweet and Sour........$8.00/quart
   Blenders......................$10.00/each

C. Extra Bartender Charge $15.00/hour
   4 hour minimum

D. Extra Barback Charge $74.00/8 hrs
   8 hour minimum

In addition to the charges listed above, it is common for properties to apply a flat service charge to functions under a certain size (typically 25 people or less). In some cases, labor and charges are waived entirely or based on the total dollar amount spent on the function. Sometimes, bartender fees are waived altogether (many meeting planners insist that they not pay bartender fees for the staffing of large hosted bars). Any specifics negotiated should be clearly spelled out in the contract.

The **cash bar**, also called a *C.O.D. bar* or *no-host bar*, is the second most common arrangement. At a cash bar, each person pays for his or her own drinks. A minimum guarantee is also specified by the hotel in this case.

Coupon sales are used at many private parties. Delegates buy tickets or coupons ahead of time and give them to the bartender when the drinks are served. The coupons may be sold by the hotel management or the host organization. Coupon sales eliminate the use of cash and the need for a cashier at the function.

Stanley Stearman, executive vice-president of the National Society of Public Accountants, said of the use of coupons for beverage functions:

> "We give everyone two drink tickets along with their banquet ticket. They are actually perforated stubs which are turned in to the bartender in return for drinks. Not only does this method limit consumption to two drinks per person, but it gives me control over my liquor costs. I pay a certain amount for each stub that has been turned in. The only disadvantage to me is that I have to pay full price even if someone redeems his stub for a soft drink."[12]

The South Coast Plaza in Costa Mesa, California, uses still a different method in servicing private parties. The **captain's bar** is a self-service or make-your-own drink bar that has been stocked with full bottles of liquor and mixes needed to make all the basic bar drinks. This bar is always hosted. The meeting planner and the convention service manager inventory the bar before and after the party, and the group is charged for how much is consumed. There is no guarantee on this type of setup because there is no bartender labor cost.

Hospitality Suites

Hospitality suites are beverage or food and beverage functions held by the sponsoring organization or by other groups (such as exhibitors at an organization's trade show). They are usually held in a suite on a sleeping room floor, which means that hospitality suites are typically sold by the catering department but serviced by room service. Larger functions, such as those offering entertainment, are held in public function rooms (in this case, they would be both sold and serviced by the catering department).

While hospitality suites have traditionally been evening hospitality functions, there has been a trend for hosting breakfast or luncheon events as well. These hospitality suites are auxiliary business, commonly referred to as in conjunction with (ICW) business, for hotels. This means that even if the ICW business is not necessarily booked directly by the meeting sponsor, it should be considered part of the group's meeting history as it increases the value of the meeting to the hotel.

Some meeting planners and exhibitors wish to avoid what they consider to be excessive prices charged by the hotel by bringing in liquor purchased outside the hotel. They then order mixers, ice and glasses from room service. Hotels have varying policies regarding such action. Some hotels have a **corkage** charge to cover the use of liquor that is purchased elsewhere.

Katie Kannapell, the banquet manager of Cipiriani 42nd Street in New York City, tells of a recent corporate event in which the champagne provided by the sponsor was $20 pricier than Cipriani's in-house stock due to the corkage charge. She says:

> "Corkage is complicated. People often think corkage is cheaper, but you
> [the meeting planner] have to ask what is included and then compare it to
> what the venue serves. Very often you are not saving anything."[13]

Union regulations often dictate the circumstances under which a bartender must be employed. Tell your client in advance about such regulations. Explain the hours involved, overtime charges and other pertinent details. Spell out the circumstances under which no such help is required. Include information about gratuities and taxes.

Brands

Most hotels offer a varied selection of liquor brands to the meeting planner. Brands are commonly offered in three categories: house (well) brands, call brands and premium brands. **House brands** are the least expensive liquors and wines and will be used for the function unless the meeting planner requests otherwise. Actual brands of liquor offered may vary from venue to venue, so be sure to inform meeting planners of the brands your hotel uses to avoid any confusion.

Call brands are brands specifically asked for by name, such as when a meeting planner requests Jim Beam Bourbon or Beefeater's Gin. These brands are generally priced in the mid-range and must be requested as replacements for house brands.

Premium brands are quality, expensive liquors, such as Crown Royal, Chivas Regal or Tanqueray Gin. When a planner selects a top-of-the line drink menu, a guest at the function will not have to settle for the one brand offered on the standard drink menu. He or she will likely be able to choose from two or three brands of quality liquor.

Be sure that the meeting planner understands these categories, his or her options (using house wines but call brands, for example) and associated charges so that he or she can make an informed decision. This will avoid complaints over liquor charges.

Pricing Methods

Meeting planners often ask advice on how much liquor will be needed. The consumption of liquor varies, of course, with the makeup of the attendees. A chart such as the one shown in Figure 14.9 should prove helpful to you and your customers in making such decisions.

Figure 14.9. GUIDE TO HELP ESTIMATE THE AMOUNT OF LIQUOR NEEDED FOR A BEVERAGE FUNCTION.

Reception Drink Estimator

Based on an all-male attendance and easy access to bars. With 50% female attendance, average is 2 1/2 to 3 per hour, with 100% female attendance, average is 2 to 2 1/2 per hour.

Number of Guests	1/2 hr	3/4 hr	One hr	1 1/4 hrs	1 1/2 hrs	1 3/4 hrs	Two hrs
25-55	2	3	3 3/4	4	4 1/4	4 1/2	4 3/4
60-104	2	3	3 3/4	4	4	4 1/2	4 3/4
105-225	1 3/4	2 1/2	3	3 1/2	4	4	4 1/2
230-300	1 1/2	2	2 1/2	2 3/4	3	3 1/4	3 1/2
315 & up	1 1/2	2	2 1/2	2 3/4	3	3 1/4	3 1/2

Drink Estimator

Bottle size	Drink size	Number of drinks
Liquor		
4/5 quart	1 oz.	25
4/5 quart	1 1/4 oz.	20
4/5 quart	1 1/2 oz.	17
Quart	1 oz.	31
Quart	1 1/4 oz.	25
Quart	1 1/2 oz.	21
Wine		
750 ml	5 oz.	5
Liter	5 oz.	6.7
Magnum	5 oz.	10.2

Source: Reprinted with permission from **The Schenley Guide to Professional Hosting**. *Published by Schenley Affiliated Brands Corp.*

Liquor charges can be figured *by the person, by the bottle* or *by the individual drink*. Whichever is used, make sure that someone on the convention staff has been designated to tally up after the affair with a designated member of the hotel staff. This will help avoid misunderstandings after the event and avoid last minute searching for someone of authority on the convention management staff to corroborate the tally.

By the Person. When liquor is priced **by the person**, a flat rate is charged for each person present during a specified period of time. This type of pricing is also referred to as the *per person/unlimited consumption plan*. Sometimes a flat rate is charged for a cocktail party of a specified time period and additional time is charged on an hourly basis. At other times the rate is given only as an hourly charge. If food is to be served, what kind and how much must be discussed and listed in the agreement.

From the meeting planner's perspective, this flat rate per person can be the simplest, but not necessarily the cheapest pricing method. Unless the group has a lot of drinkers, this is usually an expensive plan.

You will need a way to determine the number in attendance. Collecting tickets or invitations at the door is one way to do this.

Extension of the time period and the admission of people who do not have tickets require approval by an authorized person. The head count and the time period should be acknowledged immediately after the event by having the authorized person initial the tally.

By the Bottle. The convention organizer may prefer to pay **by the bottle** consumed. Liquor by the bottle can be cost-effective for large groups. If you are charging $6 per drink and serving one-ounce drinks from a fifth, the meeting group pays $150 for the bottle (25 drinks per fifth). A by the bottle charge would reduce this cost to $80 to $100 per bottle.

The by-the-bottle system is very popular for hospitality suites, both with and without bartenders. This system calls for charges on all bottles opened regardless of how much of the contents is consumed. Some hotels permit the host to keep the opened bottles; others do not. Some hotels agree to store opened bottles of liquor from one reception and use them for the group's next reception. Obviously, the bartender must be made aware of the arrangement, and it must be made part of the work order for the beverage event.

Sometimes the charges for the bartender are part of the per-bottle price. If so, this should be indicated in the work order or agreement; if not, list the rates and hours.

Make sure that the liquor supply given is stored securely. Good hotel people assist their guests in arranging storage. It is imperative that both the hotel and the convention organization have people designated to tally and record the number of bottles used and returned for credit. Meeting planners will want to ensure that they have a good inventory system in place to ensure proper billing. This means taking an inventory of the bars both before and after a function (this should always be done in the company of a hotel banquet person, who verifies the planner's totals). The inventory should not only include bottles of liquor, but also mixers, soft drinks and bottled water (as well as any other items for which the group is being charged). Sodas are usually charged at about $3 each, so it is becoming more prevalent for these items to be inventoried.

When buying liquor by the bottle, meeting planners often request the banquet bars be closed in staggered order, moving the partials from one to the other (this is termed *marrying* the bars). Their instructions also frequently call for the bartenders to pour measured drinks, as bartenders could pad the bill by overpouring.

Food may be served, but is charged separately. And, under certain conditions, there may be a room charge. Much depends on the anticipated volume and the basic agreement under which the event takes place.

By the Drink. Charges can also be made **by the drink**, based on the number of individual drinks served. This type of function always include the mandatory use of bartender service (no less than one bartender for every 75 guests is the rule of thumb). There should be an agreement on the size of the drink to be poured and the bartenders so instructed. Meeting planners often specify that portion control measuring pourers (called Posi-Pours) be used.

This arrangement is used by many meeting planners, especially those planning for small groups. Most meeting planners feel the most economical bar for receptions of under 100 persons is by the drink; for over 100 persons, by the bottle.

The guests may pay for drinks in cash or prepaid coupons, or the host may pay for it all. Food charges are a separate item, and there may be a room charge. Give the meeting planner advance notice of gratuities, taxes and a schedule of bartenders' work regulations.

Beverage Control

Rigid procedures for issuing liquor and the use of it should be maintained. The banquet department is generally responsible for issuing the liquor. Since it is impossible to judge how much or what kind of liquor will be preferred, it is customary to stock 25 percent over what the group is estimated to consume. This policy eliminates shortages, but it must be controlled.

The excess must be returned to the storeroom at the end of the function. Special banquet requisition forms are used for private parties, showing all the bottles issued, consumed and returned. Immediately after each function all bottles — full, empty and partially used — should be accounted for.

The Renaissance Hotel uses the requisition form shown in Figure 14.10. The banquet manager uses this form for each function, showing the number of bottles originally issued, any additional issues, and all returns. Each bottle issued is marked with a distinctive means of identification. At the end of the party, the banquet manager totals the requisition by determining the amount of each item consumed and its price and then making the appropriate extensions. The total is transferred to the banquet guest check, which is verified and signed by the meeting planner. A percentage of the check total is usually added to the bill as a gratuity for the staff.

Host Bar Control. Because cash is not taken with host or open bars, they are easiest to control. Opened bottles of liquor may either be returned to the storeroom for credit or bought by the meeting planner. If the meeting planner takes the open bottles, this should be noted on the requisition sheet, along with the name of the guest. Some groups buy the "cracked" bottles but prefer that the hotel hold the bottles in storage for them. Such bottles should be clearly marked and given to the guest upon request.

Cash Bar Control. This arrangement requires the most rigid controls. A bartender should not be allowed to take cash, as he would then be controlling both cash receipts and the issuing of liquor. A less-than-honest bartender could pour smaller than average drinks and pocket the cash on every fourth or fifth drink without being detected. An accurate count requires a control system.

Cash bars necessitate at least two employees — a bartender and a cashier. At the end of the party, cash sales should be equated with the amount of merchandise consumed. This system also enables the bartender to concentrate on pouring drinks and giving rapid service.

Coupon Sales Control. A cashier is not necessary if the meeting planner issues tickets prior to the event. The bartenders collect tickets for the drinks and turns them over to the banquet manager. The manager, in turn, inventories the bar before and after the function and compares the consumption of liquor with the tickets collected.

If tickets are to be sold at the party, a cashier will be needed, and cash banks must be issued. The banquet manager should issue numbered tickets to the cashier and get them

Figure 14.10. BAR REQUISITION FORM.

RAMADA RENAISSANCE HOTEL

BANQUET WINE/LIQUOR REQUISITION

NO. 001399

DATE *8-25-* DAY OF WEEK *MONDAY* TIME *6:00 PM*

FUNCTION *RECEPTION* ROOM *FOYER / RENAISSANCE BALLROOM*

ORGANIZATION NAME *SINGER* BANQUET CHECK # *06272*

BANQUET EVENT ORDER # *02135* TENDERS IN CHARGE: *Bill / Cheryle*

CLIENT'S ACCOUNT # *12948*

NUMBER OF GUESTS *275*

MANNER OF SALE: ☑ BY DRINK ☐ BY BOTTLE ☐ BY HOUR

TYPE OF BEVERAGE: ☐ PREMIUM ☑ HOUSE ☐ SPECIAL LIST

TYPE OF SALE: ☑ HOSTED ☐ CASH BAR

CODE	DESCRIPTION	ISSUED QUANT.	SIZE	RETD BOTT.	USED BOTT.	NO. DRINKS	DRINK PRICE	TOTAL	LIQUOR	WINE	MISC	% POT.
	HOUSE BOURBON	3		1.7	1.3	43	3°°	129.°°	8.35			65%
	HOUSE SCOTCH	3		1.9	1.1							
	HOUSE GIN	4		2.4	1.6							
	HOUSE VODKA	4		1.1	29							
	HOUSE BRANDY	2		1.8	.2							
	HOUSE RUM	2		1.6	.4							
	HOUSE TEQUILA	2		1.3	.7							
	HOUSE WHISKEY	2		1.8	.2							
	HOUSE WHITE WINE	18		2	16							
	HOUSE RED WINE	6		3	3							
	MILLER LITE BEER	24		5	19							
	HEINEKEN BEER											
	PREMIUM BOURBON											
	PREMIUM SCOTCH											
	PREMIUM GIN											
	PREMIUM VODKA											
	PREMIUM BRANDY											
	PREMIUM WHISKEY											
	PREMIUM TEQUILA											
	PREMIUM RUM											
TOTALS												

ISSUED BY _____ RETURNED BY _____ APPROVED BY _____

RECEIVED BY _____ RECEIVED BY _____

WHITE - FOOD AND BEVERAGE CONTROL   CANARY - BANQUET MAITRE D'   GOLDEN ROD - BEVERAGE MGR.

This form details the number of bottles issued, consumed, and returned. The form also specifies the pricing method to be used (by drink, by bottle, by hour), the type of brand (premium, house, special list), and the type of setup (hosted, cash bar).

back, along with the cash, when the function is completed. He can then verify the number of tickets issued with the cash receipts.

Automated Bars. Several hotels are making use of automated bar systems. A long-standing complaint of meeting planners is the tendency of bartenders to over-pour in host bar setups (pouring drinks without the use of shot glasses or other measuring devices is called **free pour**). They feel the staff members are encouraged to pour on the heavy side because their tips are figured as a percentage of sales. Another problem area is the counting and storing of open bottles. Both of these problems are eliminated with automated bars setups.

Automated bars operate much like soda bars, with individual push buttons for each liquor item — vodka, gin, bourbon, scotch, rye, etc. Quart bottles are placed upside down in the wells and dispensed by a vacuum system. Each bottle has its own dispensing unit and meter. The size of the drink is determined by the meeting planner, and the dispensing unit is set accordingly (this method of dispensing exact amounts of liquor per drink is known as **electronic pour**). The meters are checked and recorded before and after the party, with the difference being the amount consumed.

The control feature offered by the metered bars is what makes them attractive to both the meeting planner and the hotel. They provide a consistent drink and eliminate overpouring, but they are not without their limitations. The machine dispenses only the alcohol; mixed and blended drinks still must be prepared by a bartender. And only eight bottles can be filled on most units, limiting the choice of drinks. Some observers also say that metered bars are impersonal, lending a mechanical atmosphere to cocktail parties.

Liquor Liability. Can a hotel be held liable to an innocent third party for wrongful acts of an intoxicated attendee? The answer depends on the individual state, but due to alcohol related automobile accidents, many states have passed acts that impose liability on the dispenser of alcohol sold illegally, terming a sale is illegal if to a minor, intoxicated person or known alcoholic. Management must take reasonable care in serving alcoholic beverages at functions. Managers should be trained to be alert to potential problems with intoxicated patrons and how to deal with unruly meeting attendees. A typical contract clause might read:

If alcoholic beverages are to be served on the Hotel premises (or elsewhere under the Hotel's alcoholic beverage license) the Hotel will require that beverages be dispensed only by Hotel servers and bartenders. The Hotel's license requires the Hotel to (1) request identification (Photo ID) of any person of questionable age and refuse service if the person is either under age or proper identification cannot be produced and (2) refuse alcoholic beverage service to any person who, in the Hotel's judgment, appears intoxicated.

Some provisions are stricter, prohibiting attendees from bringing alcoholic beverages into the hotel from outside:

Alcoholic beverages may not be brought into the hotel from outside sources. The sales, service and consumption of alcoholic beverages are regulated by the State Alcoholic Beverage Commission. The Hotel, as a licensee, is subject to the regulations promulgated by the Commission, violations of which may jeopardize the Hotel's license. Consequently, it is the Hotel's policy that alcoholic beverages may not be brought into the hotel from outside sources.

Staffing and Logistics. Staff one bartender per 75 to 100 people. You will also need to staff one bar back for every three bartenders (bar backs are responsible for replenishing stocks of liquor, ice, glassware and garnishes used during the function). When food is served at receptions, staff one server per 50 people, and one waiter per 100 people for receptions without food service.

Bar locations will vary according to the room's dimensions and the placement of other provisions such as staging, dance floors and buffet tables. Generally, one bar station is required for every 75-100 guests. Avoid grouping bars too close together. With large receptions requiring several beverage stations, open those bars farthest from the entrance first in order to bring people into the room. This helps to spread the crowds. The chart below summarizes staffing requirements for receptions based on attendance.

Reception Service Estimator			
Number of Guests	Number of bartenders	Number of waiters with food	Number of waiters without food
25-100	1	2	1
105-205	2	3	2
215-325	3	3	2
350-475	4	4	3

Beverage Labor Charges. In addition to charges for the liquor and other drinks served at beverage functions, hotels also assess labor and miscellaneous fees for events. Generally, clients must hire a minimum number of bartenders for a minimum number of hours (typically for shifts of four hours). Some bartender fees, for example, are based on a sliding scale, such as $125 for the first hour, $75 for the second hour and $50 for each hour thereafter. If bartenders are hired for a four-hour shift and the function extends beyond four hours, additional overtime charges may be assessed. In addition to bartenders, beverage functions require bar backs. Some hotels include the salaries for these employees in the bartender charge, except in cases where additional bar backs are required.

Some beverage functions may also require cashiers. Many hotels do not allow clients to schedule cash bars unless at least one cashier is employed. Having a cashier eliminates the need for the bartender to handle cash, which slows down beverage production and service and can create security problems. Cashiers can be eliminated if the client sells drink tickets that guests can redeem for beverages.

Planners may also wish to employ cocktail servers, although servers can cost almost as much as bartenders. Therefore, most meeting planners eliminate the need for servers by having two or three portable bars set up in the room and having guests give their orders directly to the bartenders. If the client wishes to have cocktail servers, however, they can be used to best advantage by circulating the room with trays of poured wine or champagne. This eliminates the need for wine drinkers to slow down the flow at bar stations.

Other charges incurred at beverage functions are the costs for supplies and mixers, which are not considered part of a liquor order. It is important that all charges, whether they be for labor or supplies, be clearly spelled out in the contract in order to avoid any misunderstandings.

Post-Function Actions

Prompt action must be taken at the end of each food function to eliminate possible billing difficulties and to bring each function segment to a satisfactory close.

If billing is based on attendance, the captain in charge should tally the number of persons served or the number of tickets collected and have the authorized convention person sign an acknowledgment of the total. Make sure the person signing is designated in writing.

If beverages were served, tally the unopened bottles of liquor and/or soft drinks and have the amount acknowledged by signature. Bottles to be returned for credit must be signed for.

Most convention groups use a master billing account for the food functions. If the terms are cash, the money or check should be presented when the tally is certified as correct. If cash is collected by the organization, the hotel should provide a safe place for it or accept it in payment and give a suitable receipt.

Place a summary of the food functions in the file folder for the analysis of the convention.

In-House Coodination: Large vs. Small

We have referred to the convention service manager as the person who coordinates the convention. This person, however, does not do it all; many departments are involved. The competence of the department heads determines the extent to which the convention service manager becomes involved. If the reservations, front-desk and catering managers are on top of their jobs, the convention service manager's headaches are minimized. If not, the convention service manager must spend more time overseeing the operation.

Role of the Catering Manager

The in-house coordination at *small properties* is generally not handled the same way as at larger properties; the major difference is the role played by the *catering manager.* At larger properties, catering managers are only in charge of food and beverage; seldom do they become involved in sales and seldom are they required to account for more than the food and beverage service. But at small properties, their areas of responsibility branch out.

A property with insufficient sales volume to justify carrying a convention coordinator must nevertheless give one person that responsibility. Usually, it is the banquet or catering manager who wears two hats: head of his or her department and head of group business.

What distinguishes a large property from a small one? There is no definition, but hotels with fewer than 250 guest rooms might well handle servicing differently than larger ones.

Figure 14.11 gives a catering manager's job description adapted from the operating manual of Doubletree Hotels, whose hotels range from 140 to 300 guest rooms and are typical of such properties whose catering managers double as convention service managers.

Servicing and Selling

The division between servicing and selling is less pronounced at small hotels than at large ones. As we discussed in Chapter 10, there is wide variation among hotels in the extent to which the sales department participates in servicing.

Figure 14.11. JOB DESCRIPTION OF A CATERING MANAGER.

Catering Manager's Job Description

1. **Basic Function**
   To service all phases of group meeting/banquet functions; coordinate these activities on a daily basis; assist clients in program planning and menu selection; solicit local group catering business.

2. **General Responsibility**
   To maintain the services and reputation of Doubletree and act as management representative to group clients.

3. **Specific Responsibilities**

   a. To maintain function book. Coordinate the booking of all meeting space with the Sales Department.
   b. To solicit local food and beverage functions.
   c. To coordinate with all group meeting/banquet planners their specific group requirements with the services and facilities offered.
   d. To confirm all details relative to group functions with meeting/banquet planners.
   e. To distribute to the necessary inter-hotel departments detailed information relative to group activities.
   f. To supervise and coordinate all phases of catering, hiring and training programs.
   g. To supervise and coordinate daily operation of meeting/banquet setups and service.
   h. To assist in menu planning, preparation and pricing.
   i. To assist in referrals to the Sales Department and in booking group activities.
   j. To set up and maintain catering files.
   k. To be responsive to group requests/needs while in the hotel.
   l. To work toward achieving Annual Plan figures relating to the Catering Department (revenues, labor percentages, average checks, covers, etc.)
   m. To handle all scheduling and coverage for the servicing of catering functions.

4. **Organizational Relationship and Authority**
   Is directly responsible and accountable to the Food and Beverage Manager. Responsible for coordination with kitchen, catering service personnel and accounting.

As seen by these duties detailed by the Doubletree Hotels, the catering manager often serves as the convention service manager at small properties.
Source: Courtesy of Doubletree Hotels.

At smaller hotels, servicing and sales, particularly of food and beverage functions, are more likely to be handled by the same person. Part of the catering manager's job might be to actively solicit and schedule group banquet business. Often, the catering manager is given charge of the function book. This is fine as long as the lines of authority, responsibility and communication are clearly understood.

The problem arises when the left hand does not know what the right hand is doing; when the sales department books a convention that conflicts with the catering department's efforts. The problem is likely to be acute when the two departments are located in different areas of the hotel. In this case, the sales department rarely sees the function book and must rely on the phone or memos to communicate with the catering department. There may even be inter-departmental rivalry for function space, with each trying to show greater sales and profit.

Communication and Cooperation

Servicing requires clear communication channels at small properties. When the property has a convention service manager, there is generally good cooperation, with one independent person coordinating the efforts of other departments. But when the catering manager serves as the coordinator, there seems to be more autonomy of departments. The catering manager may be unfamiliar with the problems in the front of the house; reservation and front office departments lack understanding of the handling of food and beverage.

Such a situation is not necessarily detrimental, as long as each department does its job and there is good inter-departmental communication. The difficulty may arise when the association executive questions the hotel's handling of his or her membership's registration. If the catering manager is the planner's contact in the hotel, the planner may find little relief for the problem. Perhaps the catering manager is too busy with the upcoming dinner or has not been schooled in the procedure of registering guests. Or perhaps — and this is a more common problem — the catering manager doesn't have the authority to go to the rooms department to straighten out the situation. The meeting planner's nightmare is a contact without the muscle to get the job done.

The autonomy of departments also leads to the lack of resumes (specification sheets), which are the backbone of control and communication in servicing. Substituting for the resumes (specification sheets) are memos from the sales department to the rooms department and individual function sheets prepared by the catering manager for all meeting room and food and beverage setups. Memos and function sheets are fine ways of communicating, but a comprehensive schedule of the overall convention program is still needed.

PUTTING IT ALL TOGETHER

Your property has been approached by the corporate office of a large multi-level marketing company that wishes to hold a convention for approximately 600 distributors and spouses. While funds are unlimited, the meeting planner is totally inexperienced and will need your help to plan a successful function.

At this time, plans are sketchy. The meeting planner does want to incorporate the company's "Pot of Gold" promotion into an Awards Banquet and to stage a luau to celebrate the vacations won by the company's top five distributors. The meeting planner is open to your suggestions regarding creative menus for these two functions, but wants to serve traditional American fare for the buffets and other meal functions. The convention will run from Wednesday afternoon through Sunday afternoon. Events currently being considered are:

Wednesday	(Afternoon)	**Registration**
	(Evening)	Registration and **Hospitality Suite**
		Dinner on own
Thursday	(Morning)	**Three seminars** (Approx. 100 people each room.)
		Refreshment Break
	(Afternoon)	**Three seminars** (Approx.100 people each room)
		Refreshment Break
	(Evening)	**Buffet Dinner** (Approx. 500 attendees)
Friday	(Morning)	Same as Thursday
	(Afternoon)	**Buffet lunch** (Approx. 500 attendees)
	(Afternoon)	Same as Thursday
	(Evening)	**Directors Dinner** (24 in attendance)
		Other attendees: optional dinner show (on own)
Saturday	(Morning)	**President's Breakfast** (approx. 300 attendees)
		General Session (600 attendees)
		Lunch on own
	(Afternoon)	**Continuation of General Session**
	(Evening)	**Awards Banquet**, **Entertainment** (music and dancing)
		(600 attendees)
Sunday	(Morning)	Breakfast on own
	(Afternoon)	**Farewell Luau** (Approx. 350 attendees)

Using what you have learned in Chapters 12, 13 and 14, develop a presentation that you will use in your pre-convention planning session with the meeting planner. Cover the following areas:

1. A proposal detailing what food and beverages could be offered at the food functions (hospitality suite, refreshment breaks, buffet lunch and dinner, the directors dinner, president's breakfast, the awards banquet and luau). Include how the client could be charged for each function.
2. An outline of what your property can offer in the way of decorations, staffing, and meeting requirements (musicians, additional entertainment, staging, lighting, etc.) for the awards banquet and the luau. Provide room set-up plans detailing suggested seating, food service and entertainment area options.
3. A sample room set-up for the seminars and the general session. Include the style of seating, a list of available audiovisual equipment, and staffing (set-up, registration personnel, etc.) that your property can provide.

Summary

Food functions are an integral part of most meetings. Both association and corporate meeting planners rate the quality of foodservice as "very important" in their selection of meeting facilities. And, food and beverage functions are second only to guestrooms in generating revenue at most convention hotels.

So, while hotel sales and service people are generally primarily concerned with filling guestrooms, it is imperative that convention sales and service managers also be knowledgeable in the food and beverage area.

In addition to food and beverage functions, the success of a meeting is often judged by its impact on attendees. In today's world of high technology, it is a rare delegate who leaves a meeting whose highlight was a simple flip chart presentation. In the next chapter, we will take a look at how hotels are using today's sophisticated audiovisual equipment to enhance both large and small meetings and generate repeat sales for the property.

Endnotes:

1. Carol Bialkowski, "Emerging Trends: A Conversation with Top Hyatt F&B Executives," *Unconventional Cuisine*, © 2002, Hyatt Hotels Corporation, p. 6.
2. Ibid, p. 2.
3. Ibid.
4. *Meetings & Conventions*, March 1999, p. 21.
5. Carol Bialkowski, "Infusing Your Meeting With Local Flavor," *Unconventional Cuisine*, © 2002, Hyatt Hotels Corporation, p. 24.
6. Carol Bialkowski, "What's on the Menu?: Staying Ahead of Attendees' Food Issues," *pcma convene*, April 2004, p. 30.
7. Ibid, p. 32.
8. Bruce Myint, "Hotels Scramble to Cut Carbs," *Meetings & Conventions*, May 2004, p. 42.
9. Ruth Hill, "Association Meetings," *Meetings West*, August 2004, p. 1.
10. Jeanne O'Brien, "Sheraton Reveals New Food & Beverage Program," *Meeting News*.
11. Toni Giovanetti, "A La Carte Catering Emerges as the Favored Choice of Meeting Planners," *Hotel Business*, August 7-20, pps. 25-27.
12. Bob Skalnik, "Liquor Control," *Association and Society Manager*. Copyright Barrington Publications.
13. Cheryl-Anne Sturken, "Bar Codes: Understanding How Liquor Tabs Are Tallied," *Meetings & Conventions*, February 2004, p. 19.

Additional References:

• Alcohol and Meeting Planning, Meeting Professionals International www.mpiweb.org
• Controlling Alcohol Risks Effectively (CARE).

www.ei-alha-org/care.index.htm
- <u>Dining Room & Banquet Management, Third Edition</u>, Anthony J. Strianese and Pamela P. Strianese, Thomson Delmar Learning, 2002.
- <u>The Meeting Planner's Legal Handbook</u>, James M. Goldberg, MPI www.mpiweb.org
- <u>Meetings & Liability</u>, John S. Foster, CHSE www.mpiweb.org
- <u>On-Premise Catering</u>, Patti Shock and John Stefanelli, John Wiley and Sons, 2001.

Internet Sites:

For more information, visit the following Internet sites. Internet addresses can change without notice. If a site is no longer available at the address listed below, a search engine can be used to find the new address or additional, related sites.

The Catering Connection - www.caterconnect.com
Chef's Store - www.chefstore.com
Controlling Alcohol Risks Effectively (CARE) – www.ei-ahma.org/care.index.htm
Cuisine - www. cuisinenet.com
Food Net - www.foodnet.com
Internet Food Channel - www.foodchannel.com
National Association of Catering Executives (NACE) - www.nace.net
Training for Intervention Procedures by Servers of Alcohol (TIPS) - www.gettips.com
Virtual Vineyards - www.virtualvin.com

Study Questions:

1. Name several types of food and beverage functions commonly requested by meeting planners. Why is it necessary to have a separate function sheet for each?
2. What trends have affected the types of food served at functions? How have hotels responded to these trends?
3. What types of service are used for food functions? What factors determine the most effective type of service for a function?
4. Discuss the procedures used in establishing a guarantee for food functions. In what ways is attendance monitored to ensure the guarantee has been met?
5. What three different pricing methods are used to bill for liquor? How is control maintained for billing purposes?
6. Discuss the staffing and logistics common to beverage functions.
7. How does control of the food and beverage function differ between large and small properties? Distinguish between the role of catering manager and convention service manager.

Key Terms:

Á la carte catering. Catered events at which guests may choose from a number of different menu items.

Action station. Chefs prepare foods to order and serve them to guests. Popular items for action stations include omelets, crepes, pasta, grilled meat or shrimp, carved meats, sushi, Caesar salad and flaming desserts. Also called **Performance stations** or **Exhibition cooking**.

American/Plated service. Food is arranged on plates in the kitchen and brought to the guests.

Banquet captain. Person in charge of banquet service at food functions; supervisor of the servers. For small functions, the banquet captain also serves as maitre d'; for larger functions, he or she may be responsible for a specific area of the dining room.

Buffet service. A presentation of several food items from which the guests choose and serve themselves. Variations include **attended buffets**, at which chefs serve attendees, and **plated buffets**, at which a selection of pre-plated foods is set on a table from which attendees choose.

Butler service. At receptions, servers offer a variety of hors d'oeuvres on platters to guests. At dinners, food is presented by butlers on silver trays.

By the bottle. A charge for liquor based on full bottles served.

By the drink. A charge for liquor based on the number of drinks served.

By the person. A fixed price for liquor per attendee. This charge may cover all consumption of food and beverage (this is sometimes referred to as the **per person/unlimited consumption plan**). In some cases, beverages are charged per the person and food is ordered separately by the piece.

Call brand. Brand name liquor, distinguished from "house brand", selected by customer according to personal preference. Usually a higher quality than house brands.

Canapé. Hot or cold appetizer with a bread or cracker base.

Captain's bar. Self-service bar at which guests make their own drinks. This type of bar is always hosted.

Cash bar. Guests pay for their own drinks. Also called a **no-host bar** or **C.O.D. bar**.

Chef's tasting. The opportunity to sample a menu in advance of the event, usually in the company of the chef.

Corkage. Charge that is placed on beer, wine and liquor purchased elsewhere and brought into the facility.

Coupon sales. Attendees at a function purchase tickets for drinks from the hotel or from the host organization.

Covers. The number of meals served at a meal function.

Duoserve. A meeting service system in which food and beverage responsibilities are handled by catering while other aspects of servicing the group are handled by the convention service manager. Because responsibilities are separated, meeting planners have two hotel contacts.

Electronic pour. System of dispensing pre-determined exact amounts of liquor or non-alcoholic beverages per drink.

English/Family style service. Food is brought to the table and guests serve themselves. In some cases, the host cuts the meat and passes the tray to guests; the host may also have the meat cut by a server away from the table before it is placed before guests.

Free pour. Alcoholic drinks poured without the use of shot glasses or other measuring devices.

French service. Food service in which items are prepared tableside from a cart or gueridon. This type of service is best suited to small groups.

Guarantee. The minimum number of meals to be paid for by the client, even if some are not consumed. Usually, the hotel requires the planner to set this number no less than 48 hours prior to the event.

Head count. The actual number of people attending a food function.

Hors d'oeuvres. Small appetizers; hot and/or cold finger foods served at a reception.

Hospitality suite. Guestroom or suite used for receptions and entertainment. Usually stocked with beverages and light food. Often used by exhibitors at trade shows to entertain and sell delegates on their firm's products.

Host bar. Beverage plan for banquets or other functions in which the guests do not pay for drinks; the host is charged either by the drink or by the bottle. Also called an **open bar** or a **sponsored bar**.

House brand. Brand of wine or distilled spirits selected by a hotel or restaurant as their standard when no specific brand is specified. Also called a **well brand**.

Off-premises catering. The transportation of food, either fully prepared or in various stages of preparation, from a hotel's kitchen to a site away from the hotel.

On-premises catering. Servicing food and/or beverage functions in meeting rooms, function rooms and sleeping rooms within the hotel. Some on-premises events may extend to the hotel or restaurant grounds, but food and/or beverage is still served within the confines of the establishment.

Overset safety margin. Number of covers set over the guarantee. Billed to the client only if actually consumed.

Premium brand. Higher quality, higher priced hard liquor (spirits). The best and most expensive brands.

Pre-set service. Placement of some foods on banquet tables prior to the seating of the guests.

Reception. Stand-up social function, sometimes preceding a meal, at which beverages and light foods are served. Foods may be presented on small buffet tables or passed by servers.

Refreshment break. Short breaks between meeting sessions. Usually offering beverages and/or light food items, some are planned around a theme.

Russian service. Food is fully prepared in the kitchen and all courses are served on platters (or from tureens) to guests at their tables. A plate is placed in front of each diner and a server places food from the tray or platter on each plate.

Themed event. A function with a creative theme to make it more memorable. Themed events utilize elements that appeal to all five senses, incorporating sights (decorations and costumes), sounds, tastes (special food and beverages), touch and smells to create a unique experience for attendees.

Ticket exchange. Banquet control procedure whereby guests exchange an event coupon from their registration packet for an actual event ticket and seat assignment. This procedure increases control and tends to reduce the number of "no shows" to provide more accurate guarantees.

Uniserve. A meeting service system in which the meeting planner makes arrangements for both function space and food and beverage through one service contact, the convention service manager.

Learning Objectives:

This portion of your text introduces you to the wide variety of audiovisual equipment available to meeting planners today. We will also discuss the best options for meeting AV needs and provide guidelines for charging for audiovisual equipment and service. When you have studied this chapter, you will:

- Be able to describe the common types of audiovisual equipment and tell when each type is commonly used.

- Be able to detail the advantages and disadvantages of owning expensive audiovisual equipment versus contracting with outside sources for audiovisual needs.

- Understand how signs and notices are used by meeting planners and be able to discuss hotel procedures used to price and control the use of signage.

Outline

Outside or Inside?
- Audiovisual Specialists
- In-House Equipment

Types of Audiovisual Equipment
- Sound Systems
- Lighting
- Lecterns
- Screens
- Slide Projectors
- Overhead Projectors
- Rearview Projection
- Motion Picture Film Projectors
- Videotape and DVD Projectors
- Projection Systems for Computer Presentations
- Projector Stands
- Multimedia Presentations
- Simultaneous Interpretations
- Virtual Conferencing
- Spare Parts
- Other Presentation Devices

Charging for Audiovisual Equipment

Union Regulations

Signs and Notices
- Hotel Rules
- Sign Responsibility
- Price Schedule
- Locations

Summary

Understanding Audiovisual Requirements

Lee Sterbens
Director of Sales, Creative Services Division
Greyhound Exposition Services

"In the field of communications and information exchange, equipment and the technology used to operate it are changing rapidly. More and more people are using computers interfaced with monitors and video projectors to exchange information, compared to a few years ago when slides and transparencies were the norm. While convention service managers are rarely expected to be expert audiovisual technicians, they should be able to assist meeting planners with the selection of appropriate space and proper audiovisual equipment. Having a basic understanding of what equipment is required to achieve the desired goal will allow you to better serve your meeting groups and yourself."

15

Audiovisual Requiremnets

I t is a rare meeting today that doesn't incorporate an audiovisual presentation somewhere in its program. The more sophisticated users of AV systems require little help from the hotel staff. They know precisely what equipment they need and what is required in the facility. They may bring their own equipment or contact an AV service company for support.

In the past, most meeting needs were fairly simple. Meeting planners simply requested a few microphones, a slide projector and screen, a few flip charts and an occasional movie projector. Over the past two decades, however, technological developments in communication have led to audiovisual equipment and techniques that have greatly enhanced the meetings market. And today's sophisticated meeting planners want to take full advantage of these advanced capabilities (see Figure 15.1). It is not unusual for a meeting planner to request teleconferencing equipment, VHS/DVD players, personal computers and even multivisual synthesizers, quadraphonic sound and total immersion environments.

The meeting planner who is less knowledgeable about audiovisual systems will need support. Someone on the hotel staff should at least be familiar with, if not expert at, AV systems to provide such service or to help the planner get it locally. It is not realistic to expect convention sales and service personnel to be expert in every facet of the convention business, but all, especially the convention service manager, should keep abreast of new developments as well as be conversant in the terminology and requirements of today's AV technology.

Outside or Inside?

Since audiovisual equipment plays such a vital part in today's meetings business, properties are faced with the dilemma of how to make AV equipment available. Is it feasible to maintain a large in-house inventory, and, if so, what should be stocked? Or, would it be more cost-effective to have an outside AV firm provide the requested equipment? Or, as yet a third alternative, should the most commonly used items be stocked and outside AV firms be called upon to supply any special equipment requested by the meeting planner? In this section, we will take a look at the advantages and disadvantages of supplying AV equipment from outside sources or in-house (see box titled "Outside or Inside") and look at what factors figure into a property's decision on meeting AV requirements.

Audiovisual Specialists

Many hotel managers prefer to use a local AV service organization rather than cope with this area in-house. Outside rental firms are used when:

- the hotel lacks adequate storage space.
- equipment is used so infrequently that investment in a piece cannot be justified.
- the call for certain equipment, such as video projectors, is so heavy that it is not feasible for a hotel to inventory so many pieces.

Figure 15.1. TODAY'S "WIRED" MEETING ROOMS.

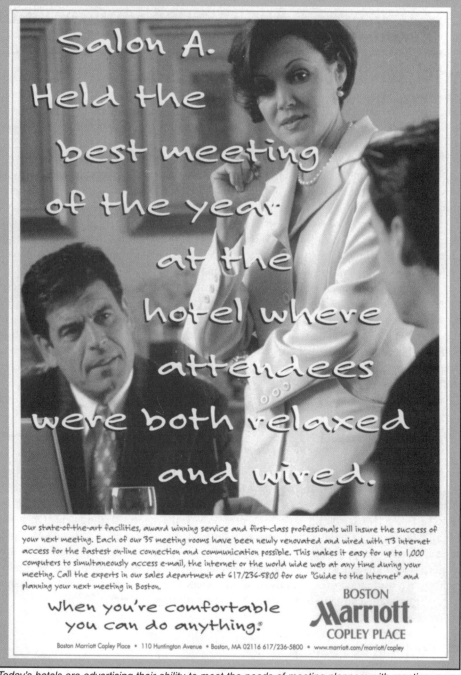

Today's hotels are advertising their ability to meet the needs of meeting planners with meeting rooms and equipment designed for the high-tech meetings common today. Note that this ad promotes T3 Internet access to enable attendees to access e-mail and the Web during the meeting.

When an outside firm is used, many convention service managers prefer to order the equipment themselves rather than have the corporation or association do it. There are three reasons for this. First, they are assured that the equipment will arrive in plenty of time to set it up. Second, they can determine how large to set the stage, since the screen is often placed on a raised platform. A third, not so admirable, reason is that AV companies often pay a commission to hotels that book them instead of the competition.

An outside company offers the hotel's client a specialist with a full staff and inventory of equipment. An expert staff can be relied upon to maintain the equipment and to handle any on-the-scene malfunctions. Many hotel managers have said that they would install an inventory of such equipment only when the volume of such rental would enable them to hire at least one full-time specialist to manage a small department. That person would assist in planning, setup, operation and service.

This is sound thinking when the hotel is in an area with good service companies. But in the more remote resort areas, the nearest AV dealer may be some distance away. If that is the case, last-minute malfunctions or additional needs can constitute a severe problem. Large conventions often contract with AV service companies that will go anywhere to handle the convention. The fees they charge are usually a small price for the convention organization to pay for a smooth AV presentation.

It is not practical to call in such organizations for the small meeting. Yet some meetings, particularly training ones, use a great deal of such equipment and need some assistance.

Outside or Inside

Hotels are faced with the decision of either owning AV equipment and leasing it to the meeting group or entrusting the AV needs of a group to an outside firm. The final decision will vary depending on individual property needs, and the following factors should be taken into consideration when making that decision.

Advantages of Using an AV Company Outside the Hotel

1. Audiovisual equipment is expensive. In the event of theft or lost items, the outside firm, rather than the hotel, would incur the loss.
2. Many audiovisual pieces are used so infrequently that the cost of maintaining an inventory would be prohibitive.
3. The cost of maintaining and repairing equipment is expensive and may not justify the hiring of a staff specialist to service audiovisual items.
4. With advances in audiovisual equipment, some items may become obsolete and require additional expenditure by the hotel.

Advantages of Owning AV Equipment and Leasing it to the Meeting Group

1. There may be a lack of suppliers in the area, or it may be difficult to rent a particular piece.
2. The property can purchase pieces that best meet its needs rather than have to rely on an outside contractor whose equipment may not be adequate.
3. The property has greater control over the quality of equipment if it owns it. Rental property may have been misused and may not function properly.
4. The property directly benefits from renting its own equipment to meeting groups, rather than turning the profits over to an outside firm.

In-House Equipment

If an arrangement with a local AV service company cannot be made, a hotel may decide to stock at least the basic AV requirements. Rick Stanfield, senior vice president of Opryland Lodging Group, cautions:

> "It is essential to track usage before investing in equipment. Do you have enough demand? Who will coordinate the AV service? These are important questions to answer. Go through a year's worth of records to see how often certain equipment is rented and calculate how many rentals will be necessary to break even. Look carefully, plot it on a graph because it's hard to get payback if your equipment is sitting on a shelf."[1]

The question might well be asked, "If a hotel is going to have its own equipment, what types and how much of each must be stocked?" Naturally, the type and quantity vary from hotel to hotel. Figure 15.2 shows the AV equipment supplied by a well-known resort

Figure 15.2. SAMPLE AUDIOVISUAL EQUIPMENT RATES.

AUDIO VISUAL

PROJECTORS
- Overhead Projector $30.00
- 35mm Slide Projector $30.00
- 35mm 50% Brighter $75.00

SCREENS
- 6' Tripod Screen $30.00
- 8' Tripod Screen $40.00
- 12' Cradle Screen $65.00

MICROPHONES
- Handheld Podium Mic. ...$15.00
- Wireless Lavalier $60.00
- Wireless Handheld $60.00

SPEAKER PHONES
- Speaker Phone (6 people) $30.00
- Polycom System (20 people) $75.00
- Gentner System (large groups) $250.00

TAPE RECORDERS
- Portable Cassette $15.00
- Stereo Cassette $40.00
- CD Player $40.00

VIDEO CAMERAS
- Camcorder $100.00
- Digital Video Camera $550.00

VIDEO MONITORS & TV's
- 25" Monitor $80.00
- 31" Monitor $150.00
- 51" Monitor $275.00

VIDEO PLAYERS/RECORDERS
- 1/2" VHS $50.00
- Beta SP $400.00

DATA & VIDEO PROJECTION
- LCD for Computer $350.00
- LCD for Video $400.00
- LCD 2000 Lumens $550.00

PRESENTATION AIDS
- Easel Only $10.00
- Flipchart (pad & easel) $25.00
- Whiteboard $20.00
- Corkboard $15.00

CARTS & STANDS
- Projection Carts $15.00
- TV/VCR Cart $20.00
- Safe Lock Stand (adjustable) $10.00

Additional Information:
Please call (435) 655-9898
Fax (435) 655-9899

WASATCH AUDIO VISUAL BUSINESS CENTER

Equipment is supplied and serviced by our on-site audio visual specialists, Wasatch A/V Business Center.

An experienced event consultant will preview your needs and arrange for hardware and technical support. This could range from the latest in giant screen projection from video or computer sources to an overhead projector and screen or a simple flipchart with colored markers.

Prices subject to change. Equipment subject to availability. This is a partial list only.

Source: Courtesy of Yarrow Hotel, Park City, Utah.

472

hotel. But no one list or rate schedule can be applied to every hotel; a hotel must consider the needs of its clients in offering the proper assortment of AV equipment.

Some hotels are reluctant to bring in local companies on a one-time rental basis for fear that the service may not be up to their own staff's standards. But if you call on a local company frequently, you have the muscle to demand *excellent service*, rather than the business-as-usual kind. After all, the malfunctions generally happen on the weekend or at night. If you can achieve a good working relationship with an alert and eager AV company, your problems are solved. If not, you had better set up some sort of department of your own.

Several hotels now contract with an AV company to set up an office at the hotel and store equipment there. Referred to as **in-house contractors**, these AV firms are often provided space rent-free but are required to pay a commission to the hotel when meeting planners contract for AV equipment. Bauer Audio Visual Inc. provides in-house services at 80 hotels. Other companies, such as AVW Audio Visual and Encore, have signed corporation-wide contracts with hotel chains. These AV firms know the facility and what will and won't work in each meeting room. Last-minute needs can be met quickly from the on-site storage of AV equipment. And, in-house companies provide convenient, consolidated billing for the planner.

Equipment used at a convention, then, can come from any of three sources — the *convening organization*, the *hotel* or an *outside AV specialist* hired by either the convention organization or the hotel. And equipment can come from any combination of the three.

The first need is to coordinate service. Another is to identify hotel equipment permanently to facilitate sorting equipment afterward. Use decals or permanent stencil imprints in paint. Many properties with in-house audiovisual departments are utilizing *bar coding* to both inventory equipment and to facilitate billing. Each type of equipment is labeled with its own bar code that can be scanned to generate reports as to where and how much is used, and charges can be instantly calculated and posted to the client's account.

Your own equipment will fare better from security and maintenance standpoints if responsibility for it is assigned to specific individuals. These people should receive special training in the care and operation of such equipment. Everyone in convention sales and service should be at home with the kind of equipment needed for most meetings. The dealer from whom the merchandise is purchased should agree to train your personnel; it requires merely some demonstration, not a lengthy course. And technical representatives of AV equipment manufacturers can be reached through the dealer to provide advice and training assistance.

Types of Audiovisual Equipment

The audiovisual equipment used for today's meetings can range from a simple flip chart to a sophisticated computer-generated multi-media presentation. In this section, we will take a look at the various types of AV equipment commonly used by meeting planners and see how each can be used to help stage a successful meeting.

Sound Systems

A sound system is the kind of AV system that most hotels own. A supply of microphones, microphone stands, amplifiers and speakers is the first purchased by a hotel staff.

Top-quality **amplifier** systems are a must. Speakers should be distributed so that there are no "dead spots" in sound. When sound systems are used with projection equipment, they should be located in the same area as the screen. Studies have shown that people tend to comprehend better when the sound and the visuals come from the same direction.

You need a variety of microphones, stands and long extension cables to handle meeting situations. It may be necessary to supply a mike for every one or two panelists at the head table or speakers at lecterns, and/or to have several microphones on the floor for questions from the audience. Ideally, the moderator and each speaker on a panel should have a microphone; if this is too costly, only then should microphones be limited to one for every two or three panelists...and they should be reminded beforehand to speak into the nearest microphone.

If you join any but a brand new facility, take inventory and have a list ready of what is available for use, in good working order. Call in a consultant on sound systems and find out what constitutes a basic inventory. Discuss this with experienced convention coordinators too.

Any basic inventory should include a variety of microphones. A **lavaliere microphone** is popular with speakers because it hooks around the neck with a ribbon or cord, leaving the hands free. It is always properly positioned. This type of mike has a variety of optional positions, such as the lapel of a business suit. It is also called a *lapel, neck,* or *pendant* microphone.

It is important that all microphones used with public address systems (lectern, table and floor mikes) be unidirectional. A **unidirectional microphone** picks up sound from only one direction (the speaker) and background noise (sounds coming from the sides and back of the microphone) is rejected. Windscreens (porous covers) also reduce the possibility of distracting sounds, such as blowing or popping.

A **standing microphone** is attached to a free-standing floor stand that is adjustable for height and angle. The stand has a sleeve or collar into which the mike can easily be placed. This type of mike, which is omni-directional (which means it picks up sounds from all directions), is typically used for questions or comments from the audience (in which case it is usually positioned in one of the aisles) or it can be used by a speaker or entertainer from the floor or stage.

A **roving microphone**, which is used to reach different parts of the audience, can also be equipped with a floor stand. Some models require a long cable to reach audience members, but some meeting planners prefer a **cordless/wireless microphone** when roving mikes are required. Cordless/wireless mikes come in two types: UHF (ultra high frequency) and VHF (very high frequency). UHF is usually preferred, but both types work well and offer freedom of movement. Wireless mikes offer the convenience of being able to move around the room without worrying about a cord (although you will want to make sure that these mikes have fresh batteries), but they are more expensive than microphones with cords and, in some cases, an audio mixer is required to control the sound if the cordless mike doesn't feature a volume adjustment.

A **table microphone** has a short stand that rests on a table, desk or lectern (the microphones, therefore, are sometimes called *lectern* or *podium mikes*). The mikes, which are usually attached to a gooseneck mike holder, are omni-directional, enabling more than one speaker to use a mike in close proximity to his or her position on the stage.

These should be tested in each room to make sure the signal doesn't come through neighboring amplifiers. Cordless microphones should only be used in situations where freedom of movement is important, as they can cause problems. Signal interference is possible from a number of sources: metal structures in the room, wire mesh in the walls, and even suspended ceiling framework can cause disruptions or distortion in the sound. And even the more expensive models can face such problems as weak signals and quality as batteries wear down. If wireless microphones are used, then, it is wise to have a backup system (such as a wired lavaliere microphone) immediately available.

All cables should be taped to the floor or carpet to avoid accidents in a darkened room. Avoid at all costs cables that run across the dais. Run such connectors along the front of the stage, hiding them in the draped skirting.

Have an attendant available during conventions. It helps to have the person on hand for the larger events and available for troubleshooting at smaller events such as workshops.

All systems should be set up and *tested* before the meeting. And spare microphones should be available; equipment is not indestructible. Find out if the meeting group plans to have someone in charge of volume control and distribution of microphones. The amplification system is crucial to the success of the meeting, and is an important part of the testing process. In cases where multiple microphones will be used, or when proceedings will be recorded, a sound technician will be needed to run a **mixer board**; the mixer board raises and lowers the volume from each input source, and will be located in the audience to enable the technician to hear exactly what the audience is hearing. In general, one mixer is required for two to four microphones and two mixers should be used for five to eight mikes.

If the hotel uses Muzak or similar background music or a paging system, make sure you can control or eliminate such distractions in each meeting room. This is essential. And many times larger rooms are subdivided by temporary walls and the controls are in only one segment. The meeting planner may not know which subdivision has the controls. Orient the convening organization staff to such control locations.

Lighting

Lighting requirements should be handled by a specialist. If the hotel has a permanent stage, a professional service company should equip it for versatile lighting. But most often, platforms are temporary and lights must be furnished on stands. If platforms are always placed in the same position in certain rooms, a permanent lighting booth may be constructed and equipped. Even smaller rooms need skillful light placement to improve visibility of screened presentations.

While the technical details should be left to a lighting professional, the convention service manager should have a working knowledge of the basic types and uses of lighting equipment.

Lighting requirements for small rooms are simple; for large rooms and audioriums they are more complex. Union regulations recognize this. Attendants are required for spotlight use when large rooms use stage lighting, and so on. They are usually not required for simple setups in small rooms. Don't forget to tell the client about union regulations and rates.

Some of the basic types of lighting include profile spots, follow spots, floodlights, and special effects lighting. **Profile spots** are also known as *ellipsoidal spots* or *lekos*, and are ceiling mounted with a range from 500 to 1,000 watts. Employing a halogen lamp, they are used to light lecterns, signs and the area of the stage nearest the audience to project background light patterns (colored filters are often used for this effect). Profile spots can also project gobo patterns, pre-cut designs that fit over the projected light to form light shapes, such as a company logo.

Follow-spots are cannon-shaped, movable lighting devices that are usually located to the rear of the auditorium. They are used to highlight and follow the speaker or performer, and require the services of a technician to ensure this added visibility is maintained. These lights are extremely brilliant, and may also be used with colored filters for a variety of effects.

Floodlights are usually used to light objects rather than people, and are often used to light backdrops (known as cycloramas) that serve as neutral backgrounds for the speakers. Floodlights are used to project a diffused, even light, and feature frames that can accommodate color filters for different effects.

Special effects lighting is used both for illumination and to "create the mood." Ballroom globes, strobe lights, ultraviolet lighting and laser lighting can be used to create a number of effects that enhance special functions — and can serve as visual centerpieces.

Dimmer switches on house lights are a must for meeting rooms. Delegates need partial illumination to take notes, while still being able to see the projection on the screen clearly. A control board is used to balance lighting to achieve the desired effect, and, depending on the complexity of the board, it may require lighting personnel or a lighting technician.

Lecterns

A **lectern** is a speaker's stand that holds notes and papers and has suitable illumination. More sophisticated lecterns have controls to enable the speaker to manipulate lighting and audiovisual equipment directly.

You should have a good inventory of table lecterns, floor models and some with self-contained sound systems. It is helpful if the lectern has a flat area that securely holds at least a water glass. This area should be large enough so that writing implements such as a pen, pencil, chalk or an electric pointer can be stored.

Lecterns should be easily accessible. They often must be approached in a relatively darkened room, so the access path must have some illumination. Cables must be taped, like those of microphones or light units. Tripping the guest speaker is not a recommended way to start a session.

Most hotels have their names or logos painted on the lectern faces. Because speakers are commonly televised and photographed, the hotel name can result in much publicity through local and national news media. It is often necessary to show some goodwill gestures to the TV people so they will compose the scene large enough to include the hotel logo.

Screens

Projection screens are often purchased by hotels. Larger ones must be tailor-made for the larger rooms, especially those hampered by a low ceiling. The charts in Figure 15.3 offer a guide to screen size selection under a variety of conditions and can help you decide where to place the projection stands when setting up.

There are several formulas used for determining seating capacity and screen placement. The two most commonly used are the *five feet rule* and the *one by six rule*.

The five feet rule states that the minimum distance from the bottom of the screen to the floor is five feet, while the average height of a seated person is four feet, six inches. Therefore, to view the screen clearly, the bottom of the screen must be a minimum of five feet off the floor.

The one by six rule states that no one should be seated closer to the screen than one times the screen's width nor farther from the screen than six times the screen's width. For example, if the meeting room's ceiling height is 15 feet, the maximum height for the projection screen is 10 feet, and if a 7-1/2 ft. high by 10 ft. wide screen is used, the farthest

Figure 15.3. GUIDE TO SCREEN SIZE SELECTION AND SEATING DISTANCE FROM SCREEN.

Choosing a screen size that takes full advantage of the specific type of projector and room size is as important as choosing the proper screen surface. Today's shorter projection lenses and larger rooms permit bigger, more lifelike projecting than ever. Now, for example, a 4" lens projects a 35mm slide to 60" height and width from a distance of only fifteen feet. And the zoom projectors need big screens to make the most of their capabilities. These charts are accurate guides to screen size selection. Make sure the screen selected is on the basis of the largest size slides or movies intended for projection.

16mm Movies

Lens Focal Length	Proj Distance	Screen Width			
		40"	50"	60"	70"
1"	D	9'	11'	13'	16'
1 1/2"	i	13'	17'	20'	23'
2"	s	18'	22'	26'	31'
2 1/2"	t	22'	27'	33'	38'
3"	a	26'	33'	40'	46'
3 1/2"	n	31'	38'	46'	54'
4"	c e	35'	44'	53'	61'

35mm Slides

Lens Focal Length	Proj Distance	Screen Width			
		40"	50"	60"	70"
3"	D	7'	9'	11'	13'
4"	i	10'	12'	15'	17'
5"	s	12'	16'	19'	22'
6"	t	15'	19'	22'	26'
7"	a	17'	22'	26'	30'
8"	n c e	20'	25'	30'	35'

Audience Capacity

Farthest Seat — 6 times screen width. First consideration when picking ideal screen for any room. (Assuming choice of lenses)
Closest Seat — Equal to screen width.
Audience Capacity — 6 sq. ft. per person after aisle space is deducted.
(Assumes ideal seating arrangement)

Screen Size	Farthest Seat from Screen	Closest Seat to Screen	Audience Capacity	Square Feet Seating Space
43" x 58"	30'	5'	88	531
54" x 74"	36'	6'	125	755
63" x 84"	42'	7'	169	1,018
72" x 96"	48'	8'	224	1,345
7 1/2' x 10'	60'	10'	350	2,100
9' x 12'	72'	12'	502	3,010
10 1/2' x 14'	84'	14'	684	4,110
13 1/2' x 18'	108'	18'	1,175	7,050
15' x 20'	120'	20'	1,400	8,400

Source: Reprinted from Basic Requirements for Meeting Room Facilities. *Used with permission by the Association of National Advertisers.*

seat from the screen should be no more than 60 feet and the closest seat no closer than ten feet.

Several other guidelines also apply to ensure maximum visibility. First, the distance from the projector to the screen should be at least 1.5 times the width of the screen. Second, the projection platform must elevate the projector to at least the bottom of the screen. Third, the projection platform should be placed at a 90-degree angle to the screen.

There are three options for placement of a screen: the center of the stage, to one side of center stage or in a corner. In deciding where to place the screen, it is important to determine which is more important in the presentation – the speaker or the information on the screen. If the speaker is conducting training, for example, the screen should be centered and the speaker should stand or sit off to the side. If the presenter is a motivational speaker or other special guest, he or she should be the focal point and the screen should be placed off to the side. Placing the screen in a corner is usually reserved as a space-saving measure when rear-screen projection is used.

You will also want to have a seating arrangement that offers an optimum relationship of the audience to the screen. The most desirable angle is between 45 and 90 degrees, although an angle of 22-45 degrees is acceptable, especially if the on-screen presentation is secondary to the speaker. Angles of less than 22 degrees are undesirable, as these angles would make it difficult to read the projected material.

When placing screens, you will also want to be sure that you do not block fire exits and that lighted exit signs or other lighting do not shine through the rear of the screen. The darker the area above the screen, the brighter the projected image will be. And, since most people are right-handed, place the screen to the speaker's right to enable the presenter to refer to projected material with his or her right hand.

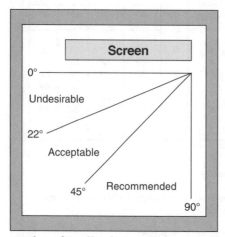

There are many types of screens available. The most popular of the larger screens is the **fastfold**, available in sizes up to 30 ft. high. The screen comes with adjustable legs to vary the height of placement off the floor (or it may be hung from the ceiling). They last a long time when taken care of and the smaller fastfolds represent a relatively minor investment. Local AV dealers may have a hard time supplying the huge screens, but no trouble supplying any number of small units.

You can give your fastfold screens a "movie theater" look by purchasing full dress kits made especially for these screens. Dress kits are curtains designed to be placed at the top and around the sides of the screen. The curtains add weight to the top of the screen, but additional support brackets will eliminate any potential problems. While using dress kits increases costs somewhat, meeting planners appreciate the "finished" look that dress kits provide for general or plenary sessions or other types of meetings for which a professional looking backdrop is important.

Wall or *ceiling screens* come in a variety of sizes and are designed to be hung from hooks or lines or mounted on the wall or ceiling. They are inexpensive and the metal tube casings make for easy storage. They are activated like the old-fashioned window shades.

Tripod screens, which come in a metal tube like the wall screen, are mounted permanently on folding tripod stands so that they can be placed anywhere. Light, portable, versatile, and inexpensive, they are extremely useful in smaller meetings. Tripod screens should be tilted forward or back at the top to avoid **keystoning**, an effect in which an image appears noticeably wider at the top than at the bottom and appears unfocused. And, for a more professional image, the bottom of the screen should be skirted.

There is a variety of screen fabric in use today. A favorite is **glass-beaded** (white), which offers great brilliance. As their name implies, the surface of these screens are covered with tiny glass beads that reflect a bright image back toward the audience. A disadvantage of this type of screen is that they have a narrow viewing angle. Smooth white **matte-surface screens** offer consistent brilliance from a wider angle, which is important in small rooms where some seats may be at a sharp angle to the screen, and are the most commonly used

SCREEN TYPE	ADVANTAGES	DISADVANTAGES	AUDIENCE SIZE
Fastfold	Excellent appearance Available in large sizes Good for rear projection Dress kits available to improve appearance	More expensive No anti-keystoning device available More labor intensive	6'x8' - up to 150 people 7.5'x10' - up to 200 people 9'x12' - up to 300 people 10.5'x14' - up to 500 people 12'x16' - up to 750 people 15'x20' - up to 1500 people
Wall/Ceiling Screens	Usually complimentary Can be large in size	Screen can't be moved Meeting room must be set around screen	Audience size will vary depending on size of screen
Tripod	Less expensive Anti-keystoning device available in sizes less than 8 ft. Fast installation	Largest size is 8-ft. Less attractive Full dress kit not available Cannot be used for rear-projection	60"x60" - up to 25 people 70"x70" - up to 50 people 84"x84" - up to 100 people 96"x96" - up to 150 people

types of screens. Silver metallic and **lenticular screens** surfaces combine the best features of both types, offering maximum brilliance and wide-angle light consistency. They are somewhat more costly than the others. Any local AV dealer can assist you in selecting the proper screens for your facility.

Slide Projectors

Slide projectors have improved tremendously over the years. The most popular tray is an 80-slide **carousel projector**. A 140-slide carousel is also in use, but it is preferable to use the 80-slide tray as much as possible; the 140-slide tray has the same diameter as the 80-slide tray, so the narrower width per slide often leads to jammed or damaged slides. Once a slide is positioned properly in the round slide tray that attaches to the top of the projector, it remains properly oriented and is not handled again. Of course, lack of rehearsals and careless tray filling still produce mishaps, but they are diminishing.

It is unfortunate that each brand of projector seems to take a different tray and the trays are not interchangeable. The situation is not as chaotic as it may seem because the Kodak Carousel slide projector is used by the vast majority of meeting presenters. It is extremely dependable and requires little maintenance and service other than lamp replacement. Spare lamps, fuses and extension cords should be on hand.

If it chooses to stock any slide projector, a hotel should select this one. There are various models under the Carousel designation but all take the common tray. Should a presenter use another brand of projector, he or she would have to specify it to an AV dealer who may be able to supply it, or just unload the trays and reload into Carousel trays, which every AV dealer has. This is a non-technical chore needing no tools and taking but a few minutes.

Such projectors are called 2 by 2 or 35mm size. They are so termed because they are designed for 35mm slide film mounted in standard frames measuring two inches by two inches. Happily, this is an industry standard. You may occasionally get a call for a projector to handle larger slide film such as 2-1/4 by 2-1/4 or 3 by 4 inch lantern slides, but not frequently.

A remote control device is often used for slide projectors. Both wired remotes and cordless remotes are available, with the wireless device giving the speaker additional mobility. When a remote device is used, it is advisable to have an assistant near the machine in case of a malfunction.

Many slide projectors can also be connected to an audiosync tape recorder. A silent electronic "cue" is added to a tape that provides music or a narrative accompaniment. As "cues" are processed, slides are automatically advanced.

A **dissolve unit** is required when two or more projectors are used in combination. A dissolve unit activates fade-in and fade-out of slides when two or more slide projectors are focused on the same screen. Dissolve units are widely used by meeting planners to avoid the light flash between slides when only one projector is used. When multiple slide projectors are used, a prerecorded tape may be synchronized with the slide sequence. The signal from the tape will activate the slide projector at the right moment.

To ensure proper functioning of equipment, the convention service manager should also have a working knowledge of the components of slide projector systems. Lenses, for example, are commonly a 4-to-6 zoom lens, but larger lenses are available if there is a need to project over longer distances. Specialized lenses are often quite expensive, but may be available from an AV company if there is a need for a non-standard lens.

Most slide projectors use a quartz-halogen bulb, but **xenon bulbs** are also available in cases where increased brilliance is required (when projecting over long distances, for example). The xenon bulb can be dangerous, however; it is filled with a high pressure gas, and its use and care is best left in the hands of an experienced operator. The availability of bulbs can be crucial to a presentation; it is wise to ensure that replacement bulbs are readily available in the event of a blowout during a presentation.

Overhead Projectors

An **overhead projector** is very popular for instructional use. Figure 15.4 illustrates how a speaker may draw or write on blank forms as he talks to his audience. The projector is positioned at the speaker and projects behind him onto a screen. Overhead projectors handle any brands of transparencies up to nine by nine inches. Such units are relatively inexpensive, rarely break, and are in great demand. Popular brands are the 3M Company, Singer, Beseler, and many others.

One of the most versatile developments in the field of overhead technology is the **computer projection panel** (also known as the LCD — liquid crystal display). This new development is an electronic device that is used instead of a transparency. The special attachment is attached to a personal computer, projecting whatever is on the computer monitor to the projection screen. Not only does this device make the image large enough for easy audience viewing, but it can also store and select data at the operator's command (see Figure 15.5)

Although most meeting planners are well versed in the layout of meeting rooms, occasionally the convention service manager will be called upon to advise in the placement of audiovisual equipment. Few things can destroy the effectiveness of a meeting more than the improper positioning of projectors and screens. No one wants to look down the

Figure 15.4. OVERHEAD PROJECTORS.

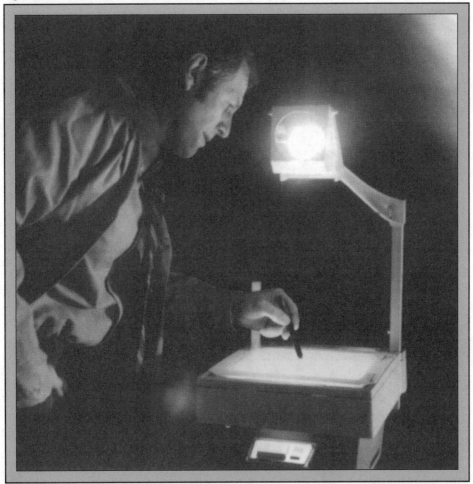

With an overhead projector, there is no need for the speaker to look at the screen to see the image being projected. The visual on the projector stage enables the speaker to see it exactly as the audience sees it. This enables the speaker to face the listeners and maintain eye contact, which stimulates audience reaction.
Source: Courtesy of the 3M Company.

back of someone's neck while the speaker explains the visuals. Obscured views can be prevented with a simple understanding of AV layout.

Figure 15.6 illustrates the proper positioning of an overhead projector so that the speaker does not block the audience's view. Figure 15.7 shows the best positioning of an overhead projector, a slide or filmstrip projector, and a movie projector. Review these illustrations thoroughly. Good visibility is foremost in communicating with visual techniques.

Rearview Projection

A visual presentation that is receiving wide use is **rearview projection**. The term "rearview" is somewhat of a misnomer because the audience still views the picture (slides, film or video visuals can be projected) from the front (see Figure 15.8). The projector, however,

Figure 15.5. LIQUID CRYSTAL DISPLAY (LCD) TECHNOLOGY.

An image may be projected from a computer monitor to a larger screen with the use of Liquid Crystal Display (LCD) technology. The LCD panel is used with an overhead projector; the LCD projector has a built-in light source.

Figure 15.6. SEATING ARRANGEMENTS WHEN USING OVERHEAD PROJECTORS.

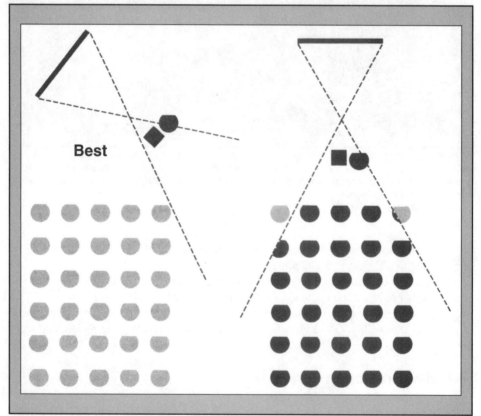

When using an overhead projector, the room should be arranged so that the audience's view of the screen is not blocked by the speaker and the projector. The seating arrangement on the left is best for viewing.
Source: Courtesy of the 3M Company.

Figure 15.7. MULTIMEDIA ARRANGEMENTS IN U-SHAPED SETUP.

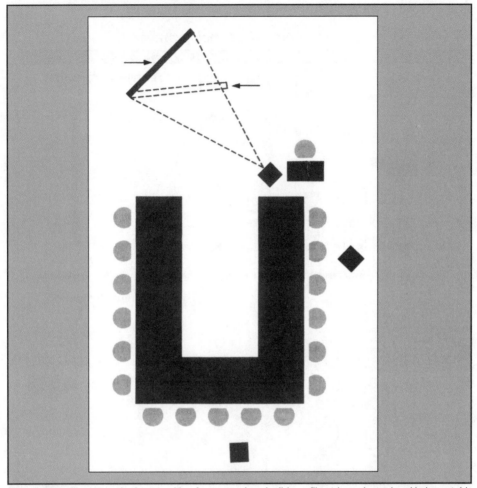

This diagram illustrates the best position for an overhead, slide or filmstrip projector in a U-shape table arrangement.

is set up behind the screen. By using a curtain or similar room divider, hotels can cut off one part of a room from the other. The audience sits on one side of the partition, the projector on the other. A **translucent rear-projection screen** is framed by the curtain, and the projection equipment is hidden on the darkened rear side.

Three of the most commonly used self-contained rear-projection units are Telex's Caramate, Kodak's Audioviewer, and Bell & Howell's Ringmaster. These units resemble small television sets with a slide tray on top; slides can be advanced manually or through the use of an audio tape programmed with silent "cues" (pulses).

The primary advantage of this technique is that all projection equipment is hidden from the audience, eliminating the need for an aisle. The disadvantage is that the room cannot be fully used for seating (rearview projection reduces the available square footage for seating up to one-third). Another disadvantage is that rear projection requires an almost completely dark projection area behind the screen, requiring complete draping of the screen -- sides, bottom and top (the area of the room where the audience is seated does not need to be darkened). In addition, if space behind the screen is limited, a more expensive wide-angle lens may be required. On the positive side, however, rearview projection can be effective as it allows the speaker more freedom of movement and the presentation can appear more dramatic as the image seems to appear out of nowhere.

Figure 15.8. COMPARISON OF COMMON PROJECTION SYSTEMS.

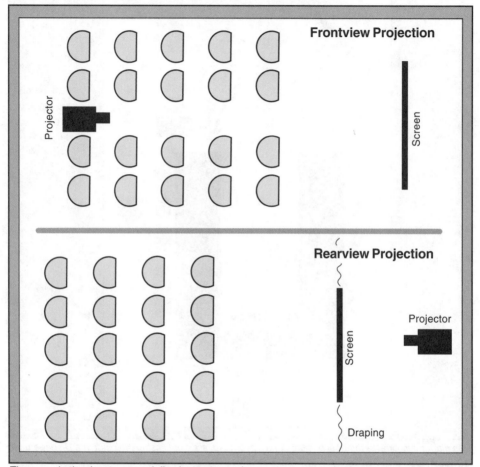

There are both advantages and disadvantages to the two common projection systems detailed in this figure. Front view projection systems do not take up a lot of space. Disadvantages include possible interference (as when attendees walk across the projected beam of light) and the danger of speakers or attendees tripping over cords or other equipment. With rearview projection systems, there is no need to dim lights, allowing attendees to take notes. The primary disadvantage of these systems is their size; not only do they take up a lot of space (typically 15 to 30 feet behind the screen), but the area behind the screen must also be completely dark, reducing the square footage available for seating.

Motion Picture Film Projectors

When movies are shown at meetings, they are most frequently the 16mm size. Fortunately, any 16mm film, sound or silent, black & white or color, can be shown on any 16mm projector. There are a number of brands on the market, and such variations as the slide trays discussed earlier for slide projectors are not found in motion picture projectors. The projectors can be used interchangeably.

The sound system built into motion picture projectors is often poor; in larger meeting rooms, an independent subsidiary sound hookup should be used. The sound from a 16mm projector can be "patched" into the property's built-in sound system for greater clarity.

Motion picture film projectors require an operator to thread the film into the projector, although some have an automatic feeding system (preferred by most convention service departments). To be on the safe side, however, a trained projectionist should be available in the event of a malfunction in the automatic system.

Another consideration when dealing with motion picture projectors is the lamp system. As with slide projectors, a higher intensity bulb is required when images must be projected over longer distances. A MARC (mazda closed arc) projector can be used when greater clarity is required, while a Xenon 16mm projector is the most powerful projector for long-distance projection (a professional projectionist is required for this equipment).

It is wise for the convention service manager to check out the room setup and the audiovisual equipment supplied before the meeting starts. He or she should check:

- the *screen*, to see if it is above the audience's heads so that all will be able to see clearly from where they sit.
- the *projector*, to see that it is secure on the stand and that an extra lamp is available.
- the *speaker*, to see that he or she is near the screen; and
- the *electrical cords*, to be sure they are out of the aisle and hidden.

Videotape and DVD Projectors

With the growing use of videotape and DVD (digital video discs) for meeting presentations, many properties are finding it imperative to provide video playback equipment and support.

Video projectors and DVD projectors are essential for viewing videotapes or digital video disks in all but small groups. A self-contained video projector has a curved six-foot screen that can easily be seen by audiences of up to 100 people.

While several of these units can be used for larger groups, it is usually more effective to use a detached video or DVD projector and a fastfold projector screen in larger rooms. This equipment offers a quality image 12 feet wide, and can be used for both front or rear projection.

For arenas and other larger areas, light-valve video projectors must be used. This type of projector projects up to 400 feet and creates an image roughly 40 feet wide. It may not be feasible to purchase this type of projector. It is more practical to rent them when the need arises.

On the other end of the meetings spectrum, television sets can be used to service small meetings. Television falls into two categories: monitors and receivers.

A **monitor** has no tuner, and interprets signals directly from a videotape player or DVD player or video camera. Monitors are more costly than television receivers, but are often requested by meeting planners due to the crisper image they produce. The next level of video monitors is high definition television (HDTV) and plasma screens. These monitors are only six inches thick and up to 50 inches in size. While available, these monitors are costly and, as yet, are not used as extensively by meeting planners.

Receivers are used to interpret and reproduce television signals, but cannot play videotapes without the use of a videotape player. And, while television receivers have built-in audio systems, these are usually of a mediocre quality; it is advisable to patch sound into the property's sound system rather than to rely on the units' audio systems.

Signals from videotapes can be split to feed a number of monitors and television receivers, and the number of units needed will depend on the size of the audience. A general rule of thumb is 25 viewers per 25-inch set and 50 viewers per 25- to 36-inch set.

Since video is widely used, it is important that the property have compatible tape equipment readily available. The basic formats available in the United States are:

- VHS (Video Home System) — uses 1/2-inch tape and is the most popular variety of tape with meeting planners.
- Betacam, Beta SP — is the common video format for presentation graphics and is the most widely used format in today's meetings market.
- U-Matic or Industrial — uses 3/4-inch tape and generates a better image than VHS. These formats are generally used for educational tapes.
- Broadcast video — 1- or 2-inch tape, used primarily by television stations and production houses; will rarely be requested by meeting planners.
- Video 8 — another Sony product that uses small cassettes (only slightly larger than standard audio cassettes). This format is rarely used, but may be found in exhibits, where space is at a premium.

It is important to note that none of these tape formats is compatible with any of the others. And, problems may also arise if speakers or presenters are from foreign countries. A NTSC standard is used for tapes in the United States, while Europe, Africa, Australia and Southeast Asia use a PAL standard, and the SECAM standard is used in Russia, France and the Middle East. It is usually impractical to stock equipment to accommodate foreign standard tapes, but the convention services department would be wise to locate audiovisual suppliers that can provide this equipment when needed.

Projection Systems for Computer Presentations

Throughout the meetings industry there has been a very rapid movement to computer-driven presentations. Slide, film, and overhead transparency projection is being replaced by computer projection at many gatherings.

There are two primary types of projection systems available for personal computer-based presentations: liquid crystal display (LCD) computer panels and computer projectors.

Liquid crystal display computer panels, discussed in the previous sections, are units that sit atop an overhead projector. The LCD panels are connected to a computer, and images on the computer screen are then displayed on the overhead projector.

A more recent innovation, and one that is preferred by many meeting planners, is the **computer data projector**. These stand alone projectors are equipped with their own built in light source into which the computer plugs directly. There is no need for an overhead projector when using this device.

Computer programs, such as Microsoft PowerPoint, are commonly used with this type of projector. These programs allow color, animation and graphics to be projected from computers onto a screen.

An even higher-end projector used in large function rooms where a large screen is required is the **DLP projector (digital light projection)**. DLPs are lighter (three to seven pounds is common), more portable, brighter (with extremely high light output of up to 15,000 lumens) and have a better image quality. While more expensive, they provide better resolution at greater distances.

Projector Stands

Projectors have to be placed on something. It may be a table or desk, but it is more versatile and convenient to have special projection tables or stands. These come in folding and rigid types. Some have casters for easy movement; with these stands projectors may be placed anywhere in a room.

There are two basic types of projector stands: the Safelock and the rolling cart. The Safelock is ideal for large projectors, and has four telescoping legs that adjust to heights up to 56 inches. Rolling carts come in several fixed heights, with the 32-inch and the 54-inch the most commonly used. The 32-inch rolling cart is ideal for overhead projectors, while the 54-inch cart is usually used for television monitors. When using rolling carts, regardless of height, **skirting** (pleated or ruffled draping) should be used to wrap the lower portion of the cart. (Skirting, which gives a professional, finished look, should also be used at the bottom of projection screens).

Permanent projection booths can be constructed for larger rooms. The screen chart in Figure 15.3 will help you choose the proper lens to fill the screen from such a fixed position. Lenses of extra-long focal lengths for long projection distance may not always be in stock but can be ordered from local AV dealers. Check local fire and union regulations regarding projection booth operations.

Multimedia Presentations

This concept uses several types of audio and visual equipment to create total sight/sound environments. **Multimedia** can range from the very simple to highly sophisticated systems, and convention service managers should have a working knowledge of the basic types of equipment commonly requested by meeting planners.

The simplest form of multimedia is the sound/slide synchronizer. This type of equipment was mentioned in the slide projector section of this chapter. It uses a sound tape that automatically advances the slides and provides music or narration during the slide presentation.

Slide projectors can also be teamed with dissolve units. Dissolve units alternate two or three slide projectors focused on the same screen. These units fade and overlap images to create a smooth multimedia presentation.

Programmers are the ultimate in multimedia equipment. The computerized control can be used to synchronize sound tracks and multiple slide projectors on multiple screens (and can even turn the lights off in the room) for a stunning audiovisual performance. And, as video continues to become a popular alternative to slides, multimedia is becoming even more exciting as a motivational and communications tool.

Simultaneous Interpretations

As meetings become more international in scope, many properties have found it necessary to provide **simultaneous interpretation** facilities. This involves having a speaker's words translated into the language(s) of the meeting participants, and requires specialized equipment and personnel.

In most cases, the speaker addresses the group and an interpreter (or interpreters) in soundproof booth(s) relays what the speaker has said to the attendees via wireless headsets.

The number of booths and headsets needed will depend on the number of languages required for the meeting.

Today's technology has enhanced this process. Loop antennas can be used within certain areas to enable attendees to hear their language within that area. And, infrared signals are also used to beam a language to attendees. Another development is multiple channel selection, which enables attendees to channel back and forth between different languages.

While simultaneous interpretation can be costly, both in terms of equipment (sound booths, headsets, antennas or infrared radiators) and personnel (interpreters and technicians), more meeting planners will require this service in today's increasingly international business world, and the properties that offer this capability can capture a share of this growing — and lucrative — market.

Virtual Conferencing

In an increasing number of cases, meeting planners have found that it is virtually impossible — or too costly — to bring all persons that should be involved in a meeting together in person. Conflicting schedules and the high cost of travel are the prime factors for the use of **virtual conferencing**. The most recent Meetings Market Report conducted by *Meetings & Conventions* found that approximately 25% of corporate meeting planners use virtual conferencing.

Virtual conferencing can be broadly defined as the electronic linking of more than two people at different sites, and falls into four basic categories: audio, audiographic, video and web conferencing.

Audio conferencing, the most basic form, is generally used when budget is a major consideration. Audio conferencing simply utilizes the telephone lines and speaker phones to connect several parties. A speaker can give a presentation to meeting "attendees" at several locations via speaker phones or special microphones and amplifier systems tied directly to the telephone lines of the participating properties or alternate remote sites.

Audiographic conferencing is generally used for planning sessions, project reviews and briefings because it combines both audio interaction and visual capabilities. Specially designed conference rooms offer the ability to "show" documents, slides, and objects via television monitors at the remote sites.

Video satellite conferencing provides full-motion, "face-to-face" networking, and is the most expensive and the most sophisticated form of virtual conferencing. Remote sites are "linked" through the use of satellite technology, and many properties now offer this type of conferencing network.

Video conferencing involves considerable expense. First, it is necessary to provide full video production, which involves multiple video cameras, technicians and special effects equipment. Second, it is necessary to provide a playback system at each location. This equipment includes multiple video monitors or video projectors. Third, uplink/downlink and satellite facilities are required. Special equipment (telephone lines, cable or a microwave system) sends the signal from the origination point to a satellite dish ("uplink" or "earth station") which beams the image to the satellite (22,000 miles or more above the earth). The signal is received by a transponder (an access point on the satellite), the frequency is changed, and the signal is beamed down to satellite dishes ("downlink") at each remote location before it travels, again via telephone line, cable or microwave system, to the remote receivers.

Figure 15.9. HIGH SPEED INTERNET SERVICES.

Today's meeting planners often require high access speed for presentations generated from remote locations for viewing on computers and projection screens. Hotels, conference facilities and convention centers are meeting this requirement by installing – and promoting – their state-of-the-art, high-speed Internet services.
Courtesy of Chaparral Suites Resort, Scottsdale. Used with permission.

While this process requires a large initial investment, many properties have found it worthwhile to purchase or lease uplink systems or find other ways to offer video-conferencing services. Sheraton Hotels and Resorts, for example, went into partnership with VueCom, which provides videoconferencing services transmitted over high-speed, fiber-optic lines. The system, which is easily adapted to various meeting sizes, is installed at approximately 140 properties.

Other chains, including Promus, Westin and Hyatt, currently offer videoconferencing or are in the process of reintroducing this service. Their investments in this technology may pay future dividends, as adverse circumstances — a fuel crisis, worsening economic trends, or other negative shifts in the business world — make video conferencing a viable alternative to costly meeting travel and accommodations.

The newest alternative to face-to-face meetings is **web conferencing**. Web conferencing refers to conducting meetings, events and seminars over the Internet. Web-based presentations utilize an Internet connection rather than satellites. While the sponsoring organizations still have the advantage of saving time and travel expenses as "attendees" can participate without leaving their offices, the Internet is less costly than satellite uplink/downlink services.

There are a number of different ways that speakers can connect to the Internet. The easiest, least expensive, but slowest connection is through a telephone line. Many planners find this access too slow and prefer the high-speed connections possible with ISDN (Integrated Services Digital Network), T1 or T3 lines (T1 lines operate at a higher capacity than an ISDN line and can be "split" to accommodate several users at once; T3 lines are even faster than T1 lines, allowing more tasks to be performed simultaneously at the higher speed). Since these lines ensure that Web information will appear very quickly on computer and projection screens, many hotels, conference facilities and convention centers are installing these types of lines throughout their meeting rooms. Figure 15.9 shows how the Chaparral Suites Resort in Scottsdale, Arizona promotes their meeting technology, including ISDN, voice and modem lines at T1 speed.

Spare Parts

If you have your own projectors — slide, movie, video, computer-based or overhead — you should maintain a stock of spare lamps. Keep fuses at hand if the hotel is not wired with circuit breakers. Someone on the convention service staff should know how to select the proper lamps, replace burnt-out ones, and instruct others in the operation of the projectors. This attention to detail can be very important to meeting planners (see Figure 15.10)

Other Presentation Devices

Not all presentation is done by film, of course. Many speakers use *chalkboards*. Some call them *blackboards*, but most of them are green these days. These may be permanently installed, hung on a wall, or used on a tripod **easel**. Make sure the chalkboard is washed clean and that chalk and *clean* erasers are supplied. To enliven the presentation, an assortment of colored chalk is preferable to white or yellow chalk only. It is the hotel's responsibility to provide the meeting planner with first-class chalkboards, blackboards and easel charts. Such equipment that is in need of repair is unsightly and difficult to work with.

A *whiteboard* is cleaner and more convenient than a chalkboard, and can be used as an impromptu projector screen as well as for easy-to-read, readily correctable presentations. Instead of chalk, dry-erase markers are used, and many whiteboards are marked like graph paper, making it easy for a speaker to write or draw in a straight line.

Whiteboards are also available in electronic versions. One model, Panasonic's Panofax, reproduces everything written on it or taped to it. When desired, a photocopy of everything on the board can be made with the push of a button. This eliminates extensive note-taking, which often distracts attendees from what the speaker is saying.

The Gemini Blackboard is another technological improvement of the whiteboard. This device has capabilities to send materials written on it to another board (sometimes

Figure 15.10. SOLVING PROBLEMS FOR MEETING PLANNERS.

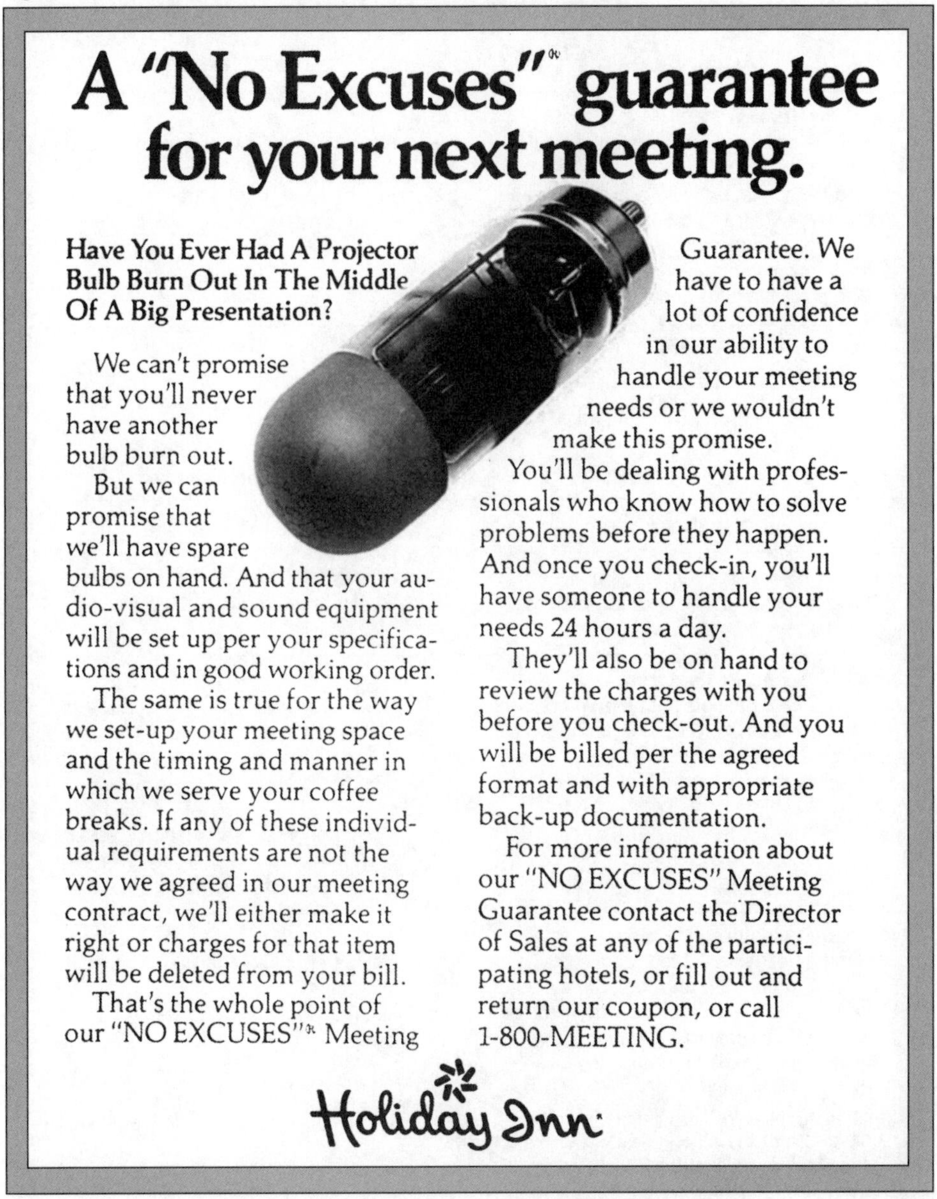

Many meeting planners worry about small details. This ad featuring Holiday Inns' "No Excuses" meeting guarantee assures meeting planners that each property is ready to handle any problem that might arise — including having spare lamps on hand to ensure that presentations can go on as planned.

thousands of miles away) via a telephone line. This application has become increasingly popular as more meeting planners are turning to teleconferences.

The SoftBoard, shown in Figure 15.11, is another example of this technology. SoftBoards are connected to a computer and store everything written on them into the computer using two infrared lasers mounted at the upper corners of the boards. Information is generated through the use of bar-coded dry erase markers, allowing the lasers to track their position and color. Information is captured stroke by stroke and can be "played back" at various speeds or stored on disks, e-mailed or cut and pasted into other files.

Advantages and Disadvantages of Popular AV Equipment

Advantages	Disadvantages
Slide Projectors 1. Can be operated with wireless remote control device. 2. Can be connected with audio-sync tape. 3. Excellent color reproduction on slides. 4. Can be computer programmed for multi-image productions. 5. Can project a larger image.	1. Limited motion capabilities compared to video. 2. Fan noise can be distracting.
Motion Picture Projectors 1. Full motion capabilities. 2. Excellent color rendition. 3. Can project large, quality images.	1. Difficult to feed unless equipment has automatic threading mechanism. 2. Built-in speakers are often of poor quality; sound may have to be "patched" to the facility's sound system.
Flip Charts and Chalkboards 1. Very inexpensive. 2. Take up very little seating space. 3. Ideal for "brainstorming" and training meetings.	1. Limited to small audiences (50 persons or less). 2. Messy and often difficult to erase.
Computer Based Projectors 1. Most are compatible with laptop computers. 2. Powerpoint and electronic graphics make for powerful presentations. 3. Possible to provide Internet connection.	1. Resolution (sharpness of image) doesn't match slides or film. 2. Technology changes about every 18 months so equipment can become obsolete. 3. Not as bright as overhead projectors so glass-beaded screens may be needed to provide a brisker image.
Overhead Projectors 1. Can be used in a lighted room. 2. Simple to operate, and transparencies can be produced quickly on a copy machine. 3. Speaker can control presentation by highlighting or marking on transparency during presentation. 4. Speakers can face audience and do not have to turn their backs (as is the case with chalkboards or flip charts).	1. Noise from built-in fans can be a distraction. 2. Limited color reproduction.
Video Projectors 1. Instant playback capabilities. 2. Full motion and color capabilities. 3. Simple to operate. 4. Video display of computer-generated information is possible.	1. Various formats of playback equipment are incompatible. 2. Difficult to project for large audiences.

Paper easel pads or **flip charts** are commonly used with broad soft-point pens, markers or crayons. These are always portable, using handy tripod easels. There are special cabinets to house them. If you have rooms used extensively for training classrooms, you may find it convenient to mount such flip-charts. The Oravisual Company has a selection of these, which are readily available from audiovisual and art supply dealers.

Figure 15.11. HIGH-TECH COMPUTER APPLICATIONS FOR PRESENTATIONS.

The SoftBoard shown above connects to a computer, which stores information written on the board with bar-coded dry erase markers. The device's playback mode works like a VCR, and information generated can also be stored on a disk, e-mailed or cut and pasted into other files.

Flip charts are generally 27x34 inches in size, and should be limited to use in small meeting rooms. When ordering flip charts, the convention services department needs to specify "flip chart easel with pad;" this will differentiate from the order for "tripod easels," which support signs but not the heavy flip chart pads. Some properties charge extra for pads and markers and supply the easels only; others include all materials needed for the presentation in the basic charge— easel, pad, and specified colors of markers.

Pointers have become more sophisticated since the days of long wooden ones. Many speakers use metal pointers that telescope down to ball-point pen size. There are also electric hand-held **laser pointers** that can project an arrowhead onto the screen from 100 feet away, allowing a greater freedom of movement for the speaker.

Another device, which is used for presentations, communication, and training, is the personal computer. Most meeting planners realize that computers can easily become damaged in transit, and look for properties that can supply personal computers for workshops and training sessions (as well as for on-site convention registration).

While the cost of stocking computers may be prohibitive, many properties make arrangements with a local computer rental center when needed. Other properties have found that the establishment of computer systems has generated sufficient bookings to prove profitable. Yet a third alternative is for the property to "link up" with a nearby computer facility.

Hotels are not expected to supply the gear for sophisticated AV presentations such as multi-screen extravaganzas. These are usually handled by specialists. Local AV dealers or service organizations can handle such needs if you get requests for such sources.

It is usually enough for hotels to be able to supply on short notice such basics as slide projectors, overhead projectors, 16mm sound projectors, screens, chalkboards, and easel

493

Sample AV Equipment List/Price Sheet

A listing such as this one can be used to give the meeting planner an at-a-glance look at exactly what audiovisual equipment will be used for a meeting or function and its overall costs. This list can also be helpful to the property's convention service department, as it provides an overview of the equipment that will be in use on specific days.

Source: Bill Masheter, "AV Bids," Association Meetings. Used with permission.

AV Flowsheet

Meeting: **American Association of Widget Waxers**
Property: **Hotel Unique**
City: **Heartland**

Room: **All**
Session:
Dates: **March 14–20, 199**

EQUIPMENT	BASE COST	Thu 14 (QTY)	Fri 15	Sat 16	Sun 17	Mon 18	Tues 19	Wed 20	TOTAL
Tripod screen 70" x 70"	$18.00		5 — $90.00	8 — $144.00	6 — $108.00	6 — $108.00	7 — $126.00		$576.00
Tripod screen 84" x 84"	$24.00		1 — $24.00	1 — $24.00	1 — $24.00	1 — $24.00	2 — $48.00	1 — $24.00	$168.00
Tripod screen 96" x 96"	$30.00							2 — $60.00	$60.00
CPE fastfold screen 10' x 10' front	$55.00		2 — $110.00	1 — $55.00	1 — $55.00	1 — $55.00	2 — $110.00		$385.00
CPE fastfold screen 12' x 12' front	$85.00		1 — $85.00	2 — $170.00	2 — $170.00	2 — $170.00	2 — $170.00	1 — $85.00	$850.00
2 x 2–35mm slide projector Kodak EKIII	$27.50		4 — $110.00	7 — $192.50	6 — $165.00	5 — $137.50	8 — $220.00		$825.00
2 x 2–35mm slide projector Kodak EKIII Britelite projector	$48.00		4 — $192.00	3 — $144.00	2 — $96.00	3 — $144.00	2 — $96.00	4 — $192.00	$864.00
2 x 2–35mm slide projector 500w xenon	$200.00			1 — $200.00	2 — $400.00	1 — $200.00	2 — $400.00	4 — $0.00	$1200.00
2 x 2 long lens	$15.00		7 — $105.00	7 — $105.00	7 — $105.00	7 — $105.00	8 — $120.00	4 — $60.00	$600.00
Safelock stand	$10.00		5 — $50.00	9 — $90.00	7 — $70.00	6 — $60.00	8 — $80.00	1 — $10.00	$360.00
Overhead projector	$27.50		5 — $137.50	10 — $275.00	6 — $165.00	5 — $137.50	8 — $220.00		$935.00
32" cart w/drape	$15.00		5 — $75.00	10 — $150.00	4 — $60.00	8 — $120.00	11 — $165.00	3 — $45.00	$615.00
16mm projector	$35.00		1 — $35.00				1 — $35.00		$70.00

pads. Beyond this, advance notice should be given and a specialist dealer called in. A meeting planner should supply a list of all AV needs in advance.

To sum up, a hotel should have a good working relationship with a local audiovisual dealer/service organization. If such a company is not available, the hotel may decide to stock a department of its own. In either case, a hotel may choose to stock a minimum number of basic items and train staff people to maintain and operate them.

Charging for Audiovisual Equipment

No single rule can be established for how much a hotel should charge for AV equipment. Competition and the availability of outside firms, the number of guest rooms occupied, the extent of food and beverage functions, and the amount invested in equipment are some of the variables that must be considered in establishing a policy.

In some cases, the client deals directly with the AV supplier if an outside supplier is used. In other cases, you may contract with the outside service and pass the charges along to the client. Whether you use outside services or provide in-house equipment, you should supply a list of your prices to the client. A form detailing the specific equipment to be used and the cost for each piece is commonly used to provide an at-a-glance overview of AV charges (see box titled "Sample AV Equipment List/Price Sheet").

Remember when figuring your prices to include any additional charges, such as delivery costs, set-up charges, labor requirements (technician, sound mixer, etc.), and other miscellaneous fees (the cost of bringing extra electricity to a room, for example). These costs may be figured into the price of the equipment, in which case you may wish to add a notation to that effect on your form. Or, additional costs may be listed separately on your form.

In any case, it is bad business to surprise the meeting planner with hidden costs; he or she must often work within an AV budget and should know exactly what will be charged for the entire meeting beforehand.

A logbook should be used to control the rental of audiovisual equipment. The log should contain the date ordered, the item, the delivery date, the guest billed, and the banquet check number. If an outside agency is billing the hotel, each invoice should be approved by the convention service manager and recorded in the logbook before sending it to accounting.

Union Regulations

One of the biggest complaints of meeting planners is the influence that unions have on the operation of audiovisual equipment. When AV equipment is ordered from outside firms, technicians are often part of the package. Projectionists, sound recording engineers, spotlight operators and other specialists with expertise in complicated equipment are required. The problem arises when the services of a projectionist really aren't needed, but the union contract calls for such a person whenever the equipment is used. One convention manager told us:

> "One of the biggest complaints by convention groups coming to our city
> is the requirement to pay the high union scale for some person to sit idly
> by and run a machine that anyone can operate. In some cities the meeting

planner or his people can't even plug the equipment in, but must wait for a union projectionist."

While this may seem a little farfetched, the situation is actually becoming more common. And it is unlikely that union restrictions will be eased. Hotels should inform meeting planners of such rigid union regulations; a violation can lead to work stoppage and a crisis in the convention.

Signs and Notices

Only the simplest meeting can make do without *signs* and *notices*. They are most obvious when absent. The convention organization has a great stake in making sure that all goes smoothly, and signs are a great help within the convention area. Many convention planners are inexperienced, so the hotel must stand ready to advise and supply. Unless you want to scramble at the last moment, you should remind the client of the need for such signs and notices and expedite the creation of them.

Hotel Rules

Hotel and convention facilities need rules about the use of signs to avoid damage to walls and doors by indiscriminate use of tapes and tacks. It is a wise hotel that builds sign holders in crucial areas of its convention space.

The best kind are permanent frames on or near doors of meeting rooms that hold standard-sized card stock for signs. Bulletin boards and other movable signboards are handled easily on short notice. Those reliable tripod easels make great sign holders and are most versatile.

A printed form outlining the hotel rules on signs should be submitted to the convention organizers to be included in their convention manuals. Figure 15.12 shows a typical sign policy regarding signs and their placement.

Hotel rules regarding distribution of notices also should be outlined clearly. Companies at trade conventions frequently request to distribute printed material at strategic points within the hotel or even to place them at the door of each delegate's room. Daily convention newspapers, newsletters and advertising material are distributed in this manner.

The hotel should inform the organization if it is willing and able to undertake such distribution and if it charges for the service. The convention organizer should be directed to inform the participants about the recommended procedure to follow for such service.

It is important to learn if the convening organization has any policy about signs and distribution of newspapers, magazines, newsletters, advertising materials or any other printed matter. The policy should be aided by the hotel staff's compliance, and all such requests should be referred to the convention staff. Hotel personnel should either handle or supervise the hanging of posters or signs.

Sign Responsibility

It is the convening organization's responsibility to create signs. The convention service manager should be alert and advise when he or she notices that they are not being planned. A discussion of signs is helpful. The inexperienced meeting planner will appreciate it; the old pro won't mind the reminder.

The program indicates the need for signs. If the organization supplies them, the hotel is freed from the responsibility. We would suggest documenting that decision with a memo or letter. Most often, however, it is easier for the organization to have the signs made through the hotel to save the bother of transporting them.

Regardless of who accepts the responsibility of supplying signs, invariably a few more are needed at the last minute. Some arrangement must be made for such service. If the hotel cannot do the job in-house, a local sign painter must be on call. In view of the fact that setup usually is on weekends and evenings, it is a wise convention hotel that sets up in-house.

Price Schedule

Establish a price schedule for all sign work, whether the hotel has an in-house shop or farms the work out. A work order should be made out for each sign; its location, if predetermined, should be noted. No verbal orders should be taken. State whether the hotel will bill the organization or the group will deal directly with a local sign company.

Figure 15.12. HOTEL SIGN POLICIES.

- All signs must be professionally printed or painted. Handwritten signs are not permitted.
- All signs must be displayed from easels.
- Placement of signs is restricted to meeting room area.
- No signs allowed in main lobby or guest room corridors. The hotel has an electronic event board in the lobby for daily meeting room and registration information, as well as electronic signs outside of each function room.
- No pins, tacks or adhesives of any sort are permitted on any hotel wall or door.
- No tape or glue permitted on painted walls. We realize that visual aids have to be displayed occasionally on the vinyl walls of our meeting rooms, but please check with your convention service manager on the type of tape to use on vinyl walls.
- The hotel's staff will be happy to assist in hanging any banners or large signs. Please check with your convention service manager for any restrictions.
- Please be advised that you will be held liable for damages if the above mentioned policies are not adhered to.

This is a typical hotel policy regarding the placement of signs.

Locations

The purpose of signs is to give information, direct pedestrian traffic and activity, and assure a smoothly flowing meeting. Thus signs are needed in logical locations. Trace the progress of attendees step by step to determine what signs are needed and where.

Start with the lobby. Large banners may be placed outside the hotel entrance or over the marquee. Or, **reader boards** listing the day's events, times and locations can either be printed or displayed on video screens. The goals are to prevent delegates from milling around and to direct traffic.

Notices on the bulletin board in the lobby, in elevators, and at crucial places in the corridors will help facilitate movement of people. The hotel staff also must be informed about events so it can answer questions intelligently. Such informed staff people should include the assistant manager, the bell captains, the door attendants and front desk personnel.

At some properties, the creation and placement of signs and notices may come under union contract. In this case, the client should be notified about any union jurisdiction to avoid difficulties.

Today's technology is also being used to convey convention information. Many hotels have an in-house television channel that is programmed to display meeting information (in most cases, there is no charge for scheduling information, and the convention organizer or vendors have the option to purchase time for additional messages or advertisements approved by the hotel). When guests awaken, they merely turn on the TV to access the schedule of events for the day. This method of communication is especially useful when last-minute changes have been made in the convention program.

Summary

Convention programs are becoming more sophisticated and often involve the services of both the hotel and a number of outside suppliers to carry them out. Today's hotels must have -- or be able to obtain -- the latest in presentation devices in addition to the traditional flipcharts and slide projectors used in the past. Today's meeting and convention attendees expect a professional presentation and come to the meeting with high expectations. In the next chapter, we will take a look at servicing meeting attendees. We will see how admission systems are set up and detail the wide variety of support services that are being used to make the convention or meeting a memorable event for all concerned.

Endnotes:

1. Vicki Meade, "Picture This," *Lodging*, September 2000, p. 94.

Additional References:

*   The Boston Handbook on Meeting Technology, Doug Fox, City of Boston and PCMA.
    Contact PCMA at (877) 827-7262.

*   Meeting Professionals' Guide to Technology. Contact EventCom Technologies by Marriott, 9550 West Higgins Rd., Suite 400, Rosemont, IL, phone 1-888-833-3572.
    www.marriott.com/eventcom

*   "What is Videoconferencing," *Videoconferencing Insight*, October 1999.
    www.videoconferencing.co.uk

Internet Sites:

For more information, visit the following Internet sites. Internet addresses can change without notice. If a site is no longer available at the address listed below, a search engine can be used to find the new address or additional, related sites.

AVW Audio Visual - www.avw.com
American Society of Training and Development - www.astd.org
Aspen Productions, Inc. - www.aspenproductions.com
Bauer Audio Visual, Inc. - www.bauerav.com
CP Communications - www.cpcom.com
In Concert Productions, Inc. - www.in-concert.com
International Webcasting Assocation - www.webcasters.org
Kodak - Meeting in a Box - www.kodak.com/90/mpi
Presentations.com - www.presentations.com
Projection Presentation Technology, Inc. - www.projection.com

Study Questions:

1. In what cases would a hotel prefer an outside AV specialist rather than coping with in-house service? What have some hotels done to offer on-site service without the expense of purchasing AV equipment?
2. Discuss the types of sound systems, lighting, lecterns and projection screens usually offered by hotels.
3. What types of projectors are commonly used in meeting presentations? When is each type typically used?
4. How has technology changed the presentation of information? What high-tech AV equipment is used today?
5. How do union regulations affect meeting presentations?
6. What factors are considered when hotels determine charges for AV equipment?
7. How do signs and notices improve convention traffic flow? Where is signage commonly posted to enhance the convention experience? What other methods are used to provide information to convention delegates?

Key Terms:

Amplifier. A device that enables sound signals to be intensified.
Audio conferencing. A conference between two or more sites using only voice transmissions.

Audiographic conferencing. Conference that combines visual capabilities with voice transmissions.

Carousel projector. Most popular 2 by 2 (35mm) slide projector. Projects images from slides in mounts measuring 2 by 2 inches, presorted in round trays.

Computer projection panel (LCD). A device that projects the image on a computer monitor onto a screen.

Computer data projector. Similar to LCD panels used with an overhead projector, except it is a self-contained unit and uses its own light source to project the computer image onto the screen.

Cordless/wireless microphone. Small, portable microphone that operates without any direct electrical connection. Often used when taking questions or comments from the audience.

DLP projector (digital light projection). High-end projector with extremely high light (up to 15,000 lumens) and scan output. Most commonly used for very large screen and room applications.

Dissolve unit. Device that activates fade-in and fade-out of slides; can be used with several projectors. Used to create a "seamless" slide presentation.

Easel. Portable three-legged stand with a rack that is used to hold signs, boards, posters, charts, cork boards, magnetic boards or other objects.

Fastfold screen. A large screen with a frame. The legs of this screen are attached at the sides to allow the screen to be folded down into a small case for storage (some fast fold screens are also suspended above the viewing area). Most popular of large viewing screens. Available in sizes up to 30 feet high.

Flip charts. Large pads on a tripod stand. Used by speakers for illustrations and drawings.

Flood lights. Lights designed to provide general illumination.

Follow-spots. Movable lights used to highlight the speaker or performance.

Glass-beaded screen. Screen on which the surface is covered with tiny glass beads that reflect a bright image back at the audience but have a narrow viewing angle.

In-house contractor. Contractor retained by a facility to provide on-site services as needed. In some cases, planners are not required to use their services, but may be charged a surcharge or facility fee for using outside contractors to provide the same service.

Keystoning. Distortion of a projected image; the image is wider on the top and narrower on the bottom. Tilting the top of the screen can correct the problem, and many data projectors allow the operator to tilt the lens to correct keystoning.

Laser pointers. Compact instruments consisting of a visible light laser. Used for pointing out features on a projected visual display.

Lavaliere microphone. A microphone that hangs around the neck, leaving the hands free. Also called a **lapel, neck or pendant microphone**.

Lectern. A speaker's stand, either "standing" (resting on the floor) or "table-top" (placed on a table) to hold papers. Most lecterns are wired to provide suitable illumination.

Lenticular screen. Screen with a silver-colored finish that has brighter reflective characteristics than a matte screen and a wider viewing angle than a beaded screen.

Matte-surface screen. Screen having a flat or matte white finish that does not reflect as effectively as a glass-bead screen but can be viewed from virtually all front angles.

Mixer board. Regulates the sound from multiple microphones. Also called a

sound board.

Monitor. Device used to view a video or computer image.

Multi-media. Refers to the use of two or more audiovisual devices for a presentation.

Overhead projector. Projects a transparency onto a screen. Speakers can write on transparencies as they are projected.

Profile spots. Adjustable spotlights used to light lecterns, signs and areas that need a tightly focused pool of light.

Reader board. A sign, either printed or displayed on a video screen, that lists the times and locations of a group's events.

Rearview projection. Movie, slide or computer image projected from a projector positioned behind the screen onto the back of a screen placed between the viewer and the projector. Also called **back projection**.

Receivers. Devices that convert electric currents or waves into visible or audible signals. Similar to a monitor, but with poorer picture quality.

Roving microphone. Hand microphone, with or without a cord, that can be moved easily through an audience to take questions.

Skirting. Pleated or ruffled draping used on audiovisual stands and stagings. Also used to drape buffet, reception and head tables for food and beverage functions.

Simultaneous interpretation. The interpretation of the presentation into another language while the speech is in progress.

Standing microphone. Microphone attached to a metal stand placed on the floor. Can be adjusted for angle and height. Also called a **floor microphone**.

Table microphone. Microphone attached to a small stand placed on a table, desk or lectern.

Translucent rear-projection screen. Plastic screen with a special gray coating that allows images to be projected from behind the screen and viewed by the audience in front.

Tripod screen. Portable projection screen with three folding legs and a pull-up surface supported by a rod on the back. Usually not larger than 10-12 feet.

Unidirectional microphone. A microphone that picks up sound from only one direction. Used for speeches, it is different from omni-directional devices, which pick up sound from all directions.

Video satellite conferencing. Two-way, full motion, full-color, interactive electronic form of communication. Various transmission technologies can be used to link groups of people at two or more communications for face-to-face meetings, seminars or conferences.

Virtual conferencing. Any meeting at which people at two or more distant locations are linked using video, audio and data for two-way communication via satellite communications or the Internet. Parties see and hear each other via TV screens or computer monitors and audio speakers.

Web conferencing. Multiple participants take part in an online, real-time meeting.

Xenon bulbs. Extremely high intensity lamps that are replacing carbon arc light sources in follow spots and long distance projectors.

Learning Objectives:

This portion of your text introduces you to a number of the details inherent to a successful meeting or convention. We will discuss convention admission systems and security, additional services provided by the hotel to enhance events and ways to build attendance by offering special programs for the adult guests and/or children of attendees or delegates. When you have studied this chapter, you will:

- Be able to describe the various types of convention registrations commonly used and detail the security systems that are put in place to control attendance at events.

- Know the other special services typically provided to convention groups by a hotel or selected suppliers.

- Be able to detail various programs that are arranged to entertain the attendees' companions or children while the meeting or convention is in progress.

Outline

Convention Registration

Convention Security
- Controlled Admission
- Ticket Arrangements
- Uncontrolled Admission
- Exhibit Security

Other Services
- Convention Headquarters Room
- Convention Hospitality Suites
- Guest Packages
- Telephones
- Printing and Duplication
- Decorations
- Entertainment
- Preferred Suppliers/Exclusives

Guest/Companion Programs
- Building Guest/Companion Attendance
- Activities for the Attendees' Guests
- Activities for Children

Checklists

Summary

Building Attendance: Mixing Business with Pleasure

Alan T. Brenner, CMP
Manager, Monterey Conference Center
Monterey, California

"Mixing pleasure into business is an attendance-builder...if the program includes pleasure along with the work, with leisure time activities and entertainment arranged and scheduled just for the fun of it...well now, there's a meeting with some of the drudgery taken out of it...Getting together just for the fun of it does more than just entertain. It refreshes the mind and uplifts the spirit...The fun times promote a different level of exchange: unstructured, open, less risky, easier to be heard, more attentive, even confidential...Managers and planners should... arrange good times ahead of time. As the working sessions march along, it's good business to mix in some pleasure!"

16 Admission Systems and Other Services

Admission at most conventions is controlled through registration of delegates. It is restricted for many reasons, such as membership, security and exclusivity. The convening organization sets the admission policy; the hotel's obligation is to help carry it out.

Convention Registration

Convention registration is different than room registration. When delegates register for guestrooms, they are given room keys and account folios to which the hotel staff will post the delegates' charges. But in the **convention registration** process, delegates receive packets outlining the convention program and pay their registration fees to the convention's sponsoring organization. In most cases, a convention registration desk is set up away from the room registration area.

The hotel's convention service manager has little control over convention registration, and yet it is extremely important that things run smoothly. The delegate who has to wait may come away with a poor image of the hotel, even if it is not the hotel's fault.

Thus convention registration is a hospitality function, as well as a control function. The delegate's first impressions of the hotel are formulated at the registration desk.

Registration also serves as a source of information. Robert Paluzzi of Caesars Palace in Las Vegas, speaking before a class of ours, defined the convention registration desk as "the headquarters place for the meeting." A directory board is placed here, listing all the meetings of the day in chronological order, as is a **message board** for memos and last minute changes.

The facility's convention service manager must be perceptive about the traffic flow and layout of this area and understand the problems that the meeting planner might face. Poorly trained registration help, a shortage of supplies, such as badges, computers or printers, and inadequate directional signs that lead to traffic bottlenecks are just a few of the potential problems. The convention service manager should try to keep these headaches from arising.

The registration area is generally broken into three areas: the packet pickup area, where the delegate receives the convention agenda; an area for the actual registration, where money changes hands and the delegate is given a badge; and an area where information and literature about tours and special services is available.

The packet pickup may occur in one of three ways. Packets may be picked up at the front desk when the delegates register for their rooms. Or, after preregistering and preassigning rooms, the hotels may leave the packets inside the guest rooms. The most popular method is to hand out the packets at a convention desk independently of the guestroom registration.

Included in the delegate's packet are complete details of the convention and instructions for registering. A prudent convention service manager can make this packet really pay off for the hotel; it is an excellent method of informing and promoting in-house sales.

Among the items the organizing group might include in the packet are:

- a list of scheduled events
- coupon tickets for all functions
- an introductory letter stating the purposes and aims of the meeting
- information about speakers and entertainers

The hotel should also provide the meeting planner with material for inclusion in the **convention packet/kit** distributed to each attendee. These items may include such information as:

- the hotel facilities available to the guest
- the times the hospitality suites and restaurants are open, and their locations
- procedures for handling hotel bills and check-out
- special favors, such as notebooks and pens with the hotel's logo

The second area in the registration process, the point where the actual registration takes place, is handled almost exclusively by the meeting planner. Three to four secretaries are normally required for large groups. Many cities provide secretaries free of charge through their convention bureaus; at other times, the hotel may be requested to find registration help, or the association may bring its own.

Figure 16.1 shows a typical example of the third stop in the registration process, the tour and special service desk. City tours, trips to local attractions, exhibit setup instructions, and similar services are provided at this point.

Figure 16.1. TOUR AND TRAVEL DESK.

The tour and travel desk is one of the stopping points in the delegate registration process.

Convention Security

Another important area of concern to meeting planners is staging a worry-free event. Meeting planners want to ensure that their attendees and exhibitors don't have to worry about their personal safety or their property. Hotels have responded to this requirement for greater security by installing electronic door locks, providing well-lighted parking and public areas, and offering high-tech alarm and surveillance systems in their exhibit halls.

In the wake of the terrorism threat following the attacks of September 11, 2001, hotels are also taking other measures to ensure the safety of their guests and their facilities. This begins with having all employees wear hotel-issued photo identification badges and putting plans in place to ensure heightened security at both front of the house and back of the house areas.

Depending on the risk level, spot checks of delegates and their luggage may be made at the front desk and in the registration area; if the risk level is elevated, inspection may be mandated for all delegates and their belongings.

There should also be plans in place for back of the house areas, such as entry points for exhibitors and loading docks. In some cases, exhibitors may be required to be accompanied from the loading docks to the exhibit area; if the security risk level is high, exhibitors may be barred from the loading docks.

To assist hotels in planning for safety and security at their convention centers and exhibit halls, the International Association of Assembly Managers (IAAM) has released such publications as Security Planning Guide (for arenas, stadiums and amphitheaters) and a Best Practices Planning Guide (for convention centers and exhibit halls).[1] Guides such as these help hotel people assess security risks and take the steps necessary to ensure a safe event.

The meeting planner can also contribute to a hassle-free meeting by controlling access to the group's functions. There are a number of ways in which this can be accomplished. The following pages will offer some insight into methods of controlling access to the event.

Controlled Admission

Most conventions insist upon registering all attendees, even when there are no charges for admission. At the very least, good mailing lists are derived from the data collected at the registration desk.

Admission often is limited to people with particular jobs or professions. People are screened at a central registration desk, fees are collected, and some sort of credential, usually a **badge**, is presented. The registrant's name and affiliation are typed, printed, or written on the badge, which then is usually placed in a plastic holder of some kind. Some holders are pinned to a garment; others clip or slip into a jacket pocket. The most popular choice with meeting planners are badges that are slipped into a plastic case and hung around the neck on a **lanyard** (when using this type of badge, be sure the name is printed on both sides so it is visible in case the badge flips over).[2] Some conventions use a self-adhering badge for one-time use.

A more sophisticated type of badge is a plastic card embossed with the registrant's name and address, similar to a charge card. Exhibitors are supplied with "lead retrieval" devices that scan the badges of the attendees. At the end of the show, the exhibitor returns the machine to the lead retrieval company and receives a printout of all the attendees who visited the booth. (Exhibitors use trade shows to develop new trade contacts, and follow-up of these new contacts may result in additional business. That's the system that feeds the exhibits, which certainly support the entire convention.)

More sophisticated systems include bar coded badges, which can be used not only for on-site registration to identify guests, but also for billing purposes. Some registrants, for example, are coded to authorize the rental of audiovisual equipment or meals and special services. The bar codes will permit instant access to these charges, making cost-accounting far more accurate and up-to-date.

Another type of sophisticated badge was introduced in April 2003 by nTAG Interactive. As the name implies, this type of badge interacts with other badges via infrared sensors; the badges "talk" to each other via a wireless network with a central server. With this type of badge, meeting planners can track session attendance, and attendees benefit as the system facilitates networking (the badges' sensors exchange data, find mutual areas of interest and display findings on the LCD screens). After the event, nTag consolidates the contact information of people the attendee has met and sends a list of them to each user via e-mail.

Figure 16.2. Sample Convention Badges.

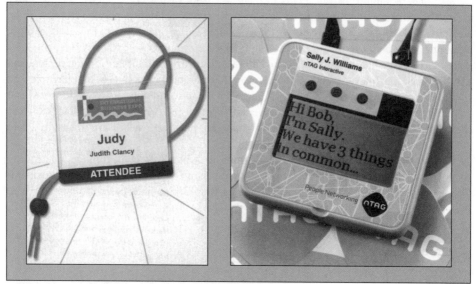

Badges for attendees and exhibitors at conventions can range from an adhesive name tag (not pictured) to a badge placed into a plastic holder and worn around the neck to today's sophisticated, interactive badges, such as the nTAG by nTAG Interactive. This badge not only displays the name of each meeting and convention attendee, but can also communicate with other badges to facilitate the tracking of attendees and provide networking opportunities.
Sources: Name badge courtesy of Corporate Meetings & Incentives; nTAG photograph courtesy of nTAG Interactive.

The convention service manager should be able to supply the names of local companies that stock different kinds of badges. However, it is generally not the hotel's responsibility to supply badges. This is the job of the convening organization. One innovative hotel stepped over this rule and designed a combination convention badge-service directory as a giveaway item. The badge-directory could be put into a suit coat pocket. The top of the badge provided space for the delegate's name and organization, and the bottom had the directory of the hotel's services.

Badges are often color-coded to sort out the different categories of registrants. In some cases, all but exhibitors are barred from the exhibit hall area except during certain show hours, and the color-coding helps the security guards police this policy. Color-coding also helps the exhibitors recognize prospective customers.

Ticket Arrangements

Tickets provide a simple way of presenting evidence on which to base charges. If the agreement is to charge ten dollars for each person served at a luncheon, each of those lunch tickets represents a ten-dollar bill. The tickets must be counted immediately after the affair, and the number verified by an authorized person from the convention staff.

Systems for collecting tickets are simple enough, but nothing should be left for the staff to improvise. Suggest one system.

If the admission is to be by ticket, a small table or two, with chairs, is set up to handle the transactions. The table is especially needed if tickets may be purchased at the door and not merely presented. Sometimes tickets or badges are to be claimed at such a table. If you expect a crowd, you'll need several table stations. It is easier to bring up the subject and discuss it in advance than to scramble for tables and chairs at the last minute.

The tables and chairs may be placed just outside or just inside the door of the function room. Space is a consideration in deciding where to put the tables.

Waiters can collect tickets at a sit-down meal, while a hotel employee can collect tickets at the door for a buffet. It is worth repeating that a person on the convention staff should be at the door, too, to troubleshoot and to identify and greet VIPs. The tables also serve as a focal point for those who have questions, for notices to be placed, and for material to be picked up.

Tickets are often sold in advance by convention organizers. The associations make money from such functions in many ways. The price they charge might be more than they pay the hotel. In addition, not every ticket is used and no refunds are made. This happens especially when the convention sells a package of tickets for all the meals of the event at a flat fee.

Lots of ruffled feathers can be avoided if the hotel staff meets with the convention staff to decide what to do when delegates lose or forget their tickets. Don't expect a security guard or a waiter to improvise in such cases. If a convention executive is authorized to approve admission at each function, make some provision for recording that number. The simplest way is for the convention executive to have extra tickets to supply when he or she sees fit to do so.

Sometimes, the count must be verified and the bill submitted to someone other than the convention organization. Many companies sponsor food functions as a way of helping an organization and to promote their image within that industry. The procedures are all the same except that you deal with another person. Arrangements should be made to ascertain who should be billed — the convention organization or the sponsor. And an authorized person should be designated to verify counts. Payment arrangements should be spelled out.

Uncontrolled Admission

There are times when the doors are open to all who care to enter. However, this is relatively rare. But it is common to permit all who have badges to enter, allowing a free flow of people into and out of the meeting and function areas. This is where color-coding helps a great deal. When admission requires only a badge, and the badge is readily available, a security guard or other hotel person, such as a captain, stationed at the door may be all that is needed.

In such uncontrolled arrangements, it is most common for all liquor and food to be paid for with cash or coupons.

Exhibit Security

Conventions accompanied by exhibitions pose a number of potential problems that can be both embarrassing and costly to a hotel. Communication is needed between the convention service manager and the person responsible for security. Coordination and cooperation are necessary to provide the protection required.

When exhibitors are involved, the hotel's security force may have to be beefed up with outside help. The extra cost should be figured into the selling price and absorbed by the organizing group. There are a number of national **security contractors** that might be called in. However, many hotels maintain an on-call list of reliable off-duty police and fire officers. They have been trained in basic security procedures and are an excellent source of help.

All security personnel, whether part-time or full-time, experienced or inexperienced, should go through a training session and orientation of the hotel's facilities. A job description such as that shown in Figure 16.3 might be given to each guard. It outlines the guard's duties and responsibilities as an employee of the hotel.

Security in the modern hotel is becoming a more complex problem. There are four critical periods involved in security: move-in; open show hours; closed show hours; and move-out. Each is different.

Move-in and move-out periods are the most critical times because of the many transitory, poorly identified persons who have access to exhibits and displays. People have been known to take anything from calculators to operating tables. Security personnel must be wary of anyone who looks suspicious. For example, it is strange to see someone wearing an overcoat when it is quite hot outside. The security guard should make tactful inquiries of such people immediately. Security guards must be alert and observant to spot the unusual.

Tight security is essential at the loading docks and truck entries during move-in. Any materials or displays that go in and out of the door should have a pass-check from show

Figure 16.3. A TYPICAL JOB DESCRIPTION FOR HOTEL SECURITY GUARDS.

Hotel Security Personnel Job Duties and Responsibility

1. *Help take care of an antagonist calmly.* Security must know how to take care of troublemakers through the use of logic or force without attracting too much attention from the guests.
2. *Watch for fire.* Security must know what to do about extinguishing small fires when fire trucks are still in transit.
3. *Report accidents.* A report must be presented to the hotel office for insurance purposes.
4. *Know how to take care of bomb threats.* Security must learn how to warn guests of bomb threats without making them panic.
5. *Emergency evacuation plan.* Security must know the hotel's exits so that in an emergency, they can direct people.
6. *Crowd control.* Security guards must know how to handle crowds during a mass panic.
7. *Policing loading areas.* Loading areas must be checked for stolen hotel property or stolen exhibits.

And in addition to these duties, a security officer must have a law enforcement background and be familiar with local and state laws.

management. Security personnel often encourage exhibitors during move-in to put their display goods in a "safe room," if one is available. If it is not available, they are encouraged to put their displays under their booths, away from the view of passing persons. This will help to eliminate theft.

It is advisable to have a roving officer rather than one who merely stands at the door; this more often is a psychological deterrent to would-be thieves.

During the show or exhibit, much of the responsibility for guarding the booths falls on the exhibitors themselves rather than the security guards; this is especially true of large conventions, where it is just not feasible to have a security guard at each exhibit. Exhibitors who decide to leave their booths for any period of time should have replacements so the booths are never left unattended.

When Burns Security Institute surveyed exhibitors and show personnel across the nation about exhibit hall security problems, more than 200 responded. According to the survey, exhibitors feel that one of the primary problems in exhibit areas is internal pilferage, with both hall workers and exhibit workers taking advantage of management trust and stealing items.

Likely times for employees to steal is during dismantling. Security needs are crucial at this time because so much is going on in the hall. The employee knows the hotel, its hiding places, and the exits that are unguarded. Because of this, employee thefts are often successful.

Exhibits are also very vulnerable to theft during the evening when exhibitors are gone. Exhibitors often leave in a hurry to join the merriment without putting expensive exhibits in the security rooms, if they are available.

Electronic surveillance is a new feature of hotel security systems. Burglar alarms and closed-circuit television are used now, but not to the extent that people might believe. Certainly there is going to be better control with such equipment, but there will be a greater expense, which the organizing group will have to bear. Thus many conventions will decide not to use such surveillance because of their tight budgets. If, however, the exhibition is a large one with highly valued items, this electronic equipment will be used.

Other Services

There are a number of other services that may have to be arranged by the convening organization or that will require your input and assistance to execute. Press facilities may have to be designated, and a source of typewriter or computer rentals found for the convention staff. Local modeling agencies, public stenographers and similar services may have to be called in. Most of these services do not require special handling, just advance notice and some thought.

Convention Headquarters Room

The administration of a large convention often requires a staff of five to ten people, so the association needs a room to work out of as an office. Hotels recognize this need and usually provide such a room free as part of the package. Ideally, this room should be adjacent to the meeting rooms and equipped with tables, typewriters, duplicating machines and perhaps a stenographer. Naturally, the hotel will charge for any such equipment supplied.

The Sonesta Hotel chain has gone a step further. A secretary is assigned to large groups free of charge to work in the headquarters room. The secretary's functions might include typing, handling messages, and arranging show tickets, among others.

Convention Hospitality Suites

Planning something for the evening hours is sometimes a real problem for meeting sponsors. One solution a convention manager might suggest to a client is a company **hospitality suite**. This calls for coffee, a bartender, card table, television — in general, a lounging atmosphere where the members may congregate informally. The advantage to the hotel is that the delegates stay in the hotel and spend their money there rather than being out on the town.

Another service provided by the hotel is what might be called "controlled hospitality suites." There is a tremendous demand for hospitality suites when a large convention and exhibition move into a hotel. Exhibitors rush for these rooms as places to entertain and transact sales. But the association executive also needs these suites for board and convention officials. When the demand for hospitality suites is greater than the number available, *the hotel's first obligation is to the meeting planner.*

Meeting planners are specific about the assigning of suites. Ground rules often state that:

- exhibitors are not to have their hospitality suites open while meetings are scheduled.
- non-exhibitors will not be allowed to have hospitality suites.

Guest Packages

Convention exhibitors and convention delegates frequently bring samples and promotional material that they would like to distribute at the meeting. Procedures for accepting these guest packages must be determined and communicated to the employees involved. If adequate storage space is available, packages are generally stored free. But it should not be a hotel's practice to store large packages or any packages for an extended period of time.

To avoid any misunderstandings, the hotel's policy can be stated in a clause, such as the following, in the organization's contract:

Storage of Exhibit Materials
The Hotel cannot accept and store shipments of exhibit materials in advance of a show. Due to County fire department regulations, crates, boxes, and other items to be used for the storage of exhibit materials cannot be stored on the Hotel premises during a show. It will be necessary for you to make arrangements with your exhibitor service to receive and store exhibits for delivery to the Hotel on the move-in date. These arrangements must also include the removal of empty crates, their storage during the show, and their subsequent return to the Hotel on the move-out date. Should any property not be removed by the designated move-out date, the Hotel management may store, or cause to be stored, any such property and your organization or the exhibitor will be charged a reasonable fee for all expenses incurred.

A package log book should be maintained, showing the date of receipt, where a package is stored, and both the addressee and addresser.

Exhibitors occasionally misdirect packages to the hotel. Such packages should be referred to the decorator's warehouse for later delivery. If exhibitors ask the hotel at the end of the convention to wrap and send out packages, the service should be provided at a charge.

Telephones

Telephone service should be discussed with the convention staff before the event; it may be necessary to bring in telephone company representatives. Many conventions want provisions made for incoming calls to meeting rooms and exhibit areas. Outgoing telephone service from meeting rooms can be abused if it is not controlled. If outgoing service is requested, it must be planned. You should discuss who is to pay and when. Figure 16.4 details the fees of the Ritz-Carlton Lake Las Vegas for telephones and other communications.

Figure 16.4. SAMPLE TELEPHONE AND COMMUNICATION CHARGES.

THE RITZ-CARLTON®
LAKE LAS VEGAS

Event Technology
CONNECTIVITY
PRICING GUIDE:

Meeting Space Connectivity:

✵ **House Phone: <u>No Charge</u> for first house phone.**
   ($25.00 per phone/per day for each additional phone.)

✵ **D.I.D. Phone Line: $50.00 per day + calls**
   (All calls billed through PBX.)

✵ **Conference Phone: $125.00**

✵ **Speaker Phone: $75.00**

✵ **T1 Connection: $700.00 Per room or location**
   Up to 5 terminals per location. (One time connection charge.)

Client Communications:

✵ **Client Walkie Talkies: $35.00 Per day.**
   (Each includes spare battery and charger.)

✵ **Nextel Communicators: $125.00 Per Week.**
   Phone capabilities $1.00 per minute
   (Includes incoming/outgoing and Long Distance.)

Most hotels prepare a detailed listing of charges for telephones and other communications equipment available for meetings and conventions. This form details the fees that the Ritz-Carlton Lake Las Vegas charges for telephones, high-speed Internet connections and other communication devices.
Source: Courtesy of the Ritz-Carlton Lake Las Vegas. Used with permission.

Printing and Duplication

Most printing is done by the organization before the event, but last-minute work is often needed. You should be able to supply the names of cooperative printers nearby who have proved their reliability. Some hotels have in-house print shops.

You should inform the convention staff of what types of duplication you can handle, what the lead time is, the costs, and the kinds of material you can handle. Have a fee schedule printed and presented beforehand or on display. You may have an in-house shop with offset printing capability, a stencil or spirit duplicator, or one of the more sophisticated models of office copiers. All of these can handle notices and the like. The convening organization is not the only one to seek such services. Many of the exhibitors look for last

---

Executive Business Center Services

Facsimile

Local Fax:	$1.00/page
Domestic Fax:	
First Page	$4.00
Additional Pages	$2.50/page
International Fax:	
First Page	$10.00
Additional Pages	$3.00/page

Computer

Workstation:

Word Processing	$25.00/hour
Printing	$0.25/page
Includes Complimentary Internet	

Clerical:

Typing	$10.00/page
Statistical Typing	$15.00/page

Rental Equipment

Fax Machine	$400/3-7 days
Copier	$400/3-7 days
Printer	$190/2 days
Color Printer	$440/2 days

Additional equipment available upon request

Comb Binding

Small Comb	$4.50/each
Medium Comb	$5.00/each
Large Comb	$6.00/each

Office Supplies

Legal Copy Paper	$12.00/ream
Formatted Diskette	$1.00/each
Legal Note Pad	$2.00/each
Name Badges	$2.00/badge
(plastic sleeve, clip, printing)	

Additional supplies available upon request

Photocopying

Black & White Copies:

Letter Size	
1-200	$0.25/page
200-500	$0.20/page
500-1000	$0.15/page
1000+	$0.10/page
Legal Size	
1-200	$0.30/page
200-500	$0.25/page
500-1000	$0.20/page
1000+	$0.15/page
Ledger Size	
1-200	$0.50/page
200-500	$0.45/page
500+	$0.40/page

Double sided copies, add $0.10/page

Color Copies:

Letter Size	
1-100	$2.50/page
100-200	$2.00/page
200-300	$1.50/page
300+	$1.00page
Legal Size	
1-100	$3.00/page
100-200	$2.50/page
200-300	$2.00/page
300+	$1.50/page

Double sided copies, add $0.50/page
Colored and Three-hole Paper, add $0.10/page

Transparencies

Black & White	$2.50/page
Color	$5.00/page

Taxes not included in copy and facsimile prices

The Ritz-Carlton, Lake Las Vegas
1610 Lake Las Vegas Parkway
Henderson, NV 89011
Phone: (702) 567-4700
Fax: (702) 567-4777

minute printing to fill needs of their exhibits and/or the sales meetings that are frequently held in conjunction with the convention.

Hotels that handle a large number of meetings and conventions often have business centers to meet printing and duplicating needs and other secretarial or business services. The box titled "Executive Business Center Services" details some of the services (and their costs) offered to meeting planners at the Ritz-Carlton Lake Las Vegas.

Decorations

From time to time you will get calls for special draperies, flowers and plants, and special flags and banners. Exhibit decorators usually handle such items; they have the expertise and the trained personnel to take care of these requests.

Hospitality suites may need floral decorations. You should have an arrangement with a florist to facilitate service and billing. Make clear to your clients whether they are to pay you or deal directly with the florist. Unless you have an arrangement with a florist for exclusive business, you really shouldn't care if the florist and your clients make their own arrangements. Often, clients are happy to be steered to firms in the house or recommended by the hotel so that they can feel sure of prompt service, especially when they are not obliged to use that particular vendor.

Entertainment

There are union regulations and tax liabilities to be considered when live entertainment is used. This varies from area to area and should be part of the general information included in the letter of agreement and discussed at the pre-event meetings.

Live entertainment will also affect your table and chair setups. Bands may call for raised platforms. Entertainers have different requirements, too. The entire stage area should be discussed to make sure you have enough space and meet all specifications.

Hotels are often called upon to supply dressing rooms for entertainers. A problem is that entertainers prefer to rehearse on the scene, which may not be possible because the room may be in use for other convention events. This should be taken into consideration when the program is arranged and rooms selected. It may not be possible to honor such requests.

Preferred Suppliers/Exclusives

Because meetings and conventions have gotten so sophisticated and complex, it is not always possible for the planner to make the necessary arrangements for each of the services described in this section. In this case, the help of an outside party is often sought. Convention decorators, drayage companies, florists, printers and duplicators, photographers, **ground operators** and audiovisual specialists are a few of the outside organizations that can be used. Over the years, the increasing use—and success of—other private services, called **destination management companies**, has led a number of properties to establish their own DMCs (see Marriott "Best Practices" box).

This can also be the case when dealing with some of the larger convention hotels. Nashville's Opryland Hotel and the Pointe Hilton Resorts, for example, own and operate services outright rather than deal with outside suppliers. They have even formed in-house destination management companies (DMCs) to keep as much as possible of the convention group's spending coming into the hotel — and offering planners the benefit of "one-stop shopping."

Receptive agents, who perform such services for delegates as guided tours and local transportation, are also extremely important to the success of a convention, as are local talent and modeling agencies, speakers bureaus, and temporary personnel services. Most hotels maintain a list of *preferred suppliers* who can provide specific services to meeting

---

BEST PRACTICES

The San Francisco Marriott: In-House Destination Management

Marriott has led the way in offering in-house destination management services. Destinations by Marriott, a new division of Marriott Lodging, has been established at several properties. Resort properties were the first to offer in-house event planning, but now a growing number of city hotels are adding it as well.

The trend toward more elaborate meetings and conventions has been on a collision course with company downsizing, forcing more meeting planners to rely on outside help for planning the myriad details associated with group functions. More and more, planners have been turning to help at the scene of their functions—destination management companies (DMCs) that can arrange for everything from ground transportation to decorations to elaborate theme perties.

Many properties, who see this type of service as a logical extension of the sales effort, are getting into the act as well; either offering hotel office space to outside DMCs or setting up their own in house DMCs. This enables the hotel to offer everything required by the meeting planner—from planning through execution of the function—with the added benefits of consolidating deposits and posting all charges to the group's master account.

Barbara Morris, director of Destinations by Marriott at the San Francisco Marriott, says her hotel's in-house destination management program (established in 1996 with a staff of six) is "awesome." She says:

> "Customers are so pleased to have the ability to work with one sup-
> plier. They like the Marriott name and the service level behind
> it...It's wonderful for the meeting planner who comes to us. They
> have a master account with everything on it. And they generally get
> a better deal if everything is done in-house."

Naturally, the entry of hotels into this area has sparked some resentment from private DMCs. They claim that the DMC staff at the hotel may not have the experience— or contacts—of established DMCs. But the entry of hotels into this arena can only make things better for meeting planners—there will be increased competition for business, resulting in even more creative options—and better service.

Meeting planners are not required to use the services of an in-house DMC; a property's service bids for the business just as outside services do. Many meeting planners, however, appreciate this "one-stop shopping" option, making it likely that the number of in-house DMCs will continue to grow—and offer more and better service to stay competitive.

Source: Ruth A. Hill, "The Entertainers: Hotels Assume the Role of Destination Managers," Lodging, *December 1998, p. 63*

planners. In many cases, the hotel receives a commission for recommending these suppliers.

Many times, hotels allow their preferred suppliers to maintain an on-site office. In this case, the supplier has a greater chance of getting most of the convention business, and pays the hotel rent and a percentage of sales. While some meeting planners appreciate the convenience of such on-site service, many are expressing concern over the growing number of properties that insist that the convening organizations use the property's preferred supplier (see box titled "Preferred Suppliers: What Meeting Planners Have to Say").

Sometimes, hotels not only have a list of preferred suppliers or their own DMCs, but also have **exclusives** with some vendors. This means that only a specified vendor is al-

---

Preferred Suppliers: What Meeting Planners Have To Say

"The value of a preferred supplier list depends on where my meeting is located. In my home area — Greater Chicago — I have my own resources and preferred suppliers. I have had experience with most suppliers or know someone else who has used the vendors and service providers.

"Away from my home base, I'd welcome a preferred supplier list to tell me who does a good job in the area, but I still would do my own calling to compare prices. I wouldn't be bound to using that list, but I would appreciate that the hotel offered it."

Roseanne M. Hoban, account executive, Association Management Systems, Naperville, IL

"I like to find my own suppliers and negotiate with them directly. I think you get a better price. If you go through the hotel to book your photographer, for example, there's going to be an added cost. The hotel is going to make some money. But it takes a lot of time to find suppliers on your own. The advantage of using a hotel's preferred suppliers are that they are familiar with the property's quirks and are likely to do a good job because their position with the hotel is at stake. And even if a planner is working with an in-house supplier, he or she can still negotiate with them directly and pay them directly."

Pat Fagan, conference service manager, Sun Life of Canada, Wellesley Hills, MA

"The issue of preferred suppliers is a hot one right now. More and more hotels are doing it, and I have even heard of hotels that are telling meeting planners that there will be a 15 percent surcharge if they do not use a preferred supplier. That's because the hotels are getting a commission from suppliers they recommend.

"I don't like it. I want to be able to choose the decorating firm, the florist, and the audiovisual company I use for my meetings. Now, if I am in a city where I have no contacts, a list of preferred suppliers might be helpful. But I don't want to be bound by it.

"Hotels that tell planners which suppliers they should use — or penalize them with a surcharge — should realize that the practice is going to cut into their business...for example, our association has a decorator we've used for the past seven or eight years. He knows our show and travels with us on site visits to cities we'll be using. While I am negotiating with the hotel, he meets with local decorators to explain exactly what we need and to find someone to contract for the job. I want his advice, not that of the hotel.

"Other groups have two- or three-year contracts with audiovisual people who will go to their meeting sites and run locally rented equipment to make sure the show goes the way it's supposed to. Now, if the hotel insists the planner employ a preferred supplier, the association is still bound to a contract with its own audiovisual firm and duplicate services could get very expensive."

Janet Balletto, national meetings coordinator, American Mathematical Society

---

lowed to provide a service or product (catered food and beverage, audiovisual equipment, decorating and/or floral service, security, cleaning services and so on) within the hotel. When a hotel has an exclusive, meeting planners do not have a choice of suppliers – and cannot bring in products or services from off-property sources.

Exclusives, which benefit hotels by generating more revenue, are becoming more common, but they are not popular with all meeting planners. Hotels can "sell" these exclusives to meeting planners by promising a better service level (hotels must select vendors that deliver, of course, and can point out vendors' familiarity with the facility and locale and his or her accessibility). Sometimes, hotels can also demonstrate that their exclusive vendors can offer services or products (such as audiovisual equipment, for example) cheaper than the organization can purchase or rent them and have them delivered to the function.

In some cases, hotels may compromise to secure the group's business; they may allow the convening organization to bring in its own decorator if it agrees to use the property's photographer, for example. Meeting planners should always be advised beforehand of existing exclusives, and all arrangements made, whether agreeing to the sole use of exclusive vendors or otherwise, should be clearly understood during the negotiating process and spelled out in the group's contract to avoid any misunderstandings.

Guest/Companion Programs

Many hotels have neglected a potentially profitable market in not promoting guest attendance at conventions. The average convention delegate spends approximately $200 per day in the hotel. If the delegate brought a guest the expenditures for both might well exceed $250 per day. It is a general conclusion that members stay longer and spend more money when a spouse or guest is along; both result in more money for the hotel. This is added revenue for the hotel and doesn't require the selling of another guestroom. For a 500-delegate convention, this could mean an *additional* $25,000 a day in sales, no small sum for any hotel.

More often than not, attendance at today's conventions includes the spouse or a guest. According to the most recent *Meetings & Conventions* Meetings Market Report, over 11 million spouses or guests attend conventions and association meetings each year. And for some groups the annual convention has become a family affair. Convention service people should make provisions for entertaining these additional guests. Special programs are usually arranged that are no different than any other program segment, as far as the hotel is concerned.

The first step, after recognizing the significance of attendance by spouses, is to sell the idea of a **guest/companion program** to the meeting planner, who after all must increase the convention budget if these programs are part of the plan. Point out that the presence of spouses and guests may be healthy for the meeting. The attendees are less likely to come to the morning session bleary-eyed after a late night on the town if their spouses or guests are accompanying them. Sessions will probably be more businesslike and delegates more alert, attentive and receptive. In addition, ticket sales for food and social functions will increase markedly with positive effects on the meeting planner's anticipated revenue.

Suggest to the meeting planner that they often determine the attendance figure. If delegates anticipate they'll have a good time, they encourage their mates or guests to attend the convention. Spouse and guest attendance at conventions fosters a close-knit family feeling, which improves the company's image. This is a strong factor in corporate decisions to invite the spouse or a guest to attend.

516

In summary, if a poll were taken, it would probably show that the most successful meetings were those at which both the husband and wife attend.

Building Guest/Companion Attendance

Once a meeting planner is convinced of the value of inviting guests, much can be done by hotels to promote their attendance. Working in conjunction with the meeting group, the convention service manager should suggest ways to create interest and thus increase attendance. The following methods might be used:

- Supply the meeting planner with the hotel's brochures and internal pieces and suggest that he or she include them with group mailings. Include such items as menus, pictures of the hotel and highlights of the city.
- In addition, you might secure a complete and up-to-date membership mailing list from the meeting planner and send personalized letters describing the planned activities. Also tell potential guests about the climate and offer suggestions on appropriate attire.
- Suggest that the convening group designate a chairperson for a guest/companion program. Offer to work with this person in arranging shows, sight-seeing and other interesting programs.
- Advertise in the popular trade journals of the conferring group. Your ad should extol the virtues of having the delegates' guests come along.

Developing Attendance With Guest/Companion Programs

Janet H. Wright, CEM
President, The Wright Organization, Inc.

"One of the most challenging aspects of meeting and exposition management is developing memorable recreational and social programs for both attendees and spouses and guests. In order to do so, you must know what the local area has to offer, and, equally important, know your audience...In some recreational areas, such as Orlando, Anaheim, etc., it is foolish to plan tours that compete with existing recreation. In those cases, we try to negotiate discounted tickets, line passes, etc. Yet in many locals where there is an abundance of activities we have found our more successful activities are those which we have created with the help of a convention service manager or a destination management company...Since we know our audience, the broad strokes of an idea are normally generated by us, with the convention service manager supplying the details and implementation. For example, one of our corporate meetings featured a 'Beach Olympics.' Since it was obvious we would lose attendees to the beach in the afternoon anyway, we made the beach part of the Corporate program...The event consisted of surfing, volleyball, sand castle building, hula dancing contests, and, during rest periods, participants heard a brief — and usually humorous, always instructive — message from the sponsor...With the tightening of tax laws, it is imperative that these supplementary activities fall within IRS guidelines as education rather than recreation to be considered tax-deductible...."

Activities for the Attendees' Guests

Hotels have recently taken positive steps to increase spouse and guest attendance; a few properties have even created guest/companion service departments with directors to meet the needs of the these attendees. Working alongside the convention service manager, the program's director helps convention committees plan and coordinate interesting programs.

Most hotels cannot afford to staff a special director for spouses and guests, but every hotel dealing in group business should at least prepare a directory of possible activities for them. This directory should be freely distributed to meeting planners. Figure 16.5 shows a list used by the prestigious Boca Raton Hotel and Club in Florida.

Shopping Trips. A very popular event that promotes goodwill is the shopping trip. Proper planning is very important. Normally, chartered buses take care of the transportation. A store guide should be scheduled to greet the attendees and, if possible, the group should be shown behind the scenes.

Timing is important. Often the attendees will break into smaller groups to go through different stores, so a rendezvous time should be clearly communicated. Also be sure that the attendees are back at the hotel in time to get ready for the evening's festivities.

Sightseeing and City Tours. Sightseeing and tours are also popular. A competent guide is paramount. The convention service manager should have a list of sightseeing and tour agencies contacted in advance.

All cities have points of interest: colleges, historic spots, gardens, and so on. One of the best-received tours is the home and garden type. Local residents open their homes for conventioneers' guests, often in an effort to raise money for charity. Generally five homes for viewing is ample. As in the case of shopping trips, timing is important. Discourage the use of cars; go by bus to keep the group together.

Guest Lecturers. Many guest/companion programs present speeches by professional people, such as doctors, lawyers, chefs, company executives and psychiatrists; questions and answers follow. Perhaps there are local speakers you might suggest to the organization. The range of these lectures is great, from flower arranging and dancing lessons to how to prepare a will.

Other Activities. Certainly the list of possibilities is nearly inexhaustible. Other suggestions gleaned from our readings and discussions with convention service managers include theatres and concerts, special business meetings for spouses and guests only and finale parties. Local cultural activities, such as visits to museums and galleries and historical districts, "behind-the-scenes" tours of the property and nearby attractions, and tours of local businesses (such as wineries, chocolate factories and manufacturers of popular products) are also popular. Or, you may wish to offer self-improvement courses, such as cooking classes and classes on time management, stress reduction, dress for success, family life, parenting, child development and so on, based on the interests of members of the group and their guests.

When planning guest activities, however, it is important to know your audience and gear your program to their specific interests and tastes. For example, the Hudson Valley Resort and Spa in Kerhonkson, New York, has developed a "menu" of ideas to customize activities to match the interests and personalities of the meeting group. Planners can choose from indoor and/or outdoor activities. A sampling of offers includes paintball battles, rock climbing excursions, and wine or antiquing tours. If possible, find our what

Figure 16.5. GUEST PROGRAMS.

Guest Entertainment

Fashion Show: A very popular attraction for the ladies — and men also — It is usually staged at the Cabana Club or Boca West Country Club at the conclusion of luncheon. A very fine show can be put on by the Hotel dress shop with eight to ten professional models.

Backgammon: Beginners' and advanced play. Matched play or Round Robin tournaments available on request.

Brushless Painting Demonstration: A nationally known artist, lecturer and teacher with a flick of her hands and arms creates graceful rhythmical and delicate shadings of color magic. This is an enjoyable as well as entirely different kind of entertainment which captures every audience. Most interesting as well as creative program. Original work done during the demonstration will be given to members of the audience. The demonstration runs approximately 45 minutes. Arrangements can also be made for groups to participate or for private lessons in painting if desired. (Available December 1 - April 1).

Golf and Tennis Clinics: Information available upon request.

Boat Trip on Inland Waterway: Many groups plan a boat trip either north or south on the inland waterway. Various boats are usually available upon advance notice. A boat from Fort Lauderdale carries 400 people. A musical combo may be taken along on one boat for dancing aboard. Bar and soft drinks are available.

Shopping Trip: Many groups enjoy a shopping trip combined with luncheon. A trip can be arranged via air conditioned 41-passenger buses to Palm Beach with a stop for luncheon at one of the nice restaurants in Palm Beach, and a few hours shopping on beautiful Worth Avenue. Prices quoted on request. Such a trip would require one hour each way and another three hours for luncheon and shopping for a total of five hours.

The Flagler Museum: A complete tour of this famous museum located in Palm Beach. Luncheon arrangements can be made at one of the fine restaurants or hotels there.

Horse Racing: Spend a delightful afternoon complete with lunch at the world famous Calder Race Track. Arrangements made through the social hostess.

Arrangements for any of the above programs can be made through the
Convention Sales Department, Boca Raton Hotel and Club.

To build attendance, guest/companion programs are often offered. This list of activities appears in the convention brochure of the Boca Raton Hotel and Club.
Source: Courtesy of the Boca Raton Hotel and Club, Boca Raton, Florida.

was done in previous years (you won't want to duplicate last year's program) and gauge which activities were most favorably received.

You will also want to schedule activities carefully. Also keep in mind that many spouses and guests consider conventions as vacations and like to sleep in; suggest that guest/companion programs be scheduled in the afternoons. Spouses and guests may also dislike being rushed from one activity to the next; ample free time should be allotted.

Activities for Children

Many organizations are also seeing the value of inviting the entire family to conventions as a way to boost attendance (see Figure 16.6). Smart meeting planners are aware that working parents want to spend more time with their children and that combining business meetings

Figure 16.6 GUEST AND CHILDREN'S PROGRAMS.

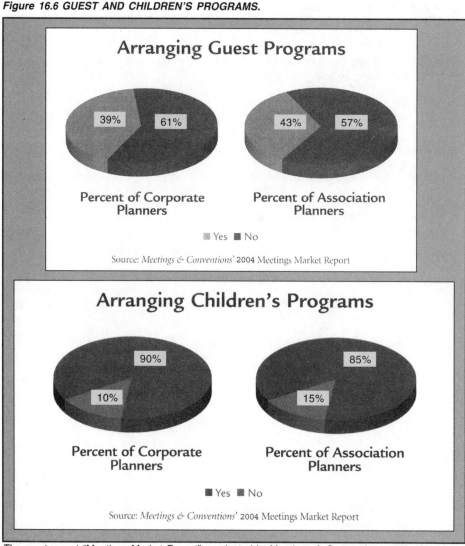

The most recent "Meetings Market Report" conducted by Meetings & Conventions *magazine shows the extent to which corporation and association planners accommodate guests and children at meetings.*

with family vacations is both practical and economical. Having to plan activities and supervision for children of varying ages, however, can prove to be a challenge.

Some hotels have established in-house programs for junior attendees. The Hyatt chain, for example, offers Camp Hyatt, a program that offers structured recreation and learning activities for several age groups. The Walt Disney World Swan offers Camp Swan, with activities (featuring Disney characters) available until midnight. There are properties that offer licensed child care facilities or lists of registered babysitters for the youngest children.

The box titled "A Rundown of Kid-Friendly Programs at the Major Hotel Chains" lists programs and activities offered by major hotel chains.

Other properties (or the sponsoring organization) look to outside sources to provide daycare and activities for children. Some of these groups, such as KiddieCorp, provide temporary childcare for conventions, while others, such as Kids Along, develop special events and programs to entertain various age groups.

A rundown of kid-friendly programs at the major hotel chains			
HOTEL CHAIN	**PROGRAM**	**AGES**	**NOTABLE FEATURES**
Doubletree	kidsCAREpak	3-12	Gift bags for children during the summer
Holiday Inn	KidSuites	All ages	Special guest rooms to give kids their own "fun" space
Hyatt	Camp Hyatt	3-12	Activities that incorporate local culture
Four Seasons	Kids for All Seasons	5-12 (may vary)	Children's bathrobes; supervised activities
Hilton	Hilton Vacation Station	2-12	Free toy rental; supervised activities at some resorts
Le Méridien	Penguin Club	4-12	Supervised activities available at offshore properties
Loews	Loews Loves Kids	10 and under	Family concierge trained to cater to children's needs
Omni	Omni Kids	13 and under	Pre-trip planning at www.omnikidsrule.com
Ritz-Carlton	Ritz Kids	4-13	Healthful kids' menu; etiquette classes for ages 8-12
Sonesta	Just Us Kids	5-12	Free activities and excursions
Westin	Westin Kids Club	12 and under	"Heavenly" cribs; free beverages and teddy bears
Wyndham	Wyndham Family Retreat	All ages	Program for families to cook and play games together

Source: Jonathan Vatner, "Family Affairs," *Meetings & Conventions*, October 2004, p. 74.

There are a wide variety of choices available, from on-site supervised recreational activities to field trips to local attractions. The wise meeting planner will schedule both children's activities to entertain young guests while their parents are tied up in meetings as well as activities for the entire family to enjoy together (one organization, for example, stages a variety show for the entire family, while others may arrange for discounted family passes to nearby attractions).

No matter which avenue is chosen, there are a number of factors to consider when hosting family-oriented groups. First and foremost is liability. The hotel must protect itself (and its guests) in regard to the safety of facilities used and the personnel supervising children. All childcare facilities should carry a minimum of $1 million in liability coverage, and most require that parents sign a waiver when dropping off children; this should also be done for any in-house programs, and especially for any field trips off-site. Background checks should be performed on all personnel having direct contact with children, and the hotel should ensure that there is a small ratio of children to staffers to ensure adequate supervision.

The accepted **adult-to-child ratio** is one adult for every three infants, one adult for every four toddlers and one adult for every six children up to eight years of age.

When the details have been worked out, it should be up to the meeting planner to communicate to the attendees exactly what will be offered—and who is responsible for paying for various activities and programs. This will eliminate any misunderstanding by participants, ensure a happier time for all involved, and establish the hotel as a family-friendly property that will likely be considered for future group activities and family vacations.

Checklists

As you can see, there are numerous details that must be worked out to ensure a successful meeting or convention. The use of checklists can help to avoid overlooking important items, and can assist in contracting for the special services that will be needed.

Figure 16.7. Convention Checklists.

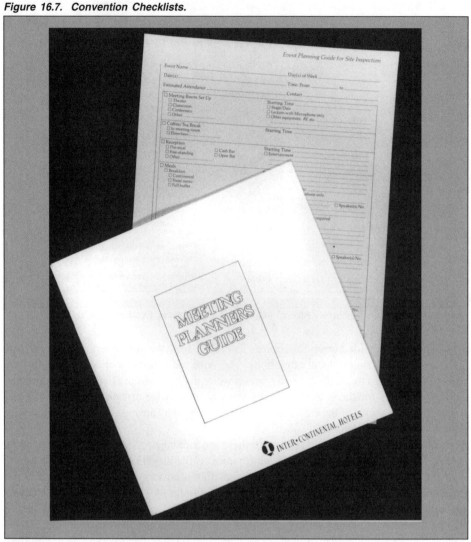

Many chains offer planning kits that include checklists that the meeting planner can use to ensure that all the details of his or her meeting or event have been covered
Source: Courtesy of InterContinental Hotels.

There should be an overall checklist giving an overview of the entire meeting as well as for each function. Many properties, such as the Sheraton Hotels and InterContinental Hotels, offer meeting planners'guides that include these types of checklists (see Figure 16.7). Save good checklists that you run across in your travels and adapt them to meet the needs of your convention clients.

Summary

Hotel personnel are often involved in a number of activities to ensure that convention programs run smoothly. When servicing a large convention, the convention service department may be involved in everything from suggesting effective admissions systems to providing security to delegates and exhibits to arranging for in-house or outsourced decorations, entertainment, and printing services. To be effective, your property must be willing to "go the extra mile" in assisting the meeting planner with these details -- as well as helping to build attendance through guest/companion and/or children's programs.

Building your skills in these areas will enable you to handle any type of meeting -- including the largest of conventions and trade shows. In the next chapter, we will take a closer look at the trade show, which provides a true test of a hotel's ability to organize and execute minute details.

Endnotes:

1. Michelle Russell, "Planning Convention Center Security," *Convene*, April 2003, p. 46.

2. From an informal poll by the Meeting Industry Mall, findings published in *Corporate Meetings & Incentives*, May 2003, p. 12.

Additional References:

- Best Practices Planning Guide for Safety and Security, International Association of Assembly Managers (IAAM). www.iamm.org

- The Convention Industry Council Manual, 7th Edition, Susan Krug, Executive Editor, 2000.

- The Dictionary of Event Management, by Joe Jeff Goldblatt and Kathy Nelson, John Wiley and Sons, 2001. www.hospitality@wiley.com

- Meeting Manager Standards and Meeting Coordinator Standards, by Don MacLurin and Ted Wykes, Meeting Professionals International. www.mpiweb.org

- Special Events: The Best Practices in Modern Event Management, 2nd Edition, by Joe Jeff Goldblatt, John Wiley and Sons. www.hospitality@wiley.com

Internet Sites:

For more information, visit the following Internet sites. Internet addresses can change without notice. If a site is no longer available at the address listed below, a search engine can be used to find the new address or additional, related sites.

Association of Destination Management Executives – www.adme.org
The DMC Network – www.dmcnetwork.com
Global Event Partners – Destination Management Companies – www.globaleventspartners.com
International Special Events Society (ISES) – www.ises.com
Kiddie Corp – www.kiddiecorp.com
Marriott Hotels, Resorts and Suites – www.marriott.com
National Speakers Association – www.nsaspeaker.org
nTAG Interactive (www.ntag.com)
PC/NAMETAG – www.pcnametag.com
USA Hosts Destination Services – www.usahosts.com

Study Questions:

1. What is the difference between hotel registration and convention registration? What three methods are used to distribute delegates' convention packets?
2. There are four critical periods for convention exhibit security. Identify them and detail the methods for control of each.
3. Why is it important for hotels to work with or to be able to recommend reliable outside suppliers? How do these arrangements benefit: the hotel? the meeting planner? the outside supplier?
4. Discuss the importance of guest/companion attendance at conventions. List possible programs for encouraging adult attendance.
5. Many conventions are planned at vacation resorts or other "family friendly" locations so delegates can bring their children along. What activities are typically planned to entertain children while their parent(s) are occupied with convention business?

Key Terms:

Adult staff-to-child ratio. The ratio of adults to children required during a childcare/youth program. Accepted ratios are 3:1 for infants, 4:1 for toddlers and 6:1 for children up to eight years old.
Badge. Identification card with registrant's name and affiliation printed on it for control and security reasons. Usually given out during convention registration, a badge can be an adhesive, pin, clip-on or necklace style or a digital interactive

badge.

Convention packet/kit. A comprehensive collection of conference documentation and/or event materials presented in a bag, binder, envelope or folder. Materials can include a program book, tickets, maps and so on, and hotels often provide information about the property for inclusion in the packet.

Convention registration. Process during which attendees pay convention registration fees and receive packets outlining the convention program.

Destination management companies (DMCs). Professional management companies that specialize in the creation and delivery of events, activities, tours, staffing and transportation utilizing their local knowledge, expertise and resources.

Exclusives. Agreements that limit who may provide specific products or services under certain conditions to only one party. A florist or a photographer, for example, may have an "exclusive" in a particular facility, meaning that no other contractor is allowed to provide the same services or products in that facility.

Ground operators. Company or person in a city that handles local transportation and/or other local travel needs.

Guest/companion program. Entertainment or activities, such as sightseeing, shopping and lectures, planned for guests and companions of those attending conventions.

Hospitality suite. Suite or room for the convenience, comfort and socialization of attendees and/or guests. Drinks and snacks are usually available.

Lanyard. A cord or string worn around the neck, as in corded badges.

Message board. Board, also sometimes called a *bulletin board*, on which convention attendees can review messages left by others and leave their own messages if they desire. May also be electronic or on-line message centers for attendees.

Receptive agents. Tour operators or travel agents who specialize in services for incoming visitors.

Security contractors. Companies hired by exhibit or event management to keep the entire event floor and individual exhibits safe during the function. Guards, closed circuit TV and other methods may be used.

Learning Objectives:

This portion of your text introduces one of the most lucrative — and most detailed — segments of the meetings and conventions industry: the exhibit and trade shows market. Trade shows require extensive planning in a number of areas, which we will cover in this chapter. When you have studied this chapter, you will:

- Be able to identify the types of exhibits and describe the usual methods of assigning exhibit space.
- Be able to describe the duties and responsibilities of key trade show personnel.
- Be able to detail the areas that are considered when planning for trade show events, including show hours and room assign-ments, labor regulations, han-dling of exhibits, and insurance.
- Be able to describe how trade shows are billed and what factors are considered when billing for exhibit space and setup.

Outline

The Scope of Exhibits and Trade Shows
- Types of Exhibits

Exhibit Planning
- Key Trade Show and Exhibit Personnel
  - The Trade Show Manager
  - Exhibition Service Contractors/Decorators
  - Exhibitors
- Scaled Drawings
- Layouts
- Photo File
- Timetable
- Show Hours and Room Assignments
- Labor Regulations
- Insurance

Exhibit Billing Procedures
- Hotel's Rental Charge
- Exhibt. Service Contractor's Fee

Convention Shipping and Receiving
- Exhibit Shipping
- Recommended Address Terminology
- Shipping Methods
- Incoming Shipping Costs

Summary

Exhibitions Require a Team Effort

Sam Lippman
President
Integrated Show Management and Marketing

"Producing trade shows is an exciting, demanding, complex challenge that requires teamwork and communications...The trade show industry is completely interdependent. Associa-tions depend on the income generated by trade shows to keep their membership fees low and still offer their members many benefits and services. Show manag-ers depend on their trade show team for the success of their trade's show. Trade show contractors depend on healthy trade shows for their livelihood. Facility man-agers depend on accurate floor plans to deliver their services to the correct booths. Exhibitors depend on qualified labor to set up and dismantle their displays. Be-cause of this interdependency, successful trade shows have a commitment to communications. Trade show managers communicate early and constantly with their exposition contractors, facilities, labor and exhibitors. This constant, interac-tive communication among all members of the trade show team helps to create shows that provide a cost-efficient marketing and education forum for exhibitors and attendees."

17 Exhibits and Trade Shows

T he exhibit is a very important part of the convention business. It is a key element in most trade conventions, with over 80 percent including an exhibition in their annual meeting, and a very important part of technical, scientific and professional conferences as well. Associations see exhibits both as a way to attract attendance and as a very essential revenue producer.

Exhibitors, in turn, consider exhibitions as unique opportunities to market their products. There is no other way they could reach so many buyers so quickly, and face to face. Most of the attendees present at the shows are decision makers, so much effort is put into exhibits as marketing tools.

The Scope of Exhibits and Trade Shows

Exhibits and trade shows are a lucrative and fast-growing segment of today's convention and meetings market. Growing at an annual rate of over four percent, an increasing number of companies are taking advantage of this excellent marketing opportunity, and some trade shows are becoming major international events (see Figure 17.1).

We explained in Chapter 4, "Selling the Association Market," that the association makes a profit from exhibits by charging exhibitors for booth space. Exhibits also offer the association a cash flow, which helps finance the convention planning. The exhibitor's reservation for booth space is usually accompanied by a check for half the cost of the space. The rest is sent in later, but still in advance of the convention.

10 Largest U.S. Exhibition Facilities

U.S. EXHIBIT HALL	
1. McCormick Place, Chicago, IL	2,200,000
2. Orange County Convention Center, Orlando, FL	2,053,820
3. Las Vegas Convention Center, Las Vegas, NV	1,984,755
4. Georgia World Congress Center, Atlanta, GA	1,370,000
5. Sands Expo & Convention Center Venetian Resort Hotel Casino, Las Vegas, NV	1,125,600
6. Ernest N. Morial Convention Center, New Orleans, LA	1,100,000
7. Kentucky Fair & Exposition Center, Louisville, KY	1,068,050
8. Dallas Convention Center, Dallas, TX	1,019,142
9. George R. Brown Convention Center, Houston, TX	930,000
10. International Exposition (I-X) Center, Cleveland, OH	902,000

© 2004 Tradeshow Week, Inc.

Top Canadian Exhibition Facilities

	TOTAL SQ. FT OF EXHIBIT SPACE
1. The National Trade Centre, Toronto, ON	1,072,000
2. Regina Exhibition Park, Regina, SK	680,000
3. International Centre, Toronto, ON	507,813
4. Toronto Congress Centre, Toronto, ON	500,000
5. Metro Toronto Convention Centre, Toronto, ON	460,000
6. Stampede Park, Calgary, AB	450,000
7. Olympic Stadium, Montreal, QC	432,500
8. Northlands Park, Edmonton, AB	350,000
9. Place Bonaventure Exhibition Hall, Montreal, QC	280,000
10. Palais des Congres de Montreal (Montreal Convention Centre), Montreal, QC	252,565

© 2004 Tradeshow Week, Inc.

The association's only costs at this stage have been for promotion of the event and payroll, a year-round burden. This advance money from exhibitors amounts to a great deal, and it literally finances the convention. The only additional revenue of any consequence comes from admission and registration fees. It, too, is solicited in advance for the same reason.

The importance of the trade show is reflected in the development of hotels with considerable convention space. These hotels have had great success in going after conventions with exhibits.

It is a rare convention organizer who does not prefer to house the entire convention under one roof. When this is not possible, separate exhibit centers are often used in conjunction with neighboring hotels. The largest exhib-

Figure 17.1. TOP TRADE SHOWS IN TERMS OF ATTENDANCE

Top Trade Shows	Attendance
1. International CES® Consumer Electronics Show	1,249,857
2. International Construction & Utility Equipment Exposition	1,113,881
3. MAGIC (Men's Apparel Guild in California) Marketplace	828,345
4. International Lawn, Garden & Power Equipment Expo	826,890
5. National Association of Broadcasters	807,000
6. International Housewares Show	786,050

Source: ©2004, Tradeshow Week, Inc.

its use huge convention centers such as McCormick Place in Chicago, which has 2,200,000 square feet, and the Las Vegas Convention Center, which boasts over 1.9 million square feet of space.

Convention hotels with built-in exhibit areas are successful even in a city with a giant convention center. In Las Vegas, for example, the attraction of a one-house event brings lots of business to individual properties, even with the convention center available. While the very largest conventions would use the convention center and several hotels near it, a somewhat smaller event might be held at the MGM Grand Hotel (5,034 rooms and 380,000 square feet of exhibit space), Wynn's (2,701 rooms and 200,000 square feet of exhibit space) or Mandalay Bay (3,220 rooms, 445 suites and an exhibit area of one million square feet). All of these hotels, as well as other hotels in the city, have the necessary supporting rooms that can accommodate conventions with exhibits.

Las Vegas enjoys as much event business as it does because of its excellent convention facilities and tourist attractions. However, trade show business is not limited to large properties only. Smaller hotels around the country use in-house exhibit areas as an asset in selling convention business and as a lucrative source of revenue. Research by the Center for Exhibition Research reveals that approximately one-third of the conventions involving trade shows have fewer than 50 exhibits per convention. A common rule of thumb is that twice the amount of space is needed for each square foot of booth space. For example, 50 eight-by-ten-foot booths need 4,000 square feet of space for the actual booths plus an additional 4,000 square feet of space for aisles, entrance and exit areas, and registration desks.[1]

Types of Exhibits

There are three basic types of exhibits: a **table top exhibit**, that is often used when there are few exhibitors or space is limited; an **area exhibit**, in which the exhibitor is assigned a specific floor space for displaying large, tall equipment or two-tier displays; and, a **booth exhibit**, which is usually constructed with either **pipe and drape** or **hardwall**.

The most common arrangement is the booth plan. Exhibit booths are ten feet wide by eight feet deep or ten feet wide by ten feet deep and limited in height to eight feet or 12 feet along the back wall with four-foot high side dividers. There are four basic types of booths: 1) *standard booths* (also known as in-line booths) are placed back-to-back with adjacent booths on the sides and have maximum heights of eight feet; 2) *perimeter booths* are located on outside walls and maximum heights of 12 feet are allowed; 3) *peninsula booths* consist of four or more spaces and are bordered on three sides with aisles; and 4) *island booths* are bordered on all four sides by aisles and include four or more spaces.

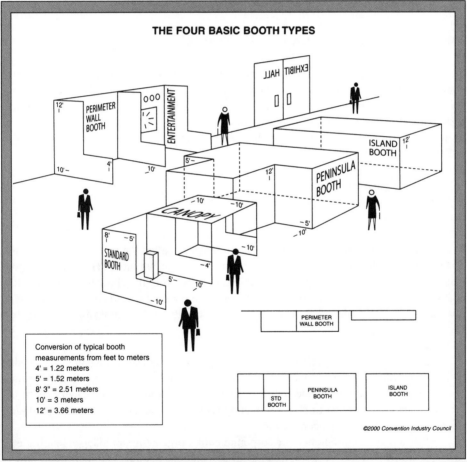

Source: Courtesy of the Convention Industry Council.

Exhibit Planning

Normally the trade show is held in conjunction with the trade association's annual meeting, but other groups or corporations may also sponsor a trade show as a profit making venture.

The association or corporation may manage the trade show from in-house, using its own personnel, or may hire an outside show manager to plan, organize, market and operate the show.

Both trade show managers who work directly for a particular association and those who work as independents are represented by the International Association for Exposition Management (IAEM), a professional association of approximately 3,000 show managers.

As mentioned in Chapter 10, some hotels with substantial dedicated exhibit space may staff a director of exhibit service. This person functions as the principal liaison between the hotel's convention service manager and the meeting group's show manager. There is a wide range of professionalism in show management. Local committees generally have little background in exposition management, while association and corporate meeting planners responsible for annual shows have developed considerable expertise in conducting a show. Hotels committed to the trade show market are well advised to employ a knowledgeable director of exhibit service with a good understanding of exhibit and trade show jargon to assist committees and meeting planners in producing a successful event.

Key Trade Show and Exhibit Personnel

Trade shows provide a forum at which companies can exhibit their products and services to convention attendees. They are, essentially, a "live" marketing event, with about sixty percent of today's trade shows held in conjunction with an association convention and forty percent sponsored by independent corporations. No matter how an exhibit is managed, if your property plays host to such an event, you will be working with a number of different people, including:

- trade show managers,
- exhibition service contractors, and
- exhibitors.

Trade Show Manager. The **trade show manager** (also called the show producer, exhibition manager, or show organizer) produces and manages the exhibition. He or she is responsible for developing a list of potential exhibitors, marketing the show to both exhibitors and attendees, contracting with an exhibition service contractor, and overseeing all logistical planning. The trade show managers you work with will be employed in one of two ways:

- directly for the organizing group, serving as an in-house staff member assigned to organize, market and manage the show for the association (the National Restaurant Association operates in this manner). Or, the trade show manager may be an outside individual or firm contracting with the association to oversee the trade show aspect of the convention.
- as a private entrepreneur or corporate entity, organizing an independent trade show for profit. A recent trend is for associations to either sell their trade show and use the invested funds to benefit the association or partner with a multi-management trade show firm and get a percentage of the profits. Examples of such trade shows include the sale of the American Booksellers Association's trade show to Reed Exhibition Companies and the sale of the National Sporting Goods show to Miller Freeman, Inc.

The show manager's first priority is to sell floor space to exhibitors. To attract exhibitors, the trade show manager prepares an **exhibit prospectus** that includes the location and dates of the show, a profile of prospective and past attendees, floor rental prices, and other pertinent information to assist potential exhibitors in making a decision as to whether to participate. High attendance figures from past shows are particularly important in recruiting exhibitors.

Exhibition Service Contractors/Decorators. It is customary for the hotel to furnish the basic exhibit area, perhaps with a floor covering, but perhaps with nothing. The trade show manager usually selects an exhibition service company to work as an "official" **exhibition service contractor** (decorator) for the event. While the trade show manager will contract with an exhibition service firm, this does not generally preclude exhibitors from using an outside contractor for the installation and dismantling of their booths. Some companies have contractual agreements with firms that travel around the country setting up the corporation's exhibits. These firms, called **exhibitor appointed contractors**, participate in several shows throughout the year. Show management and the "official" contractor require a letter of intent to use an outside contractor.

Sam Lippman, who is quoted at the start of this chapter, considers the exhibition service contractor the most important member of the trade show team. He says:

> "The exhibition service contractor's account executive is the show manager's 'eyes and ears' on the exhibit floor, allowing the show managers to focus on their many other responsibilities. From the unloading of the first truck to the dismantling of the last exhibit, a happy exhibitor is the goal of both the show manager and the exhibition service contractor. Exhibitors that have a successful show will increase their budget for the next show, for more exhibit space and more complex displays, which means more revenues for both show management and their exhibition service contractor."[2]

The contract with the show manager generally calls for general decorating of the exhibit hall (includes entrance signage, aisle carpeting, and basic construction of pipe and drape booths), the design of the **exhibition floor plan**, and on-site coordination for the show. The floor plan is a scaled, schematic drawing of the exhibit area, including dimensions, design, shape, entrances, aisles, numbered exhibit booths, lounges, concession areas, restrooms and electrical/plumbing accessibility.

It is the exhibition service contractor's job to organize, coordinate and execute all the services required to set up the exhibit area. The old-time decorator was basically a window trimmer, carpenter and sign painter whose function was to construct eight-by-ten foot booths. Decorators' work today is much more encompassing. They are in charge of labor, plumbing, electrical work, signs, cleaning, telephones, florists, booth hostesses, audiovisual information and drayage (shipping and warehouse storage of exhibits).

In fact, exhibition service contractors are key persons in the convention process. They work with meeting planners from the pre-show planning until the exhibit hall is cleaned and all the exhibitors' equipment is returned to the home offices. Decorators prepare floor plans for approval by local fire marshals. They contract with a number of suppliers, such as audiovisual dealers and florists, removing this task from the meeting planners. They provide floor managers to supervise and control the setup and dismantling of exhibit booths.

Figure 17.2. SAMPLE EXHIBITOR'S SERVICE KIT.

A typical exhibitor's service kit includes a number of forms, such as the ones above, that provide information and enable the planner to order specific products and services for various aspects of the function. The forms above can be accessed online to allow planners to quickly and easily enter required information and forward it to the convention facility. While it was previously necessary to either mail or fax requests to hotels or other convention facilities, many venues now make their forms available online to facilitate the ordering process.

Courtesy of Sands Expo, Las Vegas, NV.

Equally important, they consult with hotel convention sales and service staffs in an effort to bring about understanding and acceptance of each other's procedures and responsibilities (see box titled "Do's and Don'ts of Exhibit Planning"). This mutual understanding is best facilitated through a pre-event meeting or a series of meetings between the decorator and the convention service manager.

The exhibition service company's contract with the exhibitors is initiated through the **exhibitor's service kit** (see Figure 17.2). This kit or manual provides information, pricing and order forms for booth items including floor coverings, signage, janitorial ser-

Do's and Don'ts of Exhibit Planning

Exhibition service contractors do find fault with hotels. GES Exposition Services, a leading decorator with offices nationwide, has outlined the following hotel problem areas from actual convention situations:

1. Poor Planning for Exhibit Layout

How many times has an exhibitor walked into his assigned booth space to find a beautiful gigantic and low-hanging chandelier right smack in the middle of the booth — or a column or similar obstruction? Reason? The convention sales personnel just pulled out a basic stock floor plan and submitted it to the client — without consulting the exhibition service contractor— and nowhere did the plan indicate the column or chandelier.

2. Plumbing

Neither the plumbing contractor nor the exhibitors will ever be the same after this session — 140 booths in 30,000 sq. ft. of exhibit space...and two water and drain outlets from which to supply all the plumbing lines and connections required by the exhibitors.

3. Electrical

This was an electronics show; power load was so great that existing equipment in the hotel was inadequate to provide half the required current. Additional lines had to be brought in by the utility company at the time of the show move-in. An electronics show obviously involves a heavy power load, and the hotel could have saved everybody a lot of headaches if this had been taken into consideration while booking the show — balancing requirements against electrical facilities available — and increasing the power in advance.

4. Outdoor Tent or Patio Shows

No one at GES mentions "Patio Shows" to our production supervisor who handled this one. The exhibit area consisted of canvas carport-type awnings, on the oceanside patio of the hotel...on the windiest day of the year. A case of man against the elements...and I'm afraid "man" came out a very poor second best. It can be done, but only on a cost plus basis.

5. Labor

How many times have we set up a one hundred or two hundred booth show, all custom constructed displays, and found we would be allowed six hours for dismantle, pack-up and move out from the area? This unreasonable rush causes breakage and damage to property, misdirected shipments, and worst of all, an unhappy client who will not do business with you again.

6. Freight Move-in and Move-out

We handled a big show, involving snack food exhibits, which began dismantle at 5:00 p.m., with exhibitors for another show scheduled to begin set-up the following morning, in the same room, with different color booth drapery. The schedule didn't allow enough time for dismantle of the outgoing show, let alone the massive clean-up a food show involves with popcorn, hotdogs, mustard, ice cream and soft drink syrups on carpets and floors. We pulled out the carpet for cleaning, of course, but those slippery floors had to be scrubbed, and scrubbed thoroughly after dismantle, recrating and move-out of all freight was complete. So we worked all through the night, and throughout the morning, while the impatient incoming exhibitors watched in fascination.

7. Heavy Equipment

Heavy equipment shows do not belong on ballroom floors, nor should this heavyweight material have to be moved over marble or plush carpet. Further, the live load limit of a floor is not equal to the static load limit. One of the machines exhibited in a ballroom weighed 12,800 pounds, in a single unit 12' long and 8' wide. Not only that, but there was another part meant to be attached to the machine, weighing an additional 6,000 pounds all by itself, which was to be hoisted and attached to the top of the machine, to complete the unit, to a total height of 20'. We regret to say the hotel took a dim view of the whole operation, and refused to allow use of the hoisting rig necessary to raise the 6,000 pound attachment, so the show went on without it. A perfect show for a concrete floor, but never a ballroom.

8. Crane and Hoisting

Here is a beautiful hotel, conceived as a convention facility, with no loading dock. The primary exhibit area is on the third floor, with freight access through a removable plate glass window, also three stories above the ground. The hotel is ideal for holding a gift show, where small freight can be moved in through the receiving room and service elevators, but our show consisted of construction materials. The only way to get the freight in was to park our loaded trailers right smack under the canopy, at the hotel's main entrance, unload the freight onto specially constructed sling platforms, and hoist it up into that third floor access window by means of a two-ton crane.

9. Control of Dock

Here, we meet the drayage contractor's most serious problem. The most important single function of the drayage contractor is to get the exhibit freight in and out on schedule, a schedule not determined by him, for his convenience, but predetermined by the meeting group and the hotel. No hotel has unlimited facilities for receiving, storing and handling tons of exhibit freight. Most have limited dock space. Some much tighter than others, but none so extensive that they can accommodate miscellaneous common carriers, display house vans and independent exhibitors' vehicles, out of control of the official drayage contractor. The official drayage contractor assumes the responsibility for prompt, orderly move-in and move-out of all freight for the show, and the only way he can fulfill this obligation is by being allowed absolute control of the loading dock, and with all freight movement through his hands

As we said, a meeting of the convention service manager and the decorator before showtime is a must. Most of the difficulties outlined above could be resolved through communication and joint cooperation.

vices, electrical services, furniture rental, shipping of materials and so on. The service contractor of today frequently uses the power of technology to carry on business with exhibitors. Using the Internet, the exhibition service contractor can display the floor plan, allowing exhibitors to determine space availability. Additional linking allows the exhibitor to browse the exhibitor's service kit and complete forms for drayage, carpet, phone lines, and other needs on-line.

Often, the exhibition service contractor will subcontract special services, such as floral, catering and audiovisual, to specialty contractors. But, regardless, the exhibitor normally contracts directly with the exhibition service contractor for all services.

The exhibition service manager oversees the move-in, set-up and tear down of the trade show and is present throughout the event to service any last minute needs of either the exhibitors or the trade show manager.

Because of the tremendous coordination required in staging an annual show, many associations and independent trade show sponsors seek multi-year contracts with an exhibition service company. A good working relationship between the sponsoring organization and the exhibition service contractor is of obvious importance and should receive the very highest priority by all parties.

Exhibitors. The **exhibitor,** who can be an individual or a firm, sees the trade show as an opportunity to demonstrate products or services to prime decision makers and is therefore diligent in selecting and participating in what he or she considers to be the most important events.

Exhibitors are first contacted by the trade show manager through the prospectus. After deciding to participate, they rent floor space from the trade show manager. The exhibitors are then introduced to the exhibition service contractor via the exhibitors service kit and buy (or rent) other services and materials, such as booth signage and decorating from the exhibition service contractor.

Many participating companies appoint an **exhibit manager** to coordinate the exhibit. Large companies that participate in several shows throughout the year may assign a corporate exhibit manager to coordinate their company's exhibit. Smaller companies give sales managers or sales staff managers the additional part-time responsibility of organizing the exhibit and selling at trade shows.

While the property will not usually deal directly with exhibitors, they can have an enormous impact on the property. They require guestrooms, patronize food and beverage outlets, and often host hospitality suites. It is a wise convention service manager that works with a show organizer to ensure that the organization's overall plan includes analyzing how exhibitors will affect the overall strategy for the function.

In some cases, for example, a limited amount of guestrooms may be available at the host property, and an overabundance of exhibitors may result in convention attendees being forced to find lodging elsewhere. The convention service manager may suggest that exhibitor registration be limited to ensure that enough guestrooms are available for convention delegates. Or, the convention service manager may work with the trade show manager to find alternate accommodations for exhibitors.

In cities that host a number of conventions, such as New York, Chicago, Orlando and Las Vegas, for example, hotels have addressed this problem by building larger convention facilities so they can both provide accommodations for large groups and hold all exhibits in house. These **hotel shows**, exhibitions held entirely within the hotel rather than at a convention facility, have become increasingly common as a result of both meeting space expansion and the downsizing of some exhibits that previously required extensive floor space.

Hotel shows offer a number of advantages. Meeting planners like the idea that their attendees are somewhat of a "captive" audience in the hotel. They also like hotel shows for the financial advantages they can offer. While convention centers rely on exhibition hall and meeting room charges and other fees, the planner can often get free function space by booking blocks of rooms and other business, such as food and beverage functions. Hotels, of course, benefit from the extra business, but careful thought should be given regarding how many rooms are set aside for hotel shows - and when. Booking shows during peak times, for example, can result in the loss of large blocks of rooms that could have been sold at higher rates. Conversely, booking exhibits during valley or shoulder times can greatly contribute to the hotel's bottom line.

Scaled Drawings

We have discussed the need for the hotel to have scaled drawings of its meeting rooms. Obviously, the same need exists for the exhibit area (see Figure 17.3). Large, accurate drawings to scale should note the presence of columns, doors, windows, obstructions of any kind, the **floor load** capacity, and ceiling heights. The latter two factors are essential because some displays rise high in the air and some merchandise is heavy.

Supply the drawings to association clients in sizes that make good work sheets. It is important to keep drawings to scale. Many office copiers reduce the image to save paper or to increase sharpness. Some do it slightly; some, a great deal. But reduction destroys the key to the scale. If the scale is given as one-quarter inch equaling one foot, a *reduced* drawing carries such a notice, but a rule laid across the drawing would give a false reading. Imagine setup day with a layout that was planned on the basis of such a false print!

If you have your scaled drawings printed, perhaps in a fair quantity by the offset printing process in a convention booklet, be sure to inform your printer of the need to maintain the strict scale. Usually, printers reproduce your copy exactly as it is presented, but it doesn't hurt to make sure. Sometimes, a slight reduction in overall size helps the job get done on a specific size sheet of paper, and it usually does not affect the overall quality of a job. But not in your case. If the printer knows the importance of maintaining your scale, you might eliminate costly and aggravating problems later on.

Figure 17.3. SCALED DRAWINGS.

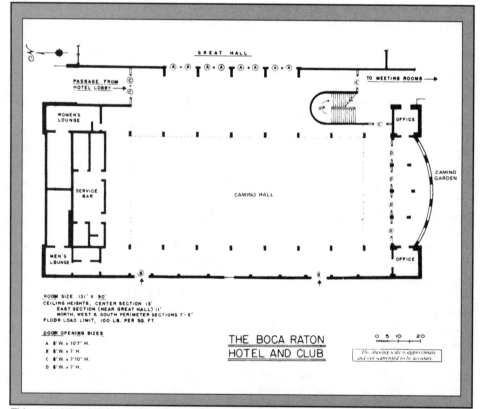

This scaled drawing for the Boca Raton Hotel and Club provides information on ceiling heights, sizes of door openings, and floor load limits. Note that although a scale is provided it is approximate.
Source: Courtesy of the Boca Raton Hotel and Club, Boca Raton, Florida.

THE INTERNATIONAL SCOPE OF TRADE SHOWS
Geneva, Switzerland, is the site of Telecom, an international telecommunications trade show held every four years. Coordinated by the International Telecommunications Union (ITU), a subcommittee of the United Nations, this high-tech exposition features exhibitors from 36 countries. It is attended by over 150,000 visitors — including ministers of communications from 77 countries and hundreds of CEOs and executives from multinational corporations.

To attract the attention of these buyers, over $900 million is spent on elaborate displays created by the foremost designers in the world. Company products are presented using today's high technology, and exhibits often feature **multi-level exhibits**, accessed by elevators and escalators. Upper level meeting rooms and hospitality lounges are available for face-to-face discussions.

Layouts

You should also offer a convention planner a variety of layout schemes for a specific hall (see Figure 17.4). An exhibit in a hall seemingly too large for it looks awful — it carries the stigma of failure on the part of the convening group to attract enough exhibitors. A different layout might provide wider aisles, or conference or rest areas; or perhaps the exhibitors could be spaced out to make for a better looking, more efficient exhibit. Screens (run-off drapes) or temporary walls could be used to block off unoccupied areas. The appearance of the exhibit is important to the hotel as well as to the convention planner. It is in your interest to make the exhibit look great.

The schematics should be presented to the convention executive early enough to help him or her prepare convention solicitation brochures. After all, the executive sells specific areas designated by numbers, not general space. It is difficult to change the layout after positions have been assigned. Exhibition service contractors might be helpful in supplying these exhibit layouts for your hall.

The service contractor will know the local fire regulations in regard to aisle width, room capacity, access to exits and anything peculiar to the area. In many places, the local fire inspector must approve exhibit layout and setup. It is so much easier to conform to local fire regulations from the very onset of the planning of the exhibit. It avoids those headache-provoking late changes and explanations that can plague a planner.

Figure 17.4. BOOTH LAYOUTS.

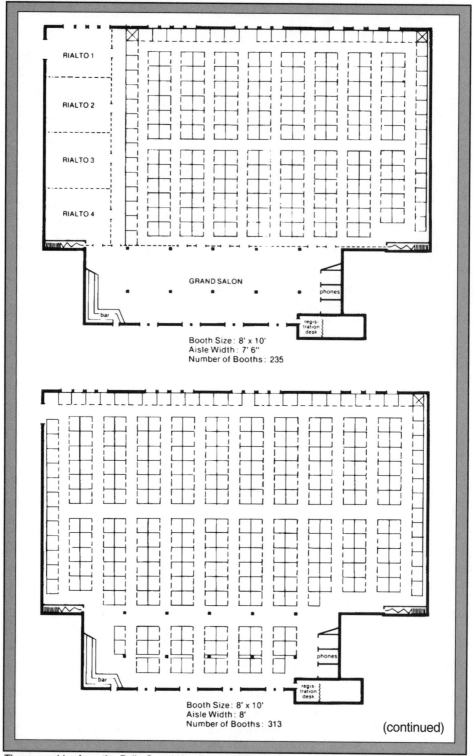

Booth Size: 8' x 10'
Aisle Width: 7' 6"
Number of Booths: 235

Booth Size: 8' x 10'
Aisle Width: 8'
Number of Booths: 313

(continued)

These graphics from the Bally Grand Hotel's convention brochure show a variety of booth layouts for the same room. Note that the layouts shown are based on both 8x10 booths and 10x10 booths. Aisle widths are also noted.
Source: Courtesy of the Bally Grand Hotel, Las Vegas.

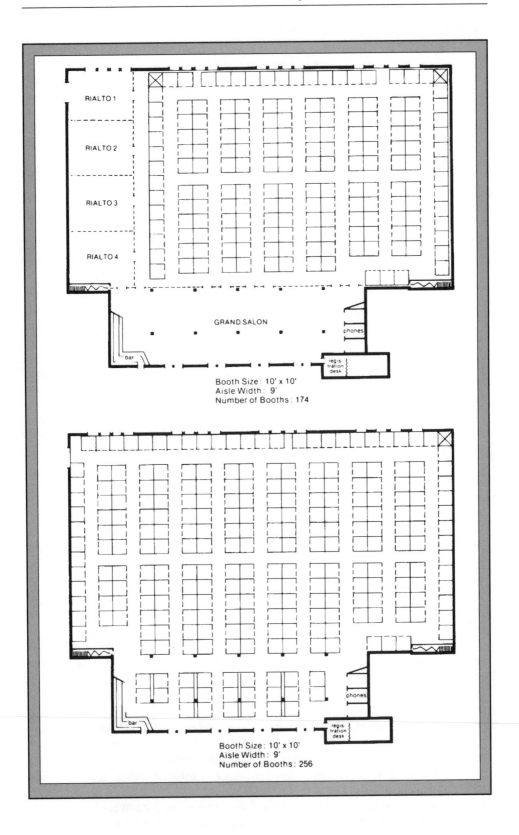

RIALTO 1

RIALTO 2

RIALTO 3

RIALTO 4

GRAND SALON

phones

bar

regis-
tration
desk

Booth Size: 10' x 10'
Aisle Width: 9'
Number of Booths: 174

phones

bar

regis-
tration
desk

Booth Size: 10' x 10'
Aisle Width: 9'
Number of Booths: 256

Photo File

It is also helpful to maintain a file of photographs of conventions held previously in your establishment. The convention executive can check out aisle width, exhibit heights and overall appearance from the photos. All too often, printed material shows only open rooms. Besides guiding the planner for his or her layout, the photos carry the endorsement of past patronage by convention organizations.

Guide the photographer by listing the characteristics you want shown clearly in the photographs. Build a file of floor setups with and without people in the scene.

Timetable

When planning for the exhibit, it is necessary to block out the time that each exhibit area will be in use. This includes the time needed to bring in the exhibit material, remove it from the crates, set it up, remove the packing cases, and clean up before the exhibit opens.

After the event, the exhibition contractor must plan the logistics of bringing in the packing cases, delivering them to the individual booth areas, dismantling the booths, arranging for shipping or storage of the units and cleaning up in time for the next exhibit to move in.

A day or two is needed for **installation and dismantle** at most exhibitions. Labor charges are important in this process. The most common complaint of exhibitors is the need to use high-priced labor at overtime rates. In an effort to negotiate the improvements they feel are needed, exhibitors have joined together to form their own trade associations.

Exhibitors in the health care industry are represented by the Healthcare Convention and Exhibitors Association (HCEA). The International Association for Exhibition Management (IAEM) is another professional association of exhibit managers. Companies and individuals who design and produce the exhibits are represented by the Exhibit Designers and Producers Association (EDPA). These groups have their own annual trade shows at which the newest ideas and designs in exhibit building are presented.

Show Hours and Room Assignments

Two other common complaints of exhibitors are the hours the exhibit hall is scheduled to be open and the method in which guestrooms are assigned. Actually, both of these are determined by the meeting group, not the hotel, but it is important for the convention service manager at least to be aware that there are complaints.

Exhibitors feel that delegates should have free time from meetings during the day to browse through the exhibit area. Many are annoyed at the long days of sitting in their booths with little delegate traffic flow. They maintain that they are too tired after sitting all day and that there is too little time left to make their important business appointments, which is why they came to the convention.

How does this all relate to the convention service manager? Bill Tobin of Caesars Palace said to a class of ours: "If I notice there is a particularly busy meeting and function schedule, I will tactfully encourage the meeting planner to give exhibitors more exposure."

The assigning of guestrooms is another source of exhibitor discontent. One of the services provided to the planners by the hotel is "controlled hospitality suites," which means the meeting group gets first choice on all hotel rooms and suites it needs. After all, it is the group's meeting. Exhibitors would like to see less of this policy, however, because it leaves many of them in hotels other than the headquarters hotel. And when forced to stay in a different hotel than the delegates, the exhibitors naturally find it more difficult to transact, and close, important evening sales.

So what can the hotel do? One solution is for the hotel to rent its smaller meeting rooms to exhibitors for evening hours. This arrangement would help delegates, exhibitors and hotels.

Labor Regulations

The trend of trade shows beginning on Sunday has made it difficult to avoid night and weekend labor charges. This overtime, added to what many exhibitors consider already exorbitant labor rates, has caused some to reconsider their commitment to exhibitions. Whenever possible, a hotel should allow exhibitors to set up early to avoid such charges.

Labor regulations in some cities prohibit exhibitors from even plugging in a projector or pounding a nail. The labor contractor does all the work, even the simple jobs that the exhibitor could easily do. Ed Johnson, past Trade Show Exhibitors Association (TSEA) president, says of this situation:

> "Every show contract specifies an official contractor and spells out certain functions the official contractor will perform exclusively. Usually these services are limited to plumbing, electrical work and drayage, but some contracts include carpenters, model agencies and photographers. We believe the exhibitor should be able to select his own florist, photographer and models rather than have to be forced to use someone who may not suit his needs. (Often these subcontracted services lead to a kickback situation.) We want to make it clear, however, that if we use someone besides the official contractor, he will be a bonafide contractor located in the show or convention city. Associations are afraid the exhibitor wants to bring in non-union help, and that just isn't true."[3]

Labor regulations vary a great deal throughout the country. Convention service managers should not close their eyes to the varying restrictions and trust to luck. Remind the association to alert its exhibitors to the labor regulations that apply to your hall. You must live with the labor contracts in your city. Most experienced convention executives are aware of the labor situations and have learned to live with them, but be wary of the inexperienced client.

Insurance

Accidents do happen, and claims do come up, so insurance coverage is absolutely essential. It should be provided by the convening organization, and smart exhibitors will carry their own as well.

The convention organization should be encouraged to contact its own insurance agents to provide full coverage for liability, fire, theft and breakage. In turn, if notified early, the convention staff should pass along such advice to exhibitors.

Too often the subject is not discussed until the need for coverage is at hand. Then someone says that he thought the hotel was covered. This is another area in which the hotel must be wary of inexperienced convention personnel.

For the protection of the hotel, each exhibitor should be presented with a contract containing a **hold harmless clause** such as the one shown in Figure 17.5. A hold harmless clause releases the hotel from liability should there be an injury, loss or breakage. These clauses also spell out exhibitor liability; if exhibitors damage hotel property, they should be held liable for repair charges.

Figure 17.5. INSURANCE AND HOLD HARMLESS CLAUSE.

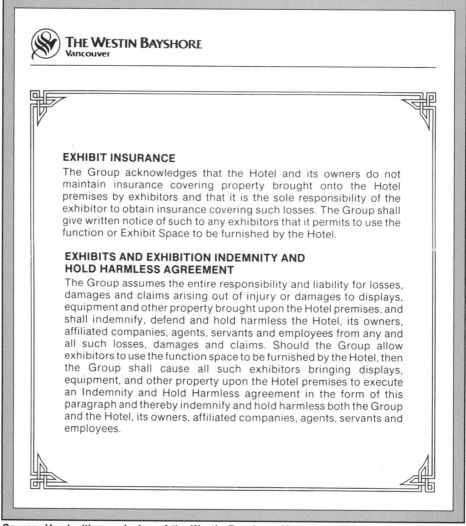

THE WESTIN BAYSHORE
Vancouver

EXHIBIT INSURANCE

The Group acknowledges that the Hotel and its owners do not maintain insurance covering property brought onto the Hotel premises by exhibitors and that it is the sole responsibility of the exhibitor to obtain insurance covering such losses. The Group shall give written notice of such to any exhibitors that it permits to use the function or Exhibit Space to be furnished by the Hotel.

EXHIBITS AND EXHIBITION INDEMNITY AND HOLD HARMLESS AGREEMENT

The Group assumes the entire responsibility and liability for losses, damages and claims arising out of injury or damages to displays, equipment and other property brought upon the Hotel premises, and shall indemnify, defend and hold harmless the Hotel, its owners, affiliated companies, agents, servants and employees from any and all such losses, damages and claims. Should the Group allow exhibitors to use the function space to be furnished by the Hotel, then the Group shall cause all such exhibitors bringing displays, equipment, and other property upon the Hotel premises to execute an Indemnity and Hold Harmless agreement in the form of this paragraph and thereby indemnify and hold harmless both the Group and the Hotel, its owners, affiliated companies, agents, servants and employees.

Source: Used with permission of the Westin Bayshore, Vancouver, B.C.

Exhibit Billing Procedures

What does the hotel charge for? There is no reason why a hotel cannot set its own policy regarding any aspect of the exhibit, providing, of course, that the client agrees to it (see Figure 17.6).

Common trade practice calls for the hotel to make a basic charge for the room. This charge may be (1) a flat fee or (2) it may be based on the number of booths sold.

This latter method of pricing is popular with meeting planners because it protects them from a poor showing by exhibitors. Of course, it means that the hotel is locked into the convention's success, or lack of it, in selling exhibit space. And the hotel's role in such sales efforts is necessarily a passive one.

Hotel's Rental Charge

Hotels historically have been paid for guestrooms and food and beverage, but only recently have they capitalized on the sale of exhibit space. Exhibitions more and more frequently are held concurrently with conventions, and hotels with adequate exhibit areas are in the best position to book these groups. Some hotels have not only been able to show profits from the rental of their exhibit areas, but they have also taken on the role of decorator, providing booths, furniture, drapery etc., for which there is an additional rental fee. This is not the rule, however; most meeting groups use independent decorating firms. There are two common types of exhibit arrangements for shows held within a hotel — the exhibit held concurrently with a convention and the exhibit held as part of a trade show. The first is sometimes termed a private trade show, with preregistration required and attendance restricted to individuals within the association. The latter, often called a **consumer show** or *gate show*, is targeted directly to consumers and open to the public, although attendees are usually charged an entrance fee at most shows. These categories require different considerations in determining rental charges.

The exhibit held concurrently with a convention is the more common type of arrangement, and rental charges vary to a greater extent. As we mentioned, it is a common hotel practice to make a basic charge for the exhibit area. Associations, which make a sizable profit reselling the space to exhibitors, are willing to pay a reasonable fee. While there are no hard numbers and fees vary from city to city, time of year and demand, it is common for the facility to charge the association or trade show company from $2.00 to $5.00 per square foot. The association or trade show company then resells the space for considerably more – in the $15-$30 per square foot range or even more.

Hotels frequently establish a figure from which they are willing to negotiate. Each group must be analyzed individually. Various factors must be considered in arriving at an agreed rate, just as in determining the charges for meeting rooms. Here are some of the considerations:

- What is the extent of the group's guestroom commitment? Its meeting room commitment?
- How much can the members be expected to spend for food and beverage?
- Is there the possibility of repeat business with this group?
- Are there any unusual problems in catering to this group (e.g., a large electronics show)?
- How great is the demand from other groups for these particular days?
- How much of an exhibit area will the group need?

The exhibit held as part of a trade show is often open to the public, as in the cases of boat, gem and antique shows. In other cases, such as the Snowsports Industry of America, the exhibit is restricted to dealers. Trade show organizers are primarily in the business for a profit and fully intend to make their profit from subleasing the hotel exhibit space. In this case, the mark up for exhibit space is considerable.

Hotels can generally command a bigger rental charge for trade show exhibitions than those used in conjunction with conventions. Meeting rooms are seldom used by trade

Figure 17.6. *EXHIBIT AND DECORATOR'S CHARGES.*

Exhibit and Decorator's Charges

There are *two charges* that you should be aware of for your budget purposes:
  A) *Hotel Exhibit Charge*   B) *Decorator Charge*

A. Hotel Exhibit Charge

Sheraton-Waikiki exhibit charge is on a *Sliding Scale Per Room basis. Sliding Scale* is based on a *Per Booth Basis Per Room Per Day,* as follows (When we use the terminology "Booth", we are speaking of an 8' x 10' area):

Sliding Scale

Number of Booths in a Room Respectively	Per Room Respectively Kauai/Maui/Molokai/Lanai
35 - 44	$30.00 per 8' x 10' booth per day.
26 - 34	$35.00 per 8' x 10' booth per day.
18 - 25	$40.00 per 8' x 10' booth per day.
10 - 17	$60.00 per 8' x 10' booth per day.
05 - 09	$180.00 per 8' x 10' booth per day.

All Foyer booths $30.00 per 8' x 10' booth per day. Entrance and exit days are full price on Fridays and Saturdays. One-half (1/2) price on Sunday through Thursday.

  Exhibit Pavilion: $2000.00 each day, plus 4.16% tax Daily charges include set-up days and exit days.

All above subject to 4.16% sales tax.

There are two *money-saving opportunities* contained in the above:
a) By careful planning of your entrance and exit dates and time, you can save money.
b) By containing your exhibits to the capacities that the respective rooms will hold offers money savings.

Kauai Room	(44) 8' x 10' exhibits	Maui Room	(44) 8' x 10' exhibits
Molokai Room	(44) 8' x 10' exhibits	Lanai Room	(37) 8' x 10' exhibits
2nd Floor Foyer	(28) 8' x 10' exhibits		

B. Decorator Charge

The decorator, when selected, also has a booth charge which includes rod and drape, electrical outlets and other specific equipment as negotiated between the decorator and the association.

The hotel agreement with the decorator is as follows:

a) The decorator will provide all chairs and tables negotiated with the association. The hotel cannot provide the tables and chairs for exhibits.
b) The respective booth electrical specifications, including spotlights, are negotiated between the decorator and the association. The hotel is not involved.
c) Storage equipment responsibility rests with the decorator. Equipment is stored in the decorator's warehouse prior to and after each convention.
d) Drayage — The decorator is responsible for the following:
  1. Receipt of exhibits from the mainland.
  2. Storing of goods.
  3. Transfer to hotel.
  4. Transfer to second floor exhibit area.
  5. Removal of exhibits back to warehouse.
  6. Shipping to mainland.

Source: Courtesy of the Sheraton Waikiki.

544

shows, and there is no assurance that attendees will stay in the hotel guestrooms. A case we know of is when antique dealers were booked into the Las Vegas Hilton. Most of the dealers were not financially able to pay the Hilton's high room rates, so they stayed in nearby budget motels.

Another consideration justifying a higher rental charge is the likelihood of damage to the hotel with the increased traffic flow. Such business, however, might well provide the hotel with increased food and beverage revenue in its restaurants and lounges.

Exhibition Service Contractor's Fee

The exhibition service contractor usually receives a flat fee of $100 to $150 for setting up each booth, using pipe frame dividers and drapery for separation on the back and sides. The service contractor charges the exhibitor extra for such furnishings as tables, chairs and wastepaper baskets. Sometimes, the exhibition service contractor will offer a **booth package** to exhibitors. In this case, the exhibitor pays a single price for the booth and such additions as a table, chair, carpet, electrical outlets and so on instead of having to pay for the added items separately.

The fees the hotel charges for the room usually include the overall lighting (but not that for individual exhibits), heating and air conditioning, and cleaning services. The individual exhibitor orders from the decorator and pays directly for extra lighting, booth decorations, the furnishings described above, electrical connections, water and gas connections, telephone service and installation, extra signs, graphics, floral decoration and photography.

Convention Shipping and Receiving

The convention service manager can avoid many frayed tempers and difficulties by advising the convention organization about shipping procedures. Such advice should be given early enough for the convention executive to include it in mailings to exhibitors.

Exhibit Shipping

Many hotels do not have adequate storage space to receive and store exhibit material prior to the event, especially since they hope to have other exhibits both before and after the event. A **drayage company** thus plays an essential role in the flow of exhibit material. Drayage refers to material handling, and is the work and cost of transferring an exhibitor's materials to and from the booth.

The drayage company receives all the exhibit material. It has adequate storage facilities in another part of town, probably where real estate is less expensive and zoning allows large warehousing operations. It also has adequate trucking equipment to move the material from its storage area to the convention site within a day or two of set up time. It is the aim of every exhibition hall manager to reduce to an absolute minimum the time the hall is not used for an active exhibit. When set up day comes, the manager wants the material moved in quickly.

Exhibit handling and storage are paid for by the exhibitors. When the exhibitor doesn't understand that the drayage company is to store all material, cases start coming to the hotel. But if the drayage company is selected early enough, such shipments are rerouted

Pictured are exhibits using only a portion of the more than 218,000 square feet of the exhibit space available at the John B. Hynes Veterans Memorial Convention Center in Boston, Massachusetts. **Source: Courtesy of the Massachusetts Convention Center Authority.**

to the drayage company facility. And the drayage company can have the convention organizer include its facility as the proper shipping address for the exhibit crates. The exhibitor then ships directly to the drayage company, which accepts the material, stores it, and starts to deliver all the crates to the convention site on set up day. When the time comes to break down, the entire process works in reverse.

Frequently, the decorator will handle all the drayage. He or she will send the exhibitor labels for any freight that will be sent to the convention. The labels are pre-stamped with the name of the convention to ensure that the service company gets the freight to the right show. The service company sometimes gives exhibitors thirty days of free storage prior to the convention; this is to make sure all freight arrives in time.

Drayage material will be delivered to the booths prior to the show. After the convention, the service company delivers the freight to a common carrier or other means of transportation, such as air or padded van.

It is important that the decorator know the truck line and invoice number of the shipment in order to trace freight if it is not received in time. Reforwarding instructions are also required by the service company.

Recommended Address Terminology

Proper address terminology facilitates handling and delivery of crates and parcels. If a drayage company is used, have all shipments addressed and consigned directly to its facility.

The *event* the shipment is intended for and the *dates* of the event should be marked clearly. This is essential even if in-house storage is provided. It is also important for small parcels sent through the mail, so there can be a logical grouping and storage within your hotel package room.

A convention service manager often will prefer to have the association address its material marked to his or her attention. Lost or misplaced crates create havoc; the first inquiries made by exhibitors are often in regard to their crates and parcels.

It is important to set up a procedure on handling material addressed to the hotel. Even if the exhibitors' manual instructed that shipments were to be sent directly to the drayage company, you'll always get some sent to the hotel. How you handle such shipments depends on how much room you have at the hotel and how much time is left before the event.

Lost shipments are always a problem. It is difficult for convention service managers to help when cases are lost en route, but they should do what they can to calm concerned and aggravated exhibitors. They, of course, should help exhibitors trace their shipments and expedite installation at the earliest moment after arrival.

Shipping Methods

You help your client and you help yourself if you indicate a preferred shipping method in your area, if there is one. From your vantage point, a preferred carrier or trucking company may mean smooth delivery of many shipments. The client is assured of delivery with little trouble.

Local companies don't all offer the same degree of service. Some truckers may have a larger installation in your city, or more trucks, or perhaps just a better, more concerned traffic manager. One desirable characteristic is delivery on weekends. Whatever the reason, recommended firms with consistently good performances ease the bottlenecks that appear on set up day. Good local trucking arrangements help a great deal.

Even using the best trucking company available does not always eliminate problems. You will also want to ensure that there are no scheduling conflicts at your **loading docks**, the area where goods are received. This is especially important if you are using your loading docks for more than one function - or if exhibitors are bringing in goods or merchandise (such as a fleet of cars, for example) that may tie up the docks for some time. The hotel's convention service manager should be aware of the number and type of deliveries expected and the amount of time required to unload incoming trucks to avoid conflicts with additional deliveries or the receipt of incoming shipments.

Incoming Shipping Costs

Some arrangements must be made to handle shipments that come in with postage or freight charges due. Drivers are not empowered to leave shipments when money is due. Without a clear arrangement, a truck might remain at the loading platform, keeping others from unloading and generally causing havoc.

Exhibitors should be advised to prepay all shipping charges, but inevitably a number of cases and cartons arrive with some money due. A procedure should be set up to pay such charges and arrange for reimbursement. This responsibility clearly belongs to the convention organization, but the hotel should make sure that some sort of system is set up. When it isn't, the hotel is generally blamed as being unable to handle incoming shipments without trouble.

Outgoing shipments should be handled properly, too. One reason so many shipments come in with charges due is the ease of shipping that way, eliminating the need to weigh and evaluate shipping costs on the scene. If exhibitors prefer to ship that way from your hotel, keep in mind that those shipments may not be going back home. Many go to other events. Similarly, the exhibit cases you receive may be coming from another event freight-collect.

Working with good shipping companies can ease your outgoing shipment problem. Alert them to the breakdown schedule of the show, and they can arrange for the trucks and drivers to be there. Those companies that work well with you to clear the cases out of your hotel are very likely the companies you'll be recommending for incoming shipments. Good local service companies are a comfort to a convention service manager, and they should be cultivated carefully.

Inform the convention staff of the time needed to set up the exhibit and to break it down. Reminding exhibitors about overtime charges works well. Some exhibitors rush to get ready for the exhibit but have to be prodded to get out quickly.

Summary

Trade shows can be a lucrative business for hotels that are willing to make the effort to organize for them. This involves developing a capable sales and service staff that under-stands the needs of both the trade show organizer and the exhibitor. While a hotel's role in the trade show may vary, it is important that its staff be able to assist meeting groups or trade show companies as needed. This may involve contracting exhibition service contractors or other outside services, such as florists, security staff, personnel to set up and dismantle booths, and drayage companies, or directly assisting with specific requirements. No matter what the hotel's involvement, the property has a stake in the success of a trade show. Trade shows bring in guestroom and food and beverage business, and satisfied exhibitors and trade show organizers often result in repeat business -- not only for future trade shows but also for other meetings and leisure stays.

 Endnotes:

1. Total number of booths = 50 booths
   Size of each booth (8'x10') = 80 square feet
   Total number of booths multiplied by the size of booths
   80 square feet x 50 booths = 4,000 net square feet
   Net square feet multiplied by 2 = 8,000 gross square feet
2. From correspondence with Sam Lippman. Used with permission.
3. Jane Chase, "Exhibitors Have Their Say," *Association & Society Manager*, copyright by Barrington Publications.

Additional References:

- <u>The Art of the Show</u>, by Sandra Morrow, Association for Exhibition Management Foundation.
  www.iaem.org
- <u>Exhibit Marketing: A Success Guide for Managers</u>, by Edward Chapman, McGraw Hill.
- <u>Expositions and Trade Shows</u>, by Deborah Robbe, John Wiley and Sons: 2000.
  www.hospitality@wiley.com
- <u>Meeting Manager Standards and Meeting Coordinator Standards</u>, by MPI Canadian Council and the Government of Canada, the Department of Human Resources Development, Meeting Professionals International.
  www.mpiweb.org

Internet Sites:

For more information, visit the following Internet sites. Internet addresses can change without notice. If a site is no longer available at the address listed below, a search engine can be used to find the new address or additional, related sites.

Canadian Association of Exposition Management - www.CAEM.ca
Center for Exposition Industry Research - www.ceir.org
EventWeb - www.eventweb.com
Exhibit Designers and Producers Association - www.edpa.com
Exhibition Service Contractors Association - www.esca.org
Exhibitor Appointed Contractors Association - www.eaca.com
Exhibitor Magazine - www.exhibitornet.com
ExhibitorNet - www.exhibitornet.com
Expo Magazine - www.expoweb.com
Expo Net: Tradeshow Marketing Resource Network - www.exponet.com
The Freeman Companies - www.freemanco.com
GES Exposition Services - www.gesexpo.com
Healthcare Convention and Exhibitors Association - www.hcea.org
International Association for Exhibition Management - www.iaem.org
National Association of Consumer Shows - www.publicshows.com
Society of Independent Show Organizers - www.siso.org
Trade Show Central - www.tscentral.com
Trade Show Exhibitors Association - www.tsea.org
Trade Show News Network - www.tsnn.com
Tradeshow Week - www.tradeshowweek.com

Study Questions:

1. Why are trade shows important to both meeting planners and hotels?
2. What are the three types of exhibits used at trade shows?
3. Who are the key personnel responsible for executing trade shows? What is the role of each?
4. Discuss how such factors as labor regulations and insurance coverage affect exhibitors.
5. What are the billing procedures typically used by hotels to bill trade show participants? What factors play a part in determining hotel charges?
6. Discuss the shipping of exhibits, including address terminology, shipping methods, and shipping costs.

Key Terms:

Area exhibit. Exhibitors are assigned specific floor space for displaying equipment and other displays.
Booth exhibit. A standard unit of exhibit space (usually 10 ft. by 10 ft.) occupied by an exhibitor. Usually constructed of pipe and draping.
Booth package. An exhibitor receives a variety of services for a single price. Carpet, a six-foot draped table, a 500-watt outlet and 500 pounds of drayage may be included in the price of each booth, for example.
Consumer show. Show open to the general public. Also called a **gate show** or **public show**, these shows may include travel destination shows, recreation shows, home and garden shows and so on. These shows are not generally connected to any convention or meeting and usually charge an entrance fee.
Drayage company. Company that receives all exhibit material, stores it and transports it to the convention site a day or two before setup starts, re-crates it at the end of the show and returns exhibit material to sender.
Exhibit manager. Person in charge of individual exhibit booth/stand.
Exhibit prospectus. Detailed guide to the exhibition prepared by the show management. Contains information about the cost of exhibitions, space, floor plan of exhibition and application for participation. Serves as a selling tool, inviting exhibitors to participate.
Exhibition floor plan. To-scale plan showing spacing of booths, aisles and design of the exhibition. Prepared by the exhibition service contractor for the show manager and approved by the fire marshal.
Exhibition service contractor. Independent firm or individual responsible for organizing, coordinating and executing all the services necessary to set up the exhibit. Sometimes referred to as a **general service contractor** or a **decorator**. Usually contracted by the planner's organization. If the sole agent, said to be the **exclusive contractor**.
Exhibitor. Person or firm that displays products or services at the show.
Exhibitor appointed contractor. Any person or firm other than the designated "official" contractor providing a service to an exhibitor. Can refer to an install and

dismantle company (I&D house). Rather than working in one city, exhibitor appointed contractors often travel throughout the country to set up and dismantle the booths for companies that exhibit at a number of shows throughout the year.

Exhibitor's service kit. Contains information about the services needed by the exhibitor for a successful convention. Usually developed by the exhibition service contractor. Contains general event information, labor/service order forms, rules and regulations pertinent to an exhibitor's participation in an exhibition. Also called an **exhibitor's manual.**

Floor load. Weight per square foot/meter that the exhibit can safely accommodate.

Hardwall. A type of exhibit construction in which the walls are made of a solid material, such as plywood, plastic or similar materials, rather than the fabric used in pipe and drape.

Hold harmless. A type of indemnity clause that requires one party to fully protect the other from a claim (this would include the payment of costs for attorney fees). States that neither party will hold the other responsible for any damages to or theft of materials or equipment.

Hotel shows. Exhibitions held in hotels as opposed to a city's convention center.

Installation and dismantle. The set up and tear down of exhibits. Also, the firm that does this work.

Loading dock. The area on premises where goods are received. Loading docks are usually raised areas that facilitate the unloading and loading of trucks.

Multi-level exhibit. An exhibit with two or more levels or stories. Often used by large companies to expand their exhibit space without taking up more floor space.

Pipe and drape. Lightweight aluminum tubing draped with fabric to create separate exhibit booths.

Table top exhibit. Used where space is limited or where there is a limited number of exhibitors.

Trade show manager. Individual who plans, organizes and operates the trade show. Responsible for renting the site and soliciting exhibitors. May work directly for the association or corporation or as an independent. Also called the **show organizer** or **show producer.**

CHAPTER APPENDIX

A BEHIND THE SCENES LOOK AT A TRADE SHOW

The Consumer Electronics Show (CES), held in January in Las Vegas, is the premier trade show for the consumer electronics industry. Sponsored by the Electronics Industries Association/Consumer Electronics Group, this trade show features audio and video-based products, multimedia, home computing, interactive, electronic gaming and cellular products. The large number of displays require the use of several facilities, including the exhibit halls of the Las Vegas Convention Center, the Convention Center parking lot, and several hotels that offer exhibit space.

Naturally, a show of this magnitude requires extensive planning and pre-show preparation. In the following photographs, we will take a "behind the scenes" look at the steps taken to prepare just one hall for this trade show.

Exhibit Hall S2 has been cleaned after a prior event and spaces for the CES exhibitors' booths have been marked and numbered. The Winter CES show will utilize over 1 million square feet of exhibit space and will host more than 1800 exhibitors

On December 28 & 29, trucks begin moving in cargos of freight, including construction material that may be used to build exhibitor booths and displays. These crates will be stacked prior to booth construction and removed as booth construction progresses.

On December 30, additional freight, including the exhibitors' merchandise and components for the display continues to arrive, the first overhead directional and exhibitor signs are hung, and booth decorating, including the laying of individual booth carpet, begins.

On January 3, booths are beginning to take shape.

By January 4, booth construction is well underway, as is booth and hall decorating, including the draping of booth and exhibit hall walls.

On January 5, the last of the freight, including rental furniture and last-minute decorating items (such as plants and flowers), is moved in. Later that evening, the aisle carpet will be laid in preparation for the next day's opening.

On January 6, the four-day show opens. Over 100,000 people, including buyers, international, and editorial press will attend.

On January 10, the day after the show, dismantling is already in progress. Aisle carpet was rolled up immediately after the show's close to facilitate the removal of freight, crates are returned for the packing of show merchandise, and booth dismantling begins.

By January 11, most of the show has been crated and is in the process of being removed from the exhibit hall.

Photographs courtesy of Stephen A. Stoney. Special thanks to the Las Vegas Convention and Visitors Bureau and the Electronic Industries Association/Consumer Electronics Shows for their help in the preparation of this Appendix.

Learning Objectives:

This portion of your text introduces you to how meetings and conventions are billed and the need for post-convention or meeting follow up to assess the performance of both the group and your property. When you have studied this chapter you will:

- Be able to detail the areas that must be covered when establishing a billing procedure for a group or a meeting.

- Know the difference between the various types of folios commonly used to bill groups.

- Recognize the need for post-event follow up and be able to describe the two types of meetings typically held and know why each is important.

Outline

Convention Billing
- The Master Account
- Time of Payment
- Guest Credit
- Gratuities and Service Charges
- HSMAI's Suggested Payment Schedule

Post-Convention Review
- Comparison with Projections
- Function Attendance
- Special Services
- Individual Comments
- Post-convention Reporting
- Final Appraisal

Summary

Establishing Convention Billing Procedures

Karen Hudson
Sales Manager, Four Seasons Hotel
Newport Beach, California

"At the Four Seasons Hotel, convention billing procedures are set up prior to the meeting. Once a contract is signed and the group requests direct billing of charges, a credit application is forwarded to the client...If the credit manager approves the credit application, a master account is established for the group. In the event credit is not approved, a deposit is then required either immediately or at some point prior to group arrival...When a master account is established in the computer system, any and all charges that the company or association is responsible for are posted to that account. These charges are processed through the front desk, which posts these charges daily. Once the group checks out, charges are collected by the credit department and compiled into one bill...If the group uses outside vendors such as entertainment or special flowers or plants, it is the responsibility of the conference service manager to post the supplier or vendor charges to the group's master account...."

18

Convention Billing and Post-Convention Review

A fter a booking has "gone definite," the convention service manager begins to collect information from the meeting planner about various aspects of the convention so that he or she can prepare the meeting **resume**. (As we explained in Chapter 12, the resume, or specification sheet, is the major internal means of communication for hotel personnel involved with the convention.) There are three basic areas that every convention service manager looks at as he or she puts together the resume: reservations, program and billing.

Open and honest communication is paramount in all three of these areas. We have already discussed the reservations and program segments. In this chapter, we will address questions about function *billings*.

Convention Billing

Convention billing is much too important to be handled haphazardly. Ranking near the top of the list of meeting planners' pet peeves are surprise billing charges. Open communications can help tremendously to have the event end on a happy note. When it is clear who pays for what, everything seems to go more smoothly.

As with most aspects of convention planning, the time to avoid billing problems is at the beginning and not at the end. Billing policy is usually established months before the group gets into the hotel, not at the end of the convention, and should address:

- What areas does the master account cover?
- How are the delegates' charges to be handled?
- Will there be more than one master account?
- Who is authorized to sign?
- What about tips and gratuities?
- How should early arrivals and late departures be handled?
- Should the hotel or the group be billed by outside service companies, such as florists and audiovisual suppliers?
- What are the charges for the various types of guestrooms? Meeting rooms? Exhibit area?
- What are the arrangements for food and beverage?
- How are transportation charges to be handled? How are special events, such as golf tournaments and tours, to be priced?
- What are the arrangements for audiovisual, electrical, and phone charges?
- Will there be a charge for security and other labor provided by the hotel?
- How does the meeting planner want the bill broken down?
- Are deposits required?
- Who will prepare and collect chits? Tickets? Banquet checks?

All of these aspects need to be prearranged, and each detail should be clearly spelled out. **Billing instructions** for each function should be clearly outlined in the resume, as shown in Figure 18.1. The accounting department, as well as the other service departments in the hotel, wants explicit instructions on the billing procedure. You definitely want to avoid the problems that arise at the check-out desk when the specification sheet doesn't deal in detail with billing arrangements.

Figure 18.1. CORPORATION AND ASSOCIATION BILLING EXAMPLES.

Example I —Arizona Biltmore Hotel, Phoenix

_____Corporation

Controller: Corporation will guarantee all personal checks up to $250 for all members.
Reserve suites 67-66-63-62-61-59-58 from 4/28. Charge 5 to Master Account — other 2 to be complimentary.

Billing: MASTER ACCOUNT to cover American plan room rate, tax and service charge of all guests.
Master Account also to cover: receptions, surcharges, recreational activities on tournament day, breakfast trail ride, cowboy hats, bandanas, refreshment breaks, entertainment, hostesses, etc.
PREPARE INCIDENTAL FOLIO for each guest. Post all incidental charges to their respective accounts. To be paid prior to departure. (LIST IN ACCOUNTING OFFICE OF ENTIRE ACCOUNTS TO BE TRANSFERRED TO M/A).

Night Auditor: NOTE: Extend $4.50 inclusive credit per person for those taking shopping tour on 4/4 or leaving prior to luncheon on 4/5. MUST NOTIFY CASHIER 24 HOURS IN ADVANCE IN ORDER TO RECEIVE THIS CREDIT. THIS CREDIT GOES TO MASTER ACCOUNT — NOT INCIDENTAL ACCOUNT.

Example II —Caesars Palace, Las Vegas

_____Association

Master Account I: All group functions should be added to the master account.
Mr._____ and Ms._____ will be the authorized signers.
NOTE: Please post a charge in the total amount of $250 to this group's master account. This charge is for the purchase of 250 Caesars Palace medallions at a cost of $1.00 per medallion.

Master Account II: A second master account is to be set up. To this master, charge the entire accounts of all _____Association Directors and Staff.
Mr. John M._____ will be the authorized signer.

Individual Account: Rooms, tax, and incidentals to be paid by the individuals.

Billing instructions from actual resumes for a corporate meeting and an association convention.
Source: Courtesy of the Arizona Biltmore Hotel and Caesar's Palace.

The Master Account

The biggest problem when working with convention billing is usually unclear communication. Therefore, an understanding of billing procedures begins with terminology.

A *folio* is a collection of charges incurred by an individual or an organization. There are three types of folios to which charges are posted:

- **Master Account Folio** — charges are paid entirely by the sponsoring organization.
- **Individual Guest Folio** — charges are paid entirely by the individual guest.
- **Split Folio** — charges are paid partially by the sponsoring organization and partially by the individual guest. Most meetings in hotels are accounted for as split folios.

A master account is generally set up to facilitate billing to the convention organization. The hotel executive and the convention executive should discuss the charges that should be billed to this account. All other charges are billed to the guests on their individual accounts.

Additional master accounts may be set up for individual program segments upon request. For example, many groups will specifiy a separate master account for group food and beverage functions, another for audiovisual, and still another for miscellaneous items such as telephone and business center use. Sometimes a participating company will sponsor a program event, such as a luncheon or cocktail party, and a separate master account is set up for this affair.

Deirdre Bourke, CMP, a senior account executive at Conferon, Inc., advises meeting planners to:

- Provide clear instructions to the hotel about specific charges that should be posted to the master account, such as room and tax, food and beverage, audiovisual, electrical, telecommunications and business center.
- Advise the hotel in advance if different master accounts are required. Establishing multiple master accounts is a simple way for meeting planners to segregate bills in advance so they don't have to be sorted out after the event.
- Confirm with the hotel that all charges posted to the master account must have backup, including invoices, signed checks and banquet event orders (BEOs).[1]

It is imperative that the convention organization put down in writing all people authorized to charge to the master account. These usually are the convention staff personnel. If *all* their charges are to be allowed on the master account, say so. The understanding is that these people are also authorized to sign charges. If this area of authority is to be limited in any way, those limitations should be spelled out.

Failure to detail the extent of charges to the master account can lead to difficulties in the case of convention guests, speakers and program presenters. The hotel doesn't care who pays what or how, so long as it is made clear who is to pay. It is the convention staff's responsibility to inform its guests about the extent of the hospitality, but it is your desk clerk or cashier who must face these people when they check out.

Ask the convention staff to inform you, as well as the guests, who will pay for rooms, food, beverage, telephone, valet charges, and other incidentals. It helps to inform the guest when he or she checks in that the room charges will be paid for by the association, but many hotels feel that this is the convention staff's task. Unfortunately, it is surprising how infrequently the convention staff follows through to tell its guests the extent to which they are responsible for charges. Bringing the matter to the attention of convention executives will at least alert them to potential embarrassing problems and maybe move them to set policy.

Such arrangements apply to corporate meetings as well those of associations, since corporate meetings may be attended by persons other than company employees. The arrangements should be spelled out completely. This applies to corporate personnel, too. Some companies pay *all* charges through the master account, while some pay only room and food charges, with the rest paid through individual expense accounts. All variations will be encountered.

The hotel should have no policy of its own, but should merely follow the *clear* instructions of the company meeting planner. These instructions should be in writing. Generally speaking, if you get the meeting planner to spell it out to you in writing, the corporate personnel stand a much better chance of receiving detailed instructional memos telling them how to check out.

The Insurance Conference Planners Association has prepared a guide providing possible solutions to problems usually associated with master account billing to be used by meeting planners and hoteliers alike. Two forms from this guide are illustrated in this chapter. Figure 18.2 illustrates a **master account billing authorization form**, which provides a comprehensive set of instructions on:

- How hotel charges are to be posted (master account or individual guest's room folio).
- The limit of financial responsibility the meeting group will accept.
- The names and specimen signatures of those who are authorized to sign for any master account expenses (only those with an **authorized signature** are permitted to sign for group charges).

Figure 18.3 illustrates a **rates and charges bulletin**, which communicates to the convention attendees the specific rates for rooms, meals, **incidental charges** and billing procedures as agreed to by the convening group and the hotel. The bulletin is sent to the convention attendees one month prior to the convention date. Use of this communication bulletin reduces disputes and speeds guest check-out.

Time of Payment

Methods and time of payment vary a great deal, depending on the policy of the hotel, the credit and reputation of the convening organization, past history, the frequency of group business and other factors.

Master accounts can add up to a considerable amount of money, and it is hard to blame hotel managers if they try to get as much of it as possible up front. This is not only because of concern about being paid, but also because of a desire to accelerate time of payment and to ease the hotel's cash flow.

The usual practice in the trade is a payment when the contract is signed, a pre-convention payment at an agreed date, on-the-scene payments, and a final payment. The final payment can be broken into two parts — one at the end of the event, and a final settlement later.

Hotels have been known to be flexible about payments, depending on what they know about the client. Political organizations certainly should not be allowed to run up large bills because the payment may be uncertain or delayed. But a prestigious local

Figure 18.2. MASTER ACCOUNT BILLING AUTHORIZATION FORM.

ICP — MASTER ACCOUNT BILLING AUTHORIZATION

Convention
Name_____
Dates_____
Food Plan_____

NOTE: Please post charges as indicated below. Master Account charges noted here apply only on meeting dates. See separate letter for exceptions and additional Master Account information.

	MA	IND		MA	IND		MA	IND
ROOM & FOOD PLAN			**HOTEL SERVICES**			**SPORTS**		
Room & Tax			Telephone • Local			Golf Greens Fees		
MAP (FAP)* Guest			• Long Distance			Golf Lessons		
MAP(FAP)* Spouse			Parking			Golf Driving Range		
Other			Valet & Laundry			Golf • Caddie Fee		
			Bellmen			Golf • Cart Rental		
FOOD & BEVERAGE			Maids			Tennis • Court Fees		
			Pool/Beach Attendants			Tennis • Lessons		
Restaurant • Food			TV Movies			Tennis • Racquet Rentals		
Restaurant • Bar			Beauty Salon			Sports Merchandise		
Room Service • Food			Barber Shop			Spa/Health Club		
Room Service • Bar			Merchandise Shops			Stables		
Bar Charges			Other			Other		
Cover Charge								
Other			**MISCELLANEOUS**			**TOURNAMENTS**		
			Airport Transfers			Refreshments		
BANQUET CHARGES			Other			Club/Racquet Rental		
						Golf/Tennis Balls		
						Greens Fees		
						Cart Rental		
						Caddie Fees		
						Court Fees		
						Other		

*Including tax & Service Charge, if any.

The _____Company
(Sponsor Organization)

1. (Is/Is not) responsible for payment of delinquent charges to individual accounts.
2. (Will/Will not) guarantee payment of its attendees' hotel bill whether paid by check or charge card.
3. (Will/Will not) guarantee personal checks cashed by its attendees up to $_____.
4. Some persons (list attached) will have entire room and incidental accounts posted to Master. These persons should be preregistered and will not check themselves out. Their room bills will be reviewed and signed by the sponsor organization's planner.
5. Authorizes these signatures (Type)_____ _____ _____
   for its MA charges   (Sign)_____ _____ _____
The hotel should consider these billing instructions definite and authorized by_____
(Planner/ Date/Telephone Number)

The meeting planner uses this form to provide the hotel with a comprehensive set of instructions on how specific charges are to be billed.
Source: Courtesy of the Insurance Conference Planners Association.

corporation that has dealt with you many times may cause your controller little concern about the bill.

Many meeting planners insist on talking with someone from the hotel's accounting department before the convention begins. The standard policy for the Hyatt Hotel chain is to take the meeting planner to the accounting office at the first mutually convenient time to go over billing procedure. The understanding agreed upon earlier is reinforced and problems are solved before the service is performed.

Figure 18.3. SPECIMEN RATES AND CHARGES BULLETIN.

SPECIMEN RATES AND CHARGES BULLETIN

To. Convention Attendees

The following rates and charges, which have been agreed to by ABC Company and the XYZ Hotel, will be in effect during your stay at the XYZ Hotel. The rates listed in this bulletin represent the maximum you should be charged for the listed services during the length of your stay at this convention.

DAILY ROOM RATE: Modified American Plan (2 meals)

$ 140.00 Per Person, per day plus
    11.00 Per Person,
        daily service charge* plus
     4.53 Daily state tax (3%)
	$ 230.00 Per Person, per day plus
	    11.00 Per Person,
	        daily service charge* plus
	     7.23 Daily state tax (3%)

$ 155.53 Daily Total	$ 248.23 Daily Total

These Rates: Include Lodging, breakfast & dinner daily, and gratuities for maids and MAP dining room personnel.

               Don't include Bellman, doorman or limo driver gratuities, parlor charges or incidental charges.

MAP CREDITS

Tavern Room   A credit of $8.00 per person will apply and the balance would be charged at a la carte prices.

Golf Club   Dinner in Golf Club carries a surcharge depending on items selected.

Main Dining Room   A few items are a la carte, depending on items selected.

All Extra Meals   (A la carte) charges will be billed to your individual hotel account.

Room Service   A room service charge of $2.00 per person ($2.50 in cottages) will apply to all room service orders.

NOTE: MAP includes dinner on check-in day, and breakfast on check-out day. Should you dine in a group, be certain that all room numbers are listed or only that person who signs will get the total charges for the group.

TRANSPORTATION

Airport to Hotel $6.50 per person
                 $3.25 per person (small children)

*Applicable if the hotel imposes a Service Charge

One month prior to the convention, a listing of specific rates and charges is sent to the convention attendee by the meeting planner. This type of communication clearly spells out exactly what is covered by the convening group and what charges the individual attendee will be responsible for, greatly reducing the chances of any misunderstandings at the time of the meeting or convention.
Source: Courtesy of the Insurance Conference Planners Association.

Convention organizers frequently complain that hotels cannot present the final accounting at the end of the event, while the convention staff is still on the premises and memories are fresh. If complete billing is not ready, they can still review the charges and initial approval. Some charges lag, but at least the bulk of the account can be settled.

A good practice, endorsed by many convention service managers, is to arrange for the meeting planner to meet with the property controller daily to go over the previous day's charges on the master account. Some hotel chains, such as the Crowne Plaza Hotels & Resorts, offer a *daily meeting debriefing* to allow meeting planners to review an itemized accounting of that day's expenditures (Figure 18.4 shows how the chain promotes this service). Daily meeting debriefings allow meeting planners to track and manage the func-

Figure 18.4. DAILY MEETING DEBRIEFINGS.

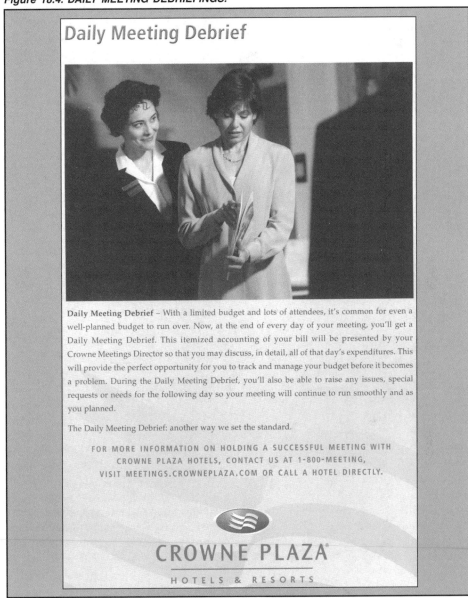

Daily Meeting Debrief – With a limited budget and lots of attendees, it's common for even a well-planned budget to run over. Now, at the end of every day of your meeting, you'll get a Daily Meeting Debrief. This itemized accounting of your bill will be presented by your Crowne Meetings Director so that you may discuss, in detail, all of that day's expenditures. This will provide the perfect opportunity for you to track and manage your budget before it becomes a problem. During the Daily Meeting Debrief, you'll also be able to raise any issues, special requests or needs for the following day so your meeting will continue to run smoothly and as you planned.

The Daily Meeting Debrief: another way we set the standard.

FOR MORE INFORMATION ON HOLDING A SUCCESSFUL MEETING WITH CROWNE PLAZA HOTELS, CONTACT US AT 1-800-MEETING, VISIT MEETINGS.CROWNEPLAZA.COM OR CALL A HOTEL DIRECTLY.

CROWNE PLAZA
HOTELS & RESORTS

The Crowne Plaza Hotels & Resorts has developed a "Meeting Success" program to assist meeting planners to plan and host successful meetings and events within their budgets. Part of this service is their Daily Meeting Debrief, which provides planners with an itemized accounting of each day's expenditures to enable them to track and manage the function budget.
Source: Courtesy of Crowne Plaza Hotels & Resorts

Best Practices:

Daily Meeting Debriefings
The Crowne Plaza Hotels & Resorts chain

To successfully attract meetings and functions business, hotels must keep abreast of the needs of meeting planners. The Crowne Plaza Hotels & Resorts chain relies on market research to ensure that they are meeting those needs. In a recent survey, the chain found that, in regard to billing, the most critical issue for the majority of the respondents was accuracy, especially in relation to correct line items and consistent formatting. Many of the planners responding suggested a pre-departure bill review meeting, an estimated pre-bill prior to the meeting, and/or a daily bill review.

Kevin Kowalski, vice president of brand management for the chain, says:

"We are currently monitoring the needs of meeting planners. These survey results reveal that services like the Crowne Meetings Director and our daily expenses debrief are directly addressing planners' needs."*

As part of its "Meeting Success" program, the chain offers a daily meeting debrief between the Crowne Meetings Director and the planner. At the meeting, an itemized accounting of charges posted to the account is presented to the planner. This enables him or her to track and manage his or her budget and also offers an opportunity to raise questions about specific items.

This daily tracking of expenditures allows the meeting planner to make any necessary changes or special requests for the next day's activities, and ensures that charges on the master account are accurate and up-to-date, facilitating the presentation of the final bill (in most cases, an accurate billing can be presented before the group leaves the hotel).

* "News Briefs", *Meetings West*, April 2004, p. 3.

tion budget on a frequent basis, and any discrepancies and questions can be addressed during these meetings. The daily reviews eliminate surprises for the meeting planner and, since issues are clarified before the group leaves the hotel, they facilitate the correct posting of master account charges (ideally, the master account can be presented before the event organizers leave the hotel).

The hotel doesn't want the entire account held up while a relatively minor matter is adjudicated, of course. One suggestion is to set this amount aside pending further investigation and/or discussion while the rest of the bill is settled. Some meeting planners ask that a certain amount be held back after the event to handle any adjustments. The amount of money held back and the time allowed should be part of the letter of agreement or other correspondence. Otherwise, the entire bill might be held up and perhaps used unfairly for leverage.

At some conventions, a considerable amount of cash is generated through registration and ticket sales. Some arrangements should be made to count this money and keep it safe. If such cash is applied against the master account, receipts should be issued for all payments. If agreed-upon payments have been made on schedule, organizations may request checks from the hotel in return for such cash. Clear such arrangements with the hotel controller.

The increasing use of the computer for accounting functions has greatly enhanced the billing process. But in addition to more efficient billing (some charges can be added instantaneously if the property uses point of sale terminals), computers increase the speed with which hotels can analyze convention groups for future billing.

One hotel sales executive sees technology helping both the hotel and the meeting planner:

> "Among the things that are different these days are that you can see the arrival/departure pattern of a group. You can see what food and beverage sales are per occupied room because they play a role in what's charged for meeting and sleeping rooms. Now the planner can get a report that will show the exact value of his or her group to the hotel. We still need to offer good meeting space, but now a lot of the competition is going to revolve around who can make the planner's job easier. And technology is helping us to accomplish that."[2]

Of course, a few hotels cannot afford the benefits of a computer, but more and more properties are making the investment. With computer systems, the bill can be broken down for each function and quickly tallied to provide the total charge within an hour of the last meeting. Confusion and long hours of labor are minimized, and the bill can be reviewed and finalized while details are still fresh in the minds of the hotel staff and the meeting planner.

Guest Credit

Another matter to be discussed by the hotel staff and the meeting planner is **guest credit**. With national credit cards, it is simply a matter of saying which cards the hotel will accept. If the hotel limits the cards it will take, this information should be given in time for inclusion in the convention brochure so the guests will be forewarned. But most national and international cards are accepted in most hotels, so this seldom constitutes much of a problem.

The extension of credit directly to the guest is more of a risk. The convention executive should be told if this is contrary to hotel policy. Then the recommended procedure by which a guest could establish credit with the hotel might be outlined.

The hotel should also state its policy about cashing checks for guests. Maximum amounts should be made clear. Cashing checks for people with no established credit is a courtesy, not an obligation. Many associations, and certainly corporations, guarantee the checks cashed for members or employees. A maximum limit, if any, should be indicated.

Gratuities and Service Charges

Gratuities and service charges are a generally accepted part of convention costs. They are covered in all sales proposals and later in the letter of agreement. Yet, few areas of convention management seem to cause as much controversy. It is important to note that while the terms **gratuity** (tip) and **service charge** are used interchangeably, they are different. A gratuity is a voluntary gift given for excellent service. A service charge is a fixed, mandatory amount given to service personnel.

Meeting planners are often confused about how much to tip, who should be tipped, and when the tip should be given. One hotelier states:

> "The end of tipping is a long way off in America. I feel the planner should settle the gratuities subject in advance. If he or she feels uncomfortable with the amount specified, he or she should go to another hotel. Likewise, if he or she feels there is dissatisfaction with the amount of the gratuities, he or she should think twice about returning to that hotel. Most of the problems with gratuities are the result of not discussing the matter with the hotel convention staff — in the beginning, when everything else is being settled. Nobody should ever feel strange about asking the hotel for advice on this matter."[3]

When hotels are approached for advice on the amounts considered fair, tipping guidelines should be suggested. Wisdom, however, should be used. Meeting planners are naturally offended by the suggestion that their gratuities are a form of remuneration rather than an expression of appreciation for good or exceptional service.

Gratuities and service charges can be categorized into four distinct groupings:

- Gratuities for hotel hourly personnel, such as bellpersons, food servers, housekeepers and door attendants.
- Service charges for group functions and banquets. These are automatic and mandatory, and are generally figured as a percentage of the bill and added to the check.
- Blanket service charges. These charges are added to the room charge and delegates are not encumbered with further tipping.
- Special gratuities given to management personnel, such as the convention service manager, banquet manager and head houseperson.

Because the issue of gratuities is often confusing to meeting planners, Howard Feiertag of the Center for Hospitality Research and Service suggests that the planner set aside one percent of the total convention costs for tips (the industry standard is one to two percent). When attendees pay tips themselves, however, there may be even more confusion. According to Feiertag, the following general guidelines apply when tipping hourly service personnel, our first classification:

Bartenders:	15 percent at the bar; 20 percent at your table
Bell Staff:	$1 per bag
Concierge:	Varies in relation to the service provided
Door Attendant:	$1 for hailing a cab or carrying bags
Housekeeping Staff:	$1 per room per night
Restaurant Server:	15 to 20 percent of the check
Room Service Staff:	15 percent unless tip is included in room charge
Valets:	$1 when your car is delivered
Wine Steward:	10 to 20 percent of the cost of the wine

Service charges for group meals and banquets, our second classification, seem to present the most problems. Many meeting planners justifiably decry the practice of a 15-percent service charge regardless of the quality of the service. However, the hotel is often following the terms of a union contract, which should be explained in the initial negotiations with the meeting planner. The flat percentage service charge is 15 to 20 percent in most cities.

It is important to note that in some states the amount will be subject to sales tax if it is listed as a service charge rather than a gratuity. If a planner hosts a lunch for 100 people at $25 per person, for example, and a service charge of 18 percent ($450) was added, the resulting total of $2,950 would be subject to the state's sales tax—not just the original cost of $2,500.

To combat this problem, some hotels eliminate the term *service charge* and replace it with *gratuity*. A gratuity can legally be added to the bill after the state sales tax has been levied on the cost of meals only. This results in major savings for meeting planners, and most of them prefer to be charged in this way.

No matter which approach is used, it is important that your hotel clearly spells out its policy to eliminate unpleasant surprises for the meeting planner. If mandatory service charges on food and beverage functions or sleeping rooms can legally be replaced with agreed-upon gratuities not subject to state taxes, this arrangement should be spelled out in the convention contract.

When there is a flat percentage on food and beverage setups, the hotel normally distributes the service charge among the service personnel. Many planners will ask the convention service manager for a breakdown of who shares in the distribution. Policies vary. While the bulk of any mandated service charge will go to the workers servicing the function, it is not uncommon for a portion to be used by management to offset labor costs. For example, one director of convention services at a well-known San Francisco hotel says:

> "The union contract specifies the apportionment of the 19 percent gratu-
> ity. No part goes to convention service staff, banquet managers, or room
> setup; but just 75 percent is equally distributed among the waiters -- the
> people who worked the function. The other 25 percent is allocated to a
> category called "salaries recovered", reducing labor costs on the profit
> and loss statement."[4]

Blanket service charges, our third classification, are becoming common. Planners and delegates often favor this form of tipping; it means they tip only once -- when they register -- and are not faced wih it again. Some resorts have used this method for years, and now commercial convention hotels are trying the system. The **American plan** has a single charge for rooms, meals and gratuities. The more common **European plan** prices rooms, meals and tips separately.

If a blanket tipping policy is to be used, this must be communicated to the delegates. Often the meeting planner will point out the policy in the registration packet. Notices declaring "Your gratuities are completely covered in the room charge; do not tip hotel personnel" are common. Similarly, the hotel must communicate this procedure to its em-ployees and discourage them from accepting tips. Again, the resume is the medium whereby the tipping policy is communicated internally.

To help clarify blanket tipping charges, we have outlined below the policies of two well-known resorts:

- The Greenbrier
  White Sulphur Springs, West Virginia

  *In lieu of gratuities for housekeeping and Modified American Plan food service
  personnel, a service charge of $12.00 per person is added daily to guests'
  accounts. Bellmen, doormen, and others who render personal services are not*

included in the service charge.

- Boca Raton Hotel and Club
  Boca Raton, Florida

  For the convenience of the convention group, the hotel adds $14.00 per day per person to cover the following hotel personnel:

- *front door and parking attendants*
- *handling of luggage on arrival and departure*
- *chamber maids*
- *dining room personnel for meals served under the meal plan*

  For a la carte food and beverages an automatic service charge of 15 percent is added to the check. Other personnel are tipped at the convention group's discretion.

The final type of gratuity is that used in rewarding special personnel. Meeting planners may ask the hotel about the accepted practice and internal policies for giving such tips. Hotels that do recommend tipping for special services will offer a suggested minimum scale. Figure 18.5 shows the results of a survey of meeting planners regarding how they tipped special service personnel.

Yet another type of service charge is the **resort fee**, charges automatically added by resorts for services ranging from in-room amenities to local telephone services to resort facilities, such as business centers, fitness centers and tennis courts. The sidebar titled "Which Amenities and Services Are Included in the Resort Fee?", which is based on the responses of 395 meeting planners, details some of the services typically included in resort fees.

WHICH AMENITIES AND SERVICES ARE INCLUDED IN THE RESORT FEE?	
Fitness center use	88%
Newspaper delivery	83%
Local phone service	78%
In-room coffee/tea	77%
Use of recreation facilities (tennis, pools)	73%
Turndown service	57%
Internet access	55%
Spa access	34%
Shuttle service	33%
Parking	32%
Housekeeping tips	26%
Bottled water	23%
Bellman tips	22%
Fax service	21%
Fitness classes	9%

Source: From a December 2004 survey conducted by M&C Research. Art Pfenning, "Who's Paying Resort Fees?", Meetings & Conventions, February 2005.

Meeting planners frequently balk at resort fees, which average $12 per day, and most feel that these fees should be eliminated. They often try to negotiate them out of the contract, or, if that is not possible, ask for a reduction in resort fees or have them rolled over into the overall room rate.

In conclusion, the handling of gratuities and service charges as with all elements of convention management, should be carefully reviewed and understood by both the meeting planner and the convention service manager. Even though tipping is a touchy area, no difficulties should arise if guidelines are clearly established at the outset.

Figure 18.5. GRATUITY STRUCTURE FOR SPECIAL TIPS.

Gratuities Vary Based On Hotel Staff Positions

Q. Assume that the following hotel personnel have been equally attentive. Indicate whether you would give them a gratuity, and if so, how much:

PERSONNEL	YES	NO	HIGH	LOW	AVERAGE
Convention Service Director (main contact)	75%	25%	$500	$25	$125
Food and Beverage Manager	68%	32%	$500	$15	$ 88
Assistant Convention Services Director	65%	35%	$150	$15	$ 58
Setup Crew Supervisor	62%	13%	$200	$10	$ 44
Hotel General Manager	0%	100%	—	—	—
Convention Sales Manager	10%	90%	$200	$35	$ 69
Account Executive on your convention	17%	83%	$400	$15	$ 80
Catering Manager	63%	37%	$400	$20	$ 78
Front Desk Supervisor*	69%	31%	$100	$10	$ 36
Head Banquet Waiter**	82%	18%	$125	$10	$ 42
Audio Visual Operator	41%	59%	$200	$ 5	$ 44
Switchboard Operator***	39%	61%	$ 50	$10	22

* Other gratuity: candy (1)
** Other gratuity: $10 per event (1); $20 per function (1)
***Other gratuity: $10 for each operator (1); $250 to PBX Fund (1); $150 to include operators (1); candy (4); and gift (1)

In a recent survey, Meeting News *asked meeting planners which hotel personnel they tipped for special service and the average amount of such tips.*
Source: Courtesy of Meeting News.

HSMAI's Suggested Payment Schedule

The Hospitality Sales & Marketing Association International offers a list of standardized procedures that help reduce problems in convention accounting. Here are the guidelines:

- Establish a formal procedure for the hotel and the meeting planner to review periodically the room block arrangements before the meeting. The recommended schedule: up to one year before the meeting; six months before; then every month; and, with one month to go, weekly. The use of rooming lists is encouraged.
- Meeting room usage and charges should be thoroughly reviewed before the meeting.
- The hotel should clearly specify what credit cards are accepted and the maximum that can be charged.
- A master statement of all functions should be organized daily.
- Night auditors and cashiers should be instructed about the details of posting convention charges.
- It is desirable to have corporate meeting planners guarantee all attendees' bills.
- The hotel should inform the company of any delinquent accounts after thirty days.
- A representative from accounting, the head cashier, and perhaps the accounts receivable department head should also attend the pre-convention meeting.
- The resume and individual function forms are to be supplied to the meeting planner before the convention; charges to be clearly specified in advance.

- At the conclusion of each function, a copy of the master statement and supporting vouchers should be furnished to the meeting planner for his or her signature.
- It is recommended that the master account be submitted in full no more than five days after the event. Prepayment of a portion of the master account is encouraged.

The emphasis of this checklist is *communication*. Every aspect of billing must be clearly and concisely communicated to the accounting department and the meeting planner.

Post-Convention Review

It is wise to review a job when it is completed. Much can be learned. Such a review should be done with an eye toward constructive improvement. The purpose of a review is to evaluate performance during the event and the forecasting and planning that preceded the convention. The goal is to improve technique so that the next event will go even smoother.

A convention service manager we interviewed about post-convention meetings said:

> "A good, thorough pre-convention meeting can lead to a very short and satisfying post-convention wrap-up."

We recommend two review sessions. The first, an intra-staff meeting, should involve the hotel staff only. The second, termed a **post-convention meeting (post-con)** should be attended by both the hotel staff and the meeting planning staff.

The hotel meeting should include the hotel sales manager, convention service manager, and all departments involved in servicing the group. The purposes of this meeting are to review the meeting's rough spots, to discuss how the event could have been expedited, and to recognize any efforts that went well as examples for the future. Often in such a meeting an internal report, called a **performance report**, is prepared. Kirby Smith, vice

Post-Convention Reporting

Mike Gamble
Sr. Vice President, Sales and Marketing
Philadelphia Convention & Visitors Bureau

"Post-convention reporting has become one of the overlooked, underrated, and irritating duties that convention professionals face everyday. Cities and hotels are still faced with inaccurate reporting of history and typically do not have the adequate information available to make a good business decision on whether or not to book a group or convention. With the fast pace of the hospitality industry, it is easy to move on to the next meeting or convention and forget about the one that has just finished....A thorough Post Convention Report...will give a much better picture of the overall value of the meeting that most times is not conveyed. During the qualifying and pre-sales activities, the hotels and convention bureaus often ask for an extraordinary amount of information about the group's history, buying habits, and ancillary spending...The irony is that typically hotels and cities are unable to provide the same amount of information back to the planner once the meeting is completed...."

president of sales skills training for Marriott says his company takes post-meeting performance reports seriously:

> "We use one form that's designed to hold people accountable in every facet of a hotel's operation, channeling to them with our bonus system. The form is broken down into the sales process -- pre-event, event, and post-event phases -- and addresses transitions from sales to service."[5]

The second meeting should involve both the meeting planner and his or her staff and the hotel staff. If the convention is city-wide, the convention bureau, exposition service contractor, destination management company, and audiovisual supplier may be invited. This meeting is also held to go over the many things that happened at the convention while they are fresh in everyone's mind. A good time to hold this meeting is when the master account gets its final review and approval. Everyone is in the hotel and relaxed after the great effort.

Don't duck discussions about the rough spots. Talk them out and try to agree on how they can be handled in the future. Both teams learn much from these inter-staff meetings.

This is also a time to begin the pitch for more business. Many hotel staff people are reluctant to start selling at this time, but if all went well, it may very well be the best time to make the pitch. If not for the convention itself, for other types of meetings. Corporations hold meetings all the time, and you should make your bid for more of their business.

Every aspect of the meeting should be reviewed and discussed candidly. Association executives should feel free to express their views on the staff's service and performance. Meeting planners appreciate having the opportunity to share their comments. If they sense the hotel is honestly concerned about improvement, they will more readily book future business.

Comparison with Projections

Compare what happened with what was expected to happen. Prepare a **pick-up report**, comparing the number of guestrooms originally blocked out with the number actually used. Review the flow into and out of the hotel. Did you have adequate help on hand to receive the guests? Were no-shows a problem? Did you overbook? If so, how did you handle it? Compare attendance with that of other years.

Early departures wreak havoc with hotel income. Yet they generally reflect at least as much on the convention programing as on the hotel attractions. If early departures were greater than in previous years, the program could be at fault; but the hotel still might give some thought to what it can do to make its facilities or area more inviting.

If this convention continually has a problem with early departures, the executive should make some effort to get members to estimate their stays more accurately and honestly. Most convention executives realize that healthy hotels are their concern, too.

Late departures create a different problem when they interfere with other group commitments that are beginning. There is enough evidence of intentional overbooking by hotels that late departures add fuel to the fire. Late departures are a problem, of course, only when the house is overfilled. Otherwise, it's a pleasant bonus.

The entire projection of arrival and departure patterns should be reviewed. The mix of rooms used — single, doubles, twins and suites — should be compared with what was blocked out in order to polish the technique for the next time. Compare the pattern with the work schedule of your front desk people and other personnel needed for heavy arrival traffic.

Function Attendance

Both the hotel staff and the convention executive are most interested in how actual attendance at special functions compared with expectations. Guarantees at food functions don't tell the whole story. If actual attendance fell below the guarantee, the convention executive still has to pay for the full number guaranteed or try to persuade the hotel to accept payment for only those served. On the other hand, if more than an extra five percent showed up, the hotel is hard pressed to seat and serve them. The convention organization is chagrined not to serve its members; the hotel is undeservedly shown in a bad light.

Review function room allocations. It is difficult to conduct a meeting in a room only 30 percent filled. A smaller room would have helped, if one were available. If not, dividers and screens could have helped. Perhaps the larger room could have been used for something else.

Special Services

Feedback on the hotel's services also is of interest. Each convention is different, but the hotel can learn from each one about room service, the restaurants, the play at the athletic facilities, the elevator service. Keep an eye on these services because hotel reputations depend on them. It is an interesting phenomenon that the people who shape the image in the hotel business are the ones who get the least pay. The telephone operator and the front desk people probably have more contact with hotel guests than anyone else on the staff. If they have been congenial throughout the convention, the customer probably will carry away a good image of the hotel.

Individual Comments

A very different picture may emerge if you take the trouble to invite comments from your own staff, too. Staff members have a different vantage point than the convention service manager. Ask the bell staff, housekeepers, and front desk people how they think the convention went.

Stand near the cashier at check-out time to get candid comments from guests. Some hotels make post-event mailings to guests. The benefits are twofold: the hotel projects a sincere desire to render good service, and it is often able to detect unspotted problem areas.

Doubletree Inns, for example, uses a service evaluation form (see Figure 18.6) to quiz the respondent on all service aspects of the meeting. An analysis of the results has proven to be very advantageous when it comes to booking repeat business.

Hyatt Hotels recently employed third-party telemarketing assistance to receive feedback from planners about service delivery. Fred Shea, vice president of sales operations, says:

> "Nobody can tell you what to do better than your customers. Hyatt commissioned the Gallup polling organization to survey meeting planners by telephone. With results of the canvassing, the company is making changes in its culture that are tied to service accountability."[6]

Whatever your approach, some effort should be made to determine the staff's and guests' feelings about how the event went and how the hotel fared.

Figure 18.6. SERVICE EVALUATION QUESTIONNAIRE.

Forms such as this one, used by the Doubletree Inn, ask delegates for a rating of the hotel's performance during a meeting or convention. Used with permission.

Post-convention Reporting

Post-convention reports have become one of the most discussed topics in today's meetings market, as accurate and thorough reports are important to both planners and hoteliers.

Meeting planners know that information is power, and when it comes to negotiating a thorough meetings history provides leverage in ensuring better rates. Catherine Roper, director of meetings for the Health Industry Distributors Association says:

"As a planner, I need help from the hotel in knowing the value of my business. This is so I have a history to bring to negotiations. For instance, my people are in the gift shops, the restaurants, playing golf and tennis and using the spa. I want to know the total picture of my meeting's value."[7]

Hotels, likewise, recognize that post-convention reports allow them to more accurately evaluate and qualify business. Convention bureaus need accurate histories when trying to establish room blocks for city-wide conventions, and hotels need them to determine their level of participation.

Accurate post-convention reports also lead to better service. For example, the convention service manager can staff to handle peak arrivals based on past experience.

To ensure they receive post-convention reports, some planners are stipulating in the contract that they won't pay until they get an accurate report. Planners are also asking hotels to provide post-convention information on **ancillary business** -- affiliates and subgroups as well as exhibitors. Planners recognize that the ancillary revenue to hotels from associations with exhibits can be huge. Not only do exhibitors utilize guestrooms, but many also hold events ranging from meals to hospitality suites to meetings.

Responding to the need for post-convention reports, most major hotel chains now have a company-wide standardized system for post-convention reporting. Hyatt, Hilton, and Marriott automatically provide post-convention reports for all groups using 100 rooms or more on peak nights.

Many in the meetings industry would like to see an industry-wide, single database of post-convention information. One possibility proposed by industry groups is to have post-convention information submitted by hotels to their convention bureaus. The information would then be stored in the **MINT** (Meeting Information Network) system, a database developed by the International Association of Convention and Visitors Bureaus, which is accessible on the Internet.

It is important to note that databases and other exchanges of information regarding a group's history should never include dollar amounts. It is a violation of antitrust law to exchange pricing information, such as room rates or banquet charges. Exchanging the number of rooms blocked, rooms picked up, number and size of food functions, and describing room service and restaurant volume as light, moderate or heavy is an acceptable practice.

Since it is so important to get accurate meeting statistics, there has been a growing consensus within the industry that standardized forms would facilitate the process. In response, the Convention Industry Council (CIC), which has been active in trying to standardize many areas of the hospitality industry, developed a post-event report template. This fourteen-page template is not only available on paper, but on computer disks and on-line as well, making it easy to enter data and get an almost immediate picture of the convention success (the on-line version can be viewed at www.conventionindustry.org/APEX/acceptedpractices/posteventreporting.htm). The box titled "Industry-Wide Post-Event Report" further explains the Post-Event Report (PER) and its importance to meeting planners and hotels alike.

Final Appraisal

Before breaking down the working file and returning appropriate correspondence to the account file, ask if you could do a better job if the clock could be turned back to give you

Industry-Wide Post-Event Report

Since compiling accurate meeting histories is essential in evaluating business, standardized information is becoming increasingly necessary. To ensure that complete, standardized data could be collected for analysis, APEX (the Accepted Practices Exchange), an initiation of the Convention Industry Council, developed a template that could be readily used for this important function.

After extensive research, the History/Post-Event Reports Panel of APEX spent a year compiling a History/Post-Event Report (PER), that meets an established set of guidelines, including:

- The necessity of a Post Event Report (PER) citing details and activities of an event—its history
- The establishment of an APEX PER template
- A face-to-face meeting between the primary event organizer and each venue or facility involved in an event that should occur immediately following the end of the event, to focus on completion of the PER
- Once the PER is complete the organizer should file report copies with each venue or facility used for the event (i.e. CVB, hotel, conference center, etc.)
- Detailed recommendations for filing the PER with each venue and facility used for the event
- The most recent PER for an event should accompany any request for proposals sent to solicit proposals for future occurrences of same
- The APEX PER should be completed for events of all sizes, especially those of 25 peak room nights or more

Approved as an "Accepted Practice" by the CIC on October 30, 2003, the 14-page template, which is available on line at www.conventionindustry.org/APEX/acceptedpractices/posteventreporting.htm and is also available on computer disks and in a paper version, includes instructions for use, forms for entering information on group event(s), contacts, hotel rooms, room blocks, food and beverage, function space, exhibit space and future event dates, a section on report distribution and tracking and Post-Event Report FAQs.

The report has proven invaluable not only for properties that had no previous reporting procedures, but also for properties and chains that had developed or were in the process of developing their own reporting systems. Dave Scypinski, senior vice president of industry relations for Starwood Hotels and Resorts, says:

"All the information we want to report on is contained in the APEX post-event report. If this to become our industry standard, we said let's get a jump on it for internal purposes."

The PER also assists meeting planners in evaluating their meetings and events. Vicky Betzig, CMP, vice president of JR Daggett and Associates, called the PER a "phenomenal" document, adding:

"I know of planners who are using it in their organizations as 'standard operating procedure.'"

One meeting planner who praises the PER is Barbara Zamora, program director for the Association of Hispanic Advertising Agencies. She says:

"It is very thorough; there is no room for error. The PER can be customized for small or large groups; I use it for both my larger meetings, and even for board meetings. Suppliers and planners can communicate much more effectively."

The popularity of the PER is evidenced by it being downloaded 432 times from the CIC website in September 2004 alone, and that the number continues to grow each month.
Sources: The APEX Post-Event Report Template, ©2003, Convention Industry Council; Christie Hicks and Christine Shimisaki, CMP, "APEX in Action: Bridging the Gap," pcma convene, June 2003, p. 18.

another chance. That question should be considered with complete frankness in the cold light of post-convention experience. If the answer discloses areas of difficulty, you should take steps to eliminate the problems in the future. The problems could deal with personnel or facilities. Solving them could help the sales manager set priorities on the kind of business you want and can handle. If the answers please you, don't forget to send a thank-you letter to the meeting planner, and to put that name in your follow-up file for some time in the very near future.

Summary

As we have seen throughout this text, selling to and servicing the conventions and meetings market requires careful planning and attention to details. The convention billing process and post-convention follow-up are important factors in building a group's goodwill and generating future business. A property must clearly spell out billing procedures and make it easy and convenient for the meeting planner to keep abreast of meeting charges. And, after the convention or meeting, follow-up is necessary to determine areas of strengths and weaknesses and to build a group history that can be used in the future to negotiate additional events.

Endnotes:

1. Deirdre Bourke, "Bill Review Made Easy", Conferon special to PCMA. www.pcma.org/templates/conferon/charts/Ch12/htm.
2. Don Nichols, "High-Tech Comes to Hotels," *Association Meetings*, January 1997, p. 46.
3. Roger Sonnabend, "The Hotelier Looks at the Business of Meetings," *3M Business Press*.
4. Julie Barker, "The Ultimate Guide to Tipping and Gratuities," *Successful Meetings*, July 1997, p. 46.
5. Ruth Hill, "Planner's Lament," *Lodging*, September 1999, p. 80.
6. Ibid.
7. Ruth Hill, "Confronting the Bull in Today's Market," *HSMAI Marketing Review*, Winter 1998, p. 35.

Additional References:

The Convention Industry Council Manual, Seventh Edition. www.conventionindustry.org

Internet Sites:

For more information, visit the following Internet sites. Internet addresses can change without notice. If a site is no longer available at the address listed below, a search engine can be used to find the new address or additional, related sites.

Caesars Palace – www.caesars.com
Conferon Special to the PCMA - www.pcma.org/templates/conferon/charts/CH12/htm.
Convention Industry Council – www.conventionindustry.org
Convention Industry Council Accepted Practices: Post-Event Reporting – www.conventionindustry.org/apex/acceptedpractices/posteventreporting.htm.
Hospitality Sales and Marketing Association International (HSMAI) – www.hsmai.org
Insurance Conference Planners – www.icpanet.com
The Original Tipping Page – www.tipping.org
Philadelphia Convention and Visitors Bureau – www.libertynet.org/phila-visitor

Study Questions:

1. Discuss the statement "As with most aspects of convention planning, the time to avoid billing problems is in the beginning and not at the end." What procedures are recommended for avoiding billing problems?
2. What are the three different folios that can be used for a meeting or convention? Who pays the charges for each?
3. What factors should be considered when determining a time of payment for a meeting group? When are charges typically billed?
4. List the four groupings for service gratuities and distinguish between blanket service charges and special tipping.
5. Outline the HSMAI's suggested payment schedule.
6. Why is a post-convention review important? Who should attend post-convention review meetings?
7. What should be included in the post-convention report? What are the benefits of post-convention reports? Design a sample report that would help your hotel to gauge the success of a convention.

Key Terms:

American plan. Charge includes room, food and beverage, and gratuities. Includes three meals per day.
Ancillary business. Affiliates and subgroups, such as exhibitors, who contribute to the overall value of the meeting. Often, this type of business that is brought to a

facility because of an event is called **in conjunction with** business.

Authorized signature. Signature of person(s) with the authority to charge to a group master account.

Billing instructions. Notice as to how charges for an event should be handled and to whom invoices should be addressed.

Blanket service charges. Service charges added into the room charge so that attendees do not have to tip during their stay. Primarily used with the American Plan (AP) system.

European plan. Guestrooms, food and beverage and tips are priced separately.

Gratuity. A voluntary payment added to a bill to signify good service. Also called a **tip**.

Guest credit. Credit extended to a guest based on information collected by the hotel's credit department. This is a courtesy of the hotel, not an obligation.

Incidental charges. Expenses other than guestroom charges and taxes. Billed to a guest's folio.

Individual guest folio. An account on which all individual guest charges not covered by the master account will be posted to be paid by the individual guest.

Master account folio. An account on which all charges incurred by delegates are accumulated to be paid by the sponsoring organization. The charges to be posted to this account should be agreed upon in advance. These may include room, tax, incidentals, food and beverage, audiovisual equipment, decor and so on. Also called a **master bill**.

Master account billing authorization form. A form that provides instructions on the types of folios to be established, limits of financial responsibility, and the names and signatures of personnel authorized to sign for group charges.

MINT (Meeting Information Network). An online database of meeting profiles maintained by the International Association of Convention and Visitors Bureaus.

Performance report. An internal report used by hotels to evaluate a convention. The hotel can use this research to determine how the convention facilities matched the client's needs.

Pick-up report. A post-meeting document detailing the number of hotel rooms used each day of an event. This report includes the total number of guestrooms originally blocked for each night and how many were actually used.

Post-convention meeting (post-con). A meeting at the primary facility at which an event occurred just after the event has ended. Attendees usually include the primary event organizer, representatives of the host organization, department heads of the facility, other facility staff as required, and event contractors. Its purpose is to evaluate the implementation of the event and to complete the post-convention report.

Post-convention report. A report of the details and activities of an event. A collection of post-convention reports over time provides a complete history for an event. Also called a **post-event report**.

Rates and charges bulletin. Communicates specific rates for rooms, meals, gratuities and billing procedures agreed upon by the various parties involved.

Resort fees. Charges automatically added by a hotel for services ranging from in-room amenities to local telephone services to resort facilities, such as business centers, fitness centers and tennis courts.

Resume. A form that provides a comprehensive overview of an entire event, from pre-convention to post-convention, for the hotel staff. These sheets detail activities from day to day (and hour by hour), and cover complete details of functions, reservations procedures, billing, recreational activities and anything else that may

require the attention of the hotel's staff. Also called a **specification sheet**.
Service charge. An automatic and mandatory amount added to standard food and beverage charges or other hotel services.
Split folio. Charges are paid partially by the sponsoring organization and partially by the guest. Communication is needed to ensure that all parties involved understand who is responsible for specific charges.

Appendix I

Directory of U.S. Trade Organizations and Publications

American Hotel & Lodging Association
(AH&LA)
1201 New York Avenue, NW, Suite 600
Washington, DC 20005
(202) 289-3100
Fax (202) 289-3199
www.ahla.com

American Society of Association
Executives
(ASAE)
1575 Eye Street, NW
Washington, DC 20005
(202) 626-2741
Fax (202) 371-0870
www.asaenet.org

American Society for Training and
Development
(ASTD)
1640 King Street/P.O. Box 1443
Alexandria, VA 22313
(703) 683-8100
www.astd.org

American Society of Travel Agents
(ASTA)
1101 King Street, Suite 200
Alexandria, VA 22314
(703) 739-2782
Fax (703) 684-8319
www.astanet.com

Association for Convention Marketing
Executives
(ACME)
2965 Flowers Road S., Suite 105
Atlanta, GA 30341
(770) 454-6111
Fax (770) 458-3314
www.acmenet.org

Association for Convention Operations
Management
(ACOM)
1819 Peachtree Street, N.E., Suite 712
Atlanta, GA 30309
(770) 454-9411
(770) 458-3314

Association of Corporate Travel
Executives
(ACTE)
515 King Street, Suite 330
Alexandria, VA 22314
800-ACTE NOW
www.acte.org

Association Management (Publication)
1575 Eye Street, NW
Washington, DC 20005
(202) 626-2711
www.asaenet.org/publications

Association Meetings (Publication)
63 Great Road
Maynard, MA 01754
(508) 897-5552
www.meetingsnet.com

Business Travel News (Publication)
1515 Broadway
New York, NY 10036
(212) 869-1300
www.btnonline.com

Center for Exhibition Industry Research
2301 Lake Shore Drive, Suite E1002
Chicago, IL 60616
(312) 808-2347
Fax (312) 949-3472
www.ceir.org

**Convention Industry Council
(CIC)**
Dept. 4490, P.O. Box 85080
Richmond, VA 23285
(703) 610-9030
Fax (703) 610-9005
www.conventionindustry.org

Corporate & Incentive Travel
(Publication)
488 Madison Avenue
New York, NY 10022
(212) 888-1500

Corporate Meetings & Incentives
(Publication)
43 L Nason Street
Maynard, MA 01754
(978) 897-5552

Convene **(Publication)**
2301 S. Lake Shore Drive
Chicago, IL 60616
(312) 423-7262
www.pcma.org/pub

**Exhibit Designers and Producers
Association
(EDPA)**
5775-G Peachtree-Dudwoody Road
Atlanta, GA 30342
(404) 303-7310
Fax (404) 252-0774
www.edpa@assnhq.com

**Exhibition Service Contractors
Association
(ESCA)**
400 S. Houston Street, Suite 210
Dallas, TX 75202
(214) 742-9217
Fax (214) 741-2519
www.esca.org

**Healthcare Convention Exhibitors
Association
(HCEA)**
5775 Peachtree-Dunwoody Road
Atlanta, GA 30342
(404) 252-3663
Fax (404) 252-0774
www.hcea.org

**Hospitality Sales and Marketing
Association International
(HSMAI)**
1300 L Street, NW, Suite 1020
Washington, DC 20005
(202) 789-0089
Fax (202) 789-1725
www.hsmai.org

HSMAI Marketing Review **(Publication)**
1300 L Street NW, Suite 1020
Washington, DC 20005
(202) 789-0089
Fax (202) 789-1725
www.hsmai.org

**Institute of Association Management
Companies
(IAMC)**
104 Wilmot Road, Suite 201
Deerfield, IL 60015-5195

Insurance Conference Planner
(Publication)
43 L Nason Street
Maynard, MA 01754
(978) 897-5552
Fax (978) 897-6824

**International Association of Assembly
Managers
(IAAM)**
635 Fritz
Coppell, TX 75019
(972) 255-8020
Fax (972) 255-9582
www.iaam.org

International Association of Conference Centers
(IACC)
243 N. Lindbergh, Suite 315
St. Louis, MO 63141
(314) 993-8575
Fax (314) 993-8919
www.iacconline.com

International Association of Convention & Visitors Bureaus
(IACVB)
2025 M Street, NW, Suite 500
Washington, DC 20036
(202) 296-7888
Fax (202) 296-7889
www.iacvb.org

International Association for Exhibition Management
(IAEM)
5001 LBJ Freeway, Suite 350
Dallas, TX 57244
(972) 458-8002
(972) 458-8119
www.iaem.org

International Association of Fairs & Expositions
(IAFE)
P.O. Box 985
Springfield, MO 65801
(417) 862-5771
Fax (417) 862-0156

Medical Meetings **(Publication)**
43 L Nason Street
Maynard, MA 01754
(978) 897-5552

Meeting News **(Publication)**
1515 Broadway
New York, NY 10036
(212) 869-1300
www.meetingsnews.com

Meeting Professionals International
(MPI)
4455 LBJ Freeway, Suite 1200
Dallas, TX 54244
(972) 702-3000
(972) 702-3036
www.mpiweb.org

Meetings & Conventions **(Publication)**
500 Plaza Drive
Secaucus, NJ 07094
(201) 902-1700
www.meetings-conventions.com

Meetings & Incentives **(Publication)**
See Appendix II.

National Coalition of Black Meeting Planners
(NCBMP)
8630 Fenton Street, Suite 126
Silver Spring, MD 20910
(202) 628-3952
Fax (301) 588-0011
www.ncbmp.com

National Association of Catering Executives
(NACE)
5565 Sterrett Drive, Suite 328
Columbia, MD 21045
(410) 997-9055
Fax (410) 997-8834
www.nace.net

National Business Travel Association
(NBTA)
1560 King Street, Suite 301
Alexandria, VA 22314
(703) 684-0836
www.mbta.org

Official Meeting Facilities Guide **(Publication)**
500 Plaza Drive
Secaucus, NJ 07094
(201) 902-1700
Fax (201) 319-1685

**Professional Convention Management
Association
(PCMA)**
2301 S. Lake Shore Drive
Chicago, IL 60616
(312) 423-7262
Fax (312) 423-7222
www.pcma.org

**Religious Conference Management
Association
(RCMA)**
1 RCA Dome, Suite 120
Indianapolis, IN 46225
(317) 632-1888
Fax (317) 632-7909
www.meetingsnet.com

Religious Conference Manager
(Publication)
43 L Nason Street
Maynard, MA 01754
(978) 897-5552

Sales and Marketing Management
(Publication)
777 Broadway
New York, NY 10003
(646) 654-7323

**Society of Corporate Meeting
Professionals
(SCMP)**
2965 Flowers Road, Suite 105
Atlanta, GA 30341
(770) 457-9212
Fax (770) 458-3314
www.scmp.org

**Society of Government Meeting Planners
(SGMP)**
908 King Street
Alexandria, VA 22314
(703) 549-0892
Fax (703) 549-0708
www.sgmp.org

**Society of Incentive Travel Executives
(SITE)**
21 West 38th Street
New York, NY 10018
(212) 575-0910
Fax (212) 575-1838
www.site-intl.org

Successful Meetings **(Publication)**
633 Third Avenue
New York, NY 10017
(212) 986-4800
www.successmtgs.com

**Trade Show Exhibitors Association
(TSEA)**
5501 Backlick Road, Suite 105
Springfield, VA 22151
(703) 941-3725
Fax (703) 941-8275
www.tsea.org

**Travel Industry Association of America
(TIAA)**
1100 New York Avenue, NW
Washington, DC 20005
(202) 408-8422
Fax (202) 408-1255

Appendix II

Directory of Canadian Trade Organizations and Publications

Canadian Association of Convention & Visitors Bureaus
c/o Tourism Winnipeg
279 Portage Avenue
Winnipeg, Manitoba, Canada, R3B 2B4
(204) 943-1970
Fax: (204) 942-4043

Canadian Association of Exposition Management
Box 82, 6900 Airport Road, Suite 239-A
Mississauga, Ontario, Canada L4V 1E8
(905) 678-9377
Fax (905) 678-9578

Canadian Association of Fairs & Exhibitions
Box 1172, Station Main
Edmonton, Alberta, Canada T5J 2M4
(780) 474-1902
Fax (780) 471-4981

Canadian Association of Professional Speakers
Box 294, 10435 Islington Avenue
Kleinburg, Ontario, Canada L0J 1C0
(905) 893-1689
Fax (905) 893-2392

Canadian Business Travel Association
5988 du Bocage
Montreal, Quebec, Canada H1M 1X2
(514) 353-4681, (888) 990-2540
Fax (514) 353-5736

Canadian Hotel Marketing & Sales Executives
84 Seventh Street
Toronto, Ontario, Canada M8V 3B4
(416) 252-9800
Fax (416) 252-7071

Canadian Society of Association Executives
10 King Street E., Suite 1100
Toronto, Ontario, Canada M5C 1C3
(416) 363-3555
Fax (416) 363-3630

Exhibit & Display Association of Canada
51A Esna Park Drive, Unit 2
Markham, Ontario, Canada L3R 1O9
(905) 943-9548
Fax (905) 943-9547

Hotel Association of Canada
130 Albert Street, Suite 1016
Ottawa, Ontario, Canada K1P 5G4
(613) 237-7149
Fax (613) 237-8928

Independent Meeting Planners Association of Canada
324 Glen Manor Drive
Toronto, Ontario, Canada M4E 2X7
(416) 686-5266
Fax (416) 686-5277

Insurance Conference Planners Association
106-206 West Esplanade
Vancouver, British Columbia, Canada V7M 3G7
(604) 988-2054
Fax (604) 988-4743

Meeting Professionals International
Box 11, 329 March Road, Suite 232
Kanata, Ontario, Canada K2K 2E1
(613) 271-8901
Fax (613) 599-7027

Meetings and Incentive Travel
(Publication)
777 Bay Street
Toronto, Ontario, Canada M5W 1A7
(416) 596-5640
Fax (416) 593-3193

Professional Convention Management Association
Canada East
2 Bloor Street W., Suite 1902
Toronto, Ontario, Canada M4W 3E2
(416) 923-2324
Fax (416) 923-7264

Canada West
1665 West Broadway
Vancouver, British Columbia, Canada V6J 1X1
(604) 736-1877
Fax (604) 736-4675

Society of Incentive & Travel Executives, Canadian Chapter
6519-B Mississauga Road
Mississauga, Ontario, Canada L5N 1A6
(905) 567-7190
Fax (905) 567-719

Appendix III

Convention Sales and Services Case Studies

The following cases have been developed through the involvement of industry leaders. The issues and problems presented in these cases illustrate the types of situations you can expect to encounter when working in convention sales and services. The discussion questions at the end of each case direct your attention to important issues, but you needn't limit your analysis to finding the answers to these questions. Examining the cases from different perspectives can help you get more out of each case.

Here are some guidelines that might be helpful in analyzing the cases:

- Read each case study carefully, noting important information and facts.

- Construct a time line of events leading to the situation being considered.

- Identify all of the significant characters in the case.

- Identify the problem presented by the case and define it. Is there more than one problem?

- Analyze the problem. What are its causes? Whom does it affect?

- List important factors in the case that affect your analysis (for example: type of property, location of property, time of year).

- List items you think should be addressed in developing a solution to the problem.

- Identify a solution (or solutions) to the problem. Remember that often times the first solution that comes to mind is not the best.

- Evaluate your solution. If your solution was implemented, would it solve the problem? What would be the possible consequences? Might it cause new problems?

- Look at the case again, taking the perspective of a different character in the case. Explore the problem and your solution(s) from that character's perspective.

Studying these cases will help you learn important lessons and develop critical thinking skills that will be valuable to you in your hospitality career.

SUMMARY OF CASE STUDIES

Chapter 2 — Leadership at the Hamilton: Impasse Between the General Manager and Director of Sales

The general manager of a 500-room first-class downtown hotels calls in a marketing consultant to shake up the sales staff. Year-to-date occupancy is down 4% with a year-end projected shortfall of $700,000 in revenue, but marketing expenses are already $55,000 over budget. The consultant's recommendations must temper the unrealistic expectations of the GM and refocus the efforts of the director of sales.

Chapter 3 — Departmental Conflict at The Ultra Hotel

This case pits marketing and sales against the rooms division in a battle over a sensitive hotel issue: how many rooms can marketing and sales have for group sales? To land an important piece of group business, the marketing and sales director wants more rooms than are usually allocated to group sales; the rooms director thinks the group's business is not worth inconveniencing the hotel's regular transient guests.

Chapter 5 – Overcoming Rate Resistance—Among the Sales Staff

The 263-room Park View Hotel has too much contracted business at a low rate. The director of sales works with the sales staff to replace a third of this business – about 5,000 room nights – with higher-rated transient and group business. They look at what business to keep, new sources of business to replace the contract business, and scripts for the sales staff to use with current clients of the preferred group rate.

Chapter 6 – Reviving Revenue Management

After surviving the opening of a competing hotel, the GM and sales staff at the Hearthstone Suites Hotel are challenged to revive the property's revenue management program. While occupancy is at budget year-to-date, average daily rate (ADR) is down by $6.00. Also, the mix of commercial business is lower than planned (40% of guest mix instead of 50%) and the SMERF segment is higher than it should be (15% of guest mix instead of 5%).

Chapter 7 – Don't Just Tell It – Sell It! or Needs Satisfaction Selling: Booking Business by Turning Features into Benefits

In this case, veteran salesperson Sandra Savvy shares techniques for combining courtesy and customers' needs satisfaction to build business, a common sense approach often overlooked in sales. New salesperson Drew Newbie also gets some tips from Sandra on how to turn property features into benefits.

Chapter 9 – No Vacancy

The negotiation process is one of the most challenging aspects of hospitality sales – particularly if both sides at the negotiation table are to be satisfied. In this case, the sales manager of the Monte Sereno Hotel negotiates with Jon Stonewall, the unyielding manager of a national computer software company, who wants to hold a regional meeting at the hotel. The challenge is to arrive at a win-win situation for the hotel and the client.

Chapter 11 – **Sales Underperforms Even While Meeting Budget**

The new general manager at a 180-room economy/business property in a booming suburb of a major city is challenged by the regional director of operations to increase the hotel's market penetration rate. The case focuses on increasing the volume of group business as well as raising the ADR for groups.

Chapter 14 – **Distributing Sales Functions Between a Hotel's Sales and Catering Departments**

Year-end projections for a 400-room first-class suburban hotel show banquet food sales will be off by $60,000 to budget and audiovisual revenues and room rental revenues will miss budget by $30,000. The director of catering learns to rely less on the hotel sales department and takes ownership of the problems.

CASE STUDY: CHAPTER 2

Leadership at the Hamilton: Impasse Between the
General Manager and Director of Sales

It was hard for Susan Fontenot to keep her mind on her driving as she made her way through the city's early morning rush-hour traffic. She was on her way to a potentially difficult meeting with Thad Johnson, the director of sales for The Hamilton, a 500-room first-class hotel right in the heart of downtown. Susan was a marketing consultant that the general manager of The Hamilton, Rick Martin, had called last week, all in a dither. "I can't believe it," Rick had said. "I just got this month's profit and loss statement, and occupancy year-to-date is down four percent, while marketing expenses are over budget by $55,000. How can that happen? Months ago I raised the sales-call quotas for our salespeople, started sending them to every trade show in sight, and re-did all of our collateral materials so they are really first class. And still we get these numbers! I don't know what else to do to help Thad — my background is in F&B, not sales. Will you come in and help us with a plan to turn things around?"

Susan knew from experience that there were two sides to every sales-are-down story, and this was no exception. When she arrived in Thad's office and sat down across the desk from him, it didn't take him long to get to the point. "Rick doesn't know what he's doing," he said bluntly. "Three months ago, when the occupancy numbers first began to go down, he started bugging me about sales calls. I told him to be patient, things would turn around. But they didn't turn around fast enough for him, and a month ago he raised our sales-call quotas. The only thing raising our call quotas did was raise everybody's stress levels in the department."

"Yes, Rick mentioned raising the quotas," Susan said, taking a yellow pad and pen from her briefcase. "Just how high did he raise them?"

"He wanted each of us to make 50 in-person client calls a week! Two breakfast site inspections, two lunch site inspections, two dinner site inspections, and four other on-site visits in between, every day. He just pulled those numbers out of the air. It's ridiculous."

"How many calls were your salespeople supposed to make before?"

Thad frowned. "I don't believe in quotas," he said. "I came up through the ranks, and I know how much I resented the director of sales I used to work for. She insisted on a certain number of calls every week, with all sorts of end-of-week and end-of-month sales call reports to fill out, and I told myself I wasn't going to operate that way. I trust my people and I don't look over their shoulders all the time. Besides, they're always busy. Because we're a first-class hotel, I emphasize personal service. I make sure the salespeople baby-sit their groups when they're in the hotel. 'Make sure the client sees you all the time and knows you care' — that's my motto. If the client has a problem, the salesperson is right there to take care of it personally."

Susan smiled. "It must make it hard for your salespeople to find time to make outside calls."

"Well, as a matter of fact, it was pretty rare for us to make an outside call before Rick handed down his quotas," Thad replied. "I never had quotas before; our hotel sells itself. Everybody know what we stand for and what we offer. If someone wants to go first-class in this city, this is the place to stay."

"How close are your salespeople coming to actually making 50 calls a week?"

"To be honest, I don't know," Thad said. "I just told them to do the best they could. Like I said, I don't believe in quotas and paperwork and I'm hoping Rick won't push it."

Susan made some notes on her yellow pad.

"Besides," That went on, "we're too busy going to trade shows! That's another thing Rick insisted on. Just between you and me, I think it's because he enjoyed going to the National Restaurant Association show in Chicago every year back when he was a food and beverage director. Now we're constantly packing and unpacking our trade show booth and making travel arrangements to travel hither and yon. Most of the time these trade shows don't generate any business. People just pick our booth clean of brochures — that's another thing!" Thad grabbed a brochure sitting on his desk. "Look at this thing! Ten pages, full color! Back at the beginning of the year Rick insisted that all of our collateral materials be in color, so he scrapped everything except for this brochure and a 30-page banquet menu collateral piece we send out to prospective banquet clients. That used to be a two-color piece, but now it's full color too. He said a first-class hotel should have first-class collateral. That sounds nice, but I don't have to tell you how expensive full-color stuff is."

"Full-color costs money, no question about it," Susan agreed.

"And while we're on the subject of expenses, how fair is it that every manager in the hotel signs for meals and drinks and it gets charged to my department as 'advertising and promotion'? If they are legitimately with a client, that's one thing. But they eat at the hotel because they don't want to eat in the employee break room, or it's raining outside, or they're short on cash this month — they even treat their spouses to dinner, and they sign the bills like it's a management perk or something. And it all gets charged to marketing. If Rick is so concerned about marketing expenses, why doesn't he do something about that? I've complained and complained about it."

"I've seen that privilege get abused at other hotels, too," Susan nodded. "How do you keep track of other department expenses, like office supplies, sales trip expenses, and so on?"

"Oh, I just wait for the profit and loss statement to come out at the end of the month and see where we are. If we're over one month, I try to cut back the next."

Susan made a note, then tapped her pen on her chin. "Let's backtrack for a moment. I'd like to know more about your staff—Rick didn't go into details with me. How many people do you have and what's their experience level?"

"I'm lucky — when I came on board two years ago, I inherited a staff of four veteran salespeople. Two had been with the hotel for five years, the other two had just come on board but had worked for other hotels for a number of years." Thad smiled. "I didn't have to do any training or coaching, I was able to just do my job and let them do theirs."

Susan smiled. "Sounds like you're pretty confident in their abilities. Have you ever gone out on a call with them?"

"No, why should I?"

"Well, because you're so confident in them, I was wondering if you had actually seem them in action, selling to a client."

"No. Up until this year, we've always made our number, and like I said earlier, we didn't make many outside sales calls anyway. People know our hotel's reputation. Most of our clients call us."

"So you don't provide your salespeople with sales targets to meet or action plans to follow?"

"Not really. Like I said, they're busy fielding all the incoming calls and taking care of clients. They're good people and they know what they're doing."

"I see." Susan made some more notes on her pad. "Well, as you know, Rick has asked me to make some recommendations to help the hotel raise its occupancy numbers. Four percent doesn't sound like much, but I'm sure you are as aware as anyone that, with your hotel's average daily rate and budgeted occupancy levels, a four-percent shortfall comes out to about $700,000 below budget for the year. I have some preliminary notions about what might be helpful, but do you have any ideas for turning things around?"

Thad leaned back in his chair and thought for a moment. "To tell you the truth, I think Rick overreacted to the situation," he said finally. "Of course I'm wiling to take a look at any ideas you come up with, but I think the numbers would eventually have come up on their own if we had just stayed our course. To my mind, personal service is the key to this market. A continued emphasis on really serving our clients once they get to the property will keep them coming back, and word-of-mouth from happy clients will keep our phones ringing." Thad paused. "I think Rick's directives are doing more harm than good, so my suggestion would be to call off the call quotas and cut way back on the trade shows."

Susan nodded and returned her pad and pen to her briefcase. "You have a point about the trade shows," she said. "Rick wants to bring marketing costs down and increase occupancy. I think I'm going to concentrate on three marketing expense areas: the trade show issue, the hotel's collateral materials, and the advertising and promotion expense account. On the occupancy side, I'm going to look at ways to determine whether your salespeople have the sales skills they need to meet the booking objectives, and I'm probably going to recommend that you give your salespeople more direction as to where you want them to focus their efforts."

Susan rose and shook hands with Thad. "I know it can be difficult to have an outsider come in to look at what you're doing, but my job really is to just try to be helpful and look for ways to make sales targets easier to make. I'm going to schedule a meeting with both you and Rick sometime next week, and I hope you'll be happy with the recommendations I come up with for you."

Discussion Questions

1. What are some recommendations Susan can make for decreasing the hotel's marketing expenses?

2. What are some recommendations Susan can make to Thad to help him evaluate his staff's sales skills?

3. What are some recommendations Susan can make to Thad to help him give his staff more direction to ensure that their efforts are focused and targeted?

Case Number: 370CI
This case was developed in cooperation with Lisa Richards of Hospitality Softnet, Inc., a marketing resources and support company.

This case also appears in <u>Contemporary Hospitality Marketing: A Service Management Approach</u> (Lansing, Mich.: Educational Institute of the American Hotel and Lodging Association), ISBN 0-86612-158-7.

CASE STUDY: CHAPTER 3

Departmental Conflict at the Ultra Hotel

A quick glance out the lobby window revealed wind-blown gray clouds bunching up over the city. "Storm's brewing out there," thought Rick Roland, the Ultra Hotel's marketing and sales director. In here, too, he thought as he walked past the lounges and restaurants on the ground floor of the 500-room, three-star convention property.

Unconsciously, Rick's pace slowed as he got closer to the meeting room where the end-of-the-month executive committee meeting was due to start. How ironic, he thought, to feel so apprehensive even though I'm almost ready to close on one of the biggest pieces of business I've landed in quite some time.

Taking a deep breath, Rick paused before entering the room. Images of the people waiting inside flashed through his mind: Fred Franklin, the general manager, a tough but fair boss who liked to give his staff members a chance to present their side of an argument; Norma Lopez, the no-nonsense controller with the laser-like focus on the bottom line; Claude van Fleet, the temperamental food and beverage director piloting a department through a terrible month; Camille Petrocelli, self-described "people person" and human resources director; and last, Jeanelle Causwell, rooms director, a fast-track performer, a favorite of Mr. Franklin's, and possibly my mortal enemy by the end of this meeting, Rick thought wryly.

Exhaling, Rick entered the meeting room. The meeting raced by for Rick until the moment he was waiting for. Mr. Franklin turned to him and said, "What have you got for us, Rick?"

"Well, gosh," Rick began, trying to inject some folksiness into a speech he had rehearsed a dozen times, "I'm about to land a nice piece of business for us. As all of you know, we've been after the ConveyorMatic meeting planner for months. The good news is, I think the guy's ready to commit in a big way. We're talking 250 rooms the second week of September, Sunday through Thursday, and — get this — it's a mandatory sales meeting for their big-spending sales staff, so filling up at least 240 of those 250 rooms is a cinch."

Seeing some nods and looks of interest, Rick went on. "Claude, you'll love this. We're getting three dinners, three lunches, three upgraded breakfasts, and two cocktail receptions with heavy hors d'oeuvres, which is big-time food and beverage sales — and that doesn't include spending in the outlets. It projects out to $130,000 in business for the hotel Last year, we had only about $80,000 the same week."

"Excuse me, Rick, but isn't it hotel policy that you're only allotted 200 rooms for group sales?" Jeanelle said, launching her first salvo.

"Good point, Jeanelle, but if I book this group this year, they could be repeat customers every year. Plus, this guy is active in Meeting Professionals International, so he could give us some great referrals."

"I love it. Let's book 'em," Claude interjected, looking relieved and grateful.

"I do have to book it today, by five o'clock. That's why I want to get us all together on this," Rick explained.

"Excuse me, again, Rick," Jeanelle said, "I'm sure you didn't make any promises to this group that would affect ourroom assignments, right?"

"Not really." Rick turned quickly to the controller. "What do you think, Norma?"

"I think we need to take a look at the numbers and make sure they're as good as you say," Norma said.

"Camille?" Rick continued eagerly.

"What?" Camille smiled, looking up from an issue of *HR Weekly*. "Oh, it sounds good; we could keep ten or fifteen people a day working for four days. Might slow down the turnover of our part-time kitchen staff."

"Rick, let's back up a minute." It was Jeanelle again, refusing to be sidetracked. "When I asked whether you'd made any promises to this group that would affect room assignments, you said 'Not really.' Could you define 'Not really' for me?"

"Well, I, uh," Rick looked down and mumbled rapidly, "I told them they could have fifty percent of their block in our new wing."

"What!" Jeanelle yelled, "You gave away my new wing! What do I tell my transient, repeat guests? My regulars stay three or four days, six times a year. You want me to tell them I'm kicking them out of the new wing? Why don't we just save time and tell them to go stay across the street from now on, because that's just what they'll do."

"But we're talking about 250 rooms!" Rick protested.

"At what rate?" Jeanelle shot back.

"Well, because of the F&B business, I gave them a discount — $79 a night."

"Wow! That's twenty percent off our regular $99 rate. Give those rooms back to me, Mr. Franklin. If we open up the corporate reservations center for discounts, I'll sell every one at $89. And I won't have to dump my best guests out of the new wing for these conveyor salesmen."

"Now, Jeanelle...", Rick pleaded.

"Now, nothing!" she snapped.

"But Jeanelle, the F&B revenue!" Claude said, dreaming of making up last month's budget shortfall. "You know as well as I do that transient guests don't eat at the hotel. This group will mean big bucks in F&B."

"Mr. Franklin, you're the general manager; it's your call," Rick said resignedly. Jeanelle and Claude nodded in agreement. The staff leaned back, waiting for the GM's decision.

Discussion Questions

1. What reasons might the GM have for deciding to turn down the business? What conflicts on the executive committee would have to be resolved if the GM decides to turn down the business?

2. What reasons might the GM have for deciding to take the business? What conflicts on the executive committee would have to be resolved if the GM decides to take the business?

Case Number 370CA
This case was developed in cooperation with Bill Flor and Randy Kinder, authors of <u>No Vacancy: A Tried & True Guide to Get More Rooms Business!</u>

This case also appears in <u>Contemporary Hospitality Marketing: A Service Management Approach</u> (Lansing, Mich.: Educational Institute of the American Hotel and Lodging Association), ISBN 0-86612-158-7.

CASE STUDY: CHAPTER 5

Overcoming Rate Resistance—Among the Sales Staff

Conversations stopped as Fran walked into the meeting room where the sales staff of the 263-room Park View Hotel had gathered. The director of sales surveyed the anxious faces that turned toward her as she approached.

"Lighten up, folks," Fran said reassuringly. "This is a strategy session, not a wake. I know you're all aware I had a meeting with the general manager last week, and he'd like us to make a few changes to our marketing plan. I'd like us to sit down together and brainstorm ways to solve some problems we identified in our meeting."

Fran passed around a handout as the salespeople took their seats. The objections started as soon as they began reading the agenda.

"Get rid of 5,000 room nights of our corporate contract business? That's crazy!" said Angela. "Most of my best accounts are corporate preferred. I worked hard to get those accounts and I'm not dropping them now."

"Where are we going to find the customers to replace these 5,000 room nights?" Michael asked. "You can't just expect that kind of new business to come strolling through the door right away."

Murmurs of agreement filled the room. "And how am I supposed to break it to my accounts that they're not going to get their preferred rate any more?" asked Tanisha. "I wouldn't know what to say, and I don't think I could sound real convincing."

Fran raised her hands. "Let's take this one step at a time. Here's the situation. The hotel has too much contracted business at a low rate. We need to replace about a third of this business – about 5,000 room nights – with higher rated transient and group business. I just want to evaluate which accounts we should keep, which ones might accept a higher – but still discounted – rate, and which ones don't make good business sense to keep."

Fran stood up next to a flip chart and uncapped a marker. "Let's set up some criteria for reviewing our contract accounts. What kinds of things should we look at? I'll start." She wrote, "Keep accounts with attractive arrival/departure patterns."

She continued to write as the staff began calling out ideas.

After a refreshment break, Fran called the group together again. "Great work, folks. Now, let's think about how we're going to replace that contract business with some new business that will bring in more revenue. I'd like to make a list of market segments and sources we could solicit more strongly. Then we can evaluate which areas we should concentrate our sales efforts on. Any ideas?" Fran worked the flip chart again.

That job done, Fran turned to the issue that Tanisha brought up earlier: how to tell clients about the change in the hotel's corporate preferred rate policy. Together, the staff decided they would be more comfortable and effective if they had scripts to work from.

Fran assigned two of the sales staff to write some scripts that everyone could use when talking with their accounts, whether they were increasing their rate or eliminating their preferred rate. As the meeting adjourned, Fran still heard grumbles from some of the sales-people. "My work's not done yet," she thought, and began planning her next steps for helping her staff accept these new rate changes.

Discussion Questions

1. What are some of the criteria the sales staff should use to evaluate whether a corporate contract account should be retained or dropped?

2. What factors should the staff consider when determining new sources of business to replace the displaced contract business?

3. What would the scripts look like that the sales staff could use when talking to clients about the rate change?

4. How can Fran help her staff become comfortable with the changes in the hotel's rate structure?

Case Number: 370CJ
This case was developed in cooperation with Lisa Richards of Hospitality Softnet, Inc., a marketing resources and support company.

This case also appears in <u>Contemporary Hospitality Marketing: A Service Management Approach</u> (East Lansing, Mich.: Educational Institute of the American Hotel & Lodging Association), ISBN 0-86612-158-7.

CASE STUDY: CHAPTER 6

Reviving Revenue Management

The Hearthstone Suites Hotel is an all-suite property with 250 rooms. A new property, the Fairmont Hotel, opened near Hearthstone Suites three months ago. Several months before the opening of the Fairmont, Laurie, the GM at the Hearthstone Suites, pushed all her front office and reservations staff to sell as many rooms as possible. As she put it, "Whatever it takes, to stay competitive." The director of sales, Pat, supported the plan from day one, but Jodie, the front office manager, had misgivings from the start. Jodie was concerned that the revenue management program that managers implemented a year and a half earlier would be totally useless because of the push for occupancy.

The most recent profit and loss statement indicates that Jodie's fears were realized. Though the occupancy is at a budget year-to-date, the average daily rate (ADR) is down by $6.00. Also, the mix of commercial business is lower than planned – 40% of guest mix instead of 50%. Also, the SMERF segment is higher than it should be – 15% of guest mix instead of 5%. SMERF is a catch-all term for group business at substantially lower rates – Social, Military, Educational, Religious, and Fraternal groups.

Jodie, Pat, and Laurie are in a meeting to discuss these latest figures.

Laurie, the general manager, opens the meeting by saying, "Well, we've weathered the storm caused by the opening of the Fairmont. We managed to hold on to our occupancy level. But it looks like we have some regrouping to do. I trust you've each received the profit and loss statement I sent you. I'm concerned about the fact that we've lost so much of our share of the commercial business. And, our ADR is much too low."

"I agree," says Jodie, "but I was just following orders when I had my staff focus on selling rooms. Our good occupancy rate has come at the cost of both yield management and revenue. It will take quite a while to regain our former position."

"We all sat down and agreed months before the Fairmont opened that we should do our best to keep our occupancy numbers, and that's what we've done," says Pat. "You and your staff have worked hard and are to be commended, Jodie."

"Hear, hear," says Laurie. "And now we have some time to re-evaluate our position and start targeting that corporate segment again."

"I just hope it's not too late to win it back from Fairmont," sighs Jodie.

Later that day, Jodie gathers her front desk and reservations team to brief them about re-implementing the revenue management program. "I know you've all been putting a lot of extra effort into filling rooms over the past several months. I'm proud of you; the whole management team is. We've met our occupancy goals. The down side is that our guest mix is off. We've lost some of our commercial segment and gained too much of the SMERF segment. And, our ADR is down a full $6. It's time we reviewed the revenue management program we use...."

"The revenue what?" blurts Jack, a fairly new front desk agent. "You never told us about that."

"Now hold on a minute," counters Jodie, "some of you are so new that you haven't been fully trained in this program, but I know I've talked about it to some extent with all of you."

"Sure, you told me a little about it," offers Tracey, a reservationist. "I never have been comfortable with it, to tell the truth. One day I quoted a guest $85 and he books a suite. A month later he calls back to book another and I quote $105. Then the guest asks why the rates went up—what am I supposed to say?"

"Well, there are things you can tell guests who ask that, but we're not going to get into that right now," says Jodie.

Bill, the most experienced front desk agent, speaks up. "I've been using the yield management program all along, just like you showed me." He turns to his co-workers. "It's really not unreasonable when you look at the big picture of the hotel's revenue. I just tell inquisitive callers that our rates depend on their arrival dates. Some periods are busier for us than others, and that affects rates."

"Bill, it's good to hear that you continued using the yield management program," Jodie says. "We can get into more detail on applying it in formal training. We've had a lot of changes since the push for volume began – changes in personnel and even changes in the yield management program itself. It's clearly time I evaluated training needs in our department in the area of yield management program execution. You can be confident, Tracey – and all of you – when you quote rates that they are competitive for what we offer. That reminds me," and here Jodie pauses a moment, "how many of you have actually been inside some of our suites?"

Three of the six employees raise their hands. "How many have seen rooms at the Fairmont or any of our other competitors?" continues Jodie. Only Bill raises his hand. "So almost none of you have seen the difference between our suites and the single rooms other properties are offering?"

"There hasn't been much time to look at what we're selling," protests Jack.

"...much less to look at what anyone else is selling," adds Linda, another reservationist.

"That's what I was afraid of," says Jodie. "In the next two weeks or so, as I'm re-evaluating training needs, I'm going to have each of you spend time gaining an appreciation of the value we offer – especially in comparison with the value of Fairmont's offerings and those of our other competition."

"Are we still going to be offering the $84 supersaver rate?" asks Tracey. "We've had a lot of repeat business because of that rate."

"I've had callers tell me we're the best deal in town," adds Linda.

But Bill cautions, "We won't need to use it next week. The Home Builders' convention is in and every room in town will be booked. We can afford to charge more next week."

"That's good thinking, Bill," says Jodie. "I know it's nice to be popular with guests and it's easy to use that discount whenever a potential guest shies away from a quoted rate; but the supersaver rate is intended to be used only as a last resort or in other special cases. We shouldn't be offering it too frequently. We also need to adjust our selling strategies when special events, like this convention, come along."

"Speaking of selling strategies, when are we going to get to go through that training module on selling skills you were talking about?" inquires Linda. "I've heard about it but I haven't gone through it yet."

Discussion Questions

1. How can the management team address the problem of low ADR?

2. What are some ways Jodie could make employees such as Jack and Tracey more familiar and comfortable with a yield management program?

3. What selling skills should training focus on for the Hearthstone Suites Hotel staff?

4. How can the Hearthstone Suites Hotel regain some of the commercial business it has lost?

Case Number: 370CF

This case was developed in cooperation with Lisa Richards of Hospitality Softnet, Inc., a marketing resources and support company.

This case also appears in <u>Contemporary Hospitality Marketing: A Service Management Approach</u> (East Lansing, Mich.: Educational Institute of the American Hotel & Lodging Association), ISBN 0-86612-158-7.

CASE STUDY: CHAPTER 7

Don't Just Tell It — Sell It! or Needs Satisfaction Selling:
Booking Business by Turning Features into Benefits

Sales at the 112-room Goodsleep Inn have been down lately. The number of room nights sold has dropped and, due to turnover, the sales staff is inexperienced. Today, the hotshot sales director, Sandra Savvy, begins training Drew Newbie, one of the new salespeople.

At their first meeting in Sandra's office, Sandra explains, "Drew, to sell our hotel you have to understand what it is you're selling and how it appeals to your potential clients."

"That's easy — we're selling rooms," Drew said.

"That's true," Sandra replied. "But it's not that simple. To be a successful salesperson, you must be able to identify the hotel features that can benefit your potential clients and satisfy their *specific* needs."

"What do you mean?"

"How would you describe the Goodsleep Inn to someone who's never been here before?" Sandra asked.

"Well," Drew said, "it has 112 rooms and is three stories high, with external corridors. Is that the kind of information you mean?"

"That's a start. What else?"

"Hmm, let's see," Drew continued. "We have a swimming pool, and our rates are pretty reasonable. We have a great, free continental breakfast, too."

"Right," Sandra said. "What about the property's location?"

"I think I see what you're getting at," Drew said enthusiastically. "We have a coin-operated laundry for guests. We're in the suburbs near the business district. The area is safe. It's also close to the interstate. And even though we don't have any food and beverage outlets at our property, there are a lot of family restaurants and convenience stores within walking distance."

"Excellent! You're getting the hang of it," Sandra said. "Some other things you may want to mention a potential client are: recent updates to the hotel, like the $150,000 guestroom renovations we just did; the free movies we offer; and our non-smoking rooms. These may seem like little things, but to some guests they mean a lot. The key is to find out what your potential guests need, then match the property's features to your guests' needs and show them how the property can benefit them."

"So, it's not just telling someone you've got rooms available, is it?" Drew asked.

"No, that's called *tell* selling," Sandra said, shaking her head. "That's what the stereotypical salesperson does — you know, the pushy person trying to sell you a used car you don't want. To really be successful in sales, you have to look for a win-win situation with clients. Find out what they really want, then describe the features of the hotel that match what they want. Keep in mind, though, that it's not just selling them a line. You don't make up stuff about the hotel that isn't true. You merely make the effort to match what you've got to what they want and describe what you have in terms of how it benefits the client. That's the way you can build long-term relationships with clients, which will increase the number of room nights sold in the long run."

Drew thought for a minute. "It sounds like common sense."

"It is. You'd be amazed at how successful you can be by simply listening to what your prospects need, describing how your hotel can meet those needs, and using a little common courtesy," Sandra said.

"Common courtesy," Drew said. "I've got that. I always say please and thank you."

"It's more than that," Sandra said. "There are simple things you can do that will really impress your potential clients and win you business for life. For example, greet potential clients at the front door, or even meet them in the parking lot and walk them to the front door; don't make them ask for you at the front desk. During the hotel tour, introduce them to the property manager and hotel employees. You'd be amazed at how little details like these can set the right tone."

"So, how do you find out what the potential clients' needs are?" Drew asked.

"That's simple — ask them! Also, take the time to get to know your markets. I do a little research before I meet with a potential client so I have some ideas about what he or she might want. Not only does it help me prepare, but it shows that I care about meeting the person's needs, not just making a sale. Then, when you give property tours, simply ask potential clients what's important to them in a hotel and give it right back to them by describing the hotel features and benefits that fit those needs."

"I guess I have my work cut out for me," Drew responded.

"Yes, Drew, but you're up for the job." Sandra picked up her planner and flipped it open. "I've got an idea. I'm giving three property tours next week. Let me tell you what I've found out about each potential client and you tell me how you would sell the property to each."

"The first tour is for the local terminal manager who handles accommodations for long-distance drivers. These guests often use a room for only eight or nine hours, just enough time to get some sleep before getting back on the road. They want time to unwind, but they don't socialize. They stay in their rooms and watch TV or sleep. They want king-size beds, clean rooms, and respect. They want to be reassured that you don't look down on them because they drive trucks or buses."

"The next tour is for a youth soccer league organizer from the parks and recreation department. She's responsible for recommending properties to out-of-town soccer teams that come here for games. Team members are usually 12- to 16-year-old boys and girls. Parents, coaches, and chaperons look for safe properties close to affordable restaurants and the soccer fields where the kids play. Luckily, we're really close to the soccer fields and we have a lot of affordable restaurants nearby. These guests want rooms with two double beds and an on-site laundry. Also, the property they choose has to be tolerant of the athletes. Everyone wants to have a good time, and the kids can get pretty rowdy."

"The third tour is for the pastor of a local church that offers a weekend couples conference twice a year. The couples attending this conference are very rate-conscious, but they want safe, clean, well-appointed rooms with king-size beds and some amenities for their weekend stay. They often do some socializing at breakfast and after the conference, although most of their time is spent away from the property."

Sandra closed her planner and looked up. "OK, Drew, it's your turn. We'll generate about 4,000 extra room nights a year if we can win the business of these potential clients. That means $125,000 in revenue. How would you present our hotel to each of these potential clients to win their business?"

Discussion Questions

1. How can Drew show common courtesy to each of these three potential clients?

2. How should Drew present the Goodsleep Inn's features and benefits to the local terminal manager?

3. How should Drew present the Goodsleep Inn's features and benefits to the soccer league organizer?

4. How should Drew present the Goodsleep Inn's features and benefits to the church pastor?

Case Number: 370CC
This case was developed in cooperation with Bill Flor and Randy Kinder, authors of <u>No Vacancy: A Tried & True Guide to Get More Rooms Business!</u>

This case also appeared in <u>Contemporary Hospitality Marketing: A Service Management Approach</u> (Lansing, Mich.: Educational Institute of the American Hotel & Lodging Association), ISBN 0-86612-158-7.

CASE STUDY: CHAPTER 9

No Vacancy

Jon Stonewall is a regional manager for IntelTech, a Seattle-based company that produces computer software. He is responsible for planning the annual meeting of his account representatives in District 12, which encompasses the entire Pacific Northwest. The meeting, normally just an opportunity for education and socializing, will be especially important this year because the company is introducing several new products. After reviewing several locations, Jon decided to have the meeting in Sacramento and asked his secretary, Chris, to gather information and solicit bids from at least five Sacramento hotels. Jon is a hard-nosed businessperson who likes to get what he wants. To waste as little time as possible, he systematically examined his choices and narrowed the selection down to two. Now it was time to make a deal.

Jon was in his office when he received a call from Julia Chavez, the sales manager of the Monte Sereno Hotel in Sacramento. She began the conversation by introducing herself and her property, a mid-range hotel with 248 rooms, 8,000 square feet of meeting space, and a 5,200-square-foot ballroom that could be divided into four equal sections.

"We're so pleased you've selected the Monte Sereno as a possible site for your next meeting," Julia continued. "I've spoken at length with your secretary and wanted to speak with you personally to be sure we understand your needs. Do you have a moment to talk?"

Jon was at the start of a busy day and was a little annoyed at the interruption, but brusquely told her to go on. Concerned by his tone, Julia thanked him for his time and proceeded cautiously.

"I understand your group will arrive Sunday afternoon and leave Thursday. You'd like 48 rooms, single occupancy, and an opening night reception with heavy hors d'oeuvres. Is that correct?"

"Yes," Jon grunted.

"Chris told me that you'll begin each morning with a continental breakfast at 8:00 a.m., followed by a general session at 8:30. The general session meeting room is to be arranged classroom-style, with a luncheon in a separate room beginning at noon. From 1:00 to 5:00 p.m., your account reps will break into groups of 10 to 15 and require separate meeting spaces."

"That's right," Jon replied, "except that everyone will be on their own at lunch time."

Julia had carefully considered this sales opportunity, weighed the options, and decided on an appropriate rate before making the call to Jon. She had taken into account the property's sales history, which showed a 92 percent occupancy rate on the particular days IntelTech had in mind. She was concerned because this meeting would use only 20 percent of the hotel's rooms while using 65 percent of the hotel's meeting space. From her standpoint, it wasn't a great piece of business. Julia wanted the business, but she wanted it on her own terms. She took a deep breath and continued.

"Well, we do have those dates available for your meeting. We can offer the guestrooms at $99, a reduction from our standard $110 rate, and offer the meeting space you need at $1,000 per day. However, I know that getting high value for your dollar is a consideration for everyone these days, so, if you can be flexible and change your dates to a Wednesday arrival and a Sunday departure, I can offer the rooms to you at $85 and waive the $1,000 charge for the meeting space — if you will hold your farewell banquet with us."

"I can't believe this!" Jon said, his voice rising. "The Salton Hotel down the street has the dates I want *and* they can give them to me at the rate you quoted! Granted, I prefer your hotel overall, but I have to consider my company. This meeting has been set for a long time;

some of my people have already made travel plans. We've even scheduled the speakers. I can't go back and change things now! Why are the rates so different later in the week?"

Julia was prepared for this response and answered him as tactfully and honestly as she could. "I'm aware of your concerns and know it would be difficult to move the meeting, but I wanted to give you the option. Since we're both businesspeople, I know you'll understand that I have to consider my property's financial position in all of this. Our sales history shows that we have our highest occupancy during the first part of the week — between 90 and 100 percent — but later in the week that number declines to around 60 percent; that's why I can give you a lower rate at that time. Because we're sold out or almost sold out from Sunday through Thursday, it doesn't make sense financially for us to offer you the lower rate early in the week."

"Look," Jon said, "I can appreciate where you're coming from, but I don't see how I can change this meeting — even if I can save a lot of money."

"I understand your situation and want to work with you in the future," Julia replied, "but I'm not sure we can meet your needs this time. Down the road, if you bring me your next meeting, I'll throw in a free cocktail party. I think you'd be very pleased with our hotel. We have outstanding food and a very friendly, courteous staff. I hope you'll come and visit us when you're in town."

Jon hesitated. Since he really wanted to stay at the Monte Sereno rather than the other hotel, he didn't want to let the matter drop. "What about this, Julia: if I agree to the higher rates and choose you over a competitor, will you do a few things for me? I'll pay the $99 room rate if you'll throw in the meeting space for nothing. I also want the free cocktail party you just mentioned. In addition, I'd like you to give us turndown service throughout our stay, a free *USA Today* in every room, and waiting for my account reps when they arrive on Sunday, a mint and a welcome note from me in every guestroom."

Discussion Questions

1. Do you think Julia should agree to host the meeting on Jon's terms? Why or why not?

2. How could Julia further negotiate each of Jon's demands and end with a win-win conclusion?

Case Number: 370CB
This case was developed in cooperation with Bill Flor and Randy Kinder, authors of No Vacancy: A Tried & True Guide to Get More Rooms Business!

This case also appears in Contemporary Hospitality Marketing: A Service Management Approach (Lansing, Mich.: Educational Institute of the American Hotel & Lodging Association), ISBN 0-86612-158-7.

CASE STUDY: CHAPTER 11

Sales Underperforms Even While Meeting Budget

The Christopher Hotel is a 180-room economy/business property of a national chain located in a booming suburb of a major city. Tony, the regional director of operations, is orienting the property's new general manager, Janice.

Generally, the hotel is close to meeting most of its budgeted targets. However, when Tony compares the hotel's activity with competing hotels in the area, the picture changes dramatically. Other hotels are enjoying much higher occupancy levels than the Christopher and they are selling rooms at higher rates. The Christopher's market penetration is only 84 percent, when its baseline goal should be to achieve at least 100 percent of its fair share of the market. Tony calculates penetration rate by dividing the hotel's actual market share by its fair share (based on the proportion of rooms available in the local market).

Tony and Janice also review the Christopher's group business. Year-to-date, the hotel sold 4,796 group room nights — short of the budgeted target of 6,500 group room nights. The average room rate (ADR) for group business is down $4 from the budget.

Tony tells Janice, "While I'm here I want to investigate these problems with you and help come up with an action plan to address them. How can we increase the Christopher's penetration rate, Janice?"

"I'd start by examining what kind of new business — group and otherwise — is being generated," says Janice. "What is the mix of corporate, leisure, government, or educational groups that is looking for rooms? I bet that new college is putting together a sports program; visiting teams will need someplace to stay."

"You could be right," says Tony. "The school is so new that you might be too early on that idea, but it couldn't hurt to get a start with the sports program developer. Let's see what the hotel has historically done with groups." He pulls out some reports. "They've got corporate groups contributing 3,000 room nights and other groups contributing the rest of their total 4,796."

"Other groups? Is that how it's listed — 'other groups'? Aren't there classifications within that 'other' category?" asks Janice.

Tony responds, "That's how it's listed."

Janice shakes her head and asks, "Do we have a group room control log to look at so we can see how individual group segments are performing? How about a pace report so we can see how group bookings kept up with budgeted amounts?"

Tony shuffles some of the papers and replies, "The previous GM did keep a GRC log and a pace report. He may not have used them to fullest advantage. He also could have kept better track of what the property's competitors were doing. That information is crucial to success, especially in this local area. In the next few months, I would like you to keep up to date on what our competitors are doing and how they're doing it."

"How good a networker was the previous director of sales?" asks Janice. "Did he have relationships with area churches, mosques, and synagogues for wedding and other special ceremony business? Was he in touch with the manager of the local convention center? How about city officials?"

"He focused more on officials of agencies serving the whole metropolitan area than on officials of this suburb." Tony replies. "Maybe he was hoping to land some of the business for conventions held downtown. He was using the right technique but on the wrong people. Our competitors here keep in touch with the city Department of Parks and Recreation. As far as wedding and ceremony groups, there's been no sales effort specifically targeting them, though some large bookings have come from that segment. I'd encourage you to pursue that option with the staff. And don't be shy about using the yellow pages of the phone book. So many salespeople use that as a last resort. Just think about all the kinds of business represented there...."

"It does sound like this is a very competitive area." Janice offers. "I wonder if our sales contacts with those buyers for groups are everything they should be. How experienced are our sales staff?"

"I'm not sure, but that's another good area to look at. Now how about this problem of the group ADR?" asks Tony.

Janice picks up a management binder labeled Rate Guidelines from the GM office bookshelf. "It's great that they had some of these, though having guidelines and making sure staff know and use them are two different things. Hmm, it doesn't have a date listed; do you know when it was last updated?"

"No, I don't," replies Tony.

"That could be important; I'll check on it. Maybe we also need to change our rooms inventory management guidelines to make sure we sell out on every night when there's potential to do so," Janice responds.

Tony closes with, "I think you've got a good handle on the most pressing issues facing the Christopher Hotel, Janice. Why don't you draft an action plan in the next couple of days and we'll refine it together."

Discussion Questions

1. What factors should Janice consider when planning to increase the hotel's market penetration rate?

2. What factors should Janice consider in relation to increasing group business?

3. What initial steps should Janice take to evaluate the low average room rate for groups?

4. How can Janice find out what the competition is doing and how they're doing it?

Case Number: 370CH
This case was developed in cooperation with Lisa Richards of Hospitality Softnet, Inc., a marketing resources and support company.

This case also appears in Contemporary Hospitality Marketing: A Service Management Approach (Lansing, Mich.: Educational Institute of the American Hotel & Lodging Association), ISBN 0-86612-158-7.

CASE STUDY: CHAPTER 14

Distributing Sales Functions Between a Hotel's Sales and Catering Departments

Carla Mills is the general manager of the Woodfield Plaza, a 400-room first-class suburban hotel. It's early July, and Carla has just reviewed the forecasted year-end profit and loss statement. A couple areas concern her. First, assuming the hotel will hit budget the rest of the year, banquet food sales will be down $60,000 to budget. Also, the audiovisual revenues and room rental revenues will miss budget by $30,000. Carla calls a meeting with her director of catering, Alan Jenkins, to discuss ways to remedy the situation.

Carla opens the meeting by contrasting the forecasted statement with the budget and asks Alan what he plans to do about the decrease in banquet food sales.

"You've been here sixty days now, Alan. You should have a good feel for the property and the community. Tell me, why are sales down in your area?"

Alan shifts in his seat. He thinks about the question for a moment, then responds. "Well, I think ultimately it comes down to a problem with selling," he says. "The sales staff knows how to sell guestrooms, but they don't seem to sell function rooms. They don't seem to be aware of opportunities to sell catering, or how to take advantage of those opportunities. I can't remember one event since I've been here that was generated by sales. And from what I've seen in past reports, this has been an ongoing problem."

"OK. That's a legitimate point," Carla replies. "Salespeople certainly could take advantage of those kinds of opportunities. Sales and catering aren't often as united as they could be when it comes to selling our services —"

"It's just that no one in sales will take ownership for selling catering," Alan interrupts.

"Then you take ownership of it," replies Carla. "Look, in fairness to sales, it's not their job to sell function rooms and banquet events, primarily. Their job *is* to sell guestrooms. In some situations they could probably work a little harder on selling function rooms. But the responsibility for selling catering events ultimately belongs to catering, not sales...and since you're so concerned about *sales* selling *functions*...how many *guestrooms* has *catering* sold? The street goes both ways."

Alan sits back in his chair, thinking about what Carla has said. "Not many, actually," he finally says. "As far as catering taking responsibility for its own sales...you're right. We need to. But we're so busy taking the calls coming in, and we're trying to process them as fast as we can. We haven't had time to focus on increasing our sales skills."

"You can't continue to be just order-takers and expect your sales to do fine," Carla says. "You need to take responsibility for your sales. You need to take an active role in this. In your own words, you need to take ownership of it. Let me ask you: Do you know where you're losing business, and why?"

"Not offhand, no."

"Do you know how you're going to solve the problem?"

"Well, I think I can come up with a solution," Alan replies.

"I know you can. And I know your staff is capable. What'd I'd like you to do is come up with a plan as to how you'll sell catering, and how you'll work with the sales staff to sell catering. Could you get that to me...let's see," Carla looks at her calendar. "Two weeks from today?"

"I think I can do that."

"Great. Now on to my next concern." Carla holds up the forecasted statement. "As you can see from this forecast, by the end of the year audiovisual revenues and room rental revenues will miss budget by $30,000 — that's if all goes well the next six months. Now, what do you suggest we do about *that*?"

Alan thinks about the problem. "With the room rentals, I think the problem is that we're giving function space away to book more room nights. I understand we have to do this, to some degree, but we're losing money doing it."

"But don't you think that's a worthy trade-off, to get more room nights?"

"I would be if it were necessary. But I don't think it is."

"What do you mean?" Carla asks.

"I think we can keep the room nights without losing the room rental completely, if we institute a sliding-scale function fee."

"Yes," Carla nods.

"For example, if the customer picks up 80 to 100 percent of a room block, there's no rental. If they pick up 50 percent of the room block, they'll get 50 percent off the rate, and so on."

"Excellent idea. That should increase room rental revenues. You may want to consider putting a similar scale in place for catering revenues."

"Hmmm...come to think of it, my staff does seem a little too eager to lower rentals. Maybe scales will help them deal more effectively with that issue."

"Good. Now, what about audiovisual rentals?"

Alan pauses. "I need to look into that. I know there are several ways to increase the AV revenues, as well as additional ways to increase room rental revenues. How about if I think about the problem in the next couple of weeks, and include my proposals in my plan?"

"I trust your judgment. Let's get together again in two weeks and see what you've come up with."

"Great. I'll see you then."

Alan leaves the room. Both he and Carla feel that they made some progress in solving their budget problems. And they're confident that in two weeks they'll have a plan in place to help prevent similar problems in the future.

Discussion Questions

1. In an ideal situation, what should the distribution of sales functions between a hotel's catering and sales departments look like?

2. Given the responsibilities of a hotel's catering department, what challenges will the director of catering face as the department shifts from simply being production-focused to being sales focused?

3. How could the catering department at the Woodfield Plaza recover more audiovisual and room rental revenues?

4. What steps should the director of catering at the Woodfield Plaza take to identify the specific causes of his budget problem? Once the specifics of the budget problem have been identified, how should he address the problem?

Case Number: 370CG

This case was developed in cooperation with Lisa Richards of Hospitality Softnet, Inc., a marketing resources and support company.

This case also appears in <u>Contemporary Hospitality Marketing: A Service Management Approach</u> (Lansing, Mich.: Educational Institute of the American Hotel & Lodging Association), ISBN 0-86612-158-7.

Index

Sidney Silverman Library
and Learning Resource Center
Bergen Community College
400 Paramus Road
Paramus, NJ 07652-1595

www.bergen.edu
Return Postage Guaranteed